Louisa Catherine

LOUISA CATHERINE

The Other Mrs. Adams

Margery M. Heffron

Edited by David L. Michelmore

Yale

UNIVERSITY
PRESS
New Haven & London

Published with assistance from the Annie Burr Lewis Fund and
the Mary Cady Tew Memorial Fund.

Yale University Press books may be purchased in quantity for
educational, business, or promotional use. For information, please
e-mail sales.press@yale.edu (U.S. office) or sales@yaleup.co.uk
(U.K. office).

Set in Electra type by IDS Infotech Ltd., Chandigarh, India.
Printed in the United States of America.

Library of Congress Cataloging-in-Publication Data

Heffron, Margery M., 1939–2011.
Louisa Catherine : the other Mrs. Adams / Margery M. Heffron ;
edited by David L. Michelmore.
pages cm
Includes bibliographical references and index.
ISBN 978-0-300-19796-9 (cloth : alk. paper) 1. Adams, Louisa
Catherine, 1775–1852. 2. Presidents' spouses — United States —
Biography. 3. Adams, John Quincy, 1767–1848. I. Michelmore,
David L., 1947– editor. II. Title.
E377.2.H44 2014
973.5'5092 — dc23   [B]   2013042868

A catalogue record for this book is available from the
British Library.

This paper meets the requirements of ANSI/NISO Z39.48-1992
(Permanence of Paper).

10 9 8 7 6 5 4 3 2

CONTENTS

Acknowledgments   VII

Introduction   1

ONE   Halcyon Days   7

TWO   Ready for Love   26

THREE   Destined for Greatness   45

FOUR   A Fine Romance   66

FIVE   At Home and Abroad   91

SIX   In Sickness and in Health   114

SEVEN   A Native in a Strange Land   137

EIGHT   Wandering Fortunes   165

NINE   A Fleeting Fairy Tale   195

TEN   Dark Days on the Baltic   218

ELEVEN   The Journey of a Lifetime   244

TWELVE   Little Boston House   272

THIRTEEN   Campaign   296

FOURTEEN   A Beautiful Plan   328

Contents

List of Abbreviations 357

Johnson Family Tree 358

Chronology 361

Notes 369

Index 407

Acknowledgments

In October 2009, my sister Margery M. Heffron was diagnosed with pancre-
atic cancer. Two years and many hours of painful treatment later, in December
2011, she died, not knowing if the book into which she had poured every last bit
of her heart and energy would ever be published. Carrying *Louisa Catherine:
The Other Mrs. Adams* to the finish line took the combined efforts of a small
army of friends, family, and fellow writers drawn to Margery's cause by her
courage and endless enthusiasm. I give them my warmest thanks, hoping that
those whose names I unwittingly omit will accept my apologies.

The book ends with John Quincy's inauguration as the nation's sixth president in March 1825, far short of where Margery had hoped to take it. She simply
ran out of time. The chronology at the end of the book provides a brief outline
of the remaining twenty-seven years of Louisa's life.

Margery wrote her first book at the age of eight, an elaborate Louisa May
Alcott imitation called *The Happy Family*, and from then on had always wanted
to be an "author." On a visit to the Old House in Quincy, she found her subject
in Louisa Catherine Adams, but, between family and career, it was another
thirty years before she found the freedom to begin writing. Even then, she kept
her ambitions largely to herself. That secrecy ended one evening at a
Massachusetts Historical Society lecture in Boston when she happened to sit
next to C. James Taylor, editor-in-chief of the Adams Papers. His immediate
enthusiasm for her idea gave her a huge boost. It led to a long and fruitful
relationship with the MHS and, eventually, to a Marc Friedlaender research
fellowship. Judith Graham, Beth Luey, and Margaret A. Hogan, editors of the
MHS's recently published two-volume *Diary and Autobiographical Writings of
Louisa Catherine Adams*, gave her unwavering support and encouragement. It's
impossible to thank them adequately. At the MHS, she also came in contact

with Catherine Allgor of the University of California, Riverside, a well-known scholar, writer, and Louisa fan whose energetic support for the project did much to buoy Margery's spirits and to allay her fears that her work was, somehow, not scholarly enough.

As she began writing, Margery leaned heavily on colleagues in the Boston Biographers Group, a small, spirited organization that she had co-founded as a kind of support group for professional writers. Members of the group—particularly Elizabeth Harris, Bernice Lerner, Melissa Nathanson, and Quincy Whitney, all of whom were working on biographies of their own—carefully read and commented on her work, chapter by chapter, just as she read and commented on theirs.

When Margery was too ill to do as much research as she needed to do, she enlisted her sister Mary Ackerman Hayes, a freshly retired school teacher, and me, a freshly retired newspaperman, to help. Mary worked tirelessly collecting and reading the Adams Papers on microfilm and providing Margery with notes and summaries and the kind of love that only a sister can provide. Mary received welcome help from Linda Madden, Interlibrary Loan Supervisor at the Mason Library of Keene State College, and Shane Harper, Resource Sharing assistant, at the Dartmouth College Library.

Elizabeth O'Connor McGurk, a college classmate of Margery's living in England, traveled to Ealing outside London to provide information for Chapter 12. Another college friend, Oriel Eaton, read every chapter as it was produced, acting as not only a proofreader/copy editor but also a general editor in addressing style and tone. And yet a third college friend, Livia Bardin, and her husband, David, a dogged researcher, dug through archival records in Washington, D.C., for new information on Louisa's family in Chapters 13 and 14. They received valuable assistance from Danny Brown at the Washington, D.C., Archives; Robert Ellis at the National Archives; and Hayden Bryan at St. John's Episcopal Church, Lafayette Square, in Washington.

Carlene Barous, a cousin, copyedited the first few chapters as Margery started treatment for her cancer. Karen Hammond, a writer and longtime friend of Margery's, copyedited the entire book before we sent it out to publishers. I would also like to thank Margery's oncologist, Dr. Elizabeth Buchbinder of Beth Israel Deaconess Medical Center in Boston, for her care and support. I believe that Margery's determination to finish this book kept her alive much longer than could have been expected.

Margery's children—Anne Sigler and John and Samuel Heffron—and her grandchildren—Keats Iwanaga and William and Phineas Heffron—should be thanked for their patience, support, and love.

Margery's husband Frank encouraged her to follow her dream in writing this book. He read and offered patient, lawyerly advice on much of it; he accompanied her on research trips to London, Nantes, St. Petersburg, and Annapolis (where she suffered a frightening and serious fall that sidelined her for months). And, in Margery's last two years, Frank stayed beside her through scores of hospital visits, physician consultations, treatments, and bad news. For all that and more he deserves all our thanks.

David L. Michelmore

Louisa Catherine

INTRODUCTION

Then it was that the little Henry, her grandson, first remembered her, from 1843 to 1848,
sitting in her panelled room, at breakfast, with her heavy silver teapot and sugar-bowl
and cream-jug. . . . By that time she was seventy years old or more, and thoroughly weary
of being beaten about a stormy world. To the boy she seemed singularly peaceful, a
vision of silver gray, presiding over her old President and her Queen Anne mahogany; an
exotic, like her Sèvres china; an object of deference to every one, and of great affection
to her son Charles; but hardly more Bostonian than she had been fifty years before, on
her wedding-day, in the shadow of the Tower of London.

—HENRY ADAMS, *The Education of Henry Adams*, 1905

The little boy had it exactly right. Although it might be argued that her entire
married life had been spent in service to the United States, Louisa Catherine
Johnson Adams was unalterably an "exotic" in Boston and a European in
America. The only First Lady to have been born and brought up outside the
United States, she did not put down permanent roots in American soil until her
forty-third year. Yet when she died in Washington in 1852, both houses of
Congress adjourned for a day in her honor—a rare tribute to a woman who
never held a political office.

What the young Henry Adams could not know was the incalculable price his
grandmother had paid for the peace and serenity she seemed to embody as—
with innate elegance—she presided over her silver tea service, Sèvres china,
Queen Anne mahogany, and the aged John Quincy Adams. Fifty years as an
Adams had left Louisa with painful emotional scars made worse by a lifetime
in the maelstrom of early and mid-nineteenth-century American politics, the
tragic loss of three adored children, and the abiding belief that she herself had
accomplished little of value.

Henry was not alone in failing to see his grandmother for the complex person
she was—she has eluded would-be biographers for more than 150 years. A

central figure in the venerable Adams dynasty, Louisa is the unknown Adams, lost in the shadow of her formidable mother-in-law, Abigail Adams, and dwarfed by the towering stature of the two presidents, John and John Quincy Adams.[1]

She deserves more. Like Jacqueline Kennedy, Louisa was a refined and lovely young woman who married into a powerful Massachusetts family with political ambitions and dynastic aspirations. Among her greatest challenges was to stake out a place within the larger-than-life Adams family. Neither John nor Abigail Adams was originally enthused with their son's choice of a privileged, English-born wife. ("I would hope for the love I bear my country that the Syren is at least *half blood*," Abigail wrote to John Quincy.) In 1801 when the young couple arrived in Quincy from Europe for the first time, it was old John who immediately became Louisa's strongest supporter, and she repaid his kindness with lifelong devotion. Although her relationship with Abigail began disastrously, Louisa's resilience in the face of personal tragedy as well as her intelligence and her devotion to John Quincy eventually won over even her intimidating mother-in-law.

In her lifetime—by virtue of her marriage—Louisa was one of the most widely known women in America. Throughout much of her seventy-seven years, stretching from the outbreak of the American Revolution to the eve of the Civil War, she was close to the center of American power and, if not an elected official, was a very shrewd observer of the politics, personalities, and issues of her day. Her sparkling descriptions of brilliant fetes, dinners, and balls at the royal courts of Tsar Alexander of Russia and the future King George IV of England and of the Washington political and social scene were relished by Abigail, and her incisive reports of Washington politics were the delight of old John's declining days. Her ball for a thousand guests in January 1824— ostensibly to honor Andrew Jackson but actually to promote John Quincy's presidential ambitions—was avidly covered by the national press. Newspaper readers throughout the country needed no further identification to recognize Louisa in a popular ditty with the refrain:

> Belles and matrons, maids and madams,
> All are gone to Mrs. Adams.[2]

But there was more to Louisa than reflected glory. At her core, she was a feminist before the term achieved currency. Throughout her life, her writings and journal entries focused on the role of women in society and within marriage. She claimed she wrote the gripping narrative of her heroic, forty-day journey in the dead of the winter of 1815 from Russia to France—following the path of Napoleon's bloody retreat, accompanied only by her terrified seven-year-old son, a hysterical lady's maid, and two rascally servants—to prove that "many undertakings which appear very difficult and arduous to my Sex, are by no means so trying as imagination forever depicts them." In the early Victorian era in which she lived, such assertive views on the role of women were becoming unfashionable and unwelcome.[3]

Louisa also anticipated—by several years—a number of causes that, as the nineteenth century progressed, would have critical social and political implications. She admired and corresponded with the feminist and abolitionist sisters Angelina and Sarah Grimké and assisted them in gathering material for a book about the politics of emancipation. She also understood and championed the rights of Native Americans: "The splendour of this Country originated in the persecution and extermination of a large portion of the aboriginal owners of this Country: and now see them rising in their strength, and struggling to maintain themselves upon the last remnants of their mighty possessions still unjustly coveted," she wrote in 1841.[4]

Louisa's assets as the wife of a senator, ambassador, secretary of state, and president were exceptional. Her fluent French—an indispensable asset in diplomatic circles of the time—made her unique among early First Ladies. Very few women in Washington, or in the country as a whole, rivaled her combination of wide reading, accomplished writing, and talent as a musician. None brought to the White House her keen understanding of diplomacy, nourished by long experience in the royal courts of Prussia, Russia, and Britain. She understood precisely how state business was routinely conducted at formal receptions and how the placement of a dinner guest could have international repercussions.

Nonetheless, Louisa is not found in the pantheon of American heroines or even on a short list of widely admired First Ladies. This may be a case of guilt by association. Despite the best efforts of his able biographers and his own voluminous, carefully polished diaries and memoirs, John Quincy has never really emerged as a likable person. Acclaimed as the hero of the *Amistad* affair, as a founder of American diplomacy, and as a great secretary of state, he is also remembered as the alleged beneficiary of a particularly unsavory political deal that installed him in the White House in 1825—despite his having lost both the popular and the Electoral College votes—and as a relatively ineffective and unsuccessful one-term president.

The less-than-flattering picture drawn of him by his contemporaries was of a cold, pinch-nosed Yankee, disdainful of others' opinions and intellectual attainments, rigid in his own beliefs, and judgmental in his moral superiority. In a tour de force of rueful self-knowledge—and acknowledging his inability to change his personality in any essential way—the sixth president said of himself, "I am a man of reserved, cold, austere, and forbidding manners. . . . My political adversaries say, a gloomy misanthropist, and my personal enemies, an unsocial savage."[5]

If we had only these negative assessments or John Quincy's extraordinary daily diary by which to assess his personality, we would have little sense of his capacity for love and ardor, his self-deprecating sense of humor, or his volatile temper. We would come upon very few direct references in his diary to Louisa and might conclude that his feelings for her were unusually passive and remote. Similarly, since Louisa's two unfinished memoirs tend to leave the reader with the false impression that much of her life was filled with self-abnegation and painful memories, we would have difficulty comprehending why she was so truly beloved by four generations of Adams men—her husband, father-in-law, three sons, and four grandsons. Late in his life John Adams wrote to an old friend that John Quincy's "marriage was the most fortunate event in his life," and it is virtually certain the sixth president would have agreed.[6]

As their lifelong correspondence abundantly shows, Louisa deeply loved John Quincy, and he loved her. But their marriage was never easy. Both were quick-tempered, ambitious for themselves and their sons, and stubborn in their beliefs. Louisa's many illnesses and bouts of depression were a perennial trial to her husband—about which he never complained. For her part, Louisa nursed resentments over a lifetime. She had good cause to do so. John Quincy refused to consult her about some of the most momentous personal, financial, and career decisions of their life together, including that of leaving their two young sons, ages six and eight, with his parents in Massachusetts for what turned out to be six years of diplomatic service in Russia—years that would be critical to the boys' education and emotional development—and his decision to return to Washington for seventeen years as a congressman following his humiliating defeat for a second term as president. Although more than one historian has attributed much of any political success her husband achieved to the vastly superior social skills of Louisa, the flinty New Englander never seemed to recognize her contribution to the achievement of what had been his and his parents' ultimate goal—the American presidency—and, especially in the early years of their marriage and during their occupancy of the White House, he was reluctant to discuss matters of state with her. After fifty years of a demanding relationship, Louisa was left with few illusions; to her son, Charles, she wryly acknowledged, "hanging and marriage [are] strongly assimilated."[7]

For her own part, Louisa is responsible for much of the dismissive way she has been viewed over the past century and a half. It was she who downplayed her role in history as negligible—the second of her two long, autobiographical fragments, written in 1840, is titled "Adventures of a Nobody." Her sense of personal frustration and failure, coupled with a palpable need to justify herself to her only surviving son as "someone who was," tarnish her memoirs with bitterness. Her reminiscences of an idyllic girlhood, which she wrote during and after the Adamses' miserable White House years, cannot be trusted for accuracy. Typically, Louisa turned to her diaries to vent her frustrations with her husband, her worries about her health, and her complaints about life in general. Navigating this negative terrain has until now discouraged even the most intrepid biographer.[8]

Louisa's story, when it has been told, has been framed in conjunction with her husband's. Because John Quincy maintained his remarkable diary from 1779 until just before his death in 1848—and indeed Louisa used his diaries to guide her in writing her own memoirs—and was a prolific letter writer and controversial public figure whose activities were widely reported as they took place, the sheer volume of material pertaining directly to him overwhelms all that is known about his wife. Henry Adams hoped to remedy this imbalance. He planned to publish his grandmother's writings in three volumes and got as far as copying out by hand some 90,000 words before he abandoned the project.[9]

In the past decade, however, Louisa has begun to move to center stage. Beginning with Catherine Allgor's scholarly *Parlor Politics* and Cokie Roberts's *Ladies of Liberty*—a study of notable American women and First Ladies in the early nineteenth century—Louisa's role in creating the social structures essential to building the enduring framework of the federal government is given full credit. Michael O'Brien's analysis of her first forty years, *Mrs. Adams in Winter*—focusing on her epic journey from St. Petersburg to Paris in 1815—brings Louisa to life against a European background roiled by war. The Massachusetts Historical Society has devoted two volumes of its monumental Adams Papers project to Louisa's diaries and autobiographical fragments.

But the full story of her life—a fascinating saga of a living contradiction—has yet to be told. Witty, talented, and charming, Louisa could also be ill-tempered, insecure, and self-pitying. She loved being the center of attention but was often agonizingly shy. A tender and loving mother, she could be painfully harsh in admonishing her sons. A feminist and abolitionist by conviction, she drew back from participating in any efforts to change the status quo. Possessing only a minimal education, she managed to develop a highly literate writing style. Born in London and raised in France and England, she mastered American electoral politics well enough to help engineer the election of her husband to the presidency. Never personally wealthy, she conquered the outrageously extravagant royal courts of Europe in ball gowns she hastily constructed herself, at least once from drawing-room draperies. She endured nine miscarriages and a stillbirth only to lose an adored toddler daughter to typhus, a son to suicide, and another to alcoholism. Dismissed at first glance by her mother-in-law as a fragile "fine lady," she became the emotional linchpin of the Adams dynasty.

Thirty years ago, in the front hallway of the Old House, the Adams family home in Quincy, Massachusetts, I came across an arresting portrait of Louisa Catherine Adams as a lovely young woman. Her level, appraising glance challenged me to pay her respect. What was it about this fiercely independent spirit, whose place in American history has, until now, gone largely unrecognized, that enabled her eventually to win the outpouring of esteem and affection that crowned her long public and private life in her adopted country? This book is my answer to that challenge.

HALCYON DAYS

All the scenes of my infancy . . . float upon my fancy like visions which never could have any reality yet like visions of delight in which all was joy and peace and love.

— LOUISA CATHERINE ADAMS, *"Record of a Life"*

Louisa wove her myth of an idyllic childhood around "the handsomest man I have ever seen," her adored father, Joshua Johnson. In his daughter's eyes, Joshua's "temper was admirable; his tastes simple; his word sacred; and his heart pure and affectionate as that of the most unsophisticated Child of Nature." Others may have harbored a more jaundiced view of Joshua's moral compass, but Louisa never wavered in her loyalty. It was, after all, her father's willingness to seize the main chance that had provided the luxurious backdrop for the "visions of delight" that warmed her memory.[1]

Sprawling, chaotic London was the place to be in 1771 if you were vigorous, restless, and hungry to make your fortune. Joshua perfectly fit the mold. A twenty-nine-year-old partner in the Annapolis mercantile firm Wallace, Davidson, and Johnson, he had arrived in London with a simple, audacious plan: cut out the middleman. If he could buy tea, calico, shoes, cutlery, and china directly from English manufacturers and suppliers, his firm would make a higher profit on sales of these products in America than if it employed London-based agents.

Joshua's task would require boldness, cunning, and charm. A stranger to the City of London's complex web of banking and trade, he first had to convince exporters to deal with him instead of with a familiar network of middlemen. He then had to identify those merchants who could offer him the most flexible and generous credit—a necessity considering the time lag in making transatlantic payments on the goods he hoped to ship overseas and sell in Annapolis.

Just before the American Revolution, Britain was coming into its own as the most powerful colonial power on earth. War with France over control of the North American colonies—called, in England, the Seven Years' War; in

America, the French and Indian War—had ended in Britain's favor just seven years earlier. London, the largest city in the world and the center of international trade, teemed with nearly a million men, women, and children, most living in heartbreaking poverty in the city's East End. But the mid-eighteenth century had also seen historic growth in middle-class prosperity, fueled by the beginnings of the Industrial Revolution and the increasing dominance of England in maritime trade. Even the top tiers of society had begun to be infiltrated by self-made men and, trailing rich dowries, their daughters.

King George III, at thirty-three nearly Joshua's contemporary, had been on the British throne for eleven years. He ruled an empire that included Canada, the American colonies, islands in the Caribbean, and outposts in India and Africa. The wealth of his realm depended on trade within the Empire—huge quantities of manufactured goods sent to North America and the West Indies in exchange for tobacco, sugar, cotton, and wheat. A flourishing triangular trade involving African slaves shipped to the West Indies and the southern American states in exchange for raw materials like tobacco and sugar was at its height. Signs of prosperity were everywhere—in the newly lighted and paved streets, the busy shops, and the leafy squares graced by stately brick townhouses.

Now playing on a world-class stage, the handsome, mercurial Joshua knew he had to look the part. Throughout his life, he cared deeply about appearances, and although Annapolis society in the 1700s was as elegant as any in America, he desperately feared being taken for an unsophisticated colonial. Within a week of arriving in England he headed for the tailor's. "I am getting clothes made and shall have more the appearance of a Londoner," he reported in his first hurried dispatch to his business partners at home.[2]

Louisa later described her father as the "descendant of an English Gentleman," and he was indeed a member of a prominent Maryland family descended from an equally well-respected clan of the same name in Great Yarmouth, Norfolk, England. Joshua (1742–1802) was the eighth of eleven children, and one of seven sons, born to Thomas Johnson II (1702–c. 1777), a Maryland planter who served from time to time in the Maryland state legislature, and Dorcas Sedgwick Johnson. Joshua's older brother, Thomas III (1732–1819), was a delegate to the first Continental Congress, where he became a good friend of John Adams. He was later elected the first Revolutionary governor of Maryland, and, briefly (1792–1793), served as an associate justice of the U.S. Supreme Court. For a younger son like Joshua, it would have been made clear early on that he was responsible for making his own way in the world. At a young age, he was apprenticed in the countinghouse, or office, of a merchant who had emigrated from Scotland. There he would probably have learned the rudiments of accounting as well as the business of transatlantic trade. In his early twenties Joshua seems to have set himself up as a retail merchant in Annapolis. He must have had some early success because, just before departing for England, he entered into partnership with the older and better-established Charles Wallace and John Davidson as a full member of the firm.[3]

Wallace and Davidson believed they could adequately maintain their young partner in London on the profits realized by not having to pay various agents' commissions and by the more advantageous credit terms they expected him to negotiate with London merchants. Crucially, their plan assumed a firm financial market in both England and America, continuing strong demand in Annapolis for European goods, and sustained high tobacco prices in Maryland to ensure full coffers from which Annapolis and Chesapeake Bay planters and professionals could pay for their goods. The strategy was initially successful. Joshua, who had been staked by the firm to £3,000, began by fulfilling the orders he had brought with him from Annapolis. A month and a half after his arrival in London, he was able to dispatch a large shipload of goods to his partners in Annapolis. Elated with his success and taking his cue from the opulence all around him, he immediately began to cast himself as a "Gentleman and a Partner." He moved from cheap lodgings to more comfortable quarters in the heart of the City's financial and mercantile district, and his living expenses quickly began to mount. In Annapolis, Wallace and Davidson protested, not for the last time, that their young partner was living extravagantly, but Joshua was not deterred: "It is a maxim with me that I had rather sink the profits of my labour than to diminish my partners and self in the good opinion of the world. It has added all the consequence to us that I wished, as it has stripped me of the appearance of a transient person," he replied to their complaints.[4]

Wallace, Davidson, and Johnson's business in London was at first limited to exporting household goods and clothing for retail sale in Maryland, but it soon expanded to include a tobacco trade in conjunction with Chesapeake Bay growers. Between 1773 and 1775, the partners handled as much as 70 percent of Maryland's tobacco exports. Joshua, meanwhile, expanded the firm's business interests to include insurance and other services and appears to have speculated privately in tobacco. As a result, he now had more than the appearance of wealth to recommend him; he was, at least temporarily, a man of property.[5]

Joshua's newfound prosperity could not have come at a more opportune moment. In December 1773, at age thirty-one, he had become the father of a baby girl, Ann (invariably called Nancy). The infant's mother was Catherine Young Nuth (or Newth) (1758?–1811), probably sixteen years old. Three months before Nancy was born, Joshua was insisting in letters home to Maryland that there was no truth to the rumor he was married. "A man must possess true courage indeed to engage in the matrimonial way. . . . I am content to let the more enterprising enjoy the charmer with all her charms." In November 1773, with Nancy's arrival imminent, Joshua informed his partners that his expenses would continue to increase and that he required a combined "dwelling house, counting house, and sample house" in which to carry on the firm's business and entertain visiting American merchants. There was no mention of raising a family in such an establishment.[6]

In fact, no record of a marriage between Joshua and Catherine around the time of Nancy's birth date has ever been located, although several biographers and genealogists, including an expert hired by Joshua's great-grandson Henry Adams, have made valiant efforts to do so. Joshua may not have been alone in wishing to keep the relationship under wraps. The prospective bride was legally a minor in 1773 and, at fifteen or sixteen, well under the average age (twenty-three) when English women of the time married. There may have been objections to a wedding on the part of her parents, who would have been required to provide their consent since a parish priest would have refused to celebrate the marriage without it. Catherine, herself, may have been illegitimate and estranged from one of her parents. Yet, as Nancy was duly baptized as legitimate in January 1774, a priest must have been convinced that a wedding had taken place before her birth.[7]

The priest was almost certainly misled. Joshua and Catherine did not marry until August 22, 1785—more than eleven years after Nancy's birth and ten years after the arrival of Louisa—at a time when they were already the parents of six living children. Their wedding, celebrated on a Monday by the curate of Saint Anne's Soho, took place in a part of London far from their Tower Hill mansion and under a civil jurisdiction distinct from that of St. Botolph Aldgate and All Hallows Barking, the two parish churches where their London-born children were baptized.[8]

Soho, then as now, was notorious for its raffish bohemianism and was home to prostitutes, music halls, and abundant pubs and bars. According to the St. Anne's Soho marriage register, curate John Jefferson affirmed that Joshua and Catherine were "of this parish" and had posted banns (typically for the three preceding weeks) before their marriage. It is possible that St. Anne's Soho, reflecting the ethos of its parish population, had a reputation as a church where few questions were asked of a prospective bride and groom and where a contribution to the curate's personal funds was not unwelcome, but precisely how Joshua and Catherine managed to marry without alerting anyone—except their two witnesses—will never be known. The small expatriate American community in London was effectively kept in the dark: no rumor of the secret wedding apparently reached the ears of John and Abigail Adams, who were living in England at the time and were occasional dinner guests of the Johnsons. Just as significantly, the Johnson children seem to have remained unaware that all but the two youngest daughters in the family had been born out of wedlock. There is no hint in any of Louisa's letters or autobiographical fragments to indicate she might have suspected there were any shadows surrounding her birth.

It may have been one of their witnesses, their longtime friend Elizabeth Hewlett, portrayed later by Louisa as "a very excentric woman of strong mind and still stronger passions," who persuaded Joshua and Catherine, after eleven years and seven children (one of whom had died), to make legal what they had successfully passed off as a fait accompli for so long. Throughout their lives together, the Johnsons had appeared in all respects to be legally married, and they were socially accepted as a married couple. They moved easily in American expatriate society and served as the London home away from home for many well-connected young men from the colonies who found themselves in London for business, study, or pleasure before and after the Revolution. Well-to-do American families would have been unlikely to have put their sons under the Johnsons' protection had there been a cloud over their marital status. All of the Johnson children were baptized as legitimate, a fact that may indicate their parents considered themselves married from the outset.[9]

Louisa idealized her parents' marital relationship, particularly, as time went on, when her own proved so different. As she remembered it, her father worshipped her beautiful, delicate, alluring mother: "My father seemed to hang on every word she uttered and gazed on her with looks of love and admiration 'as if an encrease of appetite had grown by what it fed on' never did man love woman with a devotion so perfect—His sparkling eye beamed on her with an excess of tenderness and his smile seemed to blend all those good and amiable feelings which spring spontaneous from a faithful and benevolent heart—She was his pride his joy his love and in her and his Children was concentrated all that made life desirable."[10]

Louisa also fondly recalled that her father's devotion to Catherine was so great that, if she felt unwell, he would cut her food and warm her fork, wrapping it in a napkin and heating it by the fire. It is not surprising that in later life, when her own world became achingly hard and she felt herself unloved and unappreciated, Louisa seemed to turn to illness as a way to elicit sympathy and attention.[11]

In her parents, she was also witness to a pattern in marriages that flourished at the end of the eighteenth century, went into decline during the Victorian era, and did not emerge again until the twentieth century—a union in which husband and wife were bonded not as master and servant but as loving partners and companions. (Abigail and John Adams—who addressed one another in their letters as "My Dearest Friend"—were another prime example of this marital model.) Again and again, Louisa would look back—sometimes ruefully—on the mutual respect and appreciation she called "domestic felicity" that appeared to characterize her parents' relationship and that was often missing from her own.

Though in Louisa's eyes Joshua was the strong, central personality around whom the family gathered, Catherine was much more than a delicate, lovely flower, reclining on the parlor settee while a warmed fork was held to her lips. Catherine was a force to be reckoned with. Like other gentlewomen of her time, she probably handled the family's finances, and her decisions regarding the daily management of a complex household, which eventually included eight growing children, many long-term guests, and eleven servants, would have been respected.

Ambitious for her family, Catherine was an exceptional beauty, a gracious hostess, a brilliant conversationalist, and an excellent, if extravagant, household manager. In later years, she would be welcomed to the White House by Thomas Jefferson and invited to Mount Vernon by George and Martha Washington. Louisa, writing of the way she remembered Catherine at the time when she herself was a teenager, described her charm: "My Mother had been beautiful; she was at this time very lovely, her person was very small, and exquisitely delicate, and very finely proportioned. She was lively; her understanding highly cultivated, and her wit brilliant, sometimes almost too keen."[12]

Catherine must have had some education—as had most girls, except those in the very lowest classes at the time—and her lively letters, written in a fine hand, demonstrate an easy command of spelling and composition. In later years, Abigail Adams delighted in hearing from her: "I shall be happy to learn from your pen whatever occurs worthy of observation, for tho retired from the world I like to know what is passing in it—especially if I can obtain it from one who is so capable of describing Life & Manners," the former First Lady wrote her friend in November 1809.[13]

Since Catherine's letters to Abigail are as yet missing, their special quality has to be judged by the pleasure both John and Abigail Adams took in reading them. In the former president's estimation, "She was a woman of fine Understanding and held an ingenious Pen. A constant correspondence with

[Abigail] was a high entertainment to us, full of useful information." The feisty Adams was not in the habit of praising the "fine Understanding" and "ingenious Pen" of even the most highly educated of his contemporaries, let alone a woman who died a poor widow of uncertain parentage. He recognized in Catherine Johnson a quality of mind that must have been nurtured in her youth by something finer than the street sophistication picked up from the prostitutes with whom she has sometimes been relegated. Later generations of Adamses and their biographers may have raised questions concerning Catherine's origins, but there is no hint that the former President and First Lady had anything but admiration for her.[14]

Everything about Catherine—her exquisite taste and style, her ability to manage a large household, her literacy—seems consistent with a solidly upper-middle-class background. Yet nearly every detail in her background is frustratingly vague. Even her maiden name has not been verified. Baptismal records in 1782 for Louisa's younger sister Harriet, born in France, list the child's mother's maiden name as Catherine Young, and Louisa, writing in 1825, referred to her maternal grandmother as "Miss" Young: "[In London my father] became acquainted with my Mother of whose family I knew very little as some misunderstanding had subsisted for some years indeed ever since the death of my Grandmother which had cut of[f] all communication between my father and Grandfather whose character was I am sorry to say very indifferent—My Grandmother was a Miss Young extremely beautiful and I always [heard] her represented as possessing qualities and virtues of the highest order."[15]

Later, in a brief undated genealogical note, probably for her son Charles, Louisa wrote: "My Grand Mothers name was Mary Young. She was the daughter of a Brewer . . . [and] married Mr. Nuth. They had twenty two living Children born but only reared two—My Mother Catherine Nuth and A Son who at fourteen years of Age was sent out by the East Indian Company as Cadet and was always supposed to have perished in one of the expeditions sent up into the back Country. I remember my Grandfather who died at the Age of ninety-six—I think when I was about 12 or 13 years of age."[16]

Though genealogists have so far been unsuccessful in tracking down any evidence of a young man named Nuth in the East Indian service or a brewer named Young, there is no reason to doubt that Louisa knew her grandparents—if not well—and that she accepted, as given, family accounts of her maternal antecedents.

For reasons that remain unclear, Joshua remained unwilling to announce to his partners, family, and friends the news that he was a husband and father. Or if he did, neither he nor any recipient appears to have retained such a letter.

Joshua's voluminous correspondence (of which he kept careful copies) with his Annapolis partners, ship's captains, and friends continued to spell out elaborate details regarding his health and personal expenses but contained no word of his radically changed circumstances until much later (1776) when he asked a ship's captain to bring back some linen from St. Petersburg for "Mrs. Johnson."[17]

Meanwhile, on February 12, 1775, Catherine had given birth to a second daughter, Louisa Catherine, who was duly baptized in London on March 9, 1775. Again, there seems to have been no birth announcement to friends and family. The baby was baptized in the church of St. Botolph without Aldgate, a tall, steepled, brick edifice completed just a year earlier and located in the heart of the old City of London. The address of infant and parents is listed in the parish records as Swan Street, then a narrow cross-street midway between the church and the River Thames.[18]

Louisa's baptism took place just a month before the battles at Lexington and Concord signaled the outbreak of the American Revolution. In the years leading up to the war, Joshua had found himself in a particularly delicate situation. In 1774, Parliament had passed what became known in America as the Intolerable Acts, laws that were specifically aimed at punishing Massachusetts for the Boston Tea Party. Troops were stationed in Boston, the royal governor was given near-dictatorial power, and the port was closed. Patriots up and down the Atlantic seacoast were roused to action and, in September and October 1774, the First Continental Congress (with John Adams of Massachusetts and Joshua's brother Thomas of Maryland among the fifty-five delegates attending) was held in Philadelphia.

The Continental Congress adopted a set of resolutions that committed the colonies to boycotting British goods and to ceasing exports if the Acts were not repealed. In Annapolis, Wallace and Davidson began to wrap up their overseas business, while, in London, Joshua was able to pay off their London tradesmen and make a tidy profit for the firm on the last shipments of tobacco anybody expected to see for some time. In fact, the firm ended its brief London experience on a high note: as tobacco prices soared after the outbreak of hostilities, Joshua seems to have reaped a windfall, some of which he may have retained for himself.[19]

Even as his second child was on the way, Joshua spoke out in support of the American position ("Your cause is noble; it's for liberty you struggle. Persevere, be steady and faithful to each other and the Almighty will conquer for you") and informed his partners that he wanted to come home to "share the dangers in Protecting their liberties." In March 1775, when Louisa was a month old, Joshua wrote a friend that, although he could not leave England at once, he expected to be on his way by Christmas.[20]

As a vocal pro-American, Joshua was becoming increasingly uncomfortable in England. He believed he was being watched by the British Secret Service, which had mounted an elaborate and largely successful effort to monitor the activities of Benjamin Franklin, Silas Deane, and Arthur Lee, who were attempting to secure critical military and financial assistance from France for the rebellious colonies. Joshua and the few American merchants remaining in London in the early years of the war were small fish compared to the American commissioners in France, but as they were men experienced in transatlantic communications and trade, it was prudent for the British government to keep them under surveillance. Joshua's mail was opened and reviewed even though he used a variety of pseudonyms, and a trip he made to France in 1777 was reported to the British Secret Service. When his older daughters were teenagers, Joshua loved to tell anecdotes of the risks he had run for the American cause, probably making his adventures a little more dramatic with each retelling, but whether he actually engaged in espionage is unknown.[21]

Joshua, after all, did not return to Maryland. Had he been the single man he purported to be, he would have had little trouble securing a berth on a ship back to Maryland, despite the threat of British warships on the high seas. But by the end of 1777, he had become a father twice more. Carolina Virginia Marylanda (baptized October 5, 1776, and named in a burst of patriotism) and Mary Ann (baptized December 25, 1777) had joined Nancy and Louisa in the nursery. Few responsible seamen would have agreed to transport a very young mother with four tiny girls, the eldest only four years old, through stormy winter seas across the Atlantic in the middle of a war. Catherine herself may have been reluctant to renounce the country of her birth and risk her life and that of her babies so that her husband could return to Maryland to participate in that war.

On February 6, 1778, the three American commissioners signed the long-awaited treaty "of commerce and amity" between France and the United States. Relocating to France now became more attractive for the Johnsons than remaining in London or attempting the dangerous midwinter Atlantic crossing to America. By May, the family—father, mother, and four little girls—had settled in Nantes, a bustling seaport on the River Loire, flush with success in the burgeoning slave trade.[22]

In Nantes, the Johnsons lived in baronial splendor in the city's most fashionable section, one inhabited largely by nouveau riche slave traders. Their apartment was in a magnificent building christened "Le Temple du Goût" ("The Temple of

Taste") by local citizens. Built in 1750 in an exuberant Baroque style, the majestic six-story mansion—with access both to the riverfront quay and to the narrow, cobblestoned street that bisects the tiny Ile Feydeau at the edge of the old medieval city—featured intricately designed wrought-iron balustrades lining the outer-facing balconies of each of the upper floors and massive, vaulted interior stairways. Elaborate stone carvings of heads (*mascarons*), some apparently African inspired, embellished the keystones over the floor-to-ceiling windows opening out onto each balcony. A passageway, marked by a parade of ornate marble pilasters, led into an expansive interior courtyard. Always a man to value style and sophistication, Joshua must have seen Le Temple du Goût as the ultimate emblem of his business success. Years later Louisa remembered her early experiences in France as magical, and, bathed in the glow of nostalgia, her glamorous mother and handsome father became a fairy-tale couple around whom "all was joy and peace and love."

It was a heady time for the entire family. The thriving merchant community of Nantes was wide open to foreigners and newcomers, and, compared to stratified British society, class distinctions mostly seem to have been blurred. Attracted by Joshua's warm welcome and Catherine's beauty and wit, diplomats, seafarers, and traders from around the globe regularly found their way to the Johnsons' spacious apartment in Le Temple du Goût. It was here that the couple's future reputation for gracious hospitality had its roots.[23]

Even while laying out the funds he thought were necessary to maintain the lifestyle and appearance of a rich and successful merchant, Joshua appears to have made his five-year stay in France a comparatively profitable one. Soon after the French-American treaty of cooperation was signed, the State of Maryland made him its agent in France, where he was commissioned to borrow money and conduct other business for the government in Annapolis. For a brief period, he also represented Congress in Nantes, which had become a major embarkation point for American and French officials, military personnel, and merchants traveling between the two countries.

He continued to pursue other ways to make money as well. By June 1781, three years after the family had arrived in Nantes, conditions on the high seas had become stable enough for maritime trading to resume on a more lucrative scale. Joshua, his former partner, Wallace, and another Annapolis merchant, John Muir, formed a new firm to take advantage of the business potential promised by trade between France and the new American nation created under the Articles of Confederation. Joshua was not the only member of the family moving French goods back to Annapolis; as early as July 1781, Catherine had herself become a trader. With characteristic ambition and drive, apparently using her own—possibly inherited—funds, she plunged into the mercantile business. As she recovered from the birth of her daughter Harriet in June 1781, she dictated to Joshua clear instructions to his Annapolis partners: "Inclosed we forward you an invoice . . . amounting to £502 which Mrs. Johnson [begs] you will please to receive & Dispose of on her acct. for Bills or hard money *only* & remit the net proceeds immediately in good bills of exchange on Europe. She has prepared two other parcels nearly similar to this, which we shall forward you in a few days . . . we shall at the same time write you as Mrs. Johnson's indisposition will prevent her from doing it herself. . . . Mrs. J. present[s] her compliments to you & begs you will be regular in your correspondence with her."[24]

Meanwhile, Catherine continued to give birth at regular intervals—a son, Thomas, had been born two years previously. The Johnson children now numbered five—one-year-old Mary Ann had died shortly after the family's arrival in France—and Joshua began to mention his wife and children proudly and openly in his letters home to Annapolis.

In the spring of 1779, a frequent visitor to Le Temple du Goût was the Massachusetts patriot John Adams, who had replaced Silas Deane on the three-man wartime commission delegated to represent the new American nation to France, its most important ally. Now that Congress had decided to disband the commission and retain only Benjamin Franklin as minister plenipotentiary to the Court of Louis XVI, Adams had suddenly become a private citizen and was eager to return home. With his eleven-year-old son, John Quincy, who had accompanied his father during his assignment to France, he had been scheduled to sail from Nantes in April on an American frigate. At the last minute, however, Franklin sent word that they were, instead, to travel in company with the recently designated French ambassador to the United States aboard a French ship that was not due to leave until July.

Making the best of this enforced delay, Adams's Nantes diaries report frequent meetings, either at tea or dinner, at the Johnsons, during which his host expounded on his concept of the role of a U.S. consul. Joshua seemed to be not only auditioning for the job but also seeking to make it as personally profitable as possible. He proposed that each ship entering the port should be taxed a fixed amount per ton to cover the expenses of the consul's taking care of "unfortunate Americans, Prisoners, Shipwrecked Persons, etc." and that no one should leave a ship unless cleared by the consul, presumably for a fee. Joshua promoted Nantes, rather than another port city, as the appropriate place for a consular mission: "The Advantages of the River, and of the foreign Merchants settled there, are his [Joshua's] chief Argument. You have the Productions and

Manufactures of Paris, and the whole Country, at Nantes by Water, by means of the Loire," Adams recorded in his diary.[25]

Many years later, Adams speculated that "this match [between his son and daughter-in-law] grew out of the spark that was kindled at Nantes in 1779 when he was with me frequently in the Family of Mr. Johnson," but it was unlikely that a studious eleven-year-old boy, accustomed to the conversation of adults, would have wasted a minute on a four-year-old girl. The precocious youth was kept occupied by his father in translating Cicero's first Philippic against Catiline from the Latin text and observing the work of engineers, architects, and ship-builders in the busy port. And although John Adams often reported "drinking tea at Mrs. Johnson's," he did not mention any evidence of a family.[26]

Had either Adams paid a visit to the Johnson nursery, however, they would not have found six-year-old Nancy or four-year-old Louisa. For more than a year, they had been installed in a convent-run boarding school on the upper floors of Le Temple de Goût. To place a three-year-old in a convent boarding school was not an unusual approach to upper-class child rearing in eighteenth-century France. If, as Louisa later wrote, the opulence of Le Temple du Goût had "turned the head of a beautiful and much admired young woman," Catherine may have wanted to free herself from the care of fractious toddlers. In any event, her decision to board her tiny girls away from home, even in the same building, probably raised few eyebrows—the small daughters of Louis XV, a generation earlier, had been sent to school at the abbey at Fontevrault at ages five, four, two, and one. Typically, at a convent school, very young girls from aristocratic or leading bourgeois families were taught singing, dancing, social graces, needlework, and basic literacy skills. The rigors of a classical education were available only to their brothers. Molière was only one of several theorists who argued that the two objectives of a young girl's education should be character formation to ensure moral conduct in later years and training in household management.[27]

Such training, even when it was provided, played a secondary role to religion in a convent school. When he arrived in Paris in 1784 to assist Adams and Franklin in negotiating commercial treaties, Thomas Jefferson, a religious skeptic, wasted no time in enrolling his twelve-year-old daughter Patsy in the Abbaye de Panthemont, the city's most fashionable convent school, but he negotiated a special arrangement to ensure she would not be "indoctrinated." Nevertheless, Patsy witnessed all of the school's Roman Catholic rituals, including, at least once, the taking of vows by three novice nuns. Such picturesque ceremonies designed to reinforce young girls' religious ardor and encourage their older sisters to join the teaching order, making it self-perpetuating, were central to the convent school experience. Home visits were reduced to a minimum so that the young girls in the nuns' care would remain pure and innocent.[28]

Louisa, a highly sensitive child, did not recall missing her parents or learning to read or write, but she clearly remembered "the strong impression made upon my imagination by the Roman Catholick Church the heartfelt humility with which I knelt before the Image of the tortured Jesus and the horror I felt at the thought, of mixing with hereticks. The veneration with which I entered the Convents the great affection I bore to one particular Nun who used to bring toys for sale to School."

At three, Louisa would have been barely proficient in English; of necessity she now absorbed the perfect French that would be such an asset throughout her life. She claimed that by the time she left the convent school in 1783 she had forgotten all the English she had ever known except "Yes" and "No." If that were true, it would mean that she spent no time at all with her parents, as Joshua and Catherine naturally would have conversed with their daughters in English. In reality, Louisa must have spent weeks at a time at home in Le Temple du Goût because her memories of life in the mansion were remarkably vivid for someone not yet eight years old. Describing the wedding of the family coachman, she wrote, "The Bride was a dark complexioned rosy looking woman dressed in a large flowered Calico with a most enormous bouquet—They went to Church in my fathers Carriage and had the use of it for the day. My father gave them a handsome Supper and Ball and I still seem to see the Bride and Bridegroom opening the Ball with all the gaiety of french sprightliness."[29]

It is significant that Louisa's memories are entirely of her father's generosity and that her mother did not appear in the festive wedding scene or in other recollections of her childhood. Catherine, at the peak of her beauty, seems to have been a remote presence in her daughter's early life. During the family's final months in France, Louisa became "more familiarized with the acquaintance of my Mother which was very large," a hint that Catherine may have appeared to the young girl as more glamorous and party-loving than maternal.

These last months in Nantes Louisa also remembered as a period "full of pleasure and being more at home," an acknowledgment that separation from her parents during her earliest, formative years had been difficult. As she neared her eighth birthday in February 1783, she became ill with pleurisy, which caused great "apprehensions in my dear parents for my life as they feared that consumption would ensue." When a preliminary peace agreement between Britain and the United States was signed in December 1782, Joshua was eager to be the first American merchant to return to the London mercantile market. For a year he had been depositing capital with British bankers to ensure his credit for the moment when he could begin trading again. He was convinced that by concentrating on tobacco consignments from Maryland and supplying the firm's stores in Annapolis with retail goods from England, the partnership of Wallace, Johnson, and Muir would easily outstrip their trading rivals, particularly if they got a head start. In April 1783, the entire Johnson family left Nantes for London.

On their way to England, the Johnsons stopped in Paris, where they paid a call on the distinguished diplomat John Jay, who, with Adams and Franklin, had negotiated the treaty that finally ended the American Revolution. All her life, Louisa remembered the graciousness and "unbounded kindness" of Sarah Livingston Jay in welcoming the Johnson children to her "handsome establishment," but she also never forgot how embarrassed she was that she, her sisters, and even her mother had overdressed for the occasion. Two little girls accompanying Mrs. Jay were "dressed in the plain english fashion white Frocks and Pink Sashes which appeared to me much prettier than the fine silk dress and hoop which I was used to wear." Even at eight, Louisa was more sensitive to the nuances of fashion and propriety than her mother. Catherine was known to dress extravagantly and loved nothing better than outfitting all her children alike and parading them two-by-two to church: "We were objects of general curiosity and, permit me to say, admiration to the publick. It was a goodly show and well I remember it," Louisa recalled wryly.[30]

Hoops and silk dresses were even more out of place at the boarding school where the three oldest Johnsons were dispatched almost as soon as the family had settled in a large house on Tower Hill in the heart of the City of London. The school, run by a Mrs. Carter, was in the village of Shacklewell in the nearby London borough of Hackney. It was not an easy transition, at least for Louisa, as "in consequence of our extraordinary dress and utter ignorance of English we became objects of ridicule to the whole School which consisted of forty Young Ladies from the ages of seven to twenty."[31]

Sending very young girls away to school was accepted practice among middle-class English families. Joshua and Catherine, on arriving in England after five years in France, had been advised immediately to place their three eldest daughters in Mrs. Carter's care by their friend, the strong-minded Elizabeth Hewlett. The Johnsons yielded, as they often did, to Mrs. Hewlett's advice. Other well-to-do parents sometimes sent their young daughters off to boarding schools for extended periods of time on the strength of a recommendation of a remote relative or casual acquaintance. In her *Plan of Education with Remarks on the Systems of Other Writers* (1792), the author Clara Reeve took these complacent mothers and fathers to task: "What must we think of the negligence and credulity of such parents, who entrust their most sacred treasures . . . to the care of an unknown, ignorant, too frequently unprincipled people."[32]

Jane Austen, born the same year as Louisa, also entered boarding school in 1783. Like Louisa, she was miserable: "One's heart aches for a dejected Mind of eight years old," she wrote many years later on hearing that two of her nieces were reluctantly being sent away to school at the same age. Her famous description in *Emma* of a girls' school in the countryside simultaneously skewers the typical school of the day and sketches a preferable, if not ideal, model: "Mrs. Goddard was the mistress of a school—not a seminary, or an establishment, or anything which professed, in long sentences of refined nonsense, to combine liberal acquirements with elegant morality, upon new principles and new systems—and where young ladies for enormous pay might be screwed out of health and into vanity—but a real, honest, old-fashioned boarding school, where a reasonable quantity of accomplishments were sold at a reasonable price, and where girls might be sent to be out of the way, and scramble themselves into a little education, without any danger of coming back prodigies."[33]

Writing in 1825 of her own school, Louisa's description was remarkably close to Austen's. She acknowledged Mrs. Carter's lack of academic qualifications but excused it on the grounds that parents of the time feared that overeducating their daughters would deprive them of their most desirable feminine attributes: "Mrs. Carter was an uncommonly fine Woman; exact in her discipline and Lady like in her manners. At the present day she would not have been qualified for her situation the stile of education requiring a degree of acquirement which she certainly did not possess. Many of the modern studies not then being thought requisite for the education of Women and being thought to have a tendency to render them masculine."[34]

Mischievously, Louisa also described the headmistress as "a maiden lady and one of the greatest ladies in England, most especially as she was in every respect one of the largest and fattest that England ever produced."[35]

As motherly as Mrs. Carter seems to have been, Louisa's transition from her convent school in Nantes to her boarding school in England was traumatic. Although her more outgoing sisters seem to have adapted to their new situation relatively easily, Louisa recalled "living in a state of constant torment, and being perpetually punished or mortified by those very things which had always before been subjects of admiration. . . . I became serious melancholy and almost gloomy—which caused me to be called Miss Proud by my schoolfellows, and placed me in a more painful situation than ever."[36]

Her situation was exacerbated by her mastery of the French language, which called the accent of the school's French teacher into question and resulted in the humiliation of the student rather than the teacher. "Among the most singular events of my life that of being *untaught* the language which I had acquired in its native elegance and purity, to be taught the execrable jargon then heard in the english schools, was the most extraordinary," Louisa later wrote. A much more painful adjustment to the exquisitely sensitive eight-year-old was the school's requirement that she participate in Anglican worship: "The first time I was forced to go to Church at Hackney I perfectly recollect my horror when my Governess obliged me to kneel down among what I had been taught in France to call the hereticks; which was so great that in the very act of Kneeling I fell as it were dead upon the floor and continued so ill although only eight years old that my father was obliged to take me home."[37]

Louisa's unconscious ploy to be released from school, if that's what it was, was only partially successful. She was dispatched to stay with the Hewletts in the country for two months before being taken back to Mrs. Carter's by her father who, yielding to his daughter's convent-bred religious scruples, insisted that she be allowed to leave Anglican services if they became too painful for her to bear. It was not long before she "quietly conformed to the usages and forgot insensibly all the prejudices which [she] had so early and strongly imbibed."[38]

As in his handling of this episode of religious hysteria, it was typically Joshua who was directly involved in bringing up and educating his older daughters, at least in the period before they were teenagers. If Louisa's memories were accurate, Catherine does not appear to have been influential in any major decisions regarding their early care and training nor does she seem to have been the parent the girls turned to in time of trouble. This lack of maternal oversight could easily be attributed to the fact that Catherine was regularly giving birth during her older daughters' formative years: Catherine Maria arrived in 1784, Eliza Janet in 1786, and Adelaide in 1788. The family now included seven daughters and a son, all born between December 1773 and April 1788.

Catherine was intimately involved, however, when Louisa contracted a serious illness—either typhus or a typhus-like disease—when she was nine. Both parents, she wrote, "watched me night and day with unwearied patience, and cheerfulness: and fondly supported my weary head, and soothed my aching brain." Catherine "while tears ran down her cheeks sat by my bed anxiously noting every change: seemingly busied in dressing my doll, and making its clothes" and, incidentally, ignoring a three-year-old sister watching plaintively from the doorway to the sickroom. Only when it came to administering a blister, a dangerous procedure involving placing hot plasters onto the skin to raise blisters, which were then drained, did Catherine falter. According to Louisa, the family again turned to their no-nonsense friend Elizabeth Hewlett to handle the daunting task; Catherine could not even watch the procedure. As Louisa later told the story, when the blister was drained and the prognosis for the little girl's recovery appeared positive, Mrs. Hewlett fainted for the first time in her life.[39]

Louisa was not the only young girl to become dangerously ill in a school-wide epidemic. Even the most informed parents apparently did not link sanitary conditions in schools with the sometimes fatal diseases that infected their daughters. Samuel Johnson's great friend, Hester Thrale, the wife of a wealthy brewer, was unable to save her four-year-old daughter, Harriet, who was stricken in a measles epidemic at her boarding school; Cassandra Austen nursed her nine-year-old Jane through a nearly fatal infectious fever that had spread through her school at about the same time that Louisa herself became ill. Following these near-death experiences, however, young girls were usually returned to their schools and their younger sisters later dispatched to join them.[40]

In Louisa's case, her return to Mrs. Carter's school after recovering from her illness turned out to be a life-changing decision. No longer among the youngest students, Louisa began to thrive academically, if not socially: "At school, I was universally *respected*, but I was never beloved," she later wrote, describing how the other students would never tell her of their proposed pranks for fear that she might report them. "Pride and haughteur were my predominant failings, and they had the good effect of keeping me out of bad company." She was saved from complete social ostracism, including that of her own sisters, when she made a close friend of another girl, a Miss Edwards, who also stood apart from the other students: "She was as remarkable in her temper and manners as myself: we slept in the same room; we read together, and were almost inseparable: she was an East Indian very dark, with long black indian hair; not handsome, but looked up to by all the Teachers and scholars as a girl of uncommon talents."[41]

The two lonely, "remarkable" pupils were taken in hand by the head teacher, Miss Young, who had been classically educated in the same schoolroom as boys, knew rudimentary Greek and some Latin, and was unusually well read for a woman of the time. Until Louisa was twelve, she benefited from this teacher's favoritism as well as her high academic standards: "Miss Edwards and myself were her decided favorites and we were both apt and quick in learning our different lessons, and very fond of reading; she took much pains to improve us and conversed freely with us upon the books we read, pointing out and selecting, the most beautiful and striking passages, and cultivating our taste by her judgment— Her person was masculine and her manners were forbidding; so that unless she took a particular fancy to any one; fear and dislike kept the young Ladies aloof."[42]

Thus rescued from the vacuous education afforded most young women of her generation, Louisa developed a lifelong passion for learning. In an age in which social graces were paramount and intellectual ability was something to conceal, she would later meet John Quincy Adams on something approaching his own intellectual terms, and their mutual delight in learning and literature became a bedrock of their fifty-year marriage.

Writing her memoirs in 1825, Louisa described her school friend in terms of the greatest respect, without the slightest hint of condescension. Miss Edwards may have been the daughter of an English planter, trader, or government official and an Indian woman, who may or may not have been his wife. Louisa does not comment on her friend's family background, although two homesick young girls sharing a room must have confided secrets to each other. But whatever Louisa knew or suspected about Miss Edwards's antecedents was secondary to her gratitude to her as the single school friend who shared her love of books and learning.[43]

Louisa had not been placed at Mrs. Carter's school to discover classical literature, however. She was expected to learn the arts and graces that would equip her to hold her own in the drawing rooms of her future life. Fortunately, she showed unusual aptitude for music, especially singing. She seems to have had perfect pitch, or something close to it, because she recalled driving her music masters to "despair" by being able to "execute anything at first reading" and, therefore, not needing to practice her assigned pieces. "In hymns or Anthems I was always selected to sing the Solo's or the first part in duets and by degrees acquired a great reputation in the School as a vocalist."[44]

Theatrical entertainments played a major role at the school, and Louisa was very much involved in them. Joseph Addison's *The Tragedy of Cato*, a play in five acts and surely an ambitious project for a troupe of little girls, had to be given up after several rehearsals as the students couldn't find suitable scenery and costumes. But for Hannah More's *The Search After Happiness*, "it was universally admitted that the haughty Euphemia was exactly suited to me," Louisa wrote. She remembered in detail how she planned the scenery, stitching together sheets of white pasteboard into a cottage, incorporating dining tables and green baize carpets into the set, and using houseplants to "produce a very pretty effect [that] succeeded beyond our best hopes." Louisa would rely on her knack for setting a stage with the materials she had at hand again and again throughout her life when she was called upon to entertain diplomats and politicians on a grand scale and to do it with very little money. During school vacations, the three older Johnson girls were treated to trips to the theater and the opportunity to see the great leading actresses of the time, Sarah Siddons and "the elegant Miss [Elizabeth] Farren," perform on the London stage. At home, Catherine's old gowns and hoops provided dress-up costumes for hours of pretending to be great ladies. Louisa, as shy as she was, clearly imagined her future role in life as something out of the ordinary. "I never would be anything but a *Dutchess* and never answered to any title but that of her grace."[45]

As they entered their teens, the three sisters could not have been more different. Nancy, the oldest, was, according to her sister, "vivacious," exceptionally talented on the piano, and "giving promise of great beauty," but, at fifteen, was "cadavorously pale" and so overweight as to be "unwieldy." She had to be removed from school to spend six months in the country to regain her health. Caroline, twenty months younger than Louisa, was "a lovely child, with a flow of natural spirits almost amounting to wildness blended with the most overpowering timidity of character." Whether or not Nancy's weight gain, Louisa's excessive reserve, or Caroline's wildness could be attributed to the apparent absence of their mother in their lives would be a speculative leap; what is clear is that although Louisa remembered her family life as "halcyon days of bliss long past," each of the three sisters entered adolescence with significant personal problems.[46]

Their relationships with each other were fraught with unacknowledged competitiveness as well. Louisa's descriptions of her sisters, admittedly written many years later, seem always to include a positive comment laced with a negative remark. She had not been able to rely on either sibling to stand up for her when the other girls tormented her; they, in turn, must have resented her as she became the head teacher's pet and was allotted solos to sing and star turns to perform. Simply because they were close in age did not make the three Johnson sisters alike or even compatible.

But the three would have to deal with these and other issues at home. Shortly after Louisa's triumph in *The Search After Happiness*, they were removed from Mrs. Carter's school. Joshua, facing another of his recurrent financial crises, could no longer afford to keep them there. Not yet fourteen, Louisa had completed her formal education.

READY FOR LOVE

Marriage . . . was the only honourable provision for well-educated young women of small fortune, and however uncertain of giving happiness, must be their pleasantest preservative from want.

— JANE AUSTEN, *Pride and Prejudice*

For Louisa, home always meant Number 8, Cooper's Row in the City of London. She remembered the brick, multistory mansion, steps away from the Tower of London, as "large, not sumptuous or extravagant, but such as the first Merchants in London at that day usually had: kept a neat Carriage and one pair of Horses, and every thing was conducted in the family with . . . regularity." Joshua, in his daughter's fond reminiscence, presided over a smoothly functioning machine: "My father's establishment was so perfectly regulated though large, that every thing in it moved like clock work; his household consisted of eleven Servants; three of whom had lived with him from the time of his marriage; and all of them were devotedly attached to him. He was a very indulgent Master although strict, and as every thing was methodical, every thing was easy."[1]

If Louisa's memories were accurate, the family was living very extravagantly. This was all too easy to do in postwar London. The cost of living was significantly inflated, and plain living was never Joshua's style. He had always believed that keeping up appearances was essential to his financial well-being as well as his personal self-image, and age and maturity had done nothing to dim his determination to present himself as a man of quality. Maintaining a horse and "neat" carriage, particularly in the city, was one sure sign of wealth. A horse required shelter, feeding, and daily care, all more expensive in the city than in the country. The services of a groom and coachman, as well as blacksmiths, harness makers, and saddlers, would be needed regularly. Moreover, a coach was not really necessary for transportation; hired hackney cabs were readily available in London, particularly in the area around Tower Hill.[2]

Servants, too, were an index of social standing. The eleven men and women employed in the Johnson household represented four more staff than the typical seven in a genteel home at the time. Servants had to be fed, clothed—and ideally—cared for in old age. They needed to be paid—if only a pittance—and hired, trained, and managed on a day-to-day basis. Joshua was a soft touch for hard-luck stories and frequently welcomed into his home stray souls for whom he then had to find a useful role. Louisa recalled that he once "took a french family into his House that is a man and his Wife by the name of Gallement french Emgrants in great distress and professedly Nobles. He was to be Tutor to my Brother She Governess to us Females." Earlier, a former servant, reduced to exhaustion and starvation after her husband had robbed and deserted her, appeared at the doorstep and was taken in and maintained for the rest of her life.[3]

The twenty-one regular inhabitants—master and mistress, eight children, eleven servants—plus occasional hangers-on—must have seemed like a swarming hive to the many long- and short-term visitors who nightly crowded around the dining table and lingered well into the night to hear the older daughters sing and perform on the piano and harp. The Johnsons regularly entertained key members of the fledgling American government—including, in the years when Louisa was still in school, John and Abigail Adams—as well as expatriate artists, merchants, and countless young men temporarily in London to study, represent the family business, or act as a private secretary to a public official. All of this lavish entertaining meant substantial daily expense, but few guests left the family's comfortable fireside with the impression that the Johnsons' finances were anything but solid.

The veneer of success extended to every detail. In the early 1790s, when Louisa was about seventeen, Joshua arranged for individual portraits in miniature to be painted of the entire family, except young Thomas who was away at school. The tiny, elaborate miniatures afforded Joshua an opportunity not only to display the handsome family of which he was justly proud but also to validate his (and their) social standing. Nowhere is this more obvious than in the elaborate hats and gowns worn by Catherine Johnson and her older daughters. Catherine, in the eyes of Abigail Adams, was "conspicuous" for her "taste of elegance," and she would have been determined that her daughters appear equally fashionable, particularly as they approached a marriageable age. Despite his pride in his handsome, well-dressed brood ("remarkable for their beauty," Louisa recalled), the mounting bills from dressmakers and milliners must have constituted a financial burden for their beleaguered father.[4]

How the family could afford to live and entertain in such style remains a mystery. For this model establishment, running like "clock work," was not the home of one of London's "first merchants," as Louisa described it, but a shaky vessel kept afloat by a series of deals, stratagems, and personal loans. This was a reality she could never accept. Blindly loyal to her father and desperate in later life to restore his tainted reputation, Louisa described every decision he made as benevolent and every misfortune the fault of someone else: "Noble in his sentiments; noble in his Acts; he was ever ready to befriend the unfortunate, and his temper was so open and confiding he soon became the victim of fraud and hypocrisy."[5]

But Joshua's colleagues, partners, and customers held a more jaundiced view of his honesty and candor. Always on the lookout for the main chance and perennially operating on the thin edge between bonanza and financial disaster, he missed few chances for personal gain, even if they involved cheating his partners or customers. In the early days of the American Revolution, when he remained in London after most merchants had fled, he told tobacco suppliers in Maryland that he had sold out their crop for seven pence per pound but informed an agent in Holland that he was selling his supply at twelve pence and that he still had a substantial supply on hand. He was rarely entirely candid with his partners concerning speculations he was involved in or debts he had assumed.[6]

In Louisa's memory, Joshua's decision to remove his three older daughters from Mrs. Carter's school in 1788 was based primarily on family rather than business considerations. In reality, Joshua ended his daughters' formal education at a moment in his life when his financial situation was more than usually precarious—he was facing bankruptcy. The partnership of Wallace, Johnson, and Muir had erupted into a bitter rift four years earlier when the Annapolis partners discovered that Joshua had placed the firm £240,000 in debt to the London tradesmen who supplied goods for shipment to American retailers. Fourteen years later, when the firm's affairs were still being arbitrated, Wallace and Muir claimed Joshua had understood that every shipment from London to American merchants had to be paid for within a year and that no further transactions could take place until delinquent merchants had satisfied their obligations. Yet, they said, Joshua had filled every order, whether or not the purchaser's credit was good. The Annapolis partners also complained regularly about what they saw as Joshua's sloppy business practices and questioned his extravagant lifestyle. Finally, they determined to end the partnership and replace Joshua as their overseas partner.[7]

In May 1787, Joshua, on the spot in London and faced daily with the enormous debts owed by the firm, brought together his thirteen major creditors and turned the firm's books over to them, thus avoiding arrest for bankruptcy for at least two years. These creditors became Wallace, Johnson, and Muir's London

Catherine Nuth Johnson, Louisa's mother. Oil on canvas by unidentified artist, circa 1792. Courtesy of the Massachusetts Historical Society.

trustees with authority over Joshua's decisions concerning whether to execute any new orders from Maryland. On this basis, Wallace and Muir agreed to extend the partnership until 1789. With the trustees overseeing the firm's London affairs, the partners continued in the consignment trade. By 1789,

Joshua Johnson, Louisa's father. Oil on canvas by unidentified artist, circa 1792.
Courtesy of the Massachusetts Historical Society.

however, a year after the Johnson daughters were removed from school, it had
become clear to the trustees, one of whom had gone bankrupt partly as a result
of unpaid Wallace, Johnson, and Muir debts, that the partnership could not be
sustained; as of December 31, 1789, it was dissolved.[8]

Now on his own, Joshua saw his financial affairs continue their gradual downhill slide. He moved immediately to set up an independent tobacco consignment and mercantile trading business, but times had changed. The Maryland tobacco trade was in decline, partly because the quality of the product had degenerated over the years. More important, many of Johnson's former mercantile customers no longer demanded imported goods. American manufacturers and craftsmen could now produce nearly everything that the emerging middle class wanted to buy—and at a lower cost.

Some of Joshua's mercantile activities must have been successful, and at least a few of his speculative investments had to have paid off for him to maintain the façade of a gentleman merchant, as he did, for six full years following the breakup of the firm. Louisa records no hint of economizing at No. 8, Cooper's Row, and as John Quincy later described her upbringing, she "had since infancy scarcely formed a wish, but it was instantly supplied, and where possession of fortune [had] accustomed [her] to the enjoyment of every indulgence." Such an appearance of wealth could not have been carried off for so long without some basis in fact, but, as always, Joshua operated on an extremely thin margin. The delay of a single ship could spell disaster.[9]

In the summer of 1790, Joshua's career took a new and unexpected turn—just months after the dissolution of Wallace, Johnson, and Muir—when he was appointed U.S. consul for London. It is unclear what prompted Secretary of State Thomas Jefferson to select him for what was arguably the new nation's most important consular post. As of July 21, two weeks before his appointment, Joshua's name did not appear on a handwritten list Jefferson compiled of potential consular candidates for posts ranging from Amsterdam to the island of Madeira. He does not seem to have applied for the job, nor is there any record that anyone pulled strings on his behalf. It seems a curious choice to entrust the new nation's business interests in what was then the commercial center of the world to a merchant whose former business was in the hands of trustees. Even a cursory check on the financial history of the now-defunct Wallace, Johnson, and Muir should have raised red flags in the office of the secretary of state, especially as Jefferson had available four strong candidates, each endorsed by a leading member of the new government, including one put forward by Vice President John Adams.[10]

What did Joshua have to offer that vaulted his candidacy over other, more qualified, better-connected aspirants to this most prestigious consular post? One plausible theory is that Jefferson believed him to be particularly well positioned to provide the political, military, and commercial intelligence

America desperately needed in order to survive among the wily old colonial powers.[11]

Support for this speculation is relatively easy to find. In a letter to the other newly appointed consuls from Canton in China to Cadiz in Spain, Jefferson spelled out their tasks: They were to report (in tabular form) every six months on exactly which U.S. vessels entered their ports, the names of captains and a list of their crews, the cargoes carried in and out of the harbors, and the times of arrival and departure. They were also to alert him if they observed preparations for war and to notify other consuls, merchants, and seamen in the area if a war appeared imminent. The secretary of state also strongly advised the newly appointed consuls to avoid annoying local government officials with minor problems and to "let all representations to them be concluded in the most temperate and friendly terms, never indulging in any case whatever a single expression that might irritate." No other duties were specified.[12]

To Joshua, however, Jefferson was much more precise. In addition to the usual information regarding shipping and preparations for war, Joshua was required to report in detail on the extent and geographic position of the British fishing and whaling fleets and to act forcefully to protect American seamen who had been seized and impressed into the Royal Navy. But that was not all. "In your position, we must desire something more" than the usual consular duties, Jefferson wrote in his August 7, 1790, appointment letter. "Political intelligence from that country [England] is interesting to us in a high degree; we must therefore ask you to furnish us with this as far as you shall be able."[13]

It is not known why Jefferson believed that Joshua had better access to inside government information than other Americans living in London. There is little in Joshua's correspondence to indicate that he socialized with members of Parliament or was a particularly astute observer of matters of state. It may be that he was known to Jefferson as someone who had been previously engaged in undercover activities. Louisa later recalled that "we continually heard anecdotes concerning the American Revolution, the risks my father had run ere he was obliged to quit England." What those risks were she did not say, but under all the braggadocio may have been a kernel of truth.[14]

While acting as consul, Joshua probably provided Jefferson with the intelligence he required, and he may have been paid for this service with secret funds. Typically, Joshua had made clear to Jefferson at the outset that intelligence would cost money: "You who have been in Europe . . . know how difficult it is to obtain information that can be depended on without . . . spending considerable sums of money. This would be inconsistent with my pursuits and not justifiable to my Family." If secret funds were, in fact, made available to him, it would explain why, given his chronically shaky financial situation, Joshua was willing to play the role of unpaid consul so energetically, at least at the outset. It would also explain why Jefferson, who soon clashed with Joshua over the performance of his regular consular duties, did not replace him in the position, particularly on the several occasions when Joshua threatened to resign.[15]

In August 1790, however, Joshua accepted the position of consul eagerly and immediately ordered official seals bearing the arms of the United States. He also began what became a steady drumbeat of appeals for compensation. Congress, believing that the title of consul was a sufficient honor for an American merchant living abroad and assuming that most appointees would continue to pursue their private business interests while in the consular service, had declined to pay consuls a salary or authorize them to charge fees for their services. Consuls in smaller ports apparently agreed that the title brought them the kind of prestige that could translate into lucrative connections and that the effort required to fulfill their duties was negligible.

But London was different. As Joshua regularly pointed out, he had much more work to do than did American consuls elsewhere. Louisa recalled, "Many were the Americans that he saved from imprisonment while residing in London, at his own risk furnishing them with clothes money and passage on vessels owned by him or his friends, which consigned them safe from danger either to their homes or to France."[16]

Her memories are not simply those of the adoring daughter. An independent account of Joshua's kindness to an American sea captain who had arrived in London suffering from insanity confirms them. In that case, at his own expense, Joshua saw to the captain's medical care and, in the end, paid for his burial.[17]

From time to time, Joshua also acted as a notary. Louisa later described one famous American who required his services: "A gentleman called on my father, a small neat looking man in a very handsome chariot with livery, servants, etc. He walked into the office, entered into conversation very agreeably, and then presented some papers to my father which concerned some American business to be done before the consul. My father returned the papers for signature and stood to see the name when to his utter surprize he discovered it was the traitor Arnold and he deliberately took up his *Pen* with the tongs and put it into the fire."[18]

Although ostentatious patriotism was Joshua's stock-in-trade, this encounter with Benedict Arnold seems to have been far less typical than the daily appeals he received from wretched, homesick seamen desperate to escape the clutches of the mercenaries of His Majesty's Navy. Particularly during his first year as consul, he spent countless hours appealing to officials at the Admiralty, the

Treasury, the Customs Office, and the Foreign Office on matters concerning impressed seamen, seized American vessels, sailors charging their officers with cruelty, and appeals from indigent Americans somehow stranded in London. Little of this time-consuming effort was reimbursed. Consuls dispatched to London from European powers typically received fees for their services from ship captains and merchants as well as salaries, and Joshua sought, unsuccessfully, to encourage the United States to follow their lead. He also emulated European consuls by acting in a quasi-judicial capacity in civil cases between Americans. Arbitrating his countrymen's competing claims, however, went beyond Joshua's assigned duties and never gained the secretary of state's approval.

Early on, Jefferson had reason to be concerned about Joshua's performance of the duties he had actually been assigned. In February 1791, barely six months into the job, Joshua queried the secretary of state concerning how diligent he was required to be in ascertaining the ownership of vessels purporting to be American that made anchor at British ports within his jurisdiction. Traditionally, when European wars erupted, captains of commercial ships from nations at war simply adopted the flag of a neutral nation in order to continue their trading activities unmolested by either side. When war threatened to break out between England and Spain, Jefferson was determined that the young nation not be drawn in by the "usurpation" of the American flag. Joshua was more cavalier, arguing that it made little difference which flag a vessel bore as long as American business was not hurt; he was firmly put in his place by the secretary of state.[19]

For the first two years of his appointment, Joshua was the ranking American official resident in London yet had no access to the royal court or the highest levels of the British government. As consul, he routinely dealt with second secretaries or their assistants, a situation that rankled his pride and frustrated his effectiveness. Concerned that the dignity of the new nation be established at the outset, George Washington and Jefferson refused to appoint a minister to Great Britain until a minister had been sent to represent the king in the United States. As soon as a British ambassador was established in Philadelphia, however, Thomas Pinckney of South Carolina, a planter, lawyer, and patriot who had received a classical education in England, was named minister plenipotentiary of the United States to the court of "His Britannic Majesty." But Pinckney did not arrive in London until August 1792, and, even then, his instructions from Jefferson were much more imprecise than the requests for commercial and political intelligence the secretary of state had transmitted two years earlier to Joshua. To express "that spirit of sincere friendship which we bear to the English nation" and to act in as conciliatory manner as possible made up Pinckney's major duties as far as Jefferson spelled them out.[20]

Elizabeth Motte Pinckney, the wife of the new American minister, took a particular interest in Louisa: "Mrs. Pinckney was a truly lovely woman and I became very fond of her. My father, contrary to his usual custom, allowed me to stay at her house very frequently." But two years after her arrival in London, Elizabeth Pinckney became "ill," and an eminent London doctor was called in. The clear-eyed, nineteen-year-old Louisa was skeptical: "I have always thought he mistook her complaints and she told me she was six months advanced in her pregnancy but she was determined to keep it a secret as she had always said she would not have any more children and she was ashamed to declare her situation." At the patient's request, Louisa remained with her day and night and, in fact, was present when Elizabeth—the doctor having "pronounced her out of danger although she had not been able to lie down or to sleep in any position but that of laying a pillow on a Table and resting her head on her arms to seek repose"—apparently suffered a fatal stroke.[21]

The social horizons the Pinckneys had opened to Louisa and her sisters left little time for mourning. Because of their wealth, manners, and family connections, members of the Carolina planter aristocracy, to which the minister and his late wife belonged, had easy entrée to the cream of Anglo-American society, and the Johnsons were inevitably drawn into its fringes. At the center of this rarefied atmosphere were the British businessman and member of Parliament John Barker Church and his American-born wife, Angelica, a member of New York's very wealthy and patrician van Rensselaer and Schuyler families and the sister-in-law of Alexander Hamilton. In the early 1770s Church had fled England after a duel and had served Washington as his commissary general during the Revolution. After the war, the couple, with their daughter Kitty, moved to London where they were welcomed into the highest social circles.

Angelica Church was a legendary hostess of the time. Her salons were distinguished by the presence of the statesmen William Pitt the Younger and Edmund Burke and the artists John Trumbull and Richard and Maria Cosway, who introduced Angelica to Jefferson. Kitty Church was a belle, "entirely engrossed with pleasure and formed to give as well as enjoy it," according to Louisa. The three pretty Johnson sisters—Nancy, Louisa, and Caroline—were decorative assets at the Church parties, and as they may not have represented serious competition to the wealthy and incandescent Kitty, they seem to have been called upon to appear with some regularity.[22]

Joshua did not discourage his daughters from attending the extravagant balls and dinner parties to which they were now invited, although the expenses involved in their ball gowns alone must have been considerable. And while the Johnsons may not have reciprocated with equally elaborate formal entertainments of their own, it is clear that the Tower Hill mansion continued to be a mecca for expatriate Americans of all ages and social classes and the site of numerous balls and large dinner parties. As Joshua's various business enterprises became less viable, his expenses were mounting fast.

One last opportunity to right Joshua's sinking ship existed. As Louisa recalled the circumstances, Joshua's former partners, Charles Wallace and John Muir, pressed him to return to Annapolis. Joshua believed he was owed some of the stake he had invested in the formation of the partnership of Wallace, Johnson, and Muir. "All the lawyers he had employed assured him that his presence was essential to prevent the utter destruction of his property by Mr. Muir who was even then attempting to embezzle the profits of the concern." Whether this charge against his longtime partner was justified, Joshua apparently believed that he would be in a better position to assert his rights if he confronted Wallace and Muir face to face. Unfortunately, the two Annapolis partners stipulated that Catherine and some of her children remain in England. This, Catherine refused to do. She had never been separated from her husband, and the responsibility of the Tower Hill household as well as her duty to shepherd her marriageable daughters in society was more than she could contemplate. So, although, Louisa remembered that "the ship was prepared for his departure and everything was ready," Joshua did not embark for America. "To this, however," his daughter later lamented, "all my beloved father's misfortunes must be attributed."[23]

Although her husband's financial interests may have been damaged beyond repair by her resistance to his departure for America, Catherine, the mother of seven daughters, truly did face a daunting challenge of her own: how to marry off a bevy of girls with little more than their charms to recommend them. And Catherine's bar was set especially high: Joshua had decreed that his daughters, whose entire lives had been spent in England and France, could marry only Americans. He imposed this restriction in part to please his elder brother Thomas, the renowned Maryland patriot and governor, who, in 1791, had recently become a justice of the U.S. Supreme Court. Louisa later recalled that Thomas Johnson had written her father, "telling him that he heard much of his daughters and desiring him to be careful that they should 'form connections with none but *men of note* and distinction in his own Country.' . . . This letter produced a great effect on [Joshua] and induced him to limit as much as possible our acquaintance among the English."[24]

Another factor in Joshua's determination to contain his daughters' social life within an American orbit may have been to protect his wife. Since he and Catherine had not married until two years after their return from France, he may have hoped to shield her from gossip about their previous unconventional union and what may have been her illegitimate birth. Joshua's fellow Americans, most of whom were transient visitors, might be less likely than British social arbiters to recognize the inconsistencies and gaps in Catherine's family history and be more willing to accept her as the charming and accomplished hostess she was.

Joshua had clearly been the dominant parent in his daughters' early upbringing, and he was still the central figure in the household, the person around whom all else revolved. It was he who decided where and when his children would go to school, who hired their tutors and governesses, and who established the discipline in the home. His was the final word on where his daughters visited socially and which suitors could vie for their attention. But as her three older daughters approached their mid- and late teens, it was Catherine's responsibility to guide them past the hazards that their formal entrance into society represented. They were, as Louisa later put it, "never permitted to be out of sight a moment." Their reputations had to remain spotless, and it fell to a woman who had conceived a child out of wedlock at a very young age to make certain that no hint of scandal attached itself to Nancy, Louisa, or Caroline Johnson.

The three were introduced into society—a turning point in the life of a young woman that marked her formal emergence from the schoolroom and announced her eligibility to receive suitors—almost simultaneously. Louisa, at fifteen, was somewhat younger than usual because she "came out" at the same time as sixteen-year-old Nancy, now slim, poised, and charming; once her sisters were "out," Caroline apparently could not be kept back, and she soon joined them in their social rounds and after-dinner entertainments in the Tower Hill drawing room. Placed prematurely on the marriage market, Louisa concealed her feelings of social inadequacy, but she remembered herself as an awkward teenager, set apart from the "great vivacity and much playful wit" of both her sisters: "I was timid to shyness reserved and cold—When pleased delighted to ecstacy and attached with ardour—my disposition inclined me to read the countenances of all who approached me with extreme care and my judgment of character was almost immediately stamped upon this investigation."[25]

Although her wild enthusiasms may have been typical of the average fifteen-year-old girl, it seems her exceptional wariness in society was not. Even as an adolescent, Louisa realized she possessed an unusually discerning view of the vanities and follies of others—her nickname in the family was Cassandra—that would later prove invaluable in negotiating the Byzantine intrigues of European royal courts, as well as the more rough-and-tumble but equally cutthroat politics of Washington, D.C.

Shy and reserved as she was, Louisa was not entirely immune to the attractions of the many young American males who took advantage of the Johnsons' generous hospitality. One of her father's clerks—at nineteen or twenty, an "older man"—was a first, sweet love: "My attachment to Mr. David Sterrett was very great—His character his manners, his person were all excellent; and his disposition was such as to ensure the esteem and affection of all who knew him. He was equally fond of me, and always termed me his little Wife: and every body delighted to teaze me about him until a sentiment was forming in my heart, which no one doubted, least of all myself."[26]

Flirtations aside, there is no hint in her memoirs that Louisa gave more than a passing thought to the all-important question of whom she would marry. "We were too entirely happy to make marriage a *want*, and we only looked forward to it as evidence that we were not devoid of those attractive qualities which generally are the operating causes of affection."[27]

This is nonsense, probably aimed at refuting any suggestion that she and her parents had set out to trap John Quincy Adams into matrimony. Marriage was crucially important to a young woman in England in the last decade of the eighteenth century. No public social services or private insurance policies existed to protect her as she aged or faced medical problems. On the death of her father, all family money or property, except that expressly "settled" on her, would typically devolve automatically to a woman's brothers or the nearest male relative. Unmarried middle-class women in their late twenties and thirties, thought to be beyond the marrying age, were often exploited as unpaid and unappreciated nursemaids or housekeepers in their married siblings' households or called upon to care for an elderly aunt or mother until she died. As they aged, these caretakers themselves became objects of pity in the homes of relatives.

Practically the only available alternative for a single, bright, young woman without inherited personal funds was to become a governess. But contemplating that thankless life, among unruly children and midway between the servants' hall and the drawing room, was enough to bring despair to such diverse fictional characters as Jane Fairfax in *Emma*, Becky Sharp in *Vanity Fair*, and the eponymous heroine of *Jane Eyre*. For nearly two hundred years, readers have found Jane Austen to be cynical when she referred to marriage as "the only honourable provision for well-educated young women of small fortune, and however uncertain of giving happiness, must be their pleasantest preservative from want." Yet, Catherine Johnson and her seven daughters would have recognized every word as true.[28]

For all concerned, marriage was very much a business proposition. Eldest sons, even when they expected to inherit the family property, searched for potential brides who could bring to the marriage an aristocratic title, additional land holdings, or cash to pay off existing mortgages and other debts. Younger sons, forced to take up careers in the professions and resigned to the fact that their older brother would probably inherit the family estate, also hoped to find wives who could bring significant financial assets or property to the union. A young clergyman, doctor, or solicitor, no matter how well educated, well born, or qualified in his profession, could not expect to live at the level of the gentry he served unless his wife had the means to buttress his income. Similarly, a young, upper-middle-class woman might be forced to accept a suitor who could keep her in relative comfort although her heart belonged to a struggling curate. The novels of the period are filled with vain, callous, and empty-headed—but wealthy—rivals to the deserving—but poor—hero or heroine.

Marriage was ultimately a contract that settled the central question of an adequate income for life. Divorce for middle-class couples was all but impossible. The Johnson daughters always understood that while they did not represent financial windfalls in the matrimonial game, they could each confidently expect a dowry of £5,000, a not insignificant sum. Their relative lack of fortune apparently did not discourage several young men from courting Nancy and Caroline, but all, for various reasons, were turned away by their father.

A Mr. Higginson, for example, "was a very handsome young man but my father was not very fond of the Yankeys, and they were not much encouraged to visit at our house," wrote Louisa. The beautiful Caroline was wooed in vain by a nobleman, Lord Andover, whom she met at parties at the elegant Church mansion; a "very wealthy" Mr. Gibbs of Carolina, who was rejected by Joshua for being a "great beau"; Andrew Buchanan, the man she eventually married; and a Mr. Francis, visiting from Philadelphia ("every hour increased his passion"), who, unfortunately, was already engaged to a woman at home. Nancy, too, received attentions from suitors whom her father apparently found unsuitable.[29]

Louisa, with due skepticism, reported that in later life she often met men who told her that, had they been in a position to court a woman with only a modest dowry, they would have more actively pursued her. But, as it was, "no woman, I can assure you, had fewer lovers than your mother," she wrote her sons some thirty years later. If she really had no suitors, it was not because she was unattractive. Throughout her life, Louisa was celebrated for her elegance, and it is clear in a large oil portrait, painted by Edward Savage sometime between 1792 and 1794 when she was about seventeen, that her sense of style was honed early. In the Savage painting, Louisa is wearing a flower-embroidered, gauzy muslin dress, cinched with a wide blue ribbon at the waist. Her hair is thick and simply curled and styled. A black velvet wristband is such a perfect accessory that even a single piece of jewelry would be excessive. The artist has hinted at his subject's sweetness and virginity by placing a ring of rosebuds in her hands and massing a bank of roses behind her.[30]

It is hardly a vapid upper-middle-class beauty whose dark, appraising eyes stare out at us from the portrait. Here is a young woman whose expression conveys intelligence, watchfulness, and determination. These may have been precisely the qualities that attracted her to the attention of older, accomplished men. It was they who appeared to recognize in her an intellectual curiosity lacking in the many social butterflies who surrounded her at home and in the gracious Anglo-American drawing rooms she frequented. Beginning with her childhood visits to the family's friends the Hewletts, she became the eager protégée of a succession of men charmed by her intelligence and frank admiration: "Sense and talent I almost worshipped Mr. Hewlett during my frequent visits had done much to expand my understanding and by his serious conversation had led me early to think. There was an old Gentleman by the name of Edmund Jennings who was likewise constantly at our House who was a man of fine sense whose conversation I was very fond of. . . . became a great favorite with our doctor who was somewhat of a naturalist—he delighted to show me his stuffed birds, his butterflys, his glow worms, etc. and all the beautiful varieties of the insect tribes and endeavoured to inculcate in me a taste for natural history."[31]

One "constant visitor" stood out among the others. He was the American artist and patriot John Trumbull, now known for his iconic portraits and history paintings (*The Death of General Warren at the Battle of Bunker Hill* and *The Declaration of Independence,* among many others). Trumbull had studied in England and Paris and had returned to London from Boston in 1794 as secretary to John Jay during negotiations of the final peace treaty between Great Britain and the United States. Although Louisa claimed "he was old enough to be my father," the artist was actually only nineteen years her senior, and if his self-portrait of 1793 is any indication, a youthful and handsome thirty-seven. Nevertheless, according to Louisa, the two adopted the fiction that a romantic attachment was out of the question: "I was therefore very much at my ease with him. It never entering my imagination that he could think of me but as his favorite child. This I know he did because he took every opportunity to make the distinction between myself and my sisters. He gave me some instruction in painting, but I was a poor pupil and did not profit as much as I should have done from so good a preceptor. Once in his life he said he wished he was a young man for then he should certainly pay his addresses to me; and this was the utmost that ever passed between us."[32]

Although clearly flattered by the attention paid her by eminent men, Louisa realized that the intelligence they recognized in her was less an asset in the marriage competition than the flirtatious arts and graces her sisters and their friends displayed so effortlessly. Her sense that her seriousness set her apart was reinforced by her father's singling her out as his most responsible daughter and someone in whose discretion he could invariably trust. Other young women gloried in the give and take of flirtation; Louisa seems to have sought something more.

But, bowing to the conventions of the day, she downplayed her sharp intellect, describing any attempts to improve her mind—"I was a poor pupil"—as hapless. Although at fourteen, she had used a New Year's Day cash gift from her father to buy John Milton's *Paradise Lost* and *Paradise Regained,* to which she had been introduced by her beloved teacher Miss Young, and John Mason's *A Treatise on Self-Knowledge*—three exceptionally serious and difficult books—she protested that most of the books she read were useless or worse: "My passion was reading, and I read everything I could get hold of. . . . It was all crude and undigested, ill chosen, and often of a nature to produce bad effects as it encouraged a sensibility already too keen."[33]

Books that "encouraged a sensibility already too keen" meant novels, the principal form of popular fiction in the late eighteenth century and also something of a guilty pleasure. Writing from the vantage point of a quarter-century in the Adams family, Louisa was reflecting their view that time spent reading novels was time wasted. Like today's romance novels, written to fit a publisher's template, the so-called sentimental novels of the late eighteenth century adhered to a strict formula featuring heroes in disguise, innocent young women whose virtue was constantly at risk, thwarted love, exotic locales, madness, and exaggerated emotional reactions—fainting and tears were common—at every twist and turn of the plot. By the 1790s, these novels were so full of stock characters and clichéd situations that they made easy targets for burlesque, but that did not make them any less popular, particularly among idle young women.[34]

Louisa later claimed that she grasped the distinction between novels that catered to "the lovesick sensibility of puling [whimpering] girls" and those that featured "characters of lofty excellence"—and that she chose the latter—but the novels of the day were all so hackneyed that even had she wanted to, she could not have avoided their sentimental extravagances. She also could not have escaped their message that female virtue equated with passivity and that a woman's only hope for happiness was to love and be loved by a romantic, dominating man. Crucially, she would have encountered in these novels a nearly identical denouement: the heroine united with an ideal husband with whom she would spend a lifetime of unalloyed happiness.

The promise of marital bliss conveyed by the sentimental novels Louisa read would have been reinforced by the daily example of her parents. Although she later placed much of the blame for Joshua's financial downfall on her mother's extravagant tastes, she never hinted at any tensions in the marriage itself. No matter how strenuously she denied her desire to marry, she must have dreamt of the day when she, like Catherine Johnson, would be securely placed on a pedestal.[35]

While waiting for the ideal husband to appear, Louisa prepared for what she and her parents assumed would be her future life. Immediately after removing his daughters from school, Joshua had hired a live-in governess and visiting instructors to improve their skills in music, drawing, and dancing—attributes more necessary before than after marriage—though it is not clear how long their formal lessons continued. In light of their potential future duties as mistresses of upper-class households, however, the Johnson daughters needed to know how to administer a complex domestic organization. Catherine's seemingly fragile health had limited her efforts in this sphere: "My Mother superintended the whole establishment though her health was so delicate, she was often obliged to trust to a substitute in whom she was obliged to place unlimited confidence," Louisa wrote. As they reached their late teens, their father assigned each of the older Johnson daughters responsibility for running the household for a week at a time, but he singled out Louisa for special responsibilities. This practice, Louisa later wrote, "was very beneficial to us all; and early initiated us in all the labours and troubles of family economy."[36]

Although Joshua's edict that his daughters marry only Americans was well understood within the family, the Johnson girls received essentially the same training for their future lives as their British contemporaries. Every future mistress of a well-run upper-middle-class home needed to learn how to manage an intricate household. To be successful in this role, a woman benefited from actually learning the tasks she expected her servants to perform. Louisa recalled a new cook "teaching me all she knew," a skill, she reported, that had been very valuable all her life. She also must have been taught to launder, sew, and mend clothing and household linen because she later put those abilities to good use. The role of sick nurse would also have fallen to the mistress, and she would have been expected to know the medicinal properties of the common treatments available for everything from burns to typhus. Most important, she would have supervised the household accounts, a task that included ordering food and supplies for the family and staff, paying tradesmen and others, and making certain that expenses did not exceed her household allowance.[37]

Because Joshua relied on his older daughters to take care of the family's domestic affairs as they neared adulthood, they probably had more experience in day-to-day management of an upper-middle-class household than most young women their age. Unfortunately for Louisa, her training as a household manager was based on a home organized on the British pattern, in which the eleven servants had well-defined roles for which they had long been trained. From a very young age when they entered service as a scullery maid or second footman, British house staff received constant supervision by fellow servants, as well as general oversight by the mistress of the house, and worked themselves up to positions of authority if they were able or qualified. In America, as she would later learn to her dismay, domestic helpers, when you could find them, often resented their status and received little training in their work. Most American middle-class women, particularly those of her future mother-in-law's generation, had spent their lives working alongside any servants in their employ, regularly performing every household task themselves, from spinning wool to butchering chickens. Louisa's education in the art of running a well-regulated household, although it included training in many useful domestic skills, was at a distinct distance from sustained manual labor and would later earn her only Abigail Adams's dismissive evaluation that she was too much of a "fine lady" for Massachusetts.

Although not intended as a compliment, a fine lady is exactly what the Johnson sisters were expected to become. Unlike their American contemporaries, they had been destined from birth to adorn a drawing room and to meet the very specific criteria that defined the accomplished young lady, the most important of which was to attain some proficiency in music. In both the city and country, evening entertainment in middle- and upper-middle-class homes, particularly when guests were present, routinely featured vocal and instrumental recitals by eligible young women. If virtuosity was beyond the reach of most, the daughters of the house could, at least, be trained to sing a selection of sentimental songs or perform passably on a musical instrument, either the pianoforte or, in wealthier homes, the harp. (The latter was believed ideally suited to showing off a young woman's arms and to displaying her figure to best advantage.)

Fortunately for their audiences, the older Johnson sisters appear to have possessed genuine musical talent. They had learned as schoolgirls to perform songs and dances for company: "In dancing and in musick we were put forward . . . and ballets were form'd to show *the three sisters* to advantage," Louisa remembered. She, especially, was a competent performer on both the piano and the harp and an excellent singer. After dinner each evening, her father required her "to sing and nothing but sickness could furnish an excuse for non complyance; he listened with delight to our performances which seemed to soothe his soul to peace and harmony after the labours of the day." Following these musicales, the entire family, with their guests, would often roll up the carpets for dancing.[38]

"Society at home was ever delightful to me . . . and our little unceremonious suppers were the very essence of social festivity," Louisa remembered. Reserved and serious she may have been at times, but she always delighted in sophisticated social interplay, witty conversation, and a good joke. Her memoirs are sprinkled with the kind of comic anecdotes that would have charmed a dinner companion; her ability to recall them in specific detail years later reveals how practiced she was in telling amusing stories. Her mother may have been celebrated for her "wit brilliant, sometimes almost too keen," and her sister Caroline may have been a famous mimic, but Louisa could surely hold her own in any social setting. If she listened quietly and attentively as Joshua and Catherine's eminent guests debated the great political, philosophical, and cultural questions of the day instead of seeking the spotlight for herself, Louisa was not being excessively bashful, as she was accused by her beloved father, but foresighted. She would need all the knowledge she could absorb for the life she would be called upon to lead.

Louisa had her first glimpse of that life on November 11, 1795. Arriving in London only that morning from The Hague, where he was America's resident minister to Holland, John Quincy Adams had gone almost immediately to take advantage of Joshua's services as consul to ensure that a packet of official papers be safely transmitted home. There he found Trumbull, the artist and "constant visitor," with Joshua; both men, typically, were invited to stay for the evening meal. "After Dinner Mr. Johnson's daughters entertained us with good music," John Quincy recorded in his diary that evening.[39]

The years of preparation were over. Louisa's prince had come.

3

DESTINED FOR GREATNESS

I devoted him to the Publick.

—ABIGAIL ADAMS

At first sight, the prince more nearly resembled a frog. During dinner, John Quincy "was in high spirits" and "conversed most agreeably," but when he left to go to his hotel in the Adelphi buildings, off London's Strand, the Johnson sisters, recalling the details of his unfashionable costume, were convulsed with laughter. "His dress did not impress us agreeably as it made his person appear to very great disadvantage," Louisa recalled long afterward.[1]

Their daughters could giggle, but Joshua and Catherine would have recognized at once that John Quincy was, in reality, American royalty. His father was now completing a second term as vice president of the United States. At only twenty-eight, the younger Adams had already served for more than a year as minister to Holland—an important commercial and diplomatic post in the late eighteenth century—and had spent more time in European court circles than any American of his generation. At only eleven years old, he had begun to observe at first hand the arts of statecraft and diplomacy. John and Abigail Adams had raised their eldest son to play a preeminent role in the new American nation. From an early age he had been inculcated with the belief that public service trumped all other needs and desires and that he, perhaps above all others, was destined for greatness. His ill-fitting Dutch-made waistcoat and trousers to the contrary, John Quincy was an urbane, well-educated bachelor and, as the American vice president's son, a minor celebrity on both sides of the Atlantic.

On that November evening in 1795 George Washington had not yet announced his precedent-making decision to retire from public life after two terms as president. Public opinion at home and abroad could justifiably have assumed that America's great hero, in the manner of kings and emperors, would continue to lead the new nation until his death. And as Washington had no natural heir, the line of succession could logically have led from John Adams, who stood next in line to the presidency, to his son. Some Americans, particularly Jefferson's adherents, appeared to fear that this was exactly what Vice President Adams had in mind. He had given them plenty of ammunition, arguing that a president should hold a rank and title commensurate with those of European monarchs and that one conceivably could, if reelected every four years, serve until the end of his life. Although this line of thinking ran counter to the spirit of the new U.S. Constitution and his own long-held opposition to a hereditary monarchy, Adams's point of view was not as far out of line as it appears today. In an era when power, rank, and property routinely passed from father to eldest son, the concept of a presidency passed from father to son would have seemed much more natural to most Europeans—and even to some more conservative Americans—than the quadrennial upheaval that the American political process eventually became.[2]

Whether Joshua and Catherine privately discussed John Quincy's dynastic prospects after his first visit to Tower Hill, they made no blatant moves to lure him into their family circle. For two weeks, he kept himself busy attending the theater (sometimes two plays in one evening), visiting old friends and new acquaintances, attending a trial, and writing to his family. When he finally decided to reappear at the Johnson's mansion, he got lost: "In the evening took a long walk and hunted for Mr. Johnson's, without finding the house."[3]

Finding himself at sea in the streets surrounding the Tower of London was a minor setback; what was truly worrying John Quincy was the question of what he was going to do with the rest of his life. For a quarter century, he had been on a trajectory toward something, however undefined, that would be marked by extraordinary distinction. From his vantage point in Holland, he now watched his contemporaries at home establish themselves in business or the professions, marry and begin to raise families, and find their place in the social order. Meanwhile, John Quincy's halfhearted legal career had stalled, he had not yet found a wife, and he was increasingly restless and bored. His visit to London was only a temporary hiatus from long days and nights in Holland. Although he knew he was performing an essential service by sending his father and President Washington insightful analyses of the political, military, and economic situation in Europe, he had very few meaningful official tasks and entirely too much time on his hands. "At the play in the Evening, for time must be passed, and it is impossible to read or write forever" ran a typical entry in his nightly diary.[4]

Abigail Adams had been straightforward in her ambitions for her son: "At a very early period in Life, I devoted him to the publick," she had written to Martha Washington. John Quincy Adams was born on July 11, 1767, in the village of Braintree, Massachusetts, fifteen miles southeast of Boston. His father, John, the future second president, was descended from some of the earliest families of the Massachusetts Bay Colony—he was a great-great-grandson of John and Priscilla Alden—and the only son in his immediate family to graduate from college. After Harvard, he had taught school in then-remote Worcester County by day and studied law at night. The baby's mother, the former Abigail Smith, unusually for her time, had been encouraged to read widely in the extensive library owned by her classically educated father, the Congregational minister in nearby Weymouth; her mother was a Quincy, one of the Commonwealth's most notable families. When, after a prolonged court-ship, John and Abigail married in 1764, they moved into a five-room, saltbox-style house only seventy-five feet away from the house where John had born and where his father, also John and known as Deacon Adams, had conducted both his shoemaking business and, as a nine-term selectman, the civic affairs of the town.[5]

By 1768, John's fledgling law practice, intermittently based in Boston, had started to flourish, and he had begun his lifelong practice of purchasing additional land to expand the property he had inherited from his father. Accompanying the circuit court on horseback as it made its way from Maine to Cape Cod to Worcester and back to Boston, John found himself on the road for extended periods of time. Abigail was left in Braintree to deal with the farm and with her growing family—a daughter Abigail ("Nabby") had preceded John Quincy by two years; Charles, born in 1770, and Thomas Boylston, in 1772, soon followed. (A second daughter, Susanna, died in 1770 at the age of one.) From time to time, the family moved into Boston so that John could spend more time with his children, but Abigail's health suffered in the city, and they invariably returned home to the farm.

As the author of the so-called Braintree Instructions, denouncing Britain's Stamp Act as unlawful taxation, John had gained a reputation by 1765 as a forceful advocate for colonists' rights. He had also become one of a small group of leading Bostonians who had begun to speak openly of independence from Great Britain. In 1770, he took on the extremely unpopular task of defending a British Army captain and his soldiers who had fired into a mob, killing five local men—the Boston Massacre. His was a virtuoso courtroom performance. The captain and six of his men were acquitted; two were found guilty of manslaughter but punished only with a brand on their thumbs. John's reputation was made.

He was elected that year to the Massachusetts General Court as a representative from Boston. In 1774, he was chosen by the legislature as one of its five delegates to the First Continental Congress in Philadelphia.

For the next ten years, John Adams would spend more than half his time away from home. Fortunately for posterity, his absences, first in Philadelphia and later in France and Holland, resulted in a remarkable collection of letters he wrote to his wife and she to him. Not only does their correspondence bring to life personalities and events of a crucial period in American history, it also reveals that the Adamses' concerns for their children took priority over nearly everything else, no matter how important, in their lives.

In this, they were strongly influenced by Enlightenment principles, particularly those of John Locke, whose *Some Thoughts Concerning Education*, written in 1697, was on the bookshelf in the Braintree farmhouse. Enlightenment thinkers believed that a child was born with both an essential goodness and a set of natural abilities that could be molded by education and that educating one's children was a parent's primary responsibility. The goal was to form the character of a young boy—girls were generally of secondary importance except in their roles of molding future generations of sons—so that he could use his talents for the public good and serve as a model of decorum, reason, and probity. Classical languages were essential to a boy's education as was the study of history, literature, rhetoric, and philosophy, but the well-educated man would also be familiar with geography, astronomy, science, mathematics, and fine arts. As exemplified by many of the highly literate, sophisticated Founding Fathers, a product of this educational system would carry his learning lightly, clothing it in an aura of modesty and refinement and basing his life on a strong central core of moral rectitude.[6]

From the beginning, both Adamses were determined to raise their children to be upright, accomplished paragons on the Lockean model. From York, Maine, where he was appearing in court, John wrote to Abigail concerning their six-year-old son, "I am very thoughtfull and anxious about our Johnny. What School to send him to—what Measures to take with him. He must go on learning his Latin, to his Grandfather or to you or somewhere. And he must write." The boy was not allowed to go to the local primary school because Abigail, particularly, feared that the village ruffians' coarseness would rub off on him. Instead, he was tutored by his father's law clerks and, along with Nabby, by Abigail herself. By the age of ten, he had read Smollett's two-volume *Complete History of England*, as well as a selection of Shakespeare's plays and the poetry of Pope and Thomson (*The Seasons*), and had made a futile attempt to complete Milton's *Paradise Lost*.[7]

"I have not sent Johnny [to the local school]," Abigail wrote John in Philadelphia. "I am certain that if he does not get so much good, he gets less harm, and I have always thought it of very great importance that children should in the early part of life be unaccustomed to such examples as would tend to corrupt the purity of their words and actions that they may chill with horrour at the sound of an oath, and blush with indignation at an obscene expression."[8]

As a result, young John Quincy never took part in the rough-and-tumble play of a colonial schoolyard and was rarely far from an exceptionally vigilant maternal eye. He was also routinely subjected to strongly worded letters from his father, urging him on to greater academic achievements and emphasizing the leading public role he was expected to play in the future. In August 1777, a month after he turned ten, and with the American Revolution in an extremely perilous situation, the boy was encouraged by his father to study revolutions throughout history by reading Thucydides's account of the Peloponnesian War—in English translation, at least until he had become a "perfect Master" of the original Greek. Writing from Philadelphia, where he was managing the conflict as head of Congress's Board of War, John Adams wrote: "As the future circumstances of your Country may require other wars, as well as councils and negotiations, similar to those which are now in Agitation, I wish to turn your Thoughts early to such Studies, as will afford you the most solid Instruction and Improvement for the Part which may be allotted you to act on the Stage of Life."[9]

It must have been abundantly clear to this very bright—but still extremely young—boy that his parents had destined him for something out of the ordinary. He accepted without question their high regard for his intellectual capacities, realizing that they were not making quite the same demands on his sister and brothers, and he worked hard to make his mother and father proud of him. This, too, was part of their educational philosophy. Rarely did either parent miss an opportunity to emphasize the disappointment he or she would feel if their eldest son failed to live up to the family's expectations.

In February 1778, at just ten and a half, John Quincy embarked with his father for France on the American frigate *Boston*. Congress had appointed John Adams to join Benjamin Franklin and Arthur Lee as commissioners to the Court of France, and the boy's parents had agreed that he would benefit by the example and teaching of his father as well as from early exposure to European culture. Finally landing in France after a midwinter Atlantic crossing beset by wild storms, a leaky ship with a broken mast, and the constant threat of capture by the British, John Quincy was quickly enrolled in a private boarding school at Passy, near Paris, where he studied French, Latin, dancing, music, and drawing—the subjects young French gentlemen were expected to master.[10]

Gentlemanly attributes were not, however, high on the list of accomplishments that Abigail hoped her son would acquire. She could not restrain herself from warning him to avoid becoming contaminated by the loose morals she was certain were the norm in European court circles: "You are in possession of a natural good understanding and of spirits unbroken by adversity and untamed with care. Improve your understanding for acquiring usefull knowledge and virtue, such as will render you an ornament to society, an Honour to your Country, and a Blessing to your parents. Great learning and superior abilities, should you ever possess them will be of little value and small Estimation unless Virtue, Honour, Truth, and Integrity are added to them. . . . for dear as you are to me, I had much rather you should have found your Grave in the ocean you have crossed, or any untimely death crop you in your Infant years, rather than see you an immoral profligate or a Graceless child."[11]

This letter from a mother to a little boy very far from home for the first time seems unnecessarily harsh. But Abigail's fears for the moral health of her son were directly related to bitter experience: her only brother, an alcoholic, had led an irresponsible and dissolute life. To John Quincy's former tutor, John Thaxter, who was now serving as John Adams's secretary in Paris, she reiterated her concern that her young son might fall prey to the "snares and temptations" that would beset him from all sides, but "to exclude him from temptation would be to exclude him from the World in which he is to live, and the only method which can be persued with advantage is to fix the padlock upon the mind."[12]

Exactly what temptations would require a padlock to withstand remained mainly in Abigail's imagination, but the eleven-year-old John Quincy must have understood that his mother was deeply worried that he might succumb to the lures of the luxury and dissipation she associated with Europe and Europeans. To avoid the terrible threats to his virtue she conjured up, young John Quincy naturally retreated to the safety of his books and to the company of his father. Once more, and at a crucial formative stage in his social development, Abigail had effectively denied her son the opportunity to make mistakes and had raised the bar for moral virtue and intellectual attainments to a very high level. The price John Quincy paid for attempting to meet his parents' high expectations was an ultimately tragic compulsion to set unattainable standards of excellence for himself, his wife, and his children and a deep-seated conviction that a life in public service was his sacred duty, no matter the personal cost.

Yet the young John Quincy thrived in Paris. He swiftly became fluent in French and developed a lifelong love affair with the theater. He relished sitting in on his father's conversations with Franklin and the "good doctor's" many female admirers. His father was immensely proud of him: "He has enjoyed perfect Health from first to last and is respected wherever he goes for his Vigour and Vivacity, both of Mind and Body, for his constant good Humour, and for his rapid Progress in French, as well as his general knowledge which for his age is uncommon."[13]

The boy was "the joy of [his] heart," Adams reported to Abigail, and the "Comfort of [his] Life," but, nonetheless, he did not let up on urging his son on to greater achievements, assigning him Latin odes and tightly monitoring his reading and other activities.[14]

John Adams's diplomatic achievements did not give him the same satisfaction. Franklin and Lee mistrusted and disliked one another, and their mutual ill-will extended to and was returned by Adams. The proud, easily irritated Yankee found himself increasingly isolated and impotent. He was relieved, but humiliated as well, when Congress decided to make Franklin sole minister plenipotentiary to France, and the three-person American commission was dissolved. By August 2, 1779, after many delays, including several weeks in Nantes—where they knew and visited the Johnson family—and other French ports waiting for their ship, father and son were back home in Massachusetts.

But not for long. A little more than three months later, this time with both John Quincy and nine-year-old Charles in tow, John Adams was again on his way to Paris. To his surprise, Congress had voted unanimously to appoint him to negotiate treaties of peace and commerce with Great Britain, and, with his pride restored, he had gratefully accepted the assignment. His eldest son had been extremely reluctant to return to Europe; he much preferred the family's original plan of sending him to a boarding school in Massachusetts to prepare for Harvard. Abigail, convinced that the opportunity to live and study in Europe with his father was too good for her son to pass up, strongly argued the case for returning to Paris, and she ultimately prevailed. Again, however, she felt it necessary to remind John Quincy, now twelve, of his responsibilities to his parents and to posterity: "It will be expected of you, my son, that as you are favored with superior advantages under the instructive eye of a tender parent, that your improvements should bear some proportion to your advantages. . . . The habits of a vigorous mind are formed in contending with difficulties. Great necessities call out great virtues. When a mind is raised, and animated by scenes that engage the heart, then those qualities which would otherwise lay dormant, wake into life and form the character of the hero and the statesman."[15]

A typical twelve-year-old might believe that becoming a "hero and [a] statesman" were two distinct goals, and most would prefer to dream their own dreams. John Quincy, familiar with his mother's unambiguous ambitions for his future, seems to have taken her strictures in stride and, at some level, to have adopted her standards for success. But Abigail's exhortations inevitably had a negative effect. Throughout adolescence and early adulthood, he repeatedly confided to his journals his nagging guilt that he had not accomplished as much work as he should have each day and had not organized his life with discipline and efficiency. For two years in his mid-teens, when he was in Russia and traveling independently in Scandinavia, it appears that he did not write his mother at all (and his father very rarely), a signal, perhaps, of a lingering resentment toward their overbearing interest in managing every detail of his life.[16]

It must also have seemed unfair to the boy, as he set out again on what proved to be another very dangerous journey to France, that Charles was not subject to the same level of admonishment and advice from their mother. Instead, Abigail wrote to Charles that he was missed by the entire neighborhood, "all of whom wonder how Mamma could part with you." The younger boy does seem to have had an abundance of natural charm. "Charles is well beloved here as he is at home. Wherever he goes, everybody loves him," his father wrote home to an anxious mother in Braintree. And although Charles, like John Quincy, was immediately placed in the school at Passy and quickly engaged in learning French and studying Latin, he never seems to have received the same pressure from his parents to excel.[17]

In Paris in the spring and summer of 1780, John Adams was frustrated by the French and, again, by Franklin in his diplomatic efforts. Franklin, a showman who played on his image as a rustic sage, believed in his ability to deal successfully with the French through indirection and cunning. Adams was much more confrontational, and in Franklin's view, "always an honest man, often a wise one, but sometimes, and in some things, absolutely out of his senses." After several months of no progress on peace talks, the Massachusetts patriot was happy to move temporarily to the Netherlands to seek much-needed loans for the American cause. His sons were placed as boarders in a highly regarded Dutch-speaking day school in Amsterdam, where both were desperately lonely and unhappy. When the headmaster complained of an alleged instance of John Quincy's impertinence, the angry father immediately removed his sons from the school, established them in lodgings in Leiden, and engaged private tutors in Latin and Greek. Within months, John Quincy had been admitted to attend lectures at the University of Leiden.[18]

With the same fervor with which she had warned them against the vices of the French aristocracy, Abigail advocated the virtues of Holland's sterner habits: "The universal neatness and Cleanliness of the people where you reside will cure you of all your slovenly tricks, and . . . you will learn from them industry, economy, and frugality," she wrote to John Quincy. John Adams, from Amsterdam, also resumed a steady drumbeat of advice for his older son in Leiden. On learning that John Quincy had made significant progress in Latin and Greek, he recommended that the boy also "read somewhat in the English poets every day." In the same vein, he urged him to take up ice skating, not necessarily for enjoyment, but as a way "to restrain that impetuous Ardour and violent Activity . . . which is inconsistent with your Health and Pleasure." He added, "[It] will not be amiss, to spend some of your Time in swimming, Riding, Dancing, Fencing and Skating, which are all manly Amusements, and it is as easy to learn by a little Attention, to perform them all with Taste, as it is to execute them in a slovenly, Awkward and ridiculous Manner."[19]

To twenty-first-century eyes, these parental letters to a young boy seem unnecessarily hectoring and all but devoid of tenderness. Because they had accepted so fully Locke's strictures on their primary responsibility to mold their children's minds and instill in them the purest of morals, both Abigail and John Adams would have felt remiss had they not taken every opportunity to convey timely advice and remind their eldest son of their expectations of him. The Adamses may have gone further than most, but they were not alone in what they recognized as a parent's primary duty. Delaware Congressman Henry Moore Ridgely, for example, writing contemporaneously from Washington to his nine-year-old son Charles, cautioned, "If you avoid vice and folly and devote your youth to the acquisition of learning and of wisdom, you will secure to yourself a source of future happiness and command the esteem and respect of all who know you."[20]

Days before his fourteenth birthday, John Quincy left the Netherlands for St. Petersburg, Russia, with the thirty-seven-year-old diplomat Francis Dana. (At the same time, Charles, whose homesickness had never abated and who had barely survived a serious illness, boarded a ship bound for Boston.) As Dana's secretary, John Quincy was primarily his translator since Dana spoke only rudimentary French, the language of Empress Catherine the Great's court. It was assumed that the teenager would combine his secretarial duties with continued schooling, but to everyone's apparent surprise, there proved to be no appropriate schools or tutors in the Russian capital. John Quincy attempted sporadically to teach himself German and tried to continue his Latin translations on his own; he also became a regular patron of the English Library, devouring the more than a million words of Samuel Richardson's novel *Clarissa* and copying out pages of poetry. But most of the time, without the stimulation and companionship of boys his own age, he was bored; his diary during this period consists of very brief daily entries, mainly concerning the weather.

After more than a year had passed, his father reached the end of his patience with the informal, haphazard course of his son's education: "It is a long time since you have written to me. You should think of your Father's Anxiety for the Success and Progress of your Studies. . . . You should be at Leyden or at Cambridge [Harvard]. A public [i.e., not private, tutorial] Education you must have. You are capable of Emulation, and there alone will you have it."[21]

He directed his son to leave Russia. Dana, who had been unable to secure recognition of the new nation from Catherine's court, wanted to remain in St. Petersburg a while longer, but he agreed it would be in the boy's best interests to return to his father in The Hague. John Quincy, accompanied at the outset by an Italian count of "dubious reputation," set off in October. Through the late fall, winter, and early spring, the teenager made his way by sleigh, carriage, and on horseback on a six-month odyssey through Finland, Sweden, Denmark, and Germany, finally arriving in Holland on April 21, 1783.[22]

Sometimes riding through the night, often arriving in a city or town where he knew no one, the fifteen-year-old John Quincy had to depend largely on his own charm, initiative, and resilience and on the help and kindness of people he met along the way. Armed with letters of introduction to leading citizens in the countries he visited, he found himself welcomed not only because of his father's reputation as a leading American statesman and diplomat but also for his own good looks, linguistic abilities, and the sophistication he had acquired from his years in Paris, Leiden, and St. Petersburg. Wherever he found himself, he eagerly entered into the festive activities of the "long white evenings" that composed a Nordic winter's social life. He loved the parties, informal dances, and masquerade balls, and all his life he remembered fondly the beauty of Swedish women. His Scandinavian trip was his coming of age, and he made the most of it.

The brutal northern winter played its part in delaying John Quincy's reunion with his father. On many days his diary indicates that fierce snowstorms, iced-over waterways, and impassable roads prevented him from progressing more than a mile or two. But the weather does not entirely explain a five-week stop-over in Stockholm, a two-week pause in nearby Norrkoping, and nearly a month in Hamburg in late March and early April when the roads would have cleared. Obviously, he was in no hurry to return to his former routine. For what may have been the first time in his life, John Quincy was on his own and having fun. He particularly loved Sweden: "I believe there is no Country in Europe where the people are more hospitable and affable to Strangers, or more hospitable among themselves than the Sweeds. In almost every town however small it may be they have these assemblies at least once a week during three months. . . . There one may dance Country dances, minuets, or play cards just as it pleases you; and every body is extremely polite to Strangers."[23]

"Just as it pleases you" was a novel and welcome concept to a boy now coming into manhood, particularly one for whom impromptu pleasures had long been strongly discouraged, if not forbidden. In later life he wrote his mother, possibly recalling these unsupervised six months, "If you or my father had known the *moral* dangers through which I passed, and from which by the mercy of Providence I escaped, I think neither of you would have had the courage to expose me to them." Whatever his adolescent adventures and youthful experiments, he did not confide them to his diary.[24]

When John Adams received orders in the fall of 1782 to rejoin the American team assembling in Paris to negotiate a treaty with England ending the American Revolution, his son accompanied him from Holland as private secretary. Just fifteen, John Quincy was no longer a boy. Poised, worldly, and urbane, he could record the deliberations of diplomats as competently as he could hold his own in Parisian salons. The next twenty months were to be among the happiest of his life. His mother and sister, who had sailed first to London, accompanied them to the French capital in the summer of 1784. The family was delightfully ensconced in a handsome suburban villa in Auteuil, adjoining the Bois de Boulogne. John Quincy became well acquainted with the other American peace negotiators—Franklin, John Jay, and, most of all, Thomas Jefferson. The Virginian, as John Adams noted many years later, became all but a second father to the teenage John Quincy. "He appeared to be almost your boy as much as mine," Adams wrote many years later to his longtime friend and some-time bitter political rival.[25]

In addition to his role as private secretary, John Quincy was under the academic tutelage of his father, who delighted in the precocity of his son and reveled in rereading the classic texts and exploring mathematics with him. Most of all, the young man gloried in Paris itself at the very end of the *ancien régime*. Attending the theater almost nightly—often with his sister Nabby—he also enjoyed the spectacle of the royal court in its last flowering, the city's many bookstores and art exhibitions, the highly publicized launch of a hot-air balloon, and the intoxicating conversations with French intellectuals at dinner parties and evening salons.

When his father received a long-coveted appointment as minister plenipotentiary to Great Britain, the moment had finally arrived for John Quincy to obtain the formal education he would need to earn a living and take what his parents were certain would be his rightful place in the leadership of the new nation. For that, the young-man-about-Paris needed a Harvard education. It was not an enticing prospect:

> After having been travelling for these seven years, almost all over Europe, and having been in the world and among Company for three: to return and spend one or two years in the Pale of a College, subjected to all the rules, which I have so long been freed from: then to plunge into the Dry and tedious study of the law; for three years, and afterwards not expect, (however good an Opinion I may have of myself) to bring myself into Notice, under three or four years more; if ever: it is really a Prospect somewhat discouraging for a youth of my Ambition. . . . I am determined that as long as I shall be able to get my own living, in an honorable manner, I will depend upon no one . . . which I shall never be able to do, if I loiter away my precious time in Europe and shun going home untill I am forced to it.[26]

By May 1785, John Quincy was on his way to America. On the last day of August, he appeared in Cambridge, ready to take his place as an upperclassman according to the arrangements his proud father had made from abroad. He was in for a humiliating shock: a brief examination by Harvard's president, Joseph Willard, found his skills in Greek and Latin to be deficient. He would need to be tutored and tested again in the spring before being allowed to join the junior class. For someone whose intellectual prowess had been universally celebrated, whose younger brother Charles had already matriculated, and who, in fact, was unimpressed by Harvard—"The library is good, without being magnificent"— this must have been a bitter pill. But he agreed to be tutored, along with his much younger brother Tom, by his uncle, John Shaw, the minister of the Haverhill, Massachusetts, Congregational church and a scholar renowned for his success in preparing students to enter Harvard.

John Quincy did not look forward to the next few months. As he settled down to work with his Greek textbook, he considered abandoning his diary since his daily activities "will contain nothing that even I myself may desire to remember." His months in Haverhill, however, taught him more than a mastery of classical languages. Life in the relatively uncongenial social setting of a small New England mercantile community was far from anything he had experienced over nearly half his life in the capital cities of Europe. He learned quickly that he would have to adapt his manners to customs he privately disdained and that his pronouncements on various subjects would not always be greeted by a chorus of approbation. Shaw, for example, accused him of being "obstinate, and dogmatical, and pedantic" when he vigorously questioned the minister's position on a minor issue in an apparently casual conversation. John Quincy resolved in his diary to "think more upon this Subject," which he interpreted as showing deference to the opinion of one's elders even though they were "absurd and ridiculous."[27]

And although he worked very diligently to prepare himself for retaking his exams, life in the bustling riverfront town was not all grim. Reporting on one evening in the Christmas season, he wrote, "Our time pass'd in chatting, laughing, romping, and dancing." In Haverhill that fall, for the first time in his life in daily contact with young women, he promptly fell in love with a fellow boarder, an infatuation he vigorously—and successfully—fought off: "I have heretofore more than once been obliged to exert all my Resolution, to keep myself free from a Passion, which I could not indulge, and which would have made me miserable had I not overcome it. . . . Now again, I am put to a trial. I have still more Reason, than I ever had, to repress my feelings; but I am also perswaded that I never was in greater danger."[28]

Unfortunately, the single women of Haverhill, about whom the young scholar speculated endlessly, did nothing to stem an incipient case of misogyny. Most, he claimed, were like pastel portraits, which appeared beautiful at a distance, but were actually "vile daubings"; a very few others were like oils of the great masters that became more worthy of admiration the longer and more closely they were examined. Without these exceptional women, John Quincy declared, he would "otherwise, doubt whether to hate, despise or pity [women] most." These musings may have been partly the result of a young man's almost desperate determination, despite his late-adolescent sexual awakening, to avoid an entanglement that could stand in the way of his lofty ambitions.[29]

Those ambitions were soon realized. John Quincy's many long hours with his Greek grammar, which he committed to memory, bore fruit in just a few months. On March 15, 1786, when he again appeared in Cambridge for an examination by the president and faculty, he was admitted to the junior class.

Harvard, then observing the 150th year of its founding, had not progressed far beyond its origins. The faculty consisted of the president, four tutors, three professors, and the librarian; the campus, "the Yard," comprised four buildings (of which three remain). The 140 young collegians were subjected to a rigid curriculum, conducted as daily morning recitations in which students, when called upon by their teachers, discoursed on set passages of an assigned text, an excruciating performance for which they were continuously graded. The only intellectual bright spots were a series of lectures, usually on scientific topics, scheduled whenever an appropriate faculty member could give them.[30]

Although he had virtually no respect for the faculty, referring to their "pedantic despotism" and complaining about the recitation system, John Quincy was an involved, hard-working, and apparently happy undergraduate. He immediately made new friends and by June had helped form a club in which members met to hear and discuss brief talks on various topics. His first disquisition to the group, typically, considered the proposition, "Nothing is so difficult, but that it may be overcome by Industry." Later that month, he was also made a member of Phi Beta Kappa, which he characterized as a society "established to promote friendship, and Literature." The organization seems to have met often, concluding debates on philosophical issues on at least one occasion with "a very good dinner, wit and Wine, the Bottle and the Joke [keeping] nearly and equal pace." As a change of pace from clubs formed to discuss weighty matters, John Quincy took up the flute and became a founding member of the Tea Club, "a small Society for dancing," which met in students' rooms. His attitude toward women remained tortured. Fascinated with every physical detail, he delineated in his diary the many eligible young ladies with whom he flirted through long winter evenings, particularly during the holidays, almost inevitably concluding with a negative comment ("Beauty of person, is frequently, if not always injurious to the mind").[31]

Altogether, John Quincy hated to see his brief time at Harvard come to an end the following July: "It is not without many melancholy reflections that I bid a last adieu to the walls of Harvard! The scenes through which I have past since my entrance at the university have been for the most part agreeable. I have formed an intimacy, with a number of amiable and respectable characters of my own age, and with dispositions corresponding to my own. I have never once regretted, but have frequently rejoiced that I left Europe, to come and pass a twelve-month here. It has been productive of very good effects: particularly, in reducing my opinion of myself, of my acquirements, and of my future prospects, nearer to the level of truth and reality."[32]

John Quincy graduated second in his class and, at Harvard's Commencement, delivered an oration on "The importance and necessity of public faith to the well-being of a Community." Widely reported and later reprinted for a national audience in the *Columbian Magazine*, the address was "one of the most memorable events of my life," he later recalled, even though most reviews compared his performance unfavorably to the higher-ranked speaker. Later that month, on his twentieth birthday, he wrote, "Three long years I have yet to study in order to qualify myself for business; and then—oh! How many more years to plod along, mechanically if I should live, before I shall really get into the world? . . . I sicken, at the very idea: thus is one third of a long life employ'd in preparing to act a part during another third."[33]

The "three long years" he dreaded so much were to be spent in the study of law. John Quincy understood that if he were to please his father, he had little choice of career. John Adams believed that the law was the best training for public life, and he fully intended that his three sons should follow in his footsteps. And although neither John Quincy, Charles, nor Tom Adams had any zeal for the law, each in his turn dutifully went through the necessary period of apprenticeship to a practicing lawyer, and each passed the bar and entered into practice.

John Quincy was particularly fortunate in his choice of a mentor. Theophilus Parsons of Newburyport, Massachusetts, a very successful practitioner who would become chief justice of the Supreme Judicial Court of Massachusetts, was renowned in the Commonwealth for his success in preparing young lawyers for the bar. So many young men wanted to study under him that the county bar association had to pass a rule limiting students of any practicing lawyer to three. John Quincy described Parsons as "in himself a law library and a proficient in every branch of science." After three months in the cramped little office, his enthusiasm for his teacher had not cooled. "I could not possibly have an instructor more agreeable than this gentleman," he wrote to his mother. "His talents are great; his application has been indefatigable, and his professional knowledge is surpassed by no gentleman in the Commonwealth."[34]

Parsons's strengths as an instructor did not assuage John Quincy's essential distaste for the subject. During his first year in the law office, he was assigned a heavy load of reading Blackstone, Coke, and other legal classics; at the same time, his tasks included copying out legal forms as models for future use and preparing by hand writs and other pleadings for Parsons to present in court—scribe's jobs that he found mind-numbing. When Parsons was in the office, he entertained a constant stream of visitors and passersby who loved to engage the voluble lawyer in disputation. If his clerks complained they could not concentrate on the tomes they had been assigned to read, he reminded them that it was a useful lawyerly skill to be able to work in the midst of confusion. John Quincy resorted to laboring on his reading assignments until well after midnight in his rented room two blocks from the law office. Inevitably, his health suffered, as did his spirits: "There is not one art or science, in which I have any degree of proficiency, and I have now undertaken the study of a profession, which alone ought to employ all the time I can devote to study for twenty years to come. My eyes and my health begin to fail, and I do not feel that ardor for application, which I should have."[35]

But life in Newburyport, a stately, prosperous seaport at the mouth of the Merrimack River, was not all grim toil. John Quincy's fellow clerks, as well as other young men just starting out in their professions, formed a club in which heavy drinking and 4 A.M. off-key serenades in quiet lanes played a significant part. Many times—after particularly rum-soaked parties—John Quincy could do no work at all for three or four days due to debilitating hangovers. And, as in Haverhill and Cambridge, there were many attractive, eminently marriageable young women who simultaneously bewitched and repelled the eligible young law student. All winter, he was a regular participant in balls and sleighing parties and diligently paid evening visits for tea and conversation to several young ladies and their parents.

These diversions were not enough, however, to mask the fact that John Quincy was seriously depressed. On a snowy, gray day in January, just five months after arriving in Newburyport, he lamented, "I go but little into company; and yet I am not industrious. I am recluse, without being studious. . . . I begin seriously to doubt of the goodness of my understanding, and not without my fears, that as I increase in years, the dullness of my apprehension likewise increases."[36]

His only real confidante was his sister Nabby, who, contending with a ne'er-do-well husband and frequent pregnancies, had her own cares and worries. Yet she encouraged him to persevere. In February, she wrote, "I'm sorry to find by your letter that your spirits are so low—the return of our parents will, I hope, restore them." John and Abigail, indeed, were on their way home from London, but Nabby's prescription for John Quincy's recovery turned out to be precisely the wrong one. His month-long reunion with his parents in Braintree in June and early July appears to have been a factor in making his depression even more debilitating. "What did you do to him?" his aunt, Elizabeth Shaw, in Haverhill, wrote her sister Abigail. By August, back in Newburyport, he had broken off his diary except for a line a day, more often than not referring to another sleepless night. He suffered terrible nightmares, severe stomach pains, blurry eyesight. In September he recorded that he could "neither read nor write" and on October 1 that "in the present situation of my health, I cannot possibly attend at all to study."[37]

John Quincy turned in desperation to his loving and gentle Aunt Elizabeth, who took one look at him and realized he needed a cure for both his severe sleep deprivation and his serious depression. She nursed him back to a happier frame of mind with herbal teas, a good bed, and loving care but remained apprehensive when he decided to complete his recovery in Braintree. Alerting his mother that her "son was here very sick and had alarming complaints," she wrote, "I have been very uneasy about him ever since—I think it is highly necessary for him to be exceeding careful as to Diet, Exercise, etc.—As to Study that must certainly be laid aside for the present." Soon after John Quincy's arrival home, Abigail (referred to at this point in her son's diary as "Madam") left for Long Island to be with Nabby after the birth of her second son. Even though the traditional place for a mother was to be with her daughter following childbirth, Elizabeth believed that Abigail's priorities were misplaced at this crisis point in her son's life: "I should not have thought his Mother would have left him," she wrote.[38]

John Quincy remained in Braintree, engaged in long conversations with his father, who spent the summer and fall awaiting a decision on the role he would play in the new government established when the Constitution was ratified in 1787. In March 1788, John Adams was elected vice president of the United States. By summer, he and Abigail had moved to New York, the house at Braintree was again empty, and John Quincy was back in Newburyport. Somehow, he had managed to pull himself out of his despair and could write his father in June 1789 that his "health has been restored beyond my expectations, and I have been able without injuring it, to devote a larger portion of my time to study than I hoped to when I left Braintree."[39]

Much more critical to his improved outlook on life than his ability to study law again was something he was not about to tell his mother: he was deeply in love with the exceptionally beautiful fifteen-year-old Mary Frazier and she with him. Their love affair later achieved mythic dimensions, partly because it was eventually thwarted but also because, for once, John Quincy was almost entirely silent about it. He noted the relationship only cryptically in his diary—he was restricting himself to a line a day—and he alluded to it only indirectly in correspondence with his friends. What is known from the diary is that for the next year the couple spent as much time as possible together.

In an old man's recollections, that year in the seacoast Massachusetts town was magical. At seventy-one, having come upon Mary's name on a gravestone, John Quincy recalled her as "to me the most beautiful and most beloved of her sex." During his clerkship in Newburyport, he had worked on a long, satiric poem, "The Vision," in which he described eight young ladies, in turn and at length, in mostly uncomplimentary terms. In 1790, he added a final stanza, this time a paean to the pure white skin, rosy cheeks, blue eyes, and golden hair of "Clara." The final lines constitute nothing less than a proposal of marriage:

On thee thy ardent lover's fate depends,
From thee the evil or the boon descends;
Thy choice alone can make my anxious breast
Supremely wretched, or supremely blest.[40]

In the beautiful Newburyport teenager, John Quincy may have been seeking less a strong, equal partner in marriage—as exemplified for all time by his mother—than a goddess who would never demand anything of him but his adoration. But reality, in the form of both sets of parents, intervened. To John Quincy's hints that he hoped to establish his law practice in Newburyport when his clerkship ended in the summer of 1790, both John and Abigail Adams responded that he must, instead, set up his office in Boston, a much larger, more cosmopolitan venue. Clearly, in order to earn enough income to gain his financial independence and support a wife, John Quincy needed to make a success at the law, and his parents' arguments that Boston provided the best opportunities for a thriving practice won the day.

By this time, Abigail, whom John Quincy had carefully kept ignorant of the connection, had heard rumors of the attachment between her son and Mary, and she moved swiftly to detach the couple: "Common fame reports that you are attached to a young lady. I am sorry that such a report should prevail," she wrote her son as soon as she had deduced the object of his affections. In letter after letter, she hammered home the point that no self-respecting gentleman would ask a young woman to commit herself to an engagement when he could not support her at the social level to which she had been accustomed. This was a sore point with John Quincy, who had long chafed under feelings of financial dependence on his parents; his mother's letters "added not a little to the weight of anxiety which before lay heavy on my mind."[41]

Despite his mother's unrelenting pressure and his own serious misgivings as to his money-making potential, John Quincy asked Mary to pledge herself to him informally with the understanding that the two would marry as soon as he had acquired sufficient income to support her in an appropriate style. But now her parents stepped in. Mary was made to insist on a public, formal engagement that would not leave her in limbo for an indeterminate period. In October, the lovers reached what John Quincy termed "a critical period" in their discussions, and by November 2, it was all over. They agreed never to marry unless they could find partners who equaled the qualities each had found in the other, but their rupture was understood by both to be final. Even as John Quincy began to establish himself financially, he never renewed his courtship.

Nevertheless, he seems to have resented his mother's intervention throughout his long life. Fully fifty-eight years after the event, he recalled "a genuine but not a fortunate passion" in which "the heart which . . . responded to mine was estranged from me by the intervention of a colder bosom." Although at the time he stoutly wrote Abigail that she would be relieved to know that he was now absolutely free of any attachment and would remain so, to others he confessed that his heart was very much wounded and that it would be a long time, if ever, before he bestowed it so completely again.

Meanwhile, John Quincy was faced with the imperative of earning his living. Although he had been admitted to the bar in the summer of 1790, he had no confidence in his legal skills. Technically, he had served his three-year apprenticeship to Theophilus Parsons. In fact, serious bouts of illness, long vacations, and extended visits to his parents meant that he had put far less than the requisite three years into learning the law. Few prospective clients visited his office in a house owned by his father on Court Street in Boston. He lost his first case. On December 20, his line-a-day entry read: "Succession of nothing. Read in the evening."

This time, John and Abigail Adams were alert to the unmistakable signs of an impending major depression in their eldest son. He accepted their invitation in January to visit them in Philadelphia, now the seat of the federal government. Caught up in the political life of the nation's capital and privileged, as the vice president's son, to sit at dinner nightly with the leaders of the new nation, John Quincy saw his spirits began to revive; the hopelessness that had haunted his long, lonely days and evenings in his empty Court Street office in Boston began to recede.

Over the next few years, John Quincy gradually found a place for himself in Boston. He became active in politics, serving on a committee to improve the Boston police organization and drafting the measures that would separate the north parish of Braintree, where the Adams homes were located, into a new town, Quincy, named after his great-grandfather. His widely read essays in the *Columbian Centinel*, published under the pseudonym Publicola, in rebuttal of Thomas Paine's *The Rights of Man* were reprinted throughout America and in Europe. To his immense gratification, his powers as an essayist were recognized on both sides of the political divide that would soon develop into the Federalist and Republican (Jeffersonian) parties. His social life improved, and his diary even hints at a new, ultimately unsuccessful, love ("Feel the relief of defeated hopes"). With his thoughts turning to a potential literary career, he felt less constrained by the necessity of earning his living as a lawyer. But this quiet, bookish life was not at all what his parents had pinned their hopes on.[42]

"You come into life with advantages which will disgrace you if your success is mediocre," wrote his father in April 1794, when John Quincy was twenty-six. "If you do not rise to the head not only of your profession but of your country, it will be owing to your *Laziness, Sloth, and Obstinacy*." A month later, adopting an entirely different tone, a buoyant John Adams informed his son that George Washington, favorably impressed with John Quincy's essays in support of a strong executive and in favor of the president's foreign policy, had appointed him minister to the Netherlands. No longer would he need to struggle to maintain a law practice. Denying any role in the appointment, his father wrote from Philadelphia that John Quincy's public career could now begin. "If this event should affect your sensibility as much as it does mine," the vice president assured his son, "it will make a deep impression upon your mind, both of the Importance of the Mission and of your obligation to Gratitude, Fidelity, and Exertion in the Discharge of the duties of it."[43]

John Quincy, whose wishes had not been consulted, was not nearly as delighted at the news. "I rather wish [the appointment] had not been made at all," he wrote in his diary on June 10, 1794. In September, he sailed from Boston to Holland, via London, with his younger brother Thomas as secretary.

For the next three years, John Quincy would serve as the American resident minister to a nation recently occupied by France, which was just entering its two-decade quest for dominance over Europe and England. He used his largely ceremonial post to act as America's eyes and ears on the Continent, and his detailed, cogent reports to his father provided critical intelligence and foreign policy analysis to key members of Washington's cabinet. The president himself praised the young diplomat's letters ("They contain a great deal of interesting matter, and . . . much important information and political insight") and relied on his judgment. He told the proud father, "Things appear to me exactly as they do to your son."[44]

In the early fall of 1795, just over a year after his arrival in The Hague, he was assigned by the new secretary of state, Timothy Pickering, to go to London to substitute for Ambassador Thomas Pinckney (in Spain on a special mission) at the final ratification of Jay's Treaty. A complicated agreement intended to resolve outstanding questions between England and America, the treaty covered such issues as the status of British troops in the American northwest, war reparations claimed by American merchants, and the honoring of America's neutrality in European conflicts, particularly on the high seas. John Quincy had initially been reluctant to bestir himself from The Hague to travel to London for a single ceremonial act. His mother, characteristically, urged him to seize the opportunity to shine: "You will prove yourself the Genuine Scion of the Stock from which you spring," Abigail prodded her son in September. But because he was delayed by weather in leaving Holland, the treaty was ratified before he arrived in London, and the entire trip proved unnecessary.[45]

But with Pinckney still in Spain, John Quincy claimed he was required to remain in London until orders arrived for him to return to The Hague. From late fall 1795 through the winter of 1796, any official American representation in Holland seems to have been ably handled by young Tom Adams, his older brother's secretary. Meanwhile, as the temporary senior minister on the scene in London, John Quincy tried to represent the United States at the British court. It took no time at all for the wily diplomats in the Foreign Office to seize the opportunity to take advantage of his vanity and inexperience. He put himself on the alert: "Extreme caution becomes more and more necessary. Surrounded with man-traps and spring guns, I cannot take a step without risk of error," but he knew he was making a mess of things: "Stupid blunder—Never can be satisfied with myself."[46]

His self-criticism was well placed. Gouverneur Morris, a former American minister to France and perennial favorite in British royal circles, was unimpressed with what he observed. "[He] is deeply tinctured with suspicion and sees design in everything. His mind has received an early wrong bias, and I think it will always go obliquely," Morris recorded in his diary a few weeks after John Quincy arrived in London. Two months later, Morris had no reason to revise his negative first impression of the young diplomat: "Mr. Adams . . . in his wrath and indignation at the conduct of the British Government, seemed absolutely mad. He breathed nothing but war, and was content to run into it at the hazard of our finances and even of our Constitution. Such sentiments are in him only for a moment and would not certainly influence his conduct, but such language . . . must do mischief here."[47]

By January 16, two months after his arrival from Holland, John Quincy realized his ability to perform any meaningful diplomatic work in London had been fatally compromised: "[The] papers say I took leave of the king yesterday and am going home. I suppose it is meant as a hint to me. I can certainly henceforth do no good here. But I cannot well go, without receiving further orders from home."[48]

Even to his diary, John Quincy was not being entirely honest. He had been assigned to London on a specific mission, a task that had been completed without him. Since Ambassador Pinckney had returned to London in early January, Adams's role was now redundant. He probably could have returned to Holland, resumed his diplomatic and reporting roles, and received no reprimand from the secretary of state.

But acknowledged or not, John Quincy had fallen in love. He would not leave London until he had won the hand of the sweet soprano of Tower Hill.

4

A FINE ROMANCE

I loved with all the affection of a warm and untried heart.

— LOUISA CATHERINE ADAMS, *"Record of a Life"*

Theirs was not a match made in heaven. Highly sensitive, quick-tempered, and prone to self-doubt and depression, Louisa and John Quincy mirrored and reinforced the other's least attractive and most vulnerable characteristics. The exceptional strengths they shared — intelligence, ambition, courage in adversity — would be critical to a marital bond lasting more than fifty years but did little to ease their path through an excruciatingly painful courtship and engagement period.

Although it took John Quincy more than a month after his first visit to the Johnsons to find his way back to Cooper's Row, he soon became a regular. At Nancy Johnson's birthday ball on December 22, 1795, a week after his belated return, he danced until 3 A.M. For the next four months, he spent nearly every evening (and often into the early morning) at the mansion on Tower Hill, joining the family and other guests at an early dinner and nearly always showing up later in the evening for marathon games of whist or a musical recital featuring the Johnson daughters. On other days he met the family around the dinner tables of American expatriates, escorted Catherine Johnson and her daughters to the theater, or accompanied the ladies when they were out walking or driving their carriage in Hyde Park.

Catherine realized at once that a serious campaign to win one of her daughters was under way. She was delighted, but her husband was not. "He [John Quincy] was a great favorite of my mothers, but I do not think my father admired him so much. He always had a prejudice towards the *Yankees* and insisted that they never made good husbands."[1]

Unlike previous suitors with New England roots, however, the son of the American vice president could not be denied a welcome at the home of the

The teen-aged Louisa, by Edward Savage, circa 1794, at about the time she met John Quincy. Courtesy of National Park Service, Adams National Historical Park.

nation's London consul. At first everyone was convinced that John Quincy was courting Nancy. Louisa, writing in the White House at a time when her self-esteem was at a very low point, recalled that since she typically played Cinderella to her sisters, she was not accustomed to being anyone's love interest: "It proceeded from the habit of thinking myself less attractive than my sisters. . . . My Mother was always talking to me of my awkwardness; my father of my bashfulness; my sisters made sure I was the block [model] on which all their fashions were tried and in this way I was constantly exposed to the ridicule of the whole."[2]

Secure in the universal belief that John Quincy's nightly appearances in the Johnson drawing room were due to Nancy's beauty, charm, and proficiency on the piano, Louisa "rattled on" to him without self-consciousness or self-restraint. Not for the last time did she and her lover completely misunderstand one another.

He never had any doubt where his affections lay. In a catalog of the Johnson sisters' musical accomplishments, he names only Louisa: "Evening at Mr. Johnson's. His daughters pretty and agreeable. The eldest performs remarkably well on the piano forte. The second Louisa sings. The third plays on the harp. Late home." Throughout the winter, his focus was entirely on Louisa: "Evening at Mr. Johnson's. Louisa sings prettily" (February 7); "Louisa Johnson, 21" (February 12); "Evening at Mr. Johnson's. Louisa ill" (February 14); "Evening at Mr. Johnson's. Louisa recovering" (February 15); "Covent Garden Oratorio with the ladies" (February 17).[3]

John Quincy's strong reaction to Louisa's song selections was the first indication that he had more than a brotherly—in fact, a jealous—interest in her: "I never observed any thing in Mr. Adams's conduct towards me that indicated the smallest preference but used to be surprised sometimes at his dislike of some of the songs which I used to sing. All those which he knew to be favourites of Col. [John] Trumble were so disagreeable to him he would immediately take his hat and bid us good night when I began one of them."[4]

John Quincy, believing he recognized a rival in the dashing painter and regular guest in the Johnson drawing room, deeply resented the easy familiarity, the flirtatious inside jokes, the favorite songs between the artist and the winsome twenty-one-year-old. A year later, safely engaged, he wrote Louisa that, in his jealousy, he had cursed Trumbull, then about forty, "by my Gods—Wish'd him at the D—. Innocent as he was of all I feared."[5]

Bantering with the prickly visitor about his sensitivity to certain of her performance pieces, Louisa challenged him to come up with lyrics of his own. She and everyone else were surprised when he did exactly that. One evening, he wordlessly reached across the dinner table and handed her a folded sheet of paper. Unsuspectingly, she opened the note, realized it contained the lyrics she had been promised, and began to read them aloud. Miss Henning, the family's governess and a sentimental woman steeped in the romantic novels of the day, hissed for Louisa to stop reading and snatched the paper from her hands.

Confused and embarrassed, Louisa found herself in a very uncomfortable position. She believed it entirely possible that Miss Henning's histrionics had given the verses more significance than their author had intended, but that was not how everyone else around the table interpreted the situation. For many days "the whole family [was thrown] into confusion." Having mistakenly assumed that she was the object of the young diplomat's affections, Nancy was furious and humiliated. Louisa's claim that everyone was reading too much into some simple lyrics was soon disproved. On January 27, at a ball in honor of her upcoming twenty-first birthday, John Quincy, mentioning no other partner, recorded that he "danced with Louisa" and stayed at the party until after 3 A.M. It was at this ball that he "first made his attentions decidedly publick, which brought much trouble on my head."[6]

The atmosphere in the Johnson household now became rife with tension. For months, Nancy refused to speak to her younger sister and did everything she could to make her miserable. Louisa recalled that her sisters "contrived to make me suffer so severely that even my first lesson's in the belle passion were pretty thickly strewed with thorns—love seemd to chill all the natural hilarity of my disposition, and those hours which had been spent in cheerful mirth were passed in gloom and anxiety in a sort of consciousness of some thing wrong without knowing to find the error."[7]

The first signs of "some thing wrong" came only four days after the birthday ball—if a cryptic reference in John Quincy's diary refers to Louisa: "Not in the best temper. Revolution." Two days later, a temporary peace had been established: "Evening at Drury Lane Theatre. Mrs. Johnson and her daughters at Mrs. Church's box . . . went home with the Ladies. Had a partial explanation with one of the ladies which gave some satisfaction."[8]

And so the courtship took its tortuous course throughout the winter of 1796. As a pair of lovers, the two were more like Shakespeare's Beatrice and Benedick than Romeo and Juliet. Their tiffs, misunderstandings, and reconciliations are alluded to on page after page of John Quincy's diary that winter. On February 7 ("Louisa sings prettily") and on February 10 ("Excellent music. The favorite song"), all seemed well. But a week later, following an evening at the Covent Garden Theatre to hear Handel's *L'Allegro and il Penseroso* with the Johnson women and several other escorts, John Quincy was morose: "Not much pleased with the music. Displeased with several trifling incidents. Above all dissatisfied with myself for suffering such things to possess an influence over me . . . sullen and silent the whole time."[9]

Who was it that was "sullen and silent"? John Quincy may have been referring only to his own bad humor, but if Louisa seemed remote, it might have been because she was trying to talk herself into falling in love with this proud, moody American. It should not have been such hard work. John Singleton Copley's well-known portrait of John Quincy, painted that winter, depicts a handsome man, upright and slim, with a full head of wavy hair, a direct, challenging gaze, and a mouth not yet hardened into the straight line that characterized his later likenesses. The young, attractive, worldly bachelor, already an established diplomat, and, best of all, the eldest son of a prominent American family, was obviously a prime matrimonial catch.

Louisa had long seen herself as somehow different from her sisters and the other young women she met in society. They might spend their days flirting and gossiping, but she held herself to a different standard. "Music and reading were the only things in life I thought worth living for excepting to laugh at all the oddities which fell on my way." Teased as haughty and proud by her schoolmates, she had secretly believed, even as a schoolgirl, that she was destined to play the heroine on a grander stage. As a well-bred young woman of her time, Louisa carefully denied any desire to excel, but it is clear she relished the special attention and praise she regularly received from her father and the older, distinguished artists, businessmen, and statesmen who frequented the Cooper's Row mansion. Marriage to a brilliant man of unlimited prospects would have seemed the surest way to achieve her ambition to be "somebody," and if the satisfaction of winning the race to the altar over two sisters who had for so long belittled her ability to attract the opposite sex could not be acknowledged, it could be privately relished. But Louisa, though flattered and tempted, was not yet in love, and she knew it: "Long did I contend against the probability of such an affection resting in the heart of [John Quincy], for had [Miss Henning] not argued so strongly that she had discovered it all the winter and that she had foreseen how it would end, that my vanity was enlisted, and, without a particle of affection at the time, I suffer'd myself to be coaxed into an affection that lasted probably much longer then would have done love at first sight."[10]

Love, at first sight or otherwise, brought no bliss to either Louisa or John Quincy. Her memories of the winter of 1796 focused on the jealousy that arose among the sisters, her dread of too soon being forced to leave the close family circle, and her growing recognition that her suitor's volatile temper could flare at the slightest provocation. On his part, a winter of idleness fed John Quincy's fear that he could never meet the high standards set by his parents and that he was, in fact, falling prey to the "Laziness, Sloth, and Obstinacy" his father had warned him he was prone to. As a true Adams, John Quincy was angry at himself for wasting time. He did not enjoy being in love, if that is what he was. In a typical burst of self-recrimination early in his pursuit of Louisa, he wrote in his diary, "Customary day, dull and dissipated. Pass the morning in sauntering, visiting, or lounging. Write scarce anything. Dine out almost every day and pass the Evening at Mr. Johnson's—Health low. Spirits lower. This must be reformed almost entirely."[11]

But he did not "reform." Despite his best intentions to rise early, spend his days with his books, and get to bed well before midnight, John Quincy seemed irresistibly drawn to the beauty, hospitality, and music so abundantly on display on Tower Hill.

For her part, Louisa had no idea where she stood with her purported, but undeclared, suitor. John Quincy had made his preference among the sisters clear but had given no definite indication that he intended to act on his inclinations. Louisa was left to wonder whether she was simply a distraction to beguile the evening hours while he awaited orders from the secretary of state to return to Holland, or something more. Uncertainty made her irritable, quick to take offense, and, on several occasions, physically ill. Meanwhile, John Quincy obsessed nightly—but obliquely—in his diary about Louisa's moods, his own missteps, and their frequent misunderstandings. Probably his darkest moment occurred on March 2, more than a month after he had "made his attentions decidedly publick," when something unexplained happened at a large party at the Johnsons': "Ring from Louisa's finger. Tricks play'd. A little music and dancing. Placed in a very difficult dilemma. Know not how I shall escape from it."[12]

Since Louisa did not report the ring episode in her memoirs and John Quincy's diary entries are frustratingly cryptic, we cannot know what actually happened or how it was resolved, but the incident was typical of a courtship fraught with angst on both sides.

Given Louisa's feelings at the time, there is almost no likelihood she played any part in a ploy aimed at inducing John Quincy to declare his intentions more openly than he already had. Her sisters and their prankish friends—several of whom were at the party—may have devised a plot intended to discomfit both Louisa and her beau. On the other hand, if John Quincy himself was the trickster, he had brought on himself more than he bargained for. The next night, he and Louisa had "some conversation. Did not close well." A week later, the notation "Music but no singing" indicated she was not yet appeased.[13]

After he had walked in the park with Catherine and spent the evening at Cooper's Row three days later, the "situation [was] still embarrassing." Despite this and many other contretemps ("Difference with Louisa. Repaired, however," is a characteristic diary entry), John Quincy's pursuit of his intended bride continued unabated. As he never explicitly acknowledged the courtship in his diary, to either set of parents, or to Louisa herself, his constant presence at No. 8,

Cooper's Row could have been interpreted in the expatriate community as simply a fondness for the society of the Johnson family. He was not the only young man about town attempting to maintain himself on limited funds in a sophisticated, expensive city who was attracted by the free food, wine, and evening entertainment Joshua Johnson so generously provided. Other Americans in London made the Tower Hill mansion a regular stop on their evening rounds, a source of some concern to the only serious suitor among them. His diary lists every other male visitor at the Johnson dinner table and at after-dinner music and whist parties—women guests, if there were any, went largely unreported— but only he actually seems to have been courting one of the sisters.

As the winter wore on, John Quincy's self-loathing increased. He constantly berated himself for wasting so much time, for sleeping so late, for spending so few hours in serious study. He again vowed to reform, and on April 1 embarked on a new schedule that involved reading several chapters of Gibbon's *Miscellaneous Works* each day. His resolution lasted exactly twenty-four hours; by the next evening, he was back in the Johnson drawing room and arrived home "late as usual." Even when an afternoon and evening with the Johnsons went exactly as he hoped it would, he found reason to bemoan his enjoyment: "Some music. Harp, Flute, Piano-Forte, & Voice, etc.—Wherefore must this be so pleasing?"[14]

Finally, Catherine, acting alone, had had enough. On April 13, a Wednesday, she summoned John Quincy and demanded to know exactly what he had in mind concerning her daughter. Forced to come to the point, he explained his "views and intentions" to her apparent satisfaction. Neither thought to consult Louisa or obtain Joshua's consent. To John Quincy's amazement, "something was uncommonly out of course" on Thursday, when he arrived for the evening as usual, and the chill did not lift when he "required an explanation of last night's singularities from Louisa" the next day. She was clearly furious that he had not proposed to her before talking to her mother and offended that her consent had been taken for granted so casually. She asked for time to think things over. Joshua, reluctant to lose his favorite child and, as a southerner, instinctively wary of New Englanders, no matter how cosmopolitan they appeared, also may have needed convincing. But Catherine's steely determination to bring off the match won the day. When what seems to have been a tense weekend had passed, Louisa had made her decision. She would become the bride of John Quincy Adams.

An immediate problem arose. Both Louisa and Joshua balked at John Quincy's refusal to set even an approximate wedding date ("in one year or seven") and his insistence on returning to Holland alone, there to await an unspecified change in his financial and professional situation that would enable him to support a wife. Father and daughter argued that Louisa, neither unattached nor married, would be left in an untenable situation for an indeterminate period, unable to move freely in society or to make any rational plans for her future life. But John Quincy stuck stubbornly to his guns: "Upon one point, however, the only one to which I must adhere, neither of them [Louisa or Joshua] was satisfied—the right and the reason of the thing are, however, indisputably with me, and I shall accordingly persist."15

In fact, it was Louisa, with her "horror of the banter and jests to which a young woman is exposed who is known to be engaged," who was on the side not only of right and reason but of custom and common sense. Her objections to a long, uncertain engagement were widely shared at the time. In Jane Austen's *Persuasion*, the mother of a prospective bride and an acquaintance are overheard discussing what appears to be a precipitate rush to the altar:

> "There is nothing I so abominate for young people as a long engagement. It is what I always protested against for my children. It is all very well, I used to say, for young people to be engaged, if there is a certainty of their being able to marry in six months, or even in twelve, but a long engagement!"
>
> "Yes, dear ma'am," said Mrs. Croft, "or an uncertain engagement; an engagement which may be long. To begin without knowing that at such a time there will be the means of marrying, I hold to be very unsafe and unwise, and what, I think, all parents should prevent as far as they can."16

Always the doting parent, Joshua exerted every effort to protect his beloved daughter from exactly that "unsafe and unwise" situation, but he was forced to succumb to the will of his future son-in-law. Louisa herself, under the misapprehension that the volatile political situation on the Continent, particularly the unrest emanating from France, was what primarily constrained John Quincy from taking her with him, offered to marry him at once and join him at a later date: "I urged him to give me a right to his name before he left me. . . . I had the idea in my head that as the principal reason assign'd for marriage not taking place was the then state of Holland, that as soon as things in that Country were sufficiently settled I could have join'd my husband without impropriety."17

Her offer was refused. There was no offer, in fact, that would have been accepted. In his heart, John Quincy had no real desire to become a married man. He saw a wife as an impediment to the life of quiet study and regular habits he would eagerly resume as soon as he returned to Holland and a financial burden he could ill afford. It was enough for him to know that when he married, Louisa would be his choice. Louisa, meanwhile, receiving the accurate impression that her fiancé was stalling, tried vainly to understand his insistence on indefinitely delaying the wedding.

John Quincy now roused himself to find passage back to Holland. Nine days after his "partially satisfactory" initial negotiation with Louisa and her father, and finally armed with the orders from the secretary of state to return to his post, he began seeking a shipmaster willing to take a passenger on short notice to Rotterdam. A month later he would be gone.

Meanwhile, something other than Louisa's engagement had occurred to throw the Johnson household temporarily into disarray. Catherine began to appear ill and dejected at evening parties. Her mood spread throughout the family; soon, everyone, according to John Quincy, was "unwell and dispirited." Finally, Louisa explained to him something of why the Johnsons were so distraught—almost certainly, some bad news concerning one or more of Joshua's myriad commercial ventures. Now practically a member of the family, John Quincy caught his first glimpse of the shaky financial foundation underpinning the elaborate Tower Hill establishment.

For the next few weeks, however, the old routine of afternoon promenades, musical evenings, and gala balls resumed. On May 10, less than a month after he had become engaged, John Quincy disgustedly wrote in his diary, "Time for me to go." But he did not get away soon enough. The very next day, he and Louisa quarreled bitterly.

It all began innocently enough. John Quincy and two other gentlemen agreed to escort the Johnson sisters and their mother on a tour of the pleasure gardens at Ranelagh, a twenty-three-acre wooded park in the Chelsea area of London featuring winding paths, ornamental canals, and sparkling fountains surrounding an immense wooden rotunda. In 1796, Ranelagh, the city's most fashionable venue for masquerades, concerts, and fireworks, was the perfect place for a party of young people to pass a festive May evening. The night before their excursion, Louisa playfully warned John Quincy he would have to "dress himself handsomely and look as dashy as possible" if he wanted to compete with the dandies typically on parade along Ranelagh's wooded pathways.

Louisa did not apprehend how extremely sensitive her fiancé was to the slightest remark about his grooming or attire. His mother had berated him from an early age for his "slovenly" habits and dress. When his aunt reported to her sister that the fledgling Boston lawyer "had not a pair of stockings or drawers fit to put on," Abigail had not hesitated to let him know he was disgracing the entire family by his failure to keep up appearances.[18]

Never suspecting she was walking into a hornet's nest, Louisa dressed herself "very becomingly" and the party "drove off in high spirits expecting a delightful evening." To her delight, John Quincy, as instructed, "was very handsomely dressed in blue," with "a large napoleon hat" and "altogether looked remarkably well." When the group separated to stroll in couples around the rotunda, Louisa happily took John Quincy's arm and complimented him on his appearance. That was the last straw: "He immediately took fire and assured me that *his* wife must never take the liberty of interfering in those particulars, and assumed a tone so high and lofty and made so serious a grievance of the affair, that I felt offended and told him that I resign'd all pretensions to his hand, and left him as free as air to choose a lady who would be more discreet. I then dropped his arm and joined my mother with whom I staid the remainder of the evening."[19]

The couple reconciled on the way home to Tower Hill, but the quarrel, which John Quincy noted in his diary simply as "Dress lessons," went deeper than a difference over sartorial choices. He may have believed that an apology and a "satisfactory explanation" had put the matter behind them, but Louisa knew better. For her, the barbs they hurled at one another in the Ranelagh rotunda left wounds that never fully healed: She was still smarting twenty-five years later. "If lovers' quarrels are a renewal of love, they also leave a sting behind which, however apparently behind us, opens on every trivial occasion."[20]

Louisa glimpsed in the rotunda at Ranelagh that evening "a momentary gleam of light," one of those "flashes of reason" that occur all too seldom when one is in love. Suddenly, she said, a "fear of some unknown and overhanging evil" she could not define threatened her rosy view of her future married life. If she had not seen it before, she saw it now—"a sense of unnecessary harshness and severity of character . . . which often caused me to fear something I knew not what and put a damp upon my natural spirits which I never overcame."[21]

Clearly recognizing she was entering into a lifetime relationship with a man cursed with a fragile ego, quick temper, rigid stubbornness, and a tendency to dominate, why Louisa went forward with the match is not entirely clear. Her father would certainly have supported her decision to release John Quincy from his promises. But her mother, faced with the challenge of marrying off seven daughters without fortunes, was not going to let a genuine prize get away. Catherine acknowledged, if Joshua and Louisa did not, that a ship would not be arriving any time soon to rescue the family's finances. When Louisa returned to her mother's side at Ranelagh, she probably received only the most perfunctory maternal sympathy.

Even Catherine, however, might yet have been thwarted had not her daughter finally and completely fallen in love. "I loved with all the affection of a warm and untried heart," Louisa recalled nostalgically. Her dreams of an idyllic future married life, born of the sentimental novels she had devoured and the conjugal happiness she had witnessed in her own parents, had ultimately overcome the qualms of her more rational moments. There is no doubt, moreover, that she and John Quincy were sexually attracted to one another—a passionate attachment that survived the darkest hours of their marriage—and that much of their premarital skirmishing had to do with bottled-up sexual tension. Even so, Louisa's loving nature must have been severely tested when her fiancé, on the eve of his departure, laid down a serious reading list and course of study specifically intended for the improvement of her mind. His gratuitous Pygmalion project seems to have served only to reinforce his sense of intellectual superiority and her feelings of inadequacy, however, and neither referred to it after the first month or two of their separation.[22]

At two in the morning of May 28, John Quincy noted, the lovers parted "with sensations unusually painful," and later that day he was on a ship bound for Holland. For the next thirteen months, their relationship would be conducted entirely by mail. Although the distance between them stretched only 191 miles, delivery of their letters could be delayed for more than a month, often resulting in an angry screed arriving just as the other had dispatched a love note. At first John Quincy's letters were heartfelt, even amorous. Happy in his preferred bachelor routine of writing long letters home, regular exercise, and analyzing events and trends in Continental politics, he seems to have been freed of his inhibitions. In his first letter from Holland, imploring that Louisa report to him in the minutest detail the most trivial happenings in her life, he pledged his love would cease "only with the last pulse of my heart." Louisa, however, had been so thoroughly cowed by her fiancé's apparent assumption that her mind was inferior to his that she could not bear the thought of his perusing her love letters with a judgmental eye. She put herself in the hands of the "officious" Miss Henning with the result that her early letters were embarrassingly saccharine: "Gauging of your feelings by my own I think it incumbent on me to avail myself of every opportunity of testifying my affectionate esteem for you."[23]

Mail packets from America were bringing John Quincy much less vapid communications, however. All winter, he had kept his relationship with Louisa concealed from his parents, perhaps because of indecision over whether he would finally propose to her but just as likely because he had no wish to relive the battering he had taken—from Abigail, particularly—when he had hoped to marry Mary Frazier five years earlier. He was tight-lipped in correspondence with his parents but not above dropping hints guaranteed to arouse his mother's suspicions. On the last day of March—the eve of his resolution to spend more time with Gibbon, less with the Johnsons—he wrote his mother, "I begin to think very seriously of the duty incumbent upon all good citizens to have a family—If you think this the language of a convert, perhaps you will enquire how he became so?—I am not yet prepared to answer that."[24]

Abigail leapt to the bait. Her first line of attack, on May 20, 1796, was to mock her son: "As you tell me that the enthusiasm of Youth has subsided, I will presume that reason and judgment have taken its place." Concerned that the chosen bride might be British, she admonished, "I would hope for the Love I bear my Country the Syren is at least *half blood*." Finally, in an allusion to the young Newburyport woman whose romance with John Quincy she had been instrumental in quashing, she asked, "Maria? Has she no claims?"[25]

Now thoroughly exercised and fearing that her prized son had been captivated by a London debutante whose social skills in upper-class drawing rooms would be of little help to his political career in the egalitarian United States, Abigail fired off a strongly worded letter five days later. Speculating from his broad hints that John Quincy's "flame" was one of the Johnson sisters, she asserted that although she would accept any choice he made, he should "weigh well, consider maturely of the most important action of your life." Probably at his wife's instigation, John Adams took time from his vice-presidential duties to remind his son that a young woman from a background like Louisa's "of fine parts and accomplishments, educated to drawing, dancing, and music" would most likely be captivated and then spoiled by the splendor of European courts and almost certainly would involve him in expenses far beyond his salary. "I give you a hint and you must take it," he warned.[26]

Abigail reiterated her husband's cautionary note a day later. She emphasized her potential daughter-in-law's youth and the likelihood she would be corrupted by "the licenses, dissipations, and amusements of a foreign Court," thus making her "unfit for the discharge of those domestic duties which cement the union of hearts and give it its sweetest pleasures." She reminded her son that his appointment was temporary and his salary "inadequate" in comparison with diplomats from other nations. With all the forcefulness at her command, she urged him to postpone marriage until he had reestablished himself in America sometime in the future.[27]

Although John Quincy did not yet know he had been appointed minister to Portugal—his next diplomatic assignment—both parents were well aware of this promotion in pay and prestige at the time they were raising their matrimonial red flags. They assumed that in taking up a new assignment, he would not be returning home for several years. By advising John Quincy to refrain from marrying until he could do so in America, they were, in effect, urging him to reconsider what they believed to be an extremely unwise decision and to put off acting on his choice for a very long time.

Their objections only stiffened John Quincy's resolve. He replied that his attachment was "irrevocably fixed" and that he had discussed at length with his prospective bride—whom he still did not name—the difficult adjustment she would face when at last they returned to America and he again became an impecunious lawyer. His future prospects, he said, had been described to her "in their true and not in flattering colours," and the sacrifices she would be asked to bear had been "explained, understood, and approved." As for corruption by the licentiousness of court life, he guaranteed her "delicate sense of propriety and mildness of disposition" would dispose her to follow his lead in living modestly and would shield her from the excesses of rank and wealth.[28]

Although he did not give his parents the satisfaction of acknowledging that their admonitions had hit the mark, John Quincy, in fact, had absorbed their warnings and adopted their point of view. Beginning in August, his letters to Louisa were full of advice on suppressing "some of the little attachments to splendor that lurk at your heart, perhaps imperceptibly to yourself." He began to paint their future in the bleakest terms, describing the hardships of land and sea travel, the difficulties in adapting to unfamiliar manners and customs, and the need to adopt "a cheerful conformity to things which must be endured." Most of all, he emphasized that she must "consider rank itself as an object of no consequence" and be prepared to give up "at an hour's warning" the splendor of an ambassador's station to "return to private life and no fortune." His parents themselves could not have communicated their concerns to their future daughter-in-law more emphatically.[29]

Louisa, finally, abandoned Miss Henning's stilted clichés and found her voice. She answered each of her fiancé's admonitions so fiercely that he was forced to reply immediately and shamefacedly, "Between us two, my lovely Friend, let there be Peace." She said he was wrong if he supposed her dazzled by rank ("I am and sincerely hoped to have remained a stranger to pomp"); she mentioned she had said nothing on whether or not he should accept the appointment to Lisbon, but, had he consulted her, her preference would have been an early return to America; and she claimed that the dangers and hardships of travel held no terrors for her. John Quincy was forced to backtrack ("As to the subject of pomp or parade, I will henceforth be totally silent upon it") and apologize for using the word "rank." He could not stop himself, however, from commenting on her tone ("satirical wit") and justifying his previous dire warnings on the difficulties that might lie in their path: "No, I prefer suffering the mortification even of a sneer from you rather than the future reproach of having excited false though pleasing contemplations." And then, in an all-too-prescient forecast of what lay ahead, he acknowledged, "I readily renounce all pretensions to address in the art of pleasing and hope you will find me throughout life rather a true and faithful than a complaisant friend."[30]

In this and other letters to Louisa in the fall of 1796, John Quincy made it clear he would inform her as soon her as he received final orders from Philadelphia to leave The Hague for Lisbon. He wrote that, barring unforeseen circumstances, he would travel to Portugal via London, and that, as Louisa remembered it, "our nuptials must take place immediately after his arrival as he could only spare a few days to me and family as he must proceed to his post without losing any time. Several letters came on the same subject, and my Mother began to prepare my wedding finery, which was all got ready for the expected occasion. Weeks rolled on, however, without any further intelligence and considering it as a false alarm, every thing was locked up and all the preparations concealed with as much care as if I had committed some crime in having made them."[31]

Louisa's feeling that she had done something very wrong in preparing her trousseau was not new. All summer she had been sequestered in a cottage rented by her parents in the then-fashionable London suburb of Clapham Common. Unable to move freely in society—neither bride nor belle—she seems to have been forced to endure isolation rather than risk potentially compromising situations such as dancing or conversing too freely with unattached young men. Her only social contact was with a young married woman convalescing from an injury, whom she joined two or three times a week for "lively conversation." Finally, her "painful" loneliness and boredom persuaded her parents to allow her to return home in the fall, but, predictably, her health began to suffer, especially as the family was now making definite plans to relocate to the United States and she feared she would be forced to accompany them.

Joshua, reluctant as ever to see his beloved daughter unwell and unhappy, took matters into his own hands. He wrote to John Quincy suggesting that he bring Louisa and Catherine with him to The Hague, where he had business to transact. There, he proposed, his daughter and her lover could be married, thus restoring her to "health and happiness." Such a reasonable proposal—written under the impulse of "the most honourable feelings"—was anathema to John Quincy. As Louisa recalled it, the diplomat's response was emphatic: "By return of mail [my father] received an answer so severe, so cold, and so peremptory, that his feelings were bitterly wounded and the pride of my nature was roused. I adored my father."[32]

The fiercely loyal daughter rose to her father's defense, and the lovers' correspondence almost immediately deteriorated into bitter exchanges, exacerbated by the distance separating them and the days, if not weeks, it took both attack and apology to reach the other. Although John Quincy counseled, "I hope we shall never get into a habit of writing to one another angry and kind letters alternately, for it would be far from promoting the happiness of either," neither seemed willing to yield the last word. Both Louisa and John Quincy unerringly directed their most poisonous darts exactly where they would be most hurtful, and neither waited to calm down before firing off another stinging attack.[33]

On the matter of the visit to Holland, John Quincy believed he had uncovered a devious plot. Louisa was particularly vulnerable because—although, significantly, she did not acknowledge it in her memoirs—she had opened herself up to rejection. More than a month before her father independently took it upon himself to propose a small, private, Dutch wedding, Louisa had suggested to John Quincy that the Johnson family might embark on its voyage to America via Holland, thus enabling the lovers to see one another once more before what might be a very long separation. John Quincy had turned that idea down flat. Claiming that to see her was the ardent wish of his heart, he nevertheless wrote, "The bitterness of a new separation would be so severely renewed, and the inconveniences of a double voyage to your father and family . . . and an increased distance and augmented perils upon the passage of the Atlantic, would be so great that the pleasure of a short and transient meeting cannot even in a lover's calculation be set in balance against the obstacles to your design."[34]

Unable to let practical considerations of backtracking across the North Sea before braving the Atlantic stand as enough justification for rejecting Louisa's suggestion, John Quincy felt he needed to "be candid and explicit" in letting her know he viewed her proposal as a backdoor route to marriage: "I feel myself compelled to assure you that the completion of our Union here would be impossible," he wrote, again conveying to his future bride all the cautionary advice he had received from his parents: "To connect the fortunes of any amiable woman indissolubly with mine, would be an act of absurdity towards myself and of cruelty towards her. How much would it be aggravated in your case when I should take you from the bosom of an excellent and happy family, where you have from your infancy scarcely formed a wish, but it was instantly supplied, and where possession of fortune has accustomed you to the enjoyment of every indulgence. My sentiments on the occasion therefore cannot hesitate a moment. They are paramount to every other consideration and fixed beyond the power of alteration."[35]

Her fiancé's inference that she had been plotting a wedding instead of a tender farewell roused Louisa to fury: "I have received your very decisive letter of 20th December which has astonished and mortified me so much that I can scarcely [conceive] you recollected to whom you were writing," she shot back. Continuing in the same angry vein, she attacked each of John Quincy's points: "You seem to complain of a want of confidence on my part . . . surely you cannot imagine that the authoritative stile of your letter at all calculated to inspire this confidence did I even know what you meant by it. I am very sorry to discover that we have not perfectly understood each other and to find it requisite to demand an explanation." In her own defense, she ridiculed his basic assumption: "In regard to what I did respecting our visit to Holland, you have appeared to have indulged unnecessary apprehensions." With the bitterness of a woman spurned, she evoked the "satisfaction I fondly and foolishly imagined would have been mutual" of meeting once more and protested that "had my hopes been such as your fears have magnified in my wish of seeing you in Holland, your rejection might have been softened by a declaration on your part of the probable time of our continued separation. The die is however cast. I go to America, you to your embassy, where I ardently pray the great disposer of events to grant that peace to *your* bosom which *mine* has been and will be long a stranger to."[36]

She knew her epistolary arrows, written on January 17, would find their target, and they did: "It [her letter] has given me as much pain as you expected and more than you intended," John Quincy responded less than two weeks later on January 28. Quoting her characterizations of his tone, he could not bring himself to acknowledge she might have had reason to be angry: "It has never been my intention to speak in an 'authoritative'; a 'commanding'; an 'unkind'; a 'harsh'; or a 'peremptory' stile to you and it distresses me to find that you think my letter of December 20 is deserving all those epithets. I did indeed intend to speak decisively, and I thought the occasion required it," he wrote.[37]

Before Louisa's letter reached The Hague, however, John Quincy had received her father's letter suggesting that the marriage take place in Holland before the family embarked for America. Convinced that father and daughter had acted jointly and that Louisa's protestations of innocence were suspect, John Quincy fired off a letter on January 10 reiterating and expanding upon the reasons for his adamant rejection of what he interpreted as the two Johnsons' marital designs. This time, in addition to the objections he had previously cited, he raised one especially calculated to wound a young woman raised to conform strictly to the rules of etiquette—the specter of society's disapproval: "You will be sensible what an appearance in the eyes of the world your coming here would have; an appearance consistent neither with your dignity nor my delicacy. You yourself consider it an extreme expedient . . . and I should therefore not mention my opinion of it in this point of view if I did not consider the perfect propriety and reserve of your conduct no less interesting to me than to you."[38]

In what must have seemed to Louisa like rubbing salt into her wounded ego, John Quincy was apparently more than willing to accept an indefinite delay in their matrimonial plans: "Let us my lovely friend submit with cheerfulness to the laws of necessity than to resort to unbecoming remedies for relief. Let us acquiesce with resignation in a postponement of our happiness which the course of events has rendered unavoidable, and which in all probability will prove ultimately for our own advantage rather than abandon ourselves to childish weakness or idle lamentations."[39]

Louisa's reaction was immediate and explosive:

> I regret most sincerely ever having expressed a wish to meet you in Holland, since it appears to have given you so much uneasiness, but indeed my friend you are causelessly alarmed. I really never have mentioned it to my father . . . and be satisfied that should he again offer to take me, I would immediately refuse. Believe me, I should be sorry to put it in your power or in that of the world, to say I wished to force myself upon any man or into any family—You tell me that our *visit* would neither have been consistent with your delicacy or my dignity. I rather think you ought to have reversed it and said it would have been inconsistent with your *dignity* and my *delicacy*. Whatever appearance my conduct may have to you I know not, but I am perfectly satisfied with its appearance to the world—I really am fearful that there has been a great want of dignity on my part, or I should not have had the mortification of receiving two such letters as you lately favored me with, which suffer me to say, are as unaccountable or undeserved as you seem to me have very little knowledge of my disposition, or would easily have seen that such letters would not pass unnoticed.[40]

A tipping point had been reached, and both pulled back from a final break. In an attempt to lay down ground rules and modulate the vehemence that had begun to characterize their correspondence, John Quincy wrote, "Let us understand one another, Louisa. I have always expected and intended that the communication of sentiments between you and me should be free, candid, open, and undisguised. If on either side they should occasionally give pain, I have trusted that the certainty of mutual affection would at least secure the most favourable construction; that nothing sarcastic, nothing bitter, nothing invidious, would ever pass between us; that expostulation itself would speak the language of love, and that Spirit would never be needed, or called in aid for the settlement of our differences."[41]

Apparently equating "spirit" with "temper" and describing it as a "repellent quality," he entreated his intended bride never again to use spirit against him and warned her not to test whether he could show his temper in opposition to hers.

Louisa, for her part, attempted to play the compliant female role in which her fiancé had cast her. Her subsequent letters are mostly full of sweet expressions of admiration and docility. There was nothing in her education or experience to encourage her to do anything but bow to what was generally assumed to be a man's superior understanding, reason, and knowledge of the world. Yet, from the beginning, she chafed at John Quincy's overbearing manner and only reluctantly accepted his insistence that her frequent manifestations of spirit required control and correction: "Let me again assure you, my best friend, that you shall never more be offended by an assertion of spirit that I in reality do not possess, and permit me to request you will cease to mention a subject which has already cost me so much pain, and for which I entreat your pardon. No sooner were those letters gone, than I repented my folly and was convinced my conduct was weak and ridiculous . . . and believe me, I shall carefully avoid every thing of the sort in future." She kept her word. From this point on, their letters spoke of love, admiration, and the sadness and loneliness of separation. John Quincy described walking three miles to the seashore so that he could look across the open sea and imagine he could see the coast of England. "An instant of illusion transported me to you," he wrote longingly. Responding to her lover's assertion that he had changed for the worse since she had last seen him, Louisa assured him, "No alteration can diminish my love for you."[42]

If the strains endemic to their lifetime relationship were clearly forecast in the passionate sparring that occurred around the immediate question of when the two would become man and wife, they were evident as well in running squabbles over less emotionally charged topics. Even literature, where their tastes and inclinations were remarkably similar, could become a source of dissension. Early in their yearlong separation, John Quincy urged Louisa to read Madame de Staël's *Memoirs*. She responded in surprise that he would suggest an author whose morals were so notoriously lax. Remarking that he would not soon again recommend a book to her, John Quincy defended the *Memoirs* for their literary and philosophic merit. Later, in a reversal of roles, Louisa asked for his opinion of Lord Chesterfield's *Letters to His Son*, and John

Quincy reacted with a scathing denunciation of the worldly courtier's character. Louisa, who had enjoyed the *Letters* except for its treatment of women ("He mentions the Ladies with so much severity"), responded with some asperity: "I am sorry I mentioned having read Lord Chesterfield's letters as it appears to have displeased you, which I always endeavor to avoid."[43]

Louisa also showed no hesitation in commenting on politics. She seems to have been the first to inform John Quincy of his father's election to the presidency and conveyed to him the flavor of political conversation and gossip she heard at her father's table: "It is here universally believed that your Father is elected president. If I may venture to give my opinion, I think it will be fortunate for America should he have gained his election—Mr. Jefferson, though a man of very great abilities, is not generally allowed to possess that calm, intrepid firmness, which the present period demands. Your father has always been accustomed to a public station. I make no doubt he would, as in every other, acquit himself to the satisfaction of all parties—it is certainly an arduous and difficult task, and by no means to be wished, yet the more difficult it at present appears, the more satisfaction he will enjoy from the faithful discharge of it for the welfare of his Country."[44]

Although John Quincy did not specifically discourage Louisa from expressing her political opinions, he never responded to her observations in a serious way. Instead, he emphasized what she termed his "dark side"—excessive concerns over the duties and cares as well as the vilification of the office of the presidency by the press with little indication of the pride he undoubtedly felt in the honor accorded his father: "I feel again indebted to you for mentioning the statements that you hear of concerning the American Election. . . . That so near and dear a relation of my own is personally concerned in the result, is to me a source of some of the most oppressive cares and anxieties that ever weighed upon my heart."[45]

In what may have been their true introduction to one another—and in what remains today a rare opportunity to listen in on a conversation between two intelligent, passionate individuals—the couple's weekly letters crossed the North Sea from June 1796 to June 1797. As the curtain rose on a fifty-year drama—a love story surprisingly modern and passionately played out—the voices of Louisa and John Quincy still ring exceptionally true in their courtship correspondence.

If John Quincy truly believed, as he assured his parents, that Louisa's character was distinguished by a "mildness of disposition," he has to have been surprised by the "spirit" he held against her. If he had imagined she would respond to his artfully constructed, highly literate letters with schoolgirl prattle, her cogent arguments delivered in strong, forceful language must have come as an unwelcome surprise. He took pride in his reputation as a brilliant writer, but he had met his match. Louisa's sentences have the balance and wit, if not the spelling and punctuation, that eighteenth-century essayists and letter writers strove to attain. "Your stile of writing is more than good. It is excellent," the critical John Quincy ultimately assured his fiancée. As much as he regularly attempted to patronize her—repeatedly calling her "my Louisa" and praising every instance in which she presented herself as sweet, adoring, and meekly apologetic—he could not deny that the woman he had chosen for his wife had an intellect that refused to be made subservient to his own. The question of whether a young woman who had left school—an institution with no academic pretensions—at fourteen could hold her own with a man who was as well educated as any American of his generation is answered by their correspondence. Louisa's native intelligence must have been of a very high order to have overcome her inadequate education and the years of frivolous conversation in which young ladies of her social class engaged while anticipating the arrival of their future husbands. The quiet girl in the corner, listening attentively as the eminent male visitors to the Cooper's Row mansion discussed politics, literature, science, music, and art, had received an informal higher education, and she made the most of what she had learned. On her own, Louisa had also become unusually well read. Her writing reflects an immersion in the great essayists of her time as well as an easy familiarity with Shakespeare and other notable poets and playwrights of the past.[46]

The couple's correspondence clearly foreshadowed the roles each would play—or attempt to play—in their marriage. Though each adopted a patently false persona—John Quincy, the wise counselor, Louisa the sweet, submissive acolyte—enough of their true personalities broke through to give them a foretaste of the future. John Quincy would always seek to dominate his spirited wife; Louisa would invariably resist. She would urge him to abandon his books occasionally to enjoy a taste of social life; he would respond that society was as distasteful to him as books were necessary. He would preach high-minded sermons about patience, endurance, and self-control; she would profess to agree with him but then continue to mention how difficult it was to practice exactly those virtues and how attempting to do so was playing havoc with her health, her looks, and her disposition.

John Quincy sought to portray himself as the fatherly teacher whose advice and instruction would be treasured and acted upon unquestioningly by his bright, docile, lifelong companion. He bridled whenever his judgments, language, or opinions were questioned and was quick to respond whenever Louisa held him to account or attempted to offer advice. He lashed out defensively when she quoted from his own letters to prove a point. For all his experience and achievements, John Quincy nursed deep insecurities, which he acknowledged only to his diary and which he betrayed in his letters to Louisa. Fearing to seem weak, he overplayed the dominant male, but he was quick to retreat when his "best friend" stood up against his volleys and was eager to do and say whatever was necessary to return to her good graces.

Louisa's role in the correspondence was more complicated. Torn between social pressure on a young unmarried woman to remain blissfully innocent and acquiescent to the strictures laid down by a wiser, more rational, older man and her own unquenchable need to assert herself, she wavered from defiance to submission, sometimes in a single letter. Even more than her fiancé, she nursed insecurities that limited her confidence that she could, for long, stand up for herself in the face of what she saw as John Quincy's superior intellect and worldly experience. In the worst moments of their courtship, there was no one to reassure Louisa that she was justified in calling her lover to task when he was particularly insufferable.

Even during their most bitter moments, however, John Quincy and Louisa managed, openly and lovingly, to express their deep affection for one another. Unlike the senior Adamses, who habitually greeted one another in their letters as "My Dearest Friend," John Quincy and Louisa in their early correspondence abstained from salutations of any kind. Nonetheless, they routinely referred to one another in the text as "my beloved friend" or "my most esteemed friend" (Louisa to John Quincy), "my ever dear and valued friend," "my amiable friend," or "my lovely friend" (John Quincy to Louisa), and never let an accusing or resentful letter close without fond expressions of love.

Throughout their correspondence, John Quincy's precedence was tacitly acknowledged. He regularly invoked his fiancée's name ("Such, Louisa, is the condition of human Nature"), a style that conveyed a conversational, but sometimes pedantic, tone. He signed his letters "A." Louisa obviously had much more difficulty with the problem of names. Never did she address her lover as "John." Her characteristic signature to even her most tender and romantic letters was the formal "Louisa C. Johnson." The balance of power in the marital relationship was being established: the future husband was permitted to address his future wife by her first name and to sign off casually with only his last initial. In contrast, she could refer to him only indirectly and seemed constrained, possibly by custom, to a formal mode of address, even extending to her own name.

The flow of letters back and forth across the North Sea came to a close in a way that Louisa had not dared hope for and that John Quincy had regularly claimed was out of the question. By the spring of 1797, the Johnson family was making final preparations for their projected July departure for Maryland, and Louisa fully expected to accompany her parents and siblings there. In April John Quincy finally received his orders from the secretary of state to proceed as soon as possible to the embassy in Portugal. Reversing himself on all the arguments he had been making for six months as to why Louisa could not accompany him there, he held out a hope that, perhaps, something could be worked out: "My principal embarrassment is how to make arrangements so as to render it possible for me to visit London on my way that I may have the pleasure of meeting you there, and putting an end at length to a separation so painful to us both. I have in some of my former Letters mentioned several circumstances which seem to render inexpedient your going to Lisbon; yet the moment when the possibility that you may [go] presented itself to me, all those objections lost much of their force in my mind, and my inclination to have your company almost silenced every objection that Reason and Prudence had raised."[47]

For the next month, Louisa's hopes were alternately raised and dashed as her fiancé, while claiming it was the dearest wish of his heart to marry her as soon as possible, came up with reason after reason why it would be impossible to do so. The major roadblock seemed to be logistical. John Quincy needed to travel from Rotterdam to Lisbon on a ship registered to a neutral nation because French privateers had made it a practice to harass British ships. He found a Danish ship that met his requirements, but, of course, that vessel could not make a side trip to England so that he could be married. Louisa appealed to her father, who offered to remove one of his ships, the *Mary* (of American registry and, therefore, neutral), from its regular route and send it from London to Lisbon with the honeymooning couple, Tom Adams, and two personal servants aboard. John Quincy accepted grudgingly, pointing out he thought it wasteful to devote an entire merchant schooner to transporting five passengers: "I am sorry that you concluded to send the *Mary* to Lisbon for the sole purpose of carrying us. . . . I hope you will not on that account omit any [effort] to employ her in another way."[48]

Finally, having exhausted his stock of obstacles that might indefinitely delay the marriage, John Quincy took the extraordinary step of offering Louisa one last chance to reconsider their mutual commitment: "You know the man you have chosen for the friend of your life—You know him the better for that absence which has at once shown you a trial of his affection and of his temper. He has disguised to you none of his feelings and weaknesses. You know the chances of hardship, inconvenience and danger, which you may be called to share with him. You know his inviolable attachment to his Country and his resolute determination not to continue long his absence from it. You know that upon his retirement the state of his fortune will require privations which will be painful to him only as they may affect you. Choose, Louisa, choose for yourself, and be assured that his Heart will ratify your choice."[49]

Louisa professed no doubt: "Why my beloved friend did you tell me to choose, what I have always declared, requires not a moments hesitation to determine." But her avowal of constancy and love failed to convince her pessimistic fiancé: "Be but as easily pleased my friend after marriage as you are before, and we shall live together as well as can be expected—But you have put too much gilding upon your prospects; you have promised yourself too much, and I regret already your disappointment. . . . I have always meant to leave you to your choice, until the last moment. You have made no hesitation. I hope you will have no regret."[50]

Finally, on June 28, the still reluctant bridegroom and his brother Tom left The Hague for London. Throughout the spring, John Quincy had referred to his forthcoming marriage only very obliquely in letters to his parents and not at all to his friends. His final dispatch from the Continent was typical. Before launching into a detailed account of the political situation in Europe, he wrote his father, "I left the Hague yesterday morning on my way to London from whence I hope to proceed after a very short stay there, and a great change in my personal situation, to Lisbon."[51]

John Quincy's diary for the next two weeks is filled with accounts of meeting various colleagues and acquaintances during what turned out to be a much-delayed North Sea crossing, but there is no mention of any longing to reunite with Louisa or any concern expressed about how his delay in leaving Holland might be affecting her. Detained by unfavorable winds in Rotterdam, the Adams brothers did not set sail for England until July 9—twelve days after leaving The Hague—and did not arrive in London until July 12 at about 5 P.M.

There followed a predictable, but unfortunate, decision on John Quincy's part. He chose to wait until the following day to reunite with Louisa. As consul and a ship owner, Joshua probably was aware that John Quincy was on English soil, and Louisa, also, must have realized he was in London. "I could not go out this evening and retired at an early hour," John Quincy noted in his diary. That was not how Louisa interpreted his delayed arrival: "He arrived and owing to some trifling accident on his route could not come to see me until the day after when I met him with feelings of mortified affection more bitter than I could express."[52]

The troubled courtship picked up where it had left off. Asked by her fiancé to name a wedding day, Louisa chose a date just two weeks away. Both Catherine and John Quincy appeared shocked and surprised that she seemed so anxious for the marriage to take place. Catherine rebuked her daughter for her transparent eagerness and for not having consulted her in the matter. Louisa, "naturally supposing it was what he most desired," excused herself on the grounds that she had been led to believe that her fiancé was fully as anxious as she was to act as expeditiously as possible and, in fact, was under severe time pressure to proceed to Lisbon.

But all such pressure had evaporated. En route to London, John Quincy had learned, unofficially, that his father, now president, had changed his diplomatic assignment from Portugal to Prussia, a much more prestigious post and one at the geographic heart of complex diplomatic and military events in Europe. When the bridegroom arrived in London, Rufus King, now minister plenipotentiary to England, confirmed the news.

John Quincy was furious. He had repeatedly informed his parents that he would accept no governmental position from his father. He reluctantly accepted the assignment but not before making clear exactly how angry he was: "I cannot disguise to you [President Adams] that the appointment was so totally contrary to every expectation and every wish I had formed that I have been not without hesitation with respect to accepting it. I had formed the resolution never to hold any public office under your nomination. I had explicitly declared that resolution to my mother, and I had indulged the hope that my adherence to it would never be put to so severe a trial as I have experienced." John Quincy wrote that he was agreeing to go to Berlin instead of Lisbon only under the "weight of parental authority" and his understanding that his new position would be "so much more inconvenient and troublesome"—and without additional pay— that no critic could claim his father had intended to grant him a sinecure.[53]

Not only did John Quincy object to the "degraded and humiliating aspect in which [the assignment] places me personally," he was faced with several practical implications the change in destination brought with it. His treasured books, furniture, and other household objects, as well as most of his clothes and personal items, had already been shipped to Portugal. He knew no one in Prussian diplomatic circles, and, since he would be the first-ever American minister to Berlin, he would have no previously established contacts and relationships to rely on. The *Mary* lay at anchor in the Thames, fitted up by Joshua to receive the honeymooning couple. It was an embarrassment to John Quincy that all his future father-in-law's efforts and expense had been in vain. Finally, instead of insisting on a quick turnaround time for the wedding festivities to take place, John Quincy now anticipated an extended period of waiting in London until formal instructions arrived from Philadelphia to proceed to Berlin.

The unexpected delay in the newlyweds' projected departure to their first diplomatic post provided John Quincy with one final pretext for postponing the marriage ceremony. He met with Catherine on "a matter of delicacy," which seems to have concerned where the couple would live after their vows were said since they would not be proceeding at once to board the *Mary.* On July 19, a week before the scheduled wedding, Joshua wrote to invite John Quincy to live at No. 8, Cooper's Row for the remainder of his stay in London and assured him his "acceptance (en famille) of the small comfort we have to bestow will diffuse Joy and Delight throughout our little circle." Joshua also encouraged his future son-in-law not to delay further the marriage day as the family had long planned to leave England for America in July, a departure date that had already been extended into August. John Quincy accepted his future father-in-law's gracious offer, and arrangements for the marriage ceremony went forward in haste.[54]

On July 21, John Quincy met with Joshua to discuss business. The younger man's diary does not indicate distress concerning his future father-in-law's solvency, although it must have come as a shock that Joshua was not immediately able to pay anything toward Louisa' promised dowry. John Quincy recorded only that he had received Joshua's "directions concerning his affairs with his former partners in case I should ever have occasion for them." Three days later, the two went together to purchase a special license. "I took the oath required, gave the usual bond, & obtained the license," John Quincy wrote later that evening.[55]

For better or worse, there was no turning back.

5

AT HOME AND ABROAD

Such was my honeymoon.

—LOUISA CATHERINE ADAMS, *"Record of a Life"*

On the morning of July 26, 1797, in the cool half-light of the Church of All Hallows Barking, an ancient parish church just west of the Tower of London, Louisa Catherine Johnson became the bride of John Quincy Adams. The Rev. John Hewlett—Oxford scholar, distinguished theologian, and Johnson family friend—performed the ceremony as Thomas Boylston Adams, several members of the bride's family, and two of the groom's friends, Joseph Hall and James Brooks, looked on.[1]

That so few were present for the brief Anglican ceremony uniting the twenty-two-year-old bride and thirty-year-old groom would have raised few eyebrows. Marriage ceremonies in Regency London were typically private and low key. The fact that the vicar of All Hallows Barking did not perform the ceremony himself, although somewhat unusual, was also not particularly noteworthy. In 1797 Hewlett was Morning Preacher at the Foundling Hospital, one of the most prestigious pulpits in London. The vicar of All Hallows may well have been happy to let one of England's rising young clergymen officiate at the marriage ceremony.[2]

Louisa never recounted the details of her wedding day (except to note much later that her sister Nancy, still resentful at being upstaged, took no part in adorning the bride), but she undoubtedly wore a fashionable new dress— probably white, Empire-style, fine muslin, three-quarter length sleeves—and a new bonnet and delicate shawl. In the eighteenth century a bridal gown had to serve as a best dress for special occasions long after the marriage ceremony, and its design would be comparatively informal by today's standards. Yet, Catherine Johnson, with her love of elaborate costumes, would not have stinted on lace

The twenty-eight-year-old John Quincy, by John Singleton Copley, 1796, the year before his marriage. Museum of Fine Arts, Boston, bequest of Charles Francis Adams. Photograph © 2014 Museum of Fine Arts, Boston.

and ribbon when it came to her daughter's wedding finery—all of which had been put aside a year earlier when John Quincy had indefinitely postponed the wedding date—and the petite, radiant Louisa surely made a lovely bride.[3]

For form's sake, the bridal party may have traveled by the family coach to the church, but since No. 8, Cooper's Row was just a stroll from All Hallows, the little group easily could have walked the short distance together on that warm summer morning. Immediately after the eleven o'clock ceremony, the entire party traveled by coach about ten miles northeast of Tower Hill to the edge of Epping Forest to tour a magnificent Palladian mansion, Wanstead House, which John Quincy described as "one of the splendid country seats for which this country is distinguished." They later returned home for a family dinner at which only one additional guest was present. The bridegroom remarked in his diary that "the day was a very long one and closed at about 11." Early the following morning, he was walking briskly to his old bachelor's lodgings in Osborne's Hotel in the Adelphi Buildings, two and a half miles away, where he spent the day writing and visiting with friends, a pattern he would repeat almost daily over the next month.[4]

Louisa vividly remembered her delight in the occasion: "On Wednesday, the 26th of July 1797 I became a bride under, as everyone thought, the happiest of auspices. . . . At this moment, everything seemed to combine to make my prospects brilliant." The next four weeks were a whirl of dinners, dances, and receptions given by the American diplomatic and merchant community and other friends of the Johnsons, culminating in a gala ball at the Johnsons' Tower Hill mansion on August 25 that lasted until four in the morning. This extended wedding celebration, though longer than most, was typical in the late eighteenth century and would have been expected by all concerned. It was also not unusual that the bride and groom remained in her family home during these festive weeks.[5]

John Quincy seems to have cast himself as a virtual bystander in the wedding ceremony and a very reluctant participant in the many social events that followed. He wrote that one ball was given "on the occasion of Mrs. Adams's marriage" and grumbled that the receptions and dinner parties were "among the appendages to the ceremony from which I should have been willingly relieved." Notably, there are few mentions of "we" or "us" during the first month of his wedded life in his daily diary entries. After a morning's work at his desk at Osborne's Hotel, he often spent the afternoons paying social calls, lunching with friends, or meeting with American diplomats. In the late afternoon he returned home to "Mr. Johnson's" for another evening of sociability. Each Sunday morning, he was in a pew at the Foundling Hospital, listening appreciatively to one of John Hewlett's scholarly, well-argued, and well-delivered sermons. Louisa must have accompanied him on some of these occasions, but if she did, there is no record of it.[6]

There is also little indication in his diary that marriage had affected John Quincy in any significant emotional way. Letters to his family and friends, while displaying evident self-satisfaction, seem stilted and formal. To his parents, who seem to have first learned of the marriage from the newspapers, he was particularly stiff, neglecting to mention his wife's first name and signing off with his full signature:

> My dear and honoured Parents,
>
> I have now the happiness of presenting to you another daughter, worthy as I fully believe of adding one to the number of those who already endear that relation to you. The day before yesterday united us for life. My recommendation of her to your kindness and affection I know will be unnecessary. My sentiment of her merit, will not at this moment especially boast of its *impartiality*, but if there be as I believe an inseparable chain of connection which binds together all the domestic virtues, I have the strongest pledge that she, who has in an amiable and respectable family, adorned the characters of a daughter and sister, will prove an equal ornament to that of a wife.
>
> In renewing to you the assurances of my unalterable duty and affection I would now join hers to them, but believe they will be more acceptable to you from her own hand, remaining your ever faithful son, John Q. Adams

Louisa, perhaps already inculcated with the Adams code of duty, pledged herself, in only slightly less formal terms, to earning John and Abigail's esteem:

> The day before yesterday by uniting me to your beloved Son, has given me a claim to solicit your parental affection . . . to meet the approbation of my Husband, and family is the greatest wish of my heart—Stimulated by these motives (your affection the reward) will prove a sufficient incitement never to sully the title of subscribing myself your
>
> Dutiful Daughter
Louisa C. Adams[7]

Writing to his brother Charles ("I can pass no higher eulogium upon her than to say she is worthy of being the third sister where there were already two so deserving") and a Boston friend, Daniel Sargent ("I have been about a fortnight married to Miss Johnson, a young lady, of whom I can only say to you that she is fit for the praise of any tongue but mine"), John Quincy was still self-conscious and mannered. It took Tom Adams in a letter to his mother to express some genuine joy on the occasion: "Since I wrote you . . . my brother has been married and has given me an amiable and accomplished Sister. He is very happy at present and I doubt not will continue so for the young lady has much softness of temper and seems to love as she ought. Her family have laid me under great personal obligations to them by the kindness and hospitality with which they have treated me since I have been here. I feel proud of an alliance with such worthy people. They are all to embark in the course of next month for America and will prove a great acquisition to the City of Washington, where Mr. Johnson intends to establish himself."[8]

Although Tom seems to have had no difficulty in assuring their parents that his brother was "very happy," John Quincy was doing his best to cast a gray cloud over nuptial bliss. Once again, he was in exactly the situation that made him most irritated with himself and others—an indefinite period of waiting for specific orders from the secretary of state and of spending most days and nights in frivolity. As before, his diary is full of impatient demands on himself to make better use of his time: "This course of life has too much of luxury and indolence for me. It is not however to last long."[9]

Meanwhile, in Boston, the marriage had quickly become a political issue. Rumors fomented by enemies of John Adams that Louisa was not an American citizen spread quickly. The Republican paper, the *Independent Chronicle*, on September 14 saw an easy opportunity to needle the Federalist president: "Young John Adams's negotiations have terminated in a marriage treaty with an English lady, the daughter of one Mr. Johnson, on Tower-Hill. It is a happy circumstance that he had made no other Treaty." Six days later, the Federalist *Columbian Centinel* responded: "This is an imposition upon the public, who ought to be informed, without derogating from the merits of the ladies of England, that Mrs. A. is an American lady; that her father is a citizen of Maryland, and brother to His Excellency Thomas Johnson, Esq., Late Governor of that State. All who know Mrs. A. speak of her as a lady of distinguished worth, and if every negotiation Mr. A. makes in Europe terminates as happily for his country, as this will for him, we shall have additional cause to praise the wisdom of that illustrious character [George Washington], who selected him from his fellow-citizens as one of the representatives of the United States in the Eastern hemisphere."[10]

But in the London summer of 1797, feted as a bride and still wrapped in the embrace of her family and friends, Louisa had no hint that her citizenship could prove to be grist for the partisan mills in America. Far more worrisome was her family's imminent departure for Maryland. Hanging over all the elegant dinners and lavish parties given in honor of the bridal couple that summer was her realization that it would be many years before she again saw her father and mother, or her sisters and brother (already in America). The time had long since passed for the Johnsons to leave London under auspicious circumstances. Atlantic hurricanes and inclement fall weather were already on the horizon. To have had any hope of reclaiming from his former partners the funds necessary to satisfy his London creditors, Joshua should have left for Annapolis months, if not years, earlier.

Even now, the extent of the family's financial situation was well hidden from the world. The lavish display of wealth apparent in the Johnsons' lifestyle had not diminished. Two weeks after the wedding, Tom Adams could confidently assure his parents that his brother had allied himself with "worthy people," and John Quincy himself, who had been made executor of Joshua's will and had spent an entire morning discussing financial matters with his future father-in-law, seems to have taken for granted the family's life of luxury and to have had only vague suspicions—due, perhaps, to Joshua's inability to make good on any part of Louisa's promised dowry—that the house of cards was about to collapse.

Perhaps only Joshua Johnson fully comprehended the severity of his financial situation. He alone seems to have been aware that the British government had appropriated some of his property, possibly even a ship, and that he owed his creditors, fellow merchants, tradesmen, and servants far more than he was in a position ever to pay. As he led his favorite daughter to the head of the double line of dancers on August 25, the proud father's heart must have been heavy with the knowledge that the musicians waiting to launch into the first sprightly country dance of the evening were unlikely to be compensated. News had come that very day to dash his last, fading, hope. One of his ships, overdue in port, would not arrive in time to provide him with the £500 required to tide over his creditors until he could return from America to London and finally settle all his debts.[11]

That night, John Quincy recorded in his diary that Joshua had received distressing news from America earlier in the day. He added impassively, "I should feel it more had I expected it less." Joshua, a broken man from that moment, took to his bed immediately after the ball. "Mr. Johnson ill—The cause an unhappy one," John Quincy wrote two nights later. John Quincy now decided to return immediately to the Adelphi. There is no indication that Louisa was consulted in the matter. By September 2, John Quincy had exchanged his bachelor's quarters at Osborne's Hotel for a larger suite of rooms, and he and she had moved out of her family home. During the early morning hours of September 9, the Johnson family left London for Gravesend where they intended to board a ship for America. Even John Quincy, who, by now, seemed to desire as little contact as possible with the family, was moved by his wife's palpable grief at being separated from all those she loved best; he employed her given name in his diary for the first time since the wedding: "Mr. Johnson and all his family dined with us at our house into which we have just moved. . . . After supper we had a distressing scene while the whole family took leave of Louisa." The painful impressions of that sad parting were still fresh in Louisa's memory twenty-five years later: "Never never as long as sense shall last shall I forget the worse than broken-hearted look of my adored father the last even'g he passed with me in my own house; my poor Mother too. . . . When I arose and found them gone, I was the most forlorn miserable wretch that the sun ever shined on."[12]

She had reason to be. The Johnsons had left financial chaos in their wake. As soon as it was known they had decamped under cover of darkness, creditors, tradesmen, and former servants appeared at the Adamses' door. To Louisa, "Every rap at the door made me tremble as every rap produced a dun to my father; and to me they appealed for payment believing that my father had left the means with me to settle them."[13]

According to the beleaguered bride, her new husband paid "not one shilling" on her family's debt, but *her* humiliation and *his* righteous anger are clear in everything either ever wrote about the situation. A month after the Johnsons' departure, John Quincy confessed to his diary that he "found the affairs of Mr. J. more and more adverse" and that the experience had been much harder on him personally than he had anticipated: "This trial is a strong one—More so indeed than I expected—and I expected it would be strong—I have done my duty— rigorous, inflexible duty—and no Event whatever shall convince me that by pursuing a more interested and less faithful course I should have been rewarded with greater success."[14]

John Quincy had been promised a relatively modest marriage settlement of £5,000, and Joshua's inability to pay a penny of that pledge could have provided the hesitant bridegroom with a perfectly solid justification for opting out of his engagement to marry Louisa. Doing so would have been the "more interested and less faithful course," he acknowledged to himself. Instead, he followed the demands of "rigorous, inflexible duty" and compensated by making it abundantly clear to his young, heartbroken wife that he had married her despite what would have been his own best interests.

Never known for his tact, John Quincy could not restrain himself from making Louisa feel she was included in the same deep disapprobation in which he now held her entire family. As Louisa poignantly recalled, "I loved [John Quincy] with the utmost sincerity but I learnt too quickly, in spite of his utmost exertions, how low I had sunk in his estimation without a hope of ever recovering the standing which was irreparably lost. It was strict and rigid justice, and I had nothing to complain of. Such was my honeymoon."[15]

Louisa could no longer mention her family to her husband ("bereft of that greatest of all comforts; the talking of the absent, the joys of the past, and the fond affections which had blessed all the roseate hours of infancy"). The Adamses' household accounts were turned over to John Quincy's valet, Whitcomb—an insulting signal to Louisa that she was not to be trusted with an essential responsibility normally assigned to a wife. Duly humiliated, she labored to compensate for the precipitous decline of all the Johnsons in John Quincy's estimation: "The ardent affection I bore him made me think no privation too great, no mortification too severe in mitigation of his disappointment. The mere loss of the very small property that I should have possessed I knew could not be the cause of so much bitterness. It must therefore have been the unfortunate period of my father's difficulties owing to a protested bill—a misfortune to which a merchant is liable in peculiarly hard times—that made the stroke so bitter; as his [John Quincy's] station was sufficiently prominent to produce publick attention and to shock his pride; and I am perfectly conscious that to a mind like *his* the wound could never be healed."[16]

In fact, it was Louisa's wounded psyche that would never heal. At a pivotal moment in her life, to which she obsessively returned again and again, Joshua's disgrace and John Quincy's cold, unsympathetic response critically wounded her self-esteem. Her emotions were still raw when she wrote her memoirs— "Record of a Life" in 1825 at the age of fifty, and "Adventures of a Nobody" in 1840 at the age of sixty-five. Searching for words to express adequately her unremitting pain, she described an "incubus" on her spirit and an "iron mask" of guilt that forever kept her from genuine peace of mind and blighted her prospects for a happy marriage. In her deepest heart, she was convinced that in everyone's opinion—particularly that of her husband and John and Abigail Adams—she and her family had schemed to ensnare the scion of America's first family into marriage.[17]

In this reading of the story, the Johnsons had erected a Potemkin village on Tower Hill in which the illusion of wealth had served to trick the young diplomat into believing he was marrying into a family of means and social stature. Throughout her life Louisa sought to justify her initiatives during the couple's courtship and engagement period as unmotivated by anything remotely conspiratorial. Her suggestion that she and her fiancé meet for a farewell visit in Holland and her subsequent—apparently hasty—naming of an early date for the wedding ceremony were, she said, only the natural impulses of a young woman in love. She protested, perhaps too much, that she and her parents, far from any ulterior motives where John Quincy was concerned, had even refrained from inviting him to return to Cooper's Row after his first visit there. Well aware of how her situation appeared, she accepted society's opprobrium, even as she insisted on her innocence.

Louisa's shame was made infinitely more painful by her feelings for her father. Her inordinate adoration of Joshua and her lifelong determination to clear his name and restore him to the eminence she believed he deserved went beyond the usual father-daughter bond. Louisa could admit no shred of evidence that might mar the "image of perfection" she had drawn of her father, and she seemed to fear that the slightest acknowledgment of human frailty might fatally deface that portrait. In 1840, nearly a half-century after the event, she was still fixated on the idea that her father had been ill-treated by the world: "[I had a] romantic idea of excellence, the model of which seemed practically to exist before my eyes, in the hourly exhibition of every virtue in my almost idolized father."[18]

The poor reputation that colored the remainder of Joshua's life and brought such misery upon his daughter was, she always contended, unmerited. In Louisa's mind, the situation was straightforward—her father was blameless. Again and again, throughout her life, she returned to the same story, each time emphasizing the evil inflicted on Joshua by the machinations of his partners and friends: "The man who had pretended to be my father's best friend . . . brought the heaviest calamity upon his head and stamped a wound upon that heart and that honour. . . . He was obliged to stop payment for the sum of *five hundred pounds* in consequence of the failure of a remittance and the non arrival of an East Indian ship and to quit the country with his family in a very different manner than he had ever expected."[19]

The facts surrounding the total collapse of Johnson's business and personal affairs remain murky. Among the legions of angry creditors who fruitlessly besieged the newlyweds was Frederick Delius, U.S. consul and a merchant in Bremen, Germany. Delius, who had personally ensured that the engaged couple's letters reached one another during the previous year and who considered himself a friend of both Joshua and John Quincy, now bitterly informed the latter that he and other Bremen merchants had been duped and cheated by Joshua. In what Louisa termed a "letter of the most barbarously insulting character . . . calling on my husband to save my father's forfeited honour," Delius demanded that John Quincy publish the details of Joshua's Johnson's financial dealings. Refusing the demand, John Quincy replied, "I have never had any concern of a pecuniary nature with Mr. Johnson, and am therefore not responsible either for his debts or for his credit. If all the facts alleged in your letter were true, I should be far from approving his conduct to you, but you are sensible that I am not the proper person to judge between you. . . . If you are presuming from the relation that I bear to him that I am intimately acquainted with the state of his finances, you have mistaken *my* character as much as you say you have his. . . . But, as it is, my connection, sir, was with his daughter, and not with his estate." To Joshua, John Quincy was equally cold and decisive: "I had indeed long observed your distress and that of your family. I was not particularly acquainted with its causes, nor was it a subject upon which I thought it proper or necessary to enquire. You expected that the step upon which you determined [leaving England without satisfying his creditors] would expose you to censure, but as you observe, you thought it the best you could take to do equal justice to all. The turn of affairs here has not been such as your friends could have wished. Appearances and allegations are advanced, which bring in question something more than merely your credit, and unfortunately your friends have not the means of refuting them in their power."[20]

John Quincy strongly urged Joshua to make good on all his obligations at the earliest possible moment and reminded his father-in-law of his assurances to him and others that ample funds to satisfy all his creditors would become available as soon as he reached America. Coming across her husband's papers more than forty years later, Louisa attempted to justify his manifest lack of sympathy for Joshua's distressed situation: "With the consciousness of such powers [as those possessed by John Quincy], we cannot wonder that his measure of others less gifted has often been unduly severe; and in early life when the suffering which experience brings has not taught us leniency to the casualties, the changes, and the calamities which no care can prevent, no forethought assuage, we are too apt to inveigh against the *effects* of misfortune, without a just appreciation of its causes, and all the concomitant circumstances attending it; and to censure without mercy those ills which have deserved compassion and sympathy." At the time, however, she could only suffer silently the humiliation of her husband's frigid, judgmental disdain and the aching loneliness of missing her beloved family. Her only solace was the affectionate and kind-hearted Tom Adams, in whom she confided her troubles and protested her innocence.[21]

Louisa's claim of blamelessness, though perfectly genuine, may mask unacknowledged self-reproach. Perhaps she schemed in her private moments to induce John Quincy to marry her. Perhaps in her heart she was not as immune as she claimed to be to the prospect of marrying into the presidential family. Perhaps she had suspected more about her family's financial situation than she was prepared to acknowledge. None of these private musings, however, justified the emotional burden she carried the rest of her life.

That burden consisted not only of her father's disgrace but her own wounded pride—the character fault she was always ready to acknowledge. Her self-esteem was much less stubbornly rooted than her adoration of Joshua. Christened "Miss Proud" by her schoolmates and treated as something of a paragon by her parents and their eminent friends, Louisa now had to humble herself. As she viewed her situation in the autumn of 1797 and for years afterward, there was nothing left to be proud of. Appearances were clearly against her. All too vividly could she imagine whispered conversations around the tea tables of London in which the Johnsons were pilloried for having unloaded one of their many daughters into the arms of the unsuspecting John Quincy. She may not, in fact, have overestimated her family's low repute in this regard. Two hundred years later, the author of a scholarly study on the role of Annapolis merchants in eighteenth-century Anglo-American trade could casually comment, "Johnson managed to marry off his daughter Louisa Catherine to John Quincy Adams just before disaster struck."[22]

From the day she moved from her parents' home, Louisa saw every real and imagined slight from John Quincy and others as proof that she had no respect in her husband's eyes and no standing in society other than that derived from her position as his wife. Summing up her first year in Prussia, a year in which she succeeded in captivating a rigidly formal, class-conscious royal court, she could still assert many years later that her husband must inevitably wish he had married a woman who had come to him with a significant dowry and without the stain of the Johnsons' disgrace: "His affection was all I craved, and all the Court gew gaws and vanities were as nothing to me . . . in the bitter conviction that he might have formed a connection more suitable to the Station that he filled; and with more adequate means to support its consequence."[23]

For Louisa, the loss of her father's good name and fortune as well as her own severely shaken sense of self-worth might have been bearable had she been comforted and sustained by her husband. This, John Quincy was completely unable to do. For a man whose determination to be financially independent of his parents was particularly fierce and whose primary stated reason for delaying his marriage was that he had not accumulated adequate savings to make married life economically feasible, the extent of the debts owed by his father-in-law seemed positively criminal. Not only were Joshua's financial misdeeds reprehensible on their face, according to the code of the moralistic Massachusetts Yankee, they represented an essential character flaw that John Quincy could not forgive. And, having lived most of his life in the company of boys and men, he had no experience in opening himself up to another's pain—or even recognizing it. Besieged by Joshua's creditors, John Quincy retreated into self-righteousness and may never have recognized how lonely and vulnerable his bride was.

For her part, absolutely dependent on the distant, judgmental man to whom she was pledged for the rest of her life, Louisa was close to despair. Brought up in a house full of women, she was accustomed to feminine companionship at all hours of the day and night. Although her relationship with her sisters had often been strained, there was no denying that their society (and that of their vivacious mother) had brightened her days and filled the Tower Hill mansion with gossip, laughter, and music. Now, sitting silently in rented rooms, fearfully awaiting the knock of another frustrated petitioner on the door, her household duties assigned to a manservant, and her husband visiting friends and haunting bookstalls, Louisa looked back on her former life as a sun-filled, golden era and her future as dark, lonely, and forbidding.

Louisa's emotional pain was matched by physical distress — she had become pregnant almost immediately after the wedding, and her first months were particularly difficult. Day after day, John Quincy's diary records that "Mrs. Adams" was very ill. Had her mother been on hand, Louisa's situation might have been made more comfortable and her normal fears allayed. As it was, her new husband had become her nurse, a role he was unfamiliar with and uncomfortable filling: "I find my cares accumulating as I advance in life," he remarked on October 2 when Louisa had been ill all day.

Nevertheless, in the month and a half the Adamses lived in London following the departure of the Johnson family, they truly became a married couple. Settling into a domestic routine that John Quincy acknowledged was to his liking and "could be made into something useful" were they to stay longer in London, they especially treasured the hours after dinner when the bookish husband read aloud from some very serious works (Southey's *Letters*, Bertrand's *Memoirs* in four volumes, for example) to his equally bookish wife, a nightly habit they continued for many years. John Quincy recounted in his diary a typical day in which he spent the morning reading or writing, the afternoon paying visits, doing business, or buying books, and the evening reading to Louisa. The pair walked regularly in Hyde Park and Kensington Gardens, and attended church and, occasionally, the theater. Guests, particularly John Quincy's male friends and acquaintances, typically came to dinner — which took place in midafternoon — when he was not invited out to dine with them.

Louisa's previous social connections, in contrast, had been largely severed by her family's ignominious departure for America — she later recalled the period as a time of being "unknowing and unknown." Although Elizabeth Hewlett again demonstrated her loyalty by dining with the bride and inviting her to Shacklewell and two of Catherine's other longtime friends also came forward to support her, no amount of motherly sympathy could assuage the young bride's longing for her family, her abiding sense of disgrace, and her fear of the future.

In fact, both Adamses looked with foreboding on their imminent departure to the new ministerial post in Berlin. John Quincy clearly felt inadequate to the task of representing America in what he knew was a potentially critical assignment for the future security of the United States. He had protested against the appointment not only because he hated its appearance of nepotism but also because of his "own disqualification, or at least, the much superior title of many other American citizens." He had reminded his father that since the United States had not previously assigned a minister to the Prussian court and as he, John Quincy, knew no one in Berlin, he might well encounter serious difficulties in securing entree to key diplomatic and government figures. Not one to minimize his own abilities, the young diplomat clearly felt inadequate to the task.[24]

By the end of the eighteenth century, Prussia had joined Britain, France, Russia, and Austria as one of Europe's dominant nations. Comprising three separate geographic areas spread across a wide swath of northern Germany and into present-day Poland (the area then called East Prussia), Prussia was renowned for its efficient civil service and well-trained standing army. Beginning with Frederick William, the "Great Elector," who ruled from 1640 to 1688, to Frederick the Great, whose reign spanned forty-six years from 1740 to 1786, its Hohenzollern dynasty had produced a succession of forward-thinking, effective rulers. (The twenty years between Frederick the Great's death and Napoleon's defeat of the mighty Prussian army in a single day at Jena in 1806 marked a regression in Prussia's forward progress.) Prussia, indeed, gloried in its well-earned militaristic reputation—John Quincy described it as a nation, "the only basis of whose power is military and which is little more than Nation of Soldiery"—but it also fostered a thriving culture where great philosophers like Immanuel Kant could thrive and where art, architecture, and the Golden Age of classical music could flourish.[25]

Germany at the end of the eighteenth century was composed of an intricate patchwork of principalities, mostly small and loosely confederated in the Holy Roman Empire. The dominant two states were Austria—the seat of the foundering empire—and Prussia, and the two had been in competition for power and influence for more than a century. It was a calculated decision on President Adams's part to send an envoy to Prussia—and not to Austria—and the Prussian foreign ministry recognized it as a mark of distinction. As John Quincy later reported to his father, he had been "perfectly well received everywhere. The government is very apparently pleased with this mission as a mark of attention from the government of the United States and probably specially gratified that they should have sent a Minister here not having already one at Vienna."[26]

During his four-year tenure in Berlin, the young American envoy would retain the good graces of the court, and his publicly acknowledged mission—to secure a new trade treaty with the host nation—would be accomplished after just one year of negotiation. Thereafter, in addition to his mandated court appearances, he applied himself to learning German well enough to make elegant translations of philosophical and literary works, to extensive travel within Germany, and to as much as four hours of walking every day.[27]

John Quincy's most important task, however, was to act as a listening post for his father in the heart of Europe. The president specifically instructed his son to report more fully and candidly to him than to Secretary of State Timothy Pickering, whom the president did not trust. It was a moment in history that required exactly the sophisticated worldview and analytical mind that distinguished the young diplomat. France stood poised between the chaos of the revolution, only eight years earlier in 1789, and the empire that was to come. As John Quincy and Louisa prepared to leave London in October 1797, Napoleon, following his successful campaign against Austria in northern Italy, annexed all German lands west of the Rhine. The United States—just ten years after the Constitution was adopted—needed for its very survival to remain resolutely neutral in the complex reconfiguration of power under way in Europe. President Adams depended on John Quincy to keep him abreast of every development and aware of every foreign policy implication that could threaten the new nation's perilous position.[28]

Congress was not as foresighted. Its members had taken a month to decide whether a mission to Prussia was even necessary and, if so, how little money would be required to fund it. When formal instructions finally arrived in London from the State Department, John Quincy lost no time in purchasing a traveling coach and booking passage to the port of Hamburg. Privately to his diary, he acknowledged his anxiety about the wisdom of embarking with a pregnant wife on what could be a dangerous crossing of the North Sea. Louisa, circumspectly referring to her pregnancy, remembered that "anguish of mind and deep feeling of wounded sensibility [had] reduced me to a state of health which was attended by a total loss of sleep, which with other incidental causes [pregnancy] almost unfitted me for the exertion of travel." The couple's fears extended beyond the voyage itself. They had no home to go to when they arrived in Berlin and knew no one to turn to for help. Because all John Quincy's household furnishings, books, and personal effects had been shipped three months earlier to Portugal, he and Louisa would have to set up housekeeping not knowing whether those goods would ever be reclaimed. Crucially, at the time of their arrival, neither had more than a minimal command of German; among the first books John Quincy purchased in Hamburg were an English-German dictionary and a French-German grammar.[29]

Nevertheless, they prepared to leave London on October 18 with Tom Adams again acting as his brother's secretary; Louisa's teenage maid, Elizabeth Epps; and John Quincy's manservant, Tilly Whitcomb. From the outset, the expedition did not go smoothly. As Louisa finally seated herself in the coach that was to take them to the ship, a disgruntled former servant "showered down every horrible imprecation" upon her until they drove away from their London lodgings. Due to last-minute difficulties in obtaining their passports, the captain of the merchant ship on which they had obtained passage sailed without them, and they were forced to set out on the Thames in a small open boat on a chilly autumn night to catch up. Fortunately, their ship, carrying only four other passengers, was lying anchored overnight at the mouth of the river.[30]

As violent winds rocked the ship, Louisa and most of the other passengers were constantly seasick. According to John Quincy, their situation was not improved by the "want of cleanliness on board," which he termed "very disgusting." Leaving London and all its painful recent memories behind, however, revived Louisa's naturally high spirits. "Here we began to breathe more freely, objects of novelty to me occupied my attention, and the affection and kindness of [John Quincy] and [Tom] once more cheered my drooping spirits and warm'd my sinking heart into something like hope." Continuing to delight in unfamiliar scenes and "objects of novelty," Louisa's mood became more optimistic. By the time the ship reached Hamburg, she was ready to go out to dinner and the theater and to join John Quincy and Tom on their walks around the prosperous, bustling port city. Pleased to be on solid ground and proud she had survived the stormy voyage, Louisa fondly remembered their stopover in Hamburg, although she did recall that her morning sickness was made worse by the peat the city burned for fuel.[31]

The trip to Berlin, the Prussian capital, in their own heavy English coach was, if anything, more difficult than the perilous North Sea crossing. The road, John Quincy later informed Catherine Johnson, was "a continual heap of sand" that had been reduced to bogs of mud, and they could count on traveling only 4.6 miles in two hours. The weather was wet, cold, and dreary, the inns in which the Adams party stayed were, according to Louisa, "the most miserable night accommodations," and they were immediately confronted with the difficulty that their lack of proficiency in German was going to present. On the whole, Louisa recalled, the trip was a daunting introduction to their new life: "Exhausted by fatigue, overcome by the constant danger of an overturn in consequence of the unfitness of our Carriage for the German highway, with the flurry and agitation to which a Stranger is inevitably exposed in a Country where every object is a novelty, every usage new, and the language itself unfamiliar to the ear, and difficult to the tongue; the mind is engrossed by the singularity of the Scenes thus suddenly exhibited and disgusted by its, at *first*, unpleasant aspects."[32]

After six days on the road they arrived in Berlin and settled temporarily in the Hotel de Russie, a well-regarded inn of the time on the lovely Lindenstrasse, where "everything was different in all its parts from the English habits. The House was dirty, noisy, and uncomfortable. The Beds, miserable; the Table execrable; the manners of the Mrs. of the mansion coarse though kind." Despite these unprepossessing surroundings, the travelers congratulated themselves on "having got over with so much facility an undertaking which had appeared so formidable in prospect."[33]

They had arrived in a city unlike other European capitals. Whereas London or Paris had for centuries served as royal, commercial, and cultural hubs, Berlin, until the seventeenth century, had been just one among several German cities, and one of no particular distinction. By the beginning of the eighteenth century Berlin had become important simply because it was the home of the Hohenzollern dynasty. The real transformation of the city occurred under Frederick the Great, who made Prussia into a great military power while embracing Enlightenment ideals such as religious tolerance. The epitome of the "enlightened despot," Frederick replanted the city's great park, the Tiergarten, and oversaw the construction of major late Baroque buildings throughout his capital. The prosperous city of 147,000 residents (of whom a quarter were soldiers) that Louisa and John Quincy first saw in 1797 stood as a monument to wealth and power but also to taste and refinement.[34]

While John Quincy attempted to present his official credentials to the court and Tom embarked on sightseeing in the Prussian capital, Louisa rested in the hotel. Three days later she began to suffer her first miscarriage. Immediately, John Quincy's thoughts and care were entirely for his wife. For the next ten exhausting days and sleepless nights, he and the young maid Epps stayed with Louisa constantly through what the deeply alarmed husband termed her "most excruciating pain."[35]

One of the very few diplomats John Quincy had met in his first two days in Berlin had recommended Dr. Charles Brown, an English doctor who was physician to the royal family, and John Quincy now called on him for help. Dr. Brown, who came at once to the hotel, in turn summoned an eminent German medical professor for consultation. The two agreed there was little they could do to ease Louisa's suffering and that their only hope was that she would expel the fetus before irreparable—or fatal—damage had occurred to herself. The young couple now prepared for the loss of their first child, meanwhile lamenting, in John Quincy's words, "that the worst should still be delayed." As ten days passed and Louisa became weaker, John Quincy began to fear he might lose the woman he was only just beginning to value: "A dreadful night again passed in continual expectation and with the torture of disappointment prolonged which yet continues—continued through the whole day. It is neither wise nor good to murmur at the ways of providence. I have been highly favored: beyond my deserts and even beyond my wishes. Shall I receive good and shall I not receive evil? The mind at least submits; however the heart will rebel."[36]

The miscarriage finally occurred, leaving Louisa exhausted and bedridden. John Quincy gave Dr. Brown full credit for bringing her through the crisis: "[He] attended her not only with professional skill, but with that kindness and interest which is more efficacious in sickness than medicine," the relieved young husband reported to his mother-in-law, now finally in America. Louisa, though equally grateful to Dr. Brown, never forgot John Quincy's loving care as well: "This was a new and a cruel scene for Mr. Adams and called forth all his kindness, and most gratefully do I remember his tenderness and his affection during a trial so severe."[37]

In fact, the agonizing days and nights they had shared brought the couple together in a bond that would never break. Highlighting those characteristics he knew Abigail would approve of in her daughter-in-law, John Quincy abandoned his earlier reserve in writing to his mother: "You will find by some of my late letters that we have already been brought to the trial of some unpropitious circumstances. Yet much as we have reasons to regret them, we have at least the consolation that they have only strengthened and confirmed our mutual affection. My wife is all that your heart can wish. I will not indulge myself in the panegyric which my inclination dictates for you will imagine that the lover had not yet subsided into the husband. But I will say that I am as happy as a virtuous, modest, discreet, & amiable woman can make me."[38]

As soon as he could leave his wife's bedside, John Quincy set about finding the family suitable lodgings. He settled on a small apartment over the guardhouse at the Brandenburg Gate, the grandly imposing neoclassical arch, completed only six years earlier. A pair of pavilions on either side of the gate, used by guards and customs officers, contained extra rooms for rent on the upper floors. At first the convalescent—but insatiably curious—Louisa delighted in all the activity she witnessed from her upper window "most beautifully situated between that Gate and the Thiergarten, or Park." The crowds and carriages on Unter den Linden, royal processions and military parades, and couples and families strolling in the Tiergarten provided "a source of perpetual amusement."

Her delight did not last long. Conveniently located as it was, the Brandenburg Gate lodging had some major drawbacks. Annoying enough were the military drums that beat "morning, noon, and night" at the appearance of any member of the extended royal family or an officer of rank as they passed through the gate to or from Unter den Linden. Much worse, however, for Louisa's still-fragile nerves was the apartment's proximity to the guards' assembly area where frequent corporal punishment took place. "I was exposed to see and hear all the bastinadoes which these poor fellows underwent for the slightest omission of duty." As her health recovered, the young wife became acutely aware how lonely she was. Her husband had been formally presented to the king and queen and was regularly invited to every royal dinner, ball, and card party that took place. The court was one where no evening passed without a social event at which members of the nobility and the diplomatic corps were all but required to attend, and John Quincy was zealous in his duty. But not only did Louisa receive no invitations to these soirees, she had no visitors during the day. Painfully sensitive, especially at this period in her life, Louisa assumed her husband was ashamed of her because of her father's financial disgrace and had chosen not to take her into society. "Mr. Adams never having suggested the propriety [of my being presented at court] and I supposing in the then state of my feelings that it was owing to his mortification at his marriage that he did not wish to take me out," she was afraid to raise the subject. Finally, she was visited by two young women with close ties to the royal family who informed her that since she had not been formally introduced at court, the queen was beginning to believe the Adamses were not married.

Spurred into action, the couple appeared at the theater together on the first occasion King Frederick William III and Queen Louise were expected to be in attendance, and Louisa found herself "the object of general attention." As quickly as possible, arrangements were made for her presentation to the queen, an elaborate ritual she undertook wearing a white satin dress trimmed with lace, a blue satin robe, red gloves, white satin shoes, and ostrich feathers in her hair: "So weak that my knees knocked together as I stood, frightened almost out of my senses at the idea of entering upon a stage so new; my husband not with me at this presentation, and the lady who *was* with me a total Stranger; I felt ready to sink into the floor; but the lovely Queen observing my trepidation, and probably knowing from Dr. Brown the real state of my health [possibly a second pregnancy]; came immediately almost to the door to meet me, and kindly expressed the desire she had had to become acquainted with me, and used the most encouraging expressions to set me at my ease and restore my self-confidence."[39]

Louisa remembered that her subsequent welcome by the many princes and princesses awaiting her outside the queen's reception room was "both flattering and agreeable," a reaction she attributed to relief that court gossip describing her "as having a wretched complexion, a face as long as a *horse*, very lean, and without one good feature of face or person" had proved untrue.[40]

Queen Louise invited her to stay for supper and conversed with her "several times during the supper and with great sweetness and . . . treated [her] generally with the kindest attention." For the first time since her wedding ball on Tower Hill, the party-loving Louisa had a chance to sparkle. "When I had got Home, I had a great deal to tell as the novelty of the scene had exhilarated my spirits to a great degree and afforded great diversion to both the gentlemen [John Quincy and Tom] to whom these scenes had become quite familiar."[41]

Louisa was fortunate that her debut at the royal court occurred during the reign of the most beloved queen in German history, then at the height of her popularity. The recently crowned Queen Louise (1776–1810) was gentle, charming, and, at twenty-one, just a year younger than Louisa herself. The artist Elisabeth Vigée-Lebrun was overwhelmed when she first saw the young royal: "The beauty of her figure, her neck, her arms, the dazzling freshness of her complexion, everything about her surpassed the most perfect ideal." Napoleon referred to her admiringly five years later as "my beautiful enemy." Tom Adams, who had an eye for pretty women, found the queen "remarkably beautiful and engaging." In a court where intrigues, seductions, and corruption had flourished under the late King Frederick William II (1744–1797), the new King Frederick William III (1770–1840) and his queen hoped to establish a reign where probity, naturalness, and an emphasis on family supplanted rigid protocol and illicit affairs. Queen Louise possessed a legendary ability to charm even the most cynical courtier, and her thoughtfulness when she immediately grasped how terrified Louisa was on being presented to royalty for the first time was instinctive and typical.[42]

From that moment, Louisa was unrestrained in her admiration for the queen she "so dearly loved." The queen responded in kind, genuinely concerned about Louisa's welfare—particularly during her always difficult pregnancies—and immediately ready to rescue her from uncomfortable social situations engendered by the schemes of courtiers who lived to gossip and connive for precedence. The royal signal that Louisa would be given special attention did not go unremarked by the many members of the extended Hohenzollern family, the lesser nobility, and all their hangers-on whose court status rose and fell on a smile or a frown from the king or queen. That Countess Pauline Neale, one of Queen Louise's ladies in waiting, had quickly become an intimate friend of Louisa's provided another valuable connection to the court's innermost circle. "My little friend Countess Pauline de Neale . . . well educated and well read . . . [was] full of anecdote . . . she was to me as a sort of Mentor ever ready to instruct me in the usages and customs of high life and to assist me in the duties of its performance. Whenever we met she gave an insight into the characters that passed before us; and this peep behind the Scenes was always amusing, beneficial, and instructive."⁴³

Once launched into the "giddy scenes of fashionable life," invitations ("most of which were orders from the Court") addressed to the American minister and his wife or to Louisa alone quickly followed. In keeping up the strict protocol and dress required by these royally mandated appearances, Louisa received little help, financial or otherwise, from her husband. Ordered to appear before the recently widowed dowager queen, she was forced to construct a suitable mourning costume on short notice. "Countess Neale, my maid, and myself literally basted up a dress; and although it barely held together while I wore it, by the aid of a long black veil I went through the audience with more success than could possibly have been anticipated." The old queen, who had not lived with the late king for many years before his death — having ceded her place to a succession of mistresses and two morganatic wives — had decided to yield to no one in observing the rituals of death. Her diamond-festooned mourning costume was, according to Louisa, "altogether extraordinary, and it was with the utmost difficulty that I kept my *serieux* with the dignity suited to the Wife of a foreign dignitary. When I got home [Tom Adams] laughed with all his heart at my recital of the Scene, and the gravity . . . assumed by Mr. A. who terribly dreaded some indiscretion on my part, could not controul our mirth."⁴⁴

John Quincy's fears that Louisa would disgrace him, fed by his parents, who had counseled him on the pitfalls awaiting an innocent young woman in an urbane court, were in vain. Not only did Louisa fail to commit social gaffes, she undoubtedly opened doors to her husband that he might otherwise have found closed. The real work of diplomacy went on every night at the glittering social events all across the capital city, and here Louisa's youthful beauty, natural charm, and fluent French were an indisputable asset. In the beginning, at least, John Quincy could not see her as anything but a potential embarrassment. In January, at the first ball she attended, the American minister left his bride to fend for herself: "Mr. Adams mixed in the throng of nobles, with whom he had become intimately acquainted. The Ball began with English country dances, and [Tom Adams] led me out to make my debut. The dance was long and fatiguing, but I was so extraordinarily fond of the amusement that the strangers were forgotten and he danced so well and with so much spirit, I was quite delighted. Prince Radziville then invited me, and Prince Vitgenstein for the next dances; and I had a succession of partners until two o clock in the morning—when I returned home perfectly exhausted."[45]

Her debut was a sensation. Rather sheepishly, but with a hint of triumph, Louisa acknowledged she had become a "belle." (The two princes had made her promise "to dance with them at any of the Balls where we should meet.") Refusing to let flattery turn her head, she claimed her success was due to John Quincy's reputation and standing: "Remember I was the *Wife* of a Foreign Minister, and daughter in law to the President of the United States—always addressed as your *Excellency*, and sometimes called *Princess Royal*—A capital epitome of the Bathos in *dignity*."[46]

Since the other members of the diplomatic corps were highly placed nobles in their respective countries—among others, Lord Carysfort of Britain; Viscount Anadia of Portugal; Count Panin of Russia; Baron Shultz von Ashzaden of Sweden—the Adamses, particularly in light of their personal relationship to the American president, were accorded similar distinction in court protocol. But in Louisa's eyes, the great irony—the "Bathos in dignity"—was that despite the lofty titles and distinctions bestowed upon her, she and her husband were living in very straitened circumstances. While other diplomats and their wives could easily afford to entertain lavishly and match the extravagant court standards in dress and jewels, John Quincy and Louisa were attempting with great difficulty to stretch the meager allowance Congress had reluctantly allotted them.

After six months in the Brandenburg Gate lodgings, the couple moved three blocks away to a small apartment amid huge Baroque palaces and government buildings. The front two rooms of their suite were furnished elegantly ("merely genteelly" in Louisa's opinion) so that John Quincy could conduct business and the two could occasionally entertain guests at home. The rest of the apartment reflected their tight budget: "My bedchamber had *no carpet*, a bedstead with white cotton curtains of the coarsest quality, bordered with a strip of calico cut from a striped print; and made by myself, with window curtains to match; a very common pine wood toilet table with a muslin cover; and an equally plain toilet glass—no fire in the winter; and half a dozen chairs."[47]

Louisa needed her healthy sense of the ridiculous to be bowed to as Princess Royal at a gala ball after having dressed for the party in such unheated, Spartan quarters. Luckily, she retained her sense of humor, refusing to be beguiled by flattery and immune to the superficial glamour of the royalty and nobility who now peopled her life. Prescribed nightly attendance at court soon became tedious, but, describing a typical evening card party, she managed to plumb its comic potential:

> Princess Henry was the Aunt of the King and altogether of the old school— She was upwards of seventy remarkably stiff and stately in her manners and her suppers to which I was invited every Monday Evening the dullest and most tiresome I ever was at. The company played cards after which there was a Supper consisting of all sorts of meats in great joints and in great abundance very well calculated to produce indigestion. The first time I supped there I was seated opposite to the Princess and next to Lord Granville Levison Gore one of the handsomest men I ever saw and usually celebrated for his taciturnity, but on this occasion he was mild as a maid and made so many strange remarks *a l'anglaise* that I behaved myself quite childishly [assisting Lord Levison in counting the number of helpings (nineteen) an elderly lady seated near them was consuming], with difficulty concealing my gigling from her royal highness who fortunately was too near-sighted to observe me.[48]

Much preferable for all three Adamses were the hours spent in the "unaffected, friendly, and charming society" of Dr. Brown's family, which included three young, attractive, intelligent daughters and a son. Tom Adams, who seems to have fallen in love with the middle Brown daughter and was a great friend of her brother William, recorded in his journal the many times he and Louisa abandoned John Quincy to his long solitary walks, letter writing, and reading while they enjoyed themselves with the Browns, both at their home in Berlin and at their country retreat in Charlottenburg, only a few miles outside the city.[49]

In countless critical ways, Tom was Louisa's lifeline during her first year in Berlin. "[He] was always as kind as the most affectionate brother and being less interested was of course more indulgent to my follies or my griefs than Mr. Adams whose very anxiety for my success, rendered him uneasy lest by some gaucherie I should fail." Just three years older than Louisa, Tom shared with her a love of dancing, a delight in comic stories, and a zest for life that John Quincy had either lost or never attained: "My kind brother . . . proved a solace in my moments of mental anguish and uniformly contributed to my comfort and my pleasure both in sickness and in health. He soothed me in my afflictions, corrected gently my utter want of self-confidence, flattered me judiciously and by his unerring judgement often prevented me from committing mistakes, natural to my inexperience and to which the innocence of unguarded youth is exposed in the trying scenes of a Court. I never saw so fine a temper or so truly and invariably lovely a disposition & years of intimate acquaintance will attest this fact. I have always believed that he both respected and loved me and did me justice in times when I needed a powerful friend."⁵⁰

When Tom departed for Philadelphia in September 1798 to take up the practice of law—an occupation he knew he would despise—Louisa was bereft: "I missed [him] beyond expression. If he accompanied us [to parties], he had always something amusing to relate; and we would compare notes."⁵¹

In the summer of 1798, Louisa and John Quincy observed their first anniversary. Three days later, he summed up the year in a tender tribute to his wife: "First anniversary of my marriage day. The external occurrences of the year have not been fortunate. But from the loveliness of temper and excellence of character of my wife, I account it the happiest day of my life."⁵²

Louisa's tragedy is that she did not steal a glimpse at John Quincy's diary in writing her account of the same period, "Record of a Life," in 1825, the first of four unhappy years in the White House. Instead, she recalled an entirely different memory from that summer: "At this time I heard of Mr. Adams's attachment to Miss [Mary] Frazier, and I had another reason added to the misfortunes for regretting the marriage. I had made, as it appeared, it impossible for him to view me in any other light than as a person who had known all these impediments and who determined for the sake of what is called a settlement to marry him at the expence of honour, truth, and happiness."⁵³

And with those heartbroken words, she concluded her first memoir. She could bear to write no more.

6

IN SICKNESS AND IN HEALTH

Poor little woman, how she suffers! Matrimony these are thy fruits! Bitter, bitter.

— THOMAS BOYLSTON ADAMS

As she aged, Louisa's memories of Berlin grew decidedly mixed. When depressed, she could recall every ounce of coldness she noticed in her husband, every social or marital slight she had attributed to her father's financial failure, every pang of homesickness she had felt for her struggling family far away in America. Genuinely unwell throughout much of her four years in Berlin, Louisa had every reason to appear pale and wan and to mourn the loss of her four unborn babies. "In the midst of this apparently gay life, suffering was my portion," she recalled in her poignantly titled unpublished memoir from 1840, "Adventures of a Nobody."

But the sepia tones of her retrospective self-portrait almost instantly dissolve into vivid snapshots of a shy young bride who became an overnight success at the Prussian court, an intimate of the queen, and a popular member of the small group of upper-class British expatriates living in Berlin at the turn of the nineteenth century. In the midst of what she called the court's "abundance of gorgeous display," Louisa more than held her own. "Extravagantly fond" of the English country dances, then the rage at court, and skilled at their intricate steps and turns, she was often the first woman escorted onto the ballroom floor—rarely, if ever, by her husband. She never suffered the social isolation that so many wives of other American resident ministers in European capitals endured as a result of their inability to understand and be understood in French, the language of the courts. With her ready wit, fluent French, petite beauty, and eye for the ridiculous, the wife of the American minister became a highly sought-after dinner companion for blasé courtiers, even as her gift for friendship made for close and lasting relationships with their wives and daughters. Barred from much of London's social scene by her father's edict that she and her sisters limit their acquaintance to Americans, Louisa now found herself at the nexus of British society in Berlin. Wealthy and titled English and Irish expatriate women, as well as the wives of other foreign diplomats, regularly turned to her for an introduction to Queen Louise: "There being no *lady* of the English Minister, I was a sort of substitute . . . at home the english sought *me*, abroad they flattered *me*; and I naturally felt much pleased with their acquaintance."[1]

After more than forty years as a member of a family whose code included a professed disdain for pomp and circumstance, Louisa, looking back at sixty-five, could not openly acknowledge that she reveled in the human comedy of the Prussian court, but her own recollections betray her. Her memoir describes in rapt detail the elaborate gowns, sparkling jewels, and stately royal processions daily on display. That she was never without a "princely partner" as she expertly took to the dance floor meant that even though her much-worn gown was plain by the court's standards and she owned few jewels, she had the satisfaction of knowing that she could be the belle of any ball she attended. True, there were awkward moments. John Quincy typically disappeared into the card room as soon as the couple entered a reception hall, and Louisa was forced to thread her own path through the thicket of court protocol: "I was obliged to make my way as I could—and if I staid supper at Court, he [John Quincy] was always at *home* almost before I went in to table. And in this manner he acquired the habit of leaving me to myself on almost all occasions . . . not dreaming that a woman could feel lonely in company."[2]

Comparing Louisa's accounts of royal and diplomatic events with those of John Quincy is like viewing two parallel universes. She was at a party; he was going through a tedious official duty that was keeping him away from his studies. In "Death in the Dance," a floridly written sketch perhaps composed with an eye to developing an actual event into a future piece of fiction, Louisa described a scene very familiar to her but to us reminiscent of a 1950s Hollywood costume drama:

> The Evening was to close among the fashionable world with a splendid Ball given by one of the ambassadors in honor of the birth of a prince. . . . all that money could purchase, luxury produce, or artifice invent to do honour to the fete and give zest to the pleasures of her expected guests.
>
> The House was splendidly illuminated inside with Candelabras, Chandeliers, and Lustres, reflected and multiplied by elegant Mirrors . . . [w]hile the exterior of the vast building displayed a brilliant façade of light in every variegated colour. . . . Servants in rich Liveries lined the entrys and

stair case, while in the suite of Apartments, the open folding doors of which
leading one into the other displayed their long and vast proportions.

Carriage followed Carriage and the sonorous voice of the maitre'd'hotel
echoed through the halls as he announced the arrivals. And soon the Music
sounded with merry glee; refreshments were served. . . . All was hilarity, joy
and delight, and time seemed to have shaken off his wings.[3]

Rarely in John Quincy's writings is there this rich sense of the storied
glamour and elegance of the Prussian court, and never is there an appreciation
of its spectacle. He notes the evenings and afternoons when Louisa accompanied him to formal visits, receptions, balls, and card parties—as well as those
that she did not—but seldom records any of what she did when she got there
beyond the occasional "Mrs. Adams danced." Leaving her entirely to her own
devices, he appears to have failed to witness her success in charming the
Prussian court.

Their accounts differed in other significant ways. John Quincy saw his as a
record of how he spent his time, the personages he met, and what they discussed.
He also recorded the weather, the duration of his very long walks, and the classics he was reading aloud to his wife. He noted the state of his and Louisa's
health almost daily; he listed the visits of his wife's many friends but never
related any of his own interactions with her, amicable or otherwise. In February
1801, he remarked, "Mrs. Hunter and Miss Jones called this forenoon to take
leave of Mrs. A." Louisa, describing the same event many years later using John
Quincy's diary to jog her memory, provides much more texture: "Mrs. Hunter
and Miss Jones called to take leave of me—She said 'mine was the *only House*
in which she was *not* received with chilling frigidity.' She was to leave the City
on her way to France next day. This Lady had bought a Carriage on purpose to
carry her Parrot; and Miss Jones, and her Maid, were to ride in it by turns, to
take care of it. When she *died*, she left a Legacy to this *Parrot*, of five hundred
pounds a year."[4]

Despite Louisa's strongly held belief that John Quincy harbored regret they
had married, it's noteworthy that not a word of recrimination toward his wife
can be found in his diaries. Instead, it was himself he regularly castigated for
laziness if, for example, he had not put sufficient effort into first studying the
German language and then reading as widely as possible in German literature.
Dreaming of making his living in literature rather than the law, he worked diligently on translations into English of the poet Christoph Martin Wieland's
popular romance *Oberon* and the political philosopher Friedrich Gentz's
*Origin and Principles of the American Revolution, Compared with the Origin
and Principles of the French Revolution.*

Where John Quincy's diary was centered on himself—and to a significant degree on his wife's health and activities—Louisa saw her memoir as a collection of character sketches and observations of court life: "I consider this tedious account of past times as containing a gallery of striking pictures, not hit off with the satiric keenness of a Mirabeau but more just in the likenesses," she explained early in "Adventures." Like the French diarist, she could wield a caustic pen. Describing the diplomatic corps early during her stay in Berlin, she made it clear that, though very young, she was not naïve: "Lord Elgin English; very handsome and equally presuming. Count and Countess Zinzendorf, Saxon, who had been residing there twenty two years; an excellent couple of the old School, stiff and formal as old Portraits and with faces exhibiting about as much variety of expression. The Viscount Anadia of Portugal: fat, good-humoured, and *half* agreeable."[5]

With the exception of Queen Louise, Louisa never saw individuals in "the great world of Berlin" as larger than life. The character sketches that fill "Adventures" gently skewer even the most influential members of the court with small, intimate details. She described the queen's *grande gouvernante* (mistress of ceremonies), Madame de Voss, for example, as someone who "exacted much more respect and homage" than her royal mistress and who "sidled off with her hoop shaking under her mincing step, erect as a may Pole." Louisa also found many of her required court appearances boring and inane: "the same treadmill round of ceremonious heavy etiquette." But even as she could recognize the superficiality and ordinariness of the exalted circles in which she moved, she responded to the spectacle. And she delighted in meeting—and flirting with—celebrated characters, like Beau Brummel, who teased her that reports of the queen's beauty had been exaggerated: "I insisted that it was impossible to exaggerate upon the subject and offered to bet that when [he] had seen her, [he] would be more enthusiastic than anyone else." Brummel rose to the challenge, and Louisa won the bet.[6]

Unfortunately, Louisa's clear-eyed observations were never put to the service of the American government. In this, Louisa seems to have been something of an exception. Other diplomatic wives in Berlin played an acknowledged role in their husband's careers. The Marchesa Luccassini, Louisa wrote, "knew well how to play a political game," as did Lady Elizabeth Carysfort, who "did most of the diplomacy" for Great Britain. The young queen herself was very actively employed in a diplomatic role. Although John Quincy regularly reported to his mother on the political and military situation in Europe and welcomed her analyses in return, he refused to discuss politics with his wife: "Mr. Adams had always accustomed me to believe that Women had nothing to do with politics, and as he was the glass from which my opinions were reflected, I was convinced of its truth, and sought no farther," Louisa wrote later.[7]

Had John Quincy glanced into his wife's mind, he would have discovered that whether or not he was willing to credit her with political acumen, she was, in fact, privately making trenchant observations on the important players in the Prussian court that she could recall with great detail years later: "Count Haugwitz is at the head of the Foreign Department, though second to the old Count [Finck von Finckenstein, a senior minister to the king], *apparently* in command. His manner is one of your old political deceivers, fully exemplifying the Jesuit and Machievelian doctrines, that *truth* is not needful, when false-hood will suffice. The old Count is worthy of all respect, his little peculiarities being only *tedious*, but not vicious."[8]

Louisa also cast a cool eye on the scandals of the court and was not at all shocked by the sexual escapades that enlivened the gossip that delighted her and her many visitors. Abigail Adams had no reason to fear the court's lax morals might sully her inexperienced daughter-in-law and, indirectly, John Quincy. The "presuming" Lord Elgin, for example, was famed for his ability to captivate any woman who crossed his path, but he made no progress with Louisa: "At a ball at court [he] immediately entered into conversation, and insisted on my dancing with him, which I positively refused; he persisted in urging me and at last I was obliged to point to the dress which I wore as one indicating a prede-termination not to dance and stated that I had already, contrary to established etiquette, declined to dance with two of the Princes. He laughed heartily and began to teaze me again when Madame Feitesback, a very beautiful woman with whom he had liaison not very honourable came up and took his arm. He immediately turned off, as he would not, of course, introduce her, and I never saw him afterwards. He was a remarkably handsome roué, since famous for a divorce from his Wife and as the importer of the famous Elgin Marbles."[9]

And despite Abigail's fears — "Young as she is, I hope she will never be allured by the splendour of a court, or tempted by the dissipations which prevail in them" — Louisa never was so dazzled by the splendor of the Prussian court that her vision became clouded. In a pithy summation of the conventional wisdom of the day, she described the "general formula" for the court: "The Queen lovely, the King silent, the Princesses gracious, the Princes affable . . . the enter-tainment splendid, the corps diplomatique brilliant, and the English Prince elegant."[10]

Abigail's warnings, however, had hit their mark exactly where they were directed. When Louisa was invited by the queen to take part in an elaborately staged performance at a costume ball honoring Prince Augustus of England

("The handsomest young men and the Prettiest Women had been selected"), John Quincy insisted that she refuse the honor: "Mr. Adams told me to excuse myself on the plea of ill health; but the real reason was that the expence was enormous and the constant rehearsals would have thrown me into a constant association with the gay persons of the Court, not agreeable to him and perhaps hazardous to me. The invitation was flattering nevertheless; I was the only foreign Lady so distinguished."[11]

At the risk of offending the enormously popular and powerful Queen Louise and greatly disappointing his wife, John Quincy had opted to heed his mother's admonitions. It would not be the last time. Abigail's influence from across the ocean extended even to the rouge, or lack of it, on Louisa's cheekbones. Her vehement disapproval of women wearing makeup—possibly stemming from her days in Paris in the final days of the ancien régime when both women and men were heavily powdered and "painted"—resulted in a series of incidents in which her dutiful son again defied the queen and frustrated his wife.[12]

The first rouge incident occurred one evening when Louisa, pale and weak, had returned to the social scene barely recovered from a difficult, extended pregnancy and ultimate miscarriage. Informed that the king wished her to be his partner to open a ball, she took her place at the head of the double line of dancers: "The dance formed; the king took his place, fortunately for me, next couple to the Queen, and I marched up, ready to faint, and took my place. The King walked up and spoke to me and the Queen with her usual loveliness took my hands in hers and stood and talked some minutes until I recovered myself. She told me I looked so pale she must make me a present of a box of rouge. I answered that Mr. Adams would not let me wear it. She smiled at my simplicity, and observed that if she presented me the box, he must not refuse it. And told me to tell him so. . . . I told Mr. Adams what the Queen said, but he said I must refuse the box as he should never permit me to accept it."

Queen Louise was not accustomed to having her gifts refused and at another party "insisted upon the rouge." Louisa badly wanted to accept the gift, particularly when it became de rigeur to be dressed in a style that involved a Spanish-inspired black dress, an elaborate black hat "looped up in front with diamonds and feathers of the same hue drooping lightly over the point of the hat and inclining over the left shoulder," black shoes, and a wire wound in black ribbon made to represent a lorgnette.

In Louisa's eyes, "This dress was remarkably becoming to the Ladies who wore rouge, but made those who were pale look cadaverous, particularly when not relieved by the brilliancy of diamonds. I who was remarkably pale, of course, looked a *fright* in the midst of the splendour." Finally, tired of being embarrassed by how ghastly she looked, she defied John Quincy: "Being more than usually pale, I ventured to put on a little rouge, which I fancied relieved the black and made me look quite beautiful. Wishing to evade Mr. Adams's observation, I hurried through the room telling him to put the lights out and follow me down. This excited his curiosity and he started up and led me to the table and then declared that unless I allowed him to wash my face, he would not go. He took a towel and drew me on his knee, and all my beauty was clean washed away; a kiss made the peace and we drove off to the party where I showed my pale face as usual."

In the winter of 1801, several months pregnant with the son she would finally bear, Louisa once more attempted to improve her wan appearance: "I had dressed to go to Court. The everlasting teasing about my pale face induced me to make another trial of a little rouge; and contrary to my first proceeding I walked boldly forward to meet Mr. Adams. As soon as he saw me, he required me to wash it off, which I with some temper, refused. Upon which he ran down and jumped into the carriage and left me planté là [standing there]. Even to myself appearing like a fool, crying with vexation. As soon as I had composed myself, I very coolly took off my finery, redressed myself suitably, and stepped into the carriage and joined my friends the Browns who never guessed that I had made myself so ridiculous. In those days, anger seldom lasted with me more than ten minutes, and once over all was forgotten."[13]

The rouge incidents—not entirely "forgotten" if Louisa could relate them in such detail after forty years—were unmentioned in John Quincy's diary. His records do, however, generally support Louisa's claim that she did not again attend a formal court function and instead emphasize how very ill she was during the final stages of her pregnancy. The incidents also illustrate Louisa's remarkable personal relationship with Queen Louise. Her royal highness, very much constrained by rigid protocol, could not casually visit Louisa at home or ignore Prussian and foreign dignitaries in favor of a girlish chat with her friend when they met on formal occasions. But whenever they could, the two spoke easily together. Once when they were awaiting the start of a royal christening ceremony at which Louise was to be godmother, the young queen ("elegantly dressed and loaded with diamonds, this being a state occasion") took Louisa aside to share, in private, her grief at the death of her youngest child: "The tears rolled down her cheeks as she related to me the suffering of her child, saying that it was a great trial to her to make the exertion of attending the christening but that she must perform the duty to her friend, however painful." Following his wife's lead, King Frederick William, too, was invariably kind and thoughtful to the wife of the American minister, going so far as to block off the street where

Louisa lived so that she would not be disturbed by horses' hooves on the cobble-stones as she recovered slowly from the botched birth of her first son.[14]

Another royal in Berlin, uncircumscribed by official duties or protocol, moved much more easily in the Adamses' orbit. Prince Augustus, sixth son of Britain's King George III, dispatched abroad, Louisa said, "to separate him from his wife, Lady Augusta Murray, a marriage contrary to a parliamentary law," did not appear to excite undue deference to his rank by either the Adamses or their friends, nearly all of whom were British subjects. Louisa, who prided herself on being "Brought up a *republican* and living in a Monarchy," nonchalantly described the prince, who was just two years older than she, as "good humoured and pleasant . . . a general favorite," and John Quincy, though justifiably proud of his father's role in the revolution against the prince's father, had no difficulty accepting invitations to mix with Augustus and his entourage. The prince visited regularly at Dr. Brown's home and reluctantly had to pass up a New Year's party for forty guests given by Louisa and John Quincy in 1799 in their small apartment. Louisa recalled why the prince could not join the party: "Prince Augustus sent an excuse; he was obliged to go and play at Blind man's buff with the king and queen; a diversion that the King was particularly fond of; but only play'd with the R[oyal] family and any foreign prince who might be at Berlin."[15]

The prince also rescued Louisa from an awkward protocol situation when John Quincy, as usual, was nowhere in sight:

A Ball was given in honor of Prince Augustus whose Birthday it was. The Queen Mother sat opposite to us, next [to] the young Queen; the company seated all around the room, excepting the Gentlemen who formed in half circles on each side of their majesties. The Queen Mother beckoned to *me* to come to her: I pretended to be busy talking to Mrs. Errington to avoid seeing her but she insisted; and a gentleman informed me that the Queen wished to speak to me, and I was obliged to walk across the ball room between this circle of Gentlemen, and when I got there, she only wanted to ask me "How old I was." How to get back without turning *my* back was the difficulty; but I did so with the assistance of Prince Augustus who complemented me upon extricating myself so well from the dilemma.[16]

How Louisa, whose upper-middle-class family, though sporadically wealthy, was far from noble, could move so comfortably in the extremely class-conscious society she now frequented is difficult to understand. She had been well schooled in the social graces by her mother—whose own family background remains essentially unknown—but nothing in her upbringing had prepared her for the day-to-day intercourse with royalty that was now her life. With neither title nor fortune, it is especially surprising that she was accepted so easily into the highest, rank-obsessed, court circles. She always credited her success to John Quincy. In her view, the high regard in which he was held as a result of his integrity, diplomatic skills, and immediate, familial relationship to the American president opened any doors that might have been closed to her. There is some truth to this. As Miss Johnson, the nearest she could have come to Queen Louise or Prince Augustus might have been as one in the surging crowds that cheered the royals on festive occasions. But that is not what happened. The door may have been opened by John Quincy, but, once through it, Louisa used her own elegance and grace to charm a jaded Prussian and English royal circle into welcoming her on her own merits. Other diplomats' wives, many of whom possessed both noble rank and wealth, seem never to have become as intimate as Louisa with the queen and the many princesses, duchesses, and countesses who peopled the court.

John Quincy should have been aware of the "marked distinction" with which his wife was treated by everyone from the highest to the lowest level of court society and to have realized how much less he could have accomplished had she not been at his side. From his diaries it is clear he fully appreciated the fact that most diplomacy at the time was conducted in drawing rooms and ball-rooms, but he apparently did not realize that it was in exactly these milieus that his wife's charm far outshone his. If he did, he was tragically unable to persuade Louisa of her worth. Always painfully aware of her unpaid dowry, which meant that she could not fully dress the part of a foreign minister's wife or entertain as lavishly as she wished, she never gave the smallest indication that she saw herself as an asset to John Quincy's diplomatic career.

Although unacknowledged by either partner, it was as a team that the Adamses made a success of their diplomatic posting to Berlin. John Quincy was especially fortunate in his dealings with the foreign office. At a time when Prussia's relations with France, Britain, and Russia were extremely sensitive, the attitude of Berlin's foreign ministers toward the United States was inclined to be favorable or, at a minimum, neutral. Once the treaty he had come to negotiate was signed, John Quincy's duties at court became little more than formal and social.

He endured this part of his job quite happily. At least at this moment in his career, John Quincy made more friends than enemies, and though his nightly appearances at the Prussian court were often irksome and boring to him, he never betrayed his disdain for mindless conversation and meaningless protocol. Although he seems to have made no particular effort to make friends, the American minister was a popular and sought-after companion. His diary mentions several nonobligatory social gatherings, some all-male, at which he would not have been present had he been an unwelcome or uncongenial guest. Only in his early thirties, the young diplomat had not lost his enjoyment of a convivial drinking party, a quality that had endeared him to his many friends in Newburyport and Boston. He also enjoyed playing chess with Dr. Brown and whist at what Louisa saw as the court's interminable card parties; he delighted in an evening at the opera, a musical performance, or a play; and he could always be persuaded to join excursions into the countryside. His insatiably curious mind welcomed the opportunity to meet strangers from all over Europe and the United States as they passed through. The couple's many Berlin friends would have been much more reluctant to spend time with the American minister and his wife had they not both been welcoming and amiable.

If John Quincy has been unfairly depicted as a rigid, humorless Yankee, intent on doing his grim-faced duty at social gatherings, Louisa has also suffered from her reputation as a drag on her husband's early diplomatic career. Relying primarily on their subject's diaries, some of John Quincy's biographers have drawn the conclusion that Louisa contributed very little to his success at the Prussian court. "During the first three years of their residence in Berlin, Mrs. Adams was almost continually unwell and despondent," the historian Samuel Flagg Bemis, for example, wrote.[17]

Charles Francis Adams seems to have been among the first to recognize the role his mother played in her first overseas assignment. In an appreciative essay on Louisa's place in American history written in 1839, a year before she wrote her "Adventures," he noted that American representatives at the turn of the nineteenth century were seen in European capitals as something of a curiosity, dispatched from a country that was "regarded as hardly more than successful rebels," and the first impression they made on sovereigns and court officials would be critical to the international standing of the new nation for years to come. "To Berlin, where no minister had before been acknowledged, Mr. Adams repaired, conducting his wife, as a bride, at once to play her part in the higher circles of social and political life. It need scarcely be added that she proved perfectly competent to this; and that during four years, which comprised the period of her stay at that court, notwithstanding almost continual ill-health, she succeeded in making friends and conciliating a degree of good will, the recollection of which is, even at this distance of time, believed to be among the most agreeable of the associations with her varied life."[18]

When she was well, as Charles recognized, Louisa's sweet, sparkling personality charmed its way into the hearts of everyone, from her brother-in-law Tom and her wide circle of women friends to the lofty courtiers surrounding the king and queen. But she was rarely entirely well, and her fragile health was a source of constant anxiety for her husband. Summing up his life at the turn of the century on December 31, 1799, he wrote, "The year in general would have been a pleasant one, save only for the state of my wife's health, which has been almost continually bad, and concerning which I am even now deeply concerned. The subject preys upon my spirits more than I can express." Abigail Adams did nothing to allay her son's apprehensions: "I regret that Mrs. Adams got into a Habit [miscarriages] which I fear will injure her constitution," she wrote. Louisa was fully aware of John Quincy's concerns: "My ill health was a perpetual tax upon Mr. Adams's feelings—but his kindness was unstinted in promoting my comfort. The perpetual anxiety which he displayed, however, had a tendency to defeat his wishes and to keep me in a state of disquietude beyond my strength. My nervous system became affected and the slightest agitation produced the very consequences which he so constantly apprehended."[19]

In just over two years, between November 1797 and January 1800, Louisa suffered at least four miscarriages or stillbirths. Each event extended over several days and was marked by severe, debilitating pain. Louisa and John Quincy learned to recognize the onset of the dreaded events: "Mrs. Adams was seized this afternoon about an hour after dinner, more suddenly than I have ever known before, with extreme illness. It continued with great violence until 10 o'clock at night," the agonized husband wrote in his diary. She also seems to have had frequent migraine headaches and colds.[20]

Both Louisa and John Quincy were extremely circumspect in spelling out medical details, instead referring, as was typical of the time, to her "illness" or "ill health." Two hundred years later, it is impossible to know for certain exactly why her miscarriages occurred and why they were so extended and painful. The first three months of every pregnancy were, for Louisa, extremely difficult, and morning sickness seems to have lasted throughout the day and night. Louisa's stormy crossing of the North Sea and subsequent jarring carriage ride from Hamburg to Berlin would have been the worst possible prescription for a healthy outcome of her first pregnancy. That it took nine days of excruciating pain to expel the fetus and weeks more to regain her strength may indicate that complications had occurred.

But the length of time it took for this and her other miscarriages to run their course would not have been unusual in the eighteenth century. Without medical intervention, miscarriages, such as Louisa's, could extend over a period of many days, but the more imminent danger to Louisa was always from loss of blood. It is clear from everything she wrote about her years in Berlin that she saw herself as exceptionally pale. She adamantly refused a request from her mother to have a miniature portrait painted because she thought she looked so pathetic. "I have looked so ill and ugly . . . that I have avoided sending the one Mama desired," she wrote to her sister Nancy. It seems likely that she was anemic and could ill afford to lose any more blood.[21]

It also appears likely that Louisa had debilitating menstrual periods before her marriage. Approximately once a month during their courtship, John Quincy would report that she had not appeared in the Johnson drawing room because of "illness," but she would always be back the following night. Many of the "Mrs. Adams ill" notations in John Quincy's Prussian diary may very well be attributed to severe menstrual periods. Each of her miscarriages may have contributed to her weakness and pallor, and every subsequent episode required a much longer recovery period and left her even less able to bear the strain of another pregnancy.

Another factor that may have contributed to Louisa's childbearing difficulties was the style of dress required at court. Formal dress required broad hoopskirts and cinched waist even when day dresses were simple, low-cut, Empire-waist shifts. (Louisa in her memoirs describes a comical scene at a court ball in which she and a friend were seated on either side of a hapless gentleman whose lap was filled with their hoops.) It was fashionable to hide a pregnancy as long as possible. Once confirmed, a woman was taken out of society and "confined." A burgeoning belly could be hidden under a hoopskirt, but a broadening waist could not. It must have taken extremely tight stays around a woman's midriff to disguise her situation, and a "very small woman," as Louisa described herself, would have found it particularly difficult to hide her thickening body.[22]

Louisa's repeated difficulties in carrying a baby to term added to the stress she was under in this early period of her marriage. In addition to worrying about making a social gaffe that would bring disrepute to the American mission, she continued to brood about her father's financial ruin and her own inability to contribute any funds toward household expenses. It did not help that mail from her family in America brought discouraging news. Joshua had been unable to gain access to the funds he believed were owed him by his partners, and the family was living in very distressed circumstances in Georgetown. "The Letters from America weighed me down with sorrow," she wrote many years later, "and mortification; for anguish will have vent, and the heart will breathe its sorrows to the loved ones who have participated in our blessings. It is a trite saying 'that it [crying] does no good' but it is not true; for even the momentary relief assuages the heaviness of grief, and softens its asperity."[23]

Despite a traumatic experience with her first attempt to bear a child, Louisa believed, falsely, that she was pregnant two months later in January when she was presented to the queen. ("A Second illness of the same nature had again reduced me very much, and I was still very weak.") The queen herself was pregnant at the time. She gave birth to a daughter in July; Louisa would not be as fortunate. On February 16, John Quincy mourned to his diary, "Mrs. Adams was apparently well again all the former part of the day; but in the evening—Our hopes were raised merely to be more severely dashed to the ground."[24]

Louisa was certainly pregnant a month later. On March 17, 1798, following a week of illness, John Quincy recorded that she had been sick all night. By the twenty-first, he had given up hope of a happy outcome. "Mrs. Adams ill again— My prophetic heart! I have no doubt of the cause. The cup of bitterness must be filled to the brim and drank to the dregs." Throughout April and May, Louisa's condition fluctuated almost daily between sickness and health. One day, she would be dancing at a palace ball, and on the next she would be confined to her bed. On May 26, the couple attended a play, to which they walked. John Quincy wrote that "before the first scene was finished, Mrs. A. was taken very ill and fainted—We were obliged to return home. The Prince of Weilbourg lent us his carriage. Mrs. A. continued ill an hour or two after our return but in the Evening was better." Two days later, she was back on her social rounds: "I called on the Princess of Orange and her Ladies who laughed and said they did not apprehend that my illness would prove dangerous."[25]

But it was. Throughout the last two weeks of June, John Quincy recorded day after day of Louisa's often-violent pain. By mid-July, his optimism had drained away: "Mrs. Adams again ill. It was only yesterday I was indulging some faint and feeble hopes of a better event than I had anticipated hitherto. I cannot even form an hope with impunity. The tortures of Tantalus have been inflected upon me without ceasing." On July 17 he wrote: "A dreadful night. Mrs. A. soon after going to bed was taken extremely ill and between 12 and 1 o'clock was in such extreme pain that I sent for Doctor Kibke. He was at Charlottenburg as was Dr. Brown. I sent for them both. They came between 3 and 4 in the morning. In the meantime, Mrs. A. had suffered the most excruciating pains. She was after that somewhat relieved and throughout the day easier. The doctors stayed until 6 and 8 in the morning and returned several times through the day. The case appears in almost every point similar to that of last November. Patience and resignation is all that we can have. Was up all night."[26]

Tom Adams, watching helplessly from the sidelines, was fully as anxious for Louisa as her anguished husband: "Poor little woman; how she suffers! Matrimony, these are thy fruits! Bitter, bitter," he wrote in his journal. Louisa herself refused to believe that she was about to lose another child, but John Quincy was mordantly pessimistic: "The anticipation of evils that we cannot prevent is itself a great misfortune. I have these 8 months been convinced, with scarcely the shadow of a doubt what this Event would be—yet now that it happens, I feel it with no less poignancy than if it had been unexpected. The prospects of futurity that it still holds out to me are horrible. I realize them as if present. I have no more doubt of them than of death. They poison every moment of existence, and when they come will be not less bitter for having been foretasted."[27]

By July 20, Louisa was confronted with the certainty that she would not succeed in bearing the living child she had hoped for so much, but she still had to wait for nature to take its course. John Quincy's gloom did not lift her spirits: "The heavy burthen of suspense and anxious uncertainty must still be pressed down upon us. Gloomy and terrible as the imagination in its forebodings is, the reality comes yet worse. The load upon my mind grows heavier from day to day. There is a point beyond which it can bear no more."[28]

Remarkably, only three weeks later, on August 6, the Adamses had embarked "with a large party" to Potsdam, the summer residence of the king and queen sixteen miles from Berlin, on what Louisa recalled happily as "a very pleasant and gratifying little tour." After two strenuous days of sightseeing, they returned to Berlin. On August 10, John Quincy recorded, as he so often did, "Mrs. Adams unwell."

Louisa's erratic swings between debilitating sickness and buoyant good health continued over the next six months. In March 1799, her general health took a turn for the worse. This time, John Quincy warned himself to guard against optimism: "A time of great anxiety now begins with much to fear and little to hope," he wrote in his diary on April 10, and for the following week he reported that Louisa was very ill. By May, she had regained her health and was back on the social circuit. With the Browns, she attended a massive two-day military review, a "splendid scene," in which some 10,000 men participated. John Quincy "having already seen them did not attend." That week, the couple were present at a royal ball.[29]

Soon, however, John Quincy's worst fears were realized. Louisa blamed the experience of standing at a window and watching a young child get run over by a cart as the proximate cause for another miscarriage. "I fainted and fell—The consequence was a sudden illness full of disappointment, and ruinous to my constitution—The wretchedness of Mr. Adams aggravated the evil and only made the suffering more distressingly excruciating; At such seasons women want every solace, for they endure both corporeal and mental anguish—He was kind and affectionate in his attention; but his feeling of disappointment could not be subdued."[30]

This time, possibly because of "rough handling" and excessive bleeding, Louisa did not bounce back quickly. Day after day she was confined to her bed. It was only at the end of June that her husband could write that she had "gone out for the first time and spent a couple of hours with Mrs. Brown." On July 12 he was still concerned that she was "very much fatigued by her illness and loss of sleep last night."

Something radical, Dr. Brown believed, was needed. He convinced the couple to heed the advice of many of their titled friends who routinely abandoned Berlin in the summer for the resort spa town of Töplitz, southeast of Berlin, midway between Dresden and Prague, in what is now the Czech Republic. Their five-day journey in a stagecoach from Berlin to Dresden over generally poor roads through villages that offered only the most rustic overnight accommodations would have been rigorous for a woman in the best of health. For Louisa, who was "very unwell" up to the day of their departure and had to be lifted into the carriage, it was a risky enterprise. The trip, however, turned out to be invigorating: "By the time we arrived at Dresden, I had gained sufficient strength to participate in the pleasures, which the journey presented," she wrote. Immediately on arrival in Dresden, she briskly changed her clothes and went off to visit a friend, "who I found with a sweet little Girl, who she had named Dresdina. Almost as roughly handled as myself, she had narrowly escaped with her life, but she was blessed with a fine Child, while I only lived to witness the pangs of disappointment, which so bitterly distressed my poor husband and destroyed all the comfort of my life."[31]

Töplitz, hidden in a deep mountain valley, was second only to Carlsbad in the nineteenth century as the favorite spa of European nobility and those wealthy enough to mingle with them. "Töplitz is decidedly one of the most fashionable watering places of Germany frequented not only by the nobility of Prussia, Russia, and Austria but by the sovereigns of those countries and the Dukes, Princes, etc., of smaller states as well as by the members of the royal and Imperial families of Europe," enthused an anonymous writer in *A Hand-Book for Travellers in Southern Germany*, describing a scene little changed a half-century later from what it was when the Adamses arrived.[32]

The Töplitz day began after breakfast in one's lodgings—nearly every home in the small town took in two or three boarders—followed by bathing at regularly scheduled intervals in the resort's famous hot springs. At 11 A.M., a band piped up to accompany the throng of men and women strolling along the many broad avenues and through the elaborately landscaped gardens surrounding the palace of the local eminence, Prince Clary. At 1 P.M., dinner was served at a central dining hall in the complex of buildings surrounding the palace. Afternoons were reserved for rest or carriage excursions to nearby castles and monasteries. A formal tea, hosted on the palace grounds each afternoon by one of the visiting ladies, was usually followed by a theatrical production and sometimes a ball.

The nobility came to resorts like Töplitz for weeks and months at a time in the summer for relief from various medical conditions such as gout, rheumatism, and arthritis. It was believed that bathing in the seventeen mineral-rich hot springs, and drinking the green water—"disgusting to the smell and taste," sniffed Louisa—were beneficial. Töplitz's waters were graduated from very hot—one writer claimed that if you entered the first in the series of baths, you were likely to be parboiled—to cold. Louisa, however, was spared from even having to enter a bathhouse: "The Baths are built very roughly, immediately over the Stream; at intervals; and the Physician of the place prescribes the degree of warmth proper for the complaint of the Patient. The debility under which I laboured was such, he would not permit me to attend the publick Bath's; and the Water was brought to the House and the bath's were prepared in my Chamber in Tubs, until I should be strong enough to bear the fatigue of the bath, and the exercise together. Three times a week the bath, and every day a bottle of Pyrmont Water."[33]

Louisa and John Quincy knew many of the Töplitz clientele and were immediately swept into a very active social life. Louisa loved it. "Our residence was very agreeable while at this place. The Evenings at the Gardens dancing or walking; sometimes at the Theatre. Often meeting our Berlin friends, and forming new and agreeable acquaintance among the daily arrivals." John Quincy saw it somewhat differently ("Mr. Adams found the Evening party very dull—*Too* many Grandee's to make it pleasant") but he enjoyed the opportunity to hike the nearby mountains, attend an opera or a play every evening if he wanted to, and overhear the beautifully performed choral music emanating from a Catholic church near their boardinghouse.[34]

Louisa was daily becoming stronger, and her mood was decidedly upbeat. Now it was John Quincy's turn to fall victim to a flu-like illness and high, spiking fever. Louisa nursed him tirelessly for ten days, her task not made easier by her stubborn patient's refusal to acknowledge he was ill. When John Quincy had recovered enough to resume his daily walks, Louisa was delighted to be able to join him. But he was reluctant to accept good news: "Mr. Adams, being better, began again to be anxious on my account, and forgetting the anxiety that I had suffered on his account during his sickness, seemed determined to believe that the waters had done me more harm than good." Possibly to prove the point that her health was really much improved, she accompanied him on a hike to the foot of the Schlossberg, the highest point in the vicinity—a round trip of about three hours that left her totally exhausted.

The Adamses remained in Töplitz until September 9. By then, Louisa was able to climb the Schlossberg herself and to feel superior to "Countess Panin ascending the mountain in her Carriage; a proof of what the wealthy and great of this world can accomplish." At the summit, she and John Quincy, like countless other visitors, carved their names into the walls of an ancient fortress.[35]

Louisa's health at this moment was as good as it had been for a long time. It is far more likely that the daily walks, fresh food (she mentions "new milk"), August sunshine, and cool mountain air were more efficacious than the Töplitz baths and bottled water. So, as the Adamses prepared to board a private yacht supplied by one of their titled friends for the cruise down the Elbe to Dresden—"to avoid the Geyersberg Mountain, and to vary our route"—their hearts were substantially lighter than when they arrived.

In Dresden Louisa and John Quincy again took up a life they loved. As a couple, they made wonderful travelers—curious, adaptable, always ready for a new experience. They spent days viewing the city's famed art collections, went on numerous excursions with friends to visit nearby tourist attractions, and took advantage of the great music the city had to offer. Louisa was deeply moved by a service at the Dresden Cathedral, then at the height of its Baroque glory: "There is a grandeur and awful sublimity in these buildings very striking to the imagination of young and ardent minds—and the Music, the Paintings, and ornamented Alters; with the Showy paraphernalia of the Priests; and the frank Incence; all seize upon the senses, and steal insensibly upon the heart with rapt enthusiasm. The Arts are all called into action and you gaze in wonderment at the works of man; while if you are of a reflecting mind, are led to think if man can atchieve so much, how surpassingly wonderful must the Creater be." As always, the Adamses were treated like visiting royalty. Invitations poured into their hotel room not only from the city's British colony but also from the nobles of the Saxon court. John Quincy's diary doesn't ever say, "Mrs. Adams ill." Instead, there are accounts of the many activities "we" enjoyed together, including a vigorous walk along the ramparts of the city. Louisa, in glowing good health, compared their social life in Dresden to what they had become accustomed to in Berlin: "the only difference [is] here it was all social, and that in Berlin, when I was well enough to visit the great world, it was all *State* and very laborious."[36]

It is not surprising that Louisa was pregnant again by the time they arrived home in Berlin in October 1799. Even though she was much stronger than she had been in the early stages of her previous pregnancies, a similar pattern emerged. On several days, she was too "ill" to leave the house, and John Quincy had to attend various court functions without her. Nevertheless, she seems to have been well enough to attend the theater and numerous dinners, receptions, and balls during the fall season. When Gonzalo O'Farrill arrived in Berlin as the Spanish envoy extraordinary and minister plenipotentiary to Prussia in November 1799, Louisa agreed to present Mrs. O'Farrill to the court, an extended procedure requiring formal visits to several minor royals as well as to the queen. It was at the last of these, at a party celebrating a noble wedding, that an unfortunate incident occurred:

> Mrs. [O'Farrill] was standing immediately before me, when one of the Grandees asked me to present him to her. I tapped her gently on the shoulder, and in turning she fell as gently on the Carpeted floor, and exclaimed that she had broken her Leg—I sank on one knee immediately, and rested her head on the other; when she fell into a dead fainting. She had barely recovered, when she again said she had broken the limb; which being heard by a Gentleman, who said it was only a sprain he took hold of her foot, and turned it; upon which she screamed and fainted again. Her husband had gone for a Surgeon, who raised her gently on a Sopha, and she was carried into another apartment, to which the Doctor desired me to accompany her. He then examined the *hurt*, and declared the bone to be fractured in two different places; and ordered me to cut the Stocking off, the leg being very much swollen; He gave me a pair of very sharp Scissors, and though I trembled like a leaf, I succeeded. . . . I tried to find Mr. Adams that I might get home; but ere I could succeed, I fell down in a deep fainting fit; and was carried home being attended by three or four Ladies who were alarmed at the length of time which the total insensibility continued: A succession of these fits continued nearly all night, and they kindly staid with me until I was thought out of danger: but my recovery was slow and at the end of a few weeks I suffered all the ill consequences of the fright, and again had the misery to behold the anguish of my husbands blighted hopes.[37]

John Quincy was certainly in anguish. His diary records every fainting fit and "cramps almost amounting to convulsions" as the outcome both feared hung in the balance. On January 2, Louisa was bled by Dr. Brown, a procedure intended to reduce blood flow widely advocated at the time for the cure or relief of a number of medical conditions, particularly pain in childbirth. She withstood the operation but fainted again on the way to bed that evening. Her situation did not improve, and by January 9, 1800, the exhausted husband could report to his diary: "After an uneasy, restless, and to some degree painful night, Mrs. A. has this day gone through as I hope the worst of her misfortune—She was for about three hours excessively ill. I can only pray to God that there may never again be the possibility of another like event. A better hope it would be folly to indulge for in cases like this hope is but an aggravation of misery."[38]

This time, Louisa's recovery was slower than ever before. It was not until the end of March that she could resume her social duties, and by April 22, she was playing hostess to a dinner party of fifteen distinguished guests. Still very weak, she continued to attend required receptions and balls but now often left them early. No more is said in her memoir about her love of dancing or her delight in style and spectacle. Despite John Quincy's prayer that she never again suffer another miscarriage, it seems that by spring she may have been pregnant once again and was further weakened by another—unnamed—debilitating condition. In a letter to Joshua Johnson, written in late 1800, John Quincy described Louisa's feeble condition in the spring and early summer and explained the drastic steps he had taken to correct it: "A very severe illness in the Spring of a different nature from those she had before suffered, added to a new instance of that which occurr'd at the beginning of the year left her in a state of debility as great as she had been in at any period before. I then determined to try what would be the effect of a long and fatiguing journey south into a country calculated by the variety of entertainment which it would afford to amuse the mind, to make the time seem short, and to turn weariness itself into pleasure. We therefore employed between two and three months of the last summer in making the tour of Silesia, the province which of all the Prussian domains offers the most interesting objects of nature and of human industry to the travelers' attention."[39]

As John Quincy had hoped, their two-month excursion to Silesia, with a month-long extension in Leipzig, though physically very demanding, revived Louisa. Even when two or three days of punishingly energetic sightseeing might conclude with a notation "Mrs Adams excessively fatigued," the next day's entry would record, "Masked ball in the evening." As always, the Adamses carried with them introductions to local notables who invariably escorted them to the principal neighborhood sights and entertained them at dinner. They visited industrial and crafts enterprises, attended concerts, and toured churches and art galleries. John Quincy reported the trip in a series of detailed, colorful letters to his brother Tom, who published them in forty-four installments in the Philadelphia literary journal *Port Folio*. The letters later came out in book form in London, without the author's permission, as *Letters on Silesia*.

Once more, Louisa was pregnant. In Leipzig, the usual early months of "lingering sufferring" took their toll. In late October 1800 the Adamses returned to Berlin where Louisa "was sick almost unto the death, and sadly wearisome to every one; but they bore with me with the patience of Angels, and never by look or word, made me feel the pang of *mortification*, by the most trifling indication of ennui at my complaints: but expressing the tenderest sympathy, and the most persevering and delicate attention, to an unfortunate creature; who as Mr Adams remarks in his journal 'never knew what it *was*, to be well a whole day.' "[40]

This time, John Quincy's worst fears proved unfounded. Much of the credit was due to Lady Elizabeth Carysfort, the highly born wife of the recently arrived British ambassador to Prussia, daughter of a former prime minister, and sister to another. Although Lady Carysfort was nearly two decades older than Louisa, the two became devoted friends. Louisa remembered her as "one of the finest women I ever knew—of very superior mind and cultivation: having received a Classical education like her Brothers—She was very plain in her person; somewhat masculine in her manners; and [at first] made one feel timid and afraid—But she took a fancy to me, and was so uniformly kind, and affectionate at all times; her conversation so instructive, so entertaining, and at times so delightful; I clung to her as if she had been my own mother, and loved her with equal sincerity."[41]

Their friendship marked yet another instance of Louisa's ability to bridge distinctions of class, for Lady Carysfort, by birth and marriage, was socially several insurmountable rungs above the daughter of a bankrupt American merchant and a woman of uncertain pedigree. "She kindly said that she did not know why she thus opened her heart to *me*; it was an indulgence of which she rarely availed herself, but she could not help it—and she hoped I should consider it as a proof of great attachment and respect—She then told me to apply to her on all occasions when I wanted Motherly advice, and that she would be with me in my hour of trial, if I wished it."[42]

Lady Carysfort took Louisa under her wing, encouraging—all but forcing—her to exercise daily, keep up her social engagements, eat well, and refuse to feel sorry for herself. In this, the older woman was supported by Dr. Brown, who, Louisa said, "thought it best to keep me amused—The mind too anxious for the body." No plea of illness or debility was sufficient for her ladyship. She firmly believed that Louisa did herself no good by withdrawing to a sickroom and worrying about her symptoms and prospects. More often than not, Louisa would arrive, weak and sickly, at an event engineered by Lady Carysfort and would end the evening very late in peals of laughter:

I was very ill all the morning and unable to sit up. Lady Carysfort called, and *insisted* that I should go to her in the Evening, and would not be denied; every hour or two I received a Note, intimating that she would take no denial, and at eight o'clock in the evening, as I was apparently better, Mr. Adams thought I had better go; that we could keep the Carriage, and I could return the moment I felt fatigued—I was too weak even to dress, and being in mourning, I tied a black Handkerchief round my head, with some black jet beads, in a proper don't care style; and wore a black mourning dress; and being within a Month of my confinement a black Lace Cloak. She promised me that I should not be in the Ball or receiving room, but that I should stay in a small sitting room adjoining her boudoir, where I should undergo no fatigue— When we got into the Drawing room, Lady Carysfort came to me immediately, and took my arm, and led me into the apartment provided; and there in spite of all my efforts, *laid* me on a Sopha, and left some of my young friends to amuse me—I felt very badly; but an hour or more elapsed, and no one intruded. I was lying quite at my ease, talking and laughing, when I heard a Gentleman's voice asking Lady Carysfort, "who *that* Lady was." And she answered the Lady of the American Minister. I did not dare turn my head round, the situation was altogether so ridiculous, but she brought him up to the Sopha, from which I attempted to rise; but he gently laid his hand on my Arm, and insisted that I should not move. This was Prince Adolphus, and I blushed all colours at being caught in such a position—He stood talking some time, and then sat down to the Piano, and with Madame de Caraman which I thought very odd, sung God save the King—I staid Supper and sat next to the Duke of Darmstadt, a German Lump of obesity; whose conversation kept me, and a young Lady who sat near to me . . . in "*a perfect gale.*"[43]

Throughout the holiday season and winter of 1801, Louisa and John Quincy attended the opera, countless receptions, dinner parties, and major court functions in what Louisa described as "the most splendid Winter since we have resided here." If Louisa could not go out, visitors came to dinner or to pass the evening with her; one notable dinner party in March, a month before Louisa's confinement, included Prince Adolphus, Lord and Lady Carysfort, and several other eminent guests, all crowded into the Adamses' small apartment. "The Prince received news while at Table, giving an account of the dangerous and alarming illness of his Father George III—He left us early—He would not permit me to serve the Soup, and took the ladle out of my hand, lest I should be *fatigued.*"[44]

It seems that all of society was pulling for Louisa to survive the pregnancy. Returning from the trip to Silesia, she found "a large packet from the Queen containing a charm. The packet was to be laid under my pillow every night and not to be opened until after my confinement." Throughout the winter, an anxious, exhausted John Quincy hovered over his wife. Nearly every day, he noted in his diary distressing facts about her health: "Mrs. A. had a very bad and alarming night" (February 27); "Mrs. A. was almost the whole day extremely ill—Dr. Brown and Dr. Ribke were both here" (March 6). He gave up all but the most obligatory court appearances and nearly all his writing and translation projects so that he could spend day and night with his wife. Although Lady Carysfort continued in her efforts to force Louisa to leave her sickbed, even her indomitable will was frustrated when Louisa fainted one afternoon on her way to take an afternoon drive in her ladyship's carriage.[45]

Finally, on April 12, John Quincy was able to make the diary entry he had prayed for: "I have this day to offer my humble and devout thanks to almighty God, for the birth of a son at half past three in the afternoon." Louisa's account is a little more harrowing: "on the 12th day of April, I was blessed with a *Son*— but under circumstances so distressing; and treatment so cruel on the part of the Drunken Accoucheur, that my life nearly became the forfeit."[46]

She did not exaggerate. The delivery had been managed so badly that she was temporarily paralyzed on the left side from the waist down. John Quincy hesitated even to notify their parents of the baby's birth for fear that he would have to follow his joyous news with word of Louisa's death. In a long letter to his mother that covered such diverse topics as the presidential election of 1800 and John Adams's reaction to it, the relationship of Cicero's *Republic* to Pennsylvania, the political situation in Russia, and Lord Nelson's attack on the French, he concluded, "The day before yesterday at half past three o'clock afternoon my dear Louisa gave me a Son. She has had a very severe time through the winter and is now so ill that I dare not write to her mother to give her notice of this event. I will humbly hope that in a few days I may be relieved from my anxiety on her account and enabled to announce to her mother only news of joy—The child is well."[47]

For the next five weeks, Louisa hovered between life and death. Two weeks after her child's birth, she was not only too weak to stand, she was unable to turn her body. On April 29, the desperately apprehensive husband wrote, "Mrs. A. remains immovable from and nearly so in her bed. She was the whole day as weak and faint as she has been at any period hitherto." Louisa's case roused the active concern of her many devoted friends. Lady Carysfort, Countess Neale, and Mrs. Brown came almost daily to check on her condition and to relieve John Quincy of his constant attendance at her bedside; the queen sent a messenger every day to inquire how she was. As weak as she remained, however, Louisa was not only able to nurse her infant son, she simultaneously nursed a six-month-old girl ("the daughter of a kind English woman then resident in Berlin") in what she believed was an effort to "keep the fever from my brain."[48]

As weeks went by without any real improvement in Louisa's strength, John Quincy decided to have the child christened even though the baby's mother would be unable to attend the ceremony. Lord and Lady Carysfort stood with John Quincy as godparents at the May 4 baptismal service performed by the junior Anglican chaplain attached to the British Embassy. "The child's name is George Washington, and I implore the favour of almighty God that he may live and never prove unworthy of it," the proud but solemn father wrote in his diary later that evening.[49]

John Quincy was now faced with a dilemma of timing. Just before leaving the White House in March, his father had recalled him from Berlin. Although it is not at all clear that John Adams's successor, Thomas Jefferson, had any intention of rescinding John Quincy's diplomatic appointment, the always suspicious second president did not want to afford him that option. It was now incumbent on John Quincy to make arrangements for an immediate transatlantic passage back to America. He decided to schedule the trip for midsummer and trust to fortune that his wife and newborn son would be strong enough to make the voyage. His hopes were justified. Louisa very gradually became slightly stronger, though still prone to fainting, and baby George thrived. Both would be lifted into a carriage heading out of Berlin early on the morning of June 17, 1801.

Before leaving the city of both her triumph and travail, Louisa made sad farewell visits to the Browns and Lady Carysfort. Dr. Brown entreated her to "persevere in nursing my Child for six Months; at that period my *constitution* might change—but he considered me in a deep consumption, and only trusted to this crisis to save my life. I had been fully aware of my situation and was rather pleased to learn that I might live to see my Parents, and perhaps die in their arms." She parted from Lady Carysfort with "bitter tears," recalling that "when it was thought on the 4th day of my confinement that I was dying; that a mortification had taken place. I had entreated her to *take* my Child, until Mr. Adams should leave the Country; and she had faithfully promised to perform every duty to him, as I would myself."

In the two months since the birth of her son, Louisa had faced imminent death. Certainly, many of those surrounding her bedside, and she herself, had feared the worst. But she had somehow survived, still very weak in her body but strong in her faith and triumphant in her achievement: "I received the Sacrament, with feelings I sincerely trust of devotion and gratitude for the blessings bestowed on me—I was a *Mother*—God had heard my prayer."[50]

A NATIVE IN A STRANGE LAND

I could not suit, however well inclined.

—LOUISA CATHERINE ADAMS, *"Adventures of a Nobody"*

Louisa's first sight of her "native" land was unexpectedly reassuring. After sixty days on the high seas between Hamburg and Philadelphia with an infant son in her arms, any spot on dry land would have been welcome. But Philadelphia on September 4, 1801, even in the midst of a blistering heat wave, was a pleasant surprise. Then the wealthiest city in the new nation, Philadelphia boasted a thriving free library, a hospital, the nation's first university, and a prosperous, sophisticated populace that supported theaters and several newspapers. Until very recently the nation's capital, the city basked in its role as the cradle of American independence. To Louisa, who had lived nearly all her life in large, bustling, merchant cities, the panorama of trading ships from all over the world tied up on the Delaware River waterfront was familiar and comforting, as was her first glimpse of Tom Adams, waving a welcome from the dock.[1]

The long voyage had done little to improve either her spirits or her strength. She was convinced her youth and looks were entirely gone. Her brother-in-law, she said, was "shocked and distressed" when he first glimpsed her. Nevertheless, she exerted herself to keep up with John Quincy, who immediately plunged into the city's hectic social life. Still seriously weakened from the rough handling she had undergone in childbirth, Louisa somehow managed to attend tea and dinner parties every day during the scorching week the Adamses remained in Philadelphia. Finally, utterly exhausted, she was forced to take to her bed under the care of the renowned doctor and Adams family friend Benjamin Rush.

It was not only the exceptionally hot weather and her slow postpartum recovery that was oppressing Louisa. Despite what she had written in 1825 in her memoir "Record of a Life" about an identical conversation before leaving

Prussia, she claimed in her 1840 "Adventures of a Nobody" that it was on the voyage to America that John Quincy had told her in detail—"all the history"—about his thwarted love for Mary Frazier. Self-defensively dramatizing the contrast between herself and her husband's first love, Louisa wrote, "I candidly confess however, that poor faded thing as I was, the elaborate but just account which I heard of her extreme beauty, her great attainments, the elegance of her Letters altogether made me feel *little*; and though I was not *jealous*, I could not bear the idea of the comparison that must take place, between a single woman possessing all her loveliness, and a poor broken consumptive creature, almost at the last gasp from fatigue, suffering and anxiety—It is true I had every confidence in my husbands affection, yet it was an affair of vanity on my part; and my only consolation was, that at any rate I had a *Son*."[2]

Altogether, it was not the ideal moment for John Quincy and Louisa to have one of their many disastrous misunderstandings. This one occurred because neither had considered that their first home visit in America could possibly involve the other's parents. John Quincy had not seen John and Abigail Adams for seven years—ever since leaving Boston for Holland in 1794—and he could scarcely wait to head north to New England. Louisa, on the other hand, had been living for the moment when she could surrender herself to the indulgent, loving embrace of the entire Johnson family, now living in Washington. In Berlin, her determination to stay alive until she could die in her parents' arms, she later wrote, had been a strong factor in bringing her back from the brink of death. The thought of going first to Massachusetts was anathema.[3]

The issue was not an idle spat. At the turn of the nineteenth century, transportation, even along the Eastern seaboard, was hazardous, expensive, and difficult to arrange. Once Louisa and John Quincy were headed in opposite directions, the miles between them would become an ever-greater barrier to their eventual reunion. If Louisa and the baby went first to Washington, they would eventually have to make the trip to Massachusetts without John Quincy's protective escort. Yet neither was willing to give in. On September 12, John Quincy wrote in his diary, "At 8 this morning, Mrs. A. with her child, [Louisa's maid Elizabeth] Epps and [John Quincy's valet Tilly] Whitcomb set out in the stage for Baltimore. It is the first time we have been separated since our marriage—I parted from her and my child with pain and no small concern and anxiety."[4]

By noon, he had caught his own carriage to New York, the first stage of his journey home. Louisa's party, meanwhile, made its way to Baltimore and Washington. It was unfamiliar territory: "Though this Country was to be my home, I was yet a forlorn stranger in the land of my Fathers," she wrote of her initial impressions. More troubling still was the reception she received when she finally reached her destination. Joshua Johnson, who had been waiting for her on the doorstep, gave every appearance of not recognizing her: "After he had recovered from the shock at first seeing me, he kept exclaiming that 'he did not know his own Child,' and it was some time before he could calm his feelings, and talk with me." Louisa, in turn, was appalled by how suddenly old and broken her formerly dashing father appeared. Totally spent from the long trip home, running a high fever, and concerned about the health of Joshua and her baby—who was soon sporting bug bites all over his body—Louisa gave herself completely to the restorative care of her mother and sisters.[5]

In just a few days, however, she was pleading with John Quincy to come to Washington so he could accompany her on that inevitable trip north to Quincy. In her very first letter to him, she acknowledged she had not told her family the whole truth about their plans: "They are all extremely anxious to see you and so delighted with the thoughts of your coming to fetch me that I dare not hint to them that it is not your intention." Louisa tried to temper her pleas with inducements. Singularly among most newcomers to Washington in 1801—who typically saw the federal city as little more than a stalled construction site in an unhealthy swamp—she had found much to admire and to tempt him with: "I am quite delighted with the situation of this place and think should it ever be finished it will be one of the most beautiful spots in the world. The president's house and the capitol are two most superb buildings and very well worth coming to see. The publick offices are very handsome."[6]

In less than a month, John Quincy, who was much the lonelier of the two, gave in. With a naked ardor, always surprising in a man of such controlled emotions, he wrote Louisa, "Our dear George—how I long to kiss even *his* slavering lips!—As for those of his mother I say nothing—Let her consult my heart in her own and all that pen can write or language express will shrink to nothing. . . . This day week—the 15th—I purpose to take the wings—alas! Not of the wind, but of that very earthly vehicle, the Providence Stage and thence by land or by water creep or wade or swim with all that motion give to this sluggish lump of matter my body until I can more than in wishes and imagination fly to the arms of my best beloved under her paternal roof—In the meantime with my best affections—to various people—I remain for this world and the next her devoted friend and husband."[7]

Traveling day and night, often under grueling conditions, John Quincy managed to reach Washington in just six days. In an example of his astonishing stamina, he rose early on the day after his arrival—"refreshed this morning after a good night's sleep"—and went off to pay formal visits to President Thomas

Jefferson, Secretary of State James Madison, Secretary of the Treasury Albert Gallatin, and several other cabinet officers. The next two weeks were a whirl of social activity that included a delightful two-day visit to Mount Vernon at the invitation of the widowed Martha Washington. A dinner party of "chilling frigidity" given by the president at the Executive Mansion was less enjoyable. Jefferson was still nursing his anger at the attacks from supporters of John Adams during the election of 1800, and John Quincy was not yet entirely reconciled to his father's defeat. Even the strenuous efforts of Dolley Madison, acting as Jefferson's hostess and justly celebrated for her ability to lighten any awkward social situation, proved unavailing.

Joshua and Catherine Johnson were included in the Adamses' invitations to Mount Vernon and the Executive Mansion, perhaps an indication that Joshua's disgrace was not all his daughter imagined it to be. Nevertheless, a cloud certainly hung over the Johnson family's reputation, as Abigail Adams had been quick to point out in her letter welcoming her son home. Rumors, she wrote, had followed the family to America: "Mrs. Adams is going to a place, different from all she has ever yet visited, and amongst a people where it will be impossible for her to be too guarded. Every syllable she utters will be scanned. . . . doubt not she will be prudent; but her Family has been very basely traduced."[8]

Appointed to a sinecure—Superintendent of Stamps—by former President Adams, Joshua spent most of his time pursuing what ultimately turned out to be fruitless legal claims against his former partners and in turn answering theirs against him. When he consulted John Quincy on the chances of successfully arbitrating his claims, the younger man could not offer him much hope: "Mr. Johnson gave me some of his papers to look over. He has been unfortunate in his trusts and considered prey by every man with whom he has dealt—I am strongly apprehensive of his principal causes."[9]

Louisa would have been content to remain indefinitely in Washington with her husband, baby, and family gathered around her at the Johnsons' rented house, but John Quincy was impatient to move his wife and child to Boston and get on with his new life. He knew they would face harsh November weather as they journeyed north, and the longer they delayed, the worse it would be. Finally, it was decided that Joshua and Catherine, with their two youngest daughters, would accompany John Quincy, Louisa, six-month-old George, Louisa's next-in-age sister Caroline (who was planning to live with the Adamses for several months), Epps, and Whitcomb as far as Frederick, Maryland, where the extended Johnson family—and its patriarch, former governor and Supreme Court Justice Thomas Johnson—made their home.

On November 3, the party boarded a hired carriage for what would almost immediately become a nightmare journey. Barely had they left Washington when George developed "symptoms resembling a dysentery." Not many miles further on, Joshua became violently ill. Helped to bed at an inn immediately on their arrival in Frederick, he proceeded to suffer "pain of more excessive violence than I have ever witnessed," John Quincy wrote. Joshua's brothers and sisters and their children welcomed the travelers to their various homes in the area and helped keep a vigil over the desperately ill man. Louisa was grateful that a family she had never met showed such compassion, but the visit was not a happy one: "All my relations received us with the utmost kindness, and treated Mr. Adams with the most marked attention and respect. Their Horses, their Carriages, their Houses, all were at our command, and we were *petted* in every possible way during our stay, which was in every way painful, in consequence of my dear Fathers dreadful illness."[10]

For a week, the entire family remained in Frederick, vainly hoping that Joshua would show some sign of improvement. Louisa, with a teething baby who kept both his parents awake at night, was distraught at the thought of abandoning her father. Nevertheless, John Quincy decided they must get back on the road as soon as possible. Caroline, on whom Louisa had hoped to rely for companionship and assistance in her new life, decided to remain in Frederick with their father. As the Adamses made final preparations to leave for Massachusetts, Louisa was not permitted by her husband and other family members to say farewell to Joshua. Parting, it was generally believed, would be much too excruciating for both the still-weak daughter and the gravely ill father.[11]

Determined to make up lost time, John Quincy now relentlessly pressed the travelers forward ("The Child constantly shrieking so that we could not pacify him," Louisa wrote). On the second day, they left their inn at 2 A.M. and traveled, nonstop, eighty-eight miles to Philadelphia, arriving at 5 P.M., where Louisa was "extremely overcome and very ill." Again Dr. Rush was called. Convinced her malady was rooted in her unhappiness at leaving her family, John Quincy insisted they resume what Louisa called "this dreadful journey" after only a single day's rest.

By now, a severe storm had blown up, cold, windy, and rainy. Somehow, Louisa had neglected to provide herself with appropriate winter clothing, and she suffered the consequences. Crossing the Hudson from New Jersey to New York in an open, flat-bottomed boat in a heavy rain—"only *one* man could be found, who would cross with us," she remembered—unprotected by even an umbrella and "drenched to the skin," she shivered pitiably in her fashionable pale blue satin coat "trimmed with black lace." Once in Manhattan, the soaked little party was forced to shelter in a doorway while John Quincy searched for a hackney cab for the short trip to the home of his beloved sister Nabby.[12]

But the ill-fated journey still had many miles to go. After only two days' rest in Nabby's nurturing care, the Adamses boarded a packet boat for Providence, Rhode Island. The weather had now turned wintry and rain had become snow. At noon on November 25, the wet, cold, and exhausted young family finally arrived in Quincy. John Quincy was elated: "[We] happily completed the journey commenced on the 17th of June. Here I had the pleasure of introducing my wife and child to my parents."[13]

The pleasure was not mutual.

Pale, depressed, and sickly, Louisa made a poor first impression on her Adams in-laws and their many friends and nearby relations who had crowded into Peacefields, the family's commodious new home, to meet John Quincy's bride. Louisa remembered these visits as "insupportable," and she made no secret of her unhappiness: "Quincy! What shall I say of my impressions of Quincy! Had I stepped into Noah's Ark, I do not think I could have been more utterly astonished—Dr. Tufts! Deacon French! Mr. Cranch! Old Uncle Peter! and Capt Beale!!! It was lucky for me that I was so much depressed, and so ill,

Peacefields, the Adams family home in Quincy. Drawing by Mrs. George Whitney, 1828. Courtesy of National Park Service, Adams National Historical Park.

or I should certainly have given mortal Offence — Even the Church, its forms, the snuffling through the nose, the Singers, the dressing and the dinner hour, were all novelties to me."[14]

That she was genuinely ill during her first months in New England is indisputable. It didn't help her condition that December 1801 was extremely cold — John Quincy recorded outside temperatures at $-7°$ F. Not surprisingly, exhausted from her trip north, chilled to the bone, and deeply troubled about her father's chances of recovery, Louisa developed what her husband called a "very distressing" and "incessant" cough. In late December, she was bled by Dr. Thomas Welsh in Boston, and blisters were applied. Like many physicians who saw Louisa in that fateful year, Dr. Welsh gave her only a few months to live. He was not alone. Abigail, writing to her son Tom, brusquely dismissed Louisa's chances of survival: "Mrs. Adams has had a very alarming cough & pain in her breast which confined her almost the whole time she was here and it has not left her yet. . . . Her frame is so slender & her constitution so delicate that I have many fears that she will be of short duration."[15]

Abigail, unfortunately, went on to hold Louisa's fragile health responsible for the deeply etched lines on John Quincy's face: "The constant state of anxiety which has harassed his mind upon her account has added a weight of years to his Brow, which time alone could not have effected in double the space." Abigail compensated for what appears to have been a instinctive dislike for her daughter-in-law — referring to her always as "Mrs. Adams" — by overdoing the attention she paid her. Louisa was not blind to what was happening and was clear in how it affected her: "The more particular the attentions that they thought it necessary to show me, the less I felt at *home*, and the more difficult my position became — I had a separate dish set by me of which no one was to partake; and every delicate preserve was brought out to treat me with in the kindest manner — but it always made me feel as if I was an apàrté in the family; and though I felt very grateful, it appeared so strongly to stamp me with unfitness, that often I would not eat of my delicacy, and thus gave offence — Mrs. Adams was too kind and I could not reject anything."[16]

Except for John Adams — "The old Gentleman took a fancy to *me*, and he was the only one," Louisa remembered gratefully — it seemed clear to all in the Adams orbit that John Quincy had brought home to America a woman poorly prepared to enhance his future success. Rather than an asset to the career of the man everyone expected would follow in the footsteps of his illustrious father, Louisa seemed to be a potential hindrance. "I was literally and without knowing it a *fine* Lady," she wrote many years later. "Do what I would there was a conviction on the part of others that I could not *suit*, however well inclined."[17]

How much she actually desired to adapt herself to life in Quincy is debatable. A city girl, accustomed to conversing knowledgably of music, theater, and literature, Louisa lacked any interest in farm concerns, local politics, or the health of various members of the community—all typical conversational topics in a small New England village. She had solemnly promised John Quincy she would not refer to their former glamorous life in Berlin, London, or Dresden—and she kept that promise—but she could not stop her maid Epps from talking. The good citizens of Quincy were well aware they shrank in comparison to Queen Louise of Prussia or young George's godmother, Lady Carysfort, and Epps did not let them forget it.[18]

For Louisa to be accepted in Quincy, she first had to be accepted by her mother-in-law. The strong-minded Abigail, who had managed the family property herself for the ten years her husband was away on public business, had scant patience with a weak and sickly woman who did not appear to know the bare minimum about the housework required to maintain a country establishment. Louisa had feared from Abigail's reputation as a forceful personality that she might be diminished in comparison, but she hadn't realized how much the talents and abilities she did possess would be devalued: "The qualifications necessary to form an accomplished Quincy Lady, were in direct opposition to the mode of life which I had led. . . . I tried by every means in my power to *work* as they call it; but my strength did not second the effort, and I only made matters worse—Mrs. Adams gave me instruction and advice, but I did not readily learn—and in fact on my part all went wrong, and the more I fretted the worse things grew."[19]

It came as a great relief to everyone when, on December 21, John Quincy moved his family to a small house he had purchased on Hanover Street in an older section of Boston that today is called the North End.

Boston in 1801 was enjoying renewed prosperity. The colonial town, so dependent on its West Indies commerce, had suffered badly before, during, and immediately after the American Revolution, but economic conditions had improved substantially by the turn of the nineteenth century. The population had expanded from a sparse 6,000 when the British occupied the town at the outset of the war to some 25,000 (about a third of that of Philadelphia). The old town—on a piece of land shaped like the bowl of a spoon attached to the mainland by a narrow, marshy handle—had outgrown its original footprint near the wharves fronting Boston Harbor. Its winding, narrow streets, crowded with small houses, churches, shops, and artisans' workshops—many constructed of wood and constantly at risk of fire—were becoming congested and increasingly unfashionable.

It was time for a change, and, at what proved to be a perfect moment, the young architect Charles Bulfinch returned home to Boston from his studies abroad. For three decades—from 1787 to 1817—he managed, almost single-handedly, to transform the old colonial town according to his personal—and brilliant—vision. Great brick and stone mansions, townhouses, churches, a hospital, a jail, a complete renovation of Faneuil Hall, all became part of the Bulfinch legacy to Boston. Probably his most significant achievement was the massive, new brick-and-marble State House on Beacon Hill, completed in 1798, whose great golden dome immediately dominated the skyline and would continue to do so for generations to come. This was the newly prosperous town, reminiscent in many ways of London, that welcomed Louisa in the winter of 1802.

Her "decidedly flattering" reception was as warm in Boston as it had been cool in Quincy, even though many of her new acquaintances felt the need to acquaint her with the details of John Quincy's former attachment to Mary Frazier. ("I found the latter *all* that she had been described," Louisa reported.) In an era when the Boston Brahmins were very much in the ascendancy but not, as yet, ingrown, Louisa remembered she was immediately accepted by the "Amorys, the Codmans, the Russells, the Sheaffes, the Sergeants, the Cushings . . . and many more; which formed a very large circle of acquaintance, and made me as dissipated as I had been in Berlin."[20]

It would, indeed, have been surprising if John Quincy and his sophisticated, elegant, English-born wife had not been admitted immediately to the inner circle of Boston's first families. The "late ambassador," as his brother Tom called him, was, after all, the son of the former president and a graduate of Harvard, with all that meant in terms of entrée to the town's leading citizens, but it was the couple's social skills, honed in Berlin, that ensured their continued acceptance among the elite. John Quincy's two younger brothers—both Harvard graduates—and their wives seem never to have been admitted to anything like the exclusive social scene their elder brother and Louisa almost automatically inhabited.

Louisa in 1840 remembered life in Boston at the dawn of the nineteenth century as very much to her taste: "Fortunes had not grown so large or so fast as they have since; and though living even then was luxurious; wealth was not so essential a quality as it is now, to enable the merely independent to enjoy the most extensive and general acquaintance—You were treated handsomely but not extravagantly; and the pleasures of social intercourse were more an object, than the gew-gaw display of meretricious show."[21]

Even without "meretricious show," this was a social style the Adamses could ill afford. It would have been an opportune time for John Quincy to establish a solid law practice, but he labored under at least two disadvantages: he was already several years behind his peers in building up a legal clientele, and, as he well knew, his command of the law was, at best, rusty. He acknowledged to his diary on December 29, 1801, that he was "beginning with Blackstone once more." As the church bells rang in the New Year, he wrote, "I am now returned to a private station and to my former profession—To begin anew with the common chances of good or ill success."

That success was very slow in coming. At one point early in 1802, John Quincy even toyed with the idea of moving with his family to upstate New York to make a fresh start and escape a profession that seemed to him so stultifying. He easily persuaded Tom Adams, also a very reluctant lawyer, to accompany him, but sober second thoughts and a strong dose of cold water from their parents quashed the idea before it had gone very far. The dutiful elder son turned his attention to finding clients. He attended sessions of both Suffolk and Norfolk County courts in hope of picking up litigants in urgent need of representation, and he seems to have accepted any case he was offered, no matter how mundane. Although it did not provide nearly enough to support the lifestyle he and Louisa hoped to attain, he also worked hard at a temporary appointment as a federal commissioner of bankruptcies, a position that served to guarantee a regular modest income.

But it was John Quincy's deep-seated boredom with the law that was probably the real obstacle to his professional success. After all, it had been his frustration at mastering legal tomes that had led him to a debilitating depression only a dozen years earlier. Abigail was well aware of her son's reluctance to resume a law practice that had been, at its peak, only a moderate success. John Quincy, she wrote, was "commencing anew the practice of the Law [which] is very far from being agreeable to him after a period of seven years in which his attention had been altogether occupied by other objects." The former president was less understanding. He was sure his brilliant son could be an outstanding success at the bar if he put his mind to it and clung to the conviction that success in the law would lead to a life of public service and further prestige for the family. Although John Quincy had been determined to resist his father's arguments, he acknowledged in a letter to Tom Adams that he had given up the battle almost before it had begun: "I have determined for the sake of peace, and for the want of better employment, to resume my residence and my profession in Boston—But I confirm myself more and more in the determination to have no concern whatsoever in politics."[22]

His pledge lasted just a few months. The tedium of representing clients on land claims and petty criminal complaints was fully as oppressing as John Quincy feared it would be. There was little to interest him through the long winter days when his office under the *Boston Centinel* print shop was empty of potential clients—one afternoon was spent calculating the rate of U.S. population growth. Still dreaming of a future career in science or literature, he happily joined a small group of his old Boston and Harvard friends in forming the Natural Philosophy Club, which met weekly to conduct studies of electricity and other emerging scientific fields. At one meeting, he even "took several shocks and a succession of sparks while standing on the insulation stool."[23]

Nothing, however, could quench the political ambition bred in John Quincy from birth. His impatience with the law, innate fascination with the interactions of players on the political stage, and a genuine desire to be of service to his country made it almost inevitable that he would yield to the persuasion of the many citizens who encouraged him to try for public office. On a long walk in late January 1802, less than a month after establishing his law office, he admitted to himself the hold that politics had on his heart: "Walked in the mall just before midnight. I feel strong temptation and great provocation to plunge into political controversy. But I hope to preserve myself from it by the considerations which have led me to the resolution of renouncing."[24]

By April he had been elected by the voters of Suffolk County, which included Boston, to the state senate on the Federalist slate. To his brother, who had taken seriously his many promises to remain aloof from all political activity, John Quincy justified running for the state senate as a lesser evil: "A man may as well be as busy about nothing for the public as for himself." He was not being entirely honest in downplaying how much attaining his first elected office meant to him. As soon as he was sworn in, he became fully involved in the issues before the senate and was, lamented his wife, "not much at home." In the fall of 1802, he ran for—and lost by fifty-nine votes—a seat in the U.S. House of Representatives. He claimed he was relieved he would not be forced to take up a "heavy burden and a thankless task" of representing the Boston area in Congress, but he recorded each town's vote tally in his diary and somewhat bitterly ascribed his defeat to Federalist partisans "too weak to overcome a shower of rain."[25]

Louisa, meanwhile, was coming into her own and on her own terms. Still only twenty-seven in the winter of 1802, she soon found herself at the center of a large circle of women friends, several of whom were well educated, interested in literature and world affairs, and happy to visit the little house on Hanover Street or invite her to their more elegant homes in the South End or on Beacon Hill. At first daunted by their vigorous opinions and the certainty with which they expressed them, Louisa quickly learned to appreciate the company of these intelligent women and admire their minds. In her 1840 *Adventures of a Nobody*, she wrote, "There is generally a want of feminine grace and sweetness, in these showy, strong minded Women; which produce fear in us lesser lights: and this has always been my first impression on becoming acquainted with them—yet they always appear to me to be *what God intended woman to be*, before she was carved by her Master *man*."[26]

The twelve-year-old girl who had been singled out by an exceptional teacher—and later by the classically educated Lady Carysfort—had never lost her admiration for bright and interesting members of her own sex. Although Louisa could not acknowledge being their equal—casting herself among the "lesser lights"—she was, in fact, always flattered when intellectually gifted women sought her friendship. Her resentment at the insignificant place to which "Master *man*" had relegated brilliant women as expressed in her *Adventures of a Nobody*—written eight years before the Seneca Falls Convention published its Declaration of Rights and Sentiments—was not the whim of a moment but the product of sixty-five years of observing women being forced to devalue their mental abilities.

One strong-minded woman had still to be won over. Abigail Adams remained convinced that her daughter-in-law was not only physically weak and emotionally fragile but a tragic drain on her son's energy and a threat to his ultimate happiness and fulfillment. She and the former president made it clear they expected the younger Adamses to become an integral part of the extended family circle centered on Peacefields. Thus, nearly every weekend, John Quincy managed to make the trip to Quincy to stay for a day or two. Rarely during their first winter in Boston was he accompanied by Louisa and little George. The health of one or the other was the usual excuse, but it seems clear that Louisa believed her relationship with her mother-in-law was best conducted at a safe distance.

By April matters were still strained. The occasion of George's first birthday went uncelebrated in Quincy, an omission Louisa attributed to the boy's name: "My darling boys birth day passed almost unnoticed. He was a fine Child, and I was *too vain* of him—But the name which we had given him was not liked, and perhaps we ought to have given him the name of his Grandfather," she wrote a decade after George's suicide.[27]

Two weeks after that first birthday, word came of Joshua's death in Frederick. Predictably, Louisa became "alarmingly" ill, wracked with guilt and sorrow at the news. Over and over, she grieved the tragic arc of her adored father's fortunes and lamented her own weakness in submitting to pressure to leave his side in his final days. By June, however, her mood had lightened. She began to spend more time in Quincy enjoying the lovely spring weather in the country and walking "on the hill" with John Quincy. Best of all, Catherine and Caroline Johnson had arrived in Boston. ("I was *too* happy," Louisa remembered.)[28]

Still not in robust health, Louisa seized the opportunity presented by the socially prescribed mourning period for her father to remain mostly at home in Boston under the care of her mother and sister. This regime was exactly what was needed, even if, as she believed, Abigail thought she was babying herself: "The Nature of the illnesses to which I was so constantly exposed, required repose; a thing almost incompatible hitherto with our situation; and even now, not approved. But my mourning authorized it, and it was of essential benefit to my returning strength."[29]

Meanwhile, Caroline—always the most popular of the three elder Johnson daughters and a favorite in the Adams family—had matured into an attractive, competent young woman, and she immediately took over management of the little house in the North End. Louisa was more than happy to cede her role as mistress of the household—"a thrall heavy enough to break the spirit of a Tyrant—My Experience's in this *line* in consequence of ignorance had been peculiarly painful; and my blessed Sister saved me from unspeakable discomfort."[30]

Why Louisa was so ready to acknowledge failure as a housekeeper and retire from the field so precipitously is puzzling. For her to have any future standing in the eyes of her husband, his family, and society at large, she knew she needed to master the many housewifely skills she now so sorely lacked. At the turn of the nineteenth century, the single most important role for an American woman was as a manager of household affairs, and her self-worth was bound up in her home and her children. Abigail, for one, would make herself abundantly clear on the subject in a letter to her sister Elizabeth Shaw Peabody in 1809: "I consider it as an indispensable requisite that every American wife should herself know how to order and regulate her family; how to govern her domestics, and train up her children. For this purpose, the all-wise Creator made woman an help-meet for man, and she who fails in these duties does not answer the end of her creation."[31]

Faced with this apparently holy calling, Louisa punted. It was better not to try than to try and fail. Her explanation for her inability to "*work*, as they call it" was that her physical weakness and privileged upbringing disqualified her from ever becoming the strong, capable woman her mother-in-law so obviously was. As her life went on, she had no choice but to become adept at many of the skills she at first despaired of acquiring, but her first painful experiences had given her so little confidence that she was willing to be viewed by her husband and his family as incompetent if it meant freedom from the "thrall" of household management.

In this area, as in so many others, John Quincy did little to ease her path. The abject failure she attributed to her own incompetence may simply have been Louisa's inability to meet her husband's unattainably high demands and to compete in the realm where his mother excelled. Giving up any claims to managing the household was one way to avoid constant marital fighting: "Questions of expenditure and mismanagement, highly merited on my part, caused perpetual uneasiness of a character painful to both, yet impossible to avoid," she later wrote. But it could also be argued that Louisa's ineffectiveness was directly due to John Quincy's refusal to allow her any financial discretion. Every penny he doled out to her had to be accounted for. In his account books, he itemized each purchase ("parsley, 7 cents") and, for several months, he kept a daily list of how much cash Louisa had remaining in her purse. John Quincy did not enjoy spending his mornings doing the daily marketing and keeping household accounts, but since his wife did not measure up to his perfectionist standards, he believed it was his duty to take over the essential tasks usually assigned to the mistress of the household.[32]

Louisa's apparently docile acquiescence in John Quincy's absolute control of the family's finances had its roots in her near-obsession with the shame of having been married without a dowry and under the shadow of her father's financial debacle. Having brought no money to the marriage, she believed she had no right to demand any say in how the family's funds were handled and no responsibility for helping manage the household budget. Existing on a tight allowance—she later complained she could not even buy gifts for her children—placed Louisa in a childlike, dependent status, a position that did nothing to encourage any initiatives to reclaim her rightful fiscal management duties.

She felt equally frustrated in her inability to—as her mother-in-law put it—"govern her domestics." It was almost impossible to manage a household in the nineteenth century without an extra pair of hands or two. But in America, there was no traditional servant class—except those bound under slavery. Typically, native-born "help" remained in a household for only a few months and were often as much hindrance as help. If a woman had one or two older daughters or an unmarried sister, she had built-in assistance; otherwise, even rural housewives were eager to board young girls in exchange for work around the house and garden. Unfortunately, in this sphere, as well as others, John Quincy seemed to believe Louisa failed to come up to the mark.[33]

Trained to run a London mansion equipped with eleven competent retainers who knew their jobs and took pride in their work, Louisa was unprepared to deal with the "impertinent, lazy, untrustworthy, careless, and slovenly" very young girls just off the farm who constituted the servant class in Boston. One Friday in December 1802, two girls she had recently employed announced they would be leaving her service and returning to Quincy by the next stagecoach.

In Louisa's version the two "had ventured to say that I thought they used more Sugar than was right—They insisted that they only took three piled spoonfuls in every Cup of tea, and . . . they were not accustomed to have things measured out to them. . . . It was then two o'clock and they left me at four; stupefied with astonishment and crying bitterly." Crying was not calculated to win her husband's sympathy. "Both the girls left us at two hours warning," he reported succinctly in his diary, noting that he himself had set out from Boston for a weekend in Quincy shortly after their departure, apparently leaving Louisa, Caroline, and toddler George on their own.[34]

Much of Louisa's staffing problems might have been avoided had her valuable and devoted maid Epps been by her side, but early in their first winter in Boston, the Adamses had been forced by their straitened financial circumstances to release both Epps and Whitcomb. Just when she needed a trusted guide to instruct raw trainees in basic household tasks, Louisa lost a faithful friend who had not only catered to her mistress's personal needs but also had been a loving nanny to George and an able housekeeper. "She was a dreadful loss to me, which although I have had many kind and good Servants, never has been replaced," Louisa wrote many years later.[35]

Even had Epps remained as an integral part of the Adams family, however, she might have had difficulty persuading her mistress to undertake actual housework. Despite the pressure she was under to become an "accomplished Quincy Lady," Louisa resisted learning exactly how to keep a fire going all day in the fireplace stove, how to tackle the huge copper tubs filled with dirty linen, how to sweep out rooms coated in soot and dust from the city street just outside the door. In the future, she would empathize with her destitute mother who had finally been forced to "*cook*" when, all her life, she had been served her meals. In the winter of 1802, no matter how much she protested her willingness to master household tasks, Louisa seems to have believed they were beneath her. Her early failures at housework and at directing her untrained and unmanageable helpers only confirmed her in her conviction that she was not cut out for housework and would never succeed at it.

Caroline's decision to live indefinitely with Louisa and John Quincy after Joshua's death proved to be a godsend in more ways than just her willingness to assume her sister's household responsibilities. With their mother, who remained in Boston from June to October 1802, Caroline saved her sister from loneliness in the first summer and fall in her new home. Immersed in his duties as a state senator and commissioner of bankruptcy, John Quincy was gone from Hanover Street much of every weekday and was in Quincy on most weekends—with or without his wife and son. Summing up his life in January 1803, he wrote, "When I have leisure in the afternoon or evening, I pass it at my office writing but I continue generally to spend two evenings a week at Quincy, one at the Club, one at the Society, and upon an average, one at a ball or in Company. All my time is employed." There was obviously little room for Louisa and toddler George in this busy schedule.[36]

The thirty-five-year-old lawyer was being fiercely tugged in many directions. He clearly loved the theatrics inherent in legislative debate—his diary comes alive when he includes detailed analyses of the leading characters, issues, and politics of the day. But he was also still attempting to earn a living, and at least some of his time had to be spent "plodding through" his caseload, such as it was. In July, his federal appointment as a bankruptcy commissioner was revoked when the Jefferson administration replaced Federalist appointees with Republican ones. As a result, except for his small state senate stipend and the rentals on some property he owned, John Quincy had little certain income. His twice-a-day, hour-long walks must have served as much to ward off depression about his professional future as they did to strengthen his heart and lungs.

Now firmly back within the Adams family circle, John Quincy seemed to have become as much son as husband and father. His parents—and his duty to them—loomed large in his mind. Weekly visits to them assumed such a high priority that he occasionally set out to walk the nine miles to Quincy when he could find no conveyance. His weekends there often included long hours alone, such as one Sunday afternoon spent "looking over some mathematical books and reading Amyot's translation of Plutarch." It went without saying that there were no mischievous toddlers or neglected wives to interrupt his studies. And, although he might have insisted his first loyalty was to his wife and son, John Quincy neglected to mention George's first birthday in his diary, and, as if she were just one of a number of female acolytes, he typically included Louisa in "the ladies" of the household to whom he read *Hamlet* and *Romeo and Juliet* in the evening and with whom he occasionally walked in the mall bordering Boston Common.

One certain way to secure John Quincy's immediate attention was illness. George was, from the beginning, a difficult, precocious—possibly hyperactive—child, for whom teething had been a particularly painful experience. Both Louisa and John Quincy were obsessively—by today's standards—concerned with every instance of discomfort and sickness their son exhibited. Infant mortality was so rampant in the early nineteenth century that any conscientious parent became worried when a baby ran a fever or showed a rash. What is notable is that John Quincy didn't record the usual highlights of his son's first year or two—first steps, first words—but only his illnesses. Louisa's concerns were just as high. At this point in her life, feeling herself a failure as a housekeeper, suffering in beauty—she believed—in comparison to Mary Frazier, and diminished in the eyes of her mother-in-law, her single source of pride was her handsome healthy boy, and she was determined to keep him that way.

John Quincy, having apparently learned all the wrong lessons from his own upbringing, soon became concerned about George's education. Believing perhaps that Louisa did not have her toddler son's future intellectual prowess high among her goals, he included among his evening readings learned theses on education. John Quincy, his wife said, "in the fervour of a lately acquired Parental duty; our Son being eighteen Months old; studied all the works on education; From Lock[e] to Miss Edgeworth, in which studies I participated orally—I fear without deriving the benefit which ought to have rewarded his increasing and arduous exertions for my benefit."[37]

Louisa's sardonic comment on her husband's over-anxious concern for their son's future education may reflect the apparent distance between the two in the summer and fall of 1802. In many important ways, this was one of those moments in their lives when neither seemed to need the other. Each had happily reassumed a premarital status. John Quincy had settled easily into the position of elder son, state politician, and member of the Natural Philosophy Club; Louisa had just as readily relaxed into the role of daughter and sister—one of three Johnson women in the household on Hanover Street. On either side, there was little sympathy for the other's weaknesses. Louisa could poke fun at John Quincy's "fervour," and he could, for the first time, refer to an episode "of extreme violence"—possibly her monthly menstrual period—as "cramps and hysterics."

A more deep-seated source of resentment can be traced to the matter of religion. Louisa was a devout, practicing Anglican. "I had become a Member of my

Church by reason of preference, and conviction; and my faith was fixed and unalterable," she later wrote. But now "even my religious opinions were adverse to those of all the friends of Mr. Adams, a thing altogether new to me as from the first moment of my acquaintance with him he had apparently known no creed but mine." Louisa and John Quincy had been married in an ancient Anglican church, and their son had been baptized by the Anglican chaplain in Berlin. When John Quincy was in London, he attended Anglican services at the Foundling Hospital nearly every week, and, in Berlin, he read the service from the Book of Common Prayer to Louisa on Sundays. She never suspected he would immediately revert to the Congregational faith of his ancestors as soon as he crossed the Massachusetts border. Now, he regularly attended two services every Sunday—whether in Quincy or Boston—enjoying especially the sermons that the Rev. William Emerson, the father of Ralph Waldo Emerson, preached at First Church, Boston.[38]

Sunday morning in a Congregational meetinghouse, no matter how inspiring the preacher, did not feel like church to Louisa. She missed the ritual, the music, and the familiarity of the prayer service she had grown to love. She remembered that she "joined in the Duties of [John Quincy's] religious exercises as a tribute of respect to him, and as an example to my little ones," but she also accompanied women friends to nearby Christ Church (the Episcopal Old North Church) or the nascent Trinity Church whenever she could. On the surface, the matter of religious faith seems to have been papered over in the Adams household, but in an era when one's choice of a church was a defining characteristic, Louisa's refusal to give up her Anglican beliefs and John Quincy's apparent unquestioning return to the faith of his fathers was another fissure in the bedrock of their marriage that was never bridged.

In these early years in Boston the marital tensions that dogged Louisa and John Quincy for much of their fifty years together began to assume their distinctive pattern. If John Quincy loved his wife—and he did—he didn't appear to respect her judgment. Possibly absorbing some of Abigail's assessment that Louisa was a poor household manager and altogether too prone to feeling ill and sorry for herself, he may have denigrated her in other areas as well. Louisa wrote of the "cold looks" she feared from her husband and tried to circumvent. But since her self-esteem was so fragile, she may have attributed to John Quincy negative feelings about herself and her family that he in no way harbored. There is scant trace in his voluminous diaries of any remotely negative word concerning his wife or any of the Johnsons. If he felt disappointment in Louisa's seeming inability to become a model housewife or resentment at her chronic poor health, he never expressed those feelings on paper.

Money, health, religion, in-laws, child care, career plans made without the other's knowledge—all topics that can poison any marriage—were certainly issues that haunted the Adamses' early years in America. Their sex life was apparently not. During the winter of 1803, Louisa was again pregnant. This time, thanks to the loving care she had enjoyed in the summer and fall from her mother and sister, she was much stronger than she had been during earlier pregnancies. With the party-loving Caroline, who had remained in Boston after Catherine's departure in October for Washington, Louisa happily attended the social season's festive dinners, teas, parties, and balls. In January, she herself was hostess. As would always be typical of her party-giving skills, she flouted some of the usual rules and made do with very little: "Had the first Party I ever gave in Boston—between forty and fifty. We danced until one in the morning—The House being small I opened all the rooms; and set small Tables prettily ornamented in every direction and two larger ones in the Centre of the Chambers up Stairs: all covered with refreshments—This broke the formality of a Supper and seemed to please generally."[39]

John Quincy, who recorded that he danced the whole evening, was too busy to be involved in party preparations—or clean-up. Only a few minutes after the last guest departed, he was called out for the remainder of the night to help fight a major fire—at which, as a resident of Boston, he was required to assist. Characteristically, he spent the next morning at the office and departed in the afternoon for a weekend in Quincy.

Although she was stronger than she had been during any of her previous pregnancies, Louisa was plagued throughout the spring and into early summer with what she termed "constant faintings and violent attacks of illness short in their duration" that precluded visits to Quincy. John Quincy's diary records many days and nights when his wife was indeed very ill. Louisa, in turn, was concerned about the signs of "cruel anxiety" her husband displayed as her due date approached. In a letter to Tom Adams, who was still living in Philadelphia, Abigail noted John Quincy's anxiety as well as her own deep-seated disdain for Louisa ("Madam"): "Your Brother has not been out this fortnight. He is waiting Madams confinement which is daily expected. He looks as anxious as tho he had the trouble himself to pass through. She is very well for so feeble a Body as she is. When you take a wife, it must be for better or for worse, but a healthy and good constitution is an object with those who consider, maturely."[40]

Possibly yielding to parental pressure, John Quincy decided to make up for his absence from Peacefields by a visit to the family on the Fourth of July weekend. On the evening of July 3, Louisa's labor began in Boston. Dr. Welsh was summoned at midnight, and at 3 a.m., "just as the first guns fired," a fine, healthy boy was born and placed on the carpet as neither of the two teenage "help" in attendance ("not thinking it *delicate*") could bring themselves to handle the quickly chilled baby. Fortunately, Louisa wrote, "Caroline jumped out of bed, and ran into the room almost undressed, to assist; and took the Child immediately" to clean and bundle up.

The baby, born on the Fourth of July, was appropriately named John Adams II, for the doughty old patriot who had done so much for American independence. The infant's father, after returning to Boston and thankfully receiving the news, went to the State House to hear the annual Fourth of July oration, then called on a friend and "took one turn on the Mall" before returning home for the evening. On Sunday, July 17, young John was baptized by the Congregationalist William Emerson with little ceremony. Louisa, again suffering a very long postpartum recovery, was too ill to attend, but she basked in her triumph: "He was beautiful, and I fear I was too proud of being the Mother of two fine Children."[41]

Outward pride and ambition were two cardinal sins in the eyes of the Adams family and equally as abhorrent to society at large when applied to a woman perceived to be overly pleased with herself or scheming for the advancement of her husband. The Adamses, in particular, held fast to the fiction that, if a public office were to seek them, they would willingly serve—albeit at private sacrifice—but never would they actively seek an elected position. In February 1803, following his unsuccessful run for Congress in the fall, John Quincy had been named by the Massachusetts legislature as one of the Commonwealth's two U.S. senators. Louisa denied receiving any pleasure from his election, claiming her complete freedom from ambition and repining that as she had only just become accustomed to life in Boston, "his election to the Senate yielded me no satisfaction—But there was no help for it—and such feelings were warmly disapproved by the family."[42]

John Quincy, meanwhile, was overtly despondent at his success, mourning the burden he would now have to assume and somehow forgetting that he had kept precise records of the voting on the four successive ballots it had taken for the Senate to arrive at its decision to elect him. He also neglected to mention in his diary that his election was at least partly due to a compromise the pro-Adams faction in the Massachusetts Federalist Party had struck with the anti-Adams group, which gave John Quincy the senior Senate seat but awarded the junior seat to his father's old nemesis, former Secretary of State Timothy Pickering. Nevertheless, the new senator and his family prepared for the move to Washington as soon as Louisa was well enough to travel.

Congressmen and women with young families in the twenty-first century are typically faced with a decision about whether to move their children and spouses to Washington or leave them at home in their districts; in the early nineteenth century, senators and representatives wrestled with exactly the same dilemma. Congress was in session for only five months—from November to March—but travel between the "Federal City" and elsewhere in the country was so hazardous and time-consuming that, once established either at home or in Washington, few considered making interim trips in either direction. In the Adamses' case, the decision seemed easy. To save money, the family would live with Louisa's older sister Nancy, who had married their cousin Walter Hellen, a successful tobacco merchant and a resident of Washington. An exceptionally generous man, Hellen had already welcomed the destitute, widowed Catherine Johnson with her five unmarried daughters—and sometimes her son—into his gracious home near Georgetown, a little less than three miles from Capitol Hill.[43]

When they left for Washington in late September, John Quincy and Louisa and the two boys had no home awaiting their return to Boston. Earlier in the year, the Adams family had received the shattering news that Bird, Savage & Bird, the London banking house where John Adams had deposited his savings, had failed, leaving the ex-president temporarily unable to meet his financial obligations. John Quincy, blaming himself for having encouraged his father to do business with the bank, vowed to cover the losses. He managed to sell the house on Hanover Street, as well as some insurance company stock and other equities, and friends of the family came up with loans to pay off the remainder of the elder Adams's debts. John and Abigail, grateful to their ever-responsible son, turned over to him 275 acres of their land in Quincy, land that included the little house on Penn's Hill where John Quincy was born. That humble, saltbox-style cottage was all that John Quincy and Louisa could now call home.[44]

Louisa was not sanguine at this prospect. She cried over the necessity of selling their Boston home, once again lamenting her lack of standing in the matter: "I grieved to give up my House: a fact I fear too strongly evidenced when I gave up my house, and signed the deed of Sale—I cordially approved of the Act; but I sadly regretted its necessity. I had no right to feel so it is true; for it was not my property and the total beggary of my family took away all claim. But to a Woman, her home is a blessing under every circumstance; and it is the only element in which her happiness should be fixed."[45]

Another harrowing family trip between Boston and Washington was not improved when two-year-old George dropped his own shoes and the keys to his parents' trunks overboard as the family traveled by boat between Providence and Powles Hook, New Jersey. Arriving in Newark after an excruciating, ten-mile ride on a log road, the Adamses were quarantined for several days in a single room in a crowded tavern because of a yellow fever epidemic in New York City. (Louisa, who had developed delirium and a very high fever, was presumed to have contracted the disease.) Finally, after twenty nerve-racking days on the road, the four Adamses, Caroline, and a very young nursemaid were deposited on the Hellens' doorstep at dusk on October 20, 1803.[46]

They had arrived on a historic day. As their carriage made its way along Washington's rutted, unpaved streets, they passed a friend and colleague on his way to the President's House to notify Thomas Jefferson that the Senate had just ratified the Louisiana Purchase. The news was welcome as well to the nation's newest senator. Alone among New England Federalists, John Quincy supported Jefferson's historic initiative. The new senator from Massachusetts would attend both a banquet and a ball at which Jeffersonian Republicans celebrated the acquisition of the Louisiana Territory. He would later vote to approve the funds necessary to complete the purchase and introduce an unsuccessful Constitutional amendment that would include as citizens of the United States inhabitants of these and other new territories.[47]

John Quincy's endorsement of the Louisiana Purchase was the first public indication that he had no intention of strictly adhering to the Federalist line, a strongly held point of view he had privately articulated in his diary more than a year earlier: "A politician in this country must be a man of a party, but I would fain be a man of my whole country." His Federalist colleagues saw his independence as betrayal, a bid to curry favor with the reigning Republicans, who outnumbered Federalists almost three to one when John Quincy took the oath of office. They also saw it as evidence that he placed ambition above their conservative principles.[48]

John Quincy recognized that he was trusted by neither the Federalist nor the Republican factions. He described his position as one of sitting on a field between two armies, "neither of which consider me one of their soldiers." Policy and personal considerations pulled him in opposite directions. Disagreeing with nearly every Federalist stand, he had enlisted in the party because it was the political home of his father. On the other hand, while fearing individual Republicans as radical populists, he strongly approved of Republican Secretary of State James Madison's approach to international affairs. "My conduct has given satisfaction to neither side," he wrote his mother, "and both are offended at what they consider a vain and foolish presumption of singularity."[49]

Because he expected to hold his Senate appointment for six years, John Quincy felt free to ignore the bitter opposition and personal attacks his actions and speeches stirred up at home and among his colleagues in the House and Senate. He threw himself into committee work and conscientiously attended long sessions of the Senate, chronicling in his diary and letters to his father and brother detailed accounts of debates and analyses of the issues. "Mr. Adams was entirely engrossed in his political affairs," Louisa wrote of this period many years later. At the same time, he contrived to represent some clients before the Supreme Court, devoting rare moments of spare time to preparing his cases. Leaving the Senate late each afternoon, John Quincy usually walked the three miles to the Hellen home. His daily hike along unpaved, unlighted, and muddy roads had ramifications beyond simple, healthy exercise. For one, it was relatively hazardous. Louisa described his route in the winter of 1804: "The City not being laid out; the Streets not graduated; the bridges consisting of mere loose planks; and huge stumps of Trees recently cut down intercepting every path; and the roads intersected by deep ravines continually enlarged by rain."[50]

That he walked, rather than rode horseback or took a carriage, was a strong indication of how carefully he was husbanding his available funds. Important to his political future, however, was the fact that he did not live a bachelor life among his fellow congressmen, who clustered with like-minded partisans in the many boardinghouses near the Capitol. In the first years of the nineteenth century, when the Federal City was in its earliest stage of development, much of the essential, informal business of government was conducted over a meal or a late-night, all-male discussion warmed by a roaring fire and a glass of ale. John Quincy, who stayed with the Hellens for every Congressional session of his Senate term—even when Louisa was not with him in Washington—might have benefited from the give-and-take and camaraderie inevitable in a boarding-house setting. At a minimum, he might have become a little less oblivious to political winds as they swirled around him. Instead, he retreated to the quiet of his own room in the Hellens' large home: "Spend the evenings sometimes in company; but generally reading in my chamber or to the Ladies below," he wrote.[51]

Boardinghouses were not the only places in the capital for brokering deals and forming useful alliances. The parlors and ballrooms of freshly built brick townhouses in Washington, as well as stately homes in Georgetown and Alexandria, provided politicians, ambassadors, government secretaries, newspaper editors, and their wives an opportunity to meet in more elegant surroundings. In the absence of a First Lady—Jefferson was a long-time widower—the women of the Federal City wrote their own social rules. In Louisa's eyes, this meant that "Balls, Dinners, Parties and Dejeunées Dansants succeed[ed] each other constantly; and although the roads were impassible, and but at the risk of life; the rage for pleasure, and the routine adopted by the Leaders of fashionable life in this *then* desert City 'of magnificent distances' " constituted a very active social life in which she and her husband were expected to play an important part.[52]

It was the Federal City's social scene that led to Louisa's first rapprochement with Abigail. Guessing correctly that her mother-in-law missed the gossip of the capital, she set out to provide it. "The City has been extremely gay this Winter. . . . We are become quite dissipated, scarcely an evening without producing either large Card parties or Balls which are now quite the rage. . . . We were last evening at a Ball. Madame Bonaparte who makes a great noise here was . . . almost naked." Louisa went on to describe in colorful detail a social contretemps involving the British ambassador's wife that even Dolley Madison couldn't untangle, finally concluding, "This ridiculous business destroyed the harmony of the party so completely in the beginning of the evening that we none of us knew what to do or what to say until after the M[archioness] retired when every body evinced a degree of joy and satisfaction not very complimentary to her Ladyship. . . . I cannot help smiling at all this but I think before the Lady assumes so much she should learn manners."[53]

Amidst the dreariest days of a New England winter, Louisa's lively letters would have re-created for Abigail the bright and sparkling world of dinners and balls she had left just four years earlier—and perhaps secretly missed. Louisa, on her own turf, wrote without undue deference, as if to an absent friend who would take an interest in what people were wearing and who was snubbing whom. At a safe distance from Quincy, Louisa could begin to offer her mother-in-law affection along with news of her son and grandchildren.

John Quincy, Louisa told his mother, was often too busy to attend the events that crowded the social calendar. "Mr. Adams is so much engaged he scarcely allows himself time to eat, drink or sleep. He stays at home and sends me out to make his apology." Louisa did not go unaccompanied. The charming Catherine Johnson and her personable younger daughters, too, were welcomed at balls and dinners in a city where men far outnumbered women. "Many Ladies from the different States of the Union visited the City; but accommodations were indifferent, scarce, and the inconveniences many; and only the more wealthy could afford to purchase the discomforts of the place," Louisa explained. And although Catherine had no money with which to "bring out" her younger daughters formally as she had the older three, there seemed to be no social barriers to prevent the entire family from accepting as many invitations as they could handle. "My Sisters were very pretty and attractive and their education and accomplishments rendered them objects of general admiration."[54]

Although the Hellen mansion was a carriage ride outside the center of the new city, the family entertained a constant stream of guests much the way the Johnsons had done in London: "Indeed the House was generally attractive to visitors—Mr. Adams being much courted; and my Mother and Sisters all being possessed of very popular manners with every social quality as well as my brother in Law Mr. Hellen, to make the House delightful to the leading men and foreigners of that period. The petit soupers often consisting of little more than Crackers, Butter Cake, and wine—which however gave a zest to music, dancing and wit. No one ever went there *once* that did not want to come again."[55]

Crackers, cake, and wine were a far cry from the elegant small dinners President Jefferson gave regularly at the President's House. The president used these occasions in a politically strategic way, keeping meticulous lists of who was invited and what was discussed, seating his guests at a round table to enable an easy flow of conversation, employing a dumbwaiter so that talk could range freely out of the ears of the serving staff. Louisa was impressed by his style: "The entertainment was handsome—French Servants in Livery; a French Butler, a French Cuisine, and a buffet full of choice Wine and Plate: had he had a tolerable fire on one of the bitterest days I ever experienced, we might almost have fancied ourselves in Europe." She was less impressed by the man himself: "Every thing about him was *aristocratic except* his person which was ungainly ugly and common—His manner was awkward, and excessively inelegant; and until he fairly entered into conversation, there was a sort of peering restlessness about him, which betrayed a fear of being scanned more closely by his visitors, than was altogether *agreeable* to his self complacency—While conversing he was very agreeable, and possessed the art of drawing out *others* and at the same time attracting attention to himself."[56]

Louisa's jaundiced attitude toward her host was certainly colored by her conviction that it was the president's decision to revoke Joshua's appointment in the stamp office that constituted the final blow to her father's will to remain alive. (She apparently never realized it had been Vice President Jefferson's tie-breaking vote in the Senate that had made Joshua's original appointment possible.) Undoubtedly, John and Abigail Adams's bitterness against their old friend for the ugliness of the 1800 presidential campaign had also been conveyed to their daughter-in-law as had John Quincy's disappointment at having been removed as a bankruptcy commissioner. But Louisa's immediate, instinctual dislike of Jefferson may not have been as self-generated as it seemed. For his own reasons, Jefferson may have chosen to be rude:

The dinner was agreeable enough—but when we retired to the Drawing room . . . we found a Grate of small size in the vast Circular room, the fire not rising above the second bar of this coal grate, and the coals what there were of them barely kindled; in fact in such a State, that one of the Guest's said "he could have amused himself '*by spitting out the fire*'"; Shaking with cold the company reduced to a state of . . . silence, we were under the necessity of keeping our teeth close shut, lest their chattering should proclaim that "our sufferings was intolerable," while the gallant President drew his Chair close into the centre of the hearth, and seemed impatiently to await our exit; which was sadly delayed by the neglect of the hackney Coachman. . . . After a long and dangerous ride, over the *glaciers* between the Presidents and the lone house by the river side occupied by Mr. Hellen, we had a hearty laugh at the events of the day—and a cheerful Cup of Tea, that most welcome of all restoratives round a pleasant family Table, in social chat.[57]

Telling amusing, gossipy stories around the family table over a cup of tea was what made life at the Hellens so pleasant for everyone. Reminiscent of the female-centric beehive on London's Cooper's Row, the Johnson daughters and their mother laughed, talked, made music, sewed, played with the babies, and entertained their many visitors. Louisa was in her element. There were no more complaints of poor health or "cold looks" from John Quincy. Gone was the need to measure up in the eyes of a daunting mother-in-law since responsibility for managing the large Hellen household was in the capable hands of Nancy Hellen and her husband. True, a little sisterly rivalry may well have simmered. Louisa, looking back at sixty-six, attributed what tension there was to the new nation's struggles with defining class. In traditional European societies, she wrote, one's place in society was fixed by custom and understood by everyone. In democratic America, where everyone was nominally equal, class distinctions still existed, but now they were repressed and resented: "In other Countries *Station* is so defined, and the rules of Society are so clearly understood; *feeling* is seldom unpleasantly shocked by changes which stand on the firm and fixed basis of common custom—But with us, jealousies are immediately awakened and even your children and your nearest and dearest connections, are *fearful* of being *supposed* to play a minor part on the great theatre, and despise the idea of a *secondary* place."[58]

Louisa's incisive analysis of what power and place does to relationships was mirrored by the perceptiveness with which she viewed the major players on the Washington stage. Her ability to bring these characters to life—portraying, just as she had in Berlin and Boston, both personal appearance and character in a very few words—is what makes her writing so vivid even today.[59] Here is her view from the Senate gallery, to which the ladies of the Federal City went faithfully as if to the theater:

> The Senate was at that time full of distinguished men from all parts of the Union—There was a bright Constellation of talent and learning such as is seldom concentrated in one body, and [Aaron] Burr the Vice President presided with a dignity which has never been approached since. Though a devoted Servant of the *Ladies* he never permitted a moments infringement of the Rules. And the little hammer in his graceful little hand would startle them into silence at the instant application.[60]

Here is James Madison:

> Mr. Madison was a *very* small man in his *person*, with a *very* large *head*—his manners were peculiarly unassuming; and his conversation lively, often playful, with a mixture of wit and seriousness so happily blended as to excite admiration and respect—I never saw a man with a mind so copious, so free from the pedantry and mere classical jargon of University Scholarship—but his language was chaste, well suited to occasion, and the simple expression of the passing thought, and in harmony with the taste of his hearers.

And here is Secretary of War Henry Dearborn of Maine:

> Genl Dearborn and his Wife were kind friendly excellent people. He "told of Wars and hair breadth-'scapes"; assured me that from his *own* experience when taken by the Indians in the dread affair of Genl Hull (I think) that it only required "a fortnight for men like *him* to return from *refinement* to the Savage state," and that after two Months "*he* was as much an Indian as any of them" and his good and amiable Wife, a true specimen of yankee housewifery, always kind, was for ever regretting her Milch Cows, and her Chickens at Kenebunck.

Not all her portraits were so free of malice—Jefferson did not grow in her estimation. ("His countenance indicated strongly the hypocricy of his nature and all about him his smile and his actions indicated a sort of tricky cunning, the sure attendant of a sophisticated mind devoid of a strong basis of substantial principle.") Nor did his fellow Virginian John Randolph: "Ever in extremes he was at times a delightful companion; or an insolent bully. . . . Surrounded by admirers who loved the excitement produced by his waywardness and his brilliant rhapsodies; he appeared to be the great man of his day, for he ruled the timid and amused the weak."[61]

There is no evidence that John Quincy put any store by Louisa's talent for shrewdly sizing up the great personages of the day in 1804. The young senator from Massachusetts still believed it would be the weight of his arguments and his ability to work harder than anyone that would sway both Republican and Federalist votes in his direction. Party and personality issues, in his view, were entirely secondary to superior policies and points of constitutional law. Convinced that the representatives of the people would eventually rise above their petty squabbles to do what was right, John Quincy was to be disappointed again and again. Louisa, who saw people as they were, would rarely be fooled.

Colored by years of bitter disappointment and defeat, Louisa's essentially cynical appraisal in 1840 of the difference between theory and practice in a democracy was a point of view she formed early and seems to have never rejected: "A republick of *Equality*, is a sort of *non descript* only to be realized in musty tomes generated in the unpractised and unsocial brains of needy Book Worms," she wrote in *Adventures of a Nobody*. She believed that in a country under a democratic government "where every man woman and Child is an *incompetent Sovereign*, who makes or unmakes the *efficient* and *able rulers* of the Land, according to the wisdom of party factions, the spleen and avarice of demagogues, the hireling greediness of grasping avarice, or the unprincipled recklessness of vicious profligacy," the worst rose to the top and "the best and most worthy Citizens of the Community" were ignored or reviled. This was not received wisdom but the distinctly jaundiced thinking of a woman who, reared "a republican in a monarchy," would, over a lifetime of political turmoil, apply her acute observations of politicians and the populace to advance her husband's career.[62]

8

WANDERING FORTUNES

She was called upon to follow the wandering fortunes of the wife of a
United States' senator.

—CHARLES FRANCIS ADAMS

I can neither live with or without you.

—LOUISA CATHERINE ADAMS

Senator Adams prepared to go north on April 2, 1804—alone. He would
spend the April–November Congressional recess with Abigail and John Adams
in Quincy while Louisa and the children remained in Washington with her
family. Neither wanted it that way. Badly misreading the other's views on where
the family should spend the summer, they had reached an impasse. Their
quarrel, still unresolved when they parted, followed John Quincy all the way
home and simmered for more than a month in their correspondence.

Louisa was on the attack in a letter written two days after John Quincy left
Washington. Judging from his instant and bitter response, her "painful and
unexpected" letter contained some angry observations concerning his "coldness and unkindness" as well as a caustic charge aimed at his overweening
devotion to his parents. "Our separation was very much against my inclination,
but it was your own choice," John Quincy replied loftily. "Thinking as I do that
my home is the proper and only proper home of my wife and children, I shall
always feel the sweetest satisfaction in having them with me; and shall ever
lament your determination to abide elsewhere." But, he added, as long as he
could support the expense of separate households, she would be free to live
wherever she chose.[1]

Turning to the matter of family loyalty, he first commended her love for her
mother and sisters and then turned the knife: "Your attachment to your own
family is a sentiment so amiable in itself that I can never disapprove it . . . even

when it leads you to prefer separation from me rather than separation from them." Refusing to answer directly her comments concerning his fealty to his own parents, he added, "I have naturally the same sentiments of affection and respect on my part. . . . The duties of filial, of conjugal and of paternal tenderness are all equally sacred, and I wish to discharge them all with equal fidelity."[2]

Louisa, still steaming, could not let John Quincy have the last word, especially when he accused her of preferring the society of the Hellen-Johnson household to his own. She was well aware, she said, that had she returned with him to Quincy, she would have been forced to remain there indefinitely. Attempting to sound conciliatory, she could not restrain herself from pronouncing winters in his hometown "dreary," adding: "I cannot suffer you to suppose that I remained here from choice, had I the slightest prospect of returning with you. But you have repeatedly told me that it was not in your power to take me with you after the first winter, that we must therefore be separated one half of the year for six years. The only thing left for me was to endeavor to make our separation as easy to myself as possible and I prefer'd passing the summer months with my family to living alone at Quincy through five dreary winters." Nonetheless, in the face of John Quincy's accusation that she preferred staying with her mother and sisters to living with him, Louisa offered to prove her devotion by leaving immediately for Massachusetts.[3]

The root of their quarrel seems to have been as much the couple's limited financial resources as their congenital inability to hear what the other was saying. Not for a day did Louisa forget she had brought no money to the marriage. Life with her mother and sisters under the beneficence of Walter Hellen was a constant reminder of the Johnson family's utter destitution. The final disposition of Joshua Johnson's last will and testament revealed that although the beleaguered merchant appeared confident that he had left a modest annual income to his wife, his affairs were so compromised that, in the end, he had left her and her children virtually nothing. Viewing herself as a "heavy burthen" to John Quincy, it took only a hint that she had made a selfish, costly decision in choosing to live in Washington to hurt Louisa deeply. She responded abjectly, "I brought you nothing and therefore have no claim on you whatever. My life ever has been and ever must remain a life of painful obligation."[4]

But John Quincy was equally sensitive on the matter of money. The financial independence he had worked so hard to achieve was about to be undone. To have become a United States senator and still be forced to live with one's parents would be humiliating to any thirty-six-year-old man, but it was particularly painful to one of such proud temperament. To Louisa he wrote he would not attempt to make livable the primitive saltbox cottage where he had been born until he was sure she would be willing to live there with him. The cost of repairs, he said, would only add to his worries. "Additional expence, without any prospect of additional income, would infallibly lead to my ruin; and what would be to me ten thousand times worse, to the greatest distress to you and our children."

His dilemma was real. The only money he could count on was the $6.00 per diem that senators received over the usual five-month period of a Congressional session and a small income from his remaining investments. (Most of his former savings and real property had been surrendered to assist his parents in withstanding the Bird, Savage & Bird bank failure.) During the winter, John Quincy had supplemented his salary by appearing before the U.S. Supreme Court on a few cases, but none seems to have been particularly remunerative. If the idea of taking on some short-term legal matters over the summer to ease his financial embarrassments ever occurred to him, he did not pursue it. "It is with extreme difficulty that I now find the means of defraying our necessary expences as they rise, without intrenching upon the little property which helps to support us," John Quincy informed his wife.

Four hundred miles apart, he had finally chosen to treat Louisa as a financial partner—no longer a child to whom he doled out an allowance or a "fine lady" who had to be protected from the realities of a stringent budget. Had he explained their finances to her as clearly in person as he did by letter, the pain of their separation might have been avoided. Pride and a refusal to acknowledge to her face that he was unable to provide her the elegant lifestyle she had grown up with—or even the comfortable ambiance of the Hellen ménage—may have restrained John Quincy from confronting her with what he feared she did not want to hear. Almost as much as Louisa mourned not having brought a dowry to the marriage, John Quincy regretted his inability to give his wife the comforts he believed she deserved. Her decision to remain in Washington without him only reinforced his conviction that she, too, could not face the fact of their relative penury. He apologized—but with a pointed remark regarding her preference for Washington—for the small cottage he was asking her to share: "[The house in Quincy] is not and never can be made such a place as I could wish to provide for your residence; but it may prove a shelter hereafter, and supply means of subsistence, to ourselves and our children, when we shall find none else. These considerations alone have induced me to wish that you could have reconciled your mind to this place, and to so humble a residence as that house. As however you cannot, you shall at all events reside where you yourself choose."[5]

Once her anger cooled, it did not take long for Louisa to pick up on the undertone of depression that immediately began to color all John Quincy's letters. Less than a month after he had arrived home, she informed him she would willingly join him there, even though—as she took care to point out—their life together in Quincy left something to be desired: "From the stile of your two last letters it appears to me that your spirits are unusually depressed, which gives me real uneasiness. I cannot indulge a hope that my absence can have produced this effect as we are less together at Quincy than at any other time. However, let the cause, my best friend, be what it may, I am ready and willing to return home immediately and to do every thing in my power to lessen the heavy burthen which I hourly feel I am become."

Louisa gallantly offered to make the trip with only the help of a younger sister. "I will with pleasure take charge of the Children provided you will let me bring one of my Sisters to assist me. Women frequently do such things and I am not *more timid* than the rest of my Sex," she announced to what was probably a dubious John Quincy, more accustomed to her displays of frailty than assertions of energy and courage. She declared herself perfectly capable of living in the old farmhouse ("If Mrs. Adams could reside there with four Children I can certainly live there with two") and encouraged her husband to get on with making it livable. Louisa's patently genuine offer—which John Quincy turned down—went a long way toward restoring a loving relationship between the two. For the remainder of their six-month separation, their letters betrayed no trace of bitterness or rancor.[6]

But Louisa had been correct when she sensed that John Quincy was at a very low point. Gamely attempting to farm, he planted an orchard of a hundred peach, apple, and apricot trees. Despite some early enthusiasm for grafting and planting, by May he was allotting less than an hour a day to tending his crop, and most of the peaches eventually developed a fatal case of "white worm." Instead, he spent every morning until noon analyzing the laws of the United States and the afternoon reading the collected letters of the Marquise de Sévigné or the *Odyssey* in Greek and various translations. Much of the remainder of the day was taken up with "lounging" or "at leisure." This was precisely the sort of routine calculated to drive him to bouts of self-incrimination and doubt. On July 14, even this leisurely schedule had unraveled: "This was a day of almost total intermission from serious occupations reading or writing. I wish it may not become the example of a long succession of them. But I find toil, mental or bodily, has become so wearisome that there is danger I shall shirk from it." He summed up the entire month of August 1804 as "Irregular and indolent."[7]

John Quincy's self-imposed isolation from society was almost complete. He rarely journeyed into Boston for business, accepted few invitations to join friends for dinner or meetings of his clubs—perhaps fearing the expense—and did not even accompany his parents to the funeral of a local worthy. His social life centered on Peacefields, where he spent most evenings reading *The Faerie Queene* aloud to his father or discussing politics with his parents and their many visitors. He desperately missed Louisa, George, and baby John: "To use a vulgar phrase, [I'm] like a fish out of water, without you and my children," he complained to his absent wife. Adding to John Quincy's misery, the usually ebullient Tom Adams, also now living at home, was not in the best position to lighten his brother's mood.[8]

Tom's case was a sadder—eventually more tragic—version of his older brother's. Like John Quincy, he had resisted depending on the law for his livelihood. Unfortunately, his effort to make a living simultaneously as a lawyer and as business manager and prolific writer for the literary publication *Port Folio* in Philadelphia failed, and he had remained dependent for survival on periodic infusions of cash from his parents. Sometime earlier, John Quincy had written bluntly—and thoughtfully—to his mother advising her and the former president to deal gently with their vulnerable younger son if he, in fact, yielded to their repeated entreaties to return home. Tom must be left "entirely and in the most unqualified manner to his own choice and humour in his mode of life and pursuits," John Quincy counseled his parents. At the same time, he encouraged his brother to go through the motions of becoming a Massachusetts lawyer while looking out for other more attractive opportunities.[9]

Tom, his self-confidence bruised by failure, did his best, but anything except modest success continued to elude him. Returning to Quincy in December 1803, he found the law a nightmare ("It haunts me like a spectre, for I some times start with terror from a profound reverie on writs and attachments") and missed his life in prosperous, bustling Philadelphia. He wanted to marry Ann Harrod, a young woman he had known since his school days in Haverhill, but was far from being able to support her. Nonetheless, he was willing to adopt John Quincy's advice, if only to hold depression at bay: "Your advice to keep up a *show* of my profession, I have already determined to follow, and this is all I should be likely to do for some time, with the best intentions of doing more . . . and I design to buckle to with some earnestness, to keep off the Blue Devils."[10]

Unlike the Adams brothers, Louisa was not suffering from depression in the summer of 1804. Even in hot and humid Washington, her mood was generally upbeat, and—not being pregnant—she felt the best she had in years. "My health is better than I ever remember it," she exulted. She filled her weekly letters to John Quincy, who was hungry for every homely detail, with news of the children. Although George, age three, in a mother's proud eyes, was "one of the finest children I ever saw," he was "much too clever or wise for his age. . . . He destroys all Mrs. Hellens chickens, drives the ducks to death, gets down to the Wharf and plays such pranks I am obliged to keep a person constantly running after him. I am obliged to make him *fear* me. He laughs at every body else and nobody can do any thing with him."[11]

And like most one-year-olds, baby John was not above a tantrum when he was hot, frustrated, or teething. The boys' father was uncharacteristically casual and playful in his reactions to his children's misdeeds. George was acting perfectly normally for his age, he said. John, he wrote teasingly, came by his temper naturally: "'Tis very unaccountable that [John] should be so passionate as you tell me, for you know it could not come from either of his parents. Perhaps he derives it by transmission from some former generation. But upon further recollection . . . I must confess that I can account for some degree of irritability in a child of mine, without going more than one step upwards to find its source."[12]

Separated from his wife and children and entirely free of legislative or other business, John Quincy could express his acceptance, love, and longing for them in ways that he seemed unable to do when the family was together and he, immersed in study and politics, became irritated by their noise, needs, and activities. The aching loneliness that felt to him like exile—even at home in Quincy—was not only for the children's pranks and Louisa's companionship. Candidly, he made it clear that making love with her was something he enjoyed and very much missed. Describing a woman, fashionably dressed in a low-cut diaphanous gown whom he had met at a party, he teased, "A very little cloathing you know, upon a Lady, will answer all my purposes. . . . But then for that very little I am scrupulous in exacting it. I am still of opinion that a Lady when she goes to bed at Night, should have something to do, besides opening the Sheets."[13]

By mid-June, his longing for Louisa had become almost unendurable. He copied out for her the ageless lines John Donne had written to his wife that begin

Our two souls therefore, which are one
Though I must go, indure not yet
A breach, but an expansion,
Like gold to airy thinness beat.

The poet's words, John Quincy wrote, "struck me the more forcibly as they are so peculiarly applicable to this painful separation, which we endure." Louisa responded that she would much prefer to have John Quincy with her in the flesh than even the most beautiful poetry and acknowledged that she, too, suffered from loneliness: "Your Absence begins to be insupportable and the time which yet intervenes appears to me interminable. . . . I shall know neither happiness or peace till you return."[14]

John Quincy's letters to Louisa in the summer of 1804 were conversations with an equal. He sprinkled gossip about their friends and other Boston notables with detailed commentary on Massachusetts politics, his reaction to the tragic Aaron Burr – Alexander Hamilton duel, and discussions of his reading. He even deferred to her judgment in child-raising, praising her decision to give the boys cold baths each morning and to take them out of the fetid city to the country as often as possible. From Washington, Louisa kept John Quincy informed of everything going on in the nation's new capital. When she needed money, she asked for it without apology. Even as she expressed her need for her husband's judgment and strength, she seemed to become stronger and more independent as the summer wore on. When John Quincy justified his decision to avoid memorial services for Hamilton because "neither the manner of his Death, nor his base treatment of more than one of my connections, would permit me to join in any outward demonstration of regret which I could not feel at heart," she brought him sharply to heel: "I wonder you were not there. Whatever a mans faults may have been we should not carry resentment beyond the Grave. Remember my beloved friend that as we forgive so shall we be forgiven and the opinion of the World must be favorable when we act up to the true principles of our religion."[15]

Louisa already realized "the opinion of the World" was crucial to John Quincy's political career and that his refusal to feign an emotion he did not feel would be held against him. Although she later denied their existence — "I knew nothing of Politics, and of course was without ambition," she claimed in *Adventures of a Nobody* — her shrewd political instincts and fierce ambition for her husband's political future were already at play. Writing to John Quincy, she candidly acknowledged the opposing poles of domestic tranquility and political success that, to her, clearly meant the presidency: "Form'd for domestic life my whole Soul devoted to you and my children, yet ambitious to excess, my heart and head are constantly at war. . . . I would willingly give up every future hope of your attaining the highest honors your Country admits to be assured we never should part more."[16]

Louisa's newfound confidence also came to the fore when John Quincy tersely announced the death of Mary Frazier, writing simply that "Captain D. Sargent has had the misfortune of losing his wife. . . . Her disorder I hear, was a

consumption. She has left a child about 6 months old." Accusing him of insen-
sitivity, she wrote, "You my best friend who have known her so long and once
loved her so well must indeed mourn her untimely fate and bury her faults
(if faults she had) in eternal oblivion. I never saw her but twice but the last time
I had that pleasure I was fully convinced that she still retain'd her affection for
you which she could not conceal and I pitied her from my Soul, convinced as
I am she never ceased to lament the folly she was urged to commit and to
deplore the blessing she had lost."[17]

John Quincy immediately countered that it had been ten years since he had
had any feelings for Mary other than those of "a common acquaintance,
coupled perhaps with a peculiar coldness of reserve. . . . I never felt the wish to
see her, nor was I conscious of a wish to avoid her." He also dismissed Louisa's
"fancy" that Mary had loved him to the end, blaming what he and others had
told her about his "early attachment" for Louisa's misinterpretation of what she
observed in Boston. That she felt confident enough to raise the topic of her
husband's relationship with his former love and challenge him to acknowledge
his loss, however, marked a new balance in their relationship. Her positive self-
image had come a long way from the "poor faded thing" that sailed to America
from Prussia in 1801. Now the proud and doting mother of two handsome boys,
she felt herself fulfilled, needed, and strong.[18]

Louisa's self-confidence and physical resilience were still on display when
John Quincy returned to Washington in November. Riding horseback with
him one afternoon, she was thrown to the ground while the "horse plunged and
kicked at a furious rate." Unrattled, she remounted, and though the horse
remained "restive," the two continued their canter to the Capitol and back.
More significantly, she finally felt strong enough to hold her own with Abigail
Adams. In the spring, Abigail had written Louisa how alarmed she had been to
see how pale and thin John Quincy appeared on his arrival in Quincy. She
attributed his exhaustion to his inability to "engage in any service but with his
whole attention, and the labours, and anxiety of the mind are a weariness to the
flesh." Louisa countered any inference that she had been lax in the care of her
husband's health by writing to her mother-in-law six months later that John
Quincy's health had been "extremely indifferent" when he arrived back in
Washington. "I was much surprized and grieved to see him look so ill when he
returned. I thank God he is now better though I am apprehensive while he
continues in public life there is little chance of his enjoying perfect health
owing to the extreme anxiety of his mind in the present unprosperous and
unpleasant situation of affairs."[19]

Despite their initial sparring over who could take better care of him, the two now had something on which they could agree—John Quincy's health would inevitably suffer as a result of his relentless application to his duties. Abigail, recognizing an ally, offered some practical, motherly suggestions: "I wish you would not let him go to Congress without a craker in his pocket. The space between Breakfast and dinner is so long, that his Stomack gets fill'd with flatulencies, and his food when he takes it neither dijests or nourishes him." Counting on Louisa to do for her son what she could not, she asked to be kept informed: "I want to know if his cough has left him, and whether he has any thing of the Rheumatism in his Limbs. I would have him pay particular attention to his cough, and if he is not quite relieved put a Blister between his Shoulders."[20]

Louisa, in turn, despairing that she could not persuade John Quincy to forgo his daily three-mile walk to and from the Capitol, asked his mother to intercede: "The exercise he takes so constantly is much too violent. I purchased a Horse hoping he might be induced to ride but my plan has not proved successful. It is utterly impossible to prevail on him to use it. Perhaps Madam if you were to write him on the subject he might pay more attention to it and oblige us by taking more care of himself."[21]

The two most influential women in John Quincy's life also found they had more in common than a concern for his health—they were also united in their view of his potential for political success. Although Louisa described John Quincy's situation in Congress as "irksome"—and one deleterious to his wellbeing—she reiterated her conviction that his special abilities deserved a place at the nation's highest levels: "It grieves me to see him sacrificing the best years of his life in so painful and unprofitable a way. It would however cause me infinite pain to see him give it up. His talents are so superior and he is so perfectly calculated for the station in which he is placed. His manners are so perfectly pleasing and conciliating and his understanding is so refined even his enemies envy and admire him."[22]

To this praise of her son, Abigail heartily concurred and added a bit more helpful advice: "I can readily assent to your well-drawn portrait, but there is one thing in which we must also unite, that of prevailing upon him to pay more attention to his personal appearance. Upon this Subject I have labourd to convince him of its necessity even as it conduces to his usefullness in Society. . . . It is in vain to talk of being above these little decorums—if we Live in the world and mean to serve ourselves and it, we must conform to its customs, its habits and in some measure to its fashions." Abigail had clearly ceased to think of her daughter-in-law as an obstacle on her son's path to higher office. Louisa, a safe distance away from Quincy, was just as obviously now able to take advice from her mother-in-law without resenting it. A truce, if not a capitulation, had finally been achieved.[23]

For the next few months, Louisa tried to keep Abigail abreast of the political and diplomatic gossip she knew she delighted in. As the Congressional session resumed, so did the capital's very active social scene. At its center in the winter of 1805, in lieu of a First Lady, was Dolley Madison, wife of the secretary of state. Louisa had nothing but admiration for Dolley's style and poise ("Mrs. Madison . . . was universally popular for the amenity of her manners and the suavity of her temper—She seemed to combine all the qualifications requisite to adorn the Station which she filled to the satisfaction of *all*: a most difficult performance"), but she had reservations about the housekeeping at Jefferson's executive mansion. ("The aspect of the House *below* Stairs was very handsome—Up *Stairs* there were strong indications of the want of female inspection.")[24]

Meanwhile, life in the Hellen mansion went on as before. The charm and sophistication of the Johnson women continued to attract members of the political and diplomatic community, particularly the French delegation, who were delighted to find a parlor where good music was a part of the evening's entertainment and the French language understood and appreciated. Almost upon his arrival in Washington, John Quincy plunged back into his senatorial duties and classical studies, adopting exactly the regimen his wife and mother tried to guard against. Summing up the month of January 1805 in his diary it is clear he had heard—but disregarded—their admonitions that he be less demanding of himself. Nearly every evening, he disappeared into his study: "Spend the evening from 6 to 11 or 12 in my chamber reading or writing. I cannot say this assiduity is to any great purpose and perhaps it withdraws one too much from mingling with society. But it is difficult precisely to measure the portions of Time which ought to be allotted to the world, and those which should be devoted to business."[25]

John Quincy had reached one of the many points in his life when he was painfully uncertain about his future and depressed about his prospects. On New Year's Eve, 1804, he acknowledged to his diary that, although he had "given some attention to agricultural pursuits" in the past summer, they had "soon lost their relish," especially since he could not see how he would ever make farming pay. And despite devoting most of his time in Quincy to serious reading, his studies, too, had yielded little sense of achievement. Discouraged by his inability to comprehend everything he read, he was tempted to give up books altogether. Yet he could not bring himself to do so: "When once severed from my books, I find little or nothing in life to fill the vacancy of time. I must continue to plod."[26]

A life in politics also offered little hope. In the presidential election of 1804, Jefferson had won the Electoral College vote by an overwhelming (162 to 14) mandate over his Federalist rival. Even Massachusetts had voted for the Virginian. As a nominal Federalist, John Quincy was a member of an essentially extinct political party. "My political prospects have been daily declining," he wrote in the last hours of 1804. That his son might never achieve any higher office did not disturb old John Adams, viewing from afar what he feared was the unraveling of the republic of laws he had worked so hard to design. It would be better, in his view, that John Quincy stick to his principles than bend to the Jeffersonian winds now sweeping through Washington. Once again the former president raised the chimera of success in the law: "Your Friends all know that your Talent, Learning and Application would insure you a place in the most honorable and lucrative rank at the Bar, whenever you please to take it. But you are too much disposed to gloom and despondency. Men must brave Adversity: and be modest in prosperity. If they cannot, or will not be rich and popular they must submit to be poor and obscure." The "old gentleman" would have an opportunity to reiterate his arguments in favor of the legal profession directly to his son over the spring and summer of 1805. John Quincy, Louisa, their sons, and Louisa's younger sister Eliza would be living in their cramped farmhouse just two miles from Peacefields.[27]

The trip north that spring was another exercise in endurance. Eliza Johnson, at eighteen, along to lend a hand, was of minimal assistance since she was at an age when, in Louisa's words, "circumstances of pleasure and excitement are for ever calling forth expressions of admiration and flattering attentions." By the time the group reached Philadelphia, the boys were suffering from both bad coughs and chickenpox. Because George was running a high fever, the family was compelled to stay in Philadelphia much longer than originally intended. Meanwhile, Louisa was momentarily debilitated by a cramping attack, so "violent," her husband recorded, that she required two visits from Dr. Rush in a single evening. Within a day, however, she was back on an extremely lively social round that included a grand ball, teas, dinners, and many social visits. Louisa recalled the trip on the whole as a "tedious and unpleasant journey," but her memories of fellow passenger Aaron Burr were still vivid many years later:

> He was a small man quite handsome and his manners were strikingly prepossessing and in spite of myself I was pleased with him—He appeared to fascinate every one in the Boat down to the lowest Sailor and knew every bodies history by the time we left—He was politely attentive to me, devoted to my

Sister—At Table he assisted me to help the Children with so much ease and
good nature that I was perfectly confounded. . . . At about twelve at Night we
landed and it was diverting to see Mr. Burr with my youngest Child in his
arms; a bundle in his hand and [me] leaning on his other arm to walk from
the Wharf while my Sister Mr. Adams and George followed. . . . Yet it was all
done with so little parade and with such entire good breeding that it made
you forget that he was doing any thing out of the way. He talked and laughed
all the way and we were quite intimate by the time we got to Philadelphia.[28]

Two weeks after their arrival in Quincy, the weary family moved into the old
farmhouse at Penn's Hill. Louisa always made much of her inadequacies as a
farmer's wife, but she was not quite as inept as she claimed. Her planning for
the role had begun in the winter. As early as February, she had asked Abigail to
assign someone to "do up the garden a little, that is to [sow] some different sorts
of Peas, some mustard and cress, some pepper grass, lettuce and set out some
cabbage plants." As soon as the family was installed in the cottage, she even
made an attempt at becoming a dairymaid "with the assistance of my Sister who
was more successful in milking the Cows as I confess with all my labor for want
of *knack* I could not get a drop of milk." Before the arrival of a young boy and
two farm girls to help, the two Johnson women made a sport out of their awkward
attempts to emulate accomplished New England housewives: "Never did we
laugh more heartily than while thus occupied—our perpetual blunders
rendering the whole scene so ridiculous; but we were highly gratified when
Mr. Adams pronounced his Meals excellent."[29]

As usual when they were at close quarters, Louisa found herself diminished
by her mother-in-law: "Accustomed both then and long afterwards to hear
Mrs. Adams spoken of as something much above the common standard of her
Sex, when I became acquainted with her as her daughter I felt that even my
husband must contrast [me] woefully to my disadvantage and that idea humbled
me so much in my own conceit every sense was paralysed and I felt only the
consciousness of my own inferiority." For most of the summer, Louisa seems to
have sidestepped comparisons with Abigail by remaining close to her little
farmhouse and taking her toddler sons for walks in the country, occasionally
joined by John Quincy, who could not let a potential teachable moment pass:
"Some of our time was spent in the study of Botany and our rambles among the
rocks and woods were sources of amusement under the direction and instruction of Mr. Adams who entered heart and soul in the pursuit of plants and wild
flowers while his unfruitful scholars profited very little from his lessons."[30]

Woodland rambles aside, the summer got off to rocky start. A city girl to her
bones, Louisa found the cottage remote and the neighborhood "in many

respects unpleasant, there being two or three insane persons, under no controul, of whom we were very much afraid." The house, unrenovated despite John Quincy's best intentions, was very small—four tiny rooms downstairs, three above. John Quincy typically spent most of the day with his parents, leaving Louisa at home with the children. In "wretched" health, a symptom of loneliness and unhappiness, Louisa was enjoying a generally miserable vacation.

Until midsummer, John Quincy's mood would have done nothing to lighten her gloom. He was so seriously depressed and unwell that an alarmed Abigail took him to a local doctor in the hope a remedy might be found in a pill or potion. The doctor instead prescribed "some medicine, much exercise, and a total relaxation from study." But depression was not that easily cured: "My prospects are again blasted and I have nothing left before me but Resignation!" John Quincy wrote at the end of May. Expecting he would have the discipline to apply hours of "uninterrupted leisure . . . in a manner which should be useful to myself and others," he had, in his view, wasted day after day in a "ramble about the fields." He saw little point to his compulsive studies of arcane topics and no future at the bar or in politics. Just when John Quincy's life appeared most dismal, Fate, in the form of the Harvard Corporation, stepped in with an offer to appoint him the first Boylston Professor of Rhetoric and Oratory. Suddenly, all his haphazard intellectual forays became worthwhile; now he could justify long hours spent with his books as preparation for future lectures. By July, his despair had vanished, his studies had focused on classical rhetorical models, and he had "resumed a course of very assiduous and . . . pleasing occupation."[31]

Because his arrangements with Harvard allowed him to concentrate his lectures in the months when Congress was in recess, John Quincy believed he could still pursue his Senate duties with all the zeal he had previously shown. Back in Washington that fall, he was immediately caught up in the burning foreign policy issues of the day, which he characterized to his father as "too much tameness towards France and Spain, and too much rashness with Great Britain." As before, his evenings were spent in his study, but now the ancient volumes stacked upon his reading desk were entirely devoted to a single topic: the art and history of rhetoric.[32]

No similar good fairy smiled on Louisa. Unlike her husband, she had little to look forward to in the winter of 1806. A decision had been made by John Quincy, with the strong support of his parents, that George—now four—and John—only two—would remain in Quincy for the Senate session. That their father was adamantly opposed to making another long journey with two very young children was understandable; he may also have felt their presence in the Hellen household would be a distraction to the serious scholarship he intended to pursue. Louisa had little say in the matter. A summer in rural Massachusetts had apparently battered her self-esteem and reminded her how dependent she was on her husband, financially and in every other way. The thought of leaving her boys behind was devastating: "My heart was almost broken but our finances were low and the Children were troublesome and I conceived that I had no *right* to refuse what Mr. Adams thought just—But however strong our sense of justice may be it bears very hard upon the feelings and affections when it is too strictly carried out."[33]

For a woman who gloried in her healthy, handsome boys, adored being a mother, and believed she had no other claim to respect from the world, the forced separation from her sons was fully as difficult as she had feared. In January, Louisa was still mourning them daily, bombarding their grandmother with remedies for childhood illnesses ("Should you have any apprehension of Georges having worms give him five drops of spirit of Turpentine upon a lump of Sugar every other morning") and instructions regarding their diet. She craved the smallest detail: "I have no right to urge any one on this subject but having been compelled to leave them I cannot command my feelings and must trust to your kindness to let [me] hear frequently," she wrote to Abigail.[34]

Finally, her mother-in-law briskly—and somewhat callously—took her to task. There were perfectly good reasons, Abigail wrote, for the boys to remain in Quincy: "They are much better off than they could have been at any boarding House in Washington, where they must have been confined in some degree; or have mix'd with improper persons," she wrote. In addition, "there cannot be any thing more disagreeable than transporting young Children twice a year, either by water, or in crouded Stages at such a distance, and however reluctant you might feel, at being seperated from them, I should suppose that your own judgement, experience and good sense would have convinced you of the propriety of the measure without compulsion. I have experienced seperations of all kinds from Children equally dear to me; and know how great the Sacrifice and how painfull the task, but I considered it the duty of a parent to consult the interest and benefit of their Children." Nothing in this letter assuaged Louisa's feelings. Especially hard to accept were Abigail's comparison of the Hellens' elegant and commodious home to a boardinghouse and the contention that she, Louisa, had considered her own happiness above the interest of her children.[35]

From this point on, correspondence between the two women seems to have slowed to a trickle. But in February, Abigail drew a wonderful grandmotherly picture of cherubic, two-year-old John, his sled, and the family cat, which must have delighted the boy's mother: "[The sled] employs half his time, sometimes to draw about Miss Juno, who seems to like the ride very well, and sits in it as grave and demure, as though she could never skip, and play. He has his Hammer, and his Shovel, sometimes mimicks Jobe in shoveling the Snow and at other times Hammers stoutly enough; at other times uses his needle, and sews away with Susan. . . . I devote my chamber . . . to him, and it is pretty well litter'd from morning to night." Unfortunately, she could not resist again chiding Louisa for constantly pleading for any word of her sons: "Whilst as a Mother you must be anxious to hear frequently from your Children, you will still bear in mind that they are mortal: and that no solisitude or care can at all times shield them from the common lot of Mortals."[36]

Louisa had clearly not yet endeared herself to her mother-in law. Abigail's letters to Tom Adams's new bride began, "My dear Nancy," but letters to Washington were addressed, "My dear Mrs. Adams." Louisa had undoubtedly been unable to hide her boredom and unhappiness during the summer at Penn's Hill, and her frequent headaches and other indispositions had only reinforced her sturdy mother-in-law's view that she was altogether too subject to weaknesses of mind and body. More to the point, Abigail loved Quincy and the people who lived there, and she could easily have perceived Louisa's marked distaste for life in that small New England town as personally insulting and condescending.[37]

For her part, Louisa always suspected that her Johnson family connections had fueled what she saw as Abigail's bias against her. Certain that everyone in Quincy believed she had duped the Adams heir apparent into believing he was marrying into money, Louisa retreated into a defensive—and unhelpful— posture of proud disdain: "I felt as an unwelcome intruder. . . . Who could believe or understand that I was not aware of my Fathers difficulties before I married—and the idea that I was *suspected* of having 'drawn him in,' (as is vulgarly said) seemed an incubus that was pressing me to the earth and crushing every hope of happiness." Instead, it may have been Louisa's downcast demeanor in the presence of her indomitable mother-in-law and her insistence on claiming victimhood that opened her to Abigail's scorn. Continually insisting she had been "compelled" to take actions she would have opposed had she had a dowry was a sure way to irritate a woman who had for decades strongly influenced every decision made in her extended family without any regard to her own financial standing in it.[38]

Although it would have been difficult for even the most self-confident woman to become the daughter-in-law of a legend and the wife of her favorite son, Louisa made things worse for herself by refusing to believe she was anything but a disappointment to Abigail. She would have been surprised to learn that her mother-in-law took a much more realistic view of marriage in general and the need for a husband or wife to bring a fortune into the family in particular. None of Abigail's children's spouses had any pretensions to wealth, and she was fully—if reluctantly—resigned to that fact. Louisa herself had yet to be convinced.

Desperately missing her children and once again pregnant ("My health was particularly delicate and my spirits worse"), Louisa was in a fractious mood during the winter of 1806. John Quincy was absorbed in his work—"Mr Adams was laboriously engaged all this Month in Congress and spent a large portion of his time in his Chamber"—and seemed almost unaware of her existence. Although his diary records page after page of senatorial debates and names the many evening visitors to the Hellen home, his only reference to his wife was a frequent "Mrs. Adams very unwell."[39]

The entire Washington social scene seemed to have lost its luster for Louisa that winter. Even the arrival of the Tunisian ambassador who was a "great admirer of handsome Women; and always insisted on holding them under his Cloak as it possessed many *virtues*," did not greatly amuse her; neither did a visit of a delegation of Cherokees to the Hellen home on Christmas Day. Religion offered no balm. Sunday services were then held in the Capitol and led by a variety of preachers, each declaiming according to the beliefs of his particular Protestant denomination. This was not a church service in Louisa's eyes but a defamation of one: "The preaching wretched—There is something so every way unsuitable to all religious feeling of solemnity or propriety in the Hall *itself*; independent of its intriguing and wrangling associations that you cannot think of the purity of heaven in a place so altogether worldly, where corruption faces you in every corner and where all the bad passions betrayed in the weak arise like Ghosts to haunt the imagination with the baseness of Vice or the exhibition of follies which ought to bear a harsher name."[40]

Louisa's pregnancy, with its fainting fits and many unspecified attacks of "illness," seemed entirely too reminiscent of those she had suffered through in Berlin. "Mrs. Adams was very suddenly taken ill, and with great violence about 1 o'clock this morning. . . . She continued very weak the whole day," her husband recorded in March. But as April approached, it appeared she might be able to carry the baby to term as long as she did not go north with John Quincy when the Congressional session ended. Again, Louisa framed the decision that she remain in Washington as if she had no say in the matter: "I was constantly sick and Mr. Adams determined to leave me in Washington as it was deemed dangerous for me to travel in my situation . . . the fiat of my Physician was not to be disputed and I was compelled to stay."[41]

John Quincy's departure on April 26 signaled the start of an extended exchange of loving and mutually supportive letters. A stranger intercepting their weekly correspondence would have no difficulty believing that this was a couple deeply in love, united in their aspirations, and communicating on a basis of mutual respect and trust. She was his "Dearest Louisa," to whom he sent *"les plus tendres baisers de l'Amour"*; in return, she was "ever your most tenderly affectionate wife." He asked her advice on whether to buy a two-family house overlooking Boston Common at what is now the corner of Tremont and Boylston streets, and she arose every morning at sunrise to take temperature readings so that his long-range, comparative study of Boston and Washington climates would not be interrupted. He wrote charming descriptions of their children: "George is now sitting by my side, and asks me what I am writing to you? He says he wants Mama to come home, and to go and live at the house where we lived last Summer. John calls it Papa's *beauty* House, and last Summer it certainly deserved that character. For if it had nothing else in it, there was as much *beauty* at least as in any dwelling House in New-England."[42]

While John Quincy worried about her health and counted down the weeks as she neared her delivery date, Louisa attempted to minimize her pregnancy's many complications. He assured her his maiden lecture at Harvard would be much improved were she were available to hear it ahead of time: "I regret very much your absence, for I am sure I should do better, if I could enjoy the advantage of reading my discourse to you before I speak it. In former instances I had that benefit, and know how useful it was to me; most especially in the hints of passages to be struck out." In what became a key exchange in determining the direction of John Quincy's career, Louisa argued forcefully against his somewhat serious inclination to abandon his hopes for a future in politics and settle instead for life as a Boston lawyer and Harvard professor. Balancing his teaching and Senate duties and moving twice a year between Washington and Boston had begun to look more and more arduous to John Quincy. He wrote Louisa that had she been in Boston and available for consultation, he might have resigned his Senate position immediately so that they could have some stability in their "unsettled" lives. "My temptations to break off from my connection with public affairs and resume the practice of the law, are even now so strong that if you were here, and as willing as I am, I believe I should renounce my official character at once," he confided to her.[43]

Louisa's response was complex—in her words, "prolix." At its core was a conflict between her deep yearning for the comfortable life of a middle-class matron and her equally intense belief that her husband was meant to be more than just another Boston lawyer. Acknowledging that she had long favored his return to the practice of law as the most certain career to produce a steady income, she gently suggested it was also "perhaps the most laborious and the least gratifying to a mind form'd as yours has been for a more brilliant sphere." Leaving to him the decision of whether he should resign the position for which she believed him to be "so eminently calculated to shine and to be of real and essential service to your Country," she made it clear she believed it to be his patriotic duty to retain his Senate seat: "Nature produces very few really great men. Interest and the world corrupt many of those few." Maintaining that "self and family comfort must sometimes be sacrificed for the general good," Louisa conceded it was against her own self-interest to encourage his political career: "Think not that this desire proceeds from a foolish and weak ambition which at the present crisis of affairs can hold forth but a poor compensation for the unsettled and divided life we at present lead. If I know my own heart it springs from the purest motives which banish every interest but the public welfare. . . . We are . . . bound when we possess the means to use them and to use them greatly." The woman who would later refer to ambition as a curse that tragically warped John Quincy's life—as well as the lives of their three sons—was fully as ambitious as he was at the outset of his political career and did not hesitate to raise before him the challenge of greatness. When he wavered, seduced by visions of uninterrupted hours in a book-lined study, she almost invariably reminded him of what they both regarded as his destiny—as well as his duty—cloaking her own driving ambition for him in her genuine admiration for his abilities and talents.[44]

The weekly letters traveling by coach between Washington and Quincy in the spring of 1806 shine a bright light on a complex marital relationship in a way that John Quincy's contemporaneous diary and Louisa's two unfinished memoirs do not. An unexcelled record of a remarkable life, the diary is both exceptionally complete and strangely lacking. As an account of John Quincy's life and times, it is so comprehensive a record of his public life that he could later use it as reliable substantiation for his words and actions on any given day. His account of his inner life is nearly as faithful. Not originally intended for any eyes but his own, his analysis at the end of each month and year of whether he had measured up to his personal goals and how he had allotted the hours of his days serves as a contemporary, honest assessment of his life in general and is unsparing in its self-knowledge.[45]

But Louisa—typically "Mrs. Adams"—appears seldom in her husband's diary and then primarily in connection with either her health or her visits and visitors. Her voice in conversation with him or others is silent, and the joys, quarrels, and daily concerns of their life together are entirely missing. To read only the diary is to come away, as so many biographers have, with the impression that Louisa played a minor role in John Quincy's life. But if their marriage were as distant and asymmetrical as his diary suggests, their letters in the spring of 1806 could not have been written, and we would not have John Quincy's ability to laugh at himself, his delight in the antics of his young sons, and his love and yearning for his wife.

Louisa's memoirs were even more skewed and incomplete. In recalling her husband's Senate years, she emphasized his demanding dual career as a statesman and a scholar, a life that necessarily excluded his wife and children. "Adventures of a Nobody" paints a portrait of a frequently ill, lonely, and insecure young wife, whose inclinations were for a quiet, comfortable existence, far from the excitement of politics or the glamour of society. In reality, Louisa thrived in just those arenas. Her humble protestations of gratitude in her memoirs to John Quincy for his forbearance with her whims and weaknesses and her frequent assertions that, lacking a fortune, she was undeserving of any consideration or respect—"I had no *right* to refuse what Mr. Adams thought just"—stand almost in direct contradiction to her letters of the time. Nowhere to be found in her memoirs is the woman who confidently critiqued her husband's lectures or the true believer in his ultimate role in the nation's history. That passionate, independent woman was alive and well in 1806, but by 1840 she had disappeared in Louisa's recriminations over the toll that John Quincy's passion for politics had taken on him and on his family. Without her letters, we would be justified in the impression of Louisa as a sickly woman who never adapted herself to American life and politics. We would be wrong.

As June approached, so did Louisa's due date. In warm and stifling Washington, she was confined to her bed with painful abscesses in her throat and ears, an almost total loss of the use of her right thumb, and her legs swollen to such an extent that the only stockings she could wear were her husband's. In late June, answering an urgent cry for help from her married sister Harriet, whose son was fatally ill, Louisa left her room for the first time in weeks and walked more than a mile in the heat to be at her sister's side. Walking home that night, her own labor began. Twenty hours later, with the "thermometer at 100 degrees," on June 22, she delivered a stillborn son.

Her first thoughts were for John Quincy. Still physically weak and emotionally spent, she wrote the next day to inform him of their loss. Receiving the news in Cambridge a week after the event, John Quincy broke down completely. Her letter, he wrote, was "the most excellent though the most painful . . . I ever received from you, so lovely by its tender sensibility, so admirable by its resignation and fortitude, yet so distressing to me by the affliction in which it was written, and the marks of suffering apparent even in the hand-writing that I have no words to express how much it has affected me. . . . If the tears of affliction are unbecoming a Man; Heaven will at least accept those of gratitude from me for having preserved you to me through the dangers of that heavy trial both of body and mind which it has called you to endure."[46]

John Quincy continued to mourn the death of the child he never saw. On the Fourth of July, he sent congratulations to his father but begged off taking part in the celebration. But Louisa, making a remarkable recovery and eager to reunite with her children, soon announced she was ready to venture the long trip north. Now feeling strong enough to challenge John Quincy's priorities when it came to the choice of spending time with his sons or researching and writing his lectures—always a sore point between them—she did not hesitate to express her displeasure that he had not made good on his intention to take a more active interest in the boys. And when it became clear that not only had John Quincy taken bachelor's rooms for himself in Cambridge for the summer but often could not manage to get out to Quincy to see his sons on weekends, Louisa had had enough: "I grant as you have undertaken the business [the Boylston professorship] that it is necessary to attend to it but your family have some call on you as well as the public and the place you fill will become more odious to me than ever if it is to occasion you to neglect your children and deprive you of seeing them at least once in eight days until my return."[47]

It is clear that Louisa had no patience with the "odious" Boylston professorship. To her, the prestigious Harvard chair meant the sacrifice of not only John Quincy's health but also his ability to spend time with the family. Moreover, the professorship was uncompensated by either a comfortable income or the satisfaction of service to the nation. Louisa's concerns for her husband's physical and mental well-being—although not her dismissive view of the professorship—were fully supported by Abigail. "Your mother writes me that you apply so closely to this, permit me to say, strange occupation of yours that she is fearful you will materially injure your health," she wrote from Washington, adding that she feared even her own company would be unwelcome to the cloistered scholar. Louisa was, however, not prepared to make that concession: "Having relinquished almost all claim to [your company] in the winter . . . I am the less willing to give it up in the Summer."[48]

In the end, she lost the battle. John Quincy had only limited moments to spare for his wife and sons in his highly programmed daily schedule, and at least a part of that time was devoted to teaching George to read and speak French. Furthermore, he deeply resented even the few hours he spent away from his books: "This is no longer the studious life of the two former months. I have wasted the past week and fear I shall waste the next. Nothing can be more fatal to study than petty avocations continually recurring. My lectures are already losing their value," he wrote plaintively in his summing-up for August 1806 after Louisa had been in Quincy for less than a month.[49]

Fortunately, John Quincy no longer had to deal with his wife's resentment of his avocation. When Louisa attended one of his lectures, she came away impressed. Conceding she might have too hastily dismissed the Boylston professorship, she acknowledged, "It [the trip in and out of Cambridge] was very fatiguing but the success of an experiment which I had not approved and very much mistrusted was a sufficient reward." The problem of balancing the requirements of a solitary scholar with those of family life was not as easily remedied. The small, inconvenient Penn's Hill farm house, filled to its rafters with Louisa, John Quincy, George, John, Caroline Johnson, and three live-in helpers, contained all the confusion typical of a household with small, active boys. John Quincy could — and did — escape daily to Peacefields or to Boston or Cambridge. Louisa resented being abandoned — "Mr Adams is constantly immersed in business and of course seldom at home" — but there was little she could do about it.[50]

Had Louisa been happier in Quincy, she might have accommodated herself more readily to John Quincy's absence. But she found the "frequent stiff parties" dull, and she was no closer to having any idea how to comport herself in rural society than she had been a year earlier. To a dancing master's ball, she wore "a small white french lace Cap ornamented on one side with a delicate bunch of Moss Roses; with a simple white India Muslin dress; a pink belt to match the flowers in my Cap and bouquet; and pink Satin Shoes," an ensemble that would have been very much at home in Dolley Madison's drawing room but was "much too simple for the occasion." For several days thereafter, she was "lectured" — presumably by her mother-in-law — for not dressing elaborately enough and forced to apologize "for not knowing better — The error was utter *ignorance* on my part."[51]

Louisa also found herself in the position of playing both cook and gracious hostess in primitive and cramped quarters. Guests, often Adams family members, came fairly regularly for dinner at Penn's Hill. Cooking required tending a fire in a large fireplace and managing heavy pots on long iron hooks; baking meant using a brick "beehive" oven, a notoriously intricate operation involving maintaining bricks at just the proper temperature through judicious regulation of the fire in the fireplace. When a party of ten elegant ladies and gentlemen appeared on her doorstep, Louisa was caught with ashes on her face:

"I was making and baking a Cake, and was obliged to *dress* before I could appear. The rooms of my house were literally too small to hold my company. These Ladies were the elite of Baltimore. There was something truly ridiculous in my position. The shaking off of the kitchen drapery for the parlour finery; and the assumption of the fashionable manners of my Station: was such a transition . . . and I could scarcely fancy that the smoke spots had left me *fair*; when I presented myself to the company." Gone, however, were the days when Louisa claimed an inability (and unwillingness) to accomplish household tasks. On the contrary, she had begun to take pride in her success in managing a complex household under rigorous conditions, caring for her children, and acting as a competent nurse to them and to others in need of her care.[52]

It was with her husband that she appeared most disgruntled. "Mr Adams spent most of his Evenings at his Fathers," she recalled long afterward. As fall approached and his return to the Senate neared, John Quincy became even more remote. "The cares of his family become very oppressive to him and again it is concluded that I am to stay behind," she wrote passively. John Quincy had found a house belonging to a Mr. Gulliver on Poplar Street ("a Street which we none of us ever heard of") on the outskirts of Boston where Louisa, Caroline, and the boys could board for the winter. "Every thing as usual was fixed without a word of consultation with the Family," Louisa complained.[53]

A pattern seemed to have emerged in the Adams marriage. All the ardor and warmth of their correspondence when they were apart seemed to cool when they were together. John Quincy had barely left for Washington in late November when Louisa wrote him, "I already long for your return . . . but, so it is, I can neither live with or without you."[54]

When their weekly correspondence resumed in the winter of 1806–1807, the Adamses had much to communicate. Louisa was again pregnant, and John Quincy craved every detail she could provide concerning her health and that of the boys. He was, if anything, more anxious than usual since, less than a month after his return to Washington, Nancy and Walter Hellen had lost a toddler son to an illness that began with "a fever and sore mouth." His moving account of the child's death and the devastating sorrow that had befallen the boy's parents drew from Louisa a strong plea that he allow himself to show his emotions to others and, especially, to the Hellens. Her analysis of his stiff personality was painfully acute even when her advice was couched kindly: "There are number-less little attentions, trifling in themselves, which it is in our power to offer on such occasions, and which afford the greatest consolation, to the unhappy. Forgive, my friend this observation. I know how much your mind is occupied, and how *almost impossible* it is for you to attend to such circumstances, but I likewise know the goodness of your heart, and am sure you will not feel offended at this suggestion."[55]

Louisa attempted to explain to John Quincy how his reserve could be interpreted as unkindness and how women reacted differently than men to the simplest acts of kindness: "Nancy . . . has repeatedly said, she was convinced you thought her too insignificant, to pay her any sort of attention. Our sex in general, I am convinced, however great their pretentions, can be objects of very little importance to a mind like yours, but my friend, as heaven has made us a part of the Creation, and ordain'd that men even of the *greatest abilities*, should pass the greatest proportion of their lives *with us*; as we are form'd of *such materials*, that even *seeming unkindness bitterly affects us* it ought, (even if it only proceed from a motive of compassion in your sex), to render you *anxious* to offer us those little civilities, which by raising us in our own esteem, inspires us with gratitude; and thereby render us anxiously solicitous, to return by every means in our power, those sweet, and flattering attentions, which form the basis of mans happiness."[56]

John Quincy took her words to heart ("I submit cheerfully to the voice of reproach from you") but admitted he didn't know what was required of him: "For your sake and for that of your Sisters I have often wished that I had been that man of elegant and accomplished manners, who can recommend himself to the regard of others, by *little attentions*. I have always known however that I was not, and have been sensible that I could never be made that man. It has perhaps been natural that my deficiency should be imputed to a deeper, and more inexcusable Cause—to a want of proper sensibility—to an unfeeling heart." There was just enough defensiveness in John Quincy's response, however, to prompt Louisa to confront him on the topic once more: "I was a little surprized at your appearing *so angry* at the observations made in my letter. I merely meant to insinuate that by now and then addressing *her* particularly in conversation and leading her to partake of it, she would feel herself highly flatter'd. This, my testy friend, was all I required, and you must really think me mad, if you supposed that by *little attentions*, I could possibly think of *Chesterfieldian graces*."[57]

In the end, John Quincy wrote a long, heartfelt poem to Nancy, which he portrayed to Louisa as "an attention *in my own way*." Louisa, delighted, thought the poem good enough to be published.

She, Caroline, and the little Adams boys, meanwhile, were enduring the cold of a Massachusetts winter and frequently battling hunger since their landlord regularly scrimped on their meals. The first months of 1807 were exceptionally frigid—Louisa reported the thermometer was often at minus 10° F.—and the house poorly heated. (Abigail briskly informed her son that "the Situation of Mr. Gullivers is very cold and bleak" as well as "much out of the way.") Gulliver, Louisa reported, served "Lilliputian" meals: "You know I never eat a *great deal*, and *it is fortunate*." Despite these hardships, her letters are virtually free of complaints and, instead, display an unaccustomed hardiness during a pregnancy and a steady cheerfulness. Summoned because of the "illness" of Mrs. Gulliver, Louisa found herself assisting in the delivery of the woman's first son: "I was called upon in the night to see her and *inform* her if she was ill. The extreme innocence of the ladies in this part of the Country is perfectly astonishing to me."[58]

For Louisa's thirty-second birthday, John Quincy found time to compose a long, lighthearted poem humorously detailing the events of a typical day in his life. The final stanza is an ode to his wife:

Thus, in succession pass my days,
While Time with flagging pinion flies;
And still the promis'd hour delays,
When *thou* shalt once more charm my eyes.
Louisa! thus remote from thee
Still something to each Joy is wanting;
While thy *affection* can, to me
Make the most dreary Scene enchanting.

By the first week of March, John Quincy was on his way home. Amid much confusion, including a fire on the roof, the family and Caroline moved into their new home, the house at Boylston and Tremont Streets in Boston they had purchased a year earlier. Louisa, expecting a child on a date very close to the anniversary of the birth of her stillborn child a year before, was understandably apprehensive. In her memoirs, she recalled the months after John Quincy's return from Washington with the same resentment at his apparent neglect of her in her "very delicate" condition that colored so many of her recollections: "His attendance at Cambridge [Harvard] was constant and he with my Sister participated in the pleasures of society—and passed almost every week at Quincy going early Saturday afternoon and returning on Monday."[59]

In early June, Caroline received an offer of marriage from Andrew Buchanan, a widower with four children living in Baltimore. Buchanan had first proposed to the beautiful sixteen-year-old in London in the heady days when the three older Johnson sisters were the toast of Tower Hill. Their father had turned the young suitor away, but Caroline, now thirty years old, readily accepted his offer.

After an intimate family wedding at the Adams home on July 21, the celebrations continued for several days with visits, formal dinners, and even a dance.

Less than a month before she was to give birth—still raw from her tragic experience a year earlier and always at risk for complications in pregnancy and childbirth—Louisa played hostess at all these events, even sleeping a night on the nursery floor when all the other bedrooms were given over to guests. At a formal dinner for ten men, she spent the entire time in the kitchen: "It was so essential for Ladies at that time to superintend *all* the arrangements of a dinner both in the culinary and the fixing departments; that they were often obliged to keep behind the Scenes—and though they did not publickly wait on their Lords as the Indian *Ladies* do: they certainly labored as hard and as positively: with less paint to shield their faces from the Steams of Ovens and Stewpans—O the Cakes that have been spoiled and Pies burned!!"[60]

It is a testament to her love for her sister that Louisa exerted herself so strenuously to ensure that Caroline's marriage be properly launched. In the years following her arrival in America in 1801, her bond with all her sisters had strengthened immeasurably. Forgotten were the petty jealousies and intrigues of their adolescence. Year after year in Washington, several Johnson women lived amicably in the same Washington household. Over the same period, Louisa complained about many things but almost never about her sisters and mother. Each time she went north, a sister accompanied her and was warmly welcomed in Quincy and Boston—giving the lie to her contention that the entire Johnson family was tainted in the Adams family's eyes.

Efficient, neat, personable Caroline was a special favorite and had been of particular assistance to her sister in managing both her city and country households, rescuing the infant John Adams II when he had been placed on a cold floor at birth, and appearing at countless social events that Louisa was too ill to attend. Now that Caroline was leaving for good, Louisa, emotionally fragile as childbirth neared, found it difficult to face a future without her: "The idea of losing my loved Sisters society who had ever been so especially dear to me at a moment when my situation required so much soothing care. . . . I fear I behaved very badly."[61]

Two weeks after the newlyweds left Boston for their new home, Louisa took an evening walk in the mall that runs beside Boston Common. At two in the morning, on August 18, her labor began, and as the sun rose, John Quincy was forced into the role of assisting nurse: "My Nurse towards morning was so alarmed at my Situation, that she burst into tears and was sent away and for the first time with my *fourth* Child Mr Adams was with me at the birth to see another *apparently dead Child*—in about half an hour the Child had recovered the play of his lungs, and my husband had witnessed sufferings that he had no idea of." By 9:15 A.M., John Quincy had dispatched a letter to Catherine Johnson: "I take the first moment of self-possession that I have to inform you that my dear wife at half-past eight this morning presented me a third son. The labour which commenced about 2 o'clock this morning was extremely severe, and the child and mother both suffered so much in the birth as to give us great concern." The baby, christened Charles Francis to honor his father's deceased younger brother as well as Francis Dana, whom John Quincy had accompanied to Russia, was apparently a breech birth ("born to be lucky," Louisa assured her mother). Though her baby was soon strong and healthy, Louisa, attempting to leave her bed too soon, had a difficult recovery.[62]

In less than two months, however, she was again on her way to Washington with the infant Charles Francis and John Quincy. Again, her older boys would be left behind by edict of their father. George, now six, would board with Abigail's sister Elizabeth Peabody in Haverhill and attend a school run by her husband in Atkinson, New Hampshire; John, four, would remain in Quincy with Abigail's older sister, Mary Cranch, who regularly took in very small children needing care. Louisa, still weak and absorbed in the care of her baby, protested less than she had previously but nevertheless resented the arrangements made for her two small sons without her participation.

The signs that she was to have less and less influence over the lives of George and John were becoming clear. Over the spring and summer, John Quincy had become a much more demanding parent. In his view, Louisa had been entirely too indulgent of their sons when they were under her sole care during the winter. George, especially, seemed to resist his father's insistence on mastering French and behaving as he should. Ignoring his own near nervous breakdown in his late teens, the untimely death by drinking of his brother Charles, and the "Blue Devils" of depression haunting Tom Adams, John Quincy seemed bent on repeating the parenting patterns set by John and Abigail Adams. Like them, he set virtually unattainable goals and standards for his sons and showed little patience with any failures or deviations from the paths he so clearly set out before them. Louisa, unlike Abigail, was never fully committed to this mode of parenting and thus was not made a full partner in decisions regarding the upbringing of her children. Convinced she was prone to spoiling George and John, John Quincy relegated her to a secondary role in their lives.

Back in Washington, the senior senator from Massachusetts soon placed himself in an untenable position. For nearly all of his political life, his relationship with the party that elected him—the Federalists—had been strained. In the fall of 1807, with the country facing an imminent threat from Great Britain, President Jefferson proposed a general embargo on all shipping in and out of American ports. The embargo was intended to punish Great Britain for its violations of American rights on the high seas by denying the mother country the food and raw materials it needed and to give the United States a more powerful hand in any future negotiations. John Quincy, believing the measure an alternative to outright war, reluctantly voted to support it. His fellow Federalists, influenced strongly by mercantile interests in the Northeast, protested vehemently against the embargo in general and his vote in particular. Writing to his father, whose relationship with Jefferson remained bitter, John Quincy justified his decision to support the administration's international policies and explained the difficult situation he now faced: "My views of present policy, and my sense of the course enjoined upon me by public duty, are so different from those of the federalists that I find myself in constant opposition to them. Yet I have no communication with the Administration . . . [and] the friends of the Executive in the Senate repose little confidence in me." Old John Adams understood and took the occasion to again urge a return to the practice of law: "Your Situation you think critical. I think it is clear, plain and obvious. You are supported by no Party. . . . You ought to know and expect this, and by no means to regret it. Return to your Professorship but above all to your Office as a Lawyer, devote yourself to your Profession and the Education of your Children."[63]

On January 23, John Quincy took the final step that placed him in no-man's-land between the Federalists and the Republicans: he caucused with the Jeffersonians. When Abigail heard of her son's apostasy, she refused to believe published reports: "I have considerd it as inconsistent both with your principles, and your judgment, to have countananced such a meeting by your presence," she wrote. But in his next letter to his son, the former president succinctly begged to disagree: "Your Mother has written you on the Subject of Caucus's. I am not of her opinion."[64]

Now there was nothing left for John Quincy to do but serve out the remainder of the unusually long and busy Senate session before he and Louisa returned to Boston in April. "Mr. Adams was so deeply engrossed with business he had scarcely time to speak to the family; and we had but little conversation on any subject," Louisa acidly remarked in her memoirs. It only remained for John Quincy to resign his position as senator, which he did on June 8, 1808, a day after the Massachusetts Senate named a more reliable Federalist to succeed him for the next senatorial term. Louisa was both relieved she would no longer be torn between Boston and Washington and bitter at the treatment accorded her husband, who continued to be reviled and shunned in his native state after his return: "Thus ended my travels for a time and began a system of persecution painful to our Family but disgraceful to the State of Massachusetts whose Citizens are ever Slaves to a handfull of Men who right or wrong submit to their dictation."[65]

For the next few months, Louisa, John Quincy, their three sons, and Catherine "Kitty" Johnson settled into the life that John Adams had envisioned for them. John Quincy was zealous in his preparation for his Boylston lectures, determined in his efforts to restart his law practice, and indefatigable in his efforts to teach George French.

Life in Boston appeared to be just what Louisa had long desired. "The mere commonplace routine of every day life suits me very well." Pregnant once more, she appeared less prone than usual to fainting, nausea, and other side effects. Her relations with her mother-in-law seemed more amicable even though Louisa rarely journeyed to Peacefields with John Quincy on weekends. Busy with the care of her children, managing her household, entertaining and being entertained, she looked forward to setting permanent roots in a city she had begun to feel was home.[66]

John Quincy was undergoing a much more difficult adjustment to life outside public service, an adjustment not made easier by the "most virulent and unrelenting persecutions" of his Federalist enemies. It was all very well for his father to pronounce that a career at the bar would be automatically successful; John Quincy had recognized from the beginning that the law was not his métier. Even his scholarly activities had foundered. He had written thirty-six Boylston lectures over the past three years and now was repeating the original dozen to a new generation of students. The need for tireless application to his books had passed. Typically, John Quincy fell victim to self-recrimination. ("This day has been shamefully dissipated," he wrote in his diary.)[67]

In January 1809, he seized the opportunity of taking three cases—none of which he thought he could win—to the Supreme Court, then holding its sessions at Long's Tavern on Capitol Hill. He remained in Washington until the Court adjourned in late March. Attending the Court every day, afterward dropping in at the Senate or House to hear the debates, it was clear he simply couldn't stay away from political theater. Meanwhile, the Adamses' marital relationship was unusually frosty. None of their letters that winter contains the ardent expressions of undying affection that had characterized their previous correspondence. Instead, there is a long-running barbed exchange concerning John Quincy's abrupt, "cavalier," and "cold and indifferent" departure and his reasons for it. On January 29, he concluded his letter, "Farewell my dearest *child*," which was either a joking way to let Louisa know that he thought her complaints about his departure were puerile or an insult to the mother of his three children. When she miscarried, following a bad fall on the ice, John Quincy, in nothing like the agonized tones that had greeted previous such events, wrote that, although he was saddened by the news, at least she would be spared the pain of childbirth.[68]

Throughout the winter, John Quincy vehemently denied to relatives and friends that, by being on hand in Washington in case an opening appeared, he was angling for a position in the new Madison administration. He informed his brother Tom that he was definitely not under consideration for secretary of war and assured a worried Louisa that rumors he would be named minister to Russia were false. In fact, they were not. When President Madison sent his nominations to the Senate for confirmation, the name of John Quincy Adams was on the list prominently as the nation's first minister plenipotentiary to the court of Alexander II in St. Petersburg. The Senate, however, swiftly decreed there was no need for such a position. To his mother, John Quincy tried to hide his disappointment: "This Event is I believe, the best for myself and my family; and I hope it is the best for my Country." The following day, he wrote to reassure Louisa, "I believe you will not be much disappointed, at the failure of a proposition to go to Russia—In respect to ourselves and to our Children it would have been attended with more troubles than advantage—I had as little desire as expectation of that or any other appointment, and although I feel myself obliged to the President for his nomination, I shall be better pleased to stay at home, than I should have been to go to Russia."[69]

He was fooling himself—and her. By the Fourth of July, news arrived in Boston that the appointment had been approved. Louisa was devastated. "I had been so grossly deceived, every apprehension lulled," she wrote thirty years later. "And now to come on me with such a shock!—O it was too hard! not a soul entered into my feelings and all laughed to scorn my suffering . . . crying out that it was affectation." John Quincy barely hesitated before accepting the position. On July 5, he wrote that, despite the age of his parents and the youth of his two older sons—whom he would be leaving behind—and "with a deep sense of the stormy and dangerous career upon which I enter," he had no choice but to answer the call of his country. He privately acknowledged, however, that "the satisfaction of being removed at least for a time from a situation where the deepest retirement has not sheltered me from the most virulent and unrelenting Persecution" of his former Federalist friends strongly contributed to his willingness to leave immediately for St. Petersburg.[70]

Louisa's opinion was given no weight in any of John Quincy's deliberations. Acting alone, he swiftly and efficiently engineered all arrangements for their August 5 departure for St. Petersburg. His diary records long conversations with the many young men who wished to accompany him as secretary but never mentions a discussion with his wife. "Every preparation was made without the slightest consultation with me and even the disposal of my Children and my Sister was fixed without my Knowledge until it was too late to Change," Louisa complained with some justification. A maid, Martha Godfrey, and a valet, a free Jamaican known only by his surname, Nelson, would accompany the family. Tom Adams, always a favorite, was deputized to inform Louisa of what everyone knew she did not want to hear. She would be separated from George, eight, and John, six, not for months this time but years. They would be boarded with John Quincy's aunt and uncle, Richard and Mary Cranch, in Quincy, under the broader supervision of his parents, for the duration of the Russian mission.[71]

Louisa would also be prevented from seeing the "old Gentleman" privately since everyone feared she might persuade the former president to advocate another plan. Even John Adams's intervention would have been fruitless, however. John Quincy believed that his mother was better equipped than his wife to train the boys as he wanted them trained and that Louisa belonged at his side. She never forgave him—or herself: "Oh this agony of agonies! can ambition repay such sacrifices? never!!—And from that hour to the end of time life to me will be a succession of miseries only to cease with existence—Adieu to America."[72]

A FLEETING FAIRY TALE

All this was too much like a fairy tale.

—LOUISA CATHERINE ADAMS, *"Adventures of a Nobody"*

Only an unusual woman would willingly embark on an eighty-day ocean voyage in wartime with a two-year-old child in tow. Louisa was not only unwilling, she was "broken-hearted, miserable, *alone* in every feeling." No longer was a proximity to royalty enticing. She knew from bitter experience the embarrassment of a well-worn gown in a fashionable imperial court. Even the companionship of her sister Kitty offered little comfort. Nothing but trouble, Louisa feared, could come from the combustible mix of the flirtatious, attractive Kitty and the three young male aides accompanying John Quincy to Russia.[1]

The path of the *Horace* across the North Atlantic Ocean and the North Sea, through the Skagerrak and Kattegat, and into the Baltic Sea and the Gulf of Finland was fully as hazardous and grueling as Louisa had anticipated. The *Horace* was stopped and boarded eleven times by armed Danish privateers and British sailors and was blocked by a British man-of-war as it attempted to enter the Baltic. Tossed about in terrible storms—one described by John Quincy as a "furious tempest," another as "one of the heaviest gales I ever witnessed"—the bulky merchant ship drifted perilously near the shores of Denmark and Sweden, its rigging snapped and torn, and two of its three anchors lost. By October 17, 1809, John Quincy reported, the captain, pilot, crew, and passengers were all anxious to turn back to a safe port. He declined. "I had no hope," Louisa recalled. "I knew that Mr. Adams would never give up, and we were obliged to make the best of our miserable condition."[2]

Despite everything, Louisa's irrepressible sense of the ridiculous began to reassert itself. Just off the coast of Sweden, she wrote, "in the midst of sickness, distress of mind, weariness of body, constant alarm, & not daring to put [in] our last Anchor for fear we should lose it—we received an invitation to a Ball at the Governors on the Island of [Bornholm] for eight o clock in the Evening while the Vessel was rocking, rolling and pitching as if she would go to pieces—We were obliged to decline the honor."[3]

There was more to come. Finally arriving on October 22 at Kronstadt, St. Petersburg's naval and commercial port, the Adams party was invited to meet the admiral of the fleet: "My Sister and myself wore hats which had been chosen at Copenhagen that we might appear fashionable—and we could scarcely look at one another for laughing: immense Brown Beaver . . . as much too large as our American Bonnets were too small. Thus accoutred, fancy us, immediately from the Ship, usher'd into an immense Saloon at the Admirals House full of elegantly dressed Ladies and Gentlemen staring aghast at the figures just introduced and with extreme difficulty restraining their risibility. It was exquisite beyond all description and too ridiculous in the first moments to be mortifying."[4]

The next morning, as the Adams entourage prepared to travel the last eighteen miles to the imperial capital, word came that the *Horace* had drifted overnight back out to sea with all the family's belongings on board. They were left with only the clothes they were wearing, all inappropriate for entering St. Petersburg in proper ambassadorial style in late October: "Myself in a *white Cambric* Wrapper; my Sister the same; A Child of little more than two years old with only the suit on his back, and the Minister with the Shirt he had on; solus!! We did not appear quite in the Garb of the Aberiginals of our Land but as near as possible to do it honor." Continuing in the same vein, Louisa joked that Charles's introduction to the local drinking water had already affected him so much "it required more than a philosophic Squaw to bear up."[5]

"A philosophic squaw" she was not, but confronting one of the greatest challenges of her life, Louisa demonstrated a resilience and mental toughness she didn't know she had. Hazardous journeys, separations from those she loved best, disagreeable lodgings, illness, and loneliness in an unfamiliar social setting—these were nothing new. But in St. Petersburg, Louisa would also face a harsh, unforgiving climate for much of the year, an ingrown, protocol-ridden nobility prone to extravagance, gossip, and dissipation—"the most futile and the most immoral society in the world," according to a senior diplomat—and the frustration of keeping up appearances on a pitifully inadequate budget.[6]

Separation from her children would be Louisa's heaviest cross to bear. She told Abigail that she submitted to it only because John Quincy needed to escape his unrelenting Federalist foes: "No station however high can ever atone to me for the sacrifices I have made, which nothing could have induced but the state of cruel anxiety and uneasiness in which Mr. A. passed his life in America."[7]

Despite an innate distaste for the emptiness pervading court life and her longing for her sons, Louisa found much to enjoy in St. Petersburg, especially during the family's early years there. Reprising to a lesser extent her social success in Berlin, she made friends in the expatriate community and moved easily in the exalted circles in which the Adamses soon found themselves. She marveled at the paintings and objets d'art on display in the Hermitage, enjoyed a complimentary box at the theater whenever she wished to go, and loved walking in the spectacular imperial gardens in summer. In Russia Louisa also buried her only daughter, suffered three miscarriages and chronic ill health, and endured loneliness as her husband withdrew from family life into a comprehensive study of weights and measures. The six long years she spent in Russia would be a defining experience in her life.

St. Petersburg in 1809 was a gloriously beautiful city—Pushkin's "lovely wonder of the North." Built by forced labor out of a swamp only a century earlier, the imperial capital had been intended by Peter the Great to be Russia's "window on the West." Criss-crossed by canals and bisected by the great River Neva, the city appeared, like Venice, to be rising out of water. Townhouses in pastel hues, the great, gold-domed St. Isaac's Cathedral, palatial riverfront mansions, straight, wide boulevards, and spacious gardens—all were fully as magnificent as those in any European capital.

Behind the elegant facades, however, lurked some less attractive realities. The Adamses' first lodging, the Hotel de Londres, on the city's main boulevard, the Nevsky Prospekt, was ridden with vermin. Fearing for Charles's safety, Louisa could not rest: "The Chamber I lodged in was a stone hole entered by Stone passages and so full of rats that they would drag the braid from the table by my bed side which I kept for the Child and fight all night long—and my nerves became perfectly shattered with the constant fright least they should attack the Child."[8]

Everyone in the Adams party immediately became violently ill from the city's drinking water. When they could venture out, John Quincy and Louisa, together and independently, searched the city for more suitable lodgings, but every place they saw was either inappropriate or far too expensive. Neither wished to remain at the Hotel de Londres any longer than necessary, but there were other, equally pressing concerns. On his arrival in St. Petersburg, John Quincy had been informed by the resident American consul, Levett Harris, that he needed an entirely new wardrobe in his official ministerial role. "Not a particle of the cloathing I brought with me have I been able to present myself in," he wrote his mother the following February. Within three days of setting foot in Russia—and after frenzied sessions "with tailors, hatters, wigmakers, shoemakers, milliners and the like description"—John Quincy was equipped to present his official papers to Count Nikolai Petrovich Romanzoff, the tsar's imperial chancellor. Louisa thought her husband looked "very handsome all but the Wig. O horrid! which entirely disfigured his countenance and not to his advantage." Nonetheless, America's first formal ministerial connection to the Russian government had been made, and John Quincy was launched on what would be one of the signal diplomatic achievements in his long and extraordinary career.[9]

Russia, when the Adamses arrived, was enjoying a brief period of relative quiet—the "peace" in Tolstoy's *War and Peace*. Emperor Alexander I, just thirty-two, ruled the largest state in Europe in area and population during what has been called the "apogee of Russian international power and prestige in the prerevolutionary period." The young, handsome tsar, who had come to power in 1801 when his father was assassinated—with, it was rumored, the son's tacit consent—was a man of contradictions: Abhorring the serfdom of 90 percent of his subjects, he failed during his twenty-four-year reign to produce a constitution or to improve the lot of the subservient masses; a believer in world peace, he did not hesitate to take his army into war; at first very much in love with his wife, he was later blatantly unfaithful to her; and despite being imbued by his Swiss tutor with Enlightenment principles, he became a religious mystic at the end of his life. Such was his personal charm, however, that the normally impassive John Quincy would later describe the tsar to Louisa as the "darling of the human race."[10]

In 1807 Alexander had led his army into a disastrous confrontation with Napoleon at Friedland, on the border with Prussia, in which some 25,000 Russian troops were lost. Napoleon, having already defeated Austria at Ulm and at Austerlitz in 1805 and Prussia the following year at Jena-Auerstadt, was at the peak of his domination of Europe. He decided to stop at Russia's border in order to turn his full attention to defeating his most persistent and dangerous enemy, England. The Treaty of Tilsit, signed by Alexander and Napoleon in a pavilion erected on a raft anchored in the middle of the River Nieman on July 7, 1807, placed imperial France and imperial Russia in an uneasy defensive and offensive alliance that lasted for the next five years.[11]

Although Napoleon presented the treaty as a partnership and made some minor concessions to Alexander, the agreement essentially benefited the French conqueror. Most important, Alexander pledged to join Napoleon's Continental

System, which Napoleon set up to deny Britain access to European ports. Such a strategy, had it been successful, would have wreaked havoc on the island kingdom. Using a number of stratagems and issuing trade sanctions of her own, however, Britain managed not only to survive the embargo but to profit from it.

The United States, determinedly neutral in the conflicts raging on European soil and on the world's trade routes, was primarily interested in freedom of the seas in order to conduct its maritime commerce without continual harassment by either Britain or France. Each nation presented a special threat to American shipping interests. Britain made it a practice to sail its merchant ships, complete with forged American customs and other documents, under the American flag and to board U.S. ships to seize sailors it claimed were English by birth. France and its ally Denmark, with some justification, believed that many ships flying the Stars and Stripes were actually British merchantmen intent on evading the Continental System's embargo and felt no hesitation in boarding and detaining any purportedly American vessel.

Russia, deprived by the Treaty of Tilsit of its former lively trade with Britain, was eager to promote a strong commercial alliance with America and to use U.S. merchant ships as carriers for Russian goods to the rest of the world. For the United States, Russian-American trade was particularly profitable—in 1809, one tenth of all U.S. exports went to Russia—and the cargoes of hemp, sail-cloth, and iron that left St. Petersburg for ports on America's Eastern seaboard and returned to Russia with sugar, rice, and indigo were vital to the economies of both nations.[12]

John Quincy's assignment was to foster good will between the United States and Russia and secure favorable markets in Russia for American goods. In this, he was a success from the outset. As the newly arrived minister plenipotentiary approached the tsar at his formal presentation on November 5, 1809, Alexander stepped forward to greet him warmly. "I am delighted to have the pleasure of seeing you here." Taking John Quincy by the arm, he led him to a tall window overlooking the Neva—perhaps to avoid being overheard—and laid out in detail the tenets of Russian foreign policy vis-à-vis the United States, Austria, Prussia, France, and Britain. Everything the tsar had to say was welcome to John Quincy. Alexander pronounced Madison's neutralist policy "wise and just" and said America could rely on him to do nothing to change or hinder it. "That in everything depending upon him, he should be happy to contribute towards increasing the friendly intercourse" between Russia and the United States, John Quincy reported to Secretary of State Robert Smith.[13]

Had the American mission to Russia been limited to facilitating the burgeoning trade between the two nations or ascertaining which ships entering

Russian ports under American flags were actually from America, President Madison could have dispatched another representative, preferably someone with experience in international commerce. But Madison wanted more. He chose instead a man with diplomatic experience, political acumen, and the prestige of a former president's son to represent the young American nation in St. Petersburg. In Russia the will of the tsar was absolute, especially in foreign policy. It was essential that America's minister plenipotentiary understand both the personality of the ruler and the complex relationships of the men and women who surrounded him. To obtain access to the imperial court at its highest levels, a man of stature was required. John Quincy, in many ways, was a brilliant choice. He was diligent, observant, analytical, and dogged in ensuring that the interests of the United States be taken into consideration in any foreign policy discussions that affected the young nation, and he established a relationship between Russia and the United States that remained strong well into the nineteenth century. Biographer Samuel Flagg Bemis judged his tenure a "uniform success," and the historian Alfred W. Crosby, Jr., concurred: "Never again, not even as president, did John Quincy Adams stand as near the center of the stage of world history as during his stay in St. Petersburg." The influential French ambassador by early 1811 reluctantly conceded, "It seems you are a great favorite here. You have found powerful protection."[14]

Oddly enough, it may have been John Quincy's lifelong habit of taking long daily walks that played a significant part in his warm relationship with the tsar. Alexander, too, was a solitary walker. His erect, unaccompanied figure was a regular presence along the quays that lined the city's river and canals. The two men chatted together frequently when they met. Never ostensibly about business, their brief conversations ranged from the weather to John Quincy's finances to the tsar's despair in the face of what appeared in 1812 to be inevitable war. Freed from the formalities of the court and its listening ears, both men appeared to speak naturally. Both also used their frequent informal talks to obtain or offer information. In one typical exchange, the tsar expressed surprise that a recent American arrival seemed to have no obvious business in Russia. To travel from the United States to St. Petersburg, he remarked, was not like crossing the Neva. John Quincy replied that the traveler in question was a wealthy young man with wanderlust, but added, "My countrymen, Sire, are so familiarized with the ocean that they think not much more of crossing it than going over a river." In this seemingly casual conversation, Alexander let the American know that he was kept apprised of the presence of any new foreign visitors to the capital, and John Quincy was able both to affirm the young man's bona fides and to boast of American seagoing prowess.[15]

John Quincy fit immediately into the diplomatic corps. He knew the rules of the game and was acquainted with many of the players. Within a week of his arrival, he attended a dinner at the magnificent palace that was the French embassy—"a gorgeous scene"—and reunited with many old acquaintances from his previous postings at The Hague and Berlin. Although he had no time for fools, he readily entered into conversations with those of his colleagues who read widely, especially in the classics, or who had interesting things to say on politics, science, or the arts.

It was, of course, at dinners, balls, levees, and receptions that bargains were struck, personal slights leveled, and royal or imperial favor registered. Much of the information diplomats transmitted by cipher to Paris, Vienna, Berlin, London, or Washington was gathered informally. The diplomatic community in St. Petersburg was an insular one. United by their common use of the French language, typically aristocratic backgrounds, and similar experiences in various European capitals, the group was exceptionally congenial. All held the secondary rank of minister except Armand-Augustin-Louis de Caulaincourt, Duc de Vicence, the French ambassador and close friend and confidant of Napoleon, whose influence in the capital was second only to the tsar's. Everyone was frustrated by how difficult it was to pry information from a foreign office in which lesser officials were forbidden to associate with foreign diplomats. Despite the luxurious lifestyle of the city's elite, nearly all considered an assignment to St. Petersburg a hardship post. Most refused to subject their wives to the harsh Russian winter and the exorbitant expenses associated with a diplomatic post in its glittering capital. Thus, Louisa was often the only diplomatic spouse in residence during the period the family lived in St. Petersburg.[16]

In Berlin, Louisa had almost instantly developed a wide circle of female friends—royalty and nobility, Englishwomen married to German counts, wives of diplomats assigned to the Prussian capital, and women, like Dr. Brown's wife, who provided islands of English hospitality and respite from the rigors of court life. Many of these women stayed in touch with her for years—when she passed through Berlin on her epic journey from St. Petersburg to Paris in 1815, they welcomed her as a beloved daughter and sister. But St. Petersburg was different. Russian noblewomen, Louisa explained to Abigail, were "cold and haughtily repulsive in their manners but there is at the same time a degree of freedom and unrestraint which is utterly impossible to describe. Every thing like wit or superior sense is entirely exploded and nothing but sentiment of the most languishing and susceptible kind can be tolerated."[17]

In Berlin, the distinction shown Louisa by the charismatic Queen Louise had signaled to the court that the wife of the American minister was to be made welcome. In Russia, the reigning empress, although she was unfailingly gracious to her American acquaintance, enjoyed only a fraction of the influence of the Prussian royal consort, and Louisa was never as warmly accepted by aristocratic Russian women. The few expatriate British and European women in the city, however, made Louisa immediately welcome, and, characteristically, she soon forged immediate and lasting bonds with the English-speaking Annette Krehmer, wife of the tsar's German banker, known for her hospitality to British and American visitors, and Mme. Marie Colombi, also of English heritage and the young wife of the Spanish consul. ("She is so gay; so sensible; and so attractive it is impossible to know her without loving her.") Nonetheless, her circle of friends was necessarily more constricted than it had been in Berlin.[18]

With so few kindred spirits, Louisa's life would have been unbearably lonely had Kitty Johnson not been on the scene. Pretty, sparkling Kitty had the endearing personality characteristic of so many of the Johnson women. Abigail had been completely won over during the year Kitty spent in Boston before the family embarked for Russia, and it was apparently her idea for Kitty to go to St. Petersburg. To Catherine Johnson, she wrote fondly and perceptively, "I do love Kitty sincerely. I think her a charming girl and tho not the most beautifull of your family, she is not the less amiable . . . [because of] her wit . . . the easy affibility of her manners. . . . she was noticed caressed and esteemed by all her acquaintance. I think she has stronger marks of her descent from you than any of your other daughters. I solicited and encouraged her accompanying her sister—how solitary must she have been in a foreign country without a single female companion!"[19]

Because Kitty had no official role in the American mission to St. Petersburg, she could not be formally presented to the imperial family, and although she was welcomed at diplomatic balls and at parties hosted by American merchants and others, she was not at first invited to events at the Winter Palace. Instead, she made friends with St. Petersburg's younger social set and happily flirted with John Quincy's aides. Inaccurate rumors reached Boston almost immediately that she and Francis Gray had become engaged.[20]

In the early spring of 1810, Kitty came to the attention of the tsar when he encountered her with Louisa during his—and their—regular walks along the banks of the Neva. After they had missed their promenades for a day or two, the tsar made a point of telling Louisa he expected to meet both her and her sister daily on the quay. "This was a real Imperial command in its tone and manner," she reported. Kitty thought the whole thing something of a joke, but John Quincy could see the possible political implications of the tsar's apparent interest in his wife's sister. His young aides, Kitty's self-proclaimed champions, urged her to resist the tsar's order. "The Minister looked very *grave* but said nothing—The young Gentlemen disapproved and hoped that we should not do it," Louisa recalled.[21]

Kitty may not have been completely aware of the tsar's notorious woman-izing, but the men of the American mission certainly knew of his infidelities, and it is likely that Louisa was also aware of them. Alexander's longtime mistress, Maria Naryshkina, paraded her many pregnancies at court, much to the distress of the empress, who had lost two daughters within eighteen months of their births and was apparently unable to have more children. Meanwhile, the tsar's other, shorter-lived affairs with dancers and actresses were openly acknowl-edged. John Quincy, ever a realist, had not allowed Alexander's liaison with Mme. Naryshkina to diminish his wholehearted hero worship—"The Emperor makes it a point of honor to allow no political influence to the woman by whom he has children because she is beautiful and he is young and fond of pleasure"—but he had no interest in encouraging an imperial relationship with his sister-in-law. "She has no influence at all. She is the last person in the world through whom anything could be obtained."[22]

Believing, however, that they had no choice but to take their regular walks and, necessarily, encounter the tsar, Louisa and Kitty continued to do so, often with little Charles by the hand. In May, Alexander telegraphed his interest in Kitty to the court and to the diplomatic correspondents and spies reporting to their home governments. At a grand party at the French embassy he danced the opening polonaise with Louisa—a signal honor much noticed by all in atten-dance, including John Quincy—and then informed her he was off to find her sister. "[He] took her out himself to dance and she not knowing the ettiquettes began laughing and talking to him as she would have done to an American partner, herself beginning the conversation contrary to all usages du Monde—and he was so charmed with the novelty that he detained Caulaincourt's Supper twenty-five minutes to prolong the Polonaise." With a "buzz of astonishment" the gossip mills began to grind. But summer was coming, the imperial family left St. Petersburg for their summer palace a few miles away, and the scandalous whispers died down. In October, as the winter social season resumed, however, Alexander invited the Adamses and, specifically, Kitty to attend a performance at his exclusive theater within the Hermitage and gave orders that the vivacious American should henceforth be accepted at court as if she had been formally presented. "This is considered one of the greatest honors ever conferred upon a foreign young Lady," Louisa wrote, noting also that the invitation to the Hermitage itself was an exceptional privilege for herself and John Quincy, never granted to anyone under the rank of full ambassador, and showed "the great partiality of the Emperor for my husband."[23]

With Kitty's invitation to the Hermitage, tongues again began to wag. In November, as the two sisters walked on the quay, Louisa spotted the emperor hurrying to approach them. She called for a carriage, bundled her sister into it, and left the scene before Alexander reached them. "The great distinction shown to my Sister, as the Invitation to the Hermitage had occasioned so much talk I thought it was injudicious to encourage it," Louisa wrote later. Alexander was insulted, and the next time they met, "turned his head away and did not look" at the two American women. Louisa now became concerned that John Quincy would suffer if the entire imperial establishment adopted, as it invariably did, the position of the emperor and proceeded to shun the minister plenipotentiary. But the emperor relented and again ordered Louisa and Kitty—for their health—to take daily walks where he hoped to encounter them. John Quincy stayed above it all. "The Minister took no notice," Louisa wrote, and as war with France approached, the tsar's mind moved to matters far more significant than the attractions of a sprightly American girl.[24]

Kitty continued to play an essential supporting role in the family's life in St. Petersburg, however. Always ready to accompany Louisa on the piano, attend major events with John Quincy when Louisa was ill, and play with Charles, she was also an unpaid and unheralded diplomatic asset. Other diplomatic missions, lacking pretty women, had to make do with charming young men who could perhaps woo an unsuspecting bureaucrat's wife into revealing a state secret while being waltzed around the dance floor. The wily Sardinian minister, Joseph de Maistre—a diplomat much admired for his intellect by John Quincy—requested that his sovereign, Victor Emmanuel I, send him as secretary not only a young man who was a fine dancer, conversationalist, and musician but someone "who would serve me as an informer with the women to learn the secrets of their husbands."[25]

But even as he appreciated the need to conduct business by inference and intuition in social settings, John Quincy resented the toll the effort took on his health, literary pursuits, and finances, and he found the formalities of court life inane. "So trifling and insignificant in themselves and so important in the eyes of Princes and courtiers. . . . It is not safe or prudent to despise them; nor practicable for a person of rational understanding to value them," he wrote. As the sympathetic Bemis concedes in an epic understatement, the meaninglessness of spending evening after evening in uncomfortable formal dress at court balls and diplomatic dinners "did not suit his [John Quincy's] temper perfectly." Although John Quincy's diary and Louisa's memoirs agree that there were many nights she attended gala events accompanied by one or more of the minister's aides instead of her husband, Bemis credits him with never shirking "in body or in spirit, the inevitable tours of hospitality. He talked brightly through the long dinners; he discreetly sampled the liqueurs of his Russian hosts; he walked the polonaise at the court balls and diplomatic dances."[26]

A harsher, more contemporary view was offered by one of John Quincy's well-placed young aides, John Spear Smith, a nephew of Secretary of State Robert Smith and son of Senator Samuel Smith from Maryland. Referring to John Quincy as the "mute in Siberia," he complained to his father that the older man had "never communicated to me one thing he has done." Claiming to be "on the best of terms" with the American minister, Smith continued, "He is an unfortunate appointment for this Court. He has no manners, is gauche, never was intended for a foreign Minister. . . . You would blush to see him in any society, and particularly at Court circles, walking about perfectly listless, speaking to no one, and absolutely looking as if he were in a dream. . . . Dry sense alone does not do at European Courts. Something more is necessary, which something Mr. A. does not possess."[27]

Smith was not alone. The waspish Lord William Henry Lyttelton, a British politician who knew John Quincy in St. Petersburg and later in London, was scathing in his denunciation of the American's social skills: "Of all the men whom it was ever my lot to accost and to waste civilities upon, [Adams] was the most dogged and systematically repulsive. With a vinegar aspect, cotton in his leathern ears, and hatred of England in his heart, he sat in the frivolous assemblies of Petersburg like a bull-dog among spaniels, and many were the times that I drew monosyllables and grim smiles from him and tried in vain to mitigate his venom."[28]

If John Quincy cultivated the image of the flinty and unsociable—but invariably honest—New Englander in an effort to distinguish himself from the superficial, dissolute men and women surrounding him, he was successful. He took pride in his charmlessness, but his reputation for incivility would follow him for the rest of his life. Not all of this was merited. John Quincy could not have achieved the success he did if, in fact, his manners were as boorish as Smith and Lord Lyttelton depicted. Nor, unless his contemporaries were completely blinded by their personal dislike of the man, could he have been the polished and personable—if reluctant—courtier that Bemis portrays. Lost in these assessments of John Quincy's skill in negotiating St. Petersburg's intricate social landscape lies an essential reason why America's first diplomatic mission to Russia was the success it is universally credited to be. Standing in plain sight—but unnoticed by Bemis, Smith, or Lord Lyttelton—was Louisa Catherine Adams.[29]

Louisa perfectly appreciated the political significance of the role she was to play. In her son Charles's words, "She was destined to be the first lady presented to the notice of the Russian court as a representative of American female manners and character." Most historians, relying only on John Quincy's published Russian diary—particularly the version edited by Charles, which omits many homely, personal details—have failed to recognize that Louisa's perfect French, graceful performance of the polonaise, Continental sophistication, and genuine interest in the many new people she met would turn out to be incalculable assets to the first American mission to Russia.[30]

Throughout her married life, Louisa would prove herself exceptionally adept in social situations with political implications. Her skill in coping with court etiquette and making friends at every level of society had been honed in Berlin. Now in the even loftier purlieus of the Winter Palace and the only slightly less sumptuous surroundings in which the Russian nobility, the diplomatic corps, and the foreign merchants residing in St. Petersburg passed their extravagant lives, her task was doubly difficult. Painfully conscious throughout her Russian tenure of her inability to return the hospitality she enjoyed from others and to dress in a style consistent with the court's norms, she still could appreciate the incredible opulence in which she found herself.

Her account of her presentation to the imperial family, for example, vividly describes both the theatrics of the moment and her refusal to take herself entirely seriously:

> Dressed in a Hoop with a Silver tissue skirt with a train a heavy crimson Velvet Robe with a very long train lined with White body [stiffening] and sleeves trimmed with a quantity of Blond [lace]; my hair simply arranged and ornamented with a small diamond Arrow—White Satin Shoes gloves Fan etc. and over all this *luggage* my Fur Cloak. I was attended by two footmen—and thus accoutred I appeared before the Gentlemen of our party who could not refrain from laughter at my appearance.
>
> Arrived at the Palace after ascending with great difficulty in the adjustment of my trappings I was received by a Gentleman and shown in a long and large Hall in which I found Countess Litta. . . . She placed me in the centre of the Hall fronting a large folding door and informed me that the Empress would enter by that door and that I must stand unmoved until her Imperial Majesty walked up to me—that when she came up I must affect to kiss her hand which her Majesty would not *permit* and that I must take my Glove off so as to be ready and take care in raising my head not to touch her Majesty.[31]

She went on to describe the splendidly dressed African footmen "with drawn Sabres with gold handles" who were stationed at the doors of a series of long, mirrored halls through which the emperor and empress processed, followed by a train of gentlemen and ladies-in-waiting, all in full dress. Finally, having performed the proper formalities to the imperial couple, Louisa was presented to the dowager empress, who, as a result of a law promulgated by the late emperor, actually outranked her daughter-in-law. Expecting the young American to be awed by the glories of St. Petersburg, the empress appeared to be taken aback—"*Ah mon dieu vous avez tout vue!!* [My God, you have seen everything]" she exclaimed when Louisa "expressed in strong language [her] admiration of every thing and mentioned that [she] had seen London, Paris, Berlin and Dresden, etc. but that [she] had certainly [seen] no City that equaled St Petersburg in beauty." Gloated Louisa afterward: "The Savage had been expected!!"[32]

Unlike her husband who often saw little humor and less to enjoy in his formal interactions with the imperial and diplomatic community, Louisa continued to find entertainment in her encounters with the highest levels of Russian society. Just as in Berlin, her memoirs are full of little word portraits, snippets of dialogue, and descriptions of food, décor, and costume, all recorded with evident delight. Describing one party at the French embassy, she confirmed she had inherited her mother's quick tongue: "The Ambassador told me *I* was too serious for a pretty woman; and that when 'we were at Rome we must do as Rome [does].' I told him if I should go to Rome perhaps I might."[33]

Sexual innuendoes never shocked her, but crude remarks made her angry. At a dinner at which she was seated between two desiccated courtiers who sought to amuse—or discomfit—her with their stories of former conquests, she could barely contain her revulsion: "I was perfectly enragé which was very foolish. . . . What on earth is so disgusting as two old men chuckling over their past follies and vices!!!" With the tsar, she was her natural self. At one ball, Alexander, knowing from his informants that Louisa was pregnant, assigned a courtier to escort her throughout the evening so she would not be jostled by the crowd. As the evening wore on, "he again accosted me and insisted that I should go and sit by the Empress who sat on an elevated Seat, attended by her Ladies—I thankfully declined the honor—when he insisted and said Don't you know that no one says Nay to the Emperor—I laughed and replied but I am a republican—He smiled and went on his way."[34]

Louisa loved to describe the gold and silver dinnerware, the splendid uniforms of the servants, the elaborate interiors of the grand palaces of diplomats and wealthy merchants she frequented nearly every evening during the long dark winters. At an imperial ball at the Hermitage, she was enchanted by the gorgeousness of the setting: "The illuminations exceed all description and the Pictures, vases, and rich ornaments of every description produce an effect perfectly dazzling to the eyes and the imagination." Recognizing the spectacle for what it was — "All this was too much like a fairy tale" — she could still take pleasure in the glittering social whirl while deploring its essential meaningless-ness. Night after night, the lavish parties continued. Depicting her daily life in a New Year's letter to Abigail, Louisa reported, "It is customary here to go to bed at 4 o-clock in the morn! and to rise at 11, dine at 5, take Tea at 10, and sup at one. The rest of time you are expected to pass in your Carriage paying a perpetual round of visits which are never finished and concluding the evening at some party and supper."[35]

Even two-year-old Charles was not immune. At a fancy-dress children's ball just before Christmas 1809, he appeared as an American Indian chief "to gratify the taste for Savages." Following a formal dance, the forty children under twelve were treated to "an elegant supper with oceans of champagne" while their mothers in formal evening clothes and lavish jewels stood behind their chairs. Sadly, Charles, still only two, was not allowed to take part in a lottery of "expen-sive toys" since John Quincy did not want his son either to gamble or to acquire a taste for luxury. Nonetheless, Charles had made a remarkable first impression: "He has been the admiration of Petersburg and has had the honor of being presented to their imperial Majesties who *played* with him near an hour, the Empress on her knees looking at some prints with which Charles was very much pleased. They both speak English very well and his Majesty told Mr A. he was a most charming Child," Louisa reported to the boy's proud grandmother in Quincy.[36]

Following a painful miscarriage in February 1810, Louisa quickly resumed her social obligations. After only a few months, it was clear that the pretty American wife and mother had succeeded in charming the imperial family, the diplomatic corps, and the many American and British merchants marooned for the winter in St. Petersburg whom she entertained at dinner until the ice broke in the Neva in May. Keenly appreciating the importance of her role as America's unappointed representative, Louisa was characteristically modest about her success. She claimed "neither my husband or myself ever [had] expected such distinctions" as they regularly received from the emperor and his entourage — it was all a tribute to the United States: "I presume these honors were offered as compliments to the Country, this being the first regular Mission from America."[37]

There were a few missteps. When Count Romanzoff arrived "in his State Coach with six Horses, outriders, [three] footmen with Flambeau's all in full dress" to visit not the American minister but his wife and when the empress's sister came specifically to call on her, Louisa refused to admit either visitor — "not being aware of the intended honor and our apartments very mean." Earlier, having declined an invitation from the dowager empress to a ball on the grounds of ill health but actually because she had "but one dress in which I had already appeared several times," she went off to spend "a delightful evening" with Marie Colombi. Discovering the ruse, the dowager empress made it clear the American minister's wife should not try that ploy again. Louisa accepted the reprimand ruefully, "especially as I had heard her tell a Lady who had worn the same gown several times that she 'wished that *She* (the Lady) would get another, for that *She* was tired of seeing the same colour so often.'" Louisa would not repeat these diplomatic faux pas, but the situation that prompted them — the family's "mean" lodgings and her own limited wardrobe — remained as problematic as ever.[38]

As Louisa well understood, everything she wore made a political statement, and in Russia she faced a nearly impossible dilemma. If she dressed inappropriately in homemade calico at an official function that called for silk, diamonds, and elaborate lace, the reputation of the United States would suffer in a court with little else to do but gossip about appearances. Similarly, any attempt by Louisa to scale St. Petersburg's heights of fashion would bankrupt her husband, and she — and he — would be reviled in America.

Her immediate problem was not political but financial. There was simply not enough money available to dress the entire family adequately. Even Kitty had to have proper clothes in order to go out in St. Petersburg society, and she, unfortunately, was "entirely dependent, without one sixpence in the world, not even clothed properly when she started." In a letter to his mother, John Quincy, never known to be sensitive to the niceties of fashion, acknowledged that providing himself with an entirely new wardrobe had cost much more than he had foreseen and that "the cost of a Lady's dress is far more expensive and must be more diversified than that of a man." Recognizing the importance of dress in a world where everyone was judged by appearances, he supported his wife's efforts to find a way for the family to appear minimally well dressed, but he was not prepared to spend a penny more than necessary to accomplish that goal.[39]

Louisa was forced to be creative. Her first letter home, written in great haste so that a ship leaving port before the ice set in for the winter could carry it to Boston, consisted almost entirely of a very specific list of items for Abigail to purchase: "Six pieces of Cambric Cotton at about a Dollar and 7s. 6d. a yard half Wide, 1 Piece of yd Wide Muslin for Cravats, some fine Cotton stockings, some of the Clear Net Muslins which are very fashionable here . . . in short any thing light or gauzy and 6 yd of Lace Muslin (White) with a Piece of Dimity of the Cambric kind ... Pink and blue Ginghams. P.S. I forgot to mention some knit Drawers which may be had at [Mrs.] Spragues they must be worsted yarn."⁴⁰

The desired items would not arrive for several months. Meanwhile, Louisa became desperate to find a way to make do: "I have tried every experiment even that of dressing in Mourning but it would not answer, and our motive was suspected," she lamented. Her inadequate wardrobe eventually forced John Quincy to relax his usual rule against accepting expensive gifts from anyone with whom he had business and to permit Louisa and Kitty each to accept a lovely embroidered Turkish shawl from Harris, the consul, who "had suffered agonies at the idea that american ladies should appear without such indispensables."⁴¹

Fortunately for Louisa, the prevailing fashion in the Russian court in the early years of the nineteenth century—except for formal dress like that prescribed for her presentation to the imperial family—was modeled on the Grecian style of the French Empress Josephine. High-waisted and low-necked, both day and evening gowns in light, flowing cambric or muslin fell to the floor in soft folds. This was a style Louisa and Kitty could construct for themselves or hire a relatively inexpert seamstress to make for them as long as they could obtain the requisite materials. It was also a style that depended on impressive jewels and elaborate trim to set truly wealthy, fashionable women apart from those whose family coffers were not overflowing with rubies and Brussels lace. Here the two Johnson sisters could never compete.⁴²

No one expected the new American nation to mount the same display of wealth and elegance as the triumphant French. Caulaincourt's official expenses alone were $350,000 a year in 1810 American currency. Russian officials typically lived far beyond their incomes, and the diplomatic corps was expected to keep up with their extravagant lifestyles. This was anathema to John Quincy, who was determined that he and his family would live within his salary—$9,000, with another $9,000 available for the costs of travel and getting settled in. Although the stipend paid to America's minister plenipotentiary to Russia was second only to the $25,000 salary of the president of the United States, it was a laughable sum in a city where expenses were astronomical. Offers by wealthy friends of the Adams family to underwrite expenses were turned down by the minister plenipotentiary, who spent hours each day trying to manage his household accounts.⁴³

For eight months, the family was "indifferently lodged at a public house and very expensively" in John Quincy's view. By the spring of 1810 when they finally found a suitable rental—"a very handsome house," Louisa said—the size of the household staff had surged out of control. A steward, a cook, two scullions, a porter, two footmen, a peasant to make the fires, a coachman and a postilion, a housemaid, a laundry maid, John Quincy's valet, and Louisa's personal maid constituted a barely adequate staff by St. Petersburg standards. Louisa told Abigail that the family, with only fourteen servants, had gained the reputation of living "très petitement" [very poorly] and that she was "perpetually told that [she had] not enough to do the common business of the family." Three of the Russian servants were married, and they and their children all lived with the Adamses. "I have baker's, milkman's, butcher's, greengrocerman's, poulterer's fishmonger's and grocer's bills to pay monthly, besides purchases of tea coffee, sugar, wax and tallow candles. . . . On all these articles of consumption the cook and steward first make their profits on the purchase, and next make free pillage of the articles themselves. The steward takes the same liberty with my wines," John Quincy complained in December 1810, a year after the family's arrival in St. Petersburg.[44]

Unfortunately, he didn't comprehend the extent of the fraud being perpetrated on him by his steward until more than two years later when he discovered he was missing 373 bottles of wine, including his choicest and costliest vintages. He also discovered that although his household accounts indicated that purveyors of bread, milk, and other necessities were fully paid up, in fact his steward had pocketed the cash and made off with some of the goods. As a result, merchants were clamoring to be paid. In the midst of this "trouble and anxiety," John Quincy decided to purchase an accurate set of weights and measures so he would never be cheated again. When it became clear to him that standards in such measurements varied widely, an irresistible opportunity to indulge his scientific bent presented itself. "There is something in these enquiries about weights and measures singularly fascinating to me," he wrote in his diary at the beginning of a long and fruitful investigation.[45]

Louisa, in letters home, echoed John Quincy's complaints concerning their household expenses. The costs in Russia, she wrote, were "insupportable," and every bill she presented to her husband "makes ruin stare him in the face." She offered to go home to live as simply as possible in Quincy, but John Quincy refused. Abigail, who had consistently held to the belief that the salaries paid to diplomatic representatives were insulting and damaging to the status of the United States abroad, decided to take matters into her own hands. In August 1810, she wrote to President Madison requesting that he recall her son on the basis of financial hardship. Explaining her intervention in a letter to Catherine Johnson, she wrote, "The salary of a Foreign minister, as I know by woeful experience is too narrow and constricted to reside with a family at any foreign court. . . . So that I do not see any way for Mr. Adams to save himself and his family from total ruin but by requesting a speedy recall."[46]

Madison, in a handwritten letter to the former First Lady from his home, Montpelier, in Virginia, informed her that he had agreed to her request: "I have accordingly desired the Secretary of State to let him [John Quincy] understand that as it was not the purpose of the Executive to subject him to the personal sacrifices which he finds unavoidable, he will not, in retiring from them, impair the sentiments which led to his appointment."[47]

The president also wrote a personal letter to John Quincy expressing his hope that the "peculiar urgency manifested in the letter of Mrs. Adams was rather hers than yours," but enclosing a formal letter to the tsar recalling John Quincy to the United States that the American minister could present to Alexander any time he wished. The president emphasized that although he did not want the Adamses to undergo unbearable hardship, he would much prefer that they remain in St. Petersburg.[48]

Madison apparently believed that John Quincy's recall after only a year in Russia might be misinterpreted in the United States as presidential dissatisfaction with his performance and in Russia as an indication that America was withdrawing its high-level representation in St. Petersburg because of some breach between the two nations. Neither was true, but that would not stop rumors from circulating. The president soon solved his own dilemma. In February 1811 he nominated John Quincy to fill a vacancy as an associate justice on the Supreme Court, and the Senate unanimously approved the nomination. The appointment to the high court clearly expressed Madison's regard for his minister and was intended to be read that way in both Washington and St. Petersburg.

Old John Adams saw the Supreme Court appointment as the answer to his fondest prayers. His son would be coming home to a suitably prestigious position but one that would never expose him to the level of partisan and personal attacks he had suffered in elective office. He would be safely above politics in a context in which his fine mind would find ample scope to engage the complex issues facing the still-new United States. A regular salary would be his for life. "It is a compleat Justification for your Return to your native Country," the ex-president wrote John Quincy as soon as he learned the news.

Conceding that John Quincy "did not love the law so well as other Studies" and had often been heard to express "some aversion to acting in the character of a judge," his father was undaunted: "This I hope you will easily get over." In his masterful, lawyerly way, he made the case: "There is certainly No Situation more honourable or more Usefull. There is none so independent. There is none that leads into better Company. There is none so preservative of health." Moreover, he wrote, Louisa would benefit since she would have the opportunity to visit her family in Washington at least once a year. He even introduced a heartstring-tugging note of concern regarding young George: "You will be at home with your Children . . . to oversee the Education of your Sons, and give me leave to say this is an immense Duty. Both your sons here are fine Children; but George is a Treasure of Diamonds. He has a Genius equal to any Thing, but like all other genius requires the most delicate management to prevent it from running into eccentricities."

In his summation, the former president unleashed the most forceful arguments at his command. Calling the appointment "a providential dispensation for your good, for my good, and for the preservation of your Family from Ruin," he offered his "most Serious and anxious Advice" that John Quincy would accept the appointment and "devote [himself] to the discharge of its Duties." A refusal to accept the nomination, he warned, would "create a national Disgust and Resentment. It will be imputed to Pride, oddity, Fastidiosity, and an unbridled unbounded ambition."[49]

Abigail, though far less dogmatic in expression, also clearly hoped her son would overcome his aversion to the bench and return home. Writing to John Quincy, she put the appointment in terms of an opportunity, not an obligation: "I will not impose my judgement as a law upon you, but I will say I consider it as a call of providence to you." And perhaps expressing more confidence than she in fact felt, she added, "I will take it for granted that after mature reflection you will resign yourself to the call of your Country and hold the Scales of Justice with an honest heart, and a steady hand."[50]

Although John Quincy's appointment to the Supreme Court had been approved by the Senate in February, he learned of it only on May 20 when he came across a news item in a shipment of outdated British newspapers. Two days later, he received a letter from America that "by no means removes but rather aggravates the state of painful suspense of which I must still await the issue." It would be a week more until his official appointment letter and his parents' entreaties arrived.[51]

After a single sleepless night, his decision was made. Within three days, John Quincy had replied to the president declining the position and to his parents explaining his reasons. No office, John Quincy wrote, "could tempt me to expose the lives of a wife and infant [Louisa was again pregnant] to the hardship inseparable" from a voyage through the waters of the Baltic in October—the earliest they could possibly depart. Acknowledging the honor of the appointment, the persuasive arguments advanced by his parents, and his own desire to return home, John Quincy hinted at his own deep-seated reluctance to join the Court and possibly the real reason for declining the position: "I am surely very sorry to disappoint the expectations of my Country by withholding myself from that judgement Seat where their partiality would have placed me, but how much happier for me and for them it is than it would be to disappoint their expectations." In short, he believed himself to be the wrong man for the job.[52]

Two months later, he was still attempting to justify his decision to his father. It was clear, he said, that wherever he was placed on the political map, he would be a lightning rod for controversy. Countering the argument that a seat on the high court would shield him from personal attacks, he wrote in a remarkable display of self-knowledge and *realpolitik*, "If my own Passions would allow me to stand aloof from all Politics as much as every Judge ought to, the Passions of others would involve me in them. If my heart is sufficiently impartial towards all my Countrymen to make me a proper umpire in the controversies, their hearts are not impartial enough to me to make them fit to be judged by me."[53]

Although John Quincy cited the approaching birth of a baby and the dangers to a new mother traveling with an infant across the ocean in the late fall as his primary reasons for declining the Supreme Court appointment, it appears that Louisa was not consulted in the matter. In a letter to Abigail, she said that John Quincy had "declined the acceptance of the appointment of the Judgeship from motives which I did not even Know existed but which, although I regret, are too honourable not to meet with my fullest approbation." As desperate as she was to return to America to reunite with her two older sons, she appreciated her husband's thoughtfulness in refusing to subject her and the baby to a dangerous ocean voyage. She may not have suspected that he simply was deeply opposed to accepting the Supreme Court appointment.[54]

Louisa's mind was far too occupied with personal concerns to inquire too deeply into John Quincy's career decisions. In May 1811, almost as soon as the ice broke in the Neva and mail could get through from America, she belatedly learned of the death in childbirth just before New Year's Day of her sister Nancy. The two elder Johnson sisters had been rivals in girlhood but had grown close as they matured and married. It was at Nancy's home in Washington that the Adamses had stayed for several months each year when John Quincy was in the Senate, and Louisa, now six months pregnant, fell apart at the news: "My heart collapsed with agony at the sudden shock in a dead fainting fit. . . . The fright produced alarming consequences and a premature birth was threatened with dangerous symptoms for some hours. My Physician remained with me for many hours of intense suffering when a favorable change took place and perfect quiet was relied on for recovery."[55]

Although her grief—and fear for her own safe delivery—was far from assuaged, she managed to recover her strength in time to receive the news on July 1 that the family's rented house had been sold from under them to the tsar and they would have to move within the week. After a fruitless search for a new home, they settled temporarily on a summer house on Apothecary Island on the outskirts of St. Petersburg and within sight of the sprawling vacation residences of the imperial family and most of the diplomatic corps.

Now less than a month before giving birth, Louisa superintended the move to the island. John Quincy was of limited assistance: "Slow work for he reads a page in every book that passes through his hands," Louisa complained. Once settled, the whole family delighted in the situation. John Quincy called the house "my Russian Arcadia" and described it to his mother "as pleasant a place of abode that ever fell to my lot." Two imperial bands, he said, performed twice daily on yachts moored in the river outside the nearby summer palace, so that "with the open doors and windows of warm weather we heard [the music] . . . as if it had been before our own door."[56]

Louisa was grateful for the tranquility of the riverside retreat. Years later, she remembered lazy days on the river bank, fishing with Charles. "We catch Fish not worth eating. It is an indolent sort of an amusement that just suits me for I do not think. When I look forward I tremble: but I bow down with trust in him who has mercifully saved me through a life of trouble and granted to me so many blessings."[57]

On August 12, 1811, following twelve very difficult hours of labor and to the delight of both parents, Louisa delivered a healthy baby girl. Writing immediately to his mother, a giddy John Quincy teased her about a remark she had made in an earlier letter about the rigors of a Russian winter, "I think this will convince you that 'the Climate of St. Petersburg is *not* too cold to produce an American.'" He added, more seriously, that his heart was "overflowing with gratitude to God for this new blessing that I have received at his hands."

The baby, at her father's insistence, was named Louisa Catherine. As the American flag flew over the lawn on Apothecary Island, she was baptized by the Rev. Loudon King Pitt in an Anglican ceremony on September 9. Her three sponsors were Levett Harris, the American consul; Mme. Bezarra, the wife of the Portuguese minister; and Louisa's loyal friend Annette Krehmer. "That a Quaker and a Portuguese Roman Catholic should join a church clergyman to baptize the child of a New England Congregationalist at St. Petersburg, the capital of Russia, is an incident rather extraordinary in the annals of the world," the proud father wrote his mother. Almost immediately, tiny Louisa Catherine completely won the hearts of everyone whose life she touched. In November, Louisa wrote of her three-month-old, "O she grows lovely. Such a pair of eyes! I fear I love her too well!" When they spied the baby's angelic countenance, passersby in St. Petersburg routinely exclaimed, "She is born for Heaven," a remark that deeply unsettled Louisa even while she attributed it to Russian superstition.[58]

The winter of 1812 was even harsher than usual—according to John Quincy's records, the temperature was above zero Fahrenheit on only one day in January—and brought with it almost constant illness for everyone in the family, now back in the capital in new, less spacious quarters, just around the corner from their former apartment. Like all of their rentals in St. Petersburg, this one featured thick walls, tightly sealed double windows, and close, overheated rooms. These factors, combined with the short days and frigid weather that restricted the family to inside pursuits, inevitably contributed to bad colds, fevers, and other illnesses.

All John Quincy's young aides except his nephew had left for home the previous summer, and their lively presence around the Adams dinner table was sorely missed. The family's spirits fell even lower when an onslaught of terrible news arrived by courier at the end of January: Catherine Johnson had died in an epidemic the previous September, as had Caroline's husband, Andrew Buchanan; John Quincy's aunt and uncle, Mary and Richard Cranch—who had been caring for the Adamses' two older boys—had died in October; and John Quincy's sister Nabby was suffering from a "dangerous and hopeless illness," advanced breast cancer.

Both Louisa and John Quincy, often ill themselves, worried especially when their adored daughter suffered from a variety of complaints. "I look at her with fear and trembling," Louisa wrote. Despite several spiked fevers and bad colds, the baby thrived. Writing in June to her son George, Louisa described his precocious little sister: "You have a sweet little Sister, who we think looks like Grandmama Adams, she is handsome, and has the finest pair of black eyes you ever saw. I wish you could see what a good natured little mad cap she is, she plays, all day long; and has called papa, and Mama, this six Weeks."[59]

Just after her first birthday, Baby Louisa was weaned. Almost immediately, she developed, first, dysentery and a high fever and then convulsions. By early September, a crisis had been reached. None of the drastic measures recommended by the two doctors in attendance, including lancing her gums, shaving her head, applying blisters, and administering digitalis and laudanum, did anything but make matters worse. "Language cannot express the feelings of a Parent beholding the long continued agonies of a lovely infant and finding every expedient attempted to administer relief utterly unavailing," a despairing John Quincy lamented to his diary. For days, Louisa barely left the child's side; Kitty remained by the cradle for forty-eight hours until she fainted, recovered, and returned to her post.[60]

On September 15, a heartbroken John Quincy recorded in his diary, "At twenty five minutes past one this morning expired my daughter Louisa Catherine, as lovely an infant as ever breathed the air of heaven." To his mother, a week later, his grief unabated, he was unstinting in his praise of Louisa: "Her mother—at all times and to all her children one of the tenderest and most affectionate of mothers attended her with the most unabating assiduity and vigilance night and day until the close of the scene—Faithfully did she perform every duty, and exert every faculty that God and nature had given her, to preserve the darling of her heart."[61]

Louisa, less fulsome but no less eloquent, cried out in the concluding sentence of "Adventures of a Nobody" nearly thirty years later, "My child is gone to Heaven!"[62]

DARK DAYS ON THE BALTIC

A perpetual coldness and restraint operating on a naturally warm and
affectionate disposition.

— LOUISA CATHERINE ADAMS, *"Diary, 1812–1814"*

"Eighteen twelve." Two words echoed over the centuries by the tolling bells
and booming cannons of Tchaikovsky's *1812 Overture*. In that momentous year
the entire Western world was engulfed in war. At the end of June, Napoleon led
his Grande Armée of 450,000 men across the Nieman River in what he expected
would be a three-week subjugation of the Russian Empire to his will. Meanwhile,
Russia and Great Britain, allied in opposition to Napoleon, made peace with
one another. On June 18, in a decision indirectly related to events on the
Continent, the U.S. Congress declared war on Britain. By the end of the year,
the course of history would be forever changed.[1]

Early on the morning of September 15, 1812, as Louisa and John Quincy in
St. Petersburg struggled to accept the reality of their adored daughter's death,
Napoleon rode victorious into a silent, deserted Moscow. His was a bitter
triumph. No crowds greeted his troops, no city officials were on hand to negotiate housing and feeding the exhausted and hungry soldiers, no emissaries from
Tsar Alexander arrived to sue for peace. Within hours, Russia's historic former
capital, and still its cultural heart, was entirely up in flames. That night, the
French emperor was forced to flee the fires that threatened even his safe haven
in the brick-walled Kremlin.

It had been a long march for Napoleon and the largest army the world had
ever seen. For once, the French emperor was a reluctant warrior. Anxiously, he
had watched Alexander become increasingly restive in the alliance formed in
1807 by the Treaty of Tilsit but had resisted taking any countermeasures that
could provoke Russia into active hostility. His real enemy, he continued to

believe, was Great Britain. As early as the winter of 1811, however, both John Quincy and Louisa had noted a cooling off in the close relationship between the tsar and Caulaincourt, Napoleon's close friend and trusted envoy in St. Petersburg. Describing a children's ball at the French embassy, to which Charles went dressed as the page in *The Marriage of Figaro,* John Quincy observed "a coldness and reserve about the party which I had never observed on like occasions before."[2]

By May Caulaincourt had been recalled to Paris.

The issues that led to war were both economic and political. Denied access to maritime trade with Britain under Napoleon's Continental System, Russia had reeled under inflated prices and a shortage of consumer goods. In December 1810, Alexander issued a decree effectively removing his nation from the system, a decision that eventually led to the relaxation of trade restrictions against Britain by other nations and destroyed the French emperor's grand design to bring the island kingdom to her knees through commercial sanctions. At the same time, Russia and France became rivals over the future of Poland and Turkey and clashed over Napoleon's decision to mobilize troops in areas of Poland and in several German states and principalities within easy access of the tsar's dominions.

To John Quincy the tsar expressed his deep — perhaps disingenuous — distress that war had become inevitable. Meeting the American minister in March 1812 on the Admiralty Embankment, Alexander remarked, "And so it is, after all, that war is coming that I have done so much to avoid. . . . *He* always advances. . . . He can't advance farther without attacking us." A month later, the tsar left St. Petersburg for the frontier and his troops.[3]

During the summer, as the two great armies fought pitched, deadly battles on Russian soil, peasants and landowners alike adopted a scorched-earth policy in defense of their homeland. Entire populations of cities and towns on Napoleon's projected route to Moscow were evacuated; roads were stacked with overturned carts and felled trees; the bodies of dead men and horses lay rotting in the August sun. The Russian army and populace joined in setting fire to farms, haystacks, and wheat fields. Nevertheless, the French and their allies, often marching on bare feet and empty stomachs, managed to advance toward Moscow, pillaging what little was left in the villages and fields as they moved forward.

As the weary and weakened Russian army retreated, its generals adopted the strategy of luring the French farther and farther into the heartland. To many Muscovites, the backtracking of the tsar's troops appeared to be little more than abject surrender, and the inevitable cries of cowardice and worse grew ever

louder. But neither the wily Russian general Prince Mikail Katusov nor the tsar
had any intention of admitting defeat on Russian soil. John Quincy reported
that reverses only strengthened Alexander's resolve ("His spirit stiffens with
adversity"), and Katusov, for his part, argued that strategic retreat was imperative. For its survival, his depleted army needed to regroup and avoid further
major battles while allowing the Russian climate, the harsh conditions to which
the French were subjected in abandoned Moscow, and Napoleon's precari-
ously overextended supply lines to have their disastrous effect.[4]

By October 19, Napoleon and the 95,000 troops still under his command
had left Moscow for Paris. The catastrophic events of that historic retreat, as the
Russian Cossacks chased the French and their allies — starving, frozen, dying
by the thousands — across Europe, heralded the end of Napoleon's dream of
controlling the greater part of the known world. He was forced to abdicate in
April 1814 and exiled to the island of Elba off the coast of Italy.

Concerning these dramatic events, John Quincy at first evinced little
interest. "My own spirits are so deeply affected that I am unfitted for any kind of
occupation," he wrote on September 16. The next day, he followed his "darling
infant . . . beloved child" to her grave on a rise in the "Lutheran" cemetery,
where all those who were not of the Russian Orthodox faith were buried. Louisa
and Kitty, prostrated by grief, were unable to attend either the funeral rites
conducted by the same Anglican chaplain who had baptized little Louisa or
the burial service. A week later, writing to his mother in the most moving terms
of her granddaughter's death, John Quincy uncharacteristically — because he
always salted his personal letters with news — neglected to mention the fall of
Moscow.[5]

His failure to pass along information that Russia's ancient capital was occupied and had been set afire was a conscious omission — "I can write to you of no
other subject [than his daughter's death]" — since news that the city had been
taken had already reached the diplomatic corps. The British, John Quincy
wrote in his diary, were preparing to leave St. Petersburg on the assumption that
the next logical destination for the French army would be the Russian capital.
He and Louisa had no thought of decamping. Louisa was far from ready to
leave the site of her daughter's grave, and John Quincy believed — correctly —
that the situation of the French army was desperate and that Napoleon wished
to make peace.[6]

By early October, John Quincy had returned to his former routine, resuming
his daily long walks, consultations with government officials, study of weights
and measures, and a heavy reading load of classical works and religious sermons.

Although his grief was deep and sore, he coped best by maintaining a rigid daily schedule and disciplining his mind with scholarly texts.

This was not Louisa's way. She needed to mourn openly, to rehearse the last painful weeks of her daughter's illness, to flail against the injustice of her child's death. Recognizing the depth of her loss, John Quincy was initially sympathetic toward her inability to put her grief behind her. Throughout the painful days of September 1812, his diary entries consistently refer to her as "my dear wife." Summing up the month, he wrote with rare perspicacity, "Our domestic condition is no longer the same as before. The privation and the vacuity are more heavily and more constantly felt by her [Louisa] . . . than by me. The maternal cares were the business as well as the enjoyment of her life. The loss of them is a most severe, if not an irremediable wound."[7]

A month after her baby's death, Louisa was, understandably, still distraught. "This day I have endeavour'd to keep myself constantly employed but still my mind dwells on the past and nothing can fill the dreadful void in my heart," she wrote in her diary. Exacerbating her pain was the conviction that she alone was responsible for her baby's death. The fault had been in weaning little Louisa too soon or not being prompt enough to send for medical assistance or even a fall she had taken with her infant in her arms many months earlier. Afraid she was losing her mind, she longed for death to release her—"My heart is buried in my Louisa's grave and my greatest longing is to be laid beside her"—and became obsessed with the idea that a stranger would be buried next to her child before she herself could die. Declaring that the only possession she owned was her body, Louisa prepared an informal last testament declaring her final wish to "lay me with my Infant."[8]

The death of a dearly beloved child was not an extraordinary experience in the early nineteenth century. Louisa's own sisters had lost adored, previously thriving infants and toddlers to infections and epidemics. What was exceptional in her case was her isolation from most of the female members of her extended family. Typically, when a child met an early death, sisters, aunts, and cousins— all usually living in the vicinity—rallied around the bereaved mother to provide strength and comfort. Mourning was accepted, tears encouraged. With the sustenance and support of those she loved and who loved her, a woman might eventually work through her grief and learn to bear her loss.

Louisa, bereft in St. Petersburg, was not entirely without consolation. Her sister Kitty fully empathized with her loss, and her friend Annette Krehmer, little Louisa's godmother, visited often. But their comfort and concern were not enough. Denied her husband's compassion—at least in her own mind—she seems to have given way to her grief. When she miscarried yet again in January

1813, it seemed as if there would be no break in what had become a miserable existence. John Quincy, who, despite the press of business, assured himself it would not be a dereliction of duty to "soothe and comfort" his wife, understood how much her mind affected her health: "Mrs. Adams was suddenly taken and violently ill all day. She was bled. Her illness is of an alarming nature and aggravated by the distress of mind occasioned by the heavy calamities which in a short space of time have been befallen us."[9]

In facing those calamities Louisa's religious convictions were of little comfort. Her Anglican faith was fully as judgmental as John Quincy's Congregationalism. Convinced that little Louisa had paid the ultimate price for his personal sins, John Quincy had confessed to his diary that if his daughter's "long and racking agonies" were in atonement for his sins, he could only hope that her eternal happiness would be in proportion to the "rigour of her destiny upon Earth." Louisa, too, believed a jealous God had chosen to punish her for her many transgressions: Again and again, she called upon Him to forgive her: "Humbly do I confess my sins. Great as is my punishment, I have a full conviction of the justice and mercy of my God who will not reject the petition of a contrite spirit but will grant me strength to correct the evil propensities of my nature and teach me to subdue that pride of heart from which all my errors spring."[10]

But it would be at least six months before she could acknowledge "in religion alone I have found a gleam of comfort" through "the afflictions which assail us in our passage through this vale of tears." Meanwhile, she was forced to find her path alone. By mid-October, less than a month after his daughter's death, John Quincy's initial sympathy had turned to impatience. He seems to have complained that Louisa was doing an inadequate job in teaching five-year-old Charles his "prayers and commandments" and announced he was resuming the boy's religious education and daily reading lesson himself. The incident, unmentioned in John Quincy's diary but spelled out in detail in Louisa's, prompted her to storm out of the room and reflect on her own shortcomings and, not incidentally, those of her husband: "I am peculiarly unfortunate for what I undertake with the best intentions almost always turns out exactly contrary. I read, I work, I endeavor to occupy myself usefully, but it is all in vain. My heart is almost broken, and my temper, which was never good, suffers in proportion to my grief. I strive against it and humbly implore heaven to fortify my soul and to teach me meekness and resignation. He complains of my being suspicious and jealous. These were faults once foreign to my nature, but they are insensibly acquired by a perpetual coldness and restraint operating on a naturally warm and affectionate disposition."[11]

The conflict between John Quincy's "perpetual coldness and restraint" and Louisa's "warm and affectionate disposition" began to dominate the tenor of their relationship. Louisa craved tenderness; John Quincy, peace and quiet. Had Louisa dared to steal a look into her husband's diary, she might have appreciated how deeply he ached. As it was, she could see only how eager he seemed to be to return to his former routines and pursuits. Had he, on the other hand, freely offered her comfort, she might not have felt the need to dramatize her distress. In the face of their shared loss, neither could rely for consolation on the other.

If John Quincy accused Louisa of "being suspicious and jealous," it is unlikely she thought he had his eye on another woman. Instead, she probably mistrusted the excuses he made to withdraw into the silence of his study and was jealous of anything that lured him away from the family circle, now so irreparably broken. Yet, "jealous" and "suspicious" seem to have been words spoken in anger by him and faithfully recorded by her. It was not the first time either had used words to wound the other. The tempers of both partners were notoriously short-fused, as John Quincy remarked in the only extended comment he ever offered on his marriage. On their fourteenth wedding anniversary, just before his daughter's birth, he had written dispassionately that he had enjoyed happiness greater than the "generality of mankind" and was convinced that, based on his personal experience, marriage was preferable to celibacy. Lauding Louisa as "a faithful and affectionate wife, and a careful, tender, indulgent, and watchful mother to our children, all of whom she has nursed herself," he conceded that their relationship had "not been without its trials nor invariably without dissensions between us. There are many differences of sentiment, of taste, and of opinions in regard to domestic economy and the education of children between us. There are natural frailties of temper in both of us, both being quick and irascible, and mine sometimes harsh."[12]

The harshness he acknowledged in his own temperament became, after his daughter's death, ever more hurtful to Louisa: "All I claim is a little indulgence and if I at any time desire what is unreasonable or improper, affection and gentleness will always have full effect upon my mind. It is surely enough to have the power of rejecting a request without making a rejection more painful by harshness or contempt." Since John Quincy in his diary refrained from showing any irritation at his wife's conduct, it is hard to know how much of the contempt Louisa believed he felt toward her had any basis in fact. Her choice of books to distract her mind from her loss, however, might have been the subject of a disparaging remark or two. Not for her were volume 9 of *The English Preacher*, which John Quincy read and annotated on October 4, 1812, or "several chapters" of Thomas Gisborne's *An Enquiry into the Duties of the Female Sex*, which he read a week later. Instead, she turned to a steady series of memoirs and biographies of noted figures, chiefly women, in the royal courts of France. Reading accounts of immeasurable wealth, power, and glamour evoked in Louisa no yearning to return to high life. Instead, she read in them the costs to personal integrity and human relationships brought on by insatiable ambition. These thoughts led her to reflections on Napoleon's tragic and ignominious retreat across the devastated, frozen wastes of the Russian countryside. "We behold here, the Emperor of France, after sixteen years of the most unheard of successes, in the short space of one month, plunged into all the horrors of extreme distress, flying for his life, pursued by Barbarians, a revolt in his Country, his Army totally overthrown, and surrounded by treachery, dashed instantaneously from the summit of Splendor, into such a scene of horror, and calamity. . . . The character of this man produces unceasing astonishment, and we cannot trace his rise, and see his fall, without shuddering at the length, to which a blind and inexhaustible Ambition, will lead mankind and though conscious of the justice of his fall, we shrink with pity and horror from a fate so dreadful, so hopeless."[13]

Ambition, she was beginning to believe, was an insidious evil, a character flaw "acquired insensibly and imperceptibly and . . . nursed by the adulation of the world." It was, she believed, her husband's essential and—because he would not acknowledge it—intractable failing. Addressing her remarks in her diary to "my beloved children," she warned of the price paid by those around the ambitious person—he who "came to presume that every thing that surrounds him must live for him. . . . No sacrifices however great and painful in those who are so unfortunate as to belong to him can satisfy for he is too much absorb'd in himself." Louisa returned to the subject a few pages, but four months later in her diary: "They say I am ambitious. If so, why do not the vain projects of the world occupy my thoughts and fill my Soul? When I compare myself with those to whom I am the most nearly connected, when I see every thought devoted— peace, happiness, family every thing neglected for this one object—my heart decidedly assures me that for this great end I was [not] made."[14]

Facing a loss from which she would never fully recover and without the emotional support of the man with whom her life was "most nearly connected," Louisa's physical well-being, never strong, began to disintegrate. By the first week of October 1812, she had again become the "Mrs. Adams" of her husband's diary whose appearances were marked most often by the poor state of her health. On October 8, she was "very unwell the whole day and this evening quite ill." Throughout the fall of 1812 and winter of 1813—as she lived through her worst nightmare—ill health, culminating in her miscarriage in January, took its almost inevitable toll.

Poor health appears to have been Louisa's weapon of choice—consciously or unconsciously—in her lifelong campaign to elicit "affection and gentleness" from her husband. John Quincy himself recognized that her debilitating ailments had characterized their relationship. Their marriage, he wrote in his diary on their fourteenth anniversary in 1811, had as "its greatest alloy . . . the delicacy of my wife's Constitution, the ill health which has afflicted her much of the time." Just as there is little question that Louisa was often genuinely ill, it seems equally obvious that there was a correlation between the condition of her health and the attention she was receiving from her husband or other loved ones.[15]

Early in life she had discovered that her serious childhood illnesses could single her out among her siblings for their parents' attention and care. Little in her later experience gave the lie to her perception that illness led to special kindness and concern. In Berlin, she had thrived under the insistent care of Lady Carysfort during her first successful pregnancy. Similarly, she had recovered her health almost immediately "in the restorative care of her mother and sisters" when she arrived, pale and depleted, in Washington in 1801. When she and John Quincy traveled together in Silesia—and his time and attention were not wrapped up in his own interests—Louisa found hidden reserves of strength that enabled her to maintain a rigorous schedule and withstand primitive living and traveling conditions. And although her arrival in Quincy in November 1801 was marked by a serious illness that prompted her mother-in-law to predict she would die an early death, her health improved as soon as she and John Quincy moved into their own home in Boston.

Although it is far too simplistic to trace a direct relationship between Louisa's illnesses and her psychological well-being, the evidence points to a loose correspondence between the two. Whenever she had a purpose in life, Louisa rose to meet its challenges. When, on the other hand, she felt herself unneeded and unappreciated by her husband, she seems to have sought unconsciously to command his attention through bouts of sickness.

It would be wrong, however, to pretend that Louisa's physical health was robust. Her repeated, difficult pregnancies alone were enough to weaken even the strongest constitution. During the family's residence in Russia, alone, she suffered three protracted miscarriages. Like everyone else in the family, she was subject to the colds, flu, and infections that seemed to accompany the onset of each winter in St. Petersburg. In addition, Louisa, Kitty, and John Quincy all suffered from what was diagnosed at the time as erysipelas, a bacterial infection of the skin that today would be routinely treated with antibiotics. Louisa believed that the temporary deafness she suffered during her Russian winters—a significant problem at balls and dinner parties—could be directly attributed to this disfiguring illness. By December 1812, Kitty had become so ill with what John Quincy termed arthritis that the doctor told Louisa that if she and her sister "did not make haste and return home . . . the Climate would kill us both."[16]

John Quincy, too, was far from immune to various illnesses during his Russian tenure. The longer the family stayed in St. Petersburg, the worse his health became. In the spring of 1813, a frustrated Louisa wrote to Abigail, "The health of your Son my dear Madam is a source of perpetual anxiety to us all, and I myself believe it absolutely essential to remove him to a milder Climate. I think it my duty to inform you that his breast is attacked and that although he is himself aware of it he will take no precautions whatever to check its progress." Earlier in the same year, worried about the effects of Louisa's miscarriage on her future well-being, concerned over Kitty's serious ill health, and feeling the effects of what Louisa later called his life of "inanity," John Quincy himself acknowledged to his diary that he was close to the breaking point. "My own health is deeply affected by this state of things and anxieties for the future weigh upon me with a pressure known only to almighty God," he wrote.[17]

In the long dark nights of Russian winter of 1813, Louisa's thoughts often turned to the one person she believed would understand her ongoing grief: her mother-in-law. "In Mrs. Adams I should have found a comforter, a friend who would pity sufferings which *she* would have understood," she wrote in her diary a month after baby Louisa died. Louisa was only partly referring to the death of Abigail's second daughter, Susannah, also at thirteen months, a loss the older woman had never ceased to mourn. ("Early in Life I was call'd to taste the bitter cup, forty years has not obliterated from my mind the anguish of my soul upon the occasion," Abigail recalled in her condolence letter to her daughter-in-law.) In yearning for Abigail's sympathetic shoulder to cry on, Louisa was also reflecting a critical shift in their relationship.[18]

From the moment Louisa had left Boston for Russia, she and Abigail had formed a strong bond. Abigail appeared to feel it her duty to give Louisa the encouragement she needed to endure her Russian exile. Throughout their St. Petersburg years, she directed her letters as often to her daughter-in-law as to her son and filled them with gossip, epigrams, and the loving details regarding her grandsons she knew Louisa would cherish. George and John, she wrote, "have not had a days sickness since you left them. George is steady, and Books are as much his delight as they were his Fathers passion at his Age. I see his

Father growing up in him, in a thousand of his actions. John has learnt to read so fast, that it is now a pleasure and amusement to him. His Eyes sparkle with intelligence, and he is a dear little coaxer as you can imagine." No longer did she address her correspondence to "Mrs. Adams"; Louisa was now "My dear daughter." For her part, Louisa, once she had overcome her initial homesickness, supplied Abigail with the descriptions of glittering court life she knew would make delightful reading in Quincy, emphasizing always the eminence in which John Quincy stood with the tsar.[19]

The inauspicious beginnings of their relationship and the years of resentment on Louisa's part as her husband forced her to cede her older sons' upbringing to his mother seem to have been largely forgotten. Ever a realist, Abigail had few illusions about how difficult it was to live with her eldest son. She acknowledged that the mission to Russia seemed to be his single viable career option in the summer of 1809, but she grieved the toll it would take on him and his wife. "It has ever been my opinion that Mr. Adams should not have gone abroad," she wrote to Catherine Johnson in May 1810. From her own experience Abigail appreciated how difficult it was to keep up appearances in an extravagant, sumptuous court, and she worried about the effects of a harsh climate on Louisa's fragile health.[20]

Louisa even felt herself on firm enough footing with her mother-in-law to acknowledge her inability to persuade John Quincy to commit to a return date to America. But in October 1810, she went too far: "It has however been an invariable rule with me, as I had no fortune, never to object or decline any thing which he thinks can tend to promote his ambition, his fame, or his ease, and in one instance only have I ever fail'd to observe it. That was the professorship which I firmly believe has been the cause of almost all his trouble since in his political career." Abigail kindly but firmly took her to task. She made it clear that, in her opinion, Louisa's inability to contribute to the couple's finances was well understood by John Quincy from the outset and had never been held against her by the Adams family. "The subject which preys upon your mind, and which you have repeatedly mention'd, is surely no fault of yours. It was well known to Mr. Adams before he was connected with you and can never be a complaint against you, nor was you ever reminded of it by any of his connections, nor can it, by any means lessen your influence with him. His honour and his Reputation, must be as dear to you, as tho you had possess'd ever so large a fortune, and I should esteem it a misfortune for you to have carried him a fortune, unless he had possesst sufficient to have balanced it—believe me my dear, altho you might have felt more independent, you would not have been happier."[21]

For Louisa, who had nursed both the shame of her lack of personal fortune and the grievance that she was seen by John Quincy's nearest relations as someone who had perpetrated a marital trick, Abigail's wise words had a therapeutic effect. Although she returned to the dowry theme again and again in her writings, Louisa never again repeated her timeworn excuses and complaints to her mother-in-law.

Abigail also brought her daughter-in-law up sharply in regard to John Quincy's professorship. In his mother's eyes, his tenure at Harvard had been one of the high points of his life—"The professorship will never again be fill'd with equal talents"—and had nothing to do with his political demise: "I think you are entirely mistaken with respect to your opinion of the professorship, and you must permit me to rejoice that you did not succeed, if as you say, you endeavour'd to influence him against accepting it. . . . It was not that, which raised the sum of the junto against him."[22]

Louisa was able to accept Abigail's reproaches because they were cloaked in the language of sympathy and in loving reports of her sons. Their bond was further strengthened by the sorrows they shared within a single twelve-month period when both little Louisa and John Quincy's beloved sister, Nabby, died. Losing their daughters made a mother and daughter of the two in a way they had never been before. Abigail's letter to Louisa on the death of her baby girl was so heartfelt that the younger woman could not help but feel her loss was fully appreciated: "How shall I address a Letter to you, how share and participate in your grief, without opening affresh the wound which time may in some measure have healed? Distance excluded me from knowing your distress, or sharing your sorrows, at the time when you most needed consolation but neither time, or distance has banish'd from my Bosom, that sympathy which, altho Billows rise and oceans role between us, like mercy is not confined to time or space, but crosses the Atlantic and mingles tears with you over the grave of your dear departed Babe."[23]

Louisa, in her turn, was able to open her heart to Abigail when she learned of Nabby's death on August 15, 1813. Facing her painful fate with courage and a determination to die in her parents' arms, Nabby had made a torturous three-hundred-mile journey over rutted, country roads from tiny Lebanon, in upstate New York's Chenango Valley, to Quincy. Her daughter's death shattered Abigail, a feeling Louisa well understood: "Too recently have I suffer'd the same dreadful stroke not to feel how every fibre of your heart must have been rent by this great affliction. If the tenderest sympathy could in the smallest degree assuage the anguish of maternal grief, if the assurance of the profoundest respect and affection could alleviate one pang, with what delight would I contribute by every attention in my power to ameliorate the pain which I am sensible cannot be entirely removed."[24]

Abigail's warmth toward Louisa extended to the entire Johnson family. Each of Louisa's sisters held a special place in her affections, and they, in turn, regularly turned to the older woman for advice. Even Louisa's bachelor brother, Thomas, who had settled in New Orleans as a merchant, benefited from the interest of the former First Lady. But it was Abigail's friendship with their mother, Catherine Johnson, that was a source of delight and a comfort to both women from 1809 until Catherine's death in September 1811. The two were linked, first of all, by the shared experience of having their children thousands of miles away in St. Petersburg: "Your letters my dear Madam are always entertaining and interesting to me and as we have a common bond of union, by which our hearts are drawn to a foreign country, we mutually share in all the concerns of our dear absent children," Abigail wrote in September 1810. Soon, she was writing to Catherine even when hampered by arthritis in her fingers and temporary blindness in one eye. Catherine seems to have filled her frequent, witty letters with gossip and news from the nation's capital along with keen observations of notable characters both women knew. Abigail responded with news she had received from Russia and accounts of their grandchildren: "Our grandsons are well. John is the very image of his mother—a charming boy with the best of dispositions—George is sensible and lover of books, rather positive, which years and experience will correct."[25]

Sadly, it fell to Abigail to communicate to Louisa, Kitty, and John Quincy the news of Catherine's death. Her letter of condolence was a model of its kind, sharing and appreciating Louisa's inevitable sorrow and holding out the hope of a better world. To John Quincy in November 1811, Abigail expressed her personal grief, "My own Bosom has been so lacerated with repeated Strokes of woe that I can mingle, tear for tear, with the afflicted daughters of my esteemed Friend and correspondent, whose death I most Sensibly feel, and whose loss will be long regretted by me." In an April 1813 letter to Thomas Johnson, she wrote of Catherine as "a Friend whose memory I cherish, whose loss I have not ceased to mourn, and whose frequent, and intelligent correspondence I highly valued. To her Children, who must rise up, and call her blessed, her price was far above Rubies."[26]

Catherine had lived to see five of her seven penniless daughters married. After her death, the youngest, Adelaide, cared for her late sister Nancy's three children and then, in 1813, married their wealthy father and family benefactor Walter Hellen. And in the Adamses' St. Petersburg apartment on February 17, 1813, Kitty Johnson, at twenty-nine, made the disastrous mistake of marrying

John Quincy's reprobate nephew and private secretary, William Smith, twenty-five. Whether the bride was pregnant at the time is unclear; she had been very ill and "confined to her chamber" for nearly the entire month of January, but her first child was not born until March 1814. In John Quincy's view, however, the marriage, for whatever reason, was an affair of honor. On January 18, he "had a long and very serious conversation with Mr. Smith who finally avowed a disposition to do right," but the minister plenipotentiary had to intervene twice more to wrestle from the younger man a definite commitment to marry.

Abigail, who was not apprised of the details, believed the marriage to be an "imprudent step." She thought her eldest grandson didn't deserve Kitty: "With regard to the Lady, she has the advantage of Age upon her side, and in point of understanding, accomplishments, etc, is fully his equal. I could say his superiour." Her fears were realized. Before William could leave Russia in the summer of 1814 with Kitty and their baby daughter, he was forced to use money John Quincy had given him for the family's voyage home to settle a large gambling debt. Louisa herself had to take care of smaller obligations owed by the young husband and father after the Smiths left the city. Following the Smith family's return to the United States in 1815, William embarked on a career of bad checks, debt, and alcoholism. Taken in and helped many times by the Adamses, William Smith died destitute and an alcoholic in 1853, a decade after finally abandoning Kitty.[27]

By the spring of 1813, John Quincy's career was in the doldrums. Certainly, the destructive ambition that Louisa attributed to him was far from being satisfied. He had disappeared from the American political stage in 1809, and the three-month time lag in his correspondence with Washington diminished much of any effect his long, thoughtful dispatches might have had on President Madison's foreign policy. No longer did he have regular access to the tsar, who was often abroad consulting with his fellow rulers on the future of Europe. Spending three hours a day on young Charles's lessons and taking very long walks was not enough stimulation—John Quincy's health and moods suffered from a lack of serious employment. Even Louisa began to hope for some dramatic change that would shake him out of his lethargy. "He will listen to no advice. Therefore we must hope that the natural strength of his constitution and some striking event which may give an active occupation will remove the disease he is now threaten'd with," she wrote.[28]

John Quincy was saved from obscurity by the War of 1812. In his view, it was a conflict that didn't need to happen. "I could see no good result as likely to arise from it to anyone; nothing but mischief and gratification to the makers of mischief," he recorded in his diary. As far as the United States was concerned, the justification for war was the impressments of American sailors by His Majesty's Navy and the violation of American neutral rights on the high seas. Britain, primarily concerned with events on the Continent, belatedly made important concessions to avoid armed conflict with its former colonies, but the news didn't arrive in Washington until after war had been declared by Congress on June 18, 1812. "Its principal cause and justification was removed precisely at the moment when it occurred," John Quincy mordantly confided to his brother Tom.[29]

Nothing about a war between its two great commercial partners appealed to the Russian government. On September 21, 1812, just days after his daughter's death, John Quincy was summoned to the Russian foreign minister's office and informed that the tsar himself had offered to mediate a peace between the two combatants. As soon as President Madison received the dispatch relaying Alexander's proposal, he appointed two special plenipotentiaries—Secretary of the Treasury Albert Gallatin and Senator James A. Bayard of Delaware—to serve with John Quincy as America's delegates to a peace commission. The newly appointed envoys arrived in St. Petersburg in July 1813 and remained with little to occupy their time—except visits to the Adamses—until January, when Britain, while agreeing to negotiate directly with the United States, formally declined the tsar's mediation offer. The two nonresident American commissioners left St. Petersburg with the intention of returning directly home but were detoured to London to negotiate the time and place of future direct peace talks.[30]

Louisa was not sorry to see Gallatin and Bayard depart. In her view, the two had done nothing to improve Russo-American relations or merit respect in the eyes of the American merchant community: "[They left] with every mark of disgust for the Climate, the Manners, and habits of the Russians. They were no favorites here and their manner of living did not contribute to render them comfortable or to conciliate the good will or affection of their Countrymen. Public men in general do not pay sufficient attention to this point and are not sufficiently aware that in Foreign Countries (more especially here at St Petersburg) the Americans who reside have little else to do during a large part of the year but to weigh and measure every . . . trifling error in the character of their ministers which in their own Country would pass totally unobserved and become here swelled into faults of magnitude. There are most assuredly a certain stile of manners absolutely necessary to the station and if a man is incapable of conforming to them no matter from what cause he should immediately quit it."[31]

Gallatin and Bayard, nevertheless, had sufficient diplomatic skills to negotiate a location for peace talks acceptable to both Washington and London—the city of Ghent in what is now Belgium. Madison quickly named Henry Clay,

Speaker of the House of Representatives, and Jonathan Russell, the first minister to be appointed to the court of Sweden, as additional members of the blue-ribbon peace commission and made John Quincy chairman. On April 28, 1814, John Quincy took leave of his "dear wife and Charles" and set off on what would be a signal achievement in his career.[32]

John Quincy was leaving the American legation to St. Petersburg in uncertain hands. His secretary at the time, William Smith, was not to be trusted with anything more than routine duties. The consul, Levett Harris, was a more difficult case. Like all American consuls, Harris did not receive a salary. Yet he lived in a style far more lavish than that enjoyed by John Quincy and Louisa. He apparently had made his fortune by extorting bribes from ship captains arriving in St. Petersburg under fraudulent American flags and by clearing dubiously registered cargoes, especially those intended for his business partner. John Quincy was fully aware of Harris's venality. In June 1812, he angrily confronted the consul, telling him flatly he "had reason to believe . . . vessels . . . had come here last year with fake American colours and had been admitted." He also accused Harris of slighting the complaints of American sailors impressed onto foreign, "fraudulent" ships and of ignoring specific intelligence from himself that a certain captain was sailing under false papers. Louisa had never liked the man; she had found him ridiculous in his insistence on appearances and protocol, and she did not trust his word. "I do not vouch for any thing from that quarter," she wrote John Quincy in August 1814. Harris, nonetheless, was a capable man, familiar with court politics and in touch with all corners of the commercial community. John Quincy, despite misgivings concerning the man's ethics, appointed him chargé d'affaires.[33]

Louisa was left to handle everything else. To a woman who had never been entrusted with the smallest aspect of household or financial affairs, John Quincy turned over everything relating to the family's finances, Charles's education, and management of the household and servants. He made her executrix of his will and mailed her from the road a complete memorandum of all his assets and debts as well as instructions concerning where to find leases, bills, receipts, and lists of his books, furniture, and other property. He also expected her to keep up her social contacts with the imperial court and diplomatic and merchant communities and to report to him any news or gossip she gathered in her regular social visits or at gala events.

That John Quincy was willing so cavalierly to abandon his post in St. Petersburg is a measure of his undeclared ambition to become president of the United States. Louisa was not fooled. "I feel a little anxious to know how the rival candidates for the Presidency will feel towards each other. There is some danger I think that such great interests will Clash," she teased her husband in June. There was no question that the peace commission represented several of the young nation's most able and politically ambitious men, but John Quincy was certain he could hold his own. He had been privately assured by the secretary of state that if a peace could be negotiated, he would be in line for the ambassadorship to Britain. The promise of that most coveted diplomatic assignment may have been enough to conquer his doubts about leaving his public and private affairs in St. Petersburg in hands less competent than his own.[34]

Louisa, for her part, was at first unsure about the extent of her responsibilities. Her response to John Quincy's confidence in appointing her executrix took the form of an apology, apparently for her longtime conviction that he completely lacked trust in her: "I have been labouring for many years under a false impression so painful to my heart, that I was perhaps not aware of how much it influenced my conduct. You will I am sure accept my apology, and recieve it with as much pleasure as I offer it being perfectly convinced that it is sincere, and from the Heart."[35]

John Quincy was not sure that he understood precisely what "false impression" had so wounded his wife, but he hurried to assure her that, whatever it was, it had been ill founded: "Let me repeat the wish I have so often expressed to you that if ever a *suspicion*, tending to give you disquietude should again obtrude itself upon your mind, you would disclose it at once, and give me the opportunity of proving to you, not only my confidence in you, but how much I have at heart the comfort and happiness of your life. . . . At this distance, and with that sentiment in all its ardour beating at my heart, I ask again of you never to harbour a surmise that I have not the most perfect Confidence in your intentions, and in the tenderness of your affection for myself as well as for our Children."[36]

For the nine months following John Quincy's departure from St. Petersburg, he and Louisa wrote each other at least twice a week. They addressed each other lovingly—she was his "Dearest Wife," he her "My Best Beloved Friend"—and, as so often seemed to happen, they found in letters to each other a way to express their devotion openly. John Quincy acknowledged that distance played a role: "In the affection of those who truly love, there is a fervour of Sentiment when they are separated from each other, more glowing, more unmingled and more anxious, than when being together it has the continual opportunity of manifesting itself by acts of kindness."[37]

Seeing himself as one who "truly" loved was not a foreign concept to John Quincy nor was it, apparently, to Louisa. The complicated nature of their marital relationship was never clearer than in their letters. The coldness of which Louisa regularly accused John Quincy in her memoirs and diaries could not have been his constant demeanor; if so, his loving protestations when apart would have rung hollow. Although their ability to communicate seems to have been less subject to the moods and irritations of the moment when they were separated by time and space, it appears that their daily, domestic conversation was made up of discussions of politics, world events, the arts, books, and notable personalities because those are the topics they naturally turned to in their correspondence.

John Quincy's letters contained vivid descriptions of places he visited, people he met, and entertainments and dinners he attended. They were also amusingly self-deprecating concerning his slovenly appearance, lack of gallantry, and irritation at unnecessary delays. Often slyly suggestive—so much so that he felt the need to remind himself that they might be read by Russian censors before they reached his wife—his letters made a running joke of the fact that he was sleeping in another lady's bed in her "dormeuse." He finally admitted, "There is so much gossiping in my Letters to you, that if the inspectors of the Post-Office at the Capital, take the trouble of opening and reporting them to the Government, my diplomatic gravity and dignity will be 'furieusement compromis.' But they should not open a Man's Letters to his wife."[38]

John Quincy's letters assumed that Louisa was interested in the most minute detail of the peace negotiations as well as in his character sketches of the players on both sides of the table. He addressed his detailed version of what was happening in Ghent to her with the same thoroughness and gravity he had heretofore reported world and political events to his mother. Clearly, John Quincy had come to believe that his wife's interests were his own and that her political acumen had become finely honed. He trusted her discretion completely—"You will now, my Dearest Friend receive in the mos[t] exclusive Confidence whatever I shall write you on this subject—Say not a word of it to any human being, untill the result shall be publicly known"—and saw in her an ability to understand and interpret affairs of state in light of his immediate need for information and of his future political ambitions.[39]

Louisa proved him right. From the start, her letters were filled with political intelligence and gossip. Throughout the summer and fall of 1814, she reported to him news—often erroneous—passed on by merchants and others sailing into St. Petersburg. She was not shy about expressing her own opinions on political issues raised during the peace talks. And although she claimed she was unfit for the task, she went about independently managing the household with aplomb, dealing with drunken manservants and a cook liable to strokes, taking a cottage for the summer so that Charles could play freely outdoors, and even purchasing a new carriage when the family vehicle broke down and couldn't be repaired.

In the matter of money, Louisa was always defensive. Knowing all too well John Quincy's penchant for scrutinizing even minor purchases, she seemed to feel the need to justify every ruble spent as a matter of the utmost urgency over which she had no choice. Four months after he had left St. Petersburg, she was still playing the role of the inadequate female: "I am extremely desirous of doing what would be most prudent and best but I have no one to advise with and I cannot rely at all on my own judgement more especially as I have never before been obliged to rely on *myself* and have given too many proofs of my incapacity added to which in matters of expence and management there are few people in the World so exigeant as yourself."[40]

In reality, however, she began to enjoy the power of making purchases without John Quincy's prior approval. Buying watches for her two older sons, Louisa took real pleasure in being able to send to them the first gifts she had ever purchased on her own. "I could not withstand the temptation and indulged myself with the gratification of presenting my Children a trifling souvenir," she wrote her husband in August. And when she decided to move into a much smaller apartment, she explored a number of choices and dealt with a series of landlords before finally settling on appropriate lodging. Her fears that John Quincy would second-guess her decisions were unfounded: "I am happy to find that my ideas so exactly coincide with yours, as to the propriety of taking up a smaller establishment," he wrote.[41]

The same mixed message emerged from her unescorted forays into society. Claiming that she hated to go to court events without her husband, she could not help but enjoy herself: "I hope I got through without disgracing you. On the whole I was never at a more charming party in my life," she wrote after one festive evening in the summer of 1814. Her high spirits continued after Tsar Alexander returned to St. Petersburg following Napoleon's exile to Elba. Writing of her own efforts at transatlantic diplomacy, she described a British dancing partner who "said he would astonish the World, and Show them that the English and Americans had enter'd into an alliance, by dancing a Polonaise with me. We were follow'd by the Emperor who seem'd diverted by it."[42]

Levett Harris, impressed with his own status as chargé d'affaires, attempted to assert some jurisdiction over Louisa's social life. She resisted. When he informed her it would be improper to attend royal events without her husband, since he, Harris, was the only credentialed American representative in St. Petersburg, she defied him and went anyway. "Mr. Harris, my Servants tell me, has been here twice and expressed much dissatisfaction at my having gone. You told me before you went away that I must attend all such invitations and I again repeat I thought I was *doing right*," she wrote to John Quincy.[43]

Louisa also played with Harris's ambition—obvious to her—to take over the ministerial post as soon as John Quincy vacated it. The chargé's frequent visits, she wrote to her husband, appeared to be due to his impatience "to learn what will be your *fate* and you can 'guess *why*.' . . . I am mischievous enough to flatter him with hopes one day and overset them the next." Whether the result of the long summer days at her rented cottage or at the lavish royal entertainments she frequented, Louisa's newfound joie de vivre and confidence were acknowledged by John Quincy with a slight twinge of misgiving: "That you are reconciling yourself to the inconveniences and troubles of a separation from me, cannot give me pain; on the contrary I hear it with pleasure; because present or absent the first wish of my heart is that you should enjoy life in cheerfulness and comfort—But I should deeply lament if the time should ever come that you would *like* to live absent from me. I certainly never shall *like* to live absent from you."[44]

Louisa, for her part, allowed reports of John Quincy's robust health and high spirits to begin to color her letters with a touch of self-reproach. When he was with her, she implied, he suffered from poor health and depression. Believing him to be on the way home to St. Petersburg in late August, she remarked that she hoped he would not be "in danger of falling into the *gloom* from which you seem now to be happily relieved." As fall and winter approached, her letters began to exhibit exactly the "gloom" she attributed to her husband. Deprived of sun and exercise and confined to a small, dark apartment on a side street off the Moika Canal, Louisa was again ill and out of humor. She feared that even her new quarters—as inconvenient and depressing as they were—would not satisfy John Quincy's frugal standards when he returned to St. Petersburg. In October, irritable from an attack of the flu and deprived of her husband's care and concern, she gave vent to years of frustration over John Quincy's parsimony and her inability to please him. Lashing out preemptively against an accusation that she might be spending too much money, Louisa wrote, "If from want of judgement or habit of management I have injured my Children's property, I must submit to their reproaches as I have for many years submitted to yours. Of this I am perfectly assured, I have never willfully done anything which can in the smallest degree injure you or them and that on the contrary my life has been a perpetual sacrifice of every pleasure, often of comfort, to assist in promoting what you have consider'd their welfare."[45]

John Quincy responded with judicious sweetness and calm. Dispassionately, he noted that although her spirits on one occasion had been affected by her "indisposition," she had struck a more positive note in subsequent letters. Responding to her complaint that when she had been ill at other times, he had comforted her by kissing her hand, he said he looked forward to kissing more than her hand when they were reunited "and I hope it will not be at your bed-*side*." Louisa was not so easily won. "Unless times are much changed, the one I mentioned [kissing her hand] would be sufficient to content you," she saucily replied.[46]

For weeks at a time, Louisa's bad mood was quiescent. But by late November, she had turned bitter again: "I am charmed to find by your last letter that you pass your time so agreeably at Ghent. It would be almost a pity that the Congress should break up as by all accounts you have derived so much benefit from your residence. This Climate is so injurious that the idea of your returning to sink again into the state of inanity into which you had fallen is so painful I could almost wish for anything that could prolong your absence."

Louisa described the "same insipid round" that their marriage had fallen into before John Quincy left for Ghent: "It is very fine to *talk* about only being happy in the bosom of one's family, but I confess my ideas of happiness . . . extend to something beyond the pleasure of passing every evening one hour together, the one party sleeping and the other sinking into absolute silence or gaping for want of something better to do. If this is happiness, I want both taste and sense to enjoy it." Turning her venom on herself, but indirectly on John Quincy, Louisa said she was "perfectly aware" of her incapacity to be "an agree-able companion," since she had "too often been made sensible of my incapacity not to feel it most keenly." Still ostensibly shouldering the blame for an unhappy marital relationship, she concluded, "My melancholy disposition affects all who have the misfortune to be allied to me and it is only when they [are] far removed that they find any real enjoyment."[47]

It is not hard to see what set off Louisa's display of bad temper and self-pity. The approach of another long, cold winter darkened her spirits. Her health, as usual, suffered in confined, overheated rooms. She was, she said, "sick and weary" of living alone in a country in which she could not understand the language and among a people she could not trust. John Quincy had written of the young wife of a British diplomat happily playing the role of hostess at gala dinners held jointly by both negotiating teams, and envy, along with regret for her lost youth, may also have played a part in Louisa's recriminations. But her penchant for lacerating herself for her personality flaws and general unlikable-ness seems to have gone further. At heart a social being, Louisa did not find herself an agreeable companion. Her sense of self-worth, always uncertain, suffered under the judgmental glare of her internal appraisal. Her own severest critic, she needed to see herself in the sympathetic gaze of others to avoid self-incrimination. Always, she needed reassurance—even applause—from those she loved or admired. It is to John Quincy's credit that he did not permit himself to be drawn in by Louisa's sallies. When at home, he was probably guilty of allowing her self-doubts to fester and of diminishing her self-confidence by questioning her every purchase and dismissing her abilities as a household manager or as a tutor for their son. Apart, however, he was the soul of patience. Instead of responding directly to her barbs, he typically ignored them.

As the fall dragged on, Louisa and John Quincy's separation had already lasted much longer than either had originally anticipated. The talks in Ghent, once finally begun on August 8, had quickly come to an unhappy standstill. Although America had sent five of its most notable citizens as representatives to the peace commission, Britain had relied on second-rank diplomats who were required to refer all matters back to London before reaching an agreement on the smallest point. At the outset, the British representatives seemed prepared to demand rather than negotiate, and all of their conditions were unacceptable to the United States. Meanwhile, events on land and sea favored Britain. Newspaper dispatches spoke of massive shipments of ground troops to America. American forays into Canada and Florida had been unsuccessful. John Quincy began to write of his fellow diplomats' intentions to return home to the United States immediately and his own plans for taking the most expeditious route to St. Petersburg. Louisa, communicating to him the news of the day, wrote, "the merchants of this place . . . who pretend to *know* every thing, announce that the *instructions* [to the British negotiators] are such as must break up the thing immediately as England is determined not to make Peace at all." Knowing how disappointed John Quincy would be to have failed to secure even the smallest concession, she assured him, "If this is true I shall at least have the satisfaction of soon seeing you and that will in some measure make up for the grief I must feel at your ill success."[48]

But reports of failure were premature. True, British troops had burned the Executive Mansion and other public buildings in Washington on August 24; its warships cruised almost unmolested up and down the East Coast. Yet, American naval successes on Lake Erie and Lake Champlain had blocked an invasion from the north and preserved the Ohio Valley to the United States. Under the gaze of Francis Scott Key, a British attack on Baltimore had been repulsed. It was increasingly clear that public opinion in both Britain and America had turned against an unpopular war waged for no particular purpose. The volatile political situation in Europe was Britain's most pressing concern. To those in power, the war in America had become an expensive diversion of men and resources. When even the Duke of Wellington urged peace, the British Cabinet was quick to agree to bring hostilities to an end. After four months of hard bargaining, and with much bluffing and posturing on both sides, a final peace treaty was signed on Christmas Eve 1814.[49]

The compromise agreement left none of the original issues, such as impressments or freedom of the seas, settled. But the Americans had succeeded in resisting any territorial concessions, and impressments were soon abandoned as a way to man the decks of the Royal Navy. In a letter to Louisa, John Quincy perfectly summed up the results of his negotiations: "We have obtained nothing but Peace and we have made great sacrifices to obtain it. But our honour remains unsullied. Our territory remains entire. The Peace in word and in deed has been made in terms of *perfect reciprocity* and we have surrendered not one right or pretension of our Country." The Treaty of Ghent, which would be unanimously ratified by the Senate in February, was universally popular in the United States. Thanks to it and to Andrew Jackson's magnificent victory at New Orleans on January 8, 1815—a battle fought after the treaty was signed but before word of it had reached the United States—the Ohio, the Mississippi, and the Missouri Rivers would all be open to American trade, exploration, and expansion throughout the dynamic new century.[50]

John Quincy announced the successful conclusion of the peace talks to Louisa two days after Christmas 1814 in a letter—possibly intended for the censor's eyes as well as his wife's—that was less a private communication than a proud public pronouncement: "On Saturday last, the 24th of December, the Emperor Alexander's birth-day, a treaty of Peace and Amity was signed by the British and American Plenipotentiaries in this City." His letter went on to spell out the details of the peace agreement and to hint that he might be appointed ambassador to Britain. In any case, John Quincy made clear, he would not be returning to St. Petersburg and had submitted to President Madison his request to be recalled from the Russian post. In a stunning conclusion that minimized all practical considerations, he called on Louisa to join him in Paris: "I therefore now invite you, to break up altogether our establishment at St. Petersburg, to dispose of all the furniture which you do not incline to keep, to have all the rest packed up carefully and left in the charge of Mr. Harris to be sent next Summer either to London or to Boston, and to come with Charles to me at Paris, where I shall be impatiently waiting for you."[51]

Since his own passage to Ghent had been mostly by sea in spring, the overland trip John Quincy was proposing was not one he had taken himself. His invitation downplayed the fact that it was midwinter in a harsh, northern climate, that the journey of nearly 2,000 miles would cover much the same ground that two armies had recently devastated, and that closing up their apartment and disposing of their belongings was a formidable task. Louisa's first reaction to his proposal was dismay: "Conceive the astonishment your letter caused me if you can," she responded. Yet, in her son Charles's words many years later, her decision to leave at once was "the work but of a moment. For to her mind what could be the terror of a solitary journey through the late theatre of a furious and bloody war the plains and villages still bearing palpable evidence of its horrors compared with that charming prospect of a return to more genial climes to the company of an affectionate husband and an approximation towards her long absent children?"[52]

More daunting than the trip itself, she believed, would be disposing of their belongings to John Quincy's satisfaction. As always, Louisa feared she could not meet her husband's standards—"I know not what to do about selling of the goods and I fear I shall be much imposed upon"—but she embarked on the task with furious energy. As she had suspected, it was not easy to sell their belongings for what they were worth: "I find it almost impossible to dispose of the things to any sort of advantage. Nobody has ready money." Refusing the offer of one merchant to exchange diamonds for her carriage, she immediately regretted she had been so adamant. As the month of January 1815 wore on, however, Louisa began to exhibit a skill for trade she may have inherited from her father. "I am turn'd woman of business," she wrote John Quincy proudly. She made $1,693 on sales of the family furniture to help finance her travel expenses, which John Quincy later calculated to be $1,984.99. As she organized the complex details of her projected trip, Louisa daily gained confidence in her decision-making skills and pride in her ability to function effectively in the male world of commercial transactions. Even so, she had been so thoroughly cowed by her husband that she could not acknowledge success: "If I do wrong, it is unintentional. Mon Ami, I am so afraid of cold looks," she wrote beseechingly to him just before her departure.[53]

In the midst of the confusion surrounding her departure, Louisa also embarked on a round of visits, formal and informal. John Quincy had instructed her to leave behind no hard feelings toward America since it might be some time before a new ambassador could be found willing to be assigned to St. Petersburg. Everywhere she visited, she was presented with letters of introduction to important people who could assist her all along the way to Paris; everyone, it seemed, knew a governor in one of the states and principalities she would pass through or the mayor of a city where she expected to stop. One official alerted all the postmasters along the way in Russia and its dominions to watch for Louisa's arrival and "on pain of Punishment" to provide her with good horses to speed her on her way. Gifts, too, poured in. Most of these she had boxed for shipment home or to London. But a beautiful silver cup presented to Charles by the Westphalian minister seemed too valuable to leave behind. She determined to carry it with her.[54]

John Quincy sent her very specific instructions on what to say to the dowager empress and the empress during her final audience at court. Since he himself had not been officially notified of his new appointment, she was to acknowledge only that she was leaving St. Petersburg to rejoin her husband in Paris, not that he had been reassigned to the Court of St. James's. The Tsarina Elizabeth, however, knew instinctively that Louisa was delighted by more than a temporary absence from Russia. "She saw joy sparkle in my eyes." After the farewell audience, Elizabeth remarked that she had never seen a woman "so alter'd in her life for the better."[55]

Sadder were Louisa's visits to say farewell to the intimate circle of friends who had stood by her during her nearly six-year sojourn in St. Petersburg, especially the young Countess Marie Colombi. At tea just before Louisa's departure, the two were joined by an uninvited third party, the Countess Apraxin, who was, Louisa wrote many years later, a "fat coarse woman, very talkative, full of scandal" and devoted to the practice of "bonne aventure" (fortune telling). The new arrival appeared to think it her duty to entertain Louisa and their hostess and insisted on telling Louisa's fortune. Calling for a deck of cards, she asked Louisa to choose a queen.

"You are going on a long journey," Countess Apraxin said. "You are not reluctant to leave St. Petersburg. You will soon meet those from whom you have been long separated."

There was nothing particularly prophetic in the fortune teller's tale so far, and Louisa found the whole performance comical. But the countess wasn't finished: "When you have completed half your journey, you will be much alarmed by a great change in the political world," she said. "The activities of a great man will produce an extraordinary moment in history and set all Europe into a fresh commotion. You will hear of these events while you are on the road. They will oblige you to change all your plans and will render your journey extremely difficult."

Laughing, Louisa complimented the countess on her skill in reading the cards but responded that she had no fear of becoming involved in the affairs of a "great man." There was no likelihood, she said, "of such a circumstance, as I was so insignificant and the arrangements for my journey so simple, I was quite satisfied that I should accomplish it if I escaped from accidents, without meeting with any obstacles of the kind predicted; more especially as it was a time of Peace." As Louisa remembered the conversation later, Countess Apraxin was unexpectedly serious and insistent, "She hoped I should *remember*, to which I responded I was certain I could never forget her."[56]

Just as pressing as breaking up her home and meeting her social and diplomatic obligations was Louisa's need to purchase and equip a carriage for the long trip. She and Charles would require, at a minimum, several changes of warm winter clothes, medical supplies, food and drink, and pillows and blankets, all of which had to be packed as compactly as possible. A mattress was fitted out so that Charles could sleep comfortably when they traveled at night, but Louisa evidently planned to rest while sitting up. Visits to bankers and government officials took valuable time, but it was essential that she have in hand letters of credit and passports through the various states and principalities she would have to traverse.

Finally, there was the matter of servants. John Quincy strongly advised Louisa to hire a "good man" and a female companion to accompany her. This was easier said than done. An overland trip to France in winter held little appeal for anyone, no matter how desperate he or she was to leave Russia. Through the agency of Countess Colombi, Louisa finally found an elderly French woman, Mme. Babet, a former nanny to Russian noble families, who desired to spend her final years at home in France. Louisa later described her as "a quiet and respectable person, older than myself, and very plain in her person, and manners, and very steady." John Fulling, a onetime servant to William Smith, also agreed to accompany her.[57]

At the very last minute, when it seemed she might be unable to depart for lack of adequate male protection, Harris came up with another man. Louisa later identified him as Baptiste, "a released prisoner from the remnant of Napoleons Army." From the start, Louisa was worried about Baptiste. To avoid exposing exactly how much money she carried, she hid her gold and silver coins close to her person, probably within the lining of her voluminous cloak and skirts. "I had contrived to conceal the bags of gold and silver which I carried in such a manner that neither of my Men Servants supposed that I possessed any," she later wrote. Her plan, which she assiduously put into effect, was to cash her letters of credit for small sums along the way, indicating to the men accompanying her that whatever cash she had on hand wasn't worth stealing. Meanwhile, her hidden reserves of gold and silver would be insurance that she would never face an emergency unprepared.

Throughout January 1815, a stronger, more confident woman than the relatively timid young wife who had arrived in Russia in 1809 prepared to depart St. Petersburg forever. In marked contrast to her experience during every other winter of her Russian sojourn, she did not suffer as much as a cold. Her hair now streaked with gray, Louisa had undergone a metamorphosis from a seemingly fragile "fine lady" to a woman well-seasoned in the ways of the world. With grace and efficiency she had closed out a life she had lived for nearly six years. That life, punctuated by the tragic loss of her daughter, had not been easy. There had never been enough money. She had entirely missed critical developmental years in the lives of her older sons, and she had been far from home during her mother's and older sister's final hours. Russia's harsh climate had never agreed with her, and each previous winter her health and that of every member of her family had suffered. Although her acceptance into the tsar's inner circle had gone far to overcome the coldness she found in the nobility, she was leaving behind only a small coterie of friends. Despite all this, she had survived. She was leaving Russia with her reputation unblemished, an extraordinary feat in a licentious society. If, as her son Charles later put it, her primary role was to be "the first lady presented to the notice of the Russian court as a representative of American female manners and character," there could be no question that she had set a high standard for poise and integrity.[58]

Louisa could look back on a job well done, especially over the past month. Without having to cater to John Quincy's whims and freed from working around his demands and priorities, she had met a formidable challenge. In four weeks, she had organized a journey that no woman, and few men, of her acquaintance had attempted. Now she could look to the future. In a letter left to be mailed after the carriage departed from her doorstep, Louisa wrote to John Quincy of her love for him and her eager anticipation of their reunion. "I could not celebrate my birthday in manner more delightful than in making the first step towards that meeting for which my Soul pants and for which I have hitherto hardly dared to express my desire." She was finally on her way home.[59]

THE JOURNEY OF A LIFETIME

Many undertakings which appear very difficult and arduous to my Sex, are by no means so trying as imagination forever depicts them.

—LOUISA CATHERINE ADAMS, *"Narrative of a Journey from Russia to France"*

Night falls early in the Russian winter. At five o'clock on the evening of February 12, 1815—her fortieth birthday—Louisa emerged from her small, gloomy apartment for the last time. Anxious to avoid the "disagreeable and painful feelings" of saying good-bye, she had chosen the dinner hour as her moment to slip away in darkness from the city she had called home for nearly six years. Life in Russia had never been easy, yet it was surprisingly difficult to go. "I leave Russia with regret," she acknowledged in her final letter from St. Petersburg to John Quincy. The grave of her adored daughter would remain untended. Her close circle of friends would gradually fade from memory.[1]

In the narrow side street just off the Moika Canal two vehicles stood waiting. The larger was a Russian-built, heavy, enclosed carriage—a *berline*—pulled by six horses and gliding on runners. The other was a *kibitka*, a strange-looking vehicle pulled by two horses, open on the forward side, and resembling a domed tent on a sled. The two guards would travel in the kibitka.

The wind off the canal was intensely cold. The powerful coach horses, restless to be on their way, blew ice crystals into the night air and stamped their hooves on the snow-packed cobblestones. The great bells in St. Isaac's Cathedral boomed out the hour, their deep bass notes echoing across the miles of thick ice that covered the River Neva and the city's many canals. Louisa climbed into the lead carriage; seven-year-old Charles sat at her side, excited but frightened. The elderly Frenchwoman, Mme. Babet, shrouded in a heavy shawl, would have already been seated in her corner. The small convoy headed southwest out of the imperial capital, the carriage and kibitka's slick runners making good time

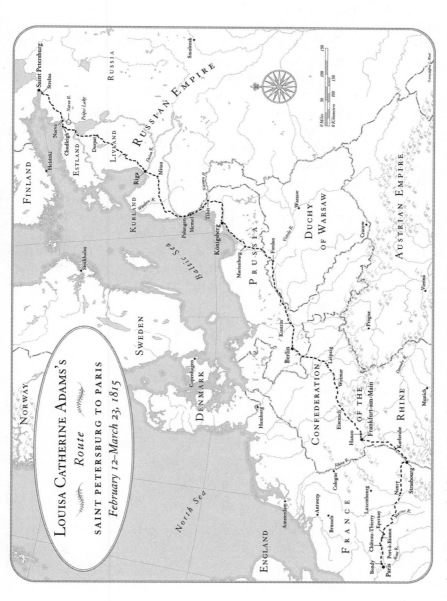

The route that Louisa traveled from St. Petersburg to Paris in the winter of 1815. By Jeffrey Ward from *Mrs. Adams in Winter*, by Michael O'Brien. Copyright © 2010 by Jeffrey Ward. Reprinted by permission of Farrar, Straus and Giroux, LLC.

on the icy roads. It was too early at night for the pale winter moon, and no stars had appeared in the great sky overhead. A blanket of darkness covered the empty fields as far as the eye could see. The stiff, leafless birches cracked in the cold. Bands of wolves began to howl.

Determined to make the trip as expeditiously as possible, Louisa gave orders to travel both night and day. This meant she slept only in naps, fully dressed, interrupted by required stops at post houses along the way. There she would show her official papers and change horses and postilions—local men who rode one or two of the horses and showed the way to the next post house. Whether day or night, the temperature was bitterly cold—Louisa recalled later that her Madeira wine had frozen in its bottles. At the provincial border town of Narva—her first real stop—she was flattered to be visited at the "very best Inn in the place" by an emissary of the governor, who informed her that an apartment had been prepared for her comfort with the hope that she would remain a few days. The governor himself then visited her at the inn, as did the Bavarian minister to Russia, who happened to be in town visiting his wife's family. The latter invited Louisa to visit his in-laws during her stopover. Declining both invitations, as she would many similar offers in the coming weeks, she replied that the urgency to reunite with her husband meant she needed to be on the road to Riga by dawn.[2]

Louisa claimed no merit in forcing the pace of her journey at the price of denying herself some of the pleasures in life she dearly loved—meeting new people at elegant dinners, attending the theater, and touring unfamiliar cities and towns. Her steady determination to decline appealing invitations, she recalled, stemmed "from a proud and fool hardy spirit and the conviction that . . . the difficulties of my path must be conquered, and it was as well to face them at once." Confronting a daunting challenge, she was afraid she might give way to her fears if she allowed herself to dwell on them in the comfort and security of a noble residence. Expense was an issue as well. Outfitting the berline and kibitka for the journey had cost more than Louisa had anticipated, and she was painfully aware that John Quincy would scrutinize every meal and purchase on her trip.[3]

Personal considerations, however, were paramount. Louisa badly missed her husband. The nine months she had spent alone in Russia had been the longest she had been without his company since their wedding day eighteen years earlier, and she had no intention of stretching their separation a day longer than necessary.

One hundred miles outside Riga, it began to rain, and Louisa's party was "overtaken by thaw." Wheels were installed on her berline, but the kibitka had to be dragged through the muddy, rutted roads on its runners. Louisa arrived in the provincial capital on February 16, four days after leaving St. Petersburg. She had gone some 350 miles, at a pace of nearly ninety miles a day. Writing her first letter of the journey to John Quincy, she blithely assured him that she had "traveled through Russia as agreeably as the Season and the nature of the roads would admit."[4]

In Riga, she found the same warm welcome she had enjoyed in Narva. Recognizing that the honors accorded her were largely a tribute to her position as the wife of the American minister, she was privately gratified at the recognition. This time, the local governor offered her both the use of his carriage and an invitation to pass her stay in the city as his guest in Riga Castle. Again, she declined to give up her room at the "tolerable lodgings" she had found but accepted the governor's invitation to dinner and the theater and to meet "all the most distinguished persons in Town."[5]

In Riga, too, she entertained the first of what would become an increasingly specific set of suspicions regarding her manservant Baptiste. The silver goblet presented to Charles in Russia by the Westphalian minister was missing from her carriage. "There was little Doubt that he had made free with it," she wrote of Baptiste, but, under the terms of the man's contract with her, she believed she was obliged to take him with her to his final destination in France. Moreover, as a woman traveling without a male companion, she needed the physical protection of both her armed guards. Admitting she had no real proof that Baptiste was the thief, Louisa decided not to press the issue.

Just two and a half days later, Louisa was on the road again, this time without the kibitka, which she had sold because of its worthlessness on anything but snow-packed roads. Her two guards now rode outside the carriage with the coachman, their belongings and the other baggage crammed on top of the carriage. But, as she headed southwest, through what is now Latvia, the snows of winter returned. More than once, the berline became stuck in wet drifts, and, Louisa reported, the passengers had to "ring up the inhabitants, who came out in numbers with shovels and pickaxes to dig us out—For this purpose the bell appeared to be commonly used, and the signal readily understood." Arriving in Mitau on the River Aa, a hospitable city with a thriving cultural life, Louisa proposed to stop only long enough to have dinner and change horses before pressing on to the next post station. At an inn she judged "the best I had found: the people very civil, and every thing comfortable," she was promptly visited by a local notable, this time a countess she had known in St. Petersburg. As always, declining an offer of an extended stay and the opportunity to see "all that was worth seeing in the Town" and to meet "some of [the countess's] distinguished friends," Louisa cited the urgency of rejoining her husband. Nonetheless, she was tempted to accept her friend's offer, especially when the noblewoman, who had broken away from "a gay party," made a second attempt to persuade her to remain for a few days in the city.[6]

The countess's two visits had not gone unnoticed by Monsieur Morel, the innkeeper. When her dinner had been cleared away, he knocked at Louisa's door and "after carefully shutting the doors and watchfully noting that no intruders were near," expressed a wish to be of service to any friend of the countess. But when Louisa asked him to sit down, Morel instead began to pace anxiously about the room: "He again examined the doors with an appearance of great anxiety, and then sat down close to me, who felt not a little uncomfortable at all this *apparently terrible preparation*—I however assumed an air of great calmness and patiently awaited the *mighty tale*, which was to thrill my nerves with horror."[7]

Morel did, in fact, have two horrific tales to tell. The first was of a "dreadful murder" that had taken place the night before on the very road Louisa intended to travel later that evening. She responded "very coolly and decidedly" that, as she had two armed servants and the road was a very well-traveled one, she felt certain she could safely reach her day's final destination by nine or ten that night. The innkeeper "looked very grave, and shook his head," and, mentioning his own daughters, said he thought it his responsibility to alert her to the danger she faced as a woman traveling at night on a route that had so recently proved deadly. Louisa thanked him for his concern but reiterated her intention of pressing forward as soon as the coach was ready.

Morel then turned to the much more sensitive subject of her manservant Baptiste. On his arrival in Mitau, Baptiste had been immediately recognized by many residents as "a desperate Villain, of the very worst character" who had lived in the city for two years prior to his capture in Russia. Louisa, displaying no sign of her own uneasiness, responded that Baptiste had "behaved very well so far; that I had felt a mistrust of him, and did not like him; but that the Gentleman who had engaged him had entered into a bond, that he should be taken to his own Country; and that I was not to part with him unless he behaved improperly—That I had no pretence to make any charge against him, as he had been particularly active and attentive; and that his conduct and manners were very respectful."[8]

Morel was placed in a difficult position. If Louisa dismissed Baptiste in Mitau, the man would suspect the innkeeper of alerting her to the details of his criminal past and, Morel feared, might seek revenge by burning down the inn. The innkeeper suggested that, as Louisa seemed determined to continue her journey as planned, she should "appear to place unlimited confidence" in Baptiste, to turn to him in an emergency, and accept his advice whenever possible. When she was nearer her destination, he counseled, she could dismiss him if the occasion warranted. Finally, Morel implored her to keep their conversation secret since to reveal they had spoken might put both of their lives in danger. She readily agreed and embarked from Mitau "under the most uneasy impressions."[9]

Much sooner than either she or Morel expected, Louisa was forced to accept the innkeeper's caution to rely implicitly on Baptiste in an emergency. The carriage had only traveled about four miles when the postilion dismounted from the lead horse and informed her he had "missed the road." He was, he said, a last-minute substitute and had never conducted a coach on that route before. Now, the heavy berline was forced to lurch from one deep rut to another "through swamps, and holes, and into valleys, into which no Carriage had surely ever passed before" as the coachman and postilion tried to find their way from the untrodden track back to the main thoroughfare. By midnight, it was clear the party was badly lost. Under the influence of Morel's dire warnings, Louisa could have collapsed in a fainting fit, as she had under bad news in earlier days. Instead, concealing her fears for the fate of her seven-year-old son, sleeping peacefully through all the commotion, she coolly assessed the situation: "I consulted Baptiste frequently, and took his advice as to the best mode of proceeding, and at twelve o'clock at night the Horses being utterly worn out, and scarce a twinkling Star to teach of living light; we determined that Baptiste should ride one of the Horses, and endeavour to find a road through which we might be extricated from our perillous situation."[10]

Suspecting Baptiste as she did, Louisa must have been more than a little discomfited to see him ride off into the night alone, leaving the lost little party in the bitter cold and deep darkness to await his return—if he ever came back. In only fifteen minutes, however, Baptiste "rode hastily" up to the carriage door and informed her that he had encountered a dwelling nearby and had roused its inhabitants. He had also come across a Russian officer who had volunteered to lead the coach back to the road "as it required great skill to keep the Carriage out of the gullies by which we were surrounded." This he did, and Louisa finally reached her intended destination at half past one in the morning. At the "very indifferent" inn she found there, she provided all the men with drink and herself and Mme. Babet with coffee. After the Russian left the inn, with a "handsome present" in hand, she briskly informed her menservants that they would be leaving very early in the morning and thanked them for "the prudence and discretion, which they had shown through this singular accident."[11]

Alone in her room sometime after 2 A.M., Louisa resolved not to "listen to any more bugbears to alarm my nerves and weaken my understanding" and prayed in thanksgiving for her successful delivery from "this hour of trial." Three days later she did not even mention the event in a letter to John Quincy except to say that "our trials have been pretty severe but I am not good at talking of our 'hairs breadth' scapes so I will say nothing more." As she was "neither young nor beautiful," she wrote later, no dramatic embellishments could be employed to make what she chose to think of as an unfortunate occurrence into a romance. She attributed the terrors she had undergone to Morel's tales of murder and warnings about Baptiste and recalled that it was only her "relief from this fearful and harassing anxiety [that] could have given an extraordinary interest, to so trifling an incident." She was being disingenuous. As a devoted reader of Gothic novels, she knew the value of a good story. This one, with its tincture of murdering brigands, a breakdown in a frozen wasteland, and eventual deliverance by an officer on horseback was much more than a routine event. Whether or not she acknowledged it, she must have felt some private satisfaction in conducting herself throughout the ordeal with unruffled composure.[12]

At daybreak, Louisa was on her way again. Now the spring thaw had set in in earnest, and progress was painfully slow. At four in the afternoon, she reached the shore of the Windau River. Here she faced a dilemma. There was no bridge, and the ice on the river was beginning to break up. She had two options. One was to take a "very long and tedious detour" to a place where she could cross confidently; the other was to make the attempt to cross on the melting ice. She decided on the riskier course. At five in the evening, as night ominously descended, men she hired from the hamlet on the east bank of the river attached the carriage to the horses by long poles in order to distribute the weight over the greatest possible area. The same men went gingerly ahead of the horses, tapping the ice to find the firmest footing. All went well until the party reached the further shore only to find to find the ice completely broken up and the waterline well below the top of the bank. "It required a violent effort in the horses, to prevent the coach from upsetting on the bank," Louisa recalled.[13]

Not at all nonplussed by the experience, Louisa directed that the coach travel through the night in order to reach the Prussian border by the next day, February 20. At the last post house in Russia, she was finally forced to use her influence. "Here I had to wait three hours for horses, and the people were so much inclined to be impudent, I was obliged to produce my Letter, and to inform the Master of the House, that I should write immediately to the Minister of the Interior, and complain of his Conduct." It worked. "The Man appeared to be much alarmed, made a great many apologies; and said the Horses should be ready immediately, and very *politely* obliged me to take a couple more than the usual compliment, as he thought the Carriage very heavy."[14]

In just eight days, Louisa had traveled 552 miles, a remarkable distance considering the condition of the roads, the heaviness of the carriage, and the necessity of stopping occasionally at an inn. Almost overnight, a petite, forty-year-old woman had gained a small measure of stature in her own eyes. Emboldened by her newfound courage, Louisa had maintained calm when lost in the wintry Russian wastes, chosen the riskier route across the Windau, and faced down a surly post master. Crossing into Prussia, she was undaunted by the officious uniformed border guards who made her go through the "formality of showing my Passports, and answering all the customary questions too tedious to enumerate."[15]

Deriding her reluctant postilions, who tried to persuade her to take a room at an inn for the night—"I enquired if there was any particular difficulty, but found that the principal objection was, that it would be *dark* before we should get across, and that it was a dreadful gloomy road"—she traveled through the night and the next day southeast to Tilsit, the town where Napoleon and Alexander II had signed their accord 1807. In Tilsit, she again turned west toward Königsberg, long the capital of East Prussia. Until now, her journey had taken her through the Baltic provinces, which had been only indirectly affected by Napoleon's march into Russia and his bloody retreat from Moscow. Beginning in Tilsit, she was retracing the paths of the French and Russian armies and seeing before her eyes the devastation of war: "Houses half burnt, a very thin population; women unprotected, and that dreary look of forlorn desertion, which sheds its gloom around on all the objects, announcing devastation and despair."[16]

When Louisa arrived in Königsberg on a cold and rainy February day, the city had barely recovered from its capture by the French in 1806 and its subsequent military occupation and role as an assembly point and procurement center for the Grande Armée's attack on Russia in the summer of 1812. The marks of the French retreat would be harder to erase. Like those in other East Prussian cities and towns on the evacuation route out of Russia after the debacle in Moscow, the citizens of Königsberg had watched with horror as the remnants of Napoleon's army passed by. Wagons bearing the sick and wounded jostled with ragged and exhausted foot soldiers for whom all military discipline was a thing of the past. The battle-weathered Prussian General Freidrich Wilhelm von Bülow later wrote that "nothing in [my] lifetime had been more shocking than the scenes in Königsberg" during November and December 1812.[17]

Yet, Königsberg by 1815 was a bustling city of 60,000 people, and Louisa was happy to spend a day exchanging her letters of credit for cash, completing arrangements for the next segment of her journey, and making "some trifling purchases of Amber," the gemstone for which the city was renowned. Had she had a male escort, she wrote later, she would have gone to the theater, a pleasure she rarely passed up.

Her sang-froid was put to the test, however, as she waited on February 23 until 3 P.M. for the heavy, wintry rains to let up enough so that her carriage could leave Königsberg for Berlin. Baptiste had begun "to assume a tone not by any means agreeable." Uneasy as to what his change in attitude meant, she imperiously called him on the carpet: "I intimated to him that he might leave me as soon as he pleased, as I was in a Country where I was very well known, as I had lived four years in Berlin, and was acquainted with the King, and all the Royal Family—He said his great desire was to return to his own Country, and that he did not wish to leave me—That he understood I had *agreed* to take him the whole way—I told him that the performance of this *agreement* depended on his good behaviour, and that if he was diligent and attentive, I should have no wish to part with him."[18]

Although Baptiste adopted a more respectful tone from then on, Louisa was not entirely satisfied. "There was something threatening in his look that did not please me, but I was afraid to notice it." She was also concerned that John Fulling, her other manservant, was clearly afraid of Baptiste and would do anything to avoid trouble with him. Both men, she decided, would bear further watching.[19]

Finally on her way again, Louisa had traveled seven miles along the road out of Königsberg and "more than a mile from any assistance," when the front wheel of the carriage "broke to pieces." The postilions advised her that the carriage could neither proceed further nor turn back. She would need an alternate means of conveyance to the nearest village since the road was in an unwalkable condition and night was closing in. One of the postilions, going for help, returned after a substantial delay, with a "miserable common cart" into which Louisa, Charles, Mme. Babet, and Baptiste crowded for the bumpy ride back to the nearest dwelling. What they discovered there brought scant comfort to Louisa. "It was a hovel consisting of two rooms and a blacksmiths shop," in which lived a "dirty, ugly, and ill natured" woman and "two or three very surly ill looking men, whose manners were far from prepossessing or kindly." Baptiste, apparently deputized to speak to the men, tried unavailingly to persuade them to convey the women and Charles back to Königsberg. The peasants suggested an alternative, however—for a price, they would make a new, temporary wheel so that the carriage could proceed in the morning. They also would house Louisa's party in the hut overnight.[20]

With one guard assigned to remain with the carriage to protect their possessions and the other standing sentry outside the door, Louisa and Mme. Babet
remained upright, hungry, and exhausted through the night inside the hovel.
Charles, meanwhile, slept soundly on his little portable bed. By morning the
party was back on the road with a new, clumsy, unpainted wheel. Soon, they
encountered a traveler, going the other way, who stopped them to inquire how
often their carriage had been overturned on the rough roadway. He had been
forced to extricate himself from the mud seven times, he informed Louisa. In
high spirits after the trials of the previous night, she found the encounter
amusing, especially as she had not met with a similar accident: "I could not
help laughing at his doleful account, and told him as I had not yet been so
roughly dealt with, I hoped to escape the pleasure altogether—He informed me
he was Count somebody . . . and that he was on his way to St. Petersburg—I
wished him better luck and we parted," she later wrote.[21]

Louisa needed all the joie de vivre she could muster when she arrived that
night at the city of Küstrin, a place that, in her view, represented even worse
aspects of war than any she had yet seen: "The desolation of this spot was unut-
terably dismal; and the guarded tone of the conversation, the suppressed sighs,
the significant shrug, were all painful indications of the miseries of unholy
Ambition, and the insatiate cravings of contaminating and soul corrupting War,
with all its train of horrors." Accustomed to stories she had heard in St. Petersburg
of the widespread ruin left in the wake of the French army, which she was more
than ready to attribute to the former emperor's "unholy Ambition," Louisa was
shocked in Küstrin to hear "nothing but praises of the gallantry of Napoleon,
and his Officers, and great regret at the damage done to this beautiful fortress."
The road she would travel the next morning, she was told, was "the most beautiful road in the world" and would have been even finer had Napoleon been
allowed to complete it. There was little sympathy for the victorious army that
had beaten the emperor back to France. Instead, horror stories about the depredations the Russian Cossacks had visited on an innocent population were on
everyone's lips: "The Cossacks! the dire Cossacks! were the perpetual theme,
and the cheeks of the Women blanched at the very name."[22]

The women of Küstrin had reason to grow pale when they recalled their
recent experiences. The Cossacks, natives of central Asia, served as irregular
Russian light cavalry and lancers. Supplying their own horses, which were fast,
small, and very easy to maneuver, they could move far ahead or behind the
regular army, weighed down as it was with heavy artillery and supply wagons.
Cossack units were therefore unrivaled as scouts and adept at cutting off enemy
supply lines and making surprise forays against unwitting rival troops. Almost as

effective as their contributions to the regular army's strategic objectives, however, was the universal terror they engendered. Their reputation for committing atrocities on men, women, and children wherever they went and their habit of plundering any manor, village, or town in their path was enough to disperse civilians and panic skittish soldiers whenever the word went out, "The Cossacks are coming!"

The scenes of war would not be far from Louisa's mind as she journeyed west. Entering Berlin on March 4 after a fourteen-year absence, she looked forward to revisiting a city where "the pleasant recollections of the past" would recapture a youthful time in her life "decked with rosy smiles, and glad antici-pations." But, even here, war had left its mark: "It was the same City that I had left in all its bearings. The beautiful Linden Strasse! the fine Brandenburg Gate; the Bridges, the Palaces, all spoke of former times; but yet it was cold, and flat, and there was a foreign air about it, which damped the pleasure I had expected, in revisiting the scenes of my youth—I missed many objects which had formerly excited my admiration, and the perfect stillness seemed to cast a gloom over all the scenes, which had once been so gay, and brilliant."[23]

Louisa lost no time in reconnecting with old friends, who "received [her] in the kindest manner possible." Beginning on the afternoon she arrived in the city, her social calendar was crowded with reunion visits to the princesses and countesses, noblewomen and expatriates with whom she had been intimate so many years before. Of the many friends and acquaintances with whom she reconnected during her single week in Berlin, she said later, she could "write a Volume." She was greeted with "unaffected warmth, and my reception was that of long separated and beloved Sister: each vied with the other in marks of attachment making my stay a succession of delights."[24]

Prussia's statesmen and military leaders were in Austria with King Frederick William III at the high-powered Congress of Vienna, where the political and geographical future of Europe was being decided. Chaired by the brilliant Austrian diplomat Prince Klemens von Metternich, the Congress comprised foreign ministers from all of Europe's major powers and minor states. In almost every case, these men represented the foremost diplomatic talent their nations and states had to offer, then or in the century to come. Countering Metternich's diplomatic skills were Talleyrand, representing the newly installed king of France, Louis XVIII; Viscount Castlereagh (and, later, the Duke of Wellington) of Britain; Count Karl Nesselrode of Russia; and William von Humboldt of Prussia. Royal heads of state deeply involved in crucial negotiations, along with Frederick William, were Tsar Alexander I of Russia and Emperor Francis I of Austria. The balance of power that came out of these deliberations established the basic diplomatic framework under which European nations operated until World War I.

Much of the Prussian court's former pomp and spectacle had been suspended in the absence of the ruler and his entourage; entertaining was temporarily on a much more informal scale. Louisa had no regrets that the stiff protocol characterizing royal entertainments when she was a young bride had given way to the simple back-and-forth of conversation among friends, but she regretted the reason for it: "The great people of Berlin had suffered so much from the War, that there was no pretention of style among them, and they were glad to see their friends socially."[25]

All of Prussia had, in fact, suffered in the years after Louisa and John Quincy returned to the United States. The vaunted Prussian army had been vanquished by Napoleon's superior logistic and strategic skills in the battles of Jena and Auerstadt in 1806. A peace agreement signed by Napoleon and Frederick William at Tilsit in 1807 placed the proud Prussians firmly under the thumb of the French emperor. Prussia lost its lands west of the Elbe, nearly all of Prussian Poland, the city of Danzig, and all its fortresses in Silesia. It was also forced to pay a large indemnity to France, thus impoverishing the national treasury, support an enormous army of occupation, and reduce its own military forces. Finally, it was compelled to join the Continental System, which resulted in a major loss of trade. Even Queen Louise, whom Napoleon had dubbed "my beautiful enemy," had been unable to persuade the emperor to lessen the terms of capitulation.[26]

There was another reason that made Berlin in the winter of 1815 so much less glamorous than it had been at the turn of the century. The young queen who, in Louisa's eyes, had singlehandedly made Berlin "so gay and brilliant" lay dead three miles away in a neoclassical mausoleum in Charlottenburg. Louise had died in 1810, at thirty-four, leaving a heartbroken husband, seven young children, and a mourning nation. Louisa took time from her many social obligations to visit the shrine: "The object of most interest [to me] was the mausoleum of the Queen at Charlottenburg in all its beauty; decorated with a bower of evergreens; emblems of the undying love and respects of her subjects."[27]

Death, like war, continued to intrude on Louisa's happiness in revisiting Berlin. On her first afternoon in the city, she announced her arrival not only to her titled friends but also to an American staying in the same hotel. He was a Captain Norman, apparently previously known to herself and John Quincy because, in a letter to her husband, Louisa did not feel she had to identify further the man she "had found dying of a fever in the upper story of the Hotel, for want of care and attention." In her *Narrative*, she wrote, "Poor Norman has been confined to his bed four months. I went to see him yesterday in his chamber and propose to do so while I stay. I much fear it will be long ere he recovers if ever. He appears to be in a deep consumption."[28]

Before Louisa left Berlin, she engaged the assistance of her old friend Pauline Neale and her family to continue oversight of Captain Norman's case. She also settled her financial accounts, ordered repairs for the carriage, and obtained a new French passport "as I was not satisfied with the one which the French Ambassador had given me at St. Petersburg." Her boundless energy all during her visit to the city, following nineteen days of grueling travel, would have been remarkable in anyone but was especially noteworthy in a woman not known for her physical endurance. Louisa believed she had come into her own. In Berlin, she said, she "felt *at home*; all the sweet sympathies of humanity had been reawakened; and the sterile heartlessness of a Russian residence of icy coldness, was thawed into life and animation."[29]

The warm welcome from her noble friends and the efficient completion of her business and official transactions buoyed Louisa's confidence in her ability to conclude her journey successfully. She would need all the self-assurance she could muster. As she prepared to leave Berlin, she realized she was, at least for the foreseeable future, entirely on her own. Much to her dismay, she had received no letter from John Quincy during her stay in Berlin and. indeed, no message from him had met her at any of her previous stops. "I am cruelly disappointed," she wrote him on March 5. Not only had she looked to him for guidance as to the best possible route for the remainder of her journey, she missed hearing from him as any loving wife would miss hearing from her husband. In former years, the thought that she would have to manage a hazardous trip on her own so that she, her son, and her servants could arrive safely in France might have overwhelmed her. In the early spring of 1815, however, she accepted the challenge with little complaint and, in fact, with remarkable alacrity.

On the morning of March 11, 1815, Louisa, Mme. Babet, and Charles again climbed into the berline, the two armed guards mounted to the coachman's seat, and the travelers headed west out of Berlin toward Frankfurt am Main. Now the roads were in much better shape than they had been in Russia and its provinces, but the matter of personal security was more disquieting. Observing straggling groups of hungry and tired disbanded soldiers along her route, Louisa adopted the stratagem at nightfall of placing Charles's toy sword and dress-up military cap along the window ledge of the carriage in an attempt to lend its occupants a military air. Fearing a random assault, she was grateful for the presence of her two guards, whether or not she trusted their honesty or loyalty.

She had reason to be on her guard. Finally stopping at an inn after a very long day on the road, Louisa "went to bed very tired, and for the first time left [her] purse with some gold in it upon the Table." She remembered later that Mme. Babet had carefully locked the doors of the bedchamber, but when they awoke in the morning, "the lamp was gone out of the chamber, my purse was there, but the gold was gone!" Even more troubling than losing some of her cash reserve was the news she heard bandied about the inn: "A rumour had arrived of the return of Napoleon to France; which . . . created many jokes, as he was *Known* to be very safe at Elba! but such a *rumour* was abroad, and in every body's mouth — I started with astonishment."[30]

"In spite of [her] reason," Louisa couldn't help feeling apprehensive about this potentially momentous change in events, especially when she recalled Countess Apraxin's prophecy that a "great man" would have a significant impact on her trip. She had never doubted that the countess's "great man" was Napoleon.[31]

Ordering an early departure, Louisa was on her way at daybreak, but now the rumors were too widespread to ignore. "Wherever we stopped to change Horses, we heard of the return of Napoleon," she wrote later. Approaching the ancient fortified city of Hanau, where an exceptionally brutal battle — "one of the most murderous in this campaign," in the words of a contemporary — had been fought between French and Austro-Bavarian troops on October 30, 1813, Louisa came upon one of the most horrifying scenes she was ever to witness: "We entered on a wide extended plain, over which was scattered remnants of Clothes; old Boots in pieces; and an immense quantity of bones, laying in this ploughed field." Always in her mind was the small boy at her side and the importance of not causing him further alarm, but she had to struggle to maintain her composure. "Conceive my horror at the sight of such a butchery! I could with difficulty keep from fainting, as fancy realized the torture, suffering, and anguish, thus brought before my eyes, with all the ghastly relics of the dead, exposed with savage barbarity to the view."[32]

With these vestiges of war fresh in her eyes, Louisa was disconcerted to learn in Hanau that there was now no doubt that Napoleon had escaped from Elba and that he had already gathered around him an army of some 14,000 recruits. And once more, she was amazed to hear that the sympathies of the German populace leaned heavily in the former French emperor's favor. Men frequenting the inn where she impatiently waited an unusual two or three hours for fresh horses "took great pains to point out . . . the wonders that had been performed by Napoleon, and his Officers. . . . They showed me where their house had been struck by three bullets or rather cannon Balls, during the Action; and informed me that the French Officers had quartered there, a fact of which they seemed very proud." It was beginning to be made clear to her that the "renowned cruelties, and barbarities of the Cossacks seemed to have whitewashed all other crimes from their minds." Even though "suffering and devastation had followed [the] steps" of the French, there was nothing but "unceasing admiration" for their exploits among the people.[33]

Hearing rumors and wild talk of the movement of armies greatly unsettled Louisa's two guards, who feared being conscripted. Louisa, in contrast, was strangely excited by all the commotion: "Soldiers were mustering in every direction; and there was a life and animation, altogether different from the dull monotony, which had pervaded all the former part of my travels," she later wrote. Concerned that her route to Paris might coincide with Napoleon's if she failed to arrive there before him, she pushed on to Frankfurt with all possible speed. Now more than ever, she was set on finishing her journey. In her son Charles's words many years later, "A less determined woman upon hearing of the condition into which France was thrown by Napoleon's return would have stopped short at some intermediate point without venturing to complete her undertaking. Not so with Mrs. Adams."[34]

Again in Frankfurt there were no letters awaiting her from John Quincy. Writing of her "severe disappointment" at not hearing from him, she proposed, in light of the news about Napoleon, to travel without any overnight stopovers in order to reach Paris ahead of the returning emperor. In that case, she wrote, John Quincy could expect her very soon. But before she sealed her letter, plans had changed. Her banker, Simon Moritz von Bethmann, rich, powerful, and influential, had come calling at her request. He convinced her that taking the direct road to Paris was far too dangerous. She must, he said, take a roundabout route through Strasbourg in order to avoid the armies mustering on one side in support of Napoleon and on the other in opposition. Louisa's immediate reaction to this plan was fear of her husband's disapproval of the extra costs such a route would entail. As well as taking longer, it would "add to the expence which has already frightened me," she wrote him apologetically on March 17.[35]

She had little choice, however, because she was in Bethmann's debt on an extremely difficult matter. That morning Baptiste and Fulling had come to her to say that they believed that only by disappearing from sight in Frankfurt could they avoid being caught up in an armed conflict in France. They had, therefore, decided to leave her service immediately. Louisa was now caught in a bind. Just as conditions became more dangerous, she would be losing her armed guards: "*Here was a situation* — I could not compel them to stay; no bribe could induce them to go on in their state of Panic."[36]

Bethmann counseled her to remain in Frankfurt until the situation settled down somewhat, and the course of Napoleon's movements became clear. "It required great prudence in my arrangements," Louisa recalled him telling her. But she stubbornly resisted his advice, protesting that it was exactly the confusion surrounding Napoleon's intentions that would work in her favor. "At present the panic itself would prove advantageous," she argued. Waiting might expose her to a situation in which two armed forces had dug in on a line she would be unable to cross. Mistakenly believing that John Quincy, realizing the danger she was in, would meet her at the Franco-German frontier, she insisted on pressing forward as soon as Bethmann could find her substitute guards.[37]

Since Louisa had given in reluctantly on the matter of the route, Bethmann yielded on the question of the immediate resumption of her journey. He agreed to attempt to find replacements for Baptiste and Fulling. After a short interval, he returned with a fourteen-year-old boy, the only male he could find willing to make the journey with her. Instead of a shield, Louisa was now saddled with another dependent. Nonetheless, she took on the youth in order to have someone to run errands, assist with baggage, and help her in and out of the berline. Afraid the boy might commit an indiscretion that would endanger the entire party, however, she decided he should ride inside the carriage with Charles, Mme. Babet, and herself. For all intents and purposes, she was now without any real protection.

The boy turned out to be, in Louisa's words, "very smart, and active." As young as he was, he had previously served as an aide to a Prussian officer and was eager to relate anecdotes from the field, particularly those "concerning Napoleon during the retreat—of his sitting among his Soldiers to warm himself! of his partaking of their Soup, when they had any! His kindness to them in the midst of their misery etc. etc." As the young aide had been serving on the allied side, his loyalty was to his Prussian officer, and he claimed he had nothing but hatred for the deposed French emperor. Always interested in meeting new people, Louisa did not make an exception of an adolescent: "It was singular to watch the workings of this young mind, swayed equally by admiration and detestation, uttered in the strong language of natural feeling."

The boy's unrepressed emotions, however, nearly involved Louisa in a compromising situation. She had stopped for dinner in Karlsruhe, planning to continue her journey later in the afternoon and evening. The innkeeper interrupted her meal to announce the—ultimately false—news, which "might be relied on as it had just come from the Palace," that Napoleon had been captured and shot. Louisa "heard an exclamation of horror; and turning round, saw the boy who I had hired, as pale as a ghost, and ready to faint—he looked piteously at me saying 'O that great Man! I did not expect that!'" Louisa considered it very fortunate that the innkeeper had just left the room or he might have "supposed me some violent Bonapartist." She was fully aware that taking sides in the conflict to come would in no way contribute to her safe passage to Paris.[38]

By four in the afternoon when she was on her way once more, signs of a looming battle were becoming more and more evident: "Waggons of every description full of Soldiers, were continually rushing towards the Frontier— roaring national Songs, and apparently in great glee at the idea of a renewal of hostilities." Observing the enthusiasm of the men for human slaughter prompted one of Louisa's strongest statements against war: "What a mere animal man may become! A machine worse than the brutes; for the instincts of the Brute creation lead only to fixed objects; while those of men termed rational may be perverted by mere accidental causes, to the worst and basest purposes, even without an adequate motive for such excesses."[39]

Louisa had little time for philosophizing. Traveling southwest, she had arrived at Kehl, a small port town on the German side of the Rhine. There, as usual, she was subjected to what she considered importunate questioning by customs officials and a search of her luggage. On the French side of the river, after somewhat less intrusive border delays, she went directly to an "excellent Hotel" in Strasbourg, recommended by a French immigration official. There, she gratefully accepted the advice and services offered by the hotel's landlord. Finding him gentlemanly in his manners and apparently trustworthy, Louisa confided the difficulty she faced in traveling without adult male protection.

She needed, she said, "a respectable and confidential person to go with me as far as Paris." Promising to pay such a person well and to underwrite his return trip to Strasbourg, she said she realized she "must rely entirely upon the discretion of this person, in the management and arrangement of my route; and should depend on him for advice, and assistance." Acknowledging that such a companion would be extremely difficult to find, the landlord claimed, however to know of a potential candidate and promised he would contact him at once. By evening he had returned with a Monsieur Dupin, whom Louisa found to be "a most respectable looking person." She hired him on the spot. A question immediately arose concerning the fourteen-year-old boy. Although Louisa offered to help him return to Frankfurt, the boy pleaded with her to let him continue on to Paris. As he had come to her aid when she was in desperate need and had rendered her "good service," Louisa thought she could not refuse his request. Dupin, however, made it a condition that the boy should be under his direct supervision or Louisa's at all times and that "he was not to talk at any of the Houses where we might stay."[40]

Having made arrangements to remain overnight in Strasbourg, Louisa took a walk with Charles to see the city sights. Poised on the border between France and Germany, Strasbourg possessed charming traces of both cultures. Medieval half-timbered buildings from the sixteenth and seventeenth centuries in the district called "La Petite France," the cathedral of Notre Dame, a Gothic marvel complete with an astronomical clock, and the lovely shaded riverbanks along the River Ill all invited the sightseeing that, under ordinary conditions, Louisa delighted in. Although she found the town "very pretty" and, surprisingly, reminiscent of Worcester, Massachusetts, time passed slowly. Her trip had lasted long enough; for the first time, she complained that her health was "dreadful."

Renewing her journey early the next day and more determined than ever to reach Paris as soon as possible, Louisa insisted that the carriage stay on the road until one in the morning. At that point, the party was passing through a relatively uninhabited area somewhere near Nancy. Very unwillingly, but obeying a signal from Dupin, she gave in to the postilions' insistence on stopping at "a very lonely house" until daylight. The inn was no better inside than it appeared from their approach: "We drove up to a miserable place in which we found a long room, with a pine Table, several very surly looking men, and nothing but common benches to sit on—Here I was obliged to sit, while they procured us a little milk, the only thing we could get—Charles seemed very much frightened as these men asked him several questions, and I was obliged to tell them the Child was too sleepy to talk."[41]

Dupin arranged for an adjoining room to be made available where Charles could rest. Louisa and Mme. Babet spent the night seated next to the sleeping seven-year-old and listening through the door to drunken boasts of what Napoleon would do to the "beggarly Crew" surrounding the Bourbon Louis XVIII. Most alarming was the fact that Louisa's own postilions were fully as vociferous in their denunciations of the Allies and the dreaded Cossacks as were their newfound drinking companions. Her experience at the inhospitable inn strengthened Louisa's confidence in Dupin. He had proved himself "judicious and discreet" and had managed a threatening situation with tact and "a quiet smoothness of manner which enforced respect, and defied suspicion." Dupin assured her that if they made good speed on the smooth roads ahead, they might reach Paris ahead of the soldiers mustering in support of Napoleon. These were words Louisa had been longing to hear. For the first time in many weeks she could feel that the successful outcome of her journey did not rest entirely with her.[42]

A woman traveling in a Russian-built coach pulled by six fast horses was extraordinary enough, however, to attract unwanted attention. At an inn where the party stopped the next evening, a suspicious gendarme seemed determined to discover who she really was and where she was going. He was "very inquisitive; expressed great astonishment at my travelling towards Paris in such a state of things, and seemed by no means contented with my answers, which were very simple." Frustrated by his inability to interrogate the mother successfully, he turned to the child, much to Charles's annoyance. Finally, the gendarme retreated to threatening the little boy by telling him he must be good and not speak a word "as little children of his age often did a great deal of mischief."[43]

Nonetheless, with the end of her journey in sight, Louisa began to feel easier. The weather was springlike, and the French roads were good. Stopping in Epernay, she treated herself to a "capital dinner" and a bottle of the local Champagne that was "superior to any that I have ever tasted before, or since." It would be her last moment of relaxation.[44]

Back on the road, she had traveled only a mile and a half when she began to hear women's voices shouting vicious obscenities. The carriage had become entangled with a mob of camp followers who had attached themselves to a troop of the Imperial Guard on its way to join Napoleon. In the cacophony of the women's curses, Louisa could make out specific threats: "Tear them out of the carriage" and "They are Russians" and "Take them out and kill them." As the cries grew louder, a party of soldiers seized the reins from her coachmen and turned their guns against them. Terrified, but keeping her head, Louisa removed her passports from safekeeping. When a general officer rode up beside the carriage, she calmly presented to him her official papers and affidavits. He called out to the unruly soldiers that the woman inside the carriage was not Russian but an American lady on her way to meet her husband in Paris. The troops then shouted "Vive les Américains" and made it clear they wanted to hear "Vive Napoléon!" in return. In the perfectly idiomatic French she learned in Nantes when she was three years old, Louisa complied, leaning out of the carriage and waving her handkerchief for good measure. The troops then repeated "Vive les Américans," adding, this time, "Ils sont nos amis."[45]

Louisa's drivers were now ordered to proceed behind a contingent of soldiers at a walking pace or risk being shot at. Meanwhile, the general's suite rode on either side of the carriage. The general himself warned Louisa that her situation was still precarious, as the army "was totally undisciplined" and would not obey orders from anyone. She must, he told her, be prepared to shout "Vive Napoléon!" at every prompt. Moreover, it was critical to her safety and that of everyone in the carriage that she appear at all times perfectly easy and unconcerned. He complimented her French accent and told her that her "perfect knowledge" of the language might well be the key to her safe passage "as no one would believe me to be a foreigner."

In one of the great dramatic performances of her life, with her son "absolutely petrified and sitting by my side like a marble statue," Louisa managed to exhibit no fear as the carriage plodded slowly on, enveloped by a crush of unruly soldiers who shouted "brutal threats" and turned their bayonets on her drivers whenever the mood struck them. The road for miles was lined with inebriated men shouting "Down with Louis XVIII" and "Vive Napoleon" and, in Louisa's words, "ripe for every species of villainy." She had heard enough of the brutalities of war in the course of her journey to understand that that disruptive behavior could certainly include rape as well as bodily harm and the loss of her possessions. It required every ounce of composure she had to maintain her erect posture, calm smile, and enthusiastic "Vive Napoleon" as the day lengthened into night.[46]

The general had promised he would seek to persuade the proprietor of the next post station to take her in, and he was as good as his word. The proprietress at first flatly refused to accommodate the besieged travelers, but the general finally "awakened her sympathy" and she agreed to comply with his request. The French woman stipulated, however, that the carriage be hidden well out of sight and that the travelers remain silent in a dark room with the shutters barred throughout the night. Louisa readily agreed to all these conditions, and the general departed. As it turned out, the room in which the little party was concealed was comfortable, a fire was made, and "a very kind old gentleman" assured her that there was reason to hope she would make it through the night "without farther molestation."[47]

By now, Mme. Babet had fallen apart completely under the strain of the day's events. In the carriage the old governess had sat "pale as death" and trembling, but now she fell prey to a form of hysteria. "She clasped her hands continually; while the tears rolled down her cheeks, crying out, that she was lost! for the Revolution was begun again, and this was only the beginning of its horrors." Fainting fits, headaches, and sickness also attacked Louisa as she sat silently in the closed, dark room, reliving the events of the day and listening to the roar of drunken soldiers crowded into the main bar of the inn. As distressed as she was, however, Louisa was still able to appreciate the fine qualities she observed in her kind landlady and to make a little word portrait of her. "She was a showy pleasant faced woman, of about forty: of an assured and prompt spirit, and who seemed to possess that readiness, and playfulness of conversation, which is often so attractive in french women."[48]

The proprietress, who had opened her casks of wine to the troops in order to prevent their marauding through the inn in search of drink, finally emptied the bar at 5 A.M. and barred the outside doors. Even though stragglers continued to demand entry, the threat of imminent danger to Louisa, Mme. Babet, and Charles had passed. The only victim of the soldiers' revelry had been the fourteen-year-old Prussian boy, who had been prodded with bayonets and made to burn his Prussian military cap. His life had been spared, Louisa believed, "with great difficulty" by the "dexterity" of the indomitable landlady.

By morning, most of the troops appeared to have passed by the inn, and, after breakfast, the exhausted travelers were on their way once more. Because the troops were moving on the most direct road to Paris, Louisa was forced to choose a slightly more roundabout route to Château-Thierry. Here she heard from passengers coming the other way from Paris that there were "forty thousand men before the Gates; and a battle was expected to take place." After consulting with Dupin, she ignored the passengers' warning to remain safely outside the capital. She was too near her destination now to give up.

In her decision to press forward, Louisa was encouraged by the fact that the canny Dupin had been careful not to refute the "whisper abroad" that she was one of Napoleon's sisters on her way to join her brother in Paris. "This idea was so favorable to the promotion of my success, that *he* was *very mysterious* and only shrugged and smiled, at the suggestion." Her six swift horses and closed carriage added substance to the rumor, which seemed to be confirmed by the fact that she—a single woman—was one of the few nonmilitary persons on the road.[49]

Stopping for dinner at Meaux on March 20, she again witnessed firsthand the ravages of war, once more perpetrated by the Cossacks. The landlady showed her the graves of six of "the most beautiful girls of the place" who had been raped and killed. "They were laid side by side, and to judge from my landlady, their relics were embalmed by the sacred tears of undying affection, and the purest sympathies of unadulterated compassion." Never again would Louisa be under any illusions—if she ever was—of the glories of war.[50]

Now the travelers were in range of Paris, but first they had to pass through the long and dark forest of Bondy. The forest for centuries had been the hideout of highwaymen who lurked behind the thickly planted trees only to spring out to steal from and sometimes murder hapless travelers. Louisa was well aware of the myths surrounding the forest and "with a mind already in some measure prepared for some catastrophe, and in the Foret de Bondy so long celebrated for Banditti exploits," the sound of hoof beats to the rear of the berline was far from reassuring.[51]

When the man she called her "imaginary highwayman" finally caught up to the carriage, it was only to tell her that for the past half hour he had observed her rear wheel coming loose. After examining the wheel, Dupin told Louisa that they could try to fasten it temporarily, but they must turn back to the place where they had had dinner to get it repaired. There she waited impatiently until late in the evening while the wheel was mended. The travelers then reentered the forest and traveled without further incident to the gates of Paris.

At eleven in the evening of March 23, 1815 — the final hour of her fortieth day on the road, Louisa arrived at the Hôtel du Nord in Paris. As she remembered it, her husband was at the theater and did not return to his lodgings until later. In his contemporaneous diary, however, John Quincy wrote that he had expected to see her carriage in the hotel yard when he returned from the play but was disappointed. His wife and son arrived, he wrote, almost immediately after he had "got into his chamber." He was happy to find Louisa and Charles both well and "delighted after an absence of eleven months to meet them again." He mentioned nothing in his diary to indicate he was aware that they had undergone more than the expected discomforts of a forty-day trip of nearly 2,000 miles.[52]

Louisa recalled their reunion differently: "I was once more happy to find myself under the protection of a husband, who was perfectly astonished at my adventures; as every thing in Paris was quiet, and it had never occurred to him, that it could have been otherwise in any other part of the Country."[53]

John Quincy may have been "astonished" at Louisa's adventures, but there is no indication beyond her characterization of his reaction that he was remotely interested in them. His diary is silent on every aspect of her trip. The young Prussian boy, Dupin, and Mme. Babet, all of whom John Quincy must have encountered before they dispersed to their final destinations, are never mentioned. There is no hint that his wife had undergone any hardships or met any particular challenges. The day after their arrival he bundled Louisa and Charles into yet another carriage to tour the Bois de Boulogne and to see the house he had lived in as a teenager with his parents and sister. That evening, John Quincy and Louisa went to the opera. Louisa seems to have had barely a minute to recover from her travails and to rest after forty days of riding in a jolting coach. In a letter to his mother a full month later, John Quincy succinctly announced the arrival in Paris of Louisa and Charles: "Mrs. Adams performed the journey from St. Petersburg in forty days and it has been of essential service both to her and Charles's health." There is no indication that the trip had been anything but efficient and bracing.[54]

Louisa was being generous in attributing John Quincy's astonishment at hearing of trouble on her trip to the fact that Paris was "quiet." In fact, the opposite was true. The city was in turmoil. Only three days before Louisa's arrival, Napoleon had reinstalled himself in the Tuilleries. After royalist troops defected to the returning emperor, Louis XVIII had escaped to Lille with his courtiers.

On the morning following Napoleon's arrival in Paris, John Quincy, hoping to catch a glimpse of the emperor, himself had "mixed with the crowd" and witnessed their exuberant cries of "Vive l'Empereur." His many personal and political contacts in Paris had spoken of little else since Napoleon had escaped from Elba. Louisa told herself for the rest of her life that John Quincy would have acted to rescue her had he thought she was in danger of any kind. But he had done nothing of the sort, even though the situation in Paris should have lent more, not less, urgency to any thoughts he had to go to her assistance.

In John Quincy's defense, he would have had no direct knowledge of the challenges his wife was facing. Under her hurried circumstances, Louisa wrote very few letters as she journeyed west. John Quincy knew she was traveling in a secure coach pulled by six horses and that she had been able to draw sufficient funds from his bankers along her route. In all his many travels around Europe, nothing approaching the escape of Napoleon from Elba and his subsequent march on Paris had ever occurred. From personal experience, John Quincy would have had no reason to connect mobs of unruly soldiers with Louisa's progress across France. Yet after Louisa left Berlin, every responsible male—whether banker or innkeeper—had forcefully urged her to delay her trip until matters had resolved themselves. John Quincy, alone, seems to have been indifferent to her danger.

It may also seem strangely detached that John Quincy wrote only three letters to Louisa while awaiting her "impatiently" in Paris. On February 19, believing she would not be leaving St. Petersburg until the following day, when in fact she had left a week earlier, he addressed a letter to her to her in care of her bankers in Königsberg. Since Louisa was in Königsberg by February 22, it would have been far too soon for her husband's letter to have come into her hands. On March 1, when John Quincy next wrote—still not having heard from his wife—he addressed his letter to Berlin. Louisa, however, had arrived in the Prussian capital on March 5 and resumed her journey on the eleventh, just ahead of the time when mail from Paris might have been expected at Berlin's poste restante. Hoping in vain for a letter from her husband, she had spent more time in Berlin than she had anticipated and was clearly vexed when she reached Frankfurt to find there was again no message from him.[55]

On March 18, three letters from his wife having finally been delivered to him, John Quincy recorded in his diary that he had sent duplicates of his letter to the post houses closest to Paris on the two roads Louisa must travel in order to reach the city gates. One of these may have been the only letter she received from him during the entire trip. Failing to take into consideration the extraordinary events under way between Berlin and Paris, he assumed Louisa had decided to take the most direct route and would be with him at any moment. His final letter, therefore, was little more than a note "to let you know where I am and with what impatience I am waiting to receive you" and ending with "no farewell but a welcome."[56]

John Quincy may have had good reason to believe that sending letters to bankers and postes restantes along Louisa's expected route was an exercise in futility. Timing his messages to correspond with her arrival at any given point would have been nearly impossible, especially when he did not know the date of her departure from St. Petersburg until a few days before her arrival in Paris. An argument can be made, however, that Louisa and Charles were not at the forefront of John Quincy's consciousness. The months he spent in Paris waiting for his wife and son to arrive, John Quincy wrote later, were "in many respects the most agreeable interlude of my life." From his youth, he had had a special love for the city. He haunted museums and bookstalls, attended the theater and the opera practically every evening, and dined with many friends and acquaintances. This was not a life he was in any hurry to give up. Its very charm may have lured him into a misplaced confidence that Louisa faced no real danger on the road. That confidence translated itself into a self-serving, matter-of-fact view that her journey from St. Petersburg to Paris had passed without incident. Unfortunately, he so convinced himself that nothing extraordinary had occurred that he could sum up the month of March 1815 in his diary without mentioning the arrival of his wife and his son.[57]

By June Louisa seems to have adopted John Quincy's nonchalant attitude toward her adventures. Writing to Abigail that "my journey from St. Petersburg was performed with as little uneasiness and as few misfortunes as could possibly have been anticipated and I have really acquired the reputation of a heroine at a very cheap rate." She conceded she had run into a spot of trouble between Strasbourg and Paris, but claimed her American passport had saved her from real peril. There was "so much of high revolutionary spirit mingled with [the trouble on the road] that I could not entirely divest myself of *fears*, which were however without any real foundation," she wrote. Such self-effacement was a pose, and Louisa knew it.[58]

She was justifiably proud of her achievement. Alone, she had been responsible for the successful outcome of a long, very dangerous journey. John Quincy had not been on hand to criticize her decisions or take responsibility away from her and onto himself. She had seen to the safety and well-being of her young son from beginning to end. She had handled money, servants, and carriage repairs with the same aplomb with which she had confronted surly peasants and rampaging soldiers. Throughout the trip, she had refrained from lapsing into the reactions that might have been expected of a highly bred lady in perilous situations—fainting, tears, and hysterics. Despite very few hours of sleep at any one time, she had maintained vigorous health and considerable energy.

In an 1839 biographical sketch, Charles Francis Adams introduced to the reading public the harrowing adventures he, as a seven-year-old, had shared with his mother. Those who knew Louisa only in her later years, he wrote, would little suspect that she had a robust or bold bone in her body. "And yet," he continued, "few women of the age ever underwent more extraordinary fatigue in her various journeys or displayed more energy in the accomplishment of her undertakings" and no journey was "so well calculated to test the strength of her nerves" as that from St. Petersburg to Paris.[59]

It took Louisa twenty-one years to acknowledge what she had accomplished. In 1836, eight years after a miserable, single term in the White House and years of unhappiness and personal tragedy, she decided to chronicle her journey for the benefit of her descendants. She had two purposes in mind. In the poignant words of a woman who feared that in some essential way she was of no significance, Louisa wrote that her "Narrative" would "perhaps at some future day serve to recall the memory of one *who was.*" But she had another goal as well. She would attempt to "show that many undertakings which appear very difficult and arduous to my Sex, are by no means so trying as imagination forever depicts them. And that energy and discretion, follow the necessity of their exertion, to protect the fancied weakness of feminine imbecility." Clearly, Louisa was challenging the women of her time to forgo the "weakness" to which she herself had so often fallen prey but had triumphantly overcome during the forty most independent days of her life. Never before had she been called upon to exhibit such reserves of strength, and never again would she accomplish anything that would give her such pride.[60]

"Narrative of a Journey from Russia to France 1815" exists today in two similar handwritten versions and as it was printed in 1903 in *Scribner's* magazine as "Mrs. John Quincy Adams's Narrative, of a Journey from St. Petersburg to Paris in February, 1815," with an introduction by her grandson Brooks Adams. In the second handwritten version, Louisa anticipated potential criticism: "I am almost ashamed of the egotism of this detailed Narrative, but a traveller cannot avoid speaking in the first person while relating his own history—and this must plead my apology." Her "Narrative," is not, however, a simple traveler's tale, a form of writing very familiar to her through John Quincy's *Travels in Silesia.* There is virtually no depiction of scenery or description of the many towns and cities through which she passed. Native costume, ethnic and religious diversity, and historical significance are all blithely ignored.

Michael O'Brien, who has meticulously retraced Louisa's route and clarified several inconsistencies in her account, does not quarrel with the basic route she described nor does he suggest that she invented any of her adventures. Louisa herself dismissed the accuracy of her reported route, blaming her own laziness: "As it is I can only give a brief sketch of the road, and I fear very often with a defective Geography. . . . Research is not in my way—Indolence wars with exertion, and is too often victorious." She must, however, have worked with a map and a calendar as it would have been impossible after more than twenty years to remember specific towns and cities in their order as well as she did. Although she always regretted not keeping a journal during her trip, specific moments seem to have come back to her with the clarity of yesterday's events. Midway through her account she refers to the "Narrative" as a chaotic document, but the momentary doubts in her literary ability immediately give way to a headlong rush into the remainder of the story. Her writing throughout is remarkably free of superfluous details, and there are few unnecessary digressions. Notably, there is only one mention of poor health.[61]

Believing throughout her life that her besetting sin was pride, Louisa was fully aware that she enjoyed the special attention she received at nearly every stop. Not every traveler was provided with a letter from the Minister of the Interior ordering priority treatment, and not every woman would have been honored by invitations to governors' palaces as, by dint of being the American minister's wife, she invariably was. The special status conveyed by the berline behind six horses—the equivalent of a stretch limousine today—marked her in every inn yard as a person of importance. Using her standing to her advantage in negotiating for fresh horses and obtaining private rooms for her dinners was critical to implementing her travel plans, but the fact that her status was so widely recognized was undeniably good for her self-esteem.

Writing an adventure story with herself as the heroine, Louisa did not yield to the temptation to overstate her own courage, poise, or resilience. Instead, she played down her bravery and belittled a frightening incident as looming unnecessarily large in her imagination. In vividly sketched episodes, she related her adventures from the first snowdrift in Russia to the wobbly wheel in the Forest of Bondy with telling detail and dialogue and let her actions under extreme stress speak for themselves. Just as there was no false bravado in her account, there was no simulation of delicacy where determination was wanted.

The secondary characters in Louisa's "Narrative" are just that. Recognizing her responsibility to them, she wrote later, "I had others under my protection to whom the example of fortitude was essential." Seven-year-old Charles, her primary consideration, was never far from his mother's side. She recounted his terror when the coach was surrounded by a volatile mob or boisterous drinkers and recalled motherly duties such as procuring him milk or arranging a bed for him to sleep on. She neglected, however, to describe how she amused a little boy closed up in a carriage for forty days or how she coped with his inevitable questions when he first glimpsed the dreadful war-ravaged sites they passed. Such details might have detracted from the essential tale of a woman, on her own, traversing the European continent in winter and how she surmounted every barrier placed in her way.[62]

Likewise, Mme. Babet is a silent passenger until—in contrast to Louisa— she succumbs to hysterics near the end of the journey. At the conclusion of her "Narrative," Louisa does lament that "the fright [Mme. Babet] had undergone was too much for her; and she was seized with a brain fever, from which she had not recovered when I left Paris two Months after." But none of the other passengers is similarly wrapped up and sent on their way. Dupin, whose services were so indispensable in the final days of her journey, disappears without a trace, as does the fourteen-year-old Prussian boy. The criminal Baptiste and the nervous Fulling are never heard from after they drop out of sight in Frankfurt.[63]

This is not egocentricity. If her purpose in 1836 was to strengthen by example the backbone of her female readers, the "Narrative" rightfully belongs to Louisa: "I was carried through my trials by the mercy of a protecting Providence; and by the conviction that weakness of either body, or mind, would only render my difficulties greater and make matters worse." Drawing a moral from her story's happy denouement, she added, "If my Sex act with persevering discretion, they may from their very *weakness* be secured from danger, and find friends and protectors: and that under all circumstances, we must never desert ourselves."[64]

Deserting herself, however, was exactly what Louisa seemed to do in the two months after her arrival in Paris. Confronted with John Quincy's total lack of interest in anything to do with her journey, she seems to have entered complicitly into his domain and accepted his priorities as her own. No period of recuperation from the effects of a lengthy and stressful adventure appeared on the schedule; little sign remained of a woman who could surmount danger and make difficult decisions with courage and grace. During the day, the couple went on long walks together and with Charles, and, often, they visited museums and other points of interest. At night they attended the theater until they had exhausted every play, opera, circus performance, and pantomime.

Only twice did Louisa assert herself. Once, after John Quincy had been ill for several days and had refused to seek medical attention, she greeted him on his return from his walk about the city with a doctor she had independently summoned to their hotel. Later in April, for unexplained reasons, she announced she would not accompany him on a visit to the Marquis de Lafayette at his family estate, an old castle outside of Paris. By the first of May, however, she had relented and agreed to make the three-day trip. Louisa's compliance with John Quincy's wishes may well have signified relief that she no longer bore heavy responsibilities, and the happiness of exploring Paris in the spring with him and Charles may have given her no reason to counter his plans for their various excursions.

Yet, when the family left Paris on May 16, traveling in "easy stages," in lovely spring weather on good roads, "Mrs. Adams was overcome by fatigue," John Quincy wrote in his diary. By the time they had crossed the channel to Dover, Louisa refused to proceed immediately to London as she was "excessively fatigued and in the Evening very unwell."[65]

What had become of the woman who had risen daily before dawn to travel over rough roads into the late night? For forty days that woman had survived on very little sleep and in extremely uncomfortable conditions but had never complained of "excessive fatigue." The "weakness of body and mind" against which Louisa later warned other women was born of her own experience. In just two months, she seems to have relinquished every ounce of strength she gained during the nine months of managing a household on her own in St. Petersburg and then in traveling across a war-ravaged northern Europe in winter. Whether Louisa decided to reinvent herself as someone incapable of making difficult decisions and surmounting hardships is impossible to know. There was nothing she wrote at the time to suggest she found it difficult to stuff the genie of self-sufficiency back into its bottle.

Twenty-one years later, however, the explicit message of her "Narrative of a Journey from Russia to France 1815" was an unqualified appeal to the women of Louisa's social class to cast off the "fancied weakness of feminine imbecility." Whether the many bouts of illness, fainting, and exhaustion that would follow her in the years after her historic journey were in reaction to the repression of her independent spirit in favor of "feminine imbecility" cannot, at this distance, be known with any confidence. The circumstances of her life and the character of the man she had chosen to share it with ensured that she would never again reach such heights of courage and ingenuity as she had in the winter of 1815. But, as she made clear in the "Narrative," she knew exactly what she had achieved. And she was proud of it.

12

LITTLE BOSTON HOUSE

One of the most delightful spots upon which I ever resided.

—*JOHN QUINCY ADAMS*

Two strangers awaited Louisa and John Quincy in their London hotel on May 25, 1815. George and John II looked like what they were—two Yankee schoolboys, painfully uncomfortable in elegant Regency London and equipped with one good suit apiece. George, fourteen, was all arms and legs, an ungainly adolescent just coming into his future height; John, who would turn twelve on the Fourth of July, was still small for his age but unrecognizable as the lively six-year-old Louisa and John Quincy had left behind in Quincy in 1809. The iced-over Baltic from November to May each winter had crucially impeded communication between the boys and their parents for six critical years of their development. Now they had to learn to become a family again.

As she prepared for their departure from Boston in care of a family friend, Abigail Adams had done her best to reintroduce her grandsons—"so long absent from you at a period in their lives when they have almost grown out of your knowledge"—to their parents. She excused George's "rusticity" on the grounds of his rapid growth and warned Louisa that "he scarcely knows what to do with himself." His mind, Abigail wrote, was a "casket which contains jewels that only want culling, refining, and burnishing in his father's crucible to render them bright." John, in old John Adams's words, was "activity itself," able to learn anything quickly but requiring a steady hand to keep him on course.[1]

Hinting at her son's unattainably high standards, Abigail warned John Quincy against demanding too much of his boys. In May she wrote, "It is an observation of a judicious writer that if we expect boys should make valuable men, they must continue some time in the state of boys or they will never make men worth forming." Three months later, she again cautioned, "You must not look for old heads on young shoulders." Abigail was especially concerned that the sensitive, talented, but awkward George be spared unwonted pressure to meet his father's demands. His health was precarious, his growth "too premature for his age," and his exceptional, "ever-active" mind, in Abigail's view, required "no common share of vigilance and attention to direct it right."

On the other hand, John, who from birth had been the apple of his grandmother's eye, could, she wrote, use a little gentle discipline. The captain of the ship on which the boys had crossed the Atlantic had reported to the anxious grandparents in Quincy that John could name every rope and every sailor "until they dubbed him Admiral." Proud as she was of "that fullblooded, enterprising, and ardent creature," Abigail conceded John had "a little too much confidence in himself and independence where experience is necessary."[2]

Neither John Quincy nor Louisa was as generous toward their older sons. In his mother's opinion, John was simply "wild"; George, his father judged, was well behind where he should have been in Greek and Latin, and his handwriting was unacceptably poor. Neither parent knew how to cope with teenage boys. Brought up in a family of girls, whose only brother at an early age had been sent off to an English boarding school and then to America, Louisa was unprepared for two noisy, ill-at-ease youths roughhousing in the small hotel suite on Cavendish Square. John Quincy, whose own adolescence had been spent mostly in the company of adults in St. Petersburg and Paris, was equally at a loss. The boys, he wrote, caused a "hurly burly of confusion" that prevented him from attending to official business.[3]

And what of Charles, who had last seen his older brothers when he himself was only two? Not yet eight years old in May 1815, he had virtually nothing in common with his older siblings. Fluent in French, Russian, and German, exposed at an early age to the ways of a decadent imperial court and fresh from two months in Paris where he regularly attended the theater and other events with his parents, Charles had lived a thoroughly sophisticated life. Accustomed to being treated as a precocious, only child, he was suddenly one of three siblings, and the youngest at that. It could not have been easy. Abigail wrote that she hoped the young boy would find himself "allied not only by the natural ties of affection and brotherly kindness but by similar pursuits in science and literature." His parents, too, seem to have assumed Charles would greet his reunion with his older, much less urbane brothers with unadulterated joy.[4]

At the end of May, just as the Adamses arrived in London, British schools began their summer vacations, which meant the restless Adams boys had to be kept occupied for at least two months. John Quincy and Louisa promptly hired tutors in mathematics and handwriting and—evidently fearing the poor impression their older sons would make in company—in fencing and dancing as well. Still, George and John had too much free time on their hands. Seeking diversions, John Quincy took George to Parliament to hear a debate on the merits of returning slaves captured in the War of 1812 to their American masters. On another occasion he helped fly the boys' kite in Regent's Park. But after only a month, he admitted to his diary that he could not manage both the duties of the American minister to the Court of St. James's and the education and amusement of his sons: "Their time is not fully employed and mine is so completely taken up that I have none left to attend to them."[5]

Into the breach stepped Louisa. Her dream of having her entire family together in one place had been fulfilled at last. Happy and healthy, she readily took over the parenting tasks John Quincy could not fulfill. Both Adamses believed strongly that vigorous exercise and fresh air were essential for growing boys. So, day after day—sometimes with her husband but often independently—Louisa took long walks or carriage rides with her sons in Hyde Park, Kensington Gardens, or Regent's Park. When John Quincy broke from his diplomatic duties in the evening, the whole family often went on another brisk trek. Keeping up with her lively sons and indefatigable husband must have been a physical challenge, but Louisa seems to have met it without complaint. There is no indication in John Quincy's diary that he lessened his pace or shortened his walks to accommodate Louisa's small frame, voluminous skirts and petticoats, and inappropriate shoes.

No number of brisk walks, however, could compensate for the stresses endemic to the family's uncomfortably close quarters in their rented city lodgings. From late May to July, John Quincy and Louisa searched for a suitable ministerial and family residence. It rapidly became obvious that the U.S. government would not be providing adequate living expenses for them to rent anything appropriate in desirable London neighborhoods. Louisa assured Abigail that, were it up to her, they would return to America immediately rather than live in such straitened circumstances as those they could afford, "viewed with contempt by all the European nations." In late July, however, another solution presented itself. "My wife went out of town seven miles to look at a house to be let for the Summer," John Quincy recorded in his diary.[6]

Louisa had found Little Boston House, the happiest home she and John Quincy would ever know.

On August 1, the Adamses moved to Little Ealing, a tiny hamlet of about 200 persons less than ten miles outside London. It was Louisa who engineered the entire move. Although John Quincy was "from breakfast time until five o'clock

. . . constantly engaged with company," the rest of the family was busy all day "in packing and loading two carts and a wagon with our baggage, furniture and wines." By midnight, he reported, they had settled in their new home, and he was halfway through sorting out his personal books and papers.[7]

It was Louisa who chose the house in which the family would live during their English sojourn and who managed the details of decorating and furnishing it, hiring servants, and moving and installing the family—all within about ten days. At some point early in the summer, she seems to have rediscovered the self-confidence and managerial skills she had acquired in nine months on her own in St. Petersburg and on her transcontinental journey but had momentarily lost in Paris. Perhaps more significantly, John Quincy had finally recognized those skills. Temporarily lacking a secretary, he had even given Louisa "constant employment" as his personal assistant. As so often happened when she had multiple responsibilities to fulfill, Louisa's health was excellent and her energy boundless.

John Quincy could not have been more pleased with her choice of a new home. The three-story, handsome brick house, he happily noted, was "not large, but neat and elegant and fitted up with all that minute attention to comfort which is characteristic of English domestic life." The name, Little Boston House, which Louisa deemed "highly appropriate," was derived from its role as the dower house on the grounds of Boston Manor House, a grand Jacobean mansion. In England at the time, a dower house was often made available to the widow of the lord of the manor when the eldest son inherited the main house, but it could also be occupied by other members of the family, usually female relatives, or rented out.[8]

Owned from the late seventeenth to the early eighteenth century by the Clitherow family, Boston Manor in 1815 was home of James Clitherow IV, known as Colonel Clitherow. In negotiating the details of the rental agreement for Little Boston House, John Quincy dealt directly with Mary Clitherow, the colonel's sister, with whom he agreed on a weekly rent of five guineas and one month's notice on either side. The rental included a coach house, a stable, and a dairy, as well as extensive walled fruit and kitchen gardens. The house itself was situated at the entrance to the manor house—a long, private drive known still as "The Ride"—and the Adamses had access to all the beautiful woodlands and parklands making up Boston Manor's grounds. As part of the rent, two pews—one for the Adams family, one for their servants—were provided at St. Mary's, the Anglican church in Great Ealing, less than a mile away.[9]

Louisa herself was elated. "The situation is beautiful, the house comfortable, and the distance from the great city supportable. . . . We are within an hour's ride of Kew, Richmond, Twickenham, Harrow, and a variety of other beautiful places, and the situation is said to be perfectly healthy," she wrote enthusiastically to Abigail, adding, "My boys are delighted at the change as they could not endure London."[10]

John and Charles, however, had little time to explore the countryside around their new home. On the family's very first day in residence, following breakfast and a walk in the garden, their parents set out to find a school for them. They turned down the first institution they visited—Orger House, a small school in Acton—but the second, Great Ealing School, located only a mile from Little Boston House, delighted them both. "We were so well satisfied upon enquiry and inspection of the school, the dining hall, and the Bed-chambers that we engaged to send the two boys [John and Charles] as soon as we could get them prepared," John Quincy wrote.[11]

Everything about Great Ealing School met the Adamses's approval. It was near enough to Little Boston House so the boys could come home easily on Sundays and school half-holidays, an important consideration to parents who were only just beginning to become reacquainted with their sons. John Hewlett, the longtime friend and scholar who had married Louisa and John Quincy in 1797, had highly recommended the school and vouched for its headmaster, Dr. George Nicholas, LL.D., a fellow graduate of Oxford. At their first meeting, both Adamses were charmed by the genial Nicholas, who seems to have run a remarkably easygoing, progressive school.

Great Ealing's 250 boys, whose ages ranged from seven to sixteen, were drawn from England's upper middle class, just the kind of boys that the Adamses hoped their sons would encounter during their formative school years. Known at the time as perhaps the premier boarding and day school for boys, Great Ealing was considered the academic equivalent of Harrow or Eton. "Ealing school at that date had a great name. It was conducted on the Eton lines; everybody sent his sons there," a friend of John Henry (later Cardinal) Newman later wrote. In the Adamses's case, however, it was not "his" but "their" sons; all references to school visits and the choice of Great Ealing School in John Quincy's diary refer to "we" and "us." Louisa was as fully involved as her husband in the educational decisions involving their younger sons—clearly something of an anomaly in a time and place when a mother's role in the education of her children typically ended in the choice of a governess for her daughters and very young sons.[12]

Only George remained under the sole purview of his father. Like his forebears, beginning with his grandfather "Deacon Adams"—who sent only his first son to college—and continuing with his own father, who seems to have become disappointed at an early age with his sons Charles and Tom, John Quincy's

John Adams II (1803–1834), by unknown artist, circa 1820s. Courtesy of National Park Service, Adams National Historical Park.

hopes for the future seem to have rested almost solely on his eldest son. He was not alone. John Adams, bereft of his grandsons in Quincy, kept up a steady stream of letters to young George ("Your studies are very near to my heart") advising him on what he ought to be studying. "You have a propensity to

Charles Francis Adams (1807–1886), by Charles Bird King, 1827. Courtesy of National Park Service, Adams National Historical Park.

modern languages, Spanish, Italian and French: but I wish to hear more of your Love of Greek. An indiscriminate Curiosity for all languages, is good for nothing but to make pedants."[13]

The plan was to send only John and Charles to Great Ealing School. John Quincy himself would tutor George in preparation for his entrance exams to

George Washington Adams (1801–1829), by Charles Bird King, circa 1820s. Courtesy of National Park Service, Adams National Historical Park.

Harvard. In order that the tutorials not take valuable time from the American minister's official duties, they would have to be conducted at daybreak. Accordingly, on the family's fifth day at Little Boston House, George was roused out of bed by his father at 6 A.M. to begin an idiosyncratic course of study: "He read three chapters in the French Bible, while I had the Latin Bible to follow him as he read," John Quincy wrote. "After which, we changed books, and I read three chapters of the French while he held the Latin Book to compare with it." This routine, hardly calculated to inspire a sleepy adolescent with a passion for learning, continued each morning. On August 22, John Quincy also assigned Cicero's Second Philippic for his son to translate. "He has not been used to this exercise and performs it very indifferently," he lamented later that day to his diary.[14]

This educational experiment lasted only two months. At the end of September, George accompanied his father to a student performance at Great Ealing School. Encountering so many boys his own age on stage and in the audience must have made him realize how lonely he was for the companionship of his contemporaries. He begged to be allowed to go to the school. John Quincy acceded reluctantly with the proviso that George live at home and continue his tutorials at an even earlier hour so that he would have time to walk a mile through the fields to arrive at school by the 7 A.M. opening bell. George readily agreed and was enrolled at the school on October 4.

The next year, despite recurrent illnesses, probably included some of the happiest moments in young George's life. He seems to have done well in his studies and to have quickly become an integral member of the school's leading group of students. He regularly brought his friends (including the "Captain of the School") home to dinner—a practice Louisa loved as it reminded her of all the young men who frequented the Tower Hill mansion when she herself was a teenager. George appeared in several school performances, took part (with John) in fencing matches, and was one of a small group of senior boys, "The Spy Club," that included the future Cardinal Newman. The club published a literary paper, *The Portfolio*, whose name, Newman recalled, was suggested by George. The paper, to which John Quincy himself contributed, ran from November 6, 1815, a month after George arrived at the school, through May 1816, when the boys returned home for summer holidays.[15]

John was even happier at Great Ealing. Naturally outgoing and full of spunk, he fit in easily with the other boys and was popular with the masters. Louisa wrote to Abigail that John excelled in mathematics, unfortunately not a subject his classically minded father and grandfather believed to be of paramount importance. The boy's report to his grandfather on how much he enjoyed sports and games prompted a sharp retort from the gruff, but loving, old president: "I approve your . . . playing Football, Crickett, running, climbing, leaping, swimming, skating and have no great Objection to your play at Marbles. . . . These are good for your Health; but what do you do for your Mind? . . . I hear enough of your gaiety and hear it with pleasure; but I do not hear enough of your studies."[16]

Only Charles, among the youngest boys at Great Ealing, had difficulty adjusting to the school. Louisa wrote Abigail that all the rambunctious activity one could expect in "a large number of boys" distracted his attention from his studies. John Quincy agreed that the size of the school would necessarily be overwhelming to such a small boy—especially one who had been mainly schooled at home—and believed Charles would have done better in a more intimate setting. But since, in his parents' opinion, the advantage of having his older brothers close at hand outweighed the benefits of moving him to a smaller school, Charles remained with Dr. Nicholas.[17]

England in the fall of 1815 was poised at the dawn of imperial greatness. Following one hundred days as the restored emperor of France, Napoleon had finally been defeated at Waterloo on June 18 by a multinational army led by Britain's "Iron Duke," Lord Wellington, and the Prussian general Prince Gebhard Blücher. The four victorious nations—Britain, Russia, Prussia, and Austria—agreed on a settlement that set the boundaries of Europe for the next forty years and restored many of its war-torn and economically depressed monarchies and duchies to their pre-Napoleonic ruling families.

Britain alone had remained untouched by battle on its own soil, but in 1815 it was mired in a severe postwar recession. By 1817, 300,000 men would be discharged from the army and navy and left to their own devices, most without pensions or any other monetary rewards for their service to the nation. Industrialists who had grown rich in the manufacture of war-related goods and the construction of warships suddenly saw government orders disappear; some were ruined, and nearly all had to discharge workers. During the Napoleonic years, English agriculture had thrived because the island nation, cut off from grain and other crops by the French emperor's Continental System, had been forced to reform its land-use and stockbreeding practices. But after the war, as cheaper grain from the Continent again became available, the landed gentry, overrepresented in Parliament, succeeded in passing the infamous Corn Law of 1815, which kept the price of grain artificially high and forbade its importation from Europe.[18]

The inevitable result was severe want and near-starvation up and down the country, particularly among the unemployed working class. Added to this burden were the crushing income taxes, passed on by employers and felt as an indirect tax on the working poor. Louisa had not been in London a month before she wrote to Abigail, "I am positively assured that the poorer classes of society do not taste meat once in several months and it is hardly possible to [take] five steps from your door without being surrounded with . . . beggars who assure you they have not a bit of bread."[19]

Many of these taxes, unfortunately, went to support the extravagant lifestyle of the self-indulgent Prince Regent, the future George IV. King George III, confined to Windsor Castle after being certified insane in 1810, reigned in name only. His eldest son, released from any parental restraint, constantly built and remodeled his many beautiful residences, collected great artworks, gems, and furniture, and entertained at lavish balls and elaborate entertainments. The English people despised him. Celebrations after Waterloo had to be organized to disguise the fact that the same London crowds who were wildly cheering the visiting Tsar Alexander and the Prussian King Frederick William were more than ready to hiss their own acting sovereign. The regent was especially unpopular among those who supported the case of his vulgar, scandal-prone wife, Princess Caroline, whom he had banished from his sight almost immediately after their wedding night—a night that he spent drunk and asleep in the fireplace. Jane Austen's attitude toward the prince and princess was typical: "Poor woman, I shall support her as long as I can, because she *is* a Woman, & because I hate her Husband."[20]

It is little wonder that the cabinet, headed by Lord Liverpool, feared a popular uprising against both the regent and the government. The prime minister himself had been present at the storming of the Bastille and never forgot the depredations of the mob. The French Revolution—an event still vivid in the memories of other senior cabinet ministers as well—turned even a minor agitation for reform among the people into a threat of total social upheaval. To avoid the threat's becoming a reality, the government badly needed to turn its attention inward. Peace abroad was less a choice than a necessity.[21]

Fortunately for Britain, the pursuit of peace entailed no diminution of power. No other nation was its rival on land or sea. Through the efforts of Foreign Secretary Viscount Lord Castlereagh, the "greatest diplomatist of British history," the island kingdom had emerged from the Congress of Vienna with matters settled largely in its favor. Castlereagh could afford to be magnanimous in his private instructions to his minister to the United States, Charles Bagot: "The avowed & true Policy of Great Britain is, in the existing state of the World, to appease controversy, & to secure if possible for all states a long interval of Repose."[22]

John Quincy, always suspicious of British intentions, found his diplomatic tasks almost ludicrously easy. He had been warned by his father that he might be stepping onto a dangerous land mine—"No man except your father was ever placed in a more delicate or dangerous situation than you are"—but the Adamses' fears proved unfounded. Because Britain needed the American market for its manufactured goods and depended on its former colonies for cotton and other agricultural imports, a commercial treaty providing reciprocal trading on an equal footing was swiftly concluded and signed on July 3, 1815, by its principal negotiators, Albert Gallatin and Henry Clay. John Quincy, only a month into his tenure as minister, readily added his signature.[23]

Thereafter, only minor fractious issues, often ameliorated or suavely turned aside by Castlereagh, ruffled the surface of Anglo-American relations. Finally, even John Quincy began to believe the British were earnest in desiring peace. "My special duty at present is to preach peace. . . . I am deeply convinced that peace is the state best adapted to the interest and the happiness of both nations," he wrote to his father a year after arriving in London.[24]

The minister's duties were thus largely taken up with his extensive correspondence with the secretary of state and American ministers and consuls throughout Europe. Writing reports and analyses had always been the part of his diplomatic assignments to which John Quincy had devoted his best efforts. Every day that he did not make the eight-mile trek from Little Ealing to the American legation office in London to pick up his mail and deal with the personal problems his fellow citizens believed only the minister could solve, he was free to write from early morning until his eyes grew too weary to continue.

This happy state of affairs would probably have gone on indefinitely had John Quincy not shot himself in the hand practicing with pistols that he had planned to present to his two older sons. Overnight, the wounds became badly infected. Since he could no longer hold a pen, he attempted to compensate by continuous reading. Ten days later, his left eye had become inflamed, and by October 15 it was causing him "severe and almost continual pain." The local doctor thought the problem was "Egyptian Opthalimia" and that blindness might be inevitable. John Quincy resisted the application of leeches but finally succumbed after a fever developed, his eye began to discharge "matter," and the pain became so excruciating he could not sleep at night and required a completely dark and silent room during the day.

Louisa cared for her husband tirelessly—waiting up with him throughout his sleepless nights, bathing his eye with a light touch of a camel's hair brush, and reading to him at those moments when the pain had subsided to a point when he could bear to hear another human voice. John Quincy acknowledged her resilience in a crisis as well as the toll her ministrations exacted from her: "My wife's kind attention was incessant but the fatigue and anxiety and alarm together with the hideous aspect of the leeches almost overpowered her strength," he later wrote. Although the infection seems to have run its course by mid-November and with no serious permanent damage to John Quincy's eyesight, it would be at least three months before he could even partially resume his customary activities. Meanwhile, he conceded, "the whole course of my life has been changed."

For once in his life, John Quincy had become the helpless partner in his marriage, utterly dependent on Louisa not only for his physical care but also for the management of their household and a major portion of his ministerial duties as well. By the end of November, he was back to taking six-mile walks but could do little that required his eyes or hands. Louisa, meanwhile, was in the process of giving a month's notice "on strong and well founded complaints" to the cook, the housemaid, and the laundry maid and "soothing a great stir and hubbub" among the remainder of the staff. She cared for the boys when they were ill, entertained their young friends at dinner, hired new staff, traveled alone into London for visiting or shopping, regularly walked for as much as an hour with her husband, and received visitors in the late afternoon.[25]

Throughout John Quincy's illness, Louisa kept a daily account of events for future entries to his diary. When his hand remained unsteady and his eyesight weak even after the infection had passed, she offered to help him keep up with his private correspondence as well. Her offer was gratefully accepted. It was no time at all before Louisa was hard at work between 10 A.M. and 4 P.M. every day except Sunday writing, at John Quincy's dictation, his official reports and responding to his voluminous public as well as private correspondence. From the start, she was completely proficient. John Quincy, therefore, had no reason to restrain his impulse toward the long, detailed compositions that had always characterized his writing. In a December letter to his mother, for example, he expounded for five closely argued pages on the controversy then raging in Massachusetts on the future direction of Unitarianism and followed up with a long concluding paragraph on politics. Louisa, later in the month, apologized to her mother-in-law for her own tardy correspondence: "Mr. Adams has written you a long letter today, which I have assisted, and I think as long as I am occupied in this way you must cease to expect any Letters from me and consider his as from us both."[26]

Abigail, however, was fully as interested in court gossip as in theological disputes, and she knew she could not expect the same shrewd comments on royal marriages and current fashion from her son that she could from her daughter-in-law. She was more curious than ever when Louisa was finally in a position to know what was happening at the highest levels of society. Queen Charlotte, wife of the unfortunate George III, resumed her formal receptions, or "drawing rooms," early in 1816, and both Louisa and John Quincy were presented to her. Thereafter, they were obliged to attend certain royal occasions, such as the elaborate wedding of the then-heir to the throne, Princess Charlotte, to Prince Leopold of Saxe-Coburg-Gotha in May 1816.[27]

Vividly recalling the moment when she herself had been presented to Queen Charlotte in 1785, Abigail was eager to hear every detail. "I should like an account of your reception and presentation to Court and the appearance of the Queen at this Age. . . . She was not esteemed a beauty 30 years ago when I was presented to her," she wrote to Louisa in May 1815, days before the younger Adamses had even arrived in London. It would be a year before Louisa could satisfy her mother-in-law's "curiosity to know whether the old fashion of Large hoops still prevails; and how the head is decorated," but then Louisa was only too happy to oblige with a detailed description of the dress Princess Charlotte wore at the royal wedding: "white net richly embroidered in silver with an elegant border in silver . . . the train blue embroidered to match and trimmed with a rich trimming of spotted net . . . the train very long, worn down, and the dress without a hoop." She wrote that she had been "thus particular" because she knew it would give Abigail pleasure. On that score, Louisa was more percep-tive than later historians who have burnished the image of the Adams family matriarch as a woman with loftier interests than the length of a princess's train or the marital scandals that swirled around the royal family. "Your Letters are a treat from which I derive pleasure unalloyed," Abigail fondly wrote her daughter-in-law in the summer of 1816.[28]

Compared to their success in engaging with royalty in earlier diplomatic postings, neither of the Adamses seems to have made any particular impression at the Court of St. James's. In Berlin Louisa had danced with the Prussian king, and in St. Petersburg John Quincy had bantered with the Russian tsar on his daily walks, but now they played the role of extras, standing uncomfortably in the shadows for endless hours at one of the Prince Regent's elaborately choreo-graphed galas or at "drawing rooms" during which the old queen and her unmarried daughters stiffly received guests. John Quincy described one such event as "five hundred persons crowded into two small chambers" where he and Louisa were "jammed up in a corner of the Drawing Room and unable equally to advance or retire."[29]

Louisa's social skills seem to have been largely wasted as a diplomatic asset in her native land. The Prince Regent never deigned to meet or appear to recognize her although she and John Quincy were regularly invited to every major social event at his official residence, Carlton House. Louisa found the prince's disdain offensive. "I have been twice to Carlton House by invitation without ever receiving a bow from its Master. I am so much of an old fashionist that I confess I feel very awkward under such circumstances and I know not how to behave. I do not like to find myself in a House where I am not acknowledged as an acquaintance."[30]

Her resentment at being ignored probably colored her report to her mother-in-law of one of the prince's most extravagant events, which took place in a large polygonal brick building with an umbrella-shaped roof he had built specifically for parties in his garden at Carlton House. The interior décor, especially the banked flowers and the bower where the musicians were stationed, Louisa wrote, created "a very pretty effect though it did not strike me very much after having witnessed the fetes in Russia . . . which were infinitely more splendid and in far better taste." Louisa was also unimpressed with the ability of Englishwomen to waltz, refusing to attribute their awkwardness in performing the newly introduced dance to "want of confidence," as a newspaper reporter had done. A lack of confidence, she wrote, was hardly a "popular failing" among the aristocracy.[31]

Britain's inflexible class system effectively assigned John Quincy and Louisa to a status below that which they had been accorded in Berlin and St. Petersburg. They seem never to have been invited for as much as a cup of tea at Boston Manor, although the Clitherow women considerately stopped by Little Boston House when John Quincy and Louisa were ill. When John Quincy called politely on his landlord early in the Adamses' tenancy of Little Boston House, he found the colonel, his wife, and sister "very much occupied," and he cut his visit short. Similarly, the family was conveniently not at home when he and Louisa, according to custom, left their visiting cards a month later. John Quincy also seems to have been unsuccessful in his efforts to meet Lady Jane Carr, the remarried widow of Spencer Perceval, the only British prime minister ever to be assassinated, who lived with her several children nearby at Elm Grove, a large mansion in Ealing. Eleven dinner invitations that the American minister and his wife sent out in October 1815 elicited, in John Quincy's words, six "excuses." Even Lord and Lady Carysfort, godparents of George and staunch friends of the Adamses in Berlin, seem to have become relatively distant now that Louisa and John Quincy were in England. Only in their early sixties, the older couple may never have made the journey out of London to visit Little Boston House.[32]

On the other hand, John Quincy and Louisa were readily accepted by their upper-middle-class neighbors and almost immediately formed congenial friendships. Just weeks after their arrival, the Adamses were invited to dine with a party of several other ladies and gentlemen of the neighborhood at the home of Dr. Nicholas. Among the guests were Major Alexander Morrison, a retired East India army officer; Alexander Copeland, a successful builder; and a Mr. Von Harten, a German whose wife—also present—was a native of Fairfield,

Connecticut. The three men, along with Dr. Nicholas, John Quincy, and the vicar of St. Mary's Church, Dr. Colston Carr, formed an informal men's group that dined together occasionally at the New Inn in Great Ealing. With their wives, they made up a social circle whose activities fitted the Adamses' tastes perfectly. After Dr. Nicholas's "most elegant and sumptuous dinner," for example, his elder daughters performed on the piano and harp while a table of guests played whist, an after-dinner entertainment reminiscent of evenings at Tower Hill in the 1790s. For the next year and a half, Louisa and John Quincy regularly gave large dinner parties, followed by music and cards, at Little Boston House. In turn, they were invited to parties and picnics, cricket matches and balls in the neighborhood.[33]

English country dancing, still extremely popular outside court circles, was featured at one ball at the New Inn attended by 162 men and women packed into two overheated rooms. Twenty-two couples in two sets went through the elaborate steps and turns that Louisa had learned to execute perfectly as a young girl. "My wife danced almost the whole evening," John Quincy—a nonpartici-pant—reported, remarking that he had felt obliged to warn her against over-taxing her energy. Two days later, Louisa proved his fears unfounded when she entertained a party of ten for dinner and performed with several young ladies who arrived after dinner for an evening of musical entertainment.[34]

Nonetheless, John Quincy chafed at his and Louisa's limited entrée into the very highest levels of British society. Because their finances dictated that they live outside the capital, he told himself that they could not ask fellow members of the diplomatic corps or aristocratic acquaintances to travel the eight miles to dine at Little Boston House. "An American Minister abroad is a perpetual lesson of humility not to say of humiliation," John Quincy wrote to his mother in June 1816. He knew the benefit of associating with "people of rank and conse-quence" but claimed it was better to shun such society than to be unable to reciprocate invitations in kind. The next day Louisa echoed his complaints. Remarking to Abigail that she and John Quincy could not "partake of [London's] pleasures in consequence of our residence in the country," she added, "We begin to find it very inconvenient and it suits our purses in many respects better than it does our inclinations."[35]

A month later, however, London called and her tune had changed. "We are here plunged into the great world notwithstanding our distance from London and between three and four times a week we are not in this house until three or four o'clock in the morning." She and John Quincy felt obliged to accept every invitation during the height of the London season, even those issued at the last minute. One night during dinner, after a very full day, John Quincy received a card from the Countess of Jersey, a former mistress of the Prince Regent and a powerful woman in society, inviting him to a party later that evening. He changed his clothes, left Little Ealing at 10 P.M., made the hour-long trip into London, mingled with the other three hundred guests, and didn't return home until almost daybreak.[36]

The Adamses recognized that their presence several times a week at these large, fashionable "routs" had little to do with John Quincy's diplomatic skills or Louisa's personal charm. Invitations to the American minister and his wife by highly placed government officials, titled hostesses, or ambassadors from wealthier nations were purely a matter of diplomatic protocol and issued primarily to swell the crowds. Their hosts did not expect invitations in return. Lost in the noise and confusion of hundreds of expensively dressed bodies pressed upon one another, substantive or witty conversations were impossible. Even Louisa's facility in French—a key diplomatic asset in Berlin and St. Petersburg—was seldom called upon in London.

Nonetheless, it is clear that, despite the crowds, the late nights, and the long carriage rides back to Little Ealing in the early morning, Louisa was enjoying herself. Her letters to Abigail depict the social season's most celebrated debutantes, portray the idiosyncrasies of the Duke of Wellington, and minutely detail ball gowns and interior decorations—all in great high spirits. John Quincy was more grudging in his reaction to a life of gaiety. Forgetting, perhaps, that an essential part of his assignment as American minister was to attend precisely these social events, no matter how meaningless, he complained to his mother that "fashionable assemblies . . . have for the last six months consumed a large portion of my time and broken in upon the regularity of my life."[37]

Surprisingly, both John Quincy and Louisa thrived on their hectic schedule. "I cannot conceive how it happens but this mode of life seems to agree perfectly well with me for I never enjoyed such health, particularly since my marriage and I am only afraid of growing too fat," Louisa informed Abigail before launching into a lively description of a ball given by the Prince Regent. John Quincy, she wrote in early September 1816, "never looked so well or so handsome as he does now."[38]

That they were both well and handsome in the summer and fall of 1816 is reflected in a pair of oil portraits painted by the twenty-one-year-old artist Charles Robert Leslie, whom Louisa described as "a young American . . . who bids fair to become a very great Artist and whom Mr. [Benjamin] West is very proud of." The young artist seems to have gloried in his virtuosic ability to depict sumptuous detail. He painted Louisa in an Empire-style, deep red, velvet gown, trimmed with white lace and beads. An embroidered lace cloak falls delicately over one shoulder. Chestnut-brown ringlets in the classical style frame her rosy complexion and dark eyes; a fashionable headpiece recalling a Roman matron's rests on her back-drawn hair. Louisa's upturned eyes and dreamy expression seem contrived, but the portrait nonetheless conveys a sense of her elegance, serenity, and intelligence.[39]

In John Quincy's view, however, Louisa's portrait was not the "excellent likeness" of his own. His is, indeed, one of the most human and approachable of the many paintings and daguerreotypes made of his face and figure during his long lifetime. With his dark hair fashionably trimmed in the ancient Roman style, the forty-nine-year-old John Quincy appears at ease in a blue cutaway waistcoat festooned with a double row of brass buttons, an immaculate, white, high-collared shirt, and a soft white cravat tied up to the chin. His index finger is inserted into a weighty volume—emblazoned with his personally designed seal—as if to signify that he has been interrupted in the act of reading. His benign facial expression has been described as "pompous," although it could as well be termed "happy" or "relaxed."[40]

Leslie perceptively interpreted his subject's mood. John Quincy was probably never more at peace with himself than in the summer and fall of 1816. He had even relinquished what he ruefully acknowledged might have been unattainable ambitions for his three sons. "I comfort myself with the reflection that they are like other children and prepare my mind for seeing them, if their lives are spared, get along in the world like other men," he wrote his mother. Even George, he concluded, was more interested in escaping his studies than pursuing them. The early morning tutorials were a thing of the past, and the three Adams boys had only to ask their father for a day off from school for it to be granted.[41]

As he relaxed at Little Boston House, John Quincy's demons of political ambition and overachievement seem momentarily to have vanished. At the end of June, he rhapsodized in his diary about the "exquisitely beautiful" countryside and the "little Paradise" that was their garden, "laid out with taste and elegance." Once the annual Parliamentary session and the attendant social season were over in August, he had little of an official nature with which to busy himself. By September, he was spending two hours a day constructing an index to his monumental diary and another hour adding to the diary itself. Once he would have passed his evenings teaching himself a new language or reading deeply in philosophy or abstract science. Now he spent crisp, fall nights happily viewing the stars and tracing the celestial constellations with George and Ellen Nicholas, the second eldest of Dr. Nicholas's five daughters, who was then on an extended stay with the Adamses.[42]

Eighteen-year-old Ellen, like her sisters, had visited regularly at Little Boston House ever since the two families met in the late summer of 1815, but this was the first time a visit had lengthened into months. Ellen was the perfect companion. She rode with Louisa on sightseeing carriage tours of the country-side, accompanied her to London for her sittings for Leslie, and fished with the whole family in the nearby Grand Junction Canal. At the Adamses' pianoforte she accompanied Louisa's sweet soprano for musical evenings of Handel arias and Italian songs. On other nights, she provided a rapt audience as John Quincy read Regency comedies and Shakespeare's plays aloud to "the Ladies."[43]

It is not hard to see why this threesome worked so well. Louisa, at forty-one, may have seen in Ellen the grown daughter she would never have. Raised in a family of women—and as a married woman, often with one of her sisters as a companion—she may simply have longed for another female to talk to in a house full of males. Ellen, just coming into bloom, may have yearned for the mother apparently missing from the crowded headmaster's quarters at Great Ealing School. Their friendship, for whatever reason, flourished over a year and a half and added an essential grace note to Louisa's happiness at Little Boston House.[44]

John Quincy's feelings toward Ellen and hers toward him may have been a little more ambiguous. Certainly, he enjoyed having her around the house. When her father came to take her home on September 29 after a long visit, he joined Louisa in an appeal "for him to leave her sometime longer." When she finally left for home in December, he wrote sadly in his diary, "Since Ellen Nicholas left us, there has been no Evening Music." Her feelings may have been more romantic. After the Adamses returned to the United States, she wrote him a warm letter at the Department of State, reminding him of her delight in his astronomy lessons and promising to treasure the little notebook into which she had copied their stellar observations. Addressing John Quincy as "my sweet Mr. Adams," she beseeched him to write her occasionally so that he could continue to instruct her by his "wisdom" and to regulate her "principles." She concluded with the hope that he would "sometimes think of your little 'favorite.'"[45]

And it was Ellen who in mid-October served as John Quincy's poetic muse, unleashing a torrent of verse from a man who acknowledged to his diary, "Could I have chosen my own genius and condition, I should have made a great poet." His poetic frenzy began when Ellen showed him some admiring verses to Louisa she had written as she sat quietly to one side during the latter's portrait sittings. Ellen and Louisa had been begging John Quincy to compose some verses that would serve as lyrics to the Italian airs they loved to perform. He could withstand their pleas no longer. Overnight he dashed off two stanzas to Ellen "in the amatory style" that he concluded in a "hyperbolic and burlesque idea" since a love poem would have been "ridiculous from me to her." Once begun, he could not stop. He added several stanzas to the original poem on his way to London the next morning and wrote the final lines the next day as he was rising from bed. The additional stanzas presented him with a dilemma. They were written "as if from a youthful and ardent lover and expressing sentiments which I neither do nor ought to feel for her. The Love is all merely poetical, but it has so much the appearance of reality that I scruple to show the lines as now are written." It is not clear that he ever did.[46]

John Quincy had soon given himself over entirely to his passion for poetry. During the many hours sitting for his portrait, commuting by carriage between Little Ealing and the American legation in London, or lying awake at night, he composed poems in every genre. He wrote ballads during sermons and revised odes as Ellen and Louisa sang in the evening. Unsurprisingly, John Quincy was not content to write short verses, however; an epistle to his mother had reached 700 lines by the end of October. In a fifty-six-line tribute to his young admirer, "To Miss Ellen Nicholas on Her Birth-Day, 14 December 1816," the aspiring poet played with the incompatibility of "lovely Ellen" born in deep winter with all the attributes of blossoming spring, finally settling on the conceit that in her complexion she had joined the "Snows of December, to Lilies of June." In another vein, he composed an admonishing verse, "A Sunday Hymn Addressed to L.C.A., and EFN, on their laughing during Divine Service," and received in return a poetic apology from Ellen, that began, "Oh! yes; thy councils have sunk deep/Within this wild and erring heart."[47]

Louisa, always reluctant to compete in intellectual contests in which her husband was a participant, finally yielded to the prevailing poetic winds and produced her first attempt, "On the Portrait of My Husband." She was proud enough of her ode to copy it out in a letter to Abigail, and on literary merit alone, it certainly ranks with the efforts of John Quincy and Ellen. Louisa's poem is an unaffected outpouring of love and respect for her husband. She praises the "Sense and sweetness join'd with ease" that distinguishes his portrait's facial expression as well as his "vast variety of mind/ Capacious, clear, and strong" and "brilliancy of wit refin'd" that "enchants the list'ning throng." Perhaps at no other moment in his life would John Quincy be distinguished by "sweetness."[48]

He, of course, responded with a poem of his own—"To My Wife," a tender and loving seventy-two-line tribute to "the best solace of my life." He extolled her "generous and kind" heart and vowed that were he to have another opportunity to choose a wife, he would not hesitate:

Louisa! Could a Mortal hand,
Break for a moment, Hymen's chain
Before the altar, I wou'd stand
And thou shoulds't be my Bride again.[49]

Even as John Quincy delighted in the "little Paradise" that was his life at Little Boston House, events outside his control were converging to bring his bucolic existence to an end. On November 1, 1816, American voters, by more than a two-to-one margin, supported James Monroe's bid for the presidency. The opposition Federalists did not formally put up a candidate, but three New England states would later give their Electoral College votes to the elderly Rufus King.

Since Jefferson's administration, a pattern had been set for the secretary of state, rather than the vice president, to move up to become president. When Monroe, then secretary of state, was nominated by a caucus of congressional Democratic-Republicans in March 1816, it was assumed—because of the weakness of the Federalists—that he would ultimately win both the popular and Electoral College vote. Speculation then turned to whom he would make next in line for the presidency. There were three outstanding candidates: Albert Gallatin, Henry Clay, and John Quincy Adams. Gallatin, in many ways, was the ablest, but he was foreign-born—a disqualification for the nation's highest office. Monroe might have been hesitant to appoint Clay because he feared losing the support of the northeastern states if a third Southerner in a row were installed in the coveted post. That left John Quincy as the obvious choice, and word came from America that it was generally understood he would be nominated immediately after Monroe's inauguration in March 1817. John Quincy dismissed this information as mere gossip and the kind of political speculation "always going on in the United States."[50]

For a man who was political to the bone, John Quincy seemed determined to convince himself that the secretary of state appointment was of little importance to him. Despite lengthy, detailed reports in his diary on his conversations with every entrepreneur and inventor who requested a visa, every letter he received, and every long walk he embarked upon, there is scant mention in the fall of 1816 concerning his future career. It was Christmas Eve before he confided to his diary that he had, in fact, discussed his potential appointment at some length with a visitor from home.

John Quincy may well have been battling the depressed spirits that a call to duty often aroused in him. Safe in idyllic Little Ealing, he may have managed to put aside thoughts of returning to the political wars in favor of indefinitely retaining the status quo. He realized that his political future was in Monroe's hands, and he probably knew he would answer a call to public service. But he would also have had foremost in his thoughts the Adams credo his mother plainly articulated in March 1817: "I know you too well and the root from whence you spring to believe you would seek for office of any kind." Therefore, he could not lift a finger to indicate an interest in becoming secretary of state.[51]

Not so Louisa. She wrote to Abigail that she had spent the month of October 1816—while John Quincy's "poetic fountain [was spouting] through all its pipes"—house hunting in London. She told her mother-in-law that Little Ealing was too far from London for either business or pleasure and that she had no intention of resuming the "serious inconvenience" of long rides from London to Ealing at three in the morning after a formal event during the long winter social season. Among its other drawbacks, visiting Americans found it "troublesome and expensive" to make the trip to Little Boston House for a short visit. "On the whole, I have thought it would be both prudent and advantageous to Mr. Adams to move into London," she wrote.[52]

Louisa knew exactly how her mother-in-law would interpret what she meant by "prudent and advantageous." With John Quincy out of sight and out of mind in the world outside Little Ealing, other presidential aspirants stood ready to seize the spotlight that the Adams family believed rightly belonged to him. Complaining that John Quincy laughed at her and told her she did not "understand his interest," Louisa appealed to Abigail to "judge between us, understanding as you do every particular that the situation demands." The "situation" seems clearly to have been the long-range goal of attaining the presidency, and Louisa, if not John Quincy, fully understood that it would not be his for the asking.

Her husband certainly showed little interest in moving from Little Ealing. "The house in which we now live is so comfortable that I despair of finding one in London even at double the Rent I pay for this, or half so convenient," John Quincy complained. Undaunted, Louisa rented a house in fashionable Gloucester Place, Portman Square, into which they could move in early December 1816. In order to further what she saw as her reluctant husband's political interests, she seemed ready to give up the congenial social life she enjoyed in the country, the family's easy accessibility to the boys' school, and the many amenities of Little Boston House for the added expense and petty annoyances of city living. What might have turned into a tug-of-war over a country or city residence ended, however, when the Portman Square rental fell through and subsequent house searches proved unsuccessful. The family settled down in Little Ealing for the remainder of the winter.[53]

Louisa seems to have retreated from her campaign to thrust John Quincy into the limelight not only because she was unable to find an appropriate London residence but also because she was once again pregnant. At forty-two, and with as many as eight miscarriages and a stillbirth behind her, she may not have welcomed this, her final pregnancy. John Quincy's diary is very circumspect, as usual, but it seems clear that by January, Louisa was experiencing many of the difficulties that had characterized her earlier pregnancies. She spent almost the entire month of February in bed "suffering much pain." Doctors were called, leeches applied, and she was bled. By March, she was feeling better, but, in John Quincy's opinion, she was still infirm.[54]

Because her health was so precarious in the winter of 1817, Louisa withdrew from all social life. John Quincy went alone to royal drawing rooms and levees. Daily visits to and from the Nicholas daughters were a thing of the past. By late March, Louisa was again attending dinners and going to the theater, but in May she wrote to Abigail—her first letter to her mother-in-law since the previous November—that her health was "very bad." When Abigail eventually heard the news of the impending birth from Louisa's sister Caroline in May, she wrote to a friend, "I never had an intimation that such a manufacture had taken place—I hope it will be of the feminine gender."[55]

John Quincy, meanwhile, was enduring a winter full of secret suspense. His diary never mentions a potential appointment in the new administration. Every rumor indicated that Monroe planned to make him secretary of state, but he had not heard directly from the president-elect himself. He took the precaution of giving three months notice to Dr. Nicholas when he paid the tuition for John and Charles in January 1817; he also informed Miss Clitherow in February that the family planned to move out of Little Boston House at the end of the month—although he extended the rental agreement by several weeks when no definitive news from Washington had arrived by March 1. The next weeks were marked by "an unsettled state of mind with anxious anticipation of the future . . . with alternatives all of which are cheerless." Finally, on April 16, John Quincy received the much-anticipated letter from the president, appointing him secretary of state and informing him that his nomination had been confirmed by the Senate.[56]

Barely hesitating, John Quincy accepted the president's offer and immediately made arrangements to return to the United States. As the family prepared to leave Little Boston House for the last time on April 28, he reminisced fondly of the happy days they had spent in Little Ealing, "one of the most delightful spots upon which I ever resided." Taking a last walk around the grounds, he wrote, "I have seldom perhaps never in the course of my life resided more comfortably than at the house which we now quit, and which I shall probably never see again." He was more prescient than he knew.[57]

Meanwhile, Louisa faced a dilemma. Now at the midpoint of her pregnancy, she would have known that she faced a serious risk of losing her baby if she embarked on a long ocean voyage. On the other hand, recalling how difficult even her successful deliveries had been in the past, she would have resisted the option of remaining alone in England without her husband or a sister to see her through what she had good reason to fear would be an ordeal. There is no indication in John Quincy's diary or in his letters that he ever entertained the thought of remaining in England until the birth of their child. He did, however, seriously contemplate the idea that Louisa would not be strong enough to make the voyage with him: "The state of Mrs. Adams's health will probably not admit of her going with us," he wrote a friend at the end of May.[58]

Whatever factors weighed in her decision, Louisa was on the ship *Washington* on June 15 with her husband, three sons, and four servants as it set sail from England to America. Accompanying the party was Daniel Pope Cook, a distant relation of Louisa's who had been sent to fetch them by President Monroe. Nearly everyone, with the exception of John Quincy, was immediately seasick, but Louisa suffered most of all. For a week, she was "continually seasick with other distressing symptoms," according to her husband. Fortunately for her, the eminent physician Dr. James Tillary, a Scotsman who had practiced for forty years in New York, was on board the *Washington*. He administered laudanum and bled his patient with little effect.[59]

On June 28, just two weeks out to sea, Louisa was "seized with great violence" to such an extent that she fully believed she was dying. Her severe pain continued, John Quincy wrote, "until near Sunset when she found herself relieved and the remainder of the evening was free from pain." What Louisa later described to Abigail as a "bad miscarriage" had taken place.[60]

Unlike his agonized diary entries after his wife's earlier miscarriages, John Quincy was remarkably cavalier—even callous—on this occasion. In his diary, he immediately followed his recording of the fact that Louisa was now free from pain with a discussion of the weather and a technical calculation of the ship's course. Using a particularly unfortunate analogy, he wrote that the weather was "changeful as a child at play," but he recorded nothing of his feelings or those of his wife and sons as he buried his unborn child at sea.[61]

On August 6, 1817, Louisa and John Quincy arrived in New York City. The most consequential years of their lives were about to begin.

13

CAMPAIGN

I have made up my mind to go on my own way.

—LOUISA CATHERINE ADAMS

In March 1818, barely six months into his term as secretary of state, John Quincy found himself in the midst of the race to succeed President Monroe in 1825, seven years later. The partisans of known candidates, he complained in his diary, "descry me as much as possible in the public opinion." Urged to strike back against one particularly egregious attack, John Quincy stood true to his vision of how an ethical presidential campaign should be conducted. Until the end, he promised, "I should do absolutely nothing."[1]

Not so Louisa. From the moment of her arrival in Washington in 1817 until her husband's disputed election in 1825, she was, in many respects, his campaign manager. How this British-born woman, who had spent most of her married life outside the country in the rarefied atmosphere of diplomatic circles, mastered American politics in a particularly chaotic political period was remarkable in itself. That she did it despite her husband's resistance to making any obvious effort to seek the presidency, her three sons' difficult passage through adolescence and early adulthood, and her own chronic ill health was an extraordinary feat of will and ambition.[2]

Leaving their three sons behind in Boston for schooling—the two younger ones at Boston Latin and George preparing for Harvard—Louisa and John Quincy arrived in Washington on September 20, 1817. They found a city that had only recently recovered from its torching by the British in August 1814. Both the President's House and the Capitol, as well as the Arsenal, the Navy Yard, the Treasury Building, and the War Office, had been set ablaze by His Majesty's celebrating troops. Once Congress decided that the federal government would

Louisa, by Charles Bird King, 1824. Courtesy of the Smithsonian American Art Museum, Washington, D.C./Art Resource, NY.

remain in Washington, reconstruction proceeded swiftly. Although it would be another seven years before the Capitol received its first dome, its two major wings were rising in a classic, monumental style reflecting the self-confidence of the new nation. By the fall of 1817, work on the executive mansion had just finished. The smell of paint and wet plaster on its walls was so overwhelming when the Adamses arrived that President James Monroe waited only long enough to swear in John Quincy as secretary of state before leaving for an extended stay at his Virginia estate.[3]

While retaining the feel of a frontier boomtown, Washington had undergone a remarkable transformation from the raw building site Louisa had first glimpsed when she returned from Prussia in 1801. Its population was in the process of expanding from 3,210 permanent residents in 1800 to the 13,247 counted in the 1820 census. When the Adamses arrived in 1817, real estate sales had increased 500 percent over 1813. Shops, particularly those of seamstresses, milliners, and bootmakers, had sprung up along Pennsylvania Avenue and its side streets. The great avenue itself, envisioned by Pierre L'Enfant and the early planners as a ceremonial boulevard both connecting and separating the constitutionally mandated centers of power, was still a rutted roadway "often filled with stagnant water." Negotiating the mile and a half between the Capitol and the President's House was a hazardous journey, as John Quincy and Louisa discovered one night when their carriage twice barely escaped tipping over. After borrowing a lantern from a guard at the Treasury Building, they were forced to wend their way home on foot, their evening clothes and shoes covered in mud.[4]

Washington was the ultimate company town, its only business government. Legislators rented rooms or suites in brick boardinghouses on Capitol Hill for the four or five months each year that Congress was in session. The boardinghouse dinner table—or "mess"—was as close to a political organizing entity as existed in an era when a single political party, the Democratic-Republicans, held absolute sway. Men from the same region and compatible political outlooks roomed, ate and frequently voted together. Not only the South and New England, but also the prosperous and populous Middle Atlantic and the new frontier states jealously guarded their regional interests and viewed with deep suspicion any attempt by another cluster of states to assume dominance. Meanwhile, members of the president's cabinet as well as the diplomatic corps and the wealthier permanent residents of the city clustered in brick townhouses near the executive mansion. These handsome, three-story mansions, on long, rectangular lots, were built close to the street and conformed to architectural criteria laid down by President Washington in 1791.[5]

John Quincy, perhaps in an effort to retain his status as an independent man, decided to rent a large house midway between the legislative and executive communities at what is now John Marshall Place but was then 4½ and C Streets. Neither he nor Louisa seems to have been particularly happy with his choice. Just two days after they moved in, the Adamses were inspecting another house that had recently come up for sale. Louisa, giving her first diplomatic dinner, for twenty distinguished guests in December, had to cope not only with "a French cook very drunk" but also with a house without "a single convenience for this sort of entertainment as there is not even an oven in the kitchen."[6]

Reflecting the new imbalance in their household management style, adopted by necessity in London and St. Petersburg, Louisa took over every detail of moving into their new quarters. John Quincy noted in his diary that for two nights in a row, she remained at their as yet-untenanted house until after 5 P.M. installing the furniture and household goods they had acquired abroad. Moving, he grumbled, had "occasioned some little interruption of my writing but not much." Two days later, he wrote contentedly that he and Louisa had spent the evening "in arranging all the letters I wrote in England in alphabetical order" and that he planned to continue the joint project for the next week or ten days.[7]

The most significant change that had taken place in the ten years Louisa had been away from the capital city was the very visible presence of women. Increasingly, the wives of cabinet members, senators, and congressmen accompanied their husbands for the congressional session—which was also the social season—and lived with them in their boardinghouses and hotels on Capitol Hill. Meanwhile, nations in addition to Britain and France had dispatched diplomats and their wives to Washington. They joined the established elite families who had long anchored the capital's social scene. Ambitious mothers, especially the wives of senators and cabinet officers, quickly realized the opportunities Washington offered their marriageable daughters and job-seeking sons, and the presence of these young people at the nightly dinners, balls, and large official presidential receptions called "drawing rooms" added to the season's gaiety. The British chargé d'affaires, Augustus Foster, considered the capital city "one of the most marrying places in the whole continent."[8]

Since nearly all cabinet positions were awarded to members of Congress or to those, like John Quincy, who had previously served in the House or Senate, an individual senator or congressman who hoped for an appointment to the president's inner circle needed to distinguish himself from his peers. This was where his wife could play an essential role. Entertaining and being entertained became a woman's most important occupation. Invitation lists and visiting became an obsessive concern. Gossip was the currency of the day. "I am

John Quincy, by Gilbert Stuart, 1818. Courtesy of White House Historical Association (White House Collection).

perfectly convinced that an angel could not escape [scandal] here," Louisa wrote in her journal on January 11, 1818, "and I have made up my mind to go on my own way."[9]

Early Washington society was governed by an informal system of protocol and precedence that reflected the social mores of the major urban areas of the

Eastern Seaboard and the patterns of behavior current among the plantation society of nearby Virginia and Maryland, along with a patina of European court manners adopted from the British and French diplomats assigned to the new capital city. President Jefferson, raised among the Virginia gentry and seasoned in the ways of the French court, knew the rules of etiquette in his bones, but he believed strongly that the rigid protocol he had observed in foreign courts was antithetical to a government for and by the people. Determined to dramatize his political beliefs, he purposely insulted the British ambassador, Anthony Merry, by greeting him during an official presentation visit in worn-down bedroom slippers and slovenly pants and coat. As the embarrassed ambassador, ceremoniously garbed in full court dress, complete with a court sword, struggled to maintain his dignity, Jefferson amused himself by tossing one of his slippers in the air and catching it with his big toe. The president followed this performance with an insult to both Merry and his wife by refusing to escort Mrs. Merry, the guest of honor, in to dinner. The so-called Merry Affair resulted in unnecessary diplomatic strains with Great Britain and, as historian Catherine Allgor observes, an etiquette war that Jefferson lost.[10]

It was a war, however, that Dolley Madison in the next administration triumphantly won. The eight years that Louisa and John Quincy were in Russia and England paralleled the domination of Washington society by the woman Louisa fondly referred to as "dear Dolley." The much-loved and admired Dolley did more than anyone to build the nation's capital as a place of both dignity and democracy. Her weekly drawing rooms, known as "squeezes" because the guests were so closely packed together, were elegant but open to almost anyone with a letter of introduction. Louisa had often remarked on the unkempt quality of the President's House under Jefferson. Dolley, beginning in 1809, completely renovated and furnished both the private and public rooms of the mansion. After everything was lost in the fires of 1814, she wasted no time in doing it again. Her aim was to combine the sophistication and style that would signal to diplomats and other overseas visitors that Americans were far from the crude savages that many believed them to be. They might be backwoodsmen, but they would never be intimidated by the mansion's gold draperies and French china service.

There was nothing in the Constitution that defined precisely how the legislative, executive, and judicial branches should interact. Through her social and political skills, Dolley made that essential connection, building a durable foundation on which the structure of a national government could rise. She accomplished this despite the constantly changing faces of the men and women who arrived in Washington for each congressional session. By personally calling on each new member of Congress and his wife and welcoming them to the

President's House, Dolley took a first and crucial step in bridging the gap between the two ends of Pennsylvania Avenue. At the same time, she established herself as a conduit to power in the capital city.

Dolley Madison left a nearly unattainable standard for future First Ladies. Few women, least of all her immediate successor, Elizabeth Monroe, had the talent or the physical vigor to maintain her relentless visiting, party giving, and acts of political patronage. In many ways the new First Lady was the polar opposite of her predecessor. During the six years that James Monroe had been secretary of state under President Madison, the Monroes had lived in relative seclusion out of society. Eight months after the couple first occupied the White House, the renowned chronicler of Washington society in the early nineteenth century, Margaret Bayard Smith, observed, "Both Mr. and Mrs. Monroe are perfect strangers not only to me but all the citizens." Elizabeth Monroe, for reasons of her own, discontinued Dolley's weekly soirees, although she did continue to give small dinner parties, open houses on the Fourth of July and New Year's Eve, and much more formal biweekly drawing rooms, which were open to anyone who had been introduced to the presidential couple. The difference was entirely in tone. Gone was Dolley's light hand on the elbow, directing a stranger to a famous senator from another part of the country. Elizabeth received guests, in Louisa's words, "not like a queen (for that is an unpardonable word in this Country) but like a goddess. Everything was brilliant and elegant."[11]

Indeed, Dolley herself might have agreed that by the time she left the President's House in 1817, her Wednesday evenings had lost something of their original brilliance. The British minister's wife, Mary Bagot—a niece of the Duke of Wellington who considered her husband's assignment to Washington tantamount to exile—was unimpressed when she attended a drawing room in the spring of 1816. Dolley's weekly parties, Mary wrote to her family in England, consisted of "a larger or smaller number of people collected—the women usually sit stuck round the room close to the wall. The men—many of whom come in boots & perfectly undone etc. with dirty hands & dirty linen—stand mostly talking with each other in the middle of the rooms. Tea & coffee & afterwards cold punch with glasses of Madeira & cakes are handed round & by ten o'clock everyone is dispersed." Dolley, however, would never have dreamed of stationing six liveried footmen at the door to the President's House for an evening drawing room, as Elizabeth Monroe did early in her tenure as First Lady, a gesture that further cemented her reputation for pretensions to royalty among the ladies of Washington.[12]

Even the introduction of footmen, however, would not have been enough to enflame Washington society to the degree that consumed both Elizabeth and

Louisa from 1818 to 1820. The uproar centered on the seemingly innocuous practice of making and receiving calls—and leaving and returning calling cards. As it
developed in the nineteenth century, the obligation of upper- and middle-class
women to make formal calls upon one another in a strict order of precedence
became more and more onerous. Modeled on rules set in Britain, the practice of
calling, at its most formal, began with a person—usually female—leaving her
engraved card at the home of someone to whom she wished to be introduced or
on whom she wished to call. If that person, typically someone of higher status,
agreed to receive the lady who had left her card, she would, in turn, leave her card
indicating the hours she would be "at home" or simply return the call in person.
At the very beginning of the process, therefore, a selective policy would be in
effect: a socially unacceptable person would never receive an invitation to visit or
be the recipient of a return call or card. No call would last more than fifteen
minutes nor would it consist of anything but prescribed conversational topics.[13]

The burgeoning city of Washington largely adopted British etiquette in
regard to calling, but with a local twist. Political status and power was the trump
that determined who called upon whom and in what order. Calling, even when
it involved simply leaving a card, was a political act, opening a dialogue between
newcomers and established residents, members of Congress and the executive
branch, and employment seekers and officials in a position to grant job requests.
Men as well as women made calling a regular practice. By December 1817, after
only three months in Washington—and before the congressional session had
even begun—Louisa had already had enough of the "usual business of visiting.
. . . All the ladies appear to think that they must visit me about once a week so
that I have no sooner got through [making return calls] than I am compelled to
begin again and even this perpetual slavery to which I seem to be doomed does
not prevent censure and [a] little jealousy. Mrs. Monroe never did a wiser thing
than give it up altogether."[14]

As it happened, Elizabeth Monroe's declaration before the social season of
1817–1818 that she would make no visits would cause Louisa acute distress. The
First Lady's decision was part of a considered plan, endorsed by her husband, to
bring more formality to the executive mansion and to set its occupants apart
from the rest of the populace. John Quincy remarked that Dolley Madison's
practice of calling on nearly everyone who arrived in the city had become a
"torture, which she felt very severely, but from which, having begun the practice, she never found an opportunity of receding." The Monroes apparently
believed that an announcement at the outset of the fifth Administration would
limit negative reaction. Instead, congressional wives turned their guns on
Louisa, an easier target than the president's wife.[15]

Four days after the president's annual New Year's Day party in 1818, two senators—John Gaillard of Mississippi, then the Senate president pro tempore, and William Smith of South Carolina—called on John Quincy at the State Department to ask "if there had been any new system of etiquette established with regard to visiting." The two were speaking not of the practice of calling itself but of precedence in the order of calling. Their complaint was that John Quincy and Louisa had not yet called on them or their wives and that Senate tradition, they claimed, held that senators paid first visits only to the president. That such high-ranking senators had come to the secretary of state's office with a question of etiquette signified its importance. They were claiming for the Senate a status just below that of the president and above that of cabinet members. John Quincy replied that that was not how he remembered visiting protocol from his years in the Senate but that he would be glad to conform, as long as the rule "that Senators would visit only the President did not extend to a requisition that the heads of departments should first visit them." That is, department heads were not required to make first visits and could visit whomever they wanted whenever they wanted. They parted in "good humor," he wrote in his diary, but clearly the issue was unresolved. John Quincy had not given in.[16]

Three weeks later, the president's wife invited Louisa to call, and again the subject was the still-simmering issue of first visits. Had the wife of the secretary of state refused to make visits to the wives of members of Congress? Louisa offered a practical excuse. Many of those women lived in boardinghouses, and it was difficult not only to locate them but also to maneuver her carriage through Washington's rutted streets in winter. "I told her that the distances were so great and the difficulty of finding the different parts of the city where ladies thought proper to take up their abode such as to make it impossible to devote the time to it. . . . It wasn't a question of etiquette at all." Louisa could readily document the difficulties she faced. Writing to her father-in-law John Adams a year later, she listed the return visits she was then committed to make: "I have now on hand a number of visits, 1 of which is nine miles from here, another 4 and ½, and three or four of 2 and 3 lying in opposite directions—with parties almost every evening and one pair of Horses—You may judge from this of the misery of morning visits and the intolerable waste of time it occasions."[17]

As she did about so many other things about Washington society, Louisa thought the whole etiquette issue absurd. "It is really laughable to see in our boasted Republic how much may be gained or lost by the failure of a morning visit between two Ladies, particularly if those Ladies are the Wives of Members of Congress." But the battle lines had been drawn, and she adopted the policy that she would return all calls paid to her but would not pay the first call.[18]

Four days after her conversation with Elizabeth Monroe, the Adamses hosted a ball, for which Louisa had sent out three hundred handwritten invitations. By eight in the evening, her reception rooms were crowded. "I had the pleasure of seeing all my friends *willing* to be amused," she reported to Abigail Adams. The crowd, however, did not include the wives of any senators. The etiquette war was under way. "Mr. A and myself are determined not to give up the point [of making first visits] and we are supported by the President and his Lady."[19]

Although Louisa held to her principles on first visits, she was scrupulous in following many of the other established rules of society, going to great lengths to make return calls, even if the return involved only the depositing of a calling card. John Quincy was conscientious as well, traveling about the capital before going to the office or on weekends, dropping his card so that the recipients (or more likely their wives) could in turn visit the Adamses. Louisa also believed it her duty to accept every ball and dinner invitation that she and John Quincy received. Whether giving parties herself or attending social occasions hosted by others, Louisa's evenings were almost entirely committed to meeting the family's social obligations.

John Quincy did not entirely share that commitment. He seems to have thought that if Louisa attended an event, it was as good as if he had attended it himself. Over one four-day period in February 1818, for example, he left her to appear unescorted at three evening parties and a ball. One party was hosted by the British minister, Charles Bagot; another by Baron Jean Guillame Hyde de Neuville, the French envoy. It might have seemed natural for the secretary of state to have some diplomatic interest in these events, but on the evening of the Bagot party, John Quincy reported to his diary, he was "deeply absorbed at home," and on the night of the ball he was occupied until midnight writing the draft of a note to the Spanish minister.[20]

Louisa didn't often complain about her husband's unsociability, at least not in her letters to Abigail and John Adams. But others, including members of Congress, did. In December 1818 a group of his supporters came to tell John Quincy that he had been widely perceived as "cold and unsocial" during the previous winter's social season and that he might "serve the publick and himself better than by remaining all this time in his closet." John Quincy's friends understood, even if he did not, that he faced stiff competition in a potential run at the presidency. If his rivals were making themselves popular by their participation in the capital's social whirl, his retreat from society was having just the opposite effect.[21]

The entire etiquette contretemps offered great amusement to former President Adams, watching it from afar in Quincy. He wrote Louisa that he hoped Henry Clay, the Speaker, would bring to the floor of the House, "a Bill to Settle the Etiquette of the United States. The debates in Congress upon that important subject will amuse, divert, instruct, and edify me to the End of my Life." In a loving tribute to his daughter-in-law he added that her "Experience in Berlin, Petersbourg, & St. James; Your Sense, Wit, and perfect fluency and Purity in the French Language" would be more trouble than help to her in any decisions on etiquette. But he realized the situation was not a laughing matter: "I pity Mrs. Monroe . . . but above all I pity you."[22]

The ex-president knew what he was talking about. Louisa could see her future in the vitriolic comments leveled at the unhappy Elizabeth Monroe. Writing to her brother Thomas in August 1818, after only a year in Washington, she cried, "Can anyone see the miserable woman who now fills that seat and not shrink with fear and disgust from a situation so wretched? To be slandered, vilified and condemned in the greatest manner merely because she has risen to the station she holds and the great bulk of mankind have not? Terrified at a look and watchful of every whisper conscious that every action however innocent or praiseworthy will be tortured into offence! Oh defend me from such a situation."[23]

The issue of first calls finally reached Cabinet-level importance at the opening of the 1819–1820 Congressional session—an election year. At Louisa's first party of the social season on December 14, 1819, sixty men and two women appeared. (Louisa herself was ill and her sister Kitty Smith presided.) Elizabeth Monroe's initial drawing room the following evening drew no more than fifty people. The atmosphere, Louisa wrote, was "cold and stiff." Clearly, a boycott was in effect. For John Quincy and President Monroe, the issue was less a matter of ladies' pique than the power of the executive vis-à-vis the legislative branch of the government. Monroe, probably eager to put the etiquette issue to rest before launching his campaign for reelection, asked John Quincy to call a meeting of the cabinet "as soon as possible" to determine a common practice among heads of departments on visiting procedures. Two days later, on December 20, the group met at the President's House to consider what John Quincy irritably characterized as "the important question of etiquette in visiting." Feelings in Congress were now running so high that not only senators but also members of the House were demanding that first visits be paid to them. The president, John Quincy reported, was inclined to "indulge this humour," but every one of his five cabinet officers balked. The meeting broke up with the issue unresolved.[24]

Louisa was unrepentant concerning her practice of not paying a first call to members of Congress and their wives and resented her position at the center of the controversy. She chose to see the contretemps as a plot to denigrate John

The east front of the White House in 1817, the year that John Quincy and Louisa
returned to the United States. Drawing is by the architect Benjamin Henry Latrobe.
Courtesy of the Library of Congress, Washington, D.C.

Quincy: "There is something so insupportable in the idea of being put as it
were upon a trial. . . . It is a very painful thing to me to be dragged into public
notice, and made an object of debate in every company—but these are the
penalties I must pay for being the Wife of a man of superior talents; who by his
real and extraordinary merits throws those who are more ambitious than himself
into the shade."[25]

Charles Francis Adams, in an editorial comment in his edition of John
Quincy's *Memoirs*, mentions—and then rebuts—another root of the offense
taken by senators and their wives on the matter of first visits, "Singularly enough,
[it] was construed as equivalent to a demand on [his parents'] part to be first
visited, and much use was made of their long residence in the Courts of Europe
to create a popular impression that they were raising questions of etiquette
never before started in American society. In point of fact, the pretension was all
on the side of the Senators."[26]

Finally, on Christmas Day 1819, John Quincy wrote to the president—and
on December 29 to the vice president for distribution to Congress—a definitive

case for the visiting policy he and Louisa had adopted. These letters are significant for their full-throated support of his wife: "She has received with pleasure
and returned the visits of all ladies who have called upon her whether connected
with members of Congress or otherwise. . . . She lays no claim, however, to the
same attention from any other lady. . . . She has invited to her house, without
waiting for formal visits, every lady of a member of Congress to whom she had
not reason to believe such an invitation would be unwelcome."[27]

The two letters, both portraying the Adamses as a simple, unassuming
couple, free of social pretensions and open to the acquaintance of anyone, official or not, may have been disingenuous, but they were effective. John Quincy's
manifestoes preempted any senatorial move to codify the practice of first calls,
and there was no one with comparable social or political standing to challenge
the markers he and Louisa had laid down. Members of Congress had too much
to lose by ignoring the man who, if recent history were any guide, had a better-
than-even chance of becoming the next president of the United States. Their
wives, many of whom were from small cities and rural areas, found it equally
hard to pass up an invitation from an Adams, a name exalted in the story of the
nation's founding. Because Louisa's parties—the food, the entertainment, the
decor—reflected the elegant good taste she had absorbed from childhood and
refined in her diplomatic postings abroad, they became the model by which
others were judged. The ladies of Washington, eager to see and be seen in such
sophisticated settings, gradually chose to forget whether or not they had been
paid a first call.

By assuming leadership of society from Elizabeth Monroe, who ceded it by
inaction, Louisa had made herself an arbiter of social protocol in the capital.
But she could not rest on announcing what she would *not* do. Never blind to
the political implications of entertaining, she blithely announced in her journal
in the fall of 1819 that her "campaign"—whether for the presidency or leadership of Washington society is not clear—had begun. Her precise goal may have
been left unexpressed, but she succeeded in becoming, over the next five years,
a powerful player in presidential politics and the capital city's leading hostess.

Her social dominance did not affect her jaundiced view of Washington and
its chief denizens. She could barely restrain herself from heavy irony when it
came to the extracurricular activities of the nation's political leaders. Of a
meeting of the trustees of the Washington Female Orphan Asylum, she wrote,

> It was laughingly proposed by one of the Ladies to encrease our buildings in
> consequence of the rapid encrease of our population, Congress having left

many females in such difficulties as to make it probable they would beg our assistance—To this I made some question and asked on what ground they could make such a claim and was informed that [as] the Session had been very long the *fathers* of the Nation had left forty cases to be provided for by the publick and that our institution was the most likely to be called upon to maintain this illicit progeny—I recommended a petition to Congress next Session for that *great* and *moral* body to found or establish a foundling institution and should certainly move that the two additional dollars a day which they have given themselves as an increase of pay may be appropriated as a fund towards the support of the Institution.[28]

The women now crowding Washington during Congressional sessions enjoyed an independence they would not have had at home. There was no reason to stay indoors, no meals to cook, no garden to tend. Freed from household duties, they could, and did, attend sessions of Congress and the Supreme Court. Speakers played to the gallery, and a session of the House, with its great orators such as Henry Clay and Daniel Webster, was the best entertainment in town. Margaret Bayard Smith describes one outing to Capitol Hill at which the galleries were so packed with ladies, foreign dignitaries, and even senators—all gathered to hear Clay—that she was forced to sit on steps in the lobby just outside the House chamber. The atmosphere of a festive occasion lasted long after Clay relinquished the floor as the "very gallant and attentive" gentlemen proceeded to pass oranges wrapped in handkerchiefs and attached to long poles up to the hundred or more ladies seated above in the gallery while other speakers droned on.[29]

Louisa yielded to no one in her fascination with the theater of Washington politics. On February 11, 1819, she managed to cover both houses of Congress and the Supreme Court in a single day: "We accordingly got ready and went to the Supreme Court which was just opened and Mr. Pinckney rose. His Oratory is of the modern theatrical School and consists chiefly of whispered breathings and bursts of vehemence. . . . We soon grew weary of this species of *exaltation* as the French say and went from there to the house where we were entertained with a very different style of oratory which I denominate the hum-drum as it produced on my ear some thing like the effect of the Cotton spinning wheel which is not dull enough to set you to sleep but sufficiently monotonous to weary your spirits."[30]

Louisa's keen description of the capital's oratorical styles was written for the benefit of John Adams, for whom she kept a daily journal that she lightly revised as biweekly letters. She began the practice in the fall of 1817 writing "journal-letters" for Abigail Adams, who had begged for news of the great world. "When your good mother was living, she kept me always informed of passing events," she wrote to Louisa. "Her letters are a history of the period in which they were written." Louisa's letters, like those of her mother, were filled with gossip—featuring the indiscretions of the British royal family, the immodest gowns worn by young women just "coming out" in society, and the minutiae of the parties the Adamses gave or attended. Abigail relished the letters, responding with news Louisa craved of the three Adams boys. The former First Lady usually added a few astute comments on Washington and Boston society and frequently pleaded for letters from her son. John Quincy, however, was too wrapped up in the cares of office to accede to his mother's—or his father's—requests for mail. He left nearly all Adams family correspondence to Louisa.[31]

Abigail spent much of the spring and summer of 1818 trying to convince a reluctant John Quincy to leave his work and make his annual summer visit to the family at the Old House in Quincy. In a letter to Louisa in May, she wrote, "I cannot bear the idea . . . that Mr. Adams and you will not make us a visit this summer. . . . How few times can he see his Father or Mother? . . . He cannot want stronger [motives] than his parents and Children." Fortunately, John Quincy relented; he, Louisa, and her ten-year-old niece Mary Hellen spent the last days of August and all of September in Quincy. Although John Quincy resented the time away from the State Department—his so-called leisure hours he saw as complete dissipation—he was afterward consoled that he had satisfied one of his mother's dearest last wishes.[32]

Sadly, on October 28, less than a month after her eldest son—in whom her earliest hopes had been realized—returned to Washington, Abigail Adams died of typhoid fever. She left behind an extended family bereft of its strong emotional center. John Adams, broken-hearted, had always assumed that he, nine years older than his wife, would be the first to die. From Monticello, Thomas Jefferson, who had lost a wife and two daughters, wrote compassionately to his old friend and rival: "Tried myself in the school of affliction by the loss of every form of connection which can rive the human heart, I know well, and feel what you have lost, what you have suffered, are suffering, and have yet to endure."[33]

There was little John Quincy and Louisa, both of whom deeply mourned Abigail's death, could do at a distance to ease the Adams patriarch's loss until the old man requested in December that Louisa resume her journal-letters. She complied immediately with a typical newsy, witty, multipage chronicle that put more emphasis on politics than on parties as in her letters to Abigail. On Christmas Eve, John Adams gratefully wrote to his son, "The recommencement of your Lady's Journal is a reviving cordial to me"; a year and a half later, he complimented Louisa on her latest dispatch, which, as usual, had "afforded me delicious entertainment."[34]

Louisa was at first somewhat apprehensive about stating her political views to a man who was, after all, among the founders of the nation: "I must begin . . . by observing that I have touched rather more largely upon political occurrences than is perhaps prudent considering how little I understand the subject. But the wish to amuse and interest you must be my apology and if the sentiments expressed are erroneous they can do no mischiefs and as nobody ought to see these effusions but yourself I rely too much on your kind indulgence to apprehend censure."[35]

She had no need to apologize. Encouraged by the flattering response she elicited from the former president and the realization that her journal-letters were being read aloud to anyone who visited the old man in Quincy, Louisa felt no hesitation in sending him page after page of her shrewd analyses of political issues, along with incisive word portraits—a skill she had developed long ago in Berlin. Reporting on the recall of the French minister Hyde de Neuville, she wrote, "He is generally liked, is too weak and flighty to be mischievous and has that immeasurable portion of *amour propre* which renders French men so happy, by making them believe in a superiority which is frequently entirely imperceptible to those who surround them and which acts as a talisman against the shafts of wit and ridicule."[36]

"Wit and ridicule" were, however, John Adams's stock in trade. His letters to Louisa—dictated to any scribe he could commandeer for the project, no matter how poor his or her spelling or orthography—resonate with his true speaking voice, booming out lighthearted quips, making wry comments as asides, and offering candid observations on national, state, and local politics. Setting the tone for his letters, the elder Adams headed them "Montezillo," a play on words meant to show how his part of the world paled in comparison to Jefferson's august country seat, Monticello. In one letter to Louisa, the old president described his New England as a region of "perfect indifference, insensibility, if not stupidity," whose residents were busy "chiseling rocks, weaving cloth, making shoes, building houses and churches out of granite . . . eating fat turkeys, roast beef and Indian Pudding and more than that, mince Pies and Plumb pudding in abundance—besides cranberry tarts."[37]

As a grandfather, John Adams was openly affectionate and much more lenient toward the three Adams boys than were either John Quincy or Louisa. In his letters to Louisa he emphasized the best in the "sons of Harvard" and joked about their foibles—George's love of cigars, John's insistence that when on vacation he owed it to himself devote his time to hunting and fishing instead

of Greek and Latin, and Charles's "wise face and sober demeanour while he is
meditating his brilliant wit and shrewd satire." He assured his son that both his
older boys were "good lads" who would "come to something" and never tired of
telling Louisa how much their frequent visits to Quincy delighted him.[38]

With his beloved wife and his only daughter gone, the old man, now well
into his eighties, relied on Louisa to fill a painful void in his life. In turn, nearly
every one of his letters overflows with love and support for her. In the winter of
1819, after she had undergone a grueling social season, he wrote, almost as if to
a wife, "The great exertions which your situation demands of you have exhausted
your strength and rendered a relaxation absolutely necessary for you . . . fly to
me as fast as your strength will bear." He added, with just a hint of sarcasm, that
John Quincy was welcome to follow his spouse when he could tear himself
away from the office. Louisa thrived on the Sage of Montezillo's strong moral
support. She especially needed his unquestioning loyalty during the first years
of their correspondence when she found herself embroiled in the "etiquette
wars." In letter after letter, he assured her that her course of action was not only
correct but the only one possible. At the same time, he emphasized how whole-
heartedly he sympathized with the dilemmas she faced.[39]

During Washington's hectic social season, three kinds of social events
were favored: dinner parties at 4 P.M., tea parties at 7 or 8 P.M., and balls, late
in the evening. In her second Washington winter—the first after the opening
of the etiquette wars—Louisa was hostess at twelve dinner parties in three
months, with from eleven to twenty-two guests each. Putting on such a
meal was a daunting and expensive undertaking. At a typical dinner party,
substantial quantities of various kinds of meat or fish, vegetables, pickles, and
sauces in large serving dishes were arrayed down the center of a long dinner
table. Two such courses were served, followed by an elaborate dessert. More
often than not at a Washington dinner party all the guests were men. Louisa, as
hostess, did not necessarily dislike being the only woman: "I sat between
Mr. Law and Mr. Vaughn and never was more amused in my life," she wrote of
one party.[40]

Tea parties were never as popular in Washington as they were in other cities,
perhaps because they were geared to women in what was still a man's town. At
a formal tea party, ladies sat chatting around the periphery of the room with
their teacups and plates of pastries balanced in their laps, waiting for the
gentlemen standing the middle of the room to break off their interesting political conversations and walk over to engage them in small talk. Most often,
"taking tea" was much more informal. Louisa went for tea at the home of one

of her sisters as often as she could and seemed to see these occasions as evenings off duty and a chance to catch up on family news.[41]

Balls were major and costly events that involved hand-writing invitations to hundreds of guests, hiring an orchestra for dancing, removing furniture and carpets from the main rooms of the house, preparing a supper, and then quickly cleaning up to make the house habitable for the family. Louisa and John Quincy gave several balls between 1819 and 1824. After one particularly successful event in January 1820, Louisa wrote to her father-in-law, "We had about three hundred, perhaps more, and the evening was more than commonly animated—I could give them no supper but substituted as well as I could all sorts of refreshments, and all my guests were apparently satisfied, but what was best of all, Mr. A. was so pleased with my success, that [afterwards] he joined in a reel with the boys and myself."[42]

Obviously, Louisa could not have entertained as regularly and as lavishly as she did without a large staff. Given the Adams family's long-held beliefs, she most likely did not own slaves, although she occasionally hired slaves owned by someone else. Unlike her recollections of earlier years, her contemporaneous journal from this period rarely names a servant—even her personal maid—or complains of the difficulties of dealing with a constantly shifting cast of untrained, sometimes unwilling men and women. In undated instructions for servants, Louisa wrote that fourteen was the minimum number needed for a well-ordered household, but it is hard to tell how many full-time workers the Adamses actually employed. It is safe to assume that, like any upper-middle-class family, they would have required a cook, a full-time maid, and a coachman—who may have doubled as a man-of-all-work—and one or two indoor servants to clean the house, polish the silver, and do the family ironing. Louisa's personal maid, Lucy Hand, and John Quincy's longtime valet, Antoine Giusta, traveled with the family from the time they arrived from Europe. Services such as laundering the linen, cleaning the fireplaces, or performing major household repairs were probably hired out to some of the many freed slaves and poor working-class families who made up much of Washington's permanent population, and extra waiters and kitchen help would have been hired for dinners, balls, and other large parties.[43]

Managing the extensive staff required to support the Adamses' very public lifestyle was entirely in Louisa's hands. Ordering food and designing menus, deciding on guest lists, writing invitations, keeping up her wardrobe, household furnishings, and correspondence, dealing with issues among the servants, practicing her harp—Louisa had a long list of tasks to accomplish each morning before she set out on her visiting rounds. Fortunately, her early training in

London had equipped her to cope with precisely these responsibilities. She was ideally suited, as were few other political wives in Washington at the time, to the demands of large-scale entertaining and the management of a complex household.

Louisa realized that teas, as they were typically structured, were unlikely to attract the influential male guests she was courting. Inventing a new format she called "sociables," she decided that she would hold a soiree every Tuesday during the congressional session. Although scheduled in the early evening so as not to conflict with balls or other late-night events, her parties included light refreshments, music, cards, entertainment, and dancing—all much more enjoyable than the usual tea party. When she could not engage a popular singer or musician to appear, she herself performed the sentimental songs of the era.

Most Washington hostesses would never dream of substituting themselves for professional musicians, but Louisa felt perfectly comfortable in doing just that. A well-known portrait done of her by Charles Bird King in 1824—at the height of John Quincy's presidential campaign—emphasizes exactly the way she chose to present herself during this period. Seated with complete composure and elegantly dressed, she rests on her large, gilded harp—the most fashionable instrument of the period. In her lap is a songbook open to "Oh! Say Not Woman's Heart Is Bought," a favorite ballad of the time and intended for performance by voice and harp. But Louisa, with her eye for significant detail, would not have chosen the song title lightly. Was she again regretting her decision to "sell" her heart to the political gods?

Louisa's innovation was an outstanding success. In the fall of 1820, in the midst of the etiquette wars, two hundred guests attended her first sociable of the season. Her goal, she said, was to make "our Congress less dependent on the foreign ministers for entertainment." But she was obviously after more than that. John Quincy needed more friends in Congress, for if no candidate won an Electoral College majority—as appeared likely even as early as 1818—the 1825 election would end up in the House. Louisa was going to help her husband woo these House voters, and John Quincy tacitly agreed with her strategy. From the beginning, he kept a nightly scorecard of "Mrs. A's tea parties"—describing them in terms such as, "numerously attended," "fully attended," "rather more than average," "about 100," and "fully attended, dancing until 10 or 11"—buried toward the end of his daily diary entries. Over the next six social seasons Louisa entertained at sixty-seven Tuesday night sociables. She also managed to "make some noise and create some jealousy" among her fellow cabinet wives, especially those whose husbands were also vying for the presidency. When these women followed her example and instituted weekly soirees of their own, Louisa upped the ante. Although her invitations were widely circulated at the beginning of the season, respondents were asked to commit themselves to attending only "Mrs. Adams's regular Tuesdays" and not those of other cabinet wives. Her guest list expanded beyond these "subscribers," however, to include diplomats, members of the military, judiciary, and Washington's permanent social elite, as well as visiting celebrities such as the Marquis de Lafayette. And despite demanding a commitment from her guests, Louisa's parties remained as popular as ever.[44]

Meanwhile, John Quincy was going from success to success. In the winter of 1819, after months of hard work and endless proposals and counterproposals, he finally won agreement with the Spanish minister in Washington on the so-called Transcontinental Treaty, which added Florida to the United States and extended the country's western boundary all the way to the Pacific Ocean. Louisa was very proud of her husband, but the political implications of his achievement were never far from her mind: "The Treaty has produced a wonderful sensation and is another proof that real unassuming ability will confound intrigue. Station is nothing when unsupported by talent and this is its only solid basis. A great Nation will never submit to be long cajoled by party factions and will learn how to appreciate unadulterated merit."[45]

Washington's attention, however, was fixed less on the treaty than on General Andrew Jackson, who was in the middle of a fight with committees in both houses of Congress over his controversial actions in Florida during the previous year. In response to a series of raids, counterraids, and the occupation of a fort by escaped slaves on the Appalachicola River, Jackson had advanced into the Spanish-held territory with a force of three thousand men. When news reached Washington in May that the general had recaptured the fort, the president immediately called his cabinet together. According to John Quincy, Monroe objected to the injudicious hanging of some of the Indian prisoners and to what he perceived as Jackson's intent to execute Alexander George Arbuthnot, a Scottish trader, and Robert Ambrister, a former British officer, both accused of giving aid to the Indians. Neither Monroe nor John Quincy knew at the time they were debating the issue that both Arbuthnot and Ambrister had already been executed.

The cabinet soon divided over Jackson's actions. Monroe and John Quincy quickly came around to his support, with the president writing only a mild reprimand reproaching Jackson for overstepping his orders. John C. Calhoun, technically the secretary of war and Jackson's superior, was incensed that the general had acted on his own; Treasury Secretary William Crawford, whose enemies in Georgia had long been allies of Jackson, saw the controversy as an opportunity to wound Calhoun, a presidential competitor, as well as Jackson; and House Speaker Henry Clay, who was stirring the pot to get the United States to ally itself more clearly with the revolutionary movements in South America against Spain, saw it as an opportunity to attack both Jackson and the administration.[46]

When Jackson was brought before Congress to face a charge of censure for his actions "on high grounds of international law and to impugn his character by suggesting that his disregard for authority outside himself presents a grave threat to the democratic process," his opponents failed to realize that the "people cared little for the letter of the law; they admired the man of action, the man of self-reliance." Jackson had simply added to his stature as a popular hero. And Jackson's actions in Florida, if they could not be approved, were not unwelcome to either Monroe or John Quincy. They helped convince Spain, already stretched thin fighting rebellions in South and Central America, that it could no longer hold onto its North American possessions. This was just the pressure the Spanish needed to agree to America's treaty demands. John Quincy, in fact, found it ironic that the Senate should vote unanimously to approve his treaty with Spain on the same day that "a committee of five members of the same body made a report severely censuring Jackson for the transactions of his campaign in Florida which have been among the most immediate and prominent causes that produced that treaty."[47]

Louisa, who enjoyed charming handsome men and being charmed by them, met Jackson for the first time in February 1819 and described him to her father-in-law in glowing terms: "He is tall and very thin and when he smiles his countenance is very agreeable. His manners are those of a Gentleman neither confidant or timid and on the whole he produced the most favourable impression—I heard much astonishment expressed by some persons not friendly to him at his being so polite as they expected to have seen him at least half *Savage.*"[48]

The jockeying of the likely 1824 presidential candidates—at that point they included John Quincy, Crawford, Clay, Calhoun, Jackson, and New York Governor DeWitt Clinton—elicited scorn from John Quincy. His diary again and again returned to the theme of "cabals and intrigues," most of them seen as emanating from the Clay forces. "Last winter Clay's principal attack was levelled against the President himself, but, finding that this only injured himself, he has this winter confined his hostilities to me. . . . All public business in Congress now connects itself with intrigues, and there is great danger that the whole Government will degenerate into a struggle of cabals."[49]

The "struggle of cabals" came at the same time as heavier issues began to weigh on Washington. One was the Panic of 1819, the first depression in the nation's history; the other was the congressional fight over admitting Missouri to the union. The Panic popped a bubble that had been built by speculation in western lands. Hundreds of banks failed, and thousands of depositors and investors were wiped out. Surprisingly, the Panic didn't upend the Monroe administration and remains, according to one historian, "the only depression in American history when the voters did not turn against the administration in Washington." The other issue—Missouri—had greater long-term significance. Both John Quincy and Louisa were deeply troubled by it. John Quincy was prescient: "I take it for granted that the present question is a mere preamble—a title page to a great tragic volume. . . . The President thinks this question will be winked away by a compromise. But so do not I. Much am I mistaken if it is not destined to survive his political and individual life and mine."[50]

Indeed, Congress and the president, of course, did manage to wink it away, admitting Maine as a state at the same time as Missouri to maintain an even balance of slave and nonslave states and prohibiting the extension of slavery in territories above Missouri's southern border but not restricting it in Missouri, which then had just a handful of slaves within its borders. The South saw the Missouri Compromise as a victory, but, more important, it revealed a "startling solidity of southern opposition to gradual emancipation in Missouri." Southerners, who, like Jefferson, thought slavery would be terminated at some point in the not-too-distant future, had been forced to align themselves with their far more radical compatriots who wished to extend it. Louisa was at her most scathing in reporting to John Adams about the compromise. "I have never pretended to understand the question in all its bearings as a political one; in a moral and religious point of view and even as a gross political inconsistency with all our boasted Institutions, liberty, and so forth, it [slavery] is so palpable a stain that the veryest dunce can see it and understand it without the foreign aid of education or art."[51]

The Missouri question was difficult politically for John Quincy, although, as secretary of state, he was not obliged to weigh in on it—at least not at first. Whatever he said was bound to offend either the antislavery or the proslavery forces. At one point, he even asked Louisa to tell her Federalist father-in-law to keep his opinions out of the public prints. "Your son requests me to beg of you as particular favour *to him* should you be addressed on the subject (which he has no doubt you will be) to refrain from giving any opinion whatever as he does not think the time has arrived in which he can with propriety take a part in the business."[52]

There is no question what John Quincy believed, however. Over a long after-noon of conversation in the winter of 1820 with Calhoun, a slaveholder, he seemed to have seen the future with awful clarity: "Slavery is the great and foul stain upon the North American Union, and it is a contemplation worthy of the most exalted soul whether its total abolition is or is not practicable: if practi-cable, by what means it may be effected, and if a choice of means be within the scope of the object, what means would accomplish it at the smallest cost of human sufferance. A dissolution, at least temporary, of the Union, as now constituted, would be certainly necessary, and the dissolution must be upon a point involving the question of slavery, and no other."[53]

In the fall of 1820 the Adamses moved out of their rented house at 4½ and C Streets and into a spacious, brick townhouse that John Quincy had purchased at 1333 F Street, within two blocks of the President's House. Louisa complained that the decision to buy the new house had been made over her objections—"I always detested [the house] as it has in my eyes no one recommendation"—and was annoyed that John Quincy claimed he had bought it to please her. The house, previously lived in by James and Dolley Madison and adapted by Dolley to accommodate her many social events, had fallen into disrepair after the Madisons moved into the President's House in 1809. Louisa wrote to her father-in-law that on visiting the property with a carpenter in June to "give orders as to what alterations and repairs" were to be made, she found the house in "miser-able condition." On reporting the same situation to her husband and listing the improvements she thought necessary, they had, she remarked sardonically, "entered, of course, into no agreement."[54]

Planning and superintending the work that needed to be done on the prop-erty was left entirely to Louisa. John Quincy's mind may have been on weightier matters when she informed him that she envisioned major renovations, but she forged ahead anyway. It came as something of a shock when he discovered what she was about: "On going to my office as I passed by the house I have purchased in F Street I was surprised to find workmen employed in pulling down the wooden shed adjoining it. Mrs. Adams has made a contract with mason named Van Cable to build an addition to the house, a measure I have acquiesced inas-much I have not expressly prevented it. I have been entangled in this and other expense almost unawares."[55]

Communication between the two seems to have reached a familiar impasse. Louisa wrote to John Adams that she was in the "midst of brick and mortar," superintending the construction of the addition while her husband continued to be "deeply immersed in weights and measures," the study of which he had begun while in Russia. The addition, which she saw as enabling her to "entertain much more agreeably and conveniently to myself than I now do," would not be finished until late January 1821. But when all the new rooms were counted, the Madisons' former home had nearly doubled in size. Louisa unveiled what she had accomplished at a "very large party" that January: "In the Eveng . . . opened my new room—It opens from the drawing room . . . and is twenty eight by 29 feet in size—It was found very convenient and tho' barely half finished answered the purpose amazingly well. The addition to my house contains two of these halls, two back rooms and six chambers with Kitchen &c. It is so planned as to make a separate house whenever we are inclined to rent it."[56]

The renovation of 1333 F Street, especially the addition of two large, new reception rooms to Dolley Madison's spacious drawing room, created a venue for the many social events Louisa's "campaign" demanded. It was a political decision, taken without her husband's open support. If her Tuesday nights were to be a success—and a spur to John Quincy's candidacy—she would need the proper space and facilities to entertain on the scale she envisioned. The bricks and mortar of the addition signified her determination to do everything in her power to see that her husband attained his lifelong ambition.

The intended beneficiary of Louisa's enormous undertaking, however, was more than usually unhelpful. In addition to acting as a general contractor, Louisa was fully in charge of the family's move to their new—and as yet unfinished—quarters in October 1820. John Quincy could only grumble, "We are repairing the house into which we have removed and at the same time building an addition to it, which multiplies inconveniences while my Report upon weights and measures allows me scarcely a moment for even thinking of anything else."[57]

The secretary of state's fascination with the arcane topic of measurements had been a major source of marital irritation for years. Since his posting to Russia, he had been engaged as a sort of hobby in a lengthy analysis of pounds, inches, coins, and other measurements. He was delighted when, on his first day at the State Department, he discovered a Senate resolution directing the secretary of state to report on the weights and measures then prevailing among the states as well as the various systems employed by other nations. The secretary was also instructed to prepare recommendations for a uniform system for the United States. Most cabinet officers, even in 1817, would have identified a scholarly clerk to whom he could assign the project. Not John Quincy. The study claimed more and more of his time and attention. In the summer of 1819, he reported to his diary: "I plunge deeper and deeper into my enquiries concerning coins, currencies, and exchange. The deeper I go, the deeper and the darker appears the deep beneath, and although the want of time will soon force me to break away from the subject without even finding its bottom, yet it now fascinates and absorbs me to the neglect of the most necessary business."[58]

As his work on the report progressed and a massive tome began to rise on his desk, John Quincy paid less and less attention to anything else. In his diary entry of December 12, 1820, he discussed at length a series of experiments he was conducting to determine how many English ounces of liquid were contained in a French liter and how his measurements could be affected by changes in the atmosphere. The final line of his entry for the day—"Mrs. Adams had her weekly tea party this evening"—certainly gives no credit to his wife's efforts to further his political career. In the summer of 1820, John Quincy ignored John Adams's appeal that he "throw the weights and measures up in the air" and take his annual vacation in Quincy. By choosing to spend the summer alone with thirteen-year-old Charles in torrid Washington—Louisa had decamped to Maryland to make her first visit to her Johnson relatives in nineteen years and to attend a family wedding—he not only ignored his lonely father's wishes but also passed up a rare opportunity to spend some leisure time with his older sons.

The *Report on Weights and Measures* was completed and submitted to Congress on February 22, 1821. John Quincy was proud of his effort—though frustrated that his exhaustive dissertations on all aspects of measurement were still incomplete. The report was erudite, and in many ways a classic, but it was far too dense to be of any practical use. Old John Adams spoke for many when he called it a "mass of historical, philosophical, chemical, metaphysical, and political knowledge" that even he had been unable to wade through. Louisa was more succinct when she wrote to her father-in-law, "Thank God we hear no more of Weights and Measures."[59]

If Louisa's primary reason for adding onto the F Street house was political, a pressing secondary concern was simply the matter of housing the many young men and women who came to live there in the years before 1825. Not only the Adams boys, but nieces and nephews of all kinds made the house their home for extended stays.

The boys at first spent very little time in Washington. In the fall of 1817 John, fourteen, and Charles, ten, had been enrolled in the Boston Latin School on School Street. They boarded nearby with family friends Dr. and Mrs. Thomas Welsh. George, sixteen, was placed with a tutor in Cambridge who would, in John Quincy's words, "give him instruction, in all the objects of study which may qualify him to enter the University as a sophomore after the winter vacation," and he was, indeed, able to enter Harvard as a second-year student in March 1818. Several months spent preparing for his examinations, however, had terrified the sensitive teenager; he had been unable to eat for ten days before appearing before Harvard's president and faculty members for his "ordeal," Abigail reported to Louisa.[60]

All three Adams boys spent as much time as they were permitted in Quincy. The Old House was the only boyhood home the two older boys had ever known; John knew every inch of its fields and woods, George every book in his grandfather's library. The old president treasured George's intellectual abilities and was ready to overlook his awkwardness and nervous insecurity; Abigail loved John's zest for life, just as she had from the time he was a toddler. Charles, at first shy, soon found himself a beloved addition to the extended family. On the day after he and John were installed at the Welsh home in Boston, they arrived back in Quincy and begged to remain until the last minute before school opened. As the fall and winter progressed, the two appeared so often at the Old House that Abigail had to declare a ban on visiting for at least a week or two "as we wanted a quiet and still house." The two aging grandparents were so accepting of their grandsons' follies, however, that they agreed to house John's bird and his dog, Booth, even though the bird sang so loudly that he was "quite a nuisance" and the dog had to be carefully shut in to keep him from going to church and "disturbing the congregation." Abigail acknowledged to Louisa that the troublesome pets were "only tollerated for the Love we bear to John."[61]

If the former president and First Lady could accept the adolescent behavior of George, John, and Charles, their father decidedly could not. The tolerance John Quincy had extended to his sons in Little Ealing had entirely dissipated. His letters to the boys became few, cold, and judgmental. Even his most admiring biographers find them "preachy . . . unbending . . . unbelievably severe" and given to asserting "pressure upon his offspring to meet high expectations." To George, particularly, he set impossibly high academic standards and decreed rigid rules of conduct. Apparently forgetting his own college years when "a very good dinner, wit and Wine, the Bottle and the Joke [kept] nearly an equal pace," he also appears to have suppressed any memories of the mental and emotional depths to which he plummeted when the pressures of the tedious study of law overwhelmed him in 1788. Even when his sons proudly reported academic success, John Quincy used the occasion to urge them on to further and more demanding challenges.[62]

Louisa was caught between the fond hopes she shared with her husband for the success of their three sons and her need to give them emotional support.

"Dear thoughtless George," she began one letter on learning that he had been part of a storied food riot between freshmen and sophomores in the college commons in the fall of 1818. But soon in the same letter she was referring to him as "my beloved son." It was important, she wrote, that he heard from her about how his part in the fracas had upset his parents as "I thought it would spare your feelings if I wrote before your father should answer your letter which has given him so much pain."[63]

Despite Louisa's concern that her boys be shielded from the worst of their father's harsh judgments and demands, she herself was not immune to giving them advice, often cloaked in the form of "words to the wise" from a loving mother. When John had not written for several months, she did not hold back: "Have you forgotten your mother? Or do you never mean to write again? I have been impatiently waiting for letters a long time and still meet with disappointment every post. What is the reason you do not write?" She frequently reminded Charles that it would be she who would be held accountable for his academic success: "My pride would be deeply wounded by any failure on your part as you have been the one of my Children who have lived the most with me."[64]

George, edgy and brilliant, seems to have made a concerted effort from time to time to live up to his father's high expectations. In his junior year he won one of the college's two Boylston prizes in rhetoric—a second-prize-winner was his classmate Ralph Waldo Emerson. His grandfather said he bore his high honor "meekly" and seemed on the way to becoming a more serious student. But his troubles with the Harvard administration did not end with the food fight of 1818. Two years later, he again barely escaped expulsion for a similar escapade. Louisa strongly suspected that many of his frequent illnesses had to do with excessive drinking and severe hangovers. "Bitter experience is the only lesson which can make any impression on some minds and I fear his mind is of that description and must be attended with much pain and suffering," she wrote to his brother John. He also had serious difficulties handling money. In August 1820, Louisa sent George ten dollars—"the utmost my limited means will allow"—which she hoped he would use "to arrange any little embarrassment you may be under when you receive it." In case he had the impression that she would be available to ease him out of future financial exigencies, she made clear that she was aware of what he was up to: "I am easily deceived *once* but cannot be so very often."[65]

As the Harvard commencement of 1821 approached, John Quincy seemed confident that his talented eldest son would graduate among the top scholars in his class. He invited the Massachusetts governor as well as Harvard's president, John T. Kirkland, and various other notables to the family's post-commencement celebration, which Louisa had presumed would be modest—"Thank God the fashion is over for giving great feasts at Commencement." But to his father's great dismay, George played only a small part in the proceedings.[66]

In the early years of Harvard, student speakers at commencement were assigned orations in rank order of their undergraduate achievement, and students are still speakers at the morning ceremonies. John Quincy had always regretted that he spoke second at his commencement. But his extended and dismissive account of the 1821 commencement program in his diary noted only that "my eldest son George Washington Adams was one of those who graduated." George spoke for three minutes—a mark of a good but unexceptional student. In her journal, Louisa wrote, "George spoke as I wished a Son of mine should speak. . . . His voice is fine, his manner easy, at times even graceful, and his emphasis, modulation, and action perfectly natural."[67]

Worse was still to come for John Quincy, a man for whom stellar achievement at Harvard was close to being the touchstone for success in life. Due to a weak performance in the Latin entrance examination, Charles, at barely fourteen, had been only conditionally admitted to the college for the fall term. His father, believing that the test results revealed a personal bias the examining tutor held against himself rather than Charles's command of the language, insisted that the boy be examined again with his father present. The youngest Adams son passed with only one error and was admitted without condition. While discussing the matter with President Kirkland, John Quincy asked to see the class standings of his two elder sons. It came as a "bitter disappointment" to learn that George had placed thirtieth in a class of fifty-nine and John only forty-fifth in a class of sixty-four students.

That night for John Quincy was a sleepless one. He lay, unable to close his eyes, as his concern for the future welfare of all his sons, George's health, and the "mortification at the discovery of how much they have wasted their time at Cambridge" warred in his mind. "I had hoped that at least one of my sons would be ambitious to excel," he lamented. Instead, they were "coming into manhood with indolent minds—flinching from study whenever they can." Louisa was far less judgmental. She saw much of herself in her eldest son: "Easily distressed, he equally magnifies his joys and sorrows until the real world in which he moves vanishes from his sight like the baseless fabrick of the visions which continually beat his imagination where all is Poetry fiction, and Love," she wrote. And although she could see the dangers that lay ahead for her beloved first-born, they were alleviated in her mind by his exceptional literary gifts. On a two-day carriage trip back to Quincy from a visit to Mount Wachusett in the north-central part of the state, beautiful in the early fall, she wrote delightedly that George's "love of Poetry and his continued quotations from the lofty descriptions so ably coloured by Lord Byron's pen gave interest to each surrounding object."[68]

Both John Quincy and Louisa worried constantly about George's poor health—emotional and physical—as did John Quincy's father. Louisa wrote that her older son was so emotionally fragile that his brother John's "perpetual flashes of *Johnson wit*" could reduce him to debilitating illness. After he had administered a particularly harsh dressing-down to the young man, John Quincy was uncharacteristically rueful: "His health is not good, and what I said affected him so much that I repented of my own unkindness." In the face of talents and weaknesses he could so readily recognize and sympathize with, why John Quincy should have chosen the law for his poetic, sensitive eldest son is almost impossible to fathom. If his own career studying law and at the bar had been notably unsuccessful and unhappy, how much worse would it be for George?[69]

John ranked even lower in his father's eyes. On the day after commencement, he competed for the Boylston Prize, which his brother had won as a junior and for which his father was sitting as a judge. Again, Louisa in the audience was proud of her boy: "I sat literally in an agony of anticipation until John's turn to speak when I was gratified beyond my best expectations by his performance which would have equalled his brother's in every respect had he spoken a little louder—For this defect he lost the prize though the Judges unanimously declared he was the best and most natural speaker of the whole." John Quincy's report of the same oration was markedly less enthusiastic: "My son John was among the unsuccessful candidates. He spoke with propriety but without sufficient force and animation."[70]

Just before returning to Washington, John Quincy met again with Kirkland in the Harvard president's office to complain of what he believed to be injustice in the class standing of his sons and the minor part played by George in the commencement ceremonies. Forced to defend the college's ranking system, Kirkland displayed records demonstrating that John had abysmal grades in Greek and was one of many students "to avail themselves of every indulgence and relaxation which could escape from actual punishment." Moreover, he was guilty of frequent absences from class. George, too, had apparently merited his mediocre standing. John Quincy beat an embarrassed retreat but warned Kirkland that if next year he should suspect any bias against his sons, he would remove them from Harvard.[71]

Kirkland wisely did not bring up the topic that was the talk of Boston's elite: Harvard's students, particularly John's classmates, were completely out of control. The Class of 1823 was "uncommonly rowdy," and liable to "forbidden dinners, battles in commons, bonfires and explosions in the Yard, cannonballs dropped from upper windows," the historian Samuel Eliot Morison wrote. It would have been unrealistic to expect the high-spirited, popular John Adams II to seclude himself in his study while his friends were pouring a mixture of water and ink on the heads of their tutors.[72]

John Quincy was not about to grant any such leeway to his sons. Stopping by John's room to say farewell—and still enraged by what he had learned from Kirkland—he laid down a series of draconian rules: Neither John nor Charles was to leave Harvard Yard—even for a weekend in Quincy—until the end of the fall term; they were forbidden to come to Washington for the Christmas holidays, a ban that would be continued in future years if their class standings were not substantially higher than forty-fifth; and all minor indiscretions would be reported to their father. These strictures were hard on both boys. Charles, very young to be just entering college, was forced to endure a punishment for sins he had not yet committed; party-loving John, eighteen, badly wanted to take part in the festive holiday social scene in Washington instead of spending three or four snowbound weeks in Quincy in the company of his grandfather and his ancient contemporaries. Both were "most affected," John Quincy wrote, but he was adamant: "My determination has been taken."[73]

Nothing could shake the secretary of state's position. Appeals from his wife and father went unheard. In December, he responded in an extraordinarily cold manner to a final plea from John that the ban on travel to Washington be lifted: "I could take no satisfaction in seeing you. I could feel nothing but sorrow and shame in your presence until you should not only have commenced but made large progress in redeeming yourself from that disgraceful standing."[74]

The boys' banishment fell hardest on Louisa. Denied the presence of her boys—and without a word of parental consultation—she became ill and morbidly depressed. In her journal entries in December 1821, she clearly assumes she will die before being reunited with her two younger sons: "I grieve night and day at my poor boys not being allowed to visit me this winter. Should it please the Almighty disposer of events that I may never see them more may their father make up to them by redoubled tenderness the loss they will sustain in an affectionate Mother—On this subject I dare not express my feelings lest a tinge of bitterness unworthy a Christian should cloud my paper—Mr. A—acts for the best I wish he may not err in his judgment."[75]

But she *was* extremely bitter. On the day she learned that John Quincy had summarily dismissed their sons' final appeal, Louisa, taking the decision personally, cried, "This day has blasted my hopes and I am absolutely refused the sight of my children—I must submit because I have no resource but it grieves me to the Soul." Again, she spoke of dying: "The separation from my children will be a grievous stroke but I endeavour to soothe myself with the conviction that they are past the age when a Mother's care is absolutely essential to their happiness or welfare and that the principles she has endeavoured to instil and the tender affection she has ever borne them will operate as safeguards and promote their future success—To God I leave them and God will protect them if they do not desert him."[76]

There is little doubt that Louisa was seriously ill in the winter of 1821–1822, stricken with a frightful attack of erysipelas: "My old friend the Erisepelas seizes on me with more than usual violence," she wrote in her journal in early December. The disease spread to her whole head and face; by December 23 she was so much worse that her doctor insisted that she be "copiously" bled. She also believed herself, at forty-six, to be pregnant and unlikely to survive the birth, a circumstance that doubtless led to her many fears for her own life and that of her "unborn Infant." Her rumored pregnancy, she complained, had become the subject of gossip: "Something or other is perpetually occurring to make me the fable of the City—Mrs. Crawford and Mrs. Calhoun have both been in the same situation . . . and had the privilege of confining themselves without any notice being taken of the matter—Alas! Poor me!"[77]

At the start of social season, Louisa substantially reduced her entertaining commitments. Too ill to sit at the foot of the table at her first all-male dinner party, she called off every sociable for the winter. She believed that the campaign she had planned so carefully only a year before would suffer, but she recognized that she had no choice. "The Winter is to be unusually brilliant but my Constellation is in eclipse and I shall only 'shine a faint satellite in the train of tinsel greatness.' I like the change as I shall have less show and more comfort."[78]

But she had very little comfort in the first six months of 1822. Her many illnesses were genuine, but, as with her son George, her feelings of self-worth were intimately bound up with her physical well-being. Entirely closed out of any decisions concerning her sons and, as a result, embittered toward her husband, it is not surprising that her chronic ailments should resurface. John Quincy had made it abundantly clear that she had failed as a mother—the role she most cherished—and that in the future he alone would take control of his sons' education and careers.[79]

Over the next few months, Louisa virtually disappears from view. Her journal-letters to her father-in-law cease. We get no glimpse of how her—actual or imagined—pregnancy ended. She neither gives nor attends any parties. All that we hear of her during the social season comes from John Quincy's laconic but frequent diary notes that "Mrs. Adams [was] quite unwell," or that he attended a ball or a dinner accompanied not by Louisa but by one of the young women then living at 1333 F Street.

Resuming her journal in December 1822, Louisa chose as her motto "Armed with fortitude let us meet the struggle and nobly rise or fall." At some point during the previous months she had summoned the strength to conquer her twin devils of bitterness and low self-worth. In so doing she had overcome the temptations of ill health that may at first have appeared as an escape from her troubles but had instead confined her to a standby role in Washington's social drama and an ineffective player in its politics. With her winter of discontent behind her, Louisa was armed and ready to resume her campaign.

14

A BEAUTIFUL PLAN

Belles and matrons, maids and madams
All are gone to Mrs. Adams.

—JOHN AGG

It took an unlikely catalyst—her weak and chronically listless only brother, Thomas Baker Johnson—for Louisa to resuscitate her "campaign" in the spring of 1822. Thomas arrived in Washington from New Orleans in May, a pitiful spectacle of a man in "a dreadful state of suffering which has reduced him to a state of debility." Often sickly and now the victim of painful hemorrhoids and severe constipation, he had been reduced to a diet composed almost entirely of "Iceland Moss," which seemed to help but which Louisa found "very nauseous to the taste."[1]

Always at her best when she was desperately needed and decisive action was called for, Louisa swung into action. By June, she had placed her brother in the hands of a noted but eccentric Philadelphia surgeon, the aptly named Dr. Philip Syng Physick, who found the case "a dreadful one" and recommended hemorrhoid surgery not only for Thomas but for Louisa as well. Until Thomas was stronger and a bout of hot weather had subsided, however, "the knife" would have to wait. Louisa, accompanied by Mary Hellen, then fifteen, settled into a boardinghouse for the summer to nurse her brother through whatever Dr. Physick held in store. Each of his meals, she wrote to John Quincy, "is of such a quality and requires so much care in the preparation as it must cook from eight to ten hours every day." She also worked at "keeping his mind employed by external objects and gently forcing him into society."[2]

Away from Washington for the summer, Louisa might have declared a reprieve from politics. Instead, she plunged into her husband's still-unacknowledged presidential campaign. Four days after her arrival in Philadelphia, she was visited by

"Mrs. John Quincy Adams's Ball, 1824," in *Harper's Bazaar*, March 18, 1871. Andrew Jackson is depicted in the center; John Quincy and Louisa (holding fan) are shown at the far right. Courtesy of Widener Library, Harvard College Library.

Robert Walsh, editor of the *National Gazette* and one of Adams's key supporters in Pennsylvania. At Walsh's behest, she urged John Quincy to come to Philadelphia to meet with potential supporters, the first of several similar entreaties that John Quincy turned down. "At this critical time, when all is warm in your favor, when the flash of superior talent has found its way into every soul susceptible of feeling," Louisa wrote to the reluctant candidate in August, "you should if possible seize the happy occasion to show yourself to your countrymen." In October, just before she returned to Washington, she made her final attempt: "Do for once gratify me I implore you; and if harm comes of it I promise never to advise again. I have already written so often on this subject that I dare not flatter myself that you will listen to me. But I really and sincerely have your interest too deeply at heart to refrain from persuading you to do that which I know will be beneficial."[3]

In a frank analysis of what John Quincy would face among the electorate in the 1824 election, she counseled: "Your enemies are hard at work to represent your reserve to your disadvantage and to attribute your coldness to aristocratic hauteur and learned arrogance; and they say they must have a President they dare speak to." But John Quincy could not bring himself to take any step that could be interpreted as campaigning. He claimed he had too much work to do as secretary of state. He was like Prometheus bound to his rock, he wrote in July, adding only half in jest, "The spirit of martyrdom seems to come upon me and I sometimes think it will be happy for me if I could die at my post."[4]

John Quincy had, indeed, spent a very busy spring on State Department business. In May, Congress approved funding for five ministers to the new nations of South America—Argentina, Colombia, Chile, Mexico, and Peru—marking the end of a long battle over an issue that had confronted John Quincy from his first weeks in Washington in 1817. In the eyes of some historians, the decision represented not a shift in U.S. foreign policy but a reversal and was more of a landmark than either the Transcontinental Treaty, which Adams had negotiated three years earlier with Spain, or the Monroe Doctrine, which the president would enunciate eighteen months later. Confronted with the collapse of Spanish power in the region, Monroe and Adams for the first time were forced to see that the nation's neighbors to the south were not just "innocuous dependencies of a weak European nation," but were separate sovereignties. John Quincy recognized the importance of recognition in shaping the eventual hands-off policy spelled out by Monroe in December 1823: "Having recognized the independence of the South American States, we could not see with indifference any attempt by European powers by forcible interposition either to restore the Spanish dominion on the American Continents or to introduce monarchical principles into those countries, or to transfer any portion of the ancient or present American possessions of Spain to any other European power," John Quincy wrote in his diary.[5]

For years, the administration had been under increasing pressure from Adams's political rival Henry Clay and others to recognize the revolutionary governments in an affirmation of republican solidarity. Adams and Monroe steadfastly balked, afraid that such a step would incite the European powers to go to war with the United States. John Quincy also doubted the new regimes were ready for republican self-government.[6]

His work at the State Department, however, was not the only reason that kept John Quincy chained to his inkwell in steaming Washington while his wife was away and the Congress in recess. Throughout the late spring and summer, he was deeply engaged in his own kind of electioneering—a long, tortured, line-by-line rebuttal of charges leveled at him by Jonathan Russell, a Massachusetts congressman and one of the five U.S. commissioners who had negotiated the Treaty of Ghent. Russell's mischievous accusations, based on falsified papers, made it appear that in the discussions ending the War of 1812 John Quincy had been ready to sell out the West in return for favors to New England fishermen. Louisa warned her husband as early as June that carrying on the feud with Russell was becoming counterproductive. Even friendly newspapers, like Walsh's *National Gazette*, had become reluctant to print every charge and counter-charge. He had already won the battle, she assured him: "Mr. Russell . . . is completely *demolished*." But John Quincy, whose stubbornness was both his strength and his weakness, could not let up. At last, he agreed to cease waging his war in the press, but in September he privately published a detailed, documentary history of the controversy, *The Duplicate Letters, the Fisheries, and the Mississippi*, which put the entire matter to a long-overdue rest but did little to endear him as an warm and accessible figure among his countrymen.[7]

Meanwhile, in Philadelphia, Louisa was busily advocating his cause. Up until the final minutes of her stay, she was indefatigable in pursuing potential political support: "This evening I am engaged to Mr. Manigault to meet all the Carolineans—I was also invited to Mr. Sauls to meet the Louisianeans; but could not go to both," she apologized to John Quincy just before leaving for Washington in October. While on her political rounds, Louisa also picked up information she thought would interest him as secretary of state. Regarding one suggestion passed on to her by a mutual acquaintance, she noted, "I mention it because it was evidently said to me for that purpose."[8]

The voluminous correspondence between Louisa and John Quincy in the summer of 1822 puts a new light on the Adamses' marriage at twenty-five.

Louisa, by Gilbert Stuart, completed in 1826. "It looks very much as I looked, like
a woman who was just attacked by the first chill of death and the features stiffening
into torpor." Courtesy of the White House Historical Association (White House
Collection).

Certainly, their many letters—Louisa's run to 270 handwritten pages—are a
more accurate gauge of their relationship than the defensive autobiographical
fragments she wrote later or the very few words John Quincy devoted to her in
his diary. Like their courtship correspondence, these pages have an immediacy

that has not faded over time despite references to largely obscure acquaintances, forgotten artists and musicians, and passing political crises. Here we see firsthand and in real time what Louisa and John Quincy talked about as a couple: art, theater, music, the health and well-being of their friends and family, and, most of all, politics.

Louisa tried all kinds of cajolery to get her Macbeth–"If chance will make me king, why chance may crown me"—to mend his political ways. Bemoaning "the illiberal attacks of any idiot that can hold a pen," Louisa worked hard to bolster his confidence: "My conviction from my long acquaintance with your conduct as a publick man is so strong that the deeper they dive, the higher they must elevate your character." These were words that the personally insecure and politically clumsy John Quincy needed to hear, but they could not move him from his pedestal.[9]

For her correspondence with John Quincy, Louisa adopted the same form she had employed so successfully in writing to his father: the journal-letter. Every day she composed several pages of lively prose. What she termed "torrents of nonsense" were, in fact, freshly observed, uninhibited depictions of the world around her and of the influential men and women she met. She knew her tone was self-confident and witty, and she acknowledged to her husband how grateful she was that she could write freely despite the inferiority that "by nature and by law" women were compelled to feel and "to which we must submit, [and] worn by us with as much satisfaction as the badge of slavery." She was flattered, she wrote, as any woman would be, by the attention of an intelligent man. To this, John Quincy responded warmly: "Whatever the cause of the confidence which you say you have but recently acquired of writing to me whatever comes into your head is, I am the principal gainer by the acquisition. I hope it will be permanent."[10]

In turn, John Quincy's letters were uniformly loving and appreciative. He regularly addressed her as "My dearest Louisa," assuring her that her letters had become a "necessity of life" to him. He agreed to withdraw his feud with Russell from the newspapers "in consequence of your good advice" and assured her that during that painful controversy she had been the single person to whom he had turned for guidance. It was not only political advice that he claimed to be grateful for. In response to Louisa's urging that he cease appearing in public as a "vegetable plant" and display more gallantry, he responded wryly that he had tried but that his initial efforts had met with less than total success: "Your letter contains such excellent advice that last evening at the theater . . . I determined to commence my practice upon it and I made myself as amiable as possible to Mrs. Gates and Miss Kitty Lee who were in the same Box with me. . . . But as

Mrs. Gates has a husband and I a wife, I thought it was time that I stay the use of my fascinating powers there, and with Miss Lee I was still less successful having only had the advantage of supplying her with a playbill." Louisa's admonitions about his slovenly dress—a lifelong problem that even his redoubtable mother had failed to correct and a topic that Louisa had been forbidden to raise since a nearly disastrous quarrel during their engagement a quarter century earlier—were more direct but just as unsuccessful. His "dress, or as I understand, *undress*" was a constant topic of conversation in Philadelphia, she reported. According to his supporters "it hurt Mr. Jefferson and they say it *injures you*." She said she had replied to attacks on her husband with a joke, but she was serious about the warning she was giving him: "I was asked if you really went to church without shoes and stockings. I replied that I had once heard you rode to your office with your head to your horse's tail and that the one was as likely as the other."[11]

How a man "so precise and methodical" in every other area of his life should care so little about his appearance had long puzzled her, but the time had now come for intervention. "When I return, I must assume command and drill you into fashion," she warned. But John Quincy failed to give serious thought to the charges against him: "As the weather is subsiding from fever heat, I have resumed my Cravat, but you know there is always room summer and Winter for ironical wags to make merry with my dress. May my graver foes never have so good reason for their charges." He would continue to dress as he pleased for the rest of his life.

On July 26, 1822, Louisa and John Quincy celebrated their twenty-fifth anniversary in separate cities. John Quincy was fulsome: "With the dawn of this morning I awaked and ejaculated a blessing to heaven upon the semi jubilee of our marriage. More than a half of your life and nearly half of mine [we] have traveled hand in hand in our pilgrimage through this valley not alone of tears. We have enjoyed great and manifold blessings and for many of them I am indebted to you." Louisa's sentiments were somewhat less wrought. Before briskly launching into political news of the day she wrote, "It is this day five and twenty years since we came together, in which time much of bad and good has fallen to our lot. But take it all in all we have probably done as well as our Neighbours, and have been much blessed as mortals usually are who cannot pretend to any extraordinary degree of perfection. I yet hope that many good years are in store for you whatever may befall myself, and that your children will long bless the day that gave them such a father."[12]

Louisa had regained her self-confidence and fully recovered from the debilitating despondency she had fallen into during the winter. Happy, independent, and purposeful, she basked in the attention she received from Philadelphia's most influential citizens and the role they ascribed to her as John Quincy's surrogate. As a woman without an escort, her evenings were circumscribed, but her days were filled with a constant stream of visitors and visits.

Louisa's health seems to have been better than it had been for a long time and her energy unflagging, but in both August and early September she suffered from a return of her dreaded "friend," erysipelas, with its attendant painful, disfiguring facial rash and fever. When she had partially recovered, she decided to accept a longstanding invitation to visit Joseph and Emily Mifflin Hopkinson at their country home in nearby Bordentown, New Jersey. She was becoming irritated with her brother Thomas, who felt "himself afflicted with every disease under the sun" and knew that she needed to get away for some moments of relaxation. By then her brother had nearly completed Dr. Physick's full course of treatments and could briefly be left alone to care for himself.

The lovely autumn days of September 1822 were to become Louisa's own Indian summer. Almost as soon as she arrived in Bordentown—up the Delaware River from Philadelphia and not far from Trenton—her hosts were visited by their neighbor, the Emperor Napoleon's older brother, Joseph Bonaparte, the exiled King of Spain and self-titled Comte de Survilliers. Joseph had managed to make his escape just before Napoleon's defeat at the Battle of Waterloo—leaving his wife in Europe but taking with him valuable paintings, gold, and other booty from Spain. Establishing himself on a thousand acres, Joseph built a mansion, Point Breeze, on a bluff overlooking a small lake he created out of the Crosswicks Creek just before it merged with the Delaware River. Now fifty-four, the count was a fine figure of a man. "He is very handsome, I think . . . very much like Napoleon but the whole countenance expressing benevolence," a somewhat giddy Louisa wrote to John Quincy. "There is so much easy good humor about him and he looks so much like a good fat substantial farmer that were we not preacquainted with his history, no one would suspect he had ever filled a throne. In this little village he is adored, for he has made the Widows hearts to sing with joy and has been a father to the fatherless; and tho a king has showered blessing around him, thus proving himself far more than a king—a good man."[13]

From their first meeting, Joseph devoted himself almost exclusively to his newest acquaintance. Louisa's perfect French would have heightened her appeal to an exile hungry to hear and speak his mother tongue, but the count needed very little to make himself appear charming. He instituted a series of breakfasts, dinners, and other social events tailored to Louisa's preferences and whims. Discovering that she enjoyed fishing, he arranged an elaborate day on the river

Joseph Napoleon, King of Spain, by Innocent-Louis Goubaud. Maison Bonaparte, Ajaccio, Corsica, France. © RMN-Grand Palais/ Art Resource, NY.

expressly for her. He monopolized her company at meals, promenaded with her in his elaborately sculptured gardens, talked knowledgably of the theater and Washington society, and gave her a private tour of his collection of Old Masters, including a Titian nude of Venus he had hung near his bed. Louisa, much to the count's surprise, failed to evince shock at the Titian: "I would not affect modesty as I said that I had seen a number of fine pictures in Europe," she wrote. Nor did she do anything but laugh heartily at "an excellent anecdote about a Quaker lady who had come across his statues of Cupid and Psyche."[14]

The count was probably playing at seduction—in his seventeen years in the United States, he is known to have fathered at least one illegitimate child—but Louisa was too worldly to be led astray by suggestive anecdotes and personal compliments. ("He is very much pleased with my wearing an American bonnet.") But there is no question that she was flattered and delighted by Joseph's attention. She acknowledged as much to John Quincy: "I hear you saying, I hope my dear your head is not quite turned by all the fine things you meet? I answer I hope not but also must ask myself the question."[15]

The Louisa who had danced the night away in the Prussian court of King Frederick William and Queen Louise and had more than held her own among the glamorous, licentious Russian aristocracy and diplomatic corps had never been unduly impressed by the level of sophistication she found in Washington. That part of her that had thrilled to gorgeous display and responded without missing a beat to urbane repartee had lain dormant for too long. In the fading days of the summer of 1822, Joseph, the Comte de Survilliers, had cracked open a door to her past that she believed was firmly shut and bolted. "This week has been one in which I have lived a year," she wrote early in her visit to Bordentown. Ten days later, when she finally returned to Philadelphia, she closed her journal wistfully, "I hope I am not spoilt, but I am almost afraid." It was time to go home.[16]

Thomas was not the only Johnson family member who came under Louisa's care and supervision. Almost as soon as she arrived in Washington in 1817, Louisa, with her parents and older sister dead, established herself as the family's matriarch. Her dominance was not universally welcomed, and, after several years had passed, she ruefully acknowledged her "reputation for loving to inter-fere in other people's concerns." The Johnson sisters, though very close, did not entirely escape family tensions. After one Christmas Day spent at Caroline's home, Louisa reported that the atmosphere had been far from festive: "We played the farce of ['] all in the wrong['] to the greatest perfection and returned tired and dissatisfied with each other, a thing not at all uncommon in intended-to-be sociable family meetings." Nevertheless, Louisa always could be relied upon to provide day-and-night nursing care during illness and childbirth, trans-portation in her carriage to Mrs. Monroe's drawing rooms, and an entree into Washington society that her younger siblings otherwise might never have enjoyed.[17]

Joshua and Catherine Johnson had settled their exiled family in Washington in 1797, and all of their children lived there at one time or another. Of their five living daughters in 1817, only Eliza, who in 1810 had married Senator John Pope of Kentucky—a successful lawyer and politician fifteen years her senior—would never see Louisa again. Pope, an opponent of the War of 1812, had paid a price for his opposition and lost his bid for a second term in 1816. He and Eliza moved back to Kentucky, where Eliza died on April 24, 1818.[18]

Nancy, the eldest, had died eight years earlier, leaving behind three children and her husband, Walter Hellen. Hellen had generously taken into his home all the Johnson women when Joshua Johnson died in 1802 and had housed John Quincy and Louisa—and occasionally their small sons—for extended periods while John Quincy served in the Senate. After Nancy's death, Hellen married the youngest Johnson sister, Adelaide, who was then caring for the children and whose continued presence in his house without marriage would have been socially unacceptable. When Walter Hellen died in 1815, he left what seemed to be an uncharacteristically harsh will. His three children by Nancy—Johnson, Mary, and Thomas—as well as his son by Adelaide—Walter—were provided with generous trust funds. Adelaide, however, received "in lieu of dower rights" only $400 a year, reimbursement for her expenses in bringing up the four children, and the right to remain living in his house as long as she remained unmarried. Walter Hellen may have assumed that his young widow would remarry, taking the infant Walter Jr. with her, and that some other provision would have to be made for his first three children. Adelaide thought this unfair and turned to Abigail Adams, who had taken charge of the young Johnson women after the death of their mother and older sister Nancy in 1811 and was not shy about sharing her opinions. Abigail immediately advised Adelaide to refuse her bequest and, instead, claim her "rightful share." This, Adelaide apparently did; she received her dower rights (property valued at about $15,000) a year and a half after Hellen's death.[19]

By the fall of 1817, Adelaide was on her own, a widow responsible for four children, ages three to seventeen. She was a regular guest at dinner parties given by her sister and brother-in-law and attracted the interest of at least one eligible bachelor about town. The widower James Joseph Monroe, the president's brother and private secretary, offered to marry Adelaide, many years his junior, in the winter of 1818. Adelaide turned him down. In a letter to Abigail Adams, Louisa didn't explain Adelaide's decision—Louisa had not thought it a good match in the first place—but the fact was that Adelaide was then pregnant with a child fathered by George Boyd, the husband of her sister Harriet and source of innumerable irritations to Louisa. The baby, named Georgiana Adelaide Hellen, was born September 27, probably in York, Pennsylvania, where Adelaide had spent the summer. Adelaide never remarried.[20]

George Boyd was appointed the Indian agent on Mackinac Island, Michigan, in December 1818 and left town alone not long after Georgiana's birth. He

returned to Washington in March 1820, where he was promptly arrested, probably for bankruptcy. By August 1820, however, Boyd, Harriet and their four children, including an infant, were living in the untamed Michigan Territory,
from which Harriet never returned. By the end of 1821, he was again in trouble:
"Boyd . . . has got himself into difficulty with the Government in consequence
of not producing vouchers for the purchase of some articles for the Army.
Harriet has applied to me to assist her in this affair. . . . Poor H[arriet] is in great
distress as he is said to be a defaulter to the amount of eight thousand dollars."
Over the years, Louisa would receive many more pitiful appeals from her
sister—who was eventually the mother of nine children—requesting that she
use her influence with John Quincy to find Boyd another position. Knowing
John Quincy's horror of the taint of nepotism, Louisa acknowledged that this
was a matter "in which . . . I can do nothing."[21]

That Louisa's petitions to her husband on behalf of her family often fell on
deaf ears had been amply proven by the fruitlessness of her efforts to ameliorate
the desperate situations in which her sister Kitty and John Quincy's nephew
William Smith repeatedly found themselves. Once burned by the feckless
William, who had left John Quincy to pay off his gambling debts in St.
Petersburg, the secretary of state was most reluctant to lift a finger on his behalf.
Kitty, who lost two children in infancy, somehow maintained her good cheer
through all her troubles. Formerly the favorite of a tsar, she was happy to wear
Louisa's hand-me-downs, sit in as hostess when Louisa was too ill to preside at
her parties, and, finally, to move into the F Street house when she no longer
had a roof over her head.

Louisa's closest sister, the beloved Caroline, also remained in Washington
after she moved there from Baltimore in 1817 with her second husband,
Nathaniel Frye Jr., chief clerk in the War Department's office of Paymaster
General. From her marriage to Andrew Buchanan of Baltimore in 1807,
Caroline had acquired four stepchildren, all under the age of nine; in 1811, the
year Buchanan died, she gave birth to Robert. It was at the Frye home that most
Johnson family gatherings took place, even though their living arrangements
were not nearly as grand as either the Adamses' large house on C Street or their
even more spacious F Street residence. When Caroline gave birth in February
1818 to premature twin boys—James and John Quincy Adams—she was
confined in a room, Louisa recounted, that was "so small that we could scarcely
turn around in it."[22]

On the day the tiny boys were born, Louisa nursed one of them with barley
water on a piece of rag through the night—"one of the most painful I ever
witnessed." Typically and heroically, she remained with her sister for the next

three days, becoming more and more ill herself. "My feet were excessively painful and on removing my stockings I found them swelled to an enormous size and very much enflamed so as to make it impossible for me to move from [my] chair." Erysipelas had come back to haunt her once more. Nevertheless, Louisa became "chief nurse to the whole family," especially as Nathaniel Frye had been brought home from the office in "in a paralytic fit and there was but small hope of recovery."[23]

Frye did, in fact, survive, but the twins, sadly, did not. Louisa, very ill, took to her bed for the next two weeks. It was good news for everyone when, in November 1820, Caroline gave birth to another son, Thomas, who by February 1821, according to Louisa, had grown "quite fat and has four teeth [and] is very lively and playful."[24]

During her first season as wife of the secretary of state, Louisa took over the task of introducing Caroline's stepdaughter, Susan Buchanan, then just nineteen, to society; a year later she performed the same service for Susan's younger sister Mary, who arrived on Christmas Day to stay for the winter with the Adamses. Both Buchanan daughters were attractive, amiable, socially adept, and ready to accompany Louisa on her calls and John Quincy to evening events when his wife was indisposed.

The same could not be said of Mary Catherine Hellen, the ten-year-old who, beginning in the fall of 1817, would spend most of the rest of her life at Louisa's side and would eventually become the grown, much-loved daughter she never had. Mary's virtual adoption by Louisa may have begun with an impromptu gesture made at the side of the sickbed of her stepmother, Adelaide Hellen. In his diary for November 2, 1817, John Quincy noted that Adelaide was extremely ill, and reported that Louisa had "brought home with her Mary Hellen . . . whom she takes to live with us." There is no indication that this was a joint decision. Louisa was not named in Walter Hellen's will or in subsequent court papers as guardian of any of his three older children, but she played a central role in their upbringing, all four of them living with the Adamses at some time or another over the next twenty years. Adelaide was made joint guardian (with Cook) of her son Walter and her stepson Thomas but not of Mary and Johnson. From time to time, Louisa and John Quincy received reimbursement from the Hellen estate for the children's expenses.[25]

From the beginning, Mary was a handful. Louisa had to remove her from school almost as soon as she had been enrolled. "I have taken [Mary] from School as I was not satisfied with the progress she made there. She now studies with me and I hope will improve more rapidly . . . [she] is a very fine Girl but a little wild." The little girl seems to have been spoiled and unruly, prone to "idleness" and inadequately educated. Louisa enthusiastically embarked upon what seemed at times to be a hopeless project. If her goal was to mold Mary's mind and behavior into that of a woman of "delicacy," she utterly failed. Mary's manners and speech remained coarse, her behavior difficult to control, and her mind seemingly set against acquiring the kind of knowledge found in books. In her teens, she flirted with and managed to entice, in turn, all the Adams boys into her web. Her flirtation with her contemporary, Charles, apparently was a teenage romance that left no lasting mark. She did become engaged, however, to George and, after throwing him over, later married John.[26]

Her brothers were almost as difficult. In March 1819 Johnson was dismissed from Princeton for "having had a leading part in . . . acts of insubordination," including the "scraping with the feet, intended as a mark of dissatisfaction, which had taken place in the refectory." Louisa, who by then felt responsible for Johnson as well as for Mary, wrote that she was "very much concerned about it and [I] do not know how to proceed." By November 1820, she had decided that he, too, would live with her. "He is an uncommonly fine young man and I think bids fair to be an honour to his family." Her optimism was misplaced. Johnson loved the lively social life at the Adamses but proved resistant to his uncle and aunt's influence. "As to Johnson Hellen there is another disappointment to my *expectations*," Louisa acknowledged after only two months. By February 5, 1821, she had given up entirely: "Johnson Hellen is this day 21 and comes into the possession of his property which he does not appear to be very willing to manage. The worst trait of his character that I perceive, is a tendency to the most pernicious indolence which he makes little or no effort to conquer." Johnson in 1829 married one of Louisa's servants, Jane Winnull, an act of which the class-conscious Louisa much disapproved. The second Hellen son, Thomas, was eight when the Adamses arrived in Washington and seems to have remained under Adelaide's guardianship, along with the toddler Walter, for some time thereafter. Eventually, however, he, too, became the responsibility of the Adamses and caused his own share of distress. He was enrolled at Phillips Exeter for 1823–1824 and 1824–1825 and then spent two years at Harvard before dropping out and joining the rest of the family as a semi-permanent resident in the White House.[27]

As difficult as the Hellen adolescents turned out to be, they were no match for Fanny Russell Johnson, twenty-two, daughter of Louisa's cousin Thomas Johnson. In his diary John Quincy described Fanny as "beautiful and fascinating, but heartless; absorbed in selfishness," adding that she "has the appetite of a Shark for Lovers, merely to display her power." From the first, Louisa, who nevertheless introduced Fanny to Washington society, was wary. "She is a lovely

Girl and I am fearful will make dreadful havoc with the hearts of one young gentleman." That Fanny did.[28]

Robert Martin, a young lawyer who had been unable to win the approval of her family and all their "connections," was one of Fanny's many ardent suitors. When she came to Washington, he followed her there; Fanny, meanwhile, was doing her best to flirt with as many young men as she could. "She has received him [Martin] here and granted him many private interviews and in public she treats him with contempt," Louisa wrote disapprovingly.

Serious trouble in the Adams household arose when Fanny played poor, luckless George off against Martin, and nearly got him horse-whipped over a supposed insult falsely reported by Fanny. John Quincy was able to find a way out of the tense situation—provoked by Fanny with no basis in fact—but not before the house fell into an uproar. Louisa was beside herself: "The day of course was passed in a manner altogether insupportable—John and Johnson exciting George to fight by every possible taunting speech and all so irritable; what with the coquettish airs of the young Lady who was alternately playing upon them all and I believe very willing to foment the discord my house was pretty much like a Bedlam broke loose." Ten days later, Louisa was very glad to see Fanny go: "Fanny Johnson went off this morning and left our young men in the depths of the *belle passion,* but relieved me by her departure of a load of care and anxiety—She is a beautiful creature; but the most accomplished Coquette I ever saw."[29]

It was not easy or particularly rewarding to be mother to as many as six adolescents and young adults in the house at one time, and the strain frequently sent Louisa to her room with a bad migraine. During the Christmas school recess of 1820–1821, she listed the "perpetual succession of noises" in a single day that had aggravated her headache: "Mary took her lesson of Music at ten o' clock accompanied by her Master on the violin. Charles then began his which lasted an hour and a half in the same manner after which the dancing master came and they danced three hours. George and Charles then played on the flute and violin for about an hour and then followed the party."[30]

Acting as surrogate mother to her younger relatives was one thing; being mother to her own three sons as they approached adulthood was another. The young Adams men had much in common. If their portraits in 1823 by Charles Bird King are at all representative, all three were slim, dark, and handsome. They all were devoted to old John Adams—who returned their love unconditionally—and found the Old House in Quincy a haven in times of trouble. The older two, especially, considered their grandfather's house their true home and their grandfather himself a source of wisdom, counsel, and comfort. When

Louisa temporarily ceased her journal-letters to the former president in the winter of 1822, George filled in. His efforts were much appreciated. "Your letter of the 28th of October has been received with pleasure . . . it is sprightly, ingenious and agreeable." While the study of law under his father as tutor proceeded slowly, the young man was an ideal correspondent for his grandfather. Widely read and eager to discuss works of history, philosophy, and poetry, George was happy to write the long, lively letters that delighted the old man as he slumbered by the fireside on frigid Quincy winter nights.[31]

If the boys deeply loved and appreciated their grandfather and often had conflicted feelings about their father, they adored their mother. Her two older sons expressed their love in poetry, but Charles confided his to his diary. Louisa, he wrote "without hesitation," was the "most pleasing woman . . . that in this country I have ever met with." Moreover, she was "delightful company"—even when unwell—and "the only fashionable woman I know."[32]

George's "sprightly" tone is evident in a tongue-in-cheek doggerel, "To My Mother," probably composed in 1822. Louisa must have been delighted by his loving characterizations of the three brothers as they approached manhood. Charles, then fourteen, was "deep and reflective . . . learned much above his years"; the "much beloved" John was "open, cheerful, gay." As for George himself, he was a "wayward boy" but remained "his mother's pride, his father's joy." Each presented Louisa with a special challenge, complicated by an approach to parenting practiced by John Quincy that conflicted with her own. When the boys were away from home, she invariably tried to soften the harsh directives she knew were coming from their father with words of support, praise, and love. Too often when they were in Washington, she found herself helplessly attempting to mediate a conflict of wills.[33]

She worried constantly about George's health as well as his excitable nature and depressed moods. As much as she recognized the special quality of his intellectual gifts, she saw that her eldest son was as stiff and awkward at a party as his father. John, socially easy and polished, had, she believed, "a character and understanding similar to my own." Unlike George, he would not, she wrote, subject her to an "hour of sophistical argument whose ingenuity may be great" but whose "hollowness" only irritated her. As Charles began his four years at Harvard, Louisa regretted that the young boy would be so far away from her immediate supervision and showered him with loving advice on his health, choice of leisure reading, and handwriting.[34]

Although incoming freshman were typically younger in the early nineteenth century than they are now, very few were as young as Charles. Out of his depth, very homesick and banned from going home for Christmas because of his brother John's poor work, Charles finished the autumn term fifty-first in a class of fifty-nine. That spring Charles had determined to leave Harvard. For once, however, John Quincy held his fire, recognizing that threats and demands that his son improve his academic standing would only hasten that decisive day. Even Charles's broad hints that he had become addicted to "depraved habits," including "billiards, drinking parties and riding," could not incite John Quincy to heavy-handedness.[35]

Without demanding that his son remain at Harvard, John Quincy asked him to reconsider. His only condition was that Charles present him with a realistic "alternative course of life." A career choice such as the Navy, he warned, might expose the boy to even greater temptations than those he had encountered in Cambridge, and it was his son's morals that gave him the most concern. John Quincy appeared ready to concede that his youngest son would fare no better academically than had George and John, but he refused to surrender any ground in the matter of character: "If I must give up all expectation of success or distinction for you in this life preserve me from the harrowing thought of your perdition in the next," he wrote the boy.[36]

Charles completed four years at Harvard, but he seems to have decided for himself the course of his education. One day in his junior year, for example, knowing that on Mondays he would be the first to be called upon to recite in his Latin class, he carried with him a copy of Molière's *La Comtesse d'Escarbagnas*, a "rather diverting work" to keep him amused while the class-mates who followed him in alphabetical order struggled with the orations of Tacitus. His diary records a steady and thoughtful reading of a wide range of literature, much of it poetry and very little of it apparently in connection with his coursework.[37]

Charles's distaste for the institution beloved by his father and grandfather was unabated by time. Eight years after he had left Harvard, he wrote bitterly that the experience had given him nothing of value. His college friendships had been transient, he recalled, and he had found his instructors cold and unin-spiring. As often as possible, he made his way to Quincy where he took his grandfather on carriage rides, helped him with his correspondence, and, in the evenings, read to him. But the Old House, in addition to the presence of his loving grandfather, had also become home to John Quincy's only living sibling, Thomas Boylston Adams, lost and angry in the fog of alcohol and unrealized dreams. Charles, never having known his uncle in his younger days, viewed him with disgust: "I had this evening the pleasure of sitting with my Uncle alone, in one of his usual fits, and I thought it somewhat singular that young girls should be invited by our ladies to this house only to see the disgrace of their father," he wrote. The spectacle of the ruined man, he believed, was meant to act as a check on the pride of an ambitious family.[38]

As Harvard's commencement of 1825 approached, John Quincy seems to have been unable to endure yet another elaborate ceremony and celebration in which his graduating son played no — or no significant — part in the proceedings. He suggested that Charles, given his standing in the lower half of his class, might be "more comfortable" away from Harvard Yard on the big day. By the end of July, Charles, eighteen, was on his way to Washington and the White House, his college years behind him.

Unlike his brother John two years ahead of him, Charles at least had a Harvard diploma in hand. John, to his parents' infinite dismay, was one of the forty-three (out of a class of seventy) members of the Class of 1823 who were expelled from the college in the Great Rebellion of 1823, just months before commencement. The class had divided itself years before into a rowdy group of "high fellows" and another of studious, rule-obeying "Blacks." When a "Black" informed on a leader of the more boisterous "high fellows" clique — causing the latter's immediate expulsion — trouble ensued. The "high fellows" swore an oath that they would leave the college until their hero was reinstated and the informer was deprived of his role in commencement. If Harvard's faculty and president had accepted these conditions, any remaining control it had over its students would have been lost. Not surprisingly, John was a prominent member of the rebelling group and was expelled with the rest.[39]

His grandfather, to whom he fled, reported to Louisa that her boy had explained the whole "hurricane or a tornado [that] has happened at College" and begged her and John Quincy to "receive him tenderly and forgive him kindly" as John had done no more to foment the uprising than had many others. Louisa had already whipped off a letter rebuking her son for his part in the rebellion, especially as it was bound to deeply anger John Quincy. She urged John to swallow his "mistaken pride" and apologize to the authorities in the hope that they would readmit him to his class before commencement. In the strongest possible language, she warned John that his "disgrace" would "render your father inflexible, give me heartfelt pain, and produce to yourself years of sorrow and repentance." She wrote again the next day, however, to say that explanations from Charles and another underclassmen had presented the episode in a new light — "one of those in which the Esprit de Corps has made it necessary for you to take your part and to act with your Class." She commended John's letter to his father recounting the reasons for his expulsion as "manly and respectful" but again warned him that if an "opportunity offers for a return to College, beware of *pride* and do not mistake it for honour." Although Louisa wrote several times to both John and Charles during this troubled period, John Quincy waited almost a month before communicating with his anxious second son. Louisa assured John that a "very kind" letter was on the way and that it had only been the pressure of business that had kept John Quincy from communicating his views.[40]

By the end of the summer, John had joined his parents in Washington. In the next nine years before his untimely death, John "devoted himself with unbounded filial affection" to helping his father, as "steward, housekeeper, secretary, social companion and kindest friend." His most thankless task was to try making a go of the Columbian Mills, a flour and corn mill along Rock Creek on what is now the grounds of the Washington Zoo. Purchasing the mill had been one of John Quincy's greatest mistakes and one he made uncharacteristically, on the spur of the moment. The mill had been owned by Louisa's uncle, Roger Johnson, whose son George, then running the enterprise, had come to John Quincy in the summer of 1823 asking for help. The banks were about to put the business in foreclosure, George said, and he was desperate. He needed $20,000 to stave off the bank and another $10,000 to $12,000 to put the mills back in operation. John Quincy, Louisa, Mary Hellen, and George rode their horses to the mills that evening to investigate what was, in John Quincy's estimation, a commercial building "in rather a neglected condition, but appear[ing] to be a valuable property."[41]

Within a week, he had sunk much of his fortune into a business in which he had no experience, no knowledge, and no time to oversee day-to-day details. Convinced that his political life was coming to an end, he decided he needed an alternative means of supporting his family. "Less than two years will terminate my political career, and leave me to the support of my private resources. Is not this a gracious offer by Providence of the means of devoting the time which may yet be allotted upon Earth to useful and respectable purposes? . . . It must be at all events, in a great degree a leap in the dark." John Quincy regretted that "leap in the dark" many times over and remained a troubled mill owner for the rest of his life.[42]

Just after his father's purchase of the mill, George, who had spent the two years following his graduation from Harvard in a dogged attempt to study law under his father's general direction, moved to Boston to prepare for the Massachusetts bar in the office of Daniel Webster. By 1824, he had been admitted to practice law. He then made a valiant attempt to fulfill the hopes of his father and grandfather and follow them into public service. Eventually elected to the state legislature in 1826, George had none of the old president's fire and none of John Quincy's taste for public life and lasted only a few months. His business career fared no better. Entrusted by John Quincy to manage his many real estate holdings in Boston and Quincy and to oversee other invest-ments, George quickly found himself losing ground and was eventually replaced by Charles.

As the election of 1824 approached, none of the three Adams sons had shown any particular aptitude for the law, the church, or business, the only professions their father considered worthwhile. Each had given Louisa and John Quincy concerns about their penchant for drinking, smoking, and high living in general. None would prove to be much of an asset in the coming campaign.

The presidential election was very much on the minds of both Louisa and John Quincy during that fall and winter of 1822–1823. In addition to the Tuesday sociables, John Quincy hosted frequent dinners for Washington's leading men, which Louisa, Mary Hellen, and the other young women of the household were expected to attend. If Louisa happened to be ill, however, none of the young unmarried and unchaperoned women could take their place at the table. "This always mortifies Mr A. very much as he conceives that his dinners are more animated and pleasant and our Gentlemen in Washington are growing so fastidious they must have handsome Girls to look at as well as a good dinner," Louisa wrote her father-in-law.[43]

As the winter went on, the electoral map became more complex. Andrew Jackson was gaining strength; John C. Calhoun had dropped out; and William Crawford, secretary of the Treasury, the man John Quincy considered the stron-gest in the field, was stumbling—out of public view. In August or early September 1823 he had traveled to the Blue Ridge Mountains to recover from ill health. There he was misdiagnosed by a doctor and given a near-fatal dose of digitalis, triggering a stroke that left him paralyzed and blind. Crawford, however, remained a candidate. The influential *National Intelligencer*, firmly in his camp, published regular reports over the next months falsely stating that he was on the road to recovery.[44]

Once more, Louisa was thrown back into Washington's social whirl, a prospect she dreaded. She was tired and discouraged and feeling more unwilling to entertain and be entertained than usual. "This Session begins with me pretty much as I suppose it will pass in Congress, that is to say with chills and fevers alternately low and high and at all times very unequal to labour in my fatiguing vocation," she wrote in the first entry in her diary in nine months. She decided to cut in half the number of her Tuesday sociables "as I am not able to undertake it oftener & what all these strangers are to do for amusement I dont know." John Quincy's chances were looking dim, and Louisa saw no point in exerting herself when the machinations of others were against her. It would be the country's loss, she was sure, and not John Quincy's: "The disgrace will not fall on him but heavily on that *very enlightened* Country and people who could not discriminate between sterling worth and base intrigue."[45]

It is in this context that on December 20, 1823, that John Quincy and Louisa—at young John's urging—decided to hold a ball honoring Andrew Jackson on January 8, the anniversary of the general's victory in the Battle of New Orleans. It was short notice to put together a party on the scale they envisioned, but timing was critical. For the ball to have its maximum effect, it had to take place before the congressional caucus, where previous presidential candidates had been chosen, was held in late January or early February. As balls were to be held in many places around the country on the anniversary of the great event, the choice of date became obvious.

At first, Louisa was reluctant to embark on this grand scheme: "I objected much to the plan but was overpowered by John's arguments and the thing was settled." John Quincy did not record his reaction, but he was then clinging naïvely to the notion that Jackson, then serving in the Senate, could be his vice presidential running mate. Both he and Louisa appeared unaware of the extent of popular sentiment building throughout the country for the Hero of New Orleans, and only by vastly underestimating Jackson's popularity and dismissing him as a serious rival could they have considered a ball in his honor.[46]

In the Adamses' eyes, the benefits to John Quincy's candidacy were the deciding factors. He would bask in the hero's popularity, and if the ball were a success, it would be the Adamses, rather than Jackson, who would be remembered afterward. "Mrs. Adams's ball" quickly came to be the most sought-after invitation in Washington. The first five hundred invitations, many of them hand-delivered by Louisa, were nearly all accepted. Those not on the original guest list besieged John Quincy at the State Department and Louisa at home for invitations. A week before the party, Louisa wrote to George in Boston that she expected a thousand guests. She was about right.[47]

The massive scale of this private party is almost impossible to conceive today. With only nineteen days to put her plans into action, Louisa warmed to the challenge. "I have a beautiful plan in my head which I shall endeavor to have executed." After clearing out as much furniture as she could, removing doors to allow movement between rooms, and transferring John Quincy's study to a small back antechamber, Louisa called in carpenters to install temporary pillars to support the second floor. The Adams family and any guests who dropped in during the holiday season were assigned to weaving garlands and wreaths of laurel, wintergreen, evergreens, and roses. Charles, in his diary, took to referring to his mother as "Madame," possibly an annoyed indication of her generalship of the coming affair. Louisa even hired a man from Baltimore to chalk the floors, following her own design, with spread eagles, flags, and the motto, "Welcome to the Hero of New Orleans." The effect must have been impressive to the few guests who saw the elaborate chalk work before the first swish of a lady's long train decimated it.[48]

The national press was caught up in the excitement surrounding the ball. One famous (and much reprinted) doggerel by the poet and newspaper editor John Agg had as its refrain "Belles and matrons, maids and madams/All are gone to Mrs. Adams." On the evening of January 8, guests began arriving at half past seven, their way lit by bonfires as far as two blocks from the F Street mansion. The *New York Statesman* correspondent described the scene: "I mingled in the multitude who were literally thronging to Mrs. Adams' party. The city was at that hour in commotion. Carriages were rolling through every street, and the sidewalks were covered with gentlemen on foot, all hastening to the same. The street opposite the Secretary's mansion was completely blocked up with carriages waiting their turn to drive to the door. It is easier to conceive than describe the scene of bustle and confusion among the crowds."[49]

"Company flocked in so early," Charles wrote in his diary, "that they could hardly get through. . . . And it was not till the upper rooms (only two were opened at first) were crowded to suffocation almost, that the lower ones were thrown open." Guests were greeted at the door by Louisa and John Quincy, the latter dressed in his usual unfashionable working attire. To the strains of sprightly tunes by members of the Marine band, the women in their ball gowns and men in evening dress, complete with medals and sashes, made their way into eight reception rooms transformed with greenery, flowers, and "small illumination lamps." When Jackson arrived at nine, the crowd pressed in to catch a glimpse of him. "The ladies climbed the chairs and benches to see General Jackson," Charles wrote in his diary.[50]

Louisa led the guest of honor through the crowd, making introductions as they went. Anticipating that she would be the center of attention, she had chosen a ball gown of light-catching steel lamé with "ornaments for head, throat, and arms" of "cut-steel," all producing a "dazzling effect." The *Statesman*'s correspondent was suitably impressed: "Mrs. Adams was elegantly but not gorgeously dressed. In her manner she unites dignity with an unusual share of ease and elegance and I never saw her appear to greater advantage than when promenading through the rooms, winding her way through the multitude by the side of the gallant General. At the approach of such a couple, the crowd involuntarily gave way as far as practicable and saluted them as they passed." As her guests bowed and curtsied before her, Louisa could have been forgiven a moment of triumph, a moment that certainly would have reminded her of the royal drawing rooms of Berlin, St. Petersburg, and London, where she had learned her lessons in "ease and elegance." An elaborate supper featuring "natural and candied fruits, pies, sweetmeats, tongues, game . . . prepared in the French style and arranged in the most exquisite taste" had been prepared. Shortly after dining, Jackson left to attend another public ball "where he expected to be greeted by the people with great joy," but where, as it turned out, only a relatively small group of supporters awaited him. Everyone, as Agg had predicted, had "gone to Mrs. Adams."[51]

The "Adams Ball," as Louisa's magnificent party was afterward known, remained unsurpassed in the annals of Washington social history. One social historian, writing in 1911, referred to it as a "brilliant ball," adding, "I have heard of it all my life." It represented the high point of the Adamses' campaign efforts, and never again would they rest so easily at the top of the political and social pyramid. For a brief moment John Quincy and Louisa had made themselves the rightful heirs to the presidency, and they had shown the world that they alone among the potential candidates and their wives possessed a sense of style and grandeur equal to that of any of the crowned heads of Europe. With the Adamses in the White House, America would stand proud in the world.[52]

That winter, Louisa continued her biweekly evening sociables and John Quincy his men-only dinners, but her spirits were on the decline. She stopped writing in her journal immediately after recording her account of the ball. She continued, however, to send journal-letters to the eighty-nine-year-old John Adams via her son George. Because the old president could no longer read, his letters were read to him by any available person and his replies dictated. Not wanting any flippant or derogatory remarks she made about Washington personalities to fall into the wrong hands, Louisa trusted George to edit her letters selectively—depending on who was present—before reading them to his grandfather and to retain in his possession everything she had written to the old man.

In June 1824, Louisa left Washington for Bedford Springs in southern Pennsylvania, a spa that had become well known for the supposed healing powers of its mineral waters. John Quincy wrote in his diary that she had made the decision to take the trip because her health was "so infirm and she has such continual severe returns of her complaints." Although the exact complaints were not specified, Louisa appeared to make a good recovery over the next five or six weeks, faithfully chronicling for her husband the comings and goings of an array of characters—from well-dressed Quakers to overemoting widows to a honeymooning couple she feared would only annoy everyone else with "their fondness." She reported early on that her headaches had disappeared, but admitted to laboring "under a depression of spirits which I can not at all control and which is perfectly unnatural to me." At forty-nine, she may have been experiencing the first signs of menopause.[53]

Despite feeling low, she, typically, found "the melange of company . . . truly diverting" and not a little grotesque: "Mr. Dawson has come for health and is laboring under a dreadful complaint such as I never before heard of. . . . The two sides of his body are gradually closing together and we ignoramuses suppose it must kill him." Of another guest, she wrote: "His history is a melancholy one. His father, mother, sister, and brother having been poisoned by a young Woman, a resident in Carlisle in a fit of jealousy; who put arsenic in the butter at breakfast, which occasioned the death of the three former, and incurable lameness in the latter, who is now an eminent lawyer at Carlisle." Three weeks into her stay, Louisa decided that she had had enough of spa life, but it was not until mid-July that her son John arrived with a carriage to ferry her, along with Mary and Johnson Hellen, back to sultry Washington and the increasingly heated contest for the presidency.[54]

Louisa had already tired of the campaign, and particularly of John Quincy's all-consuming absorption in it. She had good reason. Despite protestations that he would do nothing to advance his own cause, he was consumed by electioneering. All through the winter, his diary was filled with conjectures and conversations on his campaign and the machinations of his foes. He insisted that he wanted no part of either the congressional caucus or a rumored vice presidency.[55]

Soon, Louisa herself had become an object of interest to the opposition press. "And now it is my turn to be brought before the publick by the . . . pen of Mr. [John B.] Colvin or some of his Satellites," Louisa wrote Charles soon after her return from Pennsylvania, "with the kind intention of blackening the reputation of your father!!!" The story behind the trumped-up scandal was simple. . Louisa's hatmaker, Mary Moulton, had asked for help getting out of a financial jam. Mrs. Moulton was unable to pay her rent, and her furniture had been seized by her landlord. Louisa persuaded John Quincy to sign a note for Mrs. Moulton that allowed her to regain her goods. When she failed to make payment on the next quarter's rent, the landlord came to John Quincy for payment—but not for the $150 John Quincy thought he had signed for in

December, but for $187.50, covering an additional quarter's rent. John Quincy lost his temper and angrily charged the landlord with the worst kind of fraud.

It was that intemperate behavior that finally found its way into the anti-Adams press, specifically the *City Gazette* in Washington, which was run by Colvin, a former State Department employee who had been dismissed some years before by John Quincy and who had written venomously critical pieces about him ever since. The *City Gazette* argued that John Quincy's behavior was "highly immoral, if not positively dishonest. And that he proved on that occasion, that he is a man of an arrogant and quarrelsome temper, prone to altercations, and vehement and intemperate in his discourse upon little or no provocation." Particularly galling to Louisa was the unsavory implication she saw in the press accounts: "Mrs. Moulton is said to be a bad character and it is thought that there is a desire to make it appear that your father did '*not give the Note for Nothing*,'" she complained to Charles.[56]

When the Adamses left Washington for Quincy in late August, neither thought much of John Quincy's chances in the election. "It was probably my last bath in the Potomack," John Quincy confided gloomily to his diary on August 28 before heading off to Massachusetts. "For on my return the bathing season will have past and I shall probably never pass another summer in this city." Louisa vowed to her son Charles that she would make the coming social season her best: "As this is probably the last I should wish to be able to enjoy it and to make my exit from public life with some éclat."[57]

For John Quincy, at least, the trip to Boston and Quincy provided a bit of respite: "The uncertainty of the event continues as great as ever. It seems as if every liar and calumniator in the country was at work day and night to destroy my character. . . . It is impossible to be wholly insensible to this process while it is in operation. It distracts my attention from public business, and consumes precious time."[58]

By October, John Quincy and Louisa, accompanied by Mary Hellen and Tom Adams's daughter Elizabeth, had returned to Washington. Along the way, in Philadelphia, they had been caught up in the extraordinary traveling circus around the Marquis de Lafayette, the "Guest of the Nation," then in the second month of an eight-month visit in which he would be feted in scores of towns across the nation. Lafayette, a hero of the Revolutionary War, had endured much over the previous thirty-five years in France, including exile and imprisonment. At the time, he was out of favor at home and out of money. Congress was more than generous, eventually providing him with $200,000 and a township of land. Philadelphia, like countless other cities from Biddeford, Maine, to Baltimore and beyond had vied to give the visiting hero the grandest celebration. Newspapers could not contain their enthusiasm: "The array of beauty, decorated so as to produce the most picturesque and vivid effect, has never been surpassed in the United States. We may compute that the actors and gazers, including strangers, could not altogether have fallen short of one hundred thousand. . . . The number of troops paraded, as reported to the Inspector-General was ten thousand." Louisa and John Quincy were "unexpectedly dragged" into the festivities, Louisa wrote to George. "It was a splendid show and I whirled amid the glitter [and] confusion until my brain was almost turned."[59]

In many ways, the attention Lafayette attracted contrasted with the inattention given the ongoing presidential campaign, as if the country were thirsting for a return to the era of revolutionary heroes instead of the current spectacle of "cabals and intrigues." Nonetheless, it was cabals and intrigues that the public got, partly, at least, because the process of electing and nominating a president in 1824 was in such confusion. In some cases the state legislatures, as in Tennessee, met and endorsed a candidate simply as a publicity stunt; in others, like Pennsylvania, rump groups met to make nominations. The result was four candidates with broad support and all members of the same party.[60]

As the results of the voting were tallied in the press, it was clear that no candidate would win a majority in the Electoral College and that the decision would end up in the House. The Twelfth Amendment to the Constitution, adopted in 1804, stipulated that only the top three candidates in the Electoral College—not the top five as originally established—would go before the House for final selection. Andrew Jackson and John Quincy quickly emerged in first and second place, but the third-place finisher remained unclear until the New York legislature made its choice. The first ballot of the lame-duck legislature was inconclusive. None of John Quincy's electors secured the required votes to be selected. On the second ballot, Adams's supporters, led by the young journalist Thurlow Weed, engineered a series of deals that gave them twenty-six of the thirty-six electors for John Quincy. More important, Clay, as a result of switched votes and absences, ended up with just three electors from New York, knocking him out of third place in the Electoral College vote, behind Crawford. (The final tally: Jackson—ninety-nine; Adams—eighty-four; Crawford—forty-one; and Clay—thirty-seven.)

Clay's narrow failure to best the still ailing Crawford meant that he, as Speaker of the House, could wield enormous influence when the vote reached the House, where each state, no matter how populous, had one vote. John Quincy, now seeing more hope, had returned to Washington that fall from Quincy with renewed political hunger. Contrary to his usual habit, he was assiduous in his attendance at parties and dinners and in counting and courting votes. In December, he met with Robert P. Letcher, a friend and housemate of Clay's, ostensibly to talk over a minor federal appointment but really for Letcher to get a reading on Adams's attitude toward the influential Kentuckian. According to John Quincy, Letcher assured him that Clay would "willingly support" him if "he could thereby serve himself, and the substance of his meaning was that that if Clay's friends could know that he would have a prominent share in the Administration, that might induce them to vote for me, even in the face of instructions."[61]

Here lies the origin of what came to be known as the "corrupt bargain" that brought political ruin to both Clay and Adams and great unhappiness to Louisa. Clay was unsuccessful in his three future runs for president; Adams was limited to one presidential term and thwarted by Congress at every turn. Historians have debated since 1824 whether a quid pro quo on either side was ever demanded or offered. Recent Clay biographers insist that, with Napoleon in recent memory, he had a strong abhorrence of generals becoming president and that he left Kentucky for Washington in 1824 already determined to vote for Adams; John Quincy's diary, as full as it is of word-for-word conversations, carefully gives no hint of any bargain.[62]

Nevertheless, Adams eventually offered Clay the office of secretary of state. Clay, who was as experienced and interested in foreign affairs as anyone in Washington, in turn, was able to bring the states he had won in the Electoral College—Kentucky, Missouri, and Ohio—into the Adams column. Despite their bitter differences, the two were not unlikely allies. They both firmly believed in strengthening the union through higher tariffs and federal support for roads, canals, and manufacturing, and Clay, over the years, had been much more unfriendly to Jackson than he had been to Adams. Even with Clay's help, John Quincy would need three more states: Illinois, whose one vote would be cast by Louisa's relative and John Quincy's long-time friend Daniel P. Cook; Louisiana, where he had won one of the three electoral votes; and Maryland, which Louisa had boldly declared two years earlier was "said to be his," but where her family's influence had waned.[63]

None of this was easy. The three states, which Jackson had won, did not move easily to Adams's side. Last-minute assurances had to be given to a pair of Maryland House members that Federalists would not be excluded from federal appointments. (Jackson had won seven of Maryland's eleven electoral votes, but the House delegation was evenly split.) And even though Adams had won a majority of electoral votes from New York, his selection by the congressional delegation was deadlocked, broken only by the last-minute decision of the aging

Stephen van Rensselaer, a former Federalist thought to be a supporter of Crawford—a vote that turned out to be crucial.[64]

On February 9, 1825, a very cold day in Washington, Adams won a bare majority of thirteen states on the first ballot. Jackson, who had won eleven states in the Electoral College, ended up with just seven states in the House, and Crawford four. The result was did not sit well with the country at large. Jackson had won the largest share of both the popular and the electoral vote, but was not the eventual winner.

Unlike John Quincy, Louisa had not returned to Washington that October with renewed political vigor. Quite the opposite. In December, she wrote to Charles: "To what purpose we suffer this martyrdom, time only can prove, but I can conceive of no reward sufficiently great in the gratification of ambitions to pay for the waste of life enjoyment and comfort which must be sacrificed to attain it." She continued to hold her alternate Tuesday sociables through December and January. "This even' I resume my parties and expect to be thronged with visitors who will come to see how I behave during the ordeal which we are going through," she wrote to George in December. Despite a reluctant hostess, Louisa's parties were as popular as ever.[65]

Louisa also made herself visible to show she was impervious to any of the rumors flying around her, setting the bar high for the other candidates' wives. As soon as it got out that she had gathered a party to go to the theater, the "Crawfordites" organized a competing set of theater goers. "You must know society is now divided into separate battalions as it were," Margaret Bayard Smith wrote to her friend Mrs. Kirkpatrick in January. "Mrs. Adams collected a large party and went one night [to the theater], Mrs. Calhoun another, so it was thought by our friends that Mrs. Crawford should go too, to show our strength."[66]

Louisa's final sociable was held the night before the House vote. John Quincy reported that the party "was more fully attended than ever before. There were sixteen Senators, sixty-seven members of the House, and at least four hundred citizens and strangers."[67]

Although John Quincy and his friends had counted well and felt some confidence that he would win on the first ballot, he still feared the worst—that somehow, the supporters of Calhoun, Jackson, and Crawford would conspire to defeat him. When a House delegation came to give him the welcome news, he was naturally relieved, but, aware of the close vote and the popular and Electoral College voting, he realized he would be a minority president. Had the Constitution provided for a second election if the first ended in a virtual standoff such as this one, he insisted he would have refused the office and submitted himself to a popular referendum. As it was, he wrote to Congress, he was required to accept the will of the House.[68]

There is no evidence that the victory brought any joy to Louisa. The night before his inauguration on March 4, 1825, John Quincy wrote in his diary that he was unable to sleep because of "the unceasing excitement of many past days . . . and above all the failing and threatening state of my wife's health." The following day, despite a "long and alarming fainting fit" she was able to meet some well-wishers but she was far too ill to attend the inaugural ball, a sad but telling end to her long campaign.[69]

ABBREVIATIONS

AA	Abigail Adams
CFA	Charles Francis Adams
CJ	Catherine Nuth Johnson
GWA	George Washington Adams
JA	John Adams
JA2	John Adams II
JJ	Joshua Johnson
JQA	John Quincy Adams
LCA	Louisa Catherine Adams
TBA	Thomas Boylston Adams

JOHNSON FAMILY TREE

Joshua Johnson (1742–1811) — Catherine Nuth (1757–1811)
  m. 1785

    Ann (Nancy) (1773–1810)
        m. 1798 Walter Hellen (1766–1815) (first cousin on father's side)
        Johnson Hellen (1800–1867)
            m. 1829 Jane Winnull (maidservant)
        Washington Hellen (1802–1803)
        Walter Hellen (1804–1806)
        Mary Catherine Hellen (1807–1870)
            m. 1828 John Adams II (see below for children)
        Thomas Hellen (1809–1833)

    Louisa Catherine (1775–1852)
        m. 1797 John Quincy Adams (1767–1848)
        George Washington Adams (1801–1829)
            Eliza Dolph (did not marry)
                Daughter (name unknown) (b. 1829)
        John Adams II (1803–1834)
            m. 1828 Mary Catherine Hellen (LCA's niece)
                Mary Louisa Adams (1828–1859)
                Georgeanna Frances Adams (1830–1839)

        Charles Francis Adams (1807–1886)
            m. 1829 Abigail Brooks (1808–1889)
                Henry Adams (1828–1918)
                Louisa Adams (1831–1870)
                John Quincy Adams (1833–1894)
                Charles F. Adams Jr. (1835–1915)

Arthur Adams (1841–1846)
Mary Adams (1841–1928)
Brooks Adams (1848–1927)
Louisa Catherine Adams II (1811–1812)

Carolina Virginia Marylanda (1777–1862)
  m. 1807 Andrew Buchanan (1766–1811)
    Susan Buchanan (stepdaughter) (1798–?)
    Mary Buchanan (stepdaughter) (1800–1879)
    Robert C. Buchanan (1811–1878)

  m. 1817 Nathaniel Frye
    John Quincy Adams Frye (b./d. 1818)
    James Frye (b./.d 1818)
    Louisa Carolina (b./d. 1819)
    Thomas Baker Johnson Frye (1820–1889)

Thomas Baker (1779–1843)
  Never married; no children

Harriet (1781–1850)
  m. 1805 George Boyd (1781–1846)
    Archibald Boyd (d. 1806)
    John Quincy Adams Boyd (1806–1831)
    Joshua Johnson Boyd (d. 1832)
    Six other children

Catherine (Kitty) (1786–1869)
  m. 1813 William S. Smith (1787–1850) (son of JQA's sister Abigail)
    Unnamed child (d. 1817)
    Caroline Amelia Smith (d. 1818)

Eliza (d. 1818)
  m. 1810 John Pope (1770–1845)
    Florida (d. 1825)
    Elizabeth (1815–1835)

Adelaide (1789–1877)
  m. 1813 Walter Hellen (widowed husband of sister Nancy)
    Walter Hellen Jr. (1814–1850)

  George Boyd (married husband of sister Harriet)
    Georgiana Adelaide Hellen (1817–1863)

CHRONOLOGY

1764

John Adams and Abigail Smith marry in Weymouth, Mass.

1767

July 11: JQA born in Quincy, Mass.

1775

Feb. 12: LCA born in London.
April 19: The battles of Lexington and Concord mark outbreak of hostilities between Britain and its American colonies.

1776

July 4: Declaration of Independence.

1778

Winter or early spring: Johnson family moves to Nantes, France.
February: JA and JQA sail to France.

1779

Aug 2: JA and JQA return to Boston.
Nov. 15: JA and JQA return to France.

1781

Oct. 19: British surrender at Yorktown, Va.
Aug. 27: JQA, acting as secretary and interpreter to Francis Dana, arrives in St. Petersburg, Russia.

1783

Sept. 3: Treaty of Paris ends the Revolutionary War.

April: Johnsons return to their home at Cooper's Row, Great Tower Hill, London.

1785

Aug. 22: Joshua Johnson and Catherine Nuth are legally married. They were then parents to seven children, six of them surviving.

1787

July 18: JQA graduates from Harvard College.

1789

April 6: George Washington is elected president and JA vice president of the United States.
May: French Revolution begins.

1790

Aug. 3: JJ named first American consul in London.

1794

May 29: George Washington appoints JQA minister resident to the Netherlands.
Oct. 3: JQA and TBA, acting as his secretary, arrive at The Hague.

1795

Nov. 11: JQA visits the Johnson home for the first time and meets Louisa.

1796

May 5: LCA and JQA become engaged.
May 31: JQA returns to The Hague.

1797

March 4: JA is inaugurated as second president of the United States.
May 20: JA nominates JQA as U.S. minister plenipotentiary to Prussia.
July 26: LCA and JQA are married at the Church of All Hallows Barking in Great Tower Street, London.
Sept. 9: After the collapse of JJ's business, the Johnson family leaves London for for the United States.
Sept. 22: JQA receives word of his new assignment to Prussia.
Nov. 7: LCA, JQA, and TBA arrive in Berlin.
Nov. 19: LCA suffers the first of many miscarriages.

1800

> April 28: JA appoints JJ superintendent of the Stamp Office in the Treasury Department.
>
> July 17–Oct. 25: LCA and JQA tour Silesia.
>
> Nov. 30: Charles Adams, JQA's alcoholic brother, dies in New York City.

1801

> Feb 11: Electoral College chooses Thomas Jefferson over JA as the third president.
>
> April 12: GWA is born in Berlin.
>
> Sept. 4: LCA, JQA, with GWA return to the United States. JQA goes to Quincy; LCA, with the baby GWA, goes to Washington.
>
> Oct. 21: JQA, LCA reunite in Washington.
>
> Nov. 3: LCA, JQA, and GWA leave Washington, stopping in Frederick, Md., on their way to Quincy.
>
> Nov.3: LCA meets the Adams clan for the first time.

1802

> April 17: JJ dies.
>
> Nov. 3 JQA is defeated in a run for a seat representing Suffolk County in the U.S. House.

1803

> Feb. 7: London banking house of Bird, Savage & Bird fails, causing serious financial losses for the Adamses.
>
> Feb. 8: JQA is appointed U.S. senator by the Massachusetts legislature.
>
> July 4: JA2 is born in Boston.
>
> May 18: Napoleon is proclaimed emperor of France.
>
> June 24: JQA is appointed Boylston Professor of Rhetoric and Oratory at Harvard.
>
> Nov.11: LCA and JQA return to Washington, leaving GWA and JA2 in Quincy.

1806

> Sept. 10: Mary Catherine Hellen, daughter of Nancy Johnson Hellen, and future wife of JA2, is born.
>
> October: Prussia is conquered by Napoleon.

1807

> Aug. 18: CFA is born in Boston.
>
> Oct. 10: LCA, JQA, and CFA leave Boston, reaching Washington on

October 24. Older boys are left behind for schooling in Massachusetts.
Dec. 18: JQA expelled from the Federalist Party over his support for
Jefferson.

1808

June 2–3: Massachusetts General Court votes to replaces JQA as
senator. JQA resigns June 8 before term ends.

1809

June 26: President James Madison nominates JQA as minister
plenipotentiary to Russia.
Aug. 5: LCA, JQA, CFA and Catherine (Kitty) Johnson sail from
Boston for St. Petersburg. GWA and JA2 remain in Quincy.
Nov. 12: LCA and JQA are formally presented to Empress Elizabeth
and Emperor Alexander I of Russia.

1810

Dec. 30: Nancy Johnson Hellen, LCA's sister, dies in childbirth in
Washington.

1811

June 3: JQA declines nomination to Supreme Court.
Aug.12: Louisa Catherine Adams 2d is born in St. Petersburg.
Sept. 29: CJ, LCA's mother, dies.

1812

June 18: Congress declares war on Great Britain.
June 24: Napoleon's army invades Russia.
Sept. 15: Louisa Catherine Adams 2d dies after contracting dysentery.
Sept. 15: Napoleon's army enters Moscow.
Oct. 19: Napoleon's army leaves Moscow.

1813

Feb. 7: Catherine Johnson, LCA's sister, marries William
Steuben Smith, son of JQA's sister Abigail (Nabby) Adams Smith,
in St. Petersburg.
Aug. 14: Nabby dies of complications from breast cancer in Quincy.

1814

Jan. 14: James Madison nominates JQA, James Bayard, Henry Clay,
Albert Gallatin, and Jonathan Russell to negotiate a peace treaty with
Great Britain.
April 20: Napoleon exiled to Elba.

June 24: JQA arrives in Ghent, Belgium, to negotiate peace with Great Britain.

Aug. 24: British troops invade Washington and burn the White House, Capitol, and other public buildings.

Dec. 24: Treaty of Ghent is signed.

1815

Jan. 8: Andrew Jackson's forces defeat British troops at the Battle of New Orleans.

Feb. 12: LCA and CFA begin overland journey from St. Petersburg to Paris.

Feb. 26: Napoleon escapes from Elba.

Feb. 28: President James Madison nominates JQA as U.S. minister plenipotentiary to Great Britain.

March 23: LCA and CFA arrive in Paris and are reunited with JQA.

May 16–25: LCA, JQA, and CFA travel to London, where they meet GWA and JA2.

June 18: Napoleon defeated at Waterloo.

Aug. 1: LCA and JQA move to Boston House on Boston Lane in the London suburb of Ealing.

Oct. 30: Walter Hellen, LCA's brother-in-law, dies, leaving four children.

1816

March 21: LCA and JQA are presented to Queen Charlotte of England.

1817

March 5: President James Monroe nominates JQA as secretary of state.

June 10: LCA, JQA, and their three sons sail from London to return to United States.

Aug. 28: GWA enrolls at Harvard.

Sept. 9: CFA and JA2 enroll in the Boston Latin School.

Nov. 2: LCA brings Mary Catherine Hellen home from Adelaide Hellen's house to live with them.

1818

April 24: Eliza Johnson Pope, LCA's sister, dies in Kentucky.

Oct. 28: AA dies at the Old House in Quincy.

1819

Feb. 22: JQA signs the Adams-Onís Treaty with Spain.

Aug. 27: JA2 enters Harvard.

Dec. 14: LCA holds the first of her popular Tuesday evening "sociables."
Dec. 20: Cabinet meets to resolve so-called "etiquette war."

1820

March 20: Congress enacts the Missouri Compromise.
April 18: LCA and JQA purchase a house at 244 F Street (now 1333–1335 F Street, NW) in Washington.
Aug. 29: GWA graduates from Harvard.
September: LCA expands F Street house.
Sept. 28: CFA enrolls at Harvard.
October: JQA forbids JA2 and CFA from traveling to Washington for Christmas.

1822

June 20: LCA takes her brother Thomas Baker Johnson to Philadelphia for medical treatment.
Oct. 11: LCA returns to Washington from Philadelphia.

1823

May 2: JA2 is expelled from Harvard.
Aug 11: JQA acquires Columbian Mills.

1824

Jan. 8: LCA and JQA host a ball for Andrew Jackson on the ninth anniversary of the Battle of New Orleans.
Aug. 15: Marquis de Lafayette arrives in New York, beginning a thirteen-month journey through all twenty-four states.
Dec. 1: Electoral College meets, but with no candidate securing a majority, election is moved to the House.

1825

Feb. 9: JQA is elected president by the House of Representatives on the first ballot; he receives 13 votes, Jackson 7, and Crawford 4.
March 4: JQA is inaugurated. He appoints JA2 as his private secretary. LCA is ill and does not attend the morning inauguration or the evening inaugural ball.
July 23: LCA begins writing "Record of a Life."

1826

July 4: John Adams, LCA's beloved "old gentleman," dies in Quincy. Thomas Jefferson dies at Monticello on the same day.

1827

February: The *Saturday Evening Post* publishes an anonymously
written ten-thousand-word biography of LCA. The piece, which may
have been written by LCA herself, was meant to reestablish her family's
reputation in the face of attacks by opponents of JQA's reelection.

1828

Feb. 28: JA2 marries Mary Catherine Hellen, LCA's niece, in the White
House. All three Adams sons had been suitors of Mary Hellen at one
time or another.
Dec. 3: Andrew Jackson is elected President with 178 electoral votes to
JQA's 83, and 52 percent of the popular vote.

1829

Feb. 26–March 3: Adamses move out of the White House to a house on
Meridian Hill outside the capital. "You have no conception of how
happily we live here," LCA wrote GWA.
April 30: GWA, on his way to Washington, disappears from the deck of
a steamship on the Long Island Sound, a presumed suicide.
May 13: The Adamses learn of GWA's illegitimate child the previous
year by Eliza Dolph, a chambermaid in Thomas Welsh's house.
Sept. 3: CFA marries the well-to-do Abigail Brooks in Medford,
Massachusetts. LCA too ill to attend ceremony.

1830

Nov. 1: JQA elected to the U.S. House of Representatives, where he
serves until his death eighteen years later.

1834

Oct. 23: JA2 dies in Washington from ailments apparently brought on
by alcoholism. His widow will live with her in-laws for the rest of their
lives.

1836

June 27: LCA begins memoir of her St. Petersburg–Paris trip,
"Narrative of a Journey."

1840

July 1: LCA begins her autobiographical work "Adventures of a
Nobody."

1847

July 26: LCA and JQA celebrate their fiftieth wedding anniversary.

1848

Feb. 21; JQA collapses on the floor of the House and dies at the Capitol two days later.

1849

April 11: LCA suffers a stroke.

1852

May 15: LCA dies at her F Street home in Washington.
May 18: Congress adjourns for LCA's funeral.

NOTES

The abbreviation APM has been used throughout the notes for *Adams Papers, 1639–1889*, microfilm edition, 608 reels (Boston: Massachusetts Historical Society, 1954–1959). In some cases, punctuation and spelling have been changed from the originals for the sake of clarity. Words underlined in the originals are rendered in italics.

INTRODUCTION

Epigraph. Henry Adams, *The Education of Henry Adams, A Centennial Version*, ed. Edward Chalfant and Conrad Edick Wright (Boston: Massachusetts Historical Society, 2007), 15. Henry Adams was particularly drawn to Louisa, even fancying himself as part-southern because of her Maryland roots. See Garry Wills, *Henry Adams and the Making of America* (Boston: Houghton Mifflin, 2005), 11–32.

1. L. H. Butterfield, the longtime editor-in-chief of *The Adams Papers*, wrote: "Her story should have been told long ago, and from her own point of view, not from that of the formidable Adams men who surrounded her." L. H. Butterfield, "Tending a Dragon-Killer: Notes for the Biographer of Mrs. John Quincy Adams," *Proceedings of the American Philosophical Society* 118, no. 2 (1974): 165–178. Louisa does play a central and sympathetic role in Paul C. Nagel's *Adams Women* (New York: Oxford University Press, 1987), *Descent from Glory* (New York: Oxford University Press, 1983), and *John Quincy Adams: A Public Life, A Private Life* (New York: Oxford University Press, 1997). She is also the heroine of Jack Shepherd's *Cannibals of the Heart: A Personal Biography of Louisa Catherine and John Quincy Adams* (New York: McGraw-Hill, 1980), and is favorably viewed in Marie B. Hecht's *John Quincy Adams: A Personal History of an Independent Man* (New York: Macmillan, 1972).

2. Jon Meacham, *American Lion: Andrew Jackson in the White House* (New York: Random House, 2008), xv; "Mrs. John Quincy Adams's Ball, 1824," *Harper's Bazaar*, March 18, 1871: 166, http://hearth.library.cornell.edu/cgi/t/text/text-idx?c=hearth;i dno=4732809_1425_012.

3. "Narrative of a Journey from Russia to France," in *Diary and Autobiographical Writings of Louisa Catherine Adams*, ed. Judith S. Graham and others (Cambridge, MA: Belknap Press of Harvard University Press, 2012), 1:373.
4. "Narrative," 2:706.
5. Sarah M. Grimké to LCA, February 25 and March 27, 1838, APM Reel 506; April 13, and November 8, 1838, APM Reel 510; "Narrative," 2:706; *Memoirs of John Quincy Adams, Comprising Portions of His Diary from 1795 to 1848*, ed. Charles Francis Adams (Philadelphia, 1874) [Book digitized by Google from the library of the University of Michigan], 4:388.
6. JA to John Taylor, April 13, 1824, APM Reel 124.
7. Catherine Allgor, *Parlor Politics: In Which the Ladies of Washington Help Build a City and a Government* (Charlottesville: University Press of Virginia, 2000), 189; LCA to CFA, September 3, 1850, APM Reel 540.
8. Joan Challinor says, however, that these works are "exceptional in mid-nineteenth-century women's literature for their emotional nakedness and intensity." Joan R. Challinor, "The Mis-Education of Louisa Catherine Johnson," *Proceedings of the Massachusetts Historical Society* 95 (1986): 22. Katherine Corbett finds that "her memoirs, journals, and letters are filled with incisive, witty, and frequently sarcastic descriptions of Washington politics and political figures." Katherine T. Corbett, "Louisa Catherine Adams: The Anguished 'Adventures of a Nobody,'" in *Woman's Being, Woman's Place: Female Identity and Vocation in American History*, ed. Mary Kelley (Boston: G. K. Hall, 1979), 76.
9. Wills, *Making of America*, 16.

CHAPTER 1. HALCYON DAYS

1. "Record of a Life," in *Diary and Autobiographical Writings of Louisa Catherine Adams*, ed. Judith S. Graham and others (Cambridge, MA: Belknap Press of Harvard University Press, 2012), 1:7–8.
2. JJ to the firm, June 4, 1771, in *Joshua Johnson's Letterbook 1771–1774: Letters from a Merchant in London to His Partners in Maryland*, ed. Jacob M. Price (London: London Record Society, 1979), British History Online, http://www.british-history.ac.uk/report.aspx?compid=38787&strquery=joshua%20johnson.
3. Jacob M. Price, "Joshua Johnson in London, 1771–1775: Credit and Commercial Organization in the British Chesapeake Trade," in *Statesmen, Scholars, and Merchants: Essays in Eighteenth-Century History Presented to Dame Lucy Sutherland*, ed. Anne Whiteman, J. S. Bromley, and P. G. M. Dickson (Oxford: Clarendon Press, 1973), 158.
4. Edward C. Papenfuse, *In Pursuit of Profit: The Annapolis Merchants in the Era of the American Revolution, 1763–1805* (Baltimore: Johns Hopkins University Press, 1975), 57, 158; JJ to the firm, July 26 and November 6, 1771, in Price, *Letterbook*.
5. Papenfuse, *Profit*, 66.
6. JJ to John Davidson, September 4, 1793; JJ to the firm, November 29, 1793, in Price, *Letterbook*.

7. Lawrence Stone, *Family, Sex and Marriage in England 1500–1800* (New York: Harper & Row, 1977), 4. In 1753, the passage of Lord Hardwicke's Marriage Act meant that, as of the following year, only a church wedding was legally binding, all marriages had to be entered in the parish register and signed by both parties, and no marriage of persons under the age of twenty-one was valid without the consent of a parent or guardian. Banns concerning the forthcoming marriage had to be announced in the bride's home parish for three weeks preceding the ceremony (although so-called special licenses were available to the wealthy). Enforcement of the act was entrusted to secular courts, and there existed no legal alternative to a church wedding except to run away to Scotland — often to the notorious Gretna Green — where a wedding could take place without all the restrictions that applied in England. See Stone, 35ff; Joan R. Challinor, in "Louisa Catherine Johnson Adams: The Price of Ambition," Ph.D. dissertation, American University, 1982, 17, also 30n34, citing baptismal record, St. Botolph without Aldgate. (The name of the church stems from its ancient location outside the eastern-most gateway to the City of London wall.)

8. Challinor credits Francis James Dallett, a Fellow with the American Society of Genealogists (FASG), with discovering this information. Challinor was the first to publish the evidence. Joan R. Challinor, "Mis-Education of Louisa Catherine Johnson," *Proceedings of the Massachusetts Historical Society* 95 (1986), 24. The author has seen a copy of the marriage register, which reads:

> Joshua Johnson and Catherine Newth, both of this Parish were Married
> in this Church by Banns the 22nd day of August 1785
> By me, John Jefferson, Curate
> This Marriage was solemnized between Us /s/Joshua Johnson
> /s/Catherine Newth
> In the Presence of Us: /s/Elizabeth Hewlett /s/Jos. Palmer

The groom's distinctive signature is so clear that there can be little doubt it is that of Louisa's father. Marriage Register, St. Anne Soho, City of Westminster Archives Center.

9. "LCA Record," 1:6.

10. Ibid., 1:19–20. The casual reference here to *Hamlet*, act 1, scene II, demonstrates Louisa's easy familiarity with Shakespeare: "Must I remember? why, she would hang on him, / As if increase of appetite had grown / By what it fed on."

11. "The Adventures of a Nobody," in *Diary and Autobiographical Writings of Louisa Catherine Adams*, ed. Judith S. Graham and others (Cambridge, MA: Belknap Press of Harvard University Press, 2012), 1:177.

12. "LCA Record," 1:7.

13. Stone, *Family, Sex, and Marriage*, 359; AA to CJ, November [n.d.], 1809, APM Reel 408.

14. JA to JQA, December 10, 1811, APM Reel 412; Michael O'Brien has no hesitation in linking Catherine with prostitution: "It was a cold fact that her [Louisa's] mother . . . had once been the fondling sort." Michael O'Brien, *Mrs. Adams in Winter: A Journey in the Last Days of Napoleon* (New York: Farrar, Straus and Giroux, 2010), 76.

15. Challinor, "Mis-Education," 24; "LCA Record," 1:3.
16. LCA, undated note, APM Reel 603.
17. Challinor, *Price of Ambition*, 37.
18. Louisa's name was hyphenated on her baptismal record: "Louisa-Catharine Johnson, Dau of Joshua & Catharine . . . Swan Street," March 9, 1775. Baptismal Record Book, St. Botolph without Aldgate, Guildhall Library, London.
19. Papenfuse, *Profit*, 19, 73.
20. JJ to the firm, August 4, 1774, in Price, *Letterbook*; JJ to James Gibbs, March 22, 1775, cited in Challinor, *Price of Ambition*, 39.
21. Samuel F. Bemis, "British Secret Service and the French-American Alliance," *American Historical Review* 29, no. 3 (1924), 474–495; Challinor, *Price of Ambition*, 39; "LCA Record," 1:22.
22. Bemis, "British Secret Service," 490.
23. Challinor, *Price of Ambition*, 47.
24. JJ to the firm, July 20, 1791, *Wallace, Johnson, & Muir Letterbook, 1781–1783* (Maryland State Archives microfilm; original in Manuscript Division, New York Public Library, New York).
25. John Adams diary [electronic edition]. *Adams Family Papers: An Electronic Archive.* Massachusetts Historical Society. http://www.masshist.org/digitaladams, April 28, 14, 1779.
26. *Diary and Autobiography of John Adams*, ed. L. H. Butterfield (Cambridge, MA: Belknap Press of Harvard University Press, 1961), 2:359n3.
27. LCA, journal fragment meant for Abigail Brooks Adams, March 2, 1834, APM Reel 499; John McMasters, *Church and Society in Eighteenth-Century France*, volume 1: *The Clerical Establishment and Its Social Ramifications* (New York: Oxford University Press, 1998), 537.
28. Fawn M. Brodie, *Thomas Jefferson: An Intimate History* (New York: W. W. Norton, 1974), 187; McManners, *Church and Society*, 540.
29. "LCA Record," 1:4.
30. Ibid., 1:21, 1:5; Challinor, *Price of Ambition*, 55.
31. "LCA Record," 1:6. Hackney, now a borough of the City of London, was known for its many girls' schools. A century before Louisa arrived at Mrs. Carter's school, Samuel Pepys wrote of his August 25, 1667, visit to the local parish church: "And so I up to Putney, and there stepped into the church, to look upon the fine people there, whereof there is great store, and the young ladies." http://www.gutenberg.org/files/4184/ 4184-h/4184-h.htm#2H_4_0094.
32. Clara Reeve wrote of opening a seminary for female education, and such an establishment was "opened at Tottenham, Middlesex, by Mrs. M. Criven in the year 1788." Shirley Nelson Kersey, ed., "The Plan of a Seminary of Female Education," in *Classics in the Education of Girls and Women* (Metuchen, NJ: Scarecrow Press, 1981), 182. Also the writer and philosopher Mary Wollstonecraft, in *Thoughts on the Education of Daughters*, written just four years after Louisa entered Mrs. Carter's school, emphasized the academic deficiencies of such establishments: "Manners are too much

attended to . . . the same lessons are taught to all, and some get a smattering of things they have not the capacity ever to understand; few things are learnt thoroughly, but many follies contracted, and an immoderate fondness for dress among the rest." Mary Wollstonecraft, "Thoughts on the Education of Daughters," in Kersey, *Education of Girls and Women*, 168.

33. Claire Tomalin, *Jane Austen: A Life* (New York: Knopf, 1997), 33; Jane Austen, *Emma*, ed. R. W. Chapman (London: Oxford University Press, 1933), 21–22.

34. "LCA Record," 1:10.

35. Ibid., 1:6.

36. Ibid., 1:6.

37. Ibid., 1:13.

38. Ibid., 1:7.

39. According to the *Dictionary of Daily Wants* (1859), "A brain fever is an inflammation of the brain, or a fever (like typhus) attended by brain complications" to be treated by "blood-letting, purgatives, and cold applications to the head. . . . If the pulse is hard, a blister may be put on the head; but the great art lies in the judicious application of stimulants, such as ether, ammonia, valerian, beef-tea, wine, and opiates." From "Discovering Dickens: A Community Reading Project," http://dickens.stanford.edu/dickens/archive/tale/issue4_gloss.html.

40. Tomalin, *Jane Austen*, 36–37.

41. "LCA Record," 1:11–12.

42. Ibid., 1:12.

43. James Mayer Holzman, in his doctoral dissertation, "The Nabobs in England: A Study of the Returned Anglo-Indian, 1760–1785," Ph.D. dissertation, Columbia University, 1926. provides a list of so-called Nabobs that does not include the name Edwards. Holzman (p. 83) does cite an advertisement by a "Gentlewoman" for someone to care for two or three "little Strangers" sent home from India, an indication that at least some Anglo-Indian children may have been brought up and educated in England while their parents remained in India.

44. "LCA Record," 1:11.

45. "LCA Record," 1:10–11, 15, 12.

46. "LCA Record," 1:13, 20.

CHAPTER 2. READY FOR LOVE

1. "Record of a Life," in *Diary and Autobiographical Writings of Louisa Catherine Adams*, ed. Judith S. Graham and others (Cambridge, MA: Belknap Press of Harvard University Press, 2012), 1:8 and 1:16; Number 8, Cooper's Row, in 2009, had been replaced by a luxury hotel. Neighboring residential buildings, however, provided a clear indication of what the Johnson mansion must have looked like.

2. W. E. Lunt, *History of England*, 4th edition (New York: Harper & Brothers, 1956), 609; "He makes a monstrous deal of money, and they keep their own coach," Jane Austen, *Sense and Sensibility* (London: Oxford University Press, 1951), 275.

3. Amanda Vickery, *The Gentleman's Daughter: Women's Lives in Georgian England* (New Haven, CT: Yale University Press, 1998), 134; "LCA Record," 1:28.

4. Andrew Oliver, ed., *Portraits of John Quincy Adams and His Wife* (Cambridge, MA: Belknap Press of Harvard University, 1970), 24–26; AA to JQA, May 20, 1796, APM Reel 381.

5. "LCA Record," 1:35.

6. Edward C. Papenfuse, *In Pursuit of Profit: The Annapolis Merchants in the Era of the American Revolution, 1763–1805* (Baltimore: Johns Hopkins University Press, 1975), 75.

7. *The Papers of Thomas Jefferson*, ed. Julian P. Boyd (Princeton: Princeton University Press, 1982), ed. note, 20:486; Papenfuse, *In Pursuit of Profit*, 190.

8. Papenfuse, *In Pursuit of Profit*, 204. Joshua was not the only overextended London merchant in the late eighteenth century. "Bankruptcy was too much a part of economic normalcy in London . . . to be regarded as irrefutable proof of a trader's incompetence or improper dealings," writes Linda Colley in *The Ordeal of Elizabeth Marsh: A Woman in World History* (New York: Pantheon Books, 2007), 120. As Colley explains, "Only when the commissioners of bankruptcy were satisfied with a bankrupt's cooperation, and four-fifths of his creditors 'in number and value' had agreed to sign a special certificate, was he able securely to retain a percentage of assets, and win release from any remaining obligations and from the fear of being sued or arrested." This is apparently the action Johnson took with his thirteen major creditors.

9. JQA to LCA, December 20, 1796, APM Reel 382.

10. Boyd, *The Papers of Thomas Jefferson*, ed. note, 16:521–523.

11. Ibid., ed. note, 17:249.

12. "A circular to the Consuls and Vice Consuls of the United States," in Boyd, *The Papers of Thomas Jefferson*, 17:424, August 26, 1790.

13. Thomas Jefferson to JJ, August 7, 1790 in Boyd, *The Papers of Thomas Jefferson*, 17:119.

14. "LCA Record," 1:22.

15. JJ to Thomas Jefferson, November 2, 1790, in Boyd, *The Papers of Thomas Jefferson*, 17:667; "Johnson accepted the post and performed useful intelligence services, doing so in the same manner that William Eden employed, that is, by the use of secret service funds." Ibid., ed. note, 16:523.

16. "LCA Record," 1:23.

17. Boyd, *The Papers of Thomas Jefferson*, ed. note, 20:488.

18. "LCA Record," 1:35.

19. JJ to Thomas Jefferson, February 26, 1791; Thomas Jefferson to American Consuls, March 21, 1793, in Boyd, *The Papers of Thomas Jefferson*, 20:482.

20. Thomas Jefferson to Thomas Pinckney, June 11, 1792, in *Memoir, Correspondence, and Miscellanies from the Papers of Thomas Jefferson*, Vols. 3–4, ed. Thomas Jefferson Randolph (Charlottesville, VA: F. Carr & Co., 1829) [book digitized by Google], 178. In 1790, Gouverneur Morris was sent on an informal mission to the British Foreign Office as the personal agent of President Washington, and, as such, would have had entrée to government ministers in positions of power but would not have been credentialed as an

official representative of the United States. John Adams had served from February 24 to June 1, 1785, as minister plenipotentiary simultaneously to the court of Great Britain and to the Netherlands under the American government established by the Articles of Confederation. Pinckney was the first minister plenipotentiary to serve the nation after the adoption of the Constitution.

21. "LCA Record," 1:29, 1:31.
22. Ibid., 1:32.
23. Ibid., 1:36.
24. Ibid., 1:22.
25. Ibid., 1:19.
26. Ibid., 1:16.
27. Ibid., 1:16, 1:19, 1:34, 1:36.
28. Jane Austen, *Pride and Prejudice* (London: Oxford University Press, 1959), 122.
29. "LCA Record," 1:26, 1:36.
30. Ibid., 1:33. Savage, an American painter, was working in London between 1791 and 1794.
31. Ibid., 1:19, 1:24. Edmund Jenings (1731–1819), a wealthy Maryland native, practiced law in London. Jenings was an early patron of the American painter Charles Willson Peale and well acquainted with John Adams during the latter's diplomatic service in Paris, the Netherlands, and London and with Joshua Johnson. Following the American Revolution, Jenings was suspected of having been an agent for the British during the war. He would have been in his fifties when Louisa was a teenager. See also *Papers of John Adams*, ed. Gregg L. Lint and others (Cambridge, MA: Belknap Press of Harvard University Press, 2004), 12:x–xi. Jenings had been acquainted with Joshua Johnson since the latter's arrival in London. *Joshua Johnson's Letterbook 1771–1774: Letters from a merchant in London to his partners in Maryland*, ed. Jacob M. Price (London: London Record Society, 1979), British History Online, http://www.british-history.ac.uk/report.aspx?compid=38787&strquery=joshua%20johnson, 3.
32. "LCA Record," 1:33.
33. Ibid., 1:24.
34. Notably by Jane Austen in her early works, which were brilliant, unrestrained parodies of the novels of the day. To mock them as well as she did, however, it is clear that Austen herself was familiar with both the style and substance of the sentimental novel. Like Louisa, although she was probably rueful that she read them, she clearly did.
35. LCA, Journal Fragment meant for Abigail Brooks Adams, March 2, 1834, APM Reel 499.
36. "LCA Record," 1:16.
37. Amanda Vickery, *The Gentleman's Daughter: Women's Lives in Georgian England*, (New Haven, CT: Yale University Press, 1998), 160: "A house well regulated was a subtly burnished badge of decent gentility."
38. "LCA Record," 1:12, 1:22.
39. *The Diaries of John Quincy Adams: A Digital Collection* (Boston: Massachusetts Historical Society, 2005), http://www.masshist.org/jqadiaries, November 11, 1795.

CHAPTER 3. DESTINED FOR GREATNESS

1. "Record of a Life," in *Diary and Autobiographical Writings of Louisa Catherine Adams*, ed. Judith S. Graham and others (Cambridge, MA: Belknap Press of Harvard University Press, 2012), 1:37.
2. Richard Alan Ryerson, "'Like a Hare Before the Hunter': John Adams and the Idea of a Republican Monarchy," *Proceedings of the Massachusetts Historical Society*, 1996, 17.
3. *The Diaries of John Quincy Adams: A Digital Collection* (Boston: Massachusetts Historical Society, 2005), http://www.masshist.org/jqadiaries, November 24, 1795.
4. *JQA Diary*, August 10, 1795 [electronic edition].
5. AA to Martha Washington, June–July 1794, APM Reel 377.
6. Rosemary Keller, *Patriotism and the Female Sex: Abigail Adams and the American Revolution* (Brooklyn, NY: Carlson Publishing, 1994), 124; Locke was not alone in his views. The conservative Edmund Burke, writing about the "natural aristocracy," described very much the same goal in "Appeal from the New to the Old Whigs," http://oll.libertyfund.org/title/660/106858.
7. JA to AA, June 30, 1774, in *Adams Family Correspondence*, ed. Lyman H. Butterfield and others (Cambridge, MA: Belknap Press of Harvard University Press, 1963), 1:117; *Diary of John Quincy Adams, 1779–1786*, ed. David Grayson Allen et al. (Cambridge, MA: Belknap Press of Harvard University Press, 1981), 1:xxxv.
8. AA to JA, September 16, 1774, *AFC*, 1:153.
9. JA to JQA, August 11, 1777, *AFC*, 2:307.
10. JA to AA, September 9, 1778, *AFC*, 3:88.
11. AA to JQA, June 10, 1778, *AFC*, 3:37.
12. AA to John Thaxter, February 15, 1778, *AFC*, 2:390.
13. JA to AA, May 14, 1779, *AFC*, 3:195.
14. JA to AA June 14, 1779, *AFC*, 3:205.
15. AA to JQA, Jan. 19, 1780, *AFC*, 3:268.
16. "Why is it that I hear so seldom from my dear John; but one letter have I ever received from him since he arrived in Petersburgh." AA to JA, December 23, 1782, *AFC*, 5:54; "I have no news of my son since 8th December, when he was at Stockholm but hope every hour to hear of his arrival in the Hague," JA to AA, January 22, 1783, *AFC*, 5:74; "My dear John, my heart aches when I think how seldom I hear from him; pray direct him to write to me, he is either very negligent or I very unfortunate," AA to JA, January 10, 1783, *AFC*, 5:66.
17. AA to Charles Adams, January 19, 1780, *AFC*, 3:270; JA to AA, April–May, 1780, *AFC*, 3:332.
18. David McCullough, *John Adams* (New York: Simon & Schuster, 2001), 285.
19. AA to JQA, May 26, 1781, *AFC*, 4:36; JA to JQA, May 14, 1781, *AFC*, 4:114; JA to JQA December 28, 1780, *AFC*, 4:56.
20. Richard L. Bushman, *The Refinement of America: Persons, Houses, Cities* (New York: Knopf, 1992), 217.

21. JA to JQA, *AFC*, 4:366; "People who knew [Harvard] did not call it that." Bernard Bailyn, Donald Fleming, Oscar Handlin, Stephan Thernstrom, *Glimpses of the Harvard Past* (Cambridge, MA: Harvard University Press, 1986), 10. The authors also note (p. 11) that Harvard was supported by the state for more than two hundred years and was created as a public institution even though it was governed by a private corporation.

22. *JQA Diary*, 1:151n.

23. Ibid., 1:168.

24. JQA to AA, October 1, 1815, APM Reel 427.

25. JA to Thomas Jefferson, January 24, 1825, APM Reel 467.

26. *JQA Diary*, 1:256.

27. Ibid., 1:398.

28. Ibid., 1:351.

29. Ibid., 1:387.

30. The "Yard" included Massachusetts Hall, Harvard Hall, Holden Chapel, and Hollis Hall. (The original Stoughton Hall, seen in many early prints of Harvard buildings, had been demolished in 1781.)

31. *JQA Diary*, 2:35, 2:47, 2:52, 2:157.

32. Ibid., 2:243.

33. Ibid., 2:266n, 2:253.

34. JQA to AA, *AFC*, 8:214.

35. *JQA Diary*, 2:317.

36. Ibid., 2:345.

37. Elizabeth Smith Shaw to AA, *AFC*, 8:296–297; Abigail Adams Smith to JQA, February 1788, *AFC*, 8:229.

38. Elizabeth Smith Shaw to AA, *AFC*, 8:301; Elizabeth Smith Shaw to Mary Smith Cranch, *AFC*, 8:309.

39. *JQA Diary*, 2:434; JQA to JA, June 28, 1789, *AFC*, 8:380.

40. Paul C. Nagel, *John Quincy Adams: A Public Life, A Private Life* (Cambridge, MA: Harvard University Press, 1997), 65.

41. AA to JQA, *AFC*, 9:142; Nagel, *John Quincy Adams*, 67.

42. *JQA Diary*, April 2, 1794 [electronic edition].

43. JA to JQA, April 23, May 30, 1794, APM Reel 377.

44. George Washington to JA, Aug. 20, 1795, *The Writings of George Washington from the Original Manuscript Sources*, ed. John C. Fitzpatrick (Washington, DC, 1931–1944), Electronic Text Center, University of Virginia Library; JA to JQA, December 5, 1796, APM Reel 38.

45. AA to JQA, September 15, 1795, APM Reel 380.

46. *JQA Diary*, December 11, 1795, December 20, 1795 [electronic edition].

47. *The Diary and Letters of Gouverneur Morris*, ed. Anne Cary Morris (New York: DaCapo Press, 1988/1970), 2:138, 157.

48. *Memoirs of John Quincy Adams Comprising Portions of His Diary*, ed. Charles Francis Adams (Philadelphia: J. B. Lippincott, 1874) [Book digitized by Google from the library of the University of Michigan], 1:167.

CHAPTER 4. A FINE ROMANCE

1. "Record of a Life," in *Diary and Autobiographical Writings of Louisa Catherine Adams*, ed. Judith S. Graham and others (Cambridge, MA: Belknap Press of Harvard University Press, 2012), 1:37.
2. "LCA Record," 1:40.
3. *The Diaries of John Quincy Adams: A Digital Collection* (Boston: Massachusetts Historical Society, 2005), http://www.masshist.org/jqadiaries, December 26, 1795; line-a-day entries, February 7, 12, 14, 15, 17, 1796.
4. "LCA Record," 1:40.
5. JQA to LCA, December 5, 1798, APM Reel 382. John Quincy is quoting from Laurence Sterne's *A Sentimental Journey through France and Italy*, written in 1768.
6. "LCA Record," 1:41.
7. Ibid., 1:42.
8. *JQA Diary*, December 31, 1795; January 2, 1796 [electronic edition].
9. Ibid., February 17, 1796 [electronic edition]
10. "LCA Record," 1:40–41.
11. *JQA Diary*, February 1, 1796 [electronic edition].
12. Ibid., March 2, 1796 [electronic edition].
13. Ibid., March 3, 8, 1796 [electronic edition].
14. Ibid., March 19, 1796 [electronic edition].
15. Ibid., April 18, 1796 [electronic edition].
16. Jane Austen, *Persuasion* (London: Oxford University Press, 1951), 231.
17. "LCA Record," 1:43.
18. Paul C. Nagel, *John Quincy Adams: A Public Life, A Private Life* (Cambridge, MA: Harvard University Press, 1997), 70.
19. "LCA Record," 1:42.
20. Ibid., 1:43.
21. Ibid.
22. Ibid.
23. JQA to LCA, June 2, 1796, APM Reel 381; LCA to JQA, July 9, 1796, APM Reel 382.
24. JQA to AA, March 30, 1796, APM Reel 381.
25. AA to JQA, May 20,1796, APM Reel 381.
26. JQA to AA, November 11, 1796, APM Reel 382; JA to JQA, August 7, 1796, APM Reel 382.
27. AA to JQA, August 10, 1796, APM Reel 382.
28. JQA to AA, November 14, 1796, APM Reel 382.
29. JQA to LCA, August 13, 1796; September 12, 1796, APM Reel 382.
30. JQA to LCA, October 18, 1796, APM Reel 382.
31. "LCA Record," 1:47.
32. Ibid., 1:45. Joshua Johnson's letter to John Quincy has not been found among the Adams Papers.
33. JQA to LCA, February 20, 1797, APM Reel 383.
34. JQA to LCA, December 20, 1796, APM Reel 382.

35. Ibid.
36. LCA to JQA, January 17, 1797, APM Reel 383.
37. JQA to LCA, January 28, 1797 APM Reel 383.
38. JQA to LCA, January 10, 1797, APM Reel 383.
39. Ibid.
40. LCA to JQA, January 31, 1797, APM Reel 383.
41. JQA to LCA, February 12, 1797, APM Reel 383.
42. LCA to JQA, November 15, 1796, APM Reel 382; JQA to LCA, March 14, 1797; LCA to JQA, March 9, 1797, APM Reel 383.
43. LCA to JQA, April 21, 1797, APM Reel 384.
44. LCA to JQA, February 17, 1797, APM Reel 383.
45. JQA to LCA, February 20, 1797, APM Reel 383.
46. JQA to AA, November 14, 1796, APM Reel 128; JQA to LCA, March 6, 1797, APM Reel 383.
47. JQA to LCA, April 13, 1797, APM Reel 384.
48. JQA to JJ, June 6, 1797, APM Reel 384.
49. JQA to LCA, May 12, 1797, APM Reel 384.
50. LCA to JQA, May 26, 1797; JQA to LCA, June 6, 1797, APM Reel 384.
51. JQA to JA, June 29, 1797, APM Reel 384.
52. "LCA Record," 1:47.
53. JQA to JA, July 22, 1797, APM Reel 385.
54. JJ to JQA, July 19, 1797, APM Reel 385.
55. A special license was required whenever it was impossible to post banns for the three Sundays preceding a marriage ceremony in the bride's parish church. In this case, there was insufficient time to post banns between John Quincy's arrival in London and the wedding date—exactly the situation special licenses were designed for. Special licenses, however, had become very fashionable by the end of the eighteenth century, and to obtain one from the bishop was a mark of distinction, partly because extra expense was involved. When Mrs. Bennet in *Pride and Prejudice* learns that her daughter Elizabeth has become engaged to the extremely wealthy Mr. Darcy, she greets the news with characteristic priority to appearances. "And a special license. You must and shall be married by a special license." Austen, *Pride and Prejudice*, 378.

CHAPTER 5. AT HOME AND ABROAD

1. The Saxon Abbey of Barking founded the church of All Hallows by the Tower in 675. An arch from the original Saxon church remains. Following their execution on nearby Tower Hill, numerous beheaded bodies were brought into the church, including those of Thomas More and Archbishop William Laud. William Penn, founder of Pennsylvania was baptized at All Hallows and Samuel Pepys viewed the Fire of London from its tower in 1666.
2. The idea of a bride processing down the aisle before a large congregation of guests was offensive to upper-middle-class sensibilities like those of the novelist Fanny Burney, who, twenty years earlier, had been shocked by such a display: "I'm sure I trembled for

the bride. Oh, what a gauntlet for any woman of delicacy to run," she wrote after attending a very public and formal wedding ceremony. Quoted in Aileen Robeiro, *Dress in Eighteenth Century Europe*, (New York: Holmes & Meir Publishers, 1984), 136.

3. "Record of a Life" in *Diary and Autobiographical Writings of Louisa Catherine Adams*, ed. Judith S. Graham and others (Cambridge, MA: Belknap Press of Harvard University Press, 2012), 1:41; Robeiro, *Dress*, 136.

4. *The Diaries of John Quincy Adams: A Digital Collection* (Boston: Massachusetts Historical Society, 2005), http://www.masshist.org/jqadiaries, July 16, 1797. In his diary, JQA referred to Wanstead House as "Tilney House," as it was the seat in 1797 of the noble (and very wealthy) Tynley-Long family. A magnificent example of classical architecture on a large scale, Wanstead House featured seventy elegant rooms, fifty-eight fireplaces, and spacious, elaborately landscaped grounds. On July 27, 1797, the house would probably have been unoccupied since it was technically owned by a very young sister and brother who, due to the death of their father, the Earl, were Wards in Chancery. Peter Lawrence, "The Rise and Fall of Wanstead House in Essex, 1667–1857," www.wansteadpark.org.uk.

5. "LCA Record," 1:50; Lawrence Stone, *Family, Sex and Marriage in England, 1500–1800* (New York: Harper & Row, 1977), 335–336.

6. *JQA Diary*, August 20, July 30, 1797 [electronic edition].

7. JQA and LCA to JA and AA, July 28, 1797, APM Reel 385.

8. JQA to Charles Adams, August 1. 1797, APM Reel 130. JQA is referring here to his sister Nabby and to Charles's wife Sally Smith Adams; JQA to CA, August 1, 1797; JQA to Daniel Sargent, August 7, 1797, APM Reel 130; Thomas Boylston Adams to AA, August 17, 1797. APM Reel 385.

9. *JQA Diary*, August 19, 1797 [electronic edition].

10. Samuel F. Bemis, *John Quincy Adams and the Foundation of American Foreign Policy* (New York: W. W. Norton, 1949), 81. According to a law passed in the First Congress of 1790 (Session II, Chapter III, "An Act to establish a uniform Rule of Naturalization"), "The children of citizens of the United States that may be born beyond the sea or outside the limits of the United States may be considered as natural born citizens." Clearly, the daughter of the U.S. consul in London would qualify. See *A Century of Lawmaking for a New Nation—U.S. Congressional Documents and Debates 1774–1875*, Library of Congress, accessed at www.loc.gov.

11. In 2013, the purchasing power of £500 in 1797 would have been £42,350. Lawrence H. Officer, "Purchasing Power of the British Pounds from 1264 to 2007," Institute for the Measurement of Worth, www.measuringworth.com.

12. *JQA Diary*, August 25, 1797 [electronic edition]; "LCA Record," 1:52.

13. "LCA Record," 1:52.

14. *JQA Diary*, October 9, 1797 [electronic edition].

15. "LCA Record," 1:52.

16. "The Adventures of a Nobody," in *Diary and Autobiographical Writings of Louisa Catherine Adams*, ed. Judith S. Graham and others (Cambridge, MA: Belknap Press of Harvard University Press, 2012), 1:81.

17. Ibid., 1:77, 1:198, 1:227.
18. Ibid., 1:76. The poverty to which Louisa alludes resulted from Johnson's failure to obtain any satisfaction from his former mercantile partners. He was saved from total destitution by an appointment as superintendent of stamps by President John Adams.
19. Ibid., 1:51.
20. Frederick Delius to JQA, September 29, October 9, 1797, APM Reel 385; JQA to JJ October 11, 1797, APM Reel 386. "How Johnson got into such straitened circumstances is not clear, although Dr. Rhoda Dorsey, familiar with Johnson through his correspondence as consul in London in the 1790s, feels it was probably owing to his obtuseness when it came to speculating in matters of trade." Edward C. Papenfuse, *In Pursuit of Profit: The Annapolis Merchants in the Era of the American Revolution, 1763–1805* (Baltimore: Johns Hopkins University Press, 1975), 228n11.
21. "LCA Adventures," 1:86, 1:89.
22. Papenfuse, *Profit*, 228n11.
23. "LCA Adventures," 1:99.
24. JQA to JA, July 22, 1797, APM Reel 385.
25. JQA to JA, December 16, 1797, APM Reel 386.
26. Ibid.
27. JQA had attempted to secure a similar treaty with Sweden but was unsuccessful. Bemis, *Foundations*, 94–95.
28. Bemis, *Foundations*, 91. Also, Gerard H. Clarfield, "Pickering and Adams," in *Timothy Pickering and the American Republic* (Pittsburgh: University of Pittsburgh Press, 1980), 180–196.
29. "LCA Adventures," 1:66.
30. "LCA Record," 1:53.
31. Ibid., 1:53.
32. "LCA Adventures," 1:66.
33. Ibid., 1:67; JQA to CJ, February 7, 1798, APM Reel 387.
34. Gerhard Masur, *Imperial Berlin* (New York: Basic Books, 1970), 20–22.
35. *JQA Diary*, November 12, 1797 [electronic edition].
36. Ibid., November 17, 1797 [electronic edition]. Dr. Brown, who, like his wife, grew up in Wales, received his medical diploma from Aberdeen University in 1771 and studied in Newcastle, London, and Paris. Anthony Cross, *By the Banks of the Neva: Chapters from the Lives and Careers of the British in Eighteenth Century Russia* (Cambridge: Cambridge University Press, 1997).
37. JQA to CJ, February 7, 1798, APM Reel 387; "LCA Record," 1:55.
38. JQA to AA, February 5, 1798, APM Reel 130.
39. "LCA Adventures," 1:67–69.
40. Ibid., 1:69.
41. "LCA Record," 1:59.
42. "Elisabeth Louise Vigee Le Brun 1755–1842 — Portraits of Louise Augusta, Queen of Prussia." Reproduced from a 1992 Christies, London, catalog at www.batguano.com/xqueenofprussia.html.
43. "LCA Adventures," 1:71.

44. Ibid., 1:74.
45. Ibid., 1:79.
46. Ibid., 1:79, 1:82.
47. Ibid., 1:81.
48. "LCA Record," 1:60; "LCA Adventures," 1:78.
49. "LCA Adventures," 1:69; Thomas Boylston Adams, *Berlin and the Prussian Court in 1798*, ed. Victor H. Palsits (New York: New York Public Library, 1916), 17, http://openlibrary.org/books/OL13523359M/Berlin_and_the_Prussian_court_in_1798.
50. "LCA Adventures," 1:89.
51. Ibid., 1:93.
52. *JQA Diary*, July 26, 1798 [electronic edition].
53. "LCA Adventures," 1:61.

CHAPTER 6. IN SICKNESS AND IN HEALTH

1. "The Adventures of a Nobody," in *Diary and Autobiographical Writings of Louisa Catherine Adams*, ed. Judith S. Graham and others (Cambridge, MA: Belknap Press of Harvard University Press, 2012), 1:87.
2. "LCA Adventures," 1:95; John Adams's view: "I was never fond of Parade, Ceremony, Pomposity and Finery. . . . I always despised and detested them. . . . The World demanded them of me, but I always loathed them." JA to Thomas Boylston Adams, January 28, 1803, APM Reel 402.
3. LCA, "Death in the Dance," undated, after 1800, APM Reel 399.
4. *The Diaries of John Quincy Adams: A Digital Collection* (Boston: Massachusetts Historical Society, 2005), http://www.masshist.org/jqadiaries, February 11, 1801; "LCA Adventures," 1:147.
5. "LCA Adventures," 1:113, 73. Comte de Mirabeau (1749–1791) in 1789 published *The Secret History of the Court of Berlin*, in which he denounced the court during the last days of Frederick the Great as scandalous and corrupt. Mirabeau was savage in his portrayals of several well-known courtiers and officials.
6. "LCA Adventures," 1:73, 1:101, 1:98.
7. Ibid., 1:128, 1:140, 1:108.
8. Ibid., 1:89.
9. Ibid., 1:88, 1:89.
10. AA to CJ, June 9, 1798, APM Reel 389; "LCA Adventures," 1:96.
11. "LCA Adventures," 1:106.
12. Rouge was generally frowned upon in America. "Famous for their sophistication, the women of New Orleans were almost the only ones in America to wear makeup." Daniel Walker Howe, *What Hath God Wrought: The Transformation of America, 1815–1848* (New York: Oxford University Press, 2007), 10.
13. "LCA Adventures," 1:103, 1:104, 1:131, 1:144.
14. Ibid., 1:134.
15. Ibid., 1:85, 1:99.
16. Ibid., 1:104.

17. Samuel F. Bemis, *John Quincy Adams and the Foundation of American Foreign Policy* (New York: W. W. Norton, 1949), 90.
18. "Louisa Catherine Adams," in *The National Portrait Gallery of Distinguished Americans*, ed. James Herring and James Barton Longacre (New York: H. Perkins, 1839) [Digitized by Google Books from the Harvard University Library], 4:3. The chapter on Louisa was written by Charles Francis Adams (though not so noted in the edition), and both Louisa and John Quincy reviewed his drafts. "As to the biography it is only too good and I am perfectly satisfied with it having no wish for notoriety." LCA to CFA, March 29, 1838, APM Reel 509.
19. AA to JQA, December 2, 1798, APM Reel 392; "LCA Adventures," 1:84.
20. *JQA Diary*, January 8, 1800, December 16, 1799 [electronic edition].
21. LCA to Nancy Johnson Hellen, September 27, 1798, APM Reel 391.
22. Twenty years later, Louisa reported to John Quincy that she weighed 102 pounds. "Thus I have learnt how small a space I fill in the scale of human beings. Never mind. Little folks have been the greatest since years back; so I won't droop on this occasion." LCA to JQA, September 19, 1822, from Bordentown, NJ, to Washington, APM Reel 456.
23. "LCA Adventures," 1:113.
24. Ibid., 1:68. There is some question whether or not this was a false alarm, a miscarriage, or the beginning of Louisa's second pregnancy. John Quincy's diaries are so anguished during this period in regard to his wife's health that it is difficult to separate pregnancies from severe menstrual periods and other painful conditions.
25. Ibid., 1:84.
26. *JQA Diary*, July 14, 17, 1798 [electronic edition].
27. Thomas Boylston Adams, *Berlin and the Prussian Court in 1798*, ed. Victor H. Palsits (New York: New York Public Library, 1916), July 17, 1798 [http://openlibrary.org/books/OL13523359M/Berlin_and_the_Prussian_court_in_1798], 21; *JQA Diary*, July 18, 1798 [electronic edition].
28. *JQA Diary*, July 23, 1798 [electronic edition].
29. "LCA Adventures," 1:112.
30. Ibid., 1:110.
31. Ibid., 1:113.
32. J. Murray, ed. *A Hand-book for Travellers in Southern Germany: Being a Guide to Bavaria, Austria, Tyrol, Salzburg, and the Austrian and Bavarian Alps* (London, 1844), 382. [Digitized by Google Books from the original in the New York Public Library].
33. "LCA Adventures," 1:115.
34. Ibid., 1:116.
35. Ibid., 1:116, 1:117, 1:118, 1:120.
36. Ibid., 1:122, 1:124.
37. Ibid., 1:130. Oscar Recio Morales, "When Merit Is Not Enough: Money as a 'Parallel Route' for Irish Military Advancement in Spain," in *Irish Migration Studies in Latin America*, www.irlandeses.org/0707recio1.htm. O'Farrill became acting prime minister of Spain in 1808.
38. *JQA Diary*, January 9, 1800 [electronic edition].

39. JQA to JJ, December 10, 1800, APM Reel 399.
40. "LCA Adventures," 1:136, 1:138.
41. Ibid., 1:138. Lady Carysfort's father, George Grenville, was prime minister from 1763 to 1765. Her brother William Grenville would hold the same position from 1806 to 1807.
42. Ibid., 1:145.
43. Ibid., 1:140, 1:152. Louisa was in mourning for Charles Adams, John Quincy's younger brother, who had died penniless and an alcoholic on November 30, 1800. His older brother sincerely grieved his death; his father, the president, would not allow himself that comfort. Prince Adolphus of England (1774–1850) was the seventh son of George III.
44. Ibid., 1:153.
45. Louisa forgot about the packet until packing for the family's return to the United States. "Opening the paper [I] saw nothing but a yellow powder and to his day have no idea of what this powder consisted. . . . I write in flat contradiction to the many and oft told stories of the heartlessness of courts for there as in every class of society, the good and the bad are blended but their bad actions are engraved on brass, their good are written on the sand." LCA to CFA and Abigail Brooks Adams, December 18, 1833, APM Reel 498.
46. *JQA Diary*, April 12, 1801 [electronic edition]; "LCA Adventures," 1:154.
47. JQA to AA, April 14, 1801, APM Reel 400.
48. *JQA Diary*, April 29, 1801 [electronic edition].
49. Ibid., May 4, 1801.
50. "LCA Adventures," 1:154, 1:155.

CHAPTER 7. A NATIVE IN A STRANGE LAND

1. B. G. Smith, *Life in Early Philadelphia: Documents from the Revolutionary and Early National Periods* (University Park: Pennsylvania State University Press, 1995), 3, 10.
2. "Adventures of a Nobody," in *Diary and Autobiographical Writings of Louisa Catherine Adams*, ed. Judith S. Graham and others (Cambridge, MA: Belknap Press of Harvard University Press, 2012), 1:157.
3. "LCA Adventures," 1:155.
4. *The Diaries of John Quincy Adams: A Digital Collection* (Boston: Massachusetts Historical Society, 2005), http://www.masshist.org/jqadiaries, September 12, 1801.
5. "LCA Adventures," 1:158.
6. LCA to JQA, September 16, 1801, APM Reel 401.
7. JQA to LCA, October 8, 1801, APM Reel 401.
8. AA to JQA, September 13, 1801, APM Reel 401.
9. *JQA Diary*, October 26, 1801 [electronic edition].
10. *JQA Diary*, November 3, 1801 [electronic edition]; "LCA Adventures," 1:159.
11. "LCA Adventures," 1:159.
12. "LCA Adventures," 1:161.
13. *JQA Diary*, November 25, 1801 [electronic edition].
14. "LCA Adventures," 1:164.
15. AA to Thomas Boylston Adams, December 27, 1801, APM Reel 401.

16. "LCA Adventures," 1:164.
17. Ibid.
18. Ibid.
19. Ibid., 1:165.
20. Ibid., 1:172, 1:168; The Boston Brahmins' high opinion of themselves inspired the ditty: "And this is good old Boston/The home of the bean and the cod,/where the Lowells speak only to Cabots,/And the Cabots speak only to God."
21. "LCA Adventures," 1:190.
22. AA to Thomas Boylston Adams, December 27, 1801; JQA to Thomas Boylston Adams, September 27, 1801, APM Reel 401.
23. *JQA Diary*, March 12, 1802 [electronic edition].
24. *Diary of John Quincy Adams, 1779–1786*, ed. David Grayson Allen et al. (Cambridge, MA: Belknap Press of Harvard University Press, 1981), January 28, 1802, 1:249.
25. JQA to Thomas Boylston Adams, April 11, 1802, APM Reel 401; "LCA Adventures," 1:171.
26. "LCA Adventures," 1:175.
27. Ibid., 1:170.
28. Ibid., 1:172.
29. Ibid., 1:173.
30. Ibid.
31. Mary Beth North, *Liberty's Daughters: The Revolutionary Experience of American Women, 1750–1800* (Boston: Little, Brown, 1980), 4; AA to Elizabeth Peabody, June 5, 1809, APM Reel 407.
32. "LCA Adventures," 1:165.
33. Laurel Thatcher Ulrich, *A Midwife's Tale: The Life of Martha Ballard, Based on Her Diary, 1785–1812* (New York: Vintage Books, 1991), 81.
34. North, *Liberty's Daughters*, 22; "LCA Adventures," 1:179; *JQA Diary*, December 4, 1802 [electronic edition].
35. "LCA Adventures," 1:169. John Quincy offered to pay Epps's passage back to England, but she, instead, decided to marry Whitcomb. The two were wed on March 23, 1802; Samuel F. Bemis, *John Quincy Adams and the Foundations of American Foreign Policy* (New York: W. W. Norton, 1949), 111. On January 1, 1802, John Quincy calculated his property—including real estate, stock, and a valuable library—at the not-insignificant sum of $43,702.54. Having lived frugally during his seven years abroad, he might have been wealthier. His brother Charles, while alive, had mismanaged savings entrusted to his care, as had Dr. Thomas Welsh, who had made poor real estate investments for the absent diplomat. Until his law practice began to earn money, however, John Quincy was strapped for cash, a situation that worried him each time he dipped into his remaining savings to pay household expenses.
36. *JQA Diary*, January 31, 1803 [electronic edition].
37. "LCA Adventures," 1:174. She is probably referring to *Essays on Practical Education* (1798) by the British novelist Maria Edgeworth (1768–1849).
38. "LCA Adventures," 1:184.
39. Ibid., 1:183.
40. Ibid., 1:185; AA to Thomas Boylston Adams, June 26, 1803, APM Reel 402.

41. "LCA Adventures," 1:189.
42. Ibid., 1:185. Direct election of senators by the voters was not established until the Seventeenth Amendment was ratified in 1913.
43. Walter Hellen was the son of Joshua Johnson's eldest sister, Mary.
44. Paul C. Nagel, *John Quincy Adams: A Public Life, A Private Life* (Cambridge, MA: Harvard University Press, 1997), 141.
45. "LCA Adventures," 1:192.
46. Powles Hook is now Jersey City, New Jersey.
47. Bemis, *Foundations*, 120; "We have this day a sort of Holiday, to rejoyce for the acquisition of our new Territories. The Members of Congress of both Houses are to dine together. [The] federalists who opposed the cession however do not join in the party. Those of us who approved the measure, are to be of the feast, where we at least shall find not much congeniality." JQA to Thomas Boylston Adams, January 27, 1804, APM Reel 403.
48. *JQA Diary*, January 28, 1802 [electronic edition]; Richard Brookhiser, *America's First Dynasty: The Adamses, 1735–1918* (New York: The Free Press, 2002), 69.
49. JQA to AA, December 22, 1803, APM Reel 402.
50. "LCA Adventures," 1:204.
51. *JQA Diary*, January 31, 1804 [electronic edition].
52. "LCA Adventures," 1:207.
53. LCA to AA, February 11, 1804, APM Reel 403. Elizabeth "Betsy" Patterson Bonaparte was a Baltimore beauty who married Jerome Bonaparte, youngest brother of Napoleon Bonaparte. Napoleon eventually caused the marriage to be annulled. Betsy was renowned for diaphanous gowns that left nothing to the imagination.
54. "LCA Adventures," 1:212.
55. "LCA Adventures," 1:211.
56. Catherine Allgor, *Parlor Politics* (Charlottesville: University Press of Virginia, 2000), 26; "LCA Adventures," 1:204.
57. "LCA Adventures," 1:206; See Allgor, *Parlor Politics*, 35–47, for another instance of Jefferson's intentional rudeness—the Merry affair.
58. "LCA Adventures," 1:203.
59. Jon Meacham, *American Lion: Andrew Jackson in the White House* (New York: Random House, 2008) called Louisa "a shrewd observer of Washington politics" (xv) and her letters "witty perceptive accounts of life in the capital through several decades" (unnumbered caption with portrait of LCA).
60. "LCA Adventures," 1:215.
61. Ibid., 1:204, 1:206, 1:215, 1:212.
62. Ibid., 1:199.

CHAPTER 8. WANDERING FORTUNES

Epigraph 1. "Louisa Catherine Adams," in *The National Portrait Gallery of Distinguished Americans*, ed. James Herring and James Barton Longacre (Philadelphia: Robert E. Peterson & Co., 1853), [Digitized by Google Books from Harvard University Library], 4:3–4. The profile was written by CFA.

Epigraph 2. LCA to JQA, November 25, 1806, APM Reel 404.

1. *The Diaries of John Quincy Adams: A Digital Collection* (Boston: Massachusetts Historical Society, 2005) http://www.masshist.org/jqadiaries, April 9, 1804; JQA to LCA, April 9, 1804, APM Reel 403. Louisa's letter is not preserved in the APM.
2. JQA to LCA, April 9, 1804, APM Reel 403.
3. LCA to JQA, April 17, 1804, APM Reel 403.
4. LCA to JQA, May 13, 1804, APM Reel 403.
5. JQA to LCA, April 24, 1804, APM Reel 403.
6. LCA to JQA, May 12, 1804, APM Reel 403.
7. *JQA Diary*, July 14, 1804 [electronic edition].
8. JQA to LCA, April 15, 1804, APM Reel 403.
9. JQA to AA, November 7, 1803, APM Reel 402.
10. Thomas Boylston Adams to JQA, December 15, 1803, APM Reel 402.
11. LCA to JQA, May 29, 1804, APM Reel 403.
12. JQA to LCA June 9, 1804, APM Reel 403.
13. JQA to LCA, May 31, 1804, APM Reel 403.
14. JQA to LCA, June 17, 1804, APM Reel 403. He quotes John Donne, "A Valediction Forbidding Mourning." LCA to JQA, June 26, 1804, APM Reel 403.
15. JQA to LCA, July 28, 1804, APM Reel 403; LCA to JQA, August 5, 1804, APM Reel 403.
16. "Adventures of a Nobody," in *Diary and Autobiographical Writings of Louisa Catherine Adams*, ed. Judith S. Graham and others (Cambridge, MA: Belknap Press of Harvard University Press, 2012), 1:185; LCA to JQA, August 12, 1804, APM Reel 403.
17. JQA to LCA, August 3, 1804, APM Reel 403; LCA to JQA, August 14, 1804, APM Reel 403.
18. JQA to LCA, September 2, 1804, APM Reel 403.
19. AA to LCA, May 21, 1804, APM Reel 403; LCA to AA, November 27, 1804, APM Reel 403; JQA indicates in his diary that he rode out on horseback with LCA to the Capitol on November 5, but he does not mention an accident.
20. AA to LCA, December 8, 1804, APM Reel 403.
21. LCA to AA, December 19, 1804, APM Reel 403.
22. LCA to AA, November 27, 1804, APM Reel 403.
23. AA to LCA, December 8, 1804, APM Reel 403.
24. "LCA Adventures," 1:219. Jefferson was a widower, and neither of his daughters, who sometimes acted as his hostess, was in town.
25. *JQA Diary*, January 31, 1805 [electronic edition].
26. Ibid., December 31, 1804 [electronic edition].
27. JA to JQA, February 7, 1805, APM Reel 404.
28. "LCA Adventures," 1:223–224.
29. LCA to AA, February 11, 1805, APM Reel 404; "LCA Adventures," 1:225, 226. Peppergrass is a bitter spring green.
30. "LCA Adventures," 1:225, 226.
31. *JQA, Diary*, May 31, 1805 [electronic edition]. This prestigious chair has been held by many distinguished persons and was in the last half of the twentieth century graced by the poets Archibald MacLeish, Robert Fitzgerald, and Seamus Heaney. Jay Heinrichs,

"Why Harvard Destroyed Rhetoric," *Harvard Alumni Magazine*, July–August 1995. http://inpraiseofargument.squarespace.com/harvard.

32. JQA to JA, December 6, 1805, APM Reel 404.
33. "LCA Adventures," 1:228.
34. LCA to AA, January 6, 1806, APM Reel 404.
35. AA to LCA, January 19, 1806, APM Reel 404.
36. AA to LCA, February 15, 1806, APM Reel 404.
37. Thomas Boylston Adams and Ann Harrod had married in Haverhill in May 1805.
38. "LCA Adventures," 1:227.
39. Ibid., 1:232.
40. Ibid., 1:229, 231.
41. *JQA, Diary*, March 22, 1806 [electronic edition]; "LCA Adventures," 1:235.
42. JQA to LCA, May 18, 1806, APM Reel 404.
43. JQA to LCA, June 8, 1806, APM Reel 404.
44. LCA to JQA, June 15, 1806, APM Reel 404; Joan R. Challinor, "Louisa Catherine Johnson Adams: The Price of Ambition" (Ph.D. dissertation, American University, 1982), 9–10.
45. *Diary of John Quincy Adams, 1779–1786, Vol. 1*, ed. David Grayson Allen et al. (Cambridge, MA: Belknap Press of the Harvard University Press, 1981), xxii.
46. JQA to LCA, June 30, 1806, APM Reel 404. LCA's letter, which JQA enclosed in one to his father announcing the infant's death, is not now among the Adams Papers even though JQA specifically requested that JA preserve it for him.
47. LCA to JQA, July 20, 1806, APM Reel 404.
48. Ibid. The salary was $348 a quarter, but John Quincy taught only when the Senate was not in session. Bemis, *Foundations*, 133.
49. *JQA Diary*, August 31, 1806 [electronic edition].
50. "LCA Adventures," 1:238.
51. Ibid., 1:241.
52. Ibid., 1:242; Susan Strasser, *Never Done: A History of American Housework* (New York: Pantheon Books, 1982), 36. "Only constant fire tending—poking, shifting logs, and adding wood—could keep a hot fire going in brick ovens and fireplaces."
53. "LCA Adventures," 1:242, 244.
54. LCA to JQA, November 25, 1806, APM Reel 404.
55. LCA to JQA, December 28, 1806, APM Reel 404.
56. Ibid.
57. JQA to LCA, January 6, 1807, APM Reel 405; LCA to JQA, January 16, 1807, APM Reel 405.
58. AA to JQA, January 16, 1807, APM Reel 405; "LCA Adventures," 1:247; LCA to JQA, January 29, 1807, APM Reel 405.
59. "LCA Adventures," 1:249.
60. Ibid., 1:252.
61. Ibid., 1:253.
62. Ibid., 1:255; JQA to CJ, August 18, 1807, APM Reel 405.

63. JQA to JA, December 27, 1807, APM Reel 405; JA to JQA, January 8, 1808, APM Reel 405.
64. JA to JQA, February 19, 1808, APM Reel 405.
65. "LCA Adventures," 1:269, 274.
66. Ibid., 1:277.
67. Donald M. Goodfellow, "The First Boylston Professor of Rhetoric and Oratory," *New England Quarterly* 19, no. 3 (September 1946); *JQA Diary*, January 3, 1809 [electronic edition].
68. JQA to LCA, February 13, 1809, APM Reel 407. "I am very much afraid that I shall lose them all."
69. JQA to AA, March 8, 1809; JQA to LCA, March 9, 1809, APM Reel 407.
70. "LCA Adventures," 1:274; *JQA Diary*, July 5, 1809 [electronic edition].
71. "LCA Adventures," 1:283.
72. Ibid., 1:284.

CHAPTER 9. A FLEETING FAIRY TALE

1. "The Adventures of a Nobody," in *Diary and Autobiographical Writings of Louisa Catherine Adams*, ed. Judith S. Graham and others (Cambridge, MA: Belknap Press of Harvard University Press, 2012), 1:285. The aides included William Steuben Smith, whom John Quincy had hired to be his private secretary as a favor to his sister Nabby, the young man's mother; Alexander Everett, a former student of John Quincy's; and Francis C. Gray, a son of the merchant who owned the *Horace*. Everett and Gray were traveling at their own expense. In April 1810, they would be joined by John Spear Smith, nephew of then-Secretary of State Robert Smith.
2. *Memoirs of John Quincy Adams, Comprising Portions of His Diary from 1795 to 1848*, ed. Charles Francis Adams (Philadelphia: J. B. Lippincott, 1874) [Book digitized by Google from the library of the University of Michigan] September 27, 1809, 2:30; "LCA Adventures," 1:290.
3. "LCA Adventures," 1:290.
4. Ibid., 1:291.
5. Ibid., 1:292. *Solus*, Latin for alone, was used as a stage direction for an actor alone on a stage.
6. Joseph DeMaistre to Victor Emmanuel of Sardinia, August 19, 1803, in Patricia Kennedy Grimsted, *The Foreign Ministers of Alexander I: Political Attitudes and the Conduct of Russian Diplomacy 1801–1825* (Berkeley: University of California Press, 1969), 21.
7. LCA to AA, October 13, 1814, APM Reel 417.
8. *Alexander Pushkin*, trans. and ed. A. D. P. Briggs (London: J. M. Dent, 1997), 91; "LCA Adventures," 1:293.
9. JQA to AA, February 8, 1810, APM Reel 409; "LCA Adventures," 1:293.
10. David Saunders, *Russia in the Age of Reaction and Reform, 1801–1881* (London: Longman, 1992), 10; Grimsted, *Foreign Ministers*, viii; JQA to LCA, July 2, 1814, APM Reel 418. The population of Russia in 1811 was 42.5 million.

11. Janet M. Hartley, *Alexander I* (London: Longman, 1994), 75.

12. Catherine Allgor, "'A Republican in a Monarchy'; Louisa Catherine Adams in Russia," *Diplomatic History* 21 (Winter 1997): 15–43; David Mayers, *The Ambassadors and America's Soviet Policy* (New York: Oxford University Press, 1995), 17.

13. *The Diaries of John Quincy Adams: A Digital Collection* (Boston: Massachusetts Historical Society, 2005), http://www.masshist.org/jqadiaries, November 5, 1809; Nina Bashkina and others, eds., *The United States and Russia: The Beginning of Relations 1765–1815* (Washington, DC: Government Printing Office, 1980).

14. Allgor, "'Republican in a Monarchy,'" 24; Grimsted, *Foreign Ministers*, 11; Samuel F. Bemis, *John Quincy Adams and the Foundations of American Foreign Policy* (New York: W. W. Norton, 1949), 162; Alfred W. Crosby, Jr., *America, Russia, Hemp, and Napoleon: American Trade with Russia and the Baltic, 1783–1812* (Columbus: Ohio State University Press, 1965), 150–151; *JQA Diary*, February 15, 1811 [electronic edition].

15. *JQA Diary*, October 11, 1811 [electronic edition]

16. Grimsted, *Foreign Ministers*, 19.

17. LCA to AA, January 7, 1810, APM Reel 409.

18. "LCA Adventures," 1:342.

19. AA to CJ, November [n.d.], 1809, APM Reel 408.

20. AA to CJ, December 19, 1810, APM Reel 408.

21. "LCA Adventures," 1:316.

22. *JQA Diary*, January 9, 1810 [electronic edition].

23. "LCA Adventures," 1:318, 326.

24. Ibid., 1:333.

25. Grimsted, *Foreign Ministers*, 21, citing Joseph de Maistre to Victor Emmanuel I, August 19, 1803; Maistre, *Mémoires politiques et correspondance diplomatique de Joseph de Maistre*, ed. A. Blanc (Paris, 1858), 383–385.

26. *JQA Diary*, November 4, 1809 [electronic edition]; Bemis, *Foundations*, 163.

27. Bashkina, *The United States and Russia*, 666.

28. Crosby, *American Trade*, 152; "W. H. Lyttleton to Sir Charles Bagot," January 22, 1827, in Josceline Bagot, ed., *George Canning and His Friends* (New York: E. P. Dutton, 1909). 2:362. [Digitized by Google Books from the original at Indiana University]. William Henry Lyttelton, Third Baron Lyttelton (1782–1837), "enjoyed a reputation as a wit." *Oxford Dictionary of National Biography*, ed. H. C. G. Matthew and Brian Harrison,34:378 (Oxford: Oxford University Press, 2004).

29. I am indebted in the section that follows to the insights of Catherine Allgor in "'A Republican in a Monarchy.'"

30. "Louisa Catherine Adams," in *The National Portrait Gallery of Distinguished Americans*, ed. James Herring and James Barton Longacre (Philadelphia: Robert E. Peterson & Co., 1853), [Digitized by Google Books from Harvard University Library], 4:4.

31. "LCA Adventures," 1:297.

32. Ibid., 1:298.

33. Ibid., 1:302.

34. Ibid., 1:341, 1:336.

35. Ibid., 1:300, 1:307; LCA to AA, January 7, 1810, APM Reel 409.
36. LCA to AA, June 2, 1810, APM Reel 409. Years later, Charles reported encountering a young secretary of the Russian legation in Washington whom he had known as a child "and who stamped himself upon my remembrance by maliciously giving me a glass of brandy and water instead of claret and water at a childs ball in St. Petersburg whereby I was completely upset." CFA to Abigail Brooks, his future wife, September 25, 1828, APM Reel 487.
37. "LCA Adventures," 1:310.
38. Ibid., 1:310, 1:305.
39. Ibid., 1:284; JQA to AA, February 8, 1810, APM Reel 409.
40. LCA to AA, October 28, 1809, APM Reel 408.
41. "LCA Adventures," 1:315, 1:302.
42. Louisa was perfectly capable of sewing elaborate garments. On short notice, she prepared Charles for a visit to the Winter Palace "to see the Emperor and Empress who would be there on Monday Morning at twelve o clock. Thus I was obliged to make him a suitable dress. It consisted of a white Satin Frock over which was worn a sprigged Muslin dress white Satin Pantelets. The Shoulders and bosom bare and the Sleeves tied up with Satin Ribbon with a white Satin Sash to fasten the waist of the Frock and white Satin Slippers." "LCA Adventures," 1:311.
43. Bemis, *Foundations*, 164.
44. JQA to AA, February 8, 1810, APM Reel 409; LCA to AA, July 9, 1810, APM Reel 410; *JQA Diary*, December 17, 1810 [electronic edition]. The house, where they stayed for only a year, was located where the Moika Canal met New Street. Michael O'Brien, *Mrs. Adams in Winter: A Journey in the Last Days of Napoleon* (New York: Farrar, Straus and Giroux, 2010), 29.
45. *JQA Diary*, February 16, 1812 [electronic edition].
46. LCA to AA, May 13, 1810; AA to CJ, May 4, 1810, APM Reel 409.
47. James Madison to AA, August 15, 1810, APM Reel 410.
48. James Madison to JQA, October 16, 1810, APM Reel 410.
49. JA to JQA, March 4, 1811, APM Reel 411.
50. AA to JQA, March 4, 1811, APM Reel 411.
51. *JQA Diary*, May 22, 1811 [electronic edition].
52. JQA to JA, May 30, 1811, APM Reel 411.
53. JQA to JA, July 21, 1811, APM Reel 412.
54. LCA to AA, June 10, 1811, APM Reel 411.
55. "LCA Adventures," 1:344.
56. JQA to AA, October 2, 1811, APM Reel 412.
57. "LCA Adventures," 1:348.
58. JQA to AA, September 10, 1811; "LCA Adventures," 1:351.
59. LCA to GWA, June 14, 1812, APM Reel 413.
60. *JQA Diary*, September 12, 1812 [electronic edition].
61. Ibid.; JQA to AA, September 21, 1812, APM Reel 414.
62. "LCA Adventures," 1:355.

CHAPTER 10. DARK DAYS ON THE BALTIC

1. A *grande armée* in French military usage referred to Napoleon's main operational force but the term is associated more generally with the army sent to Moscow in 1812. This, the largest army the world had ever seen, included soldiers from almost every nation in Europe. Adam Zamoyski, *Moscow 1812: Napoleon's Fatal March* (New York: HarperCollins, 2004), 84, 298.

2. Zamoyski, *Moscow 1812*, 61, 84; *The Diaries of John Quincy Adams: A Digital Collection* (Boston: Massachusetts Historical Society, 2005), http://www.masshist.org/jqadiaries, February 8, 1811.

3. *JQA Diary*, March 19, 1812 [electronic edition].

4. Ibid., September 30, 1812.

5. Michael O'Brien, *Mrs. Adams in Winter: A Journey in the Last Days of Napoleon* (New York: Farrar, Straus and Giroux, 2010), 252.

6. JQA to AA, September 21, 1812, APM Reel 414.

7. *JQA Diary*, September 30, 1812 [electronic edition].

8. "Diary of Louisa Catherine Adams, 1812–1814," in *Diary and Autobiographical Writings of Louisa Catherine Adams*, ed. Judith S. Graham and others (Cambridge, MA: Belknap Press of Harvard University Press, 2012), 1:357. Louisa began a diary October 22, 1812 and continued it, irregularly, through February 14, 1814.

9. *JQA Diary*, January 15, 1813 [electronic edition].

10. JQA to AA, September 21, 1812, APM Reel 414; "LCA Diary, 1812–1814," October 22, 1812, 1:357.

11. LCA to AA, April 4, 1813, APM Reel 415; "LCA Diary, 1812–1814," October 25, 1812, 1:358.

12. *Memoirs of John Quincy Adams, Comprising Portions of His Diary from 1795 to 1848*, ed. Charles Francis Adams (Philadelphia: J. B. Lippincott, 1874) [Book digitized by Google from the library of the University of Michigan], 2:282–283.

13. "LCA Diary, 1812–1814," October 25, 1812, 1:358; November 27, 1812, 1:361.

14. Ibid., December 23, 1812, 1:366; August 14, 1812, 1:369.

15. *JQA Diary*, July 26, 1811 [electronic edition].

16. Ibid., December 5, 1812, 1:362.

17. LCA to AA, April 4, 1813, APM Reel 415; *JQA Diary*, January 21, 1813 [electronic edition].

18. "LCA Diary," October 25, 1812, 1:358; AA to LCA, January 30, 1813, APM Reel 415.

19. AA to LCA, February 20, 1810, APM Reel 409.

20. AA to CJ, May 4, 1810, APM Reel 409.

21. LCA to AA, October 23, 1810, APM Reel 410; AA to LCA, January 21, 1811, APM Reel 411.

22. AA to LCA, January 21, 1811, APM Reel 411.

23. AA to LCA, January 30, 1813, APM Reel 415.

24. LCA to AA, January 1, 1815, APM Reel 421.

25. AA to CJ, September 13, 1810, August 18, 1810, APM Reel 410.

26. AA to JQA, November 17, 1811, APM Reel 412; AA to Thomas Johnson, April 3, 1813, APM Reel 415.

27. AA to Elizabeth Peabody, June 26, 1813, Shaw Family Papers (Elizabeth Smith Shaw Letters, folios 185–186); Paul C. Nagel, *Adams Women: Abigail and Louisa Adams, Their Sisters and Their Daughters* (New York: Oxford University Press, 1987), 233. The child, named Caroline Amelia, died of measles after reaching the United States. A second child, their last, died September 19, 1817.

28. O'Brien, *Mrs. Adams in Winter*, 9, refers to "the cul-de-sac that was Saint Petersburg, the place that had come close to burying [JQA's] career." "LCA Diary, 1812–1814," April 4, 1813, 1:369.

29. *JQA Diary*, September 21, 1812 [electronic edition]; JQA to Thomas Boylston Adams, September 29, 1812, APM Reel 139.

30. Samuel F. Bemis, *John Quincy Adams and the Foundations of American Foreign Policy* (New York: W. W. Norton, 1949), 186.

31. *JQA Diary*, June 2, 1812; "LCA Diary, 1812–1814," post–January 25, 1814, 1:371.

32. Bemis, *Foundations*, 188.

33. LCA to JQA, August 5, 1814, APM Reel 419; Bemis, *Foundations*, 188. John Quincy would later give a deposition against Harris in a libel case in American courts. "Mr A—is teazed to death again giving a Deposition in the Case of Harris and Lewis which occupies every Even'g he can spare and that is four out of seven until twelve o'clock." "Diary, 1819–1849," in *Diary and Autobiographical Writings of Louisa Catherine Adams*, ed. Judith S. Graham and others (Cambridge, MA: Belknap Press of Harvard University Press, 2012), 2:661.

34. LCA to JQA, June 13, 1814, APM Reel 418.

35. LCA to JQA, May 19, 1814, APM Reel 418.

36. JQA to LCA, June 14, 1814, APM Reel 418.

37. Ibid.

38. JQA to LCA, June 11 and May 14, 1814, APM Reel 418. A *dormeuse* was a carriage fitted out with a mattress, a conveyance that John Quincy said was "so unusual a Spectacle on this road, that it assembled a crowd of gazers, at almost every Stage, where I stopp'd."

39. JQA to LCA, August 9, 1814, APM Reel 419.

40. LCA to JQA, August 30, 1814, APM Reel 419.

41. LCA to JQA, August 15, 1814; JQA to LCA, August 12, 1814, APM Reel 419.

42. LCA to JQA, July 5, August 5, 1814, APM Reel 419.

43. LCA to JQA, August 7, 1814, APM Reel 419.

44. JQA to LCA, August 12, 1814, APM Reel 419.

45. LCA to JQA, August 22, 1814, APM Reel 419; LCA to JQA, October 16, 1814, APM Reel 420.

46. JQA to LCA, November 11, 14, 1814, APM Reel 420; LCA to JQA, December 6, 1814, APM Reel 421.

47. LCA to JQA, November 22, 1814, APM Reel 420.

48. LCA to JQA, August 30, 1814, APM Reel 420.

49. Bemis, *Foundations*, 216; Samuel Eliot Morison, *The Oxford History of the American People* (New York: Oxford University Press, 1965), 398.

50. Bemis, *Foundations*, 215; Morison, *American People*, 398; JQA to LCA, January 3, 1815, APM Reel 422.

51. JQA to LCA, December 27, 1814, APM Reel 421.
52. "Louisa Catherine Adams," in *The National Portrait Gallery of Distinguished Americans*, eds. James Herring and James Barton Longacre (Philadelphia: Robert E. Peterson & Co., 1853) [Digitized by Google Books from Harvard University Library], 4:5.
53. LCA to JQA, February 7, January 31, February 1, 1815, APM Reel 422; Michael O'Brien has calculated the overall cost of the journey in 2010 currency at about $28,000. O'Brien, *Mrs. Adams in Winter*, 58.
54. "Narrative of a Journey from Russia to France," in *Diary and Autobiographical Writings of Louisa Catherine Adams*, ed. Judith S. Graham and others (Cambridge, MA: Belknap Press of Harvard University Press, 2012), 1:378.
55. LCA to JQA, March 5, 1815, APM Reel 422.
56. "LCA Narrative," 1:387–388.
57. In her "Narrative," Louisa remembered that she had not secured the services of Mme. Babet until the day of her departure, but in a January 31 letter to John Quincy, she informed him that she had been able to make an arrangement with a Frenchwoman. The onetime Smith servant is identified by Michael O'Brien as John Fulling based on evidence from LCA's Russian passport. That passport, however, misidentifies the other two passengers as Maria Blot and a man called Englebert. O'Brien, *Mrs. Adams in Winter*, 306n2.
58. "Louisa Catherine Adams," 4:4.
59. LCA to JQA, February 12, 1815, APM Reel 422.

CHAPTER 11. THE JOURNEY OF A LIFETIME

1. LCA to JQA, February 7, 1815, APM Reel 442.
2. Narva is located in what is now Estonia. Riga was the capital of Livland, a province of the Russian empire. It is now the capital of Latvia.
3. "Narrative of a Journey from Russia to France," in *Diary and Autobiographical Writings of Louisa Catherine Adams*, ed. Judith S. Graham and others (Cambridge, MA: Belknap Press of Harvard University Press, 2012), 1:381.
4. Michael O'Brien, *Mrs. Adams in Winter: A Journey in the Last Days of Napoleon* (New York: Farrar, Straus and Giroux, 2010), 88–89; LCA to JQA, February 17, 1815, APM Reel 422.
5. "LCA Narrative," 1:378.
6. O'Brien, *Mrs. Adams in Winter*, 91; "LCA Narrative," 1:378. Mitau is now Jelgava, Latvia.
7. O'Brien, *Mrs. Adams in Winter*, 104; "LCA Narrative," 1:379.
8. "LCA Narrative," 1:380.
9. Ibid., 1:381.
10. Ibid.
11. Ibid., 1:382.
12. LCA to JQA, February 17–20, 1815, APM Reel 422; "LCA Narrative," 1:382.

13. O'Brien, *Mrs. Adams in Winter*, 113, has convincingly argued that the river in question must be the Windau and not the Vistula, as Louisa remembered it.
14. "LCA Narrative," 1:383.
15. O'Brien, *Mrs. Adams in Winter*, 114; "LCA Narrative," 1:383.
16. "LCA Narrative," 1:383, 384. Königsberg is now Kaliningrad, a forlorn piece of Russian territory isolated between Poland and Lithuania. For centuries it had been fought over by France, Germany, Russia, and Sweden; in World War II it was bombed heavily.
17. Michael V. Leggiere, *Napoleon and Berlin: The Franco-Prussian War in North Germany* (Norman: University of Oklahoma Press, 2002), 26.
18. "LCA Narrative," 1:385.
19. O'Brien, *Mrs. Adams in Winter*, 306n2.
20. "LCA Narrative," 1:385.
21. Ibid., 1:386.
22. Küstrin, now Kostrzyn, Poland; "LCA Narrative," 1:386.
23. "LCA Narrative," 1:389.
24. Ibid.
25. Ibid.
26. Constance Wright, *Beautiful Enemy: A Biography of Queen Louise of Prussia* (New York: Dodd, Mead & Company, 1969), 174; Leggiere, *Napoleon and Berlin*, 20.
27. "LCA Narrative," 1:390.
28. Ibid., 1:391; LCA to JQA, March 5, 1815, APM Reel 422.
29. "LCA Narrative," 1:391.
30. Ibid., 1:392. The inn was in Eisenach, according to O'Brien, *Mrs. Adams in Winter*, 193, but Louisa does not identify it.
31. "LCA Narrative," 1:392.
32. O'Brien, *Mrs. Adams in Winter*, 197; "LCA Narrative," 1:394.
33. "LCA Narrative," 1:395.
34. Ibid.; "Louisa Catherine Adams," in *The National Portrait Gallery of Distinguished Americans*, ed. James Herring and James Barton Longacre (Philadelphia: Robert E. Peterson & Co., 1853) [Digitized by Google from Harvard University], 4:6.
35. O'Brien, *Mrs. Adams in Winter*, 202; LCA to JQA, March 17, 1815, APM Reel 422.
36. "LCA Narrative," 1:395.
37. Ibid., 1:395, 396.
38. Ibid., 1:397.
39. Ibid.
40. Ibid., 1:399.
41. O'Brien, *Mrs. Adams in Winter*, 277; "LCA Narrative," 1:400.
42. "LCA Narrative," 1:400.
43. Ibid., 1:401.
44. Ibid.
45. Identified by O'Brien in *Mrs. Adams in Winter*, 284, as Claude Etienne Michel.
46. "LCA Narrative," 1:402.
47. Ibid. The proprietress is identified by O'Brien in *Mrs. Adams in Winter*, 287, as Gabrielle Victoire Larangot.

48. "LCA Narrative," 1:403.
49. Ibid., 1:404.
50. Ibid., 1:405.
51. Ibid., 1:404.
52. *JQA Diary*, March 23, 1815 [electronic edition].
53. "LCA Narrative," 1:405.
54. JQA to AA, April 22, 1815, APM Reel 423.
55. JQA to LCA, December 27, 1814; O'Brien, *Mrs. Adams in Winter*, 165.
56. JQA to LCA, March 18, 1815, APM Reel 422.
57. JQA to AA, March 4, 1816, APM Reel 430; Joan R. Challinor, "Louisa Catherine Johnson Adams: The Price of Ambition" (Ph.D. dissertation, American University, Washington D.C., 1982), 545.
58. LCA to AA, June 12, 1815, APM Reel 424.
59. "Louisa Catherine Adams," 4:6.
60. "LCA Narrative," 1:375.
61. Ibid., 1:406, 1:398n1.
62. Ibid., 1:406.
63. Ibid.
64. Ibid.
65. *JQA Diary*, May 24, 1815 [electronic edition].

CHAPTER 12. LITTLE BOSTON HOUSE

1. AA to LCA, April 14, 1815; JA to JQA, April 8, 1815, APM Reel 423.
2. AA to JQA, August 15, May 20, 1815, APM Reel 423.
3. *The Diaries of John Quincy Adams: A Digital Collection* (Boston: Massachusetts Historical Society, 2005), http://www.masshist.org/jqadiaries, "Summary," May 1815.
4. AA to CFA, July 12, 1815, APM Reel 425.
5. *JQA Diary*, "Summary," June 1815 [electronic edition].
6. LCA to AA, July 8, 1815, APM Reel 425; *JQA Diary*, July 21, 1815 [electronic edition].
7. *JQA Diary*, August 1, 1815 [electronic edition].
8. *JQA Diary*, August 2, 1815 [electronic edition]; LCA to AA, August 6, 1815, APM Reel 426.
9. *JQA Diary*, January 11, 1816 [electronic edition]. Rent equaled approximately US$25 at the time.
10. LCA to AA, August 6, 1815, APM Reel 426.
11. *JQA Diary*, August 2, 1815 [electronic edition].
12. *The Letters and Diaries of John Henry Newman, Vol. I, Ealing, Trinity, Oriel, February 1801 to December 1826*, ed. Ian Ker and Thomas Gornall, S.J. (Oxford: Clarendon Press, 1978), 10. "The Times Obituary of Cardinal John Henry Newman," originally published August 12, 1890, Times Online, Times Newspapers, London, refers to Great Ealing School as "the best private school in England."
13. JA to GWA, October 3, 1815, APM Reel 427.

14. *JQA Diary*, August 15, 22, 1815 [electronic edition].
15. *JQA Diary*, December 17, 1815 [electronis edition]. The boy, unidentified, may have been Newman, who was the head boy at the school at this time. Newman wrote of *Portfolio*: "There is nothing in it worth preserving. I have kept, however, Mr. Adams's lines, 'The Grasshopper and the Ant.'" *Letters and Diaries*, 10.
16. JA to JA2, July 31, 1816, APM Reel 432.
17. LCA to AA, October 2, 1815, APM Reel 427.
18. John W. Derry, *Reaction and Reform 1793–1798* (London: Blandford Press, 1963) reproduced as *A Short History of Nineteenth Century England, 1793–1868* (New York: Mentor Books, 1963), 58.
19. LCA to AA, June 12, 1815, APM Reel 424.
20. Christopher Hibbert, *George IV: The Rebel Who Would Be King* (New York: Palgrave Macmillan, 2007), 409–410. Letter from Jane Austen to Martha Lloyd, February 16, 1813, http://www.pemberley.com/janeinfo/jprncwal.html. See also Jane Aiken Hodge, *Only a Novel: The Double Life of Jane Austen* (Greenwich, Conn.: Fawcett World Library, 1973), 182.
21. Derry, *Reaction and Reform*, 72.
22. Samuel F. Bemis, *John Quincy Adams and the Foundations of American Foreign Policy* (New York: W. W. Norton, 1949), 228; Bradford Perkins, *Castlereagh and Adams: England and the United States 1812–1823* (Berkeley: University of California Press, 1964), 197.
23. JA to JQA, May 1, 1815, APM Reel 432.
24. Perkins, *Castlereagh and Adams*, 212; JQA to JA, May 29, 1816, APM Reel 431.
25. *JQA Diary*, October 24, 27, November 14, 20, 1815 [electronic edition].
26. LCA to AA, December 23, 1815, APM Reel 428.
27. Princess Charlotte (1796–1817), the only child of the Prince Regent and Princess Caroline, was at the time of her death on November 6, 1817, immediately after the mismanaged birth of a stillborn son, the only legitimate grandchild of George III.
28. AA to LCA, May [n.d.], 1815, APM Reel 423; AA to LCA, May 2, 1816, LCA to AA, May 17, 1816, APM Reel 431; AA to LCA, August 8, 1816, APM Reel 433.
29. *JQA Diary*, June 17, 1816 [electronic edition].
30. LCA to AA, July 4, 1816, APM Reel 432.
31. Hibbert, *George IV*, 459; LCA to AA, July 4, 1816, APM Reel 432.
32. Paul Fitzmaurice, "Ealing Civic Society Newsletter," Spring 2009. Also information provided by Fitzmaurice to Elizabeth O'Connor McGurk, July 20, 2010.
33. *JQA Diary*, September 1, 1815 [electronic edition].
34. *JQA Diary*, November 4, 6, 1816 [electronic edition].
35. JQA to AA, June 6, 1816, APM Reel 432; LCA to AA, June 7, 1816, APM Reel 432.
36. LCA to AA, July 4, 1816, APM Reel 432; Hibbert, *George IV*, 177ff.
37. JQA to AA, August 16, 1816, APM Reel 433.
38. LCA to AA, July 4, 1816, APM Reel 432; September 11, 1816, APM Reel 434.
39. LCA to AA, September 11, 1816, APM Reel 434. The companion portraits now hang in the John Quincy Adams State Drawing Room at the U.S. State Department, a handsome room used by the secretary of state to receive diplomats and other guests. The

paintings were commissioned by Thomas Baker Johnson, brother of Louisa Catherine Adams, and passed on to CFA in 1836 and probably later to his son, Charles Francis Adams II. Thereafter, they were bequeathed to Mrs. Robert Homans and finally to her son, Robert Homans Jr. They were given to the nation by Robert Homans Jr., Miss Lucy Aldrich Homans, and Miss Abigail Homans in memory of their father. (Correspondence to the author from Lynn M. Turner, Registrar, Collections Manager Diplomatic Reception Rooms and State Rooms, U.S. Department of State, November 10, 2010). Benjamin West (1738–1820) was an eminent American painter of historical scenes, whose successful career was largely spent in London. Louisa's beauty is almost entirely lost in later engravings made of Leslie's oil portrait. In the engravings, which inevitably lack the shaping of her cheekbones, mouth, and chin created by the painter's brush, her face is flat and her expression more strained than serene.

40. Andrew Oliver, *Portraits of JQA and His Wife* (Cambridge, MA: Belknap Press of Harvard University Press, 1970), 63.
41. JQA to AA, June 12, 1816, APM Reel 432.
42. *JQA Diary*, June 30, 1816 [electronic edition].
43. Fitzmaurice to the author, November 9, 2010. The canal is now called the Grand Union Canal.
44. In addition to his five daughters, Dr. Nicholas was the father of three sons. A ward also lived with the family. Correspondence to the author from Elizabeth O'Connor McGurk, August 9, 2010. Neither Louisa nor John Quincy ever mentions meeting a Mrs. Nicholas.
45. *JQA Diary*, "Summary," December 1816 [electronic edition]. Ellen Nicholas to JQA August 4, 1817. Ellen died on October 22, 1818, "in the 21st year of her age," according to her memorial relief in St. Mary's Perivale, West London.
46. *JQA Diary*, October 12, 15, 1816 [electronic edition]; Ellen Nicholas, "Lines Addressed to Mrs. Adams while sitting for her Portrait," October 14, 1816, APM Reel 271.
47. JQA, "To Miss Ellen Nicholas on Her Birth-Day, December 14, 1816," October 13, 1816, APM Reel 271; Ellen Nicholas, "To J. Q. Adams," APM Reel 271.
48. LCA, "To My Husband," in LCA to AA, November 11, 1816, APM Reel 434.
49. JQA, "To My Wife," [n.d.], APM Reel 272.
50. Bemis, *Foundations*, 244–245; *JQA Diary*, December 5, 1816 [electronic edition].
51. AA to JQA, March 17, 1817, APM Reel 436.
52. *JQA Diary*, October 19, 1816 [electronic edition]; LCA to AA, November 11, 1816, APM Reel 434.
53. *JQA Diary*, November 16, 1816 [electronic edition].
54. *JQA Diary*, February 5, 1817 [electronic edition].
55. AA to Harriet Welsh, May 30, 1817, APM Reel 437.
56. *JQA Diary*, "Summary," March 1817 [electronic edition].
57. *JQA Diary*, April 23, 28, 1817 [electronic edition].
58. JQA to William Rae Wilson, May 29, 1817, APM Reel 143.
59. *JQA Diary*, June 25, 1817 [electronic edition].
60. LCA to AA, August 14, 1817, APM Reel 438.
61. *JQA Diary*, June 28, 1817 [electronic edition].

CHAPTER 13. CAMPAIGN

1. *Memoirs of John Quincy Adams, Comprising Portions of His Diary from 1795 to 1848,* ed. Charles Francis Adams (Philadelphia: J. B. Lippincott, 1874) [Book digitized by Google from the library of the University of Michigan], 4:64.
2. See the profile of LCA at http://millercenter.org/president/jqadams/essays/firstlady/louisa: "If John Quincy Adams was a candidate for President of United States in 1824, his wife was, without a doubt, his unofficial campaign manager" as an example of recent opinion on the role she played in his election.
3. *JQA Memoirs,* 4:7. A low, wooden dome covered in copper, designed by Charles Bulfinch, was completed in 1824. The familiar ironwork dome we know today was installed in its place between 1855 and 1866.
4. Catherine Allgor, *Parlor Politics* (Charlottesville: University Press of Virginia, 2000), 104; Anne Hollingsworth Wharton, *Social Life in the Early Republic,* 2nd ed. (Philadelphia: J. B. Lippincott, 1903), 58, quoting the architect Benjamin Latrobe (uncited) [Book digitized by Google from the library of the University of Michigan]; *JQA Memoirs,* 4:74. Decennial U.S. Census numbers for Washington (not including Georgetown or Alexandria, which were separate): 1800—3,210; 1810—8,208; 1820—13,247.
5. Pamela Scott, "Residential Architecture of Washington, D.C., and Its Suburbs," Library of Congress, http://www.loc.gov/rr/print/adecenter/essays/Scott.html.
6. LCA to AA, December 16, 1817, APM Reel 441.
7. *The Diaries of John Quincy Adams: A Digital Collection* (Boston: Massachusetts Historical Society, 2005), http://www.masshist.org/jqadiaries, October 12, 14, 1817.
8. Jehanne Wake, *Sisters of Fortune: America's Caton Sisters at Home and Abroad* (New York: Simon & Schuster, 2010), 63, quoting Foster, uncited.
9. James Sterling Young, *The Washington Community 1800–1828* (New York: Columbia University Press, 1966), 223; LCA to AA, January 11, 1818, APM Reel 442.
10. Cynthia D. Earman, "Remembering the Ladies: Women, Etiquette, and Diversions in Washington City, 1800–1814," *Washington History* 12, no. 1 (Spring–Summer, 2000), 104; Allgor, *Parlor Politics,* 47.
11. Margaret Bayard Smith, *The First Forty Years of Washington Society,* ed. G. Hunt (New York: C. Scribner's Sons, 1906) [Book digitized by Google from the library of the University of California], 141; LCA to AA, January 1, 1818, APM Reel 442.
12. David Hosford, "Exile in Yankeeland: The Journal of Mary Bagot, 1816–1819," *Records of the Columbia Historical Society* 51 (1984), 30–50.
13. Elizabeth Cleghorn Gaskell, *Cranford* (Boston: L. C. Page and Co., 1898) [Book digitized by Google from the library of Harvard University], 5. In *Cranford,* first published in 1851, the rules are spelled out to a young visitor: " 'You are never to stay longer than a quarter of an hour.'
" 'But am I to look at my watch? How am I to find out when a quarter of an hour has passed?'
" 'You must keep thinking about the time, my dear, and not allow yourself to forget it in conversation.'

"As everybody had this rule in their minds, whether they received or paid a call, of course no absorbing subject was ever spoken about. We kept ourselves to short sentences of small talk, and were punctual to our time."

14. LCA to AA, December 30, 1817, APM Reel 441.
15. *JQA Memoirs*, 4:45.
16. Susan Radomsky, "The Social Life of Politics: Washington's Official Society and the Emergence of a National Political Elite, 1800–1876" (Ph.D. dissertation, University of Chicago, 2005), 119; *JQA Memoirs*, 4:35.
17. LCA to AA, January 24, 1818, APM Reel 442; "Diary of Louisa Catherine Adams, 1819–1849," in *Diary and Autobiographical Writings of Louisa Catherine Adams*, ed. Judith S. Graham and others (Cambridge, MA: Belknap Press of Harvard University Press, 2012), 2:447.
18. LCA to AA, January 20, 1818, APM Reel 442.
19. LCA to AA, January 27, 1818, APM Reel 442.
20. *JQA Diary*, February 16–17, 1818 [electronic edition].
21. LCA to JA, December 13, 1818, APM Reel 445.
22. JA to LCA, December 28, 1818; JA to LCA, December 24, 1818, APM Reel 445.
23. LCA to Thomas Johnson, August 17, 1818, APM Reel 438.
24. "LCA Diary, 1819–1849," December 15, 1819, 2:444; *JQA Memoirs*, 4:480.
25. LCA to JA, December 10, 1818, APM Reel 442.
26. *JQA Memoirs*, 4:482.
27. Ibid., 4:490.
28. "LCA Diary, 1819–1849," June 6, 1820, 2:516.
29. Smith, *The First Forty Years*, 146.
30. "LCA Diary, 1819–1849," February 11, 1819, 2:415. LCA is referring to Sen. Charles Pinckney of South Carolina.
31. AA to LCA, December 12, 1817, APM Reel 441.
32. AA to LCA, May 20, 1818, APM Reel 443.
33. AA to LCA, May 20, 1818, APM Reel 443; Thomas Jefferson to JA, November 13, 1818, APM Reel 445.
34. JA to JQA, December 24, 1818, APM Reel 445; JA to LCA, May 8, 1820, APM Reel 449.
35. LCA to JA, January 2, 1819, APM Reel 446.
36. Ibid.
37. JA to LCA, January 1, 1820, APM Reel 446. In a letter to Francis Van der Kamp (September 23, 1814, APM Reel 122), JA described how he came up with the name: "Mr. Jefferson lives at Monticello, the lofty mountain. I live at *Montezillo*, a little hill." JA was apparently unaware that both words mean "little mountain." David McCullough, *John Adams* (New York: Simon & Schuster, 2001), 606.
38. JA to LCA, June 21, 1820, APM Reel 449; JA to JQA, September 8, 1820, APM Reel 450.
39. JA to LCA, March 1, 1819, APM Reel 446.
40. Barbara Carson, *Ambitious Appetites: Dining, Behavior, and Patterns of Consumption in Federal Washington* (Washington, D.C.: American Institute of Architects Press, 1990), 48; "LCA Diary, 1819–1849," February 25, 1819, 2:424.
41. Carson, *Ambitious Appetites*, 125.

42. "LCA Diary, 1819–1849," 2:457.
43. Carson, *Ambitious Appetites*, 94; "LCA Diary, 1819–1849," 2:448n. The 1820 census for JQA's household lists one slave, probably hired, and ten free white persons.
44. "LCA Diary, 1819–1849," January 18, 1820, 2:444.
45. Ibid., February 26, 1820, 2:425.
46. Samuel F. Bemis, *John Quincy Adams and the Foundations of American Foreign Policy* (New York: W. W. Norton, 1949), 315.
47. J. William Ward, *Andrew Jackson: Symbol for an Age* (New York: Oxford University Press, 1962), 59; Bemis, *Foundations*, 316; *JQA Memoirs*, 4:278.
48. "LCA Diary, 1819–1849," February 3, 1819, 2:411.
49. *JQA Memoirs*, 4:212.
50. Daniel Walker Howe, *What Hath God Wrought* (New York: Oxford University Press), 147; *JQA Memoirs*, 4:503.
51. Howe, *What Hath God Wrought*, 155; "LCA Diary, 1819–1849," March 4, 1829, 2:482.
52. LCA to JA, January 22, 1820, APM Reel 449.
53. *JQA Memoirs*, 4:531.
54. LCA to JA2, August 8, 1820, APM Reel 450; "LCA Diary, 1819–1849," June 8, 1820, 2:517.
55. *JQA Diary*, September 14, 1820 [electronic edition].
56. LCA to JA, October 15, 1820, APM Reel 450; "LCA Diary, 1819–1849," January 23, 1821, 2:549.
57. *JQA Diary*, October 25, 1820 [electronic edition].
58. *JQA Memoirs*, 4:402.
59. "LCA Diary, 1819–1849," January 6, 1821, 2:504.
60. *JQA Diary*, September 3, 1817 [electronic edition]; AA to LCA, February 20, 1818, APM Reel 442. Boston Latin was then known as "Mr. Gould's school." The headmaster was Benjamin A. Gould.
61. AA to LCA, February 27, 1818, APM Reel 442.
62. Bemis, *Foundations*, 249–250; Paul C. Nagel, *John Quincy Adams: A Public Life, A Private Life* (Cambridge, MA: Harvard University Press, 1997), 276; *JQA Diary*, September 5, 1786 [electronic edition].
63. LCA to GWA, November 17, 1818, APM Reel 445; William Bentinck-Smith, *The Harvard Book* (Cambridge, MA: Harvard University Press, 1986) includes an epic poem on the riot, "The Rebelliad," 122–126.
64. LCA to JA2, June 19, 1820; LCA to CFA, April 20, 1820, APM Reel 449.
65. LCA to JA2, May 1, 1820, APM Reel 449; LCA to GWA, August 10, 1820, APM Reel 450.
66. "LCA Diary, 1819–1849," August 22, 1821, 2:598.
67. *JQA Diary*, August 29, 1821 [electronic edition]; "LCA Diary, 1819–1849," August 30, 1821, 2:601.
68. *JQA Diary*, September 30, 1821 [electronic edition]; "LCA Diary, 1819–1849," September 18, 1821, 2:610; August 16, 1821, 2:599.
69. "LCA Diary, 1819–1849," August 16, 1821, 2:594; *JQA Diary*, September 29, 1821 [electronic edition].

70. "LCA Diary, 1819–1849," August 30, 1821, 2:602; *JQA Diary*, August 30, 1821 [electronic edition].
71. *JQA Diary*, October 1, 1821 [electronic edition].
72. Samuel Eliot Morison, *Three Hundred Years of Harvard* (Cambridge, MA: Harvard University Press, 1936), 231.
73. *JQA Diary*, October 1, 1821 [electronic edition].
74. JQA to JA2, December 15, 1821, APM Reel 453.
75. "LCA Diary, 1819–1849," December 6, 1821, 2:614.
76. "LCA Diary, 1819–1849," December 17, 18, 1821, 2:618–619.
77. "LCA Diary, 1819–1849," December 13, 1821, 2:616. Today, Louisa's attacks of erysipelas would be treated with penicillin. The infection, which afflicted her scores of times over her life, produced blisters, fever, shaking, and chills along with very painful, very red and swollen skin.
78. "LCA Diary, 1819–1849," December 8, 1821, 2:615. LCA is quoting Jane West, *A Tale of the Times*, 2d ed. (London, 1799), 18.
79. Ann Douglas Wood, "'The Fashionable Diseases': Women's Complaints and Their Treatment in Nineteenth-Century America," *Journal of Interdisciplinary History* 4, no. 1 (Summer 1973), 27. "One could multiply examples almost endlessly of women of this period who never expected to live through the next year and survived into their eighties and nineties. Still this evidence, like all the evidence in this area, is ambiguous. There are many diseases and ailments which, in the absence of sufficient medical knowhow, can become chronic and make their victim's life a torment without ending it."

CHAPTER 14. A BEAUTIFUL PLAN

1. LCA to JA2, May 21, 1822, APM Reel 455. Thomas Johnson had been postmaster of New Orleans since 1808. "Traditionally, Iceland moss was considered to be strongly antibiotic, antiemetic. . . . [It] has been principally recommended in chronic pulmonary and digestive conditions . . . such as dyspepsia, and chronic diarrhea." http://www.herbal-supplement-resource.com/iceland-moss.html.
2. LCA to JQA, June 24, 1822; LCA to JQA, July 31, 1822; LCA to JQA, August 2, 1822, APM Reels 455, 456.
3. LCA to JQA, August 1, 1822; LCA to JQA, October 2–4, 1822, APM Reel 456.
4. LCA to JQA, October 2–4, 1822; JQA to LCA, July 10, 1822, APM Reels 456, 455.
5. James E. Lewis Jr., *American Union and the Problem of Neighborhood* (Chapel Hill: University of North Carolina Press, 1998), 156.
6. *Memoirs of John Quincy Adams, Comprising Portions of His Diary from 1795 to 1848*, ed. Charles Francis Adams (Philadelphia: J. B. Lippincott, 1874) [Book digitized by Google from the library of the University of Michigan]), 6:200; "[JQA] doubted that a people who were Catholic, mixed-race or Spanish, and inured to tyranny could govern themselves. It seemed more likely that they would increase European influence, political tyranny, and commercial restrictions in the New World." Lewis, *American Union*, 102.

7. LCA to JQA, June 28, 1822, APM Reel 455.

8. LCA to JQA, October 7, 1822, APM Reel 456.

9. LCA to JQA, September 9, 1822, APM Reel 456. Joseph Hopkinson, the influential Philadelphia lawyer, congressman, and author the lyrics for "Hail Columbia," spoke often with Louisa in the summer of 1822 about her husband's reluctance to do anything to advance his candidacy. Hopkinson labeled this the "Macbeth policy." He spelled it out in a letter to Louisa that he knew she would show her husband. "The Macbeth policy . . . will not answer where little is left to chance or merit, but kings are made by politicians and newspapers; and the man who sits down waiting to be crowned, either by chance or just right, will go bareheaded all his life." John Quincy wrote a lengthy response defending himself. "Merit and just right in this country will be heard. And in any case, if they are not heard—'without my stir'—I shall acquiesce in the conclusion that it is because they do not exist." *JQA Memoirs*, 6:130.

10. LCA to JQA, August 8–9, 1822; JQA to LCA, August 12, 1822, APM Reel 456.

11. JQA to LCA, September 6, 1822; JQA to LCA, August 5, 1822; LCA to JQA, August 18, 1822, APM Reel 456.

12. JQA to LCA, August 28, July 26, 1822; LCA to JQA, July 26–27, 1822, APM Reel 456.

13. LCA to JQA, September 17, 1822, APM Reel 456.

14. Ibid., September 23, 24, 1822, APM Reel 456.

15. Patricia Tyson Stroud, *The Man Who Had Been King* (Philadelphia: University of Pennsylvania Press, 2005), 56; LCA to JQA, September 21, 27, 1822, APM Reel 456.

16. LCA to JQA, September 20, October 1, 1822, APM Reel 456.

17. LCA to JQA, August 19, 1822, APM Reel 456; "Diary of Louisa Catherine Adams, 1819–1849," in *Diary and Autobiographical Writings of Louisa Catherine Adams*, ed. Judith S. Graham and others (Cambridge, MA: Belknap Press of Harvard University Press, 2012), December 26, 1820, 2:537. *All in the Wrong* is the title of a comedy by Arthur Murphy published in London in 1761, ibid., 2:537n1.

18. The Popes had returned to Lexington in 1813 where they built a brick Palladian mansion, one of three private homes ever designed by Benjamin Latrobe, architect of the U.S. Capitol. John and Eliza Pope had two daughters, Elizabeth and Florida. Florida died in 1825 "after nine months of severe suffering. . . . Her complaints originating in a trifling accident appears not to have been understood and she has been gradually wasting away and sinking into her grave." LCA to GWA, August 6, 1825, APM Reel 471. Pope later served in Congress with JQA and was a frequent guest of the Adamses.

19. Adelaide Hellen to AA, January 3, 1816, APM Reel 429; AA to LCA, March 20, 1816, APM Reel 430. The Walter Hellen estate was not finally settled until 1835, having been "postponed until the youngest child, Walter, should come of age." *JQA Diary*, April 21, 1835 [electronic edition]. John Quincy had become executor when the original executor, Thomas Cook, died in 1826. Documents and accounts related to Walter Hellen's will are located in the National Archives, Washington, D.C.

20. LCA to AA, March 13, 1818, APM Reel 442; *The Diaries of John Quincy Adams: A Digital Collection* (Boston: Massachusetts Historical Society, 2005) http://www.masshist.org/jqadiaries April 29, 30, May 12, 1818; "Register of Baptisms in St. John's Church Washington City by William Hawley Rector," lists Georgiana's birthdate as

September 27, 1818, and her parents as George Boyd and Adelaide Hellen. She was baptized May 21, 1820. Louisa is listed as sponsor but was not in attendance: "at home for good reason." Adelaide went on what John Quincy described as "a tour to Philadelphia, and elsewhere, for the summer" in early May. Boyd escorted her and returned after two weeks from "little York." Georgiana, known as Adele, kept the Hellen name up to her marriage in 1838 to Thomas Lyman Moody.

21. "LCA Diary, 1819–1849," December 11, 1821, 2:616; February 11, 1821, 2:559.

22. LCA to AA, February 20, 1818, APM Reel 442.

23. Ibid., February 22, 1818.

24. "LCA Diary, 1819–1849," February 10, 1821, 2:558.

25. *JQA Diary*, November 2, 1817 [electronic edition]. Receipts exist at the National Archives for reimbursements to Adelaide (signed by Adelaide) for board for the children; also receipts for reimbursements to Louisa (signed by Louisa) for board for Thomas and Mary and to JQA for expenses for these children.

26. LCA to CFA, March 22, 1818, APM Reel 442.

27. "LCA Diary, 1819–1849," 2:437n1; November 28, 1821, 2:526; February 15, 1821, 2:546; January 13, 1821, 2:554; Jack Shepherd, *The Adams Chronicles* (Boston: Little, Brown, 1975), 297. John Quincy was reimbursed by the Hellen estate for Exeter's fees: $162.30 for the year 1824; $150 for 1825. Reviewed by David Bardin, Esq. in the Thomas Hellen Guardianship files, National Archives.

28. *JQA Diary*, January 24, 1821 [electronic edition]; "LCA Diary, 1819–1849," December 9, 1820, 2:531.

29. "LCA Diary, 1819–1849," January 24, 1821, 2:549; January 12, 1821, 2:543; January 14, 1821, 2:545.

30. "LCA Diary, 1819–1849," January 9, 1821, 2:542.

31. JA to GWA, November 3, 1821, APM Reel 453.

32. "Diary of Charles Francis Adams," Vol. 1, September 8, 1824, in *Founding Families: Digital Editions of the Papers of the Winthrops and the Adamses*, ed. C. James Taylor (Boston: Massachusetts Historical Society, 2007) http://www.masshist.org/publications/apde/portia.php?id=DCA01d279.

33. GWA to LCA, April 12, 1822, APM Reel 266.

34. LCA to JA2, December 2, 1821, APM Reel 453.

35. "CFA Diary," May 10, 1824 [electronic edition]. Charles was recollecting his freshman year habits in this journal entry composed two years later.

36. JQA to CFA, May 18, 1822, APM Reel 455.

37. Ibid.

38. Martin Duberman, *Charles Francis Adams 1807–1886* (Stanford: Stanford University Press, 1960), 427n19; "CFA Diary," May 27, June 3, 1824 [electronic edition].

39. JQA to CFA, July 17, 1825, APM Reel 471; Samuel Eliot Morison, *Three Hundred Years of Harvard* (Cambridge, MA: Harvard University Press, 1936), 231. John Adams II, along with twenty-eight of his classmates, received his degree posthumously in 1873.

40. JA to LCA, May 10, 1823, APM Reel 460; LCA to JA2, May 10, 11, 1823, APM Reel 463.

41. Samuel F. Bemis, *John Quincy Adams and the Union* (New York: Alfred A. Knopf, 1965), 199; *JQA Diary*, July 11, 1823 [electronic edition]. When JA2 died in 1834 after a three-year illness probably tied to alcoholism, his grief-stricken father wrote, "I controuled as far as I was able the unutterable anguish of my own soul endeavoring to sooth the yet more aggravated affliction of his widowed wife." *JQA Diary*, October 23, 1834 [electronic edition].

42. *JQA Diary*, July 12, 1823 [electronic edition]; Bemis, *Union*, 198.

43. LCA to JA, February 13, 1823, APM Reel 458.

44. David S. Heidler and Jeanne T. Heidler, *Henry Clay, the Essential American* (New York: Random House, 2010), 163.

45. "LCA Diary, 1819–1849," November 30, 1823, 2:669.

46. Ibid., December 20, 1823, 2:680.

47. *New York Statesman*, republished in *Newburyport Herald*, January 23, 1824, Newsbank.

48. "LCA Diary, 1819–1849," December 14, 1823, 2:681.

49. Ibid., December 20, 1823, 2:680; *New York Statesman*, republished in *Newburyport Herald*, January 23, 1824, Newsbank.

50. "CFA Diary," January 8, 1824 [electronic edition].

51. "Mrs. John Quincy Adams's Ball, 1824," *Harper's Bazaar* March, 18, 1871: 166 http://hearth.library.cornell.edu/cgi/t/text/text-idx?c=hearth;idno=4732809_1425_012; *New York Statesman*, republished in *Newburyport (Mass.) Herald*, January 23, 1824, Newsbank.

52. Marian Campbell Gouverneur, *As I Remember: Recollections of American Society During the Nineteenth Century* (Boston: D. Appleton and Co., 1911), 279.

53. *JQA Diary*, June 1, 1824 [electronic edition]; LCA to JQA, June 18, July 2–5, 1824, APM Reel 465.

54. LCA to JQA, July 14, June 22–23, 1824, APM Reel 465.

55. *JQA Diary*, January 25, 1824 [electronic edition].

56. *Washington City Gazette*, republished in *Richmond Enquirer*, August 3, 1824, Newsbank; LCA to CFA, July 29, 1824, APM Reel 465.

57. *JQA Diary*, August 28, 1824 [electronic edition]; LCA to CFA, July 22, 1824, APM Reel 465.

58. *JQA Diary*, August 31, 1824 [electronic edition].

59. *National Gazette* (Philadelphia), October 5, 1824, reprinted in the *Rhode Island American*, Newsbank; LCA to GWA, October 10, 1824, APM Reel 466.

60. Robert P. Hay, "The American Revolution Twice Recalled: Lafayette's Visit and the Election of 1824," *Indiana Magazine of History* 69, no. 1 (1973): 61, http://www.jstor.org/stable/27789869.

61. *JQA Memoirs*, 6:447.

62. "An inescapable logic drove what Clay did, if not how he did it, suggesting that his decision to have Mr. Adams as president was inevitable, regardless of its timing." Heidler and Heidler, *Henry Clay*, 179.

63. Lynn Hudson Parsons, *The Birth of Modern Politics: Andrew Jackson, John Quincy Adams, and the Election of 1824* (New York: Oxford University Press, 2009), 293.

64. Bemis, *Union*, 45.

65. LCA to GWA, December 14, 1824, APM Reel 466.

66. Margaret Bayard Smith, *The First Forty Years of Washington Society*, ed. G. Hunt (New York: C. Scribner's Sons, 1906) [digitized by Google from the library of the University of California], 170.

67. LCA to GWA, December 14, 1824, APM Reel 466; *JQA Diary*, February 8, 1825 [electronic edition].

68. *JQA Diary*, February 9, 1825 [electronic edition]; copy of acceptance letter, APM Reel 467.

69. *JQA Diary*, March 3, 1825 [electronic edition].

INDEX

Adams, Abigail (Nabby): birth of, 47; death of, 228–229; illness of, 216; as JQA's confidante, 60; LCA visits, 142; travels to Paris, 55

Adams, Abigail Smith (AA): ambitions for JQA, 47, 50, 51–52, 146, 184, 211–212, 213; corresponds with LCA, 160–161, 284–286, 309–310; death of, 310; on Europe, 52–53, 118–119; as grandmother, 272–273, 321; on household management, 149; and Johnson family, 11, 12–13, 27, 140, 202, 227, 229, 310, 338; and JQA's engagement to LCA, 77–78; and JQA's engagement to Mary Frazier, 62; and JQA's health, 172–173; on JQA's politics, 191; JQA writes poetry for, 291; LCA compares self to, 176; on LCA's health, 124, 143, 155; in Paris, 55; relationship with LCA, 2, 143–144, 148, 149, 172–174, 178–179, 185, 226–229; returns to Quincy, 60

Adams, Brooks, 268

Adams, Charles: birth of, 47; death of, 190, 384n43; education of, 52, 56, 59; JQA corresponds with, 94; returns to Boston, 53; travels to Paris, 51–52

Adams, Charles Francis (CFA): birth of, 189–190; and brothers, 273; childhood of, 2–3; education of, 222, 276, 281, 296;

320, 323, 343–344; on etiquette controversy, 307; and grandparents, 312, 344; health of, 196; on journey to Paris, 268–270; and JQA's investments, 347; on LCA, 123, 205–206, 258, 343; marries Abigail Brooks, 367; and Mary Hellen, 341; portrait of, 278; in Russia, 208, 219, 391nn36, 42; in Washington, 345, 349

Adams, Elizabeth, travels to Washington, 352

Adams, George Washington (GWA): birth of, 135; career of 346–347; child of, 367; childhood of, 170, 190, 194, 226–227, 229; christened, 136, 148; death of, 367; education of, 184, 192, 213, 276–280, 289, 296, 320–324; and Fanny Johnson, 342; and grandparents, 177–179, 311, 321, 343, 350; health of, 139, 141, 153, 175, 324; LCA on, 323–324, 343; in London, 272–273; and Mary Hellen, 341; portrait of, 279; "To My Mother," 343

Adams, Henry, on LCA, 1, 5, 369

Adams, John (JA): ambitions for JQA, 46, 146, 175, 191, 212–213; appoints JQA to Prussia, 89, 103; elected vice-president, 61; on etiquette controversy, 305–306; finances of, 157; fondness for LCA, 2, 143, 311–312; as grandfather, 277–278, 280, 311–312, 321, 322, 342–345; and

Adams, John (JA) (*Continued*)
  Johnson family, 11, 12–13, 17–18, 27, 140;
  on JQA's engagement, 77–78; LCA
  corresponds with, 304, 309–311, 317, 350;
  minister to Great Britain, 55, 375n20; in
  Netherlands, 52; and neutrality, 104; on
  New England, 311; in Paris, 51–52, 55;
  political career of, 47–48; recalls JQA
  from Berlin, 136; returns to Quincy, 60;
  on weights and measures, 320
Adams, John II (JA2): birth of, 155–156;
  childhood of, 170, 190, 194, 226–227, 229;
  at Columbian Mills, 346–347; death of,
  405n41; education of, 276, 280, 296, 320,
  323, 324, 345–346; and grandparents,
  177–179, 311–312, 321; health of, 175; LCA
  on, 343; in London, 272–273; marries
  Mary Hellen, 341; portrait of, 277
Adams, John Quincy (JQA): and
  Alexander I, 199–200, 203; ambitions of,
  46, 181–182, 232–233; ancestors of, 47;
  appearance of, 45, 74–75, 173–174,
  197–198, 334; appointed secretary of
  state, 292–295; appointed to Great
  Britain, 241, 282–283; appointed to
  Portugal, 77, 78, 79, 87; appointed to
  Prussia, 89–90; appointed to Russia,
  193–194; church attendance of, 154;
  corresponds with AA, 284; corresponds
  with LCA, 76–88, 94, 181–183, 186–187,
  192–193, 233–239, 266–267, 331–337;
  courts LCA, 68–72; courts Mary Frazier,
  61–63; as Dana's secretary, 53–54; death
  of, 368; declines appointment to
  Supreme Court, 213–214; depression of,
  60–61, 63, 66, 146, 167–169, 174–175, 177,
  236, 292–293; diaries of, 116–117, 182–183,
  223, 289, 354; *The Duplicate Letters, the
  Fisheries, and the Mississippi*, 331;
  education of, 48–50, 52, 53, 56–57, 58,
  60–61; 1824 election of, 3, 331, 351–356;
  as father, 184–185, 189–190, 273–274,
  276–280, 289, 321–322, 324, 325, 346;
  finances of, 152, 157, 166–167, 209,

210–213, 287, 385n35; Harvard career of,
  177, 184–185, 192, 227, 228; health of, 129,
  172–173, 226, 270–271, 283–284, 288; as
  JA's secretary, 55; and Johnson family,
  17–18, 44, 66, 97, 99–100, 101, 140; legal
  career of, 3, 63, 146–147, 152, 159, 167,
  192; *Letters on Silesia*, 132; in
  Massachusetts Senate, 147; in
  Netherlands, 63–65, 72–73, 74, 76;
  poetry of, 188, 290–292; portraits of, 70,
  92, 288–289; as "Publicola," 63; reading
  of, 49, 51, 72, 102, 116, 152, 153, 159, 168,
  169, 174, 177, 220–221, 223–224, 290;
  "Report on Weights and Measures," 211,
  220, 318–320; reputation of, 3–4,
  204–205; runs for Congress, 147; in
  Scandinavia, 54–55; Senate career of,
  156, 158–159, 174, 177, 190–192;
  temperament of, 70–72, 95, 167–169,
  177, 186–187, 222–223, 292–293, 305; and
  Treaty of Ghent, 232; on women, 57, 58,
  60, 61
Adams, Louisa Catherine (LCA's
  daughter), 215–217, 220
Adams, Louisa Catherine Johnson (LCA):
  and AA, 94, 160–161, 173–174, 226–230,
  284–286, 288, 293; "Adventures of a
  Nobody," 5, 98, 114, 117, 148, 183; advises
  JQA, 181–182, 184–185, 330, 331, 333–334;
  and Alexander I, 203, 207; birth of, 14;
  citizenship of, 95, 380n10; and CJ, 11–12,
  19, 22–23, 44; Congress honors, 1, 368;
  corresponds with JQA, 76–88, 94,
  181–183, 186–187, 192–193, 233–239,
  266–267, 331–337; corresponds with
  sons, 322; "Death in the Dance," 15–16;
  death of, 368; début of, 37; depression
  of, 4, 66, 142–143, 236, 325–327, 351;
  dowry of, 39, 97, 228; education of,
  18–19, 20–25, 42–43, 85; engagement of,
  72–73, 75, 79; entertains, 2, 134, 155, 287,
  305, 308, 312, 313–315, 318–319, 348–350,
  355; friendships of, 109–110, 112–113,
  114–115, 116, 120, 123–124, 129–130,

133–135, 147–148, 197, 201–202, 241, 254, 256, 286–287, 290; health of, 124–128, 142–143, 153, 155, 158, 175, 224–226, 236, 325–327, 335, 347–348, 350–351, 356, 383n22; and Hellen children, 340–341; as household manager, 149–152, 176, 185–186, 234–236, 275, 284, 299, 313–314; and JA, 2, 143, 304, 309–312, 317, 350; and JJ, 7, 11–12, 19, 97–101; as JQA's secretary, 275, 284; mourns daughter, 221–222; musical talent of, 3, 24, 43–44, 68, 69, 287, 290, 314; "Narrative of a Journey," 2–3, 267–270; nurses JQA, 283–284; portraits of, 6, 39–40, 288–289, 297, 314, 332, 397–398n39; pregnancies of, 102, 106–107, 119, 120, 124–128, 131–132, 133–136, 155–156, 180–181, 183, 186, 188–190, 192, 193, 207, 208, 213, 214–215, 221–222, 225, 294–295, 326; press coverage of, 2, 95, 349, 351–352; reading of, 3, 41–42, 70, 223–224, 371n10; "Record of a Life," 98; religious beliefs of, 19, 22, 153, 222; reunited with family, 138–139; *Saturday Evening Post* biography of, 367; self-confidence of, 86, 108, 112, 150, 171–172, 236, 238, 240, 256, 275, 333, 334–335; separated from sons, 178–179, 190, 194, 196–197, 325–326; and sisters, 25, 67–68, 70, 101–102, 162, 165–166, 189, 214, 312–313, 337–340; stillborn child of, 183–184; wardrobe of, 5–6, 27, 115, 196, 208–210, 288–289, 349–350; wedding of, 79, 89, 91–93; on women's abilities, 2–3, 117–118, 147–148, 168, 268, 271; writing of, 84–85, 115–118, 162–163, 207, 291, 309–311, 333

Adams, Susanna, 47, 226

Adams, Thomas Boylston (TBA): attends LCA's wedding, 91; in Berlin, 106, 109, 112; birth of, 47; career of, 146, 169; CFA on, 344–345; depression of, 190; friendship with LCA, 94–95, 100, 110, 112–113, 126; as JQA's secretary, 65, 87, 88, 105; returns to America, 113; studies law, 59; mentioned, 137, 194

"Adams Ball," 2, 329, 348–350

Adelphi Buildings, 93, 96

Adolphus, Prince, 134

Agg, John, 349

Alexander I: and Adamses, 199–200, 203, 207, 208; at Congress of Vienna, 254; and Kitty Johnson, 202–204; reign of, 198; returns to St. Petersburg, 235; and War of 1812, 231

All Hallows Barking, 10, 91

Allgor, Catherine, *Parlor Politics*, 5

Ambrister, Robert, executed, 315

Amistad, JQA and, 3

Anadia, João, Viscount, 111, 117

anemia, 125

Anglican Church, LCA and, 153–154

Apothecary Island, 215

Apraxin, Countess, 241–242, 257

Arbuthnot, Alexander George, executed, 315

Argentina, U.S. minister to, 330–331

Arnold, Benedict, 33

Augustus Ferdinand, Prince of Prussia, 121

Babet, Mme. (servant), 242, 263, 270

Bagot, Charles, 282, 305

Bagot, Mary, on Washington society, 302

Baptiste (servant), 242, 247, 248–249, 252, 258

Bayard, James A., appointed to peace commission, 231

Bedford Springs, LCA visits, 350–351

Bemis, Samuel Flagg, 123, 200, 204–205

Berlin: Adamses' residences in, 106–108, 111; growth of 106; LCA revisits (1815), 254–256; social life in, 108–109, 110–112, 114–115, 127, 134, 201

Bethmann, Simon Moritz von (banker), 258–259

Bezarra, Mme., sponsors LCA's daughter, 215

Bird, Savage & Bird, failure of, 157

Blücher, Gebhard, 281
boarding schools, 20–21, 276
Bonaparte, Elizabeth "Betsy" Patterson,
    386n53
Bonaparte, Jerome, 386n53
Bonaparte, Joseph, 335–337
Bonaparte, Napoleon. *See* Napoleon
Bondy, forest of, 264–265
Bordentown, N.J., LCA visits, 335–337
Boston: Adamses move to (1806), 186;
    Adamses return to (1808), 191–192;
    expansion of, 144–145; social life in,
    145–146; Tremont Street house, 188
Boston Latin School, 320
Boyd, George, 338–339
Boyd, Harriet, 17, 161, 183, 338–339
Boylston Prize, 322, 324
Brandenburg Gate, 107–108
Brooks, Abigail, marries CFA, 367
Brooks, James, attends LCA's wedding, 91
Brown, Dr. Charles: in Berlin, 381n36;
    entertains Adamses, 112, 120; treats
    LCA, 106–107, 126, 128, 131, 133,
    135, 136
Brown, Mrs., nurses LCA, 135
Brummel, Beau, 117
Buchanan, Andrew, 39, 188–189, 216
Buchanan, Mary, 340
Buchanan, Robert, 339
Buchanan, Susan, 340
Bulfinch, Charles, 145
Bülow, Friedrich Wilhelm von, 251
Burr, Aaron, 163, 175–176
Butterfield, Lyman H., 369n1

Calhoun, John C., 315–316, 347
calling cards, 303–308
Caroline of Brunswick, 282
Carr, Dr. Colston, 287
Carter, Mrs., LCA attends school of, 20–25
Carysfort, John Joshua Proby, Earl of, 111,
    136, 286
Carysfort, Lady Elizabeth, 117, 133–135,
    136, 225, 286

Castlereagh, Viscount, at Congress of
    Vienna, 254, 282, 283
Catholic Church, LCA on, 18–19, 130
Caulaincourt, Armand-Augustin-Louis de,
    Duc de Vicence, 200, 201–202, 210,
    218–219
Challinor, Joan, 370n8
Charlotte, Princess of Wales, 285
Charlotte, Queen of England, Adamses
    presented to, 284–285
Chesterfield, Lord, *Letters to His Son*,
    83–84
Chile, U.S. minister to, 330
Church, Angelica, 35
Church, John Barker, 35
Church, Kitty, 35
City Gazette, attacks JQA, 352
Clapham Common, LCA moves to, 79
Clay, Henry, 231–232, 283, 309, 316, 331,
    353–355
Clinton, DeWitt, 316
Clitherow family, 275, 286
clothing: appropriateness of, 20, 185, 196,
    209, 334; at court, 108, 110, 111, 119–120,
    206–207, 208, 209–210, 285; for
    mourning, 134; styles of, 91–92; trade in,
    9; and women's health, 125
Colombi, Marie, 202, 209, 241, 242
Colombia, U.S. minister to, 330–331
Columbian Centinel, 63, 95
Columbian Magazine, 58
Columbian Mills, 346
Colvin, John B., attacks JQA, 351–352
Congregational Church, LCA on, 143, 154
Continental System, 198–199, 219, 255
convent schools, 18–19
Cook, Daniel Pope, 295, 354
Copeland, Alexander, 286
Copley, John Singleton, portrait of JQA,
    70, 92
Corbett, Katherine, 370n8
Corn Law of 1815, 281
"corrupt bargain" of 1824/25, 353–355
cosmetics, 119–120, 382n12

Cossacks, 253–254, 258, 264

Cranch, Richard and Mary, LCA's sons board with, 194, 216

Crawford, William, 315–316, 347, 353–355

Crosby, Alfred W., Jr., 200

Dana, Francis, 53–54

dancing, LCA's love of, 110–11

Davidson, John, 9

Dearborn, Henry, LCA on, 163

Delius, Frederick, 99–100

democracy, LCA on, 164

diplomatic corps: in Berlin, 111; in St. Petersburg, 201; in Washington, 299

Dolph, Eliza, bears GWA's child, 367

Dresden, Adamses visit, 128, 130

Dupin, M. (servant), 260–261, 264

education: JQA's interest in, 48, 153; of women, 12, 42–43, 372–373nn 31, 32

Electoral College (1824), 353

Elgin, Thomas Bruce, Lord, LCA on, 117, 118

Elizabeth (servant), 313

Elizabeth Alexeievna, Empress of Russia, 202, 203, 208, 241

Emerson, Rev. William, 154, 156

Epernay, LCA stops in, 262

Epps, Elizabeth, 105, 106, 138, 140, 144, 151, 385n35

erysipelas, 225, 326, 335, 340, 402n77

etiquette controversy, 303–308

Everett, Alexander, 389n1

Farren, Elizabeth, 24

feminism, LCA's, 2–3, 147–148. *See also* women

Finck von Finckenstein, Count, 118

Florida, Andrew Jackson in, 315–316

Foster, Augustus, 299

Francis I, at Congress of Vienna, 254

Frankfurt, LCA arrives in, 258–259

Franklin, Benjamin, 49, 51, 52

Frazier, Mary, 61–63, 77, 113, 138, 145, 171–172

Frederica Louise of Prussia, 110, 121

Frederick, Md., Adamses visit, 140–141

Frederick the Great, 103, 106

Frederick William III, 108, 109, 119–121, 254, 282

Frye, Carolina Virginia Marylanda Johnson Buchanan. *See* Johnson, Carolina Virginia Marylanda (Caroline)

Frye, Nathaniel, 339, 340

Frye, Thomas, 340

Fulling, John, 242, 252, 258

Gaillard, John, 304

Gallatin, Albert, 140, 231, 283, 292

George III, 282

George IV, 282, 285–286

Ghent, Treaty of, 234–237, 239, 331

Giusta, Antoine, 313

Godfrey, Martha, 194

Goubard, Innocent-Louis, portrait of Joseph Napoleon, 336

Gray, Francis C., 202, 389n1

Great Britain: ambassadorship to, 233; 1815 recession in, 281–282; Secret Service of, 15; in 1770s, 8; U.S. relations with, 282–283. *See also* London; War of 1812

Great Ealing School, Adams sons attend, 276

Grimké, Angelina and Sarah, LCA and, 3

Hackney, 372n31

Hall, Joseph, attends LCA's wedding, 91

Hamburg, Adamses visit, 105

Hamilton, Alexander, death of, 171

Hanau, 257

Harris, Levett, 21, 197, 210, 215, 232, 235, 393n33

Harrod, Ann, TBA courts, 169

Harvard: CFA on, 343–345; expels students, 345; GWA attends, 320–321; JQA attends, 57–58; JQA teaches at, 177,

184–185, 192, 227, 228; student riots at, 322, 324–325

Haugwitz, Count, LCA on, 118

Hellen, Adelaide, 22, 161, 229, 338

Hellen, Ann (Nancy). *See* Johnson, Ann (Nancy)

Hellen, Georgiana Adelaide, 338, 403–404n20

Hellen, Johnson, 338, 341, 351

Hellen, Mary Catherine: birth of, 363; inheritance of, 338; lives with Adamses, 310, 340–341, 367; marries JA2, 341; mentioned, 347; travels with LCA, 328, 351, 352

Hellen, Thomas, 338, 341

Hellen, Walter, 157, 174, 229, 338

Hellen, Walter, Jr., inheritance of, 338

Henning, Miss (LCA's governess), 68–69, 70, 76

Hermitage, LCA visits, 203–204, 207–208

Hewlett, Elizabeth, 11, 20, 22–23, 102

Hewlett, John, 40, 91, 93

Hohenzollern dynasty, 103

Holy Roman Empire, 103

Hopkinson, Emily Mifflin, 335

Hopkinson, Joseph, 335–337, 403n9

Horace, Adamses sail on, 195–196

Hotel de Russie (Berlin), Adamses lodge at, 106

Humboldt, William von, at Congress of Vienna, 254

Hyde de Neuville, Jean Guillaume, Baron, 305, 311

Independent Chronicle, on LCA, 95

Jackson, Andrew: and Battle of New Orleans, 239; Congress and, 315–316; in 1824 election, 316, 347, 353–355; LCA's ball for, 2, 329, 348–350

Jay, Sarah Livingston, LCA on, 20

Jefferson, Patsy, 18

Jefferson, Thomas: on AA's death, 310; and CJ, 12; and daughter's education, 18; and JJ, 31–34; and JQA, 55,139–140; LCA on, 84, 161–162, 163, 174; and protocol, 301

Jennings, Edmund, 40, 375n31

Jersey, Countess of, entertains, 287–288

Johnson, Adelaide, 22, 161, 229, 338

Johnson, Ann (Nancy): birth of, 9, 10; birthday ball of, 66; death of, 214, 338; début of, 37; entertains, 161; and JQA, 67–68, 69, 186–187; and LCA's wedding, 91; marries Walter Hellen, 157; as teenager, 25

Johnson, Carolina Virginia Marylanda (Caroline): birth of, 15; début of, 37; JQA on, 68; lives with LCA, 140, 149, 152; marries Andrew Buchanan, 188–189; marries Nathaniel Frye, 339–340; social activities of, 155; suitors of, 39; as teenager, 25, 44

Johnson, Catherine Maria (Kitty): birth of, 22; cares for LCA, 217, 221; health of, 226; lives with Adamses, 339; marries William Steuben Smith, 229–230, 339; in Russia, 195, 202–204; in Washington society, 161, 306

Johnson, Catherine N. (CJ): and AA, 12–13, 229, 310; ancestors of, 13; in Boston, 149; business activities of, 16–17; death of, 216; health of, 42; and JQA, 66, 71–72, 75; LCA's memories of, 11–12, 19, 44; marriage of, 9–11, 13–14, 36–37; nurses LCA, 22–23; portrait of, 29; stylishness of, 20, 91–92; in Washington, 155, 157, 160–161, 337

Johnson, Dorcas Sedgwick, 8

Johnson, Eliza Janet Dorcas, 22, 175–176, 337–338, 403n18

Johnson, Fanny Russell, 341–342

Johnson, George, 346

Johnson, Harriet, 17, 161, 183, 338–339

Johnson, Joshua (JJ): ancestors of, 8; business of, 8–9, 14–15, 16–17, 28, 31, 74, 90, 95–102, 125, 140; and daughters'

marriages, 36–37, 39, 66; death of, 149; diplomatic activities of, 16, 31–34; estate of, 166; health of, 139, 141; hospitality of, 27, 72, 93; and JQA, 72, 73, 79, 87, 89, 90; LCA's memories of, 7, 11–12, 19, 99; lifestyle of, 8, 9, 15–16, 26–27, 35–36; marriage of, 9–11, 13–14, 36–37; patriotism of, 14–15, 33–34; portrait of, 30; returns to America, 79, 87, 90, 96–97; in Washington, 337
Johnson, Mary Ann, 15, 17
Johnson, Roger, 346
Johnson, Thomas, II, 8
Johnson, Thomas, III, 8, 36, 95, 140–141
Johnson, Thomas Baker, 17, 229, 328, 335, 397–398n39, 402n1

Karlsruhe, LCA stops in, 259–260
Katusov, Prince Mikail, 220
Kehl, LCA stops in, 260
King, Charles Bird, portraits by, 278, 279, 297, 314
King, Rufus, 89
Kirkland, John, 322, 323, 324
Königsberg, LCA stops in, 251–252
Krehmer, Annette, 202, 215, 221
Küstrin, LCA arrives in, 253

Lafayette, Marquis de, 271, 315, 352–353
Latrobe, Benjamin Henry, 307, 403n18
Leipzig, Adamses visit, 132–133
Leopold, Prince of Saxe-Coburg-Gotha, 285
Leslie, Charles Robert, portraits by, 288–289, 397–398n39
Letcher, Robert P., in 1824 election, 354
Litta, Countess, 206
Little Boston House, 275–276
Little Ealing, 274–275, 286–287, 294–295
Liverpool, Lord, 282
London: Adamses' lodgings in, 273–274; Johnson family in, 15–16, 19–20, 26–27; mercantile role of, 7–8; social life in, 285–286, 287–288
Louis XIII, at Congress of Vienna, 254

Louis XVIII, 265–266
Louise, Queen of Prussia: death of, 255; diplomatic role of, 117; LCA presented to, 108–109; LCA's friendship with, 109–110, 118–120, 134–135; and Napoleon, 255; pregnancy of, 126
Louisiana Purchase, 158
Luccassini, Marchesa, diplomatic role of, 117
Lyttelton, Lord William Henry, on JQA, 205

Madison, Dolley, 140, 174, 301–302, 303, 318
Madison, James: appoints JQA to Russia, 193, 199–200; appoints peace commission (1812), 231–232; JQA calls on, 140; JQA supports, 158; LCA on, 163; nominates JQA to Supreme Court, 212–214
Maine, admission of, 317
Maistre, Joseph de, 204
Maria Feodorovna, Dowager Empress of Russia, 207, 209
Marriage Act (Great Britain, 1753), 371n7
Martin, Robert, 342
Massachusetts Historical Society, publishes LCA's writings, 5
Meaux, LCA stops at, 264
medical care: bleeding, 131, 143, 222, 294, 295, 311, 326; blisters, 22–23, 143, 173, 216, 373n39; for depression, 177; for hemorrhoids, 328; for infants, 216–217; for miscarriage, 124–125; at spas, 129; women's role in, 42
Merry, Anthony, 301
Metternich, Prince Klemens von, at Congress of Vienna, 254
Mexico, U.S. minister to, 330–331
migraines, 124, 342
miscarriages. *See* LCA, pregnancies of
Missouri Compromise, 317–318
Mitau, LCA's reception in, 247–249

Monroe, Elizabeth, entertains, 302,
    303–304, 306, 308
Monroe, James, 292, 306, 315–316
Monroe, James Joseph, and Adelaide
    Johnson, 338
Monroe Doctrine, 330–331
More, Hannah, *The Search After
    Happiness*, 24
Morel, M., in Mitau, 247–249
Morison, Samuel Eliot, on Harvard riots,
    324–325
Morris, Gouverneur, 65, 374–375n20
Morrison, Major Alexander, 286
Moulton, Mary, 351–352
Mount Vernon, LCA visits, 140
music, LCA's talent for, 3, 24, 43–44, 68,
    69, 287, 290, 314

Nantes: JA and JQA visit, 17–18; Johnsons
    move to, 15–20
Napoleon: abdication and exile of, 220;
    death rumored, 258–259; escapes from
    Elba, 257–258, 261, 262; German
    campaigns of, 104; at Jena 103; LCA on,
    224; in Paris, 265–266; and Queen
    Louise, 109; reputation of, 253; in
    Russia, 198–199, 218–220; at Waterloo,
    281
Napoleonic wars, effects of, 251–255,
    257–258, 281
Narva, LCA's reception in, 246
Naryshkina, Maria, and Alexander I, 203
National Gazette, 330, 331
National Intelligencer, 347
Native Americans, 3, 315–316
Natural Philosophy Club, JQA forms, 147
Neale, Pauline, 109–110, 135, 256
Nelson (servant), 194
Nesselrode, Count Karl, at Congress of
    Vienna, 254
New York Statesman, 349–350
Newark, N.J., Adamses quarantined in, 158
Newman, John Henry, Cardinal, 280
newspapers. *See* press

Newth, Catherine Young, marriage of,
    9–11
Nicholas, Dr. George, 276, 286–287
Nicholas, Ellen, 289–291
Norman, Captain, LCA assists, 255–256
Nuth, Catherine Young, marriage of, 9–11

O'Brien, Michael: *Mrs. Adams in Winter*,
    5, 269, 371n14
O'Farrill, Gonzalo, 131
O'Farrill, Mrs., LCA presents at court, 131
opera, 123, 265

Panic of 1819, 317
Panin, Count, 111
Paris, 20, 265–266
Parsons, Theophilus, JQA studies with, 59
Peru, U.S. minister to, 330–331
Philadelphia, Adamses visit, 137, 175,
    328–330, 331–337
Physick, Dr. Philip Syng, 328
Pickering, Timothy, 64, 104, 156
Pinckney, Charles, as orator, 309
Pinckney, Elizabeth Motte, 35
Pinckney, Thomas, 34–35, 64–65
Pitt, Rev. Loudon King, 215
poetry: CFA reads, 344; GWA's love of,
    323–324, 343; about Harvard riot,
    401n63; about Jackson ball, 349; by JA2,
    343; JQA and, 48, 53, 61, 116, 170, 187,
    188, 290–292; LCA reads, 85
Pope, Eliza, 22, 175–176, 337–338,
    403n18
Pope, John, 337–338
Portfolio, The, 280
Potsdam, Adamses travel to, 127
press: on JQA, 330–331, 352; on Lafayette's
    visit, 353; on LCA, 2, 95, 349, 351–352
Prussia, 102–106, 250–251. *See also* Berlin
"Publicola" (JQA), 63

Quincy, Mass.: Adamses move to, 157;
    Adamses summer in, 176–177, 310, 352;
    LCA on, 142–143, 185–186

Randolph, John, LCA on, 163
Ranelagh, outing to, 74–75
reading: JQA's, 49, 51, 72, 83–84, 102, 116, 152, 153, 159, 168, 169, 174, 177, 220–221, 223–224, 290; LCA's, 3, 41–42, 70, 83–84, 223–224, 371n10; as shared interest, 102
religion, LCA on, 19, 22, 153, 222
Rensselaer, Stephen van, in 1824 election, 354–355
Riga, LCA's reception in, 247
Roberts, Cokie, *Ladies of Liberty*, 5
Romanzoff, Nikolai Petrovich, 198, 208
Rush, Benjamin, treats LCA, 137, 141, 175
Russell, Jonathan, 232, 331, 333
Russia: Napoleon invades, 218–220; trade with United States, 199–200. *See also* St. Petersburg

St. Anne's Soho, 10–11
St. Botolph without Aldgate, 10, 14
St. Petersburg: Adamses' lodgings in, 197, 210–211, 215, 216; climate of, 196, 197, 216; court of, 196; social life in, 201–202, 203–205, 207–210, 235
Sargent, Daniel, 94
Scribner's, publishes "Narrative," 268
seasickness, 105, 295
servants, 27, 43, 150–151, 211, 242, 313–314
Shakespeare, LCA's knowledge of, 85, 371n10
Shaw, Elizabeth, 60–61
Shaw, John, 56–57
Shultz von Ashzaden, Carl Gustav, 111
Siddons, Sarah, 24
Silesia, Adamses visit, 132–133, 225
slavery: LCA on, 3, 117; and Missouri Compromise, 317
slaves, LCA hires, 313
Smith, Abigail Adams. *See* Adams, Abigail (Nabby)
Smith, Catherine Maria (Kitty). *See* Johnson, Catherine Maria (Kitty)
Smith, John Spear, 205, 389n1
Smith, Margaret Bayard, 302, 309, 355

Smith, Robert, 199, 205
Smith, William (of South Carolina), 304
Smith, William Steuben, 229–230, 232, 339, 389n1
South America, U.S. policy on, 330–331
Stael, Mme. de, *Memoirs*, 83
Sterrett, David, 38
Strasbourg, LCA visits, 260–261
Stuart, Gilbert, portrait of LCA, 332

Talleyrand, Charles-Maurice de, at Congress of Vienna, 254
"Temple du Goût" (Nantes), 15–16
theater: in Berlin, 108; JQA's love of, 46, 50, 55, 123; LCA and JQA attend, 270; in LCA's childhood, 24
Tillary, Dr. James, treats LCA, 295
Tilsit, LCA reaches, 251
Tilsit, Treaty of, 198–199
tobacco, trade in, 8, 9, 14, 20, 28, 31
Töplitz, Adamses visit, 128–130
Transcontinental Treaty, 315–316, 330
travel, LCA on, 105–106, 130
Trumbull, John, 35, 40, 44, 68

United States: and Napoleonic wars, 199–200; South American policy, 330–331; trade with Russia, 199–200
United States, Congress: in 1824 election, 353–355; honors LCA, 1, 368; LCA visits, 309; morals of, 308–309; regional interests in, 298
United States, Supreme Court: JQA declines appointment to, 213–214; LCA visits, 309

Vienna, Congress of, 254–255, 281, 282
Von Harten, Mr. and Mrs., 286–287
Voss, Sophie Marie, LCA on, 117

Wallace, Davidson, and Johnson, 7, 9
Wallace, Johnson, and Muir, 16, 28–29, 30, 36. *See also* JJ, business of
Walsh, Robert: supports JQA, 328–330

Wanstead House, 93, 380n4
War of 1812, 230–232, 238–239, 296–298;
    Treaty of Ghent ends, 234–237, 239, 331
Washington, D.C.: Adamses' homes in,
    299, 318–319; boardinghouses in, 298;
    LCA on, 139, 308–309; reconstruction
    of, 296–298; social life in, 159–162, 180,
    299, 305, 312–313
Washington, George: appoints JQA to
    Netherlands, 63–64; and CJ, 12
Washington, Martha, 12, 140
Washington Female Orphan Asylum,
    308–309
Waterloo, Battle of, 281
Webster, Daniel, 309, 346
Weed, Thurlow, in 1824 election, 353
Wellington, Duke of, 254, 281, 288
Welsh, Abigail, JA2 and CFA board with,
    320–321
Welsh, Dr. Thomas, and JQA's
    investments, 385n35; treats LCA, 143,
    155–156

Whitcomb, Tilley: handles household
    accounts, 98; leaves Adamses' service,
    151; marries Elizabeth Epps, 385n35;
    travels with Adamses, 105, 138, 140
White House: Latrobe drawing of, 307;
    restoration of, 298
Windau River, LCA crosses, 250
Winnull, Jane, marries Johnson Hellen,
    341
women: as audience for "Narrative,"
    268, 270, 271; in diplomacy, 117–118,
    204–205; education of, 12, 42–43,
    372–373nn31, 32; health of, 402n79;
    LCA on, 2–3, 147–148, 333; provide
    medical care, 42; in Washington,
    299–300, 303–308, 309

yellow fever, 158
Young, Mary (LCA's grandmother), 13
Young, Miss (teacher), 23

Zinzendorf, Count and Countess, 117